WHAT'S *New* TO THIS EDITION?

- **Communication Unplugged** offers practical tips for communicating without technology
- **Career Frontier** features enhance career development
- **Original SAGE Video** brings concepts to life
- **New contemporary examples** and **updated references** appear throughout
- **Additional coverage of the "dark side" of technology** offers a balanced view of mediated communication

ASSESS YOUR COMMUNICATION

INTERPERSONAL COMMUNICATION COMPETENCE

INSTRUCTIONS: Here are some statements about how people interact with other people. For each statement, circle the response that best reflects your communication with others. Be honest in your responses and reflect on your communication behavior carefully.

	ALMOST NEVER	SELDOM	SOMETIMES	OFTEN	ALMOST ALWAYS
1. I allow friends to see who I really am.	1	2	3	4	5
2. I can put myself in others' shoes.	1	2	3	4	5
3. I am comfortable in social situations.	1	2	3	4	5
4. When I have been wronged, I confront the person who wronged me.	1	2	3	4	5
5. I let others know that I understand what they say.	1	2	3	4	5
6. My conversations are characterized by smooth shifts from one topic to the next.	1	2	3	4	5
7. My friends can tell when I'm happy or sad.	1	2	3	4	5
8. My communication is usually descriptive, not evaluative.	1	2	3	4	5
9. My friends truly believe that I care about them.	1	2	3	4	5
10. I accomplish my communication goals.	1	2	3	4	5

TOTAL

Add your responses for all 10 items. Scores may range from a low of 10 (low interpersonal communication competence) to a high of 50 (high interpersonal communication competence).

As you can see from the statements, interpersonal communication competence involves mastering the skills associated with self-disclosure, empathy, social relaxation, assertiveness, interest in others, interaction management, expressiveness, supportiveness, approachability, and control of your environment.

Reflect on each item that you scored as a 1 (almost never), 2 (seldom), or 3 (sometimes). Can you see how improving that behavior might enrich your interpersonal communication? Are there ways in which you can apply the content of this chapter to help you incorporate that behavior more often?

Source: Adapted from Rubin, R. B. & Martin, M. M (1994). Development of a measure of interpersonal communication competence. Communication Research Reports, 11, 33–44. doi: 10.1080/08824099409359936

- **Assess Your Communication** engages students by providing a self-inventory to prepare them for a variety of communication contexts

- **Communication How-To** creatively directs students to apply readings to real-life situations

  COMMUNICATION HOW-TO
MANAGE INTERPERSONAL CONFLICT

Conflict in relationships is inevitable and can be both a positive and a negative force. Conflict allows us to solve problems and potentially make the relationship work better for all involved. Below are some basic tips on managing interpersonal conflict.

 1. **Talk face to face about the conflict.** Text messages and online chat will not allow us to take advantage of nonverbal characteristics.

 2. **Use inclusive language when possible.** It notes that the couple is in this conflict together and can solve the issue. "We will work this out."

 3. **Put yourself in their shoes.** Most of the time, each person is correct about at least part of the problem. Express empathy.

 4. **Use "I" language to express your own feelings and thoughts.** Avoid blaming the other person for how you feel. Say, "I feel sad about the fight." Don't say, "You made me feel sad about the fight."

 5. **Listen.** Instead of thinking of the next argument, truly listen to the other person before you even think about what to say next.

• **Career Frontier** presents examples and suggestions for using communication skills to enhance career development

• **Communication Unplugged** encourages students to put their devices down and offers practical tips for communicating without the assistance of technology

• **Make a Difference** features promote student civic engagement and activism

• **Ethical Connection** uniquely emphasizes the importance of ethical communication

• **Communication in Action** and **Speeches in Action integrated video features** include real student speech samples, communication scenarios, and exclusive content from the SAGE Video collection to bring communication concepts and skills to life for today's students. In-text discussion questions and multiple-choice questions available through the study site and interactive ebook help students connect video and chapter content and test their own comprehension.

The Communication Age is *Interactive*

This dynamic **interactive eBook** version of *The Communication Age* goes way beyond highlighting and note taking! Read your mobile-friendly eBook anywhere, any time with **easy access across desktop, smartphone, and tablet devices**. Using the VitalSource Bookshelf® platform, **download your book to a personal computer** and read it offline, **share notes and highlights with instructors and classmates** who are using the same eBook, and "follow" friends and instructors as they make their own notes and highlights. Simply click on icons and links in the eBook to experience a broad array of multimedia resources as well as access to academic articles.

Get **FREE** access to the interactive eBook with the purchase of the new edition. **Bundle ISBN: 978-1-5063-4071-5**

$SAGE edge™

SAGE edge offers a robust online environment featuring an impressive array of tools and resources for review, study, and further exploration, keeping both instructors and students on the cutting edge of teaching and learning. SAGE edge content is open-access and available on demand. Learning and teaching has never been easier!

Learn more at **edge.sagepub.com/edwards2e**

Tools that help students become confident and effective public speakers

SpeechPlanner

This interactive, web-based tool guides you through the process of planning and preparing your speech, one step at a time. Featuring practical tips, strategies, and useful examples designed to explain and illustrate every step of the speech-making process, this valuable planner makes it simple and easy to create highly effective, successful speeches, anywhere, any time. SpeechPlanner includes video examples of effective speeches with time-coded references to highlight best practices. Its unique practice timer feature allows students to practice delivering speeches within allotted time limits, promoting effective and appropriately paced delivery.

For details on packaging SpeechPlanner with your text and for additional information, speak with a SAGE representative or visit **speechplanner.sagepub.com**

PACKAGE your book with SpeechPlanner
ISBN: 978-1-5063-3890-3

Looking for a solution to share and assess student speech videos for your course?

Contact your SAGE sales representative to review our options.

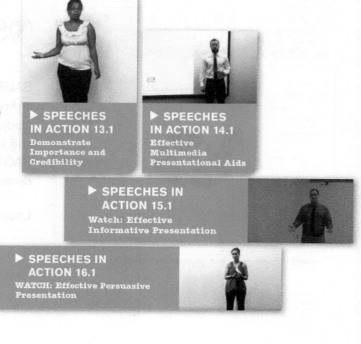

▶ SPEECHES IN ACTION 13.1
Demonstrate Importance and Credibility

▶ SPEECHES IN ACTION 14.1
Effective Multimedia Presentational Aids

▶ SPEECHES IN ACTION 15.1
Watch: Effective Informative Presentation

▶ SPEECHES IN ACTION 16.1
WATCH: Effective Persuasive Presentation

THE
COMMUNICATION
AGE
2

THE COMMUNICATION AGE

CONNECTING & ENGAGING 2

AUTUMN EDWARDS
Western Michigan University

CHAD EDWARDS
Western Michigan University

SHAWN T. WAHL
Missouri State University

SCOTT A. MYERS
West Virginia University

$SAGE

Los Angeles | London | New Delhi
Singapore | Washington DC

Los Angeles | London | New Delhi
Singapore | Washington DC

FOR INFORMATION:

SAGE Publications, Inc.
2455 Teller Road
Thousand Oaks, California 91320
E-mail: order@sagepub.com

SAGE Publications Ltd.
1 Oliver's Yard
55 City Road
London EC1Y 1SP
United Kingdom

SAGE Publications India Pvt. Ltd.
B 1/I 1 Mohan Cooperative Industrial Area
Mathura Road, New Delhi 110 044
India

SAGE Publications Asia-Pacific Pte. Ltd.
3 Church Street
#10-04 Samsung Hub
Singapore 049483

Acquisitions Editor: Matthew Byrnie
Associate Editor: Natalie Konopinski
Editorial Assistant: Janae Masnovi
eLearning Editor: Gabrielle Piccininni
Production Editor: Olivia Weber-Stenis
Copy Editor: Talia Greenberg
Typesetter: C&M Digitals (P) Ltd.
Proofreader: Theresa Kay
Indexer: Sheila Bodell
Cover Designer: Gail Buschman
Marketing Manager: Ashlee Blunk

Copyright © 2017 by SAGE Publications, Inc.

Printed in the United States of America.

ISBN 978-1-4833-7370-6

This book is printed on acid-free paper.

15 16 17 18 19 10 9 8 7 6 5 4 3 2 1

Brief CONTENTS

Detailed CONTENTS

01 COMMUNICATION IN THE 21ST CENTURY   1

Thinkstock

02 PERCEPTION, SELF, AND COMMUNICATION   24

iStock

03   VERBAL COMMUNICATION   50

Thinkstock

04   NONVERBAL COMMUNICATION   76

iStock

05 LISTENING 104

Thinkstock

08 SMALL GROUP AND TEAM COMMUNICATION 180

Thinkstock

09 WORKPLACE AND ORGANIZATIONAL COMMUNICATION 212

Canstock

10 COMMUNICATION AND NEW MEDIA 240

iStock

11 SELECTING YOUR TOPIC AND KNOWING YOUR AUDIENCE 268

Thinkstock

12   RESEARCHING YOUR PRESENTATION   292

Thinkstock

15 INFORMATIVE PRESENTATIONS 368

16 PERSUASIVE PRESENTATIONS 392

INTERVIEWING IN THE COMMUNICATION AGE   418

Preface

We are thrilled to share the second edition with you! This edition is updated with new chapter openers, new research, and two new features: Communication Unplugged and Career Frontier. These features offer timely advice for students both to consider their communication choices and gain valuable career skills in communication.

The Communication Age: Connecting and Engaging provides students a contemporary and relatable textbook with a solid foundation in the fundamentals of communication. The textbook's driving theme is life in the Communication Age. In the Communication Age, technology, media, and communication converge and deeply permeate daily life. The dramatic rise in social media, social networking sites, mobile computing, and general online activity has led to increased complexities between face-to-face communication and mediated communication, increasing the need for communication competencies and critical thinking across life contexts.

We wrote this textbook because we noticed that most textbooks in the "introduction to communication" market are written from an "Information Age" perspective, in which people connect *with* and *to* the Internet and technology, not *through* it, as do today's students. Furthermore, in the few years since publication of the first edition, more scholars are discussing HMI: human communication "with" machines.

In such textbooks, social networking sites, like Facebook or Twitter, or text messaging are given a "text box," or are treated as a special case. This textbook treats virtual spaces and communication technologies as places and ways where students develop, maintain, and foster connection and engage with others. In short, this textbook couples traditional instruction on the fundamentals of face-to-face communication with the latest research on mediated communication.

As an author team, we considered the questions instructors have when planning an introductory communication course. First, we examined the broader conceptual questions:

- What do we want our students to learn?

- How can this information be applied to their current and future life?

- How can we make this material meaningful, useful, and interesting to students considering the presence of new media and convergence across communication contexts?

- How can all of the important information, skills, and competencies relevant to the basics of communication be covered in one term?

Next, we focused on the critical questions that emerge about how to organize core communication skills and competencies in a way that addresses the blend of face-to-face and mediated experience. Instructors often grapple with questions like

- Should I include a social media component?
- How much attention should be given to topics like listening, interviewing, and public speaking?
- How can the course be relevant due to the influence of new media?

The last six chapters of the textbook focus on giving presentations in the Communication Age. Because of the integration of media and technology into all of life's spheres, the Communication Age is one in which presentations are not simply "public speeches," but multimedia efforts to persuade and inform in a variety of settings and across time. Today's communicators must be able to present in multiple contexts, both virtual and real, for synchronous and asynchronous audiences. This textbook provides instruction relevant to traditional public speaking, along with the additional presentational opportunities and challenges of today's students.

ORGANIZING THEME: CONVERGENCE IN THE COMMUNICATION AGE

We believe that developing an organizing theme lends clarity to a textbook. The Convergence in the Communication Age theme of this textbook is one that encourages students to focus on communication competency in both face-to-face and mediated contexts. We believe that one of the strengths of *The Communication Age: Connecting and Engaging* is that it links the research base on new media to basic communication skills in order to promote competency and engaged citizenship. As the various communication contexts and skills are covered, we work to constantly balance the material between the face-to-face and mediated communication experience.

FEATURES OF THE TEXTBOOK

The Communication Age: Connecting and Engaging presents several pedagogical features that students will be able to use and to which they will immediately relate. Each of these features is based on the most current research and information.

Career Frontier

In the Career Frontier feature we offer strategies and tips that focus on career preparation and emphasize the importance of communication competence in a student's work life. We encourage application of knowledge to a variety of professional contexts and situations. This feature also discusses employment possibilities for students in communication careers.

Communication Unplugged

The Communication Unplugged feature emphasizes communication choices in important face-to-face contexts in light of the constant shifts in human communication between mediated and face-to-face communities. These boxes offer scenarios and topics for students to explore the tensions between online and offline communication experiences with a focus on important communication skills relevant across life contexts.

Make a Difference

The Make a Difference feature addresses the vital relationship between communication and civic engagement by weaving together conceptual material with real-world examples, and showcasing how students, organizations, scholars, and everyday citizens have used communication to address important social issues. These boxes offer ways for students to actively participate in their local communities using communication skills.

Ethical Connection

Each chapter includes an Ethical Connection feature that is a brief, real-world case study tackling an ethical issue connected to chapter content. The feature is driven by the National Communication Association's "Credo for Ethical Communication," and it encourages students to communicate with respect to self, others, and surroundings, giving careful consideration to the ways in which our words construct our social realities. Ethical Connection boxes promote class discussion, critical analysis, and self-inventory by taking a careful look at real-world case studies that resonate with students.

Assess Your Communication

Chapters include the Assess Your Communication feature, which encourages communication competency and self-inventory. This feature includes scales, assessments, and self-reports established by leading researchers in the communication discipline, designed in a way that is easy to understand. The Assess Your Communication feature is directly related to chapter content and encourages students to personalize information and to focus directly on communication competency across life contexts.

Writing Style and Examples

The writing style used in this book is designed to connect with students on a personal level. Reviewers and students found the style to be accessible, warm, and engaging while still maintaining a scholarly focus. The examples used in the textbook are taken from popular culture and real-life scenarios. Woven throughout the text seamlessly, these examples are taken from both face-to-face communication and the virtual world to highlight life in the age of communication.

Introductory and Summary Sections

Each chapter begins with a What You'll Learn section that lists the top five important concepts or ideas in the chapter. Each chapter concludes with a parallel What You've Learned section that provides a summary of the top five things students have learned through reading the chapter. In classroom testing, students find this organization helpful for focusing their reading and studying for exams. These statements are designed to be used in your assessment of student outcomes.

Chapter Openers

At the beginning of each chapter is a recent current event or popular culture item that highlights the basic ideas of the chapter, but does so in a way to demonstrate life in the Communication Age. These chapter openers are a great way to lead a discussion about the material presented.

Pictures

A cutting-edge visual program is featured across chapters. Pictures are related to chapter content and invite students to visualize real-world experiences related to communication. The photo program is culturally sensitive and designed to enhance chapter content and application of knowledge.

ANCILLARIES

The Communication Age: Connecting and Engaging includes a comprehensive ancillary package that utilizes new media and a wide range of instructional technologies designed to support instructor course preparation and student learning.

Student Study Site

edge.sagepub.com/edwards2e

- Mobile-friendly eFlashcards to strengthen understanding of key concepts
- Mobile-friendly practice quizzes to encourage self-guided assessment and practice

- Carefully selected video and multimedia content that enhance exploration of key topics
- EXCLUSIVE access to full-text SAGE journal articles and other readings, which support and expand on chapter concepts

Instructor Teaching Site

http://edge.sagepub.com/edwards2e

- Course Management System integration to make it easy for student test results and graded assignments to seamlessly flow into instructor gradebooks
- Test banks built on Bloom's Taxonomy to provide a diverse range of test items
- Chapter activities for individual or group projects, providing lively and stimulating ideas for use in and out of class to reinforce active learning
- iClickr Questions to poll students before class or lecture to stimulate conversation and participation
- Sample course syllabi with suggested models for structuring your course
- Editable, chapter-specific PowerPoint® slides to offer you flexibility when creating multimedia lectures
- Access to full-text SAGE journal articles that expose students to important research and scholarship tied to chapter concepts
- Video and multimedia content to enhance student engagement and appeal to different learning styles, including exclusive access to video clips from the SAGE Video collection for use in course lectures

Interactive eBook

The Communication Age is also available as an Interactive eBook, which can be packaged free with the book or purchased separately. The interactive eBook offers integrated video clips of sample speeches and communication scenarios, as well as links to additional web, audio, and video resources. The interactive eBook also includes unique student quiz material that can feed to instructors' gradebooks.

Acknowledgments

There are many people who did amazing work on the creation of this textbook.

First, thank you to our Executive Editor at SAGE, Matt Byrnie, for his encouragement and vision for this project. Special thanks go to Natalie Konopinski, Associate Editor at SAGE, for her support, help, and wisdom. She learned a great deal about the four of us for this edition. Matt and Natalie: It has been a joy and privilege to work with you. We could not ask for a better pair to guide us. We also would like to thank Janae Masnovi, Gabrielle Piccininni, Ashlee Blunk, and Talia Greenberg for their amazing work. And we would like to thank Felicia Weathers and several graduate students who did a beautiful job working on various tasks: Travis Covill, Eric Mishne, Brett Stoll, Kierstin Toth, and Tucker Robinson.

Finally, we wish to thank all of the reviewers who contributed greatly to this second edition through excellent suggestions, creative insights, and helpful critiques: Jaime Bochantin, *DePaul University*; Tim Chandler, *Hardin-Simmons University*; Aaron Duncan, *University of Nebraska–Lincoln*; Paul R. Edleman, *Sauk Valley Community College*; William H. Foster, *Naugatuck Valley Community College*; Sara Holmes, *Richland College*; Theodoros Katerinakis, *Drexel University*; Amy K. Lenoce, *Naugatuck Valley Community College*; Aimee E. Miller-Ott, *Illinois State University*; Jennifer Millspaugh, *Richland College*; Faith Mullen, *Liberty University*; Laura Oliver, *The University of Texas at San Antonio*; Chris R. Sawyer, *Texas Christian University*; Deborah Sheffield, *William Paterson University*; Yasmin Shenoy, *University of Hartford*; and Christopher Sweerus, *William Paterson University*.

Autumn Says Thanks to . . .

I feel so grateful to have a network of friends, teachers, students, colleagues, and family who awaken my passions, support my endeavors, sharpen my mind, and nurture my spirit. I would like to express my appreciation to the cohorts of Western Michigan University students, both undergraduate and graduate, whose insights and questions have stretched my thinking and inspired my writing. My deepest gratitude goes out to Chad Edwards—my best friend and partner—for filling my life with love, laughter, and adventure. To our daughters, America and Emerson, I thank you for being living daily proof of the joy communication brings. Finally, thank you Shawn Wahl and Scott Myers for bringing such fun and integrity to this project. Our friendship means the world to me.

Chad Says Thanks to . . .

First, I need to thank my students for their support and guidance. The students in the Communication and Social Robotics Labs are so helpful to both Autumn and myself. My special thanks to Shawn Wahl and Scott Myers, who are two of the best friends I could ask for. It has been a crazy 20 years together! I would like to thank our daughters for their love and ideas: America Edwards for telling us more about growing up in the Communication Age; Emerson Edwards for making me laugh and being the perfect example of a kid using technology and face-to-face communication to converse with the world. Last, I would like to thank my best friend, wife, and partner, Autumn Edwards, for her support, wisdom, courage, and love. You are amazing.

Shawn Says Thanks to . . .

I would first like to thank my friends and coauthors Autumn Edwards, Chad Edwards, and Scott Myers for their continued commitment to this project. The three of you are incredibly special to me and it is difficult for me to express how grateful I am to have you all in my personal and professional life. I would like to thank my colleagues, friends, and students in the School of Communication and the College of Arts and Letters at Missouri State University. I am especially grateful to Gloria Galanes for her leadership, friendship, and constant support. I would like to thank my research assistants Travis Covill and Tucker Robinson for their creativity and contributions to this project. Finally, I want to thank my family and friends for their support and belief in this book and my passion for teaching and studying communication. Thanks to my mother, Evelyn Wahl, who was always there to listen and provide support during the writing process; my brothers, Larkin Wahl and Shannon Wahl, for their confidence and support; my pug dogs, Jake and Bentley, for loving me in every moment; and my dearest friends and collaborators Steve Beebe, Karla Bergen, Dawn O. Braithwaite, Jason Hausback, Terry Lewis, Shad Tyra, Kelly M. Quintanilla, Phyllis Japp, Ron Lee, and Chad McBride.

Scott Says Thanks to . . .

I would like to thank Autumn Edwards, Chad Edwards, and Shawn Wahl for inviting me to be part of such a special project. I don't think any of us knew that a chance meeting on a sidewalk at NCA so many years ago would evolve into working together and developing such a wonderful friendship. I have enjoyed sharing many laughs with the three of you as we completed this second edition. This time, my writing companion was my iPad, which, despite holding over 60 hours of music, repeatedly blared the last 25 songs I had purchased, including many songs recorded by Britney Spears, Lady Gaga, and Sia. I now know the words to all these songs and I can stop composing my own lyrics, for which I'm sure my work colleagues are grateful. And speaking of my work colleagues, I am extremely fortunate to work with such great people. Thank you all for all the support you have provided me over the past few years.

SAGE gratefully acknowledges the contributions of the following reviewers:

Jaime Bochantin, *DePaul University*

Tim Chandler, *Hardin-Simmons University*

Aaron Duncan, *University of Nebraska–Lincoln*

Paul R. Edleman, *Sauk Valley Community College*

William H. Foster, *Naugatuck Valley Community College*

Sara Holmes, *Richland College*

Theodoros Katerinakis, *Drexel University*

Amy K. Lenoce, *Naugatuck Valley Community College*

Aimee E. Miller-Ott, *Illinois State University*

Jennifer Millspaugh, *Richland College*

Faith Mullen, *Liberty University*

Laura Oliver, *The University of Texas at San Antonio*

Chris R. Sawyer, *Texas Christian University*

Deborah Sheffield, *William Paterson University*

Yasmin Shenoy, *University of Hartford*

Christopher Sweerus, *William Paterson University*

Autumn Edwards (PhD, Ohio University) is an associate professor in the School of Communication at Western Michigan University. Her scholarly interests include interpersonal communication, communication and technology, and communication theory. Her research focuses on the influence of interpersonal message design on aspects of community life, relational health, and personal well-being, in both face-to-face and mediated contexts. Autumn directs (jointly with Chad Edwards) the Communication and Social Robotics Labs at Western Michigan University. Recently published work appears in journals such as *The Journal of Computer Mediated Communication, Computers in Human Behavior, Communication Education,* and *Communication Studies,* as well as in several edited books. She is the recipient of an Outstanding Teaching Award and the Kim Giffin Research Award from the University of Kansas, and was designated a Claude Kantner Research Fellow at Ohio University. She is the recipient of a Distinguished Teaching Award from Western Michigan University.

Chad Edwards (PhD, University of Kansas) is an associate professor of communication in the School of Communication at Western Michigan University. Previously, he was a Hartel Fellow at Marietta College. Chad's research interests include communication in the teacher–student relationship, human–robot interaction, and computer-mediated communication. Recent publications include articles in *Communication Education, Communication Research Reports, Computers in Human Behavior, Basic Communication Course Annual,* and other communication and education studies journals. He serves on numerous editorial boards, including that of *Communication Education.* He has held offices at both national and regional communication conferences and is a past president of the Central States Communication Association. In 2009, Chad received the Distinguished Teaching Award from Western Michigan University (the highest teaching award given by WMU). He also has been awarded teaching awards from the College of Arts and Sciences at Western Michigan University, the University of Kansas, and Texas Tech University. Additionally, Chad has received several top paper awards for his research.

Shawn T. Wahl (PhD, University of Nebraska, Lincoln) is a professor of communication and head of the Department of Communication in the School of Communication Studies at Missouri State University (MSU). Prior to his work at MSU, he served as head of the Department of Communication, Mass Media, and Theatre at Angelo State University and as the director of graduate studies at Texas A&M University, Corpus Christi. He is coauthor of *Nonverbal Communication for a Lifetime; Business and Professional Communication: KEYS for Workplace Excellence; Persuasion in Your Life; Communication and Culture in Your Life;* and *Public Relations Principles: Strategies for Professional Success.* Shawn has published articles in *Communication Education, Communication Research Reports, Communication Teacher, Journal of Family Communication,* and *Basic Communication Course Annual.* Shawn was a faculty participant in the National Communication Association Learning Outcomes in Communication project and is the 2016 president of the Central States Communication Association. In addition, Shawn has worked across the nation as a corporate trainer, communication consultant, and leadership coach in a variety of industries. Outside of his professional work, he enjoys spending time with his family and two Chinese pugs (Jake and Bentley).

Scott A. Myers (PhD, Kent State University) is a professor and Peggy Rardin McConnell Chair of Communication Studies in the Department of Communication Studies at West Virginia University (WVU), where he teaches courses in instructional communication, organizational communication, and communication pedagogy. His research interests center primarily on the student–instructor relationship in the college classroom and the adult sibling relationship, with his research appearing in outlets such as *Communication Education, Journal of Family Communication, Communication Research Reports,* and *Communication Quarterly,* among others. At WVU, he was recognized by the Eberly College of Arts and Sciences as a Woodburn Professor (2005–2007) and as an Outstanding Teacher in 2010. He is a former editor of *Communication Teacher,* a former executive director of the Central States Communication Association (CSCA), and a past president of CSCA.

01

COMMUNICATION IN THE 21ST CENTURY

WHAT YOU'LL LEARN   After studying this chapter, you will be able to:

1 Describe the nature and characteristics of the Communication Age.

2 Define communication.

3 Identify the various contexts within which communication occurs.

4 Describe metaphors used to describe communication.

5 Explain the importance of considering the ethics of communication.

Communication is the key to achieving many of the positive outcomes each of us desires. On the collective level, we may hope to build truly global communities, to achieve groundbreaking levels of civic participation, and to make lasting social change. On the more personal level, we may hope to fully and freely express ourselves, to stay connected with a vast network of family and friends, to build and nurture satisfying intimate relationships, to thrive in our careers, and to become our best versions of ourselves.

Communication is also central to overcoming the serious and unprecedented social and personal challenges we face. Some of you may be troubled by uncaring corporations, the economic downturn, cynical news media, or leaders who divide us and prevent us from getting things done. You may be concerned about environmental issues or social inequality. You may worry about cultural and religious extremism and fear what may happen if we are unable to work through our differences. You may be anxious about living up to expectations and finding true love. And, in our rapidly changing high-tech social landscape, you may wonder how you will balance the multiple and sometimes competing demands of everyday life: to find work that is both meaningful and profitable, to integrate your social life and your work life, to successfully prioritize how you spend your time and energy, and all the while to live up to your potential and make a difference. Whether you worry about a few of these issues or all of them, an understanding of communication equips you with the power to create the best possible outcomes.

Luckily, we do not face the future alone or unarmed. A rich past accompanies us on our journey. Centuries' worth of wisdom and knowledge are at our fingertips. For over 2,000 years, communication has been the subject of serious study.

Philosophers and scientists have grappled with fundamental communication issues that are as relevant today as they were in the past. What is the nature of communication? What can communication accomplish? What characterizes communication as ethical, moral, and good? What makes communication successful for attaining goals? What degrades communication and robs it of its potential? In addition, communication has long played a starring role in understandings of identity, relationships, and community formation.

Many of the communication issues we face today are strikingly similar to those faced by generations long past. For instance, the dramatic increase in the use of digital communication technology—including text messaging, instant messaging, social networking, e-mailing, and blogging—is a cause of concern for many people. They worry that we may be paying a price for all this convenience, speed, and access in terms of losing the intimacy of face-to-face encounters, privacy, and control over our information. It might surprise you to learn that the ancient Greeks had similar concerns about the first communication technology: writing! The point is that the history of communication study is useful precisely because it teaches us about current issues. Therefore, we approach the history of communication as a living conversation that awaits our perspectives and voices, not as a collection of dead facts and lifeless laws. Our challenge is to align the fundamentals of communication with the present moment and, in the process, to shed some new light on both. The following section paints a fuller picture of our present moment, by describing some seismic shifts in contemporary life.

THE COMMUNICATION AGE

Connection is everything, and the way we connect is changing. The Communication Age is an age in which communication, technology, and media converge and deeply permeate daily life. Convergence refers to the ways in which the many forms of technologically mediated and face-to-face communication overlap and intersect in our daily lives. For example, you continue a conversation with a friend in person that you began on Facebook about the TV shows *Orange Is the New Black* or *Grey's Anatomy,* which you both streamed online. Your friend refers you to a good blog that poses a theory about the show's next episode, which prompts you to text her with your reaction to the post. Face-to-face communication and mediated communication were once treated as distinct and separate modes of interaction. Today, they are intimately interconnected. Perhaps no activity is considered as heavily face to face as falling in love. Yet more than one third of recently married couples in the United States met online (Cacioppo, Cacioppo, Gonzaga, Ogburn, & VanderWeele, 2013).

Online activity is beginning to replace some traditional forms of meeting a mate, such as introductions through friends, family, or religious organizations, and this is especially true for same-sex couples (Rosenfeld & Thomas, 2011).

This unprecedented level of convergence affects not only what we do, but also what we are. For the first time in history, people have a bodily existence as well as a digital existence. We maintain a presence in both physical and virtual space. Think about it. Here you are, in the flesh, holding this book and reading its pages. You are physically present for anyone who happens to be near you. But your boundaries and your effects on the world extend far beyond the physical space you occupy. Digitally, you stretch across the

Look familiar? How does this interaction demonstrate communication convergence?

vastness of space and time. The fact that you are reading right now does not stop your friends, family, and acquaintances from sending you an e-mail or posting on your social media pages in virtual space. And, at this very moment, any number of people may be reading your latest posts, liking your images on Instagram, swiping your profile on Tinder, or viewing your résumé through LinkedIn.

One of the main effects of communication convergence is a massive increase in the number and types of opportunities to connect with others. Obviously, the positive potential of convergence is tremendous. On the other hand, convergence also introduces new challenges. As we multitask to take full advantage of technology, media, and communication, we may feel easily distracted, overcommitted, or spread too thin. Simply put, dividing our attention scatters our focus. As a case in point, reflect on how you felt when reading the previous paragraph. If you are like us, the mere mention of online activities or mobile applications is enough to cause momentary distraction. We are willing to bet that quite a few of you checked social networking sites or glanced at your phones for notifications. Even more of you let your minds temporarily drift to consider what you might be missing while you read this chapter.

The second characteristic of the Communication Age is that communication, technology, and media deeply permeate daily life. To permeate daily life means to saturate or infuse it. Many of you are digital natives, or people for whom digital technologies such as computers, cell phones, video games, and digital cameras already existed when they were born (Prensky, 2001). If so, you grew up in a permeated world. Those of you who are a bit older are sometimes called digital immigrants, a term used to refer to people who have adopted and learned digital technologies later in life. Digital immigrants have seen firsthand how communication technologies have become more and more prevalent in everyday life. Regardless of who we are, what we do, or where we go, we are never far from the presence of technology, media, and communication (see "Career Frontier: Life in the Communication Age").

According to the Pew Research Center, 83% of teenagers and young adults sleep with their cell phones. The average American teenager sends over 60 texts per day (Lenhart, 2012).

▶ **COMMUNICATION IN ACTION 1.2**

WATCH: Convergence and Distraction

Communication technology gets in the way as this couple attempts to have a face-to-face conversation. What could they do differently to connect and engage one another more effectively?

CAREER FRONTIER: LIFE IN THE COMMUNICATION AGE

FOR A BRIEF and entertaining illustration of the ways in which communication, media, and technology converge and deeply permeate daily life to influence business and careers, watch the YouTube video "Did You Know 6.0: Change to Thrive." As you will see, communication technologies and behaviors are dramatically reshaping global economies and individual prospects.

1. Were you surprised by the information presented?

2. What facts or statistics did you find most striking?

3. After watching the video, what does your picture of the future look like?

Sixty-three percent of all teens say they exchange text messages every day with people in their lives, which far surpasses the frequency with which they turn to other forms of *daily* communication, including face-to-face socializing outside of school (35%) (Lenhart, 2012).

This trend is only increasing. By 2020, mobile devices are predicted to be the primary Internet connection tools for most of the world. Furthermore, futurists who are field experts at tracking current trends predict that we will quickly see even more radical levels of communication convergence and permeation. We might be the first generation to inhabit both the physical universe and a metaverse (a separate but complementary virtual world intimately interconnected with the real world).

Virtual worlds and augmented realities (a blend of physical and virtual realities) are already popular formats for games and other forms of entertainment. In the near future, our lifestyles may involve a seamless transition from virtual reality, artificial reality, and what we call "real life." As you read each chapter in this book, you will encounter a feature titled "Communication Unplugged," which discusses situations in which the older, more traditional mode of communicating face to face, through the basic media of body and voice, may be preferable to using newer, computer-mediated forms of communication. Face-to-face communication is a powerful but potentially underutilized form of relating with others.

The permeation of communication, technology, and media into everyday life has advantages and disadvantages. Being able to instantly access information and stay in touch with people throughout your daily activities is convenient and often efficient. However, the ability to access information and people on demand has introduced new social problems. Families may worry about how "texting at the table" affects the quality of mealtimes. Lovers may worry about the hurtfulness of getting "dumped by text." Employers may worry that the time employees spend on social networking sites harms productivity. And, in extreme cases, the permeation of communication

Corbis

Communication increasingly involves technologically augmented realities.

technologies into everyday life poses a public safety hazard. Cell phone dialing and text messaging while driving are responsible for a number of traffic accidents, injuries, and fatalities (Distraction.gov, 2015). In 2013, some 3,154 people were killed and an estimated 424,000 injured on U.S. roadways by crashes involving driver distraction (Distraction.gov, 2015). Fortunately, following multimedia awareness campaigns led by the U.S. Department of Transportation and several tough new laws, the number of distraction-related fatalities has decreased significantly since 2009. In this case, communication technologies and new media are being used to address a problem created by those same technologies.

Distracted driving is a problem both caused and solved by communication technology.

In this textbook, we treat face-to-face communication and computer-mediated communication as integrated counterparts of our daily lives. That is to say, we try not to favor one over the other, and we recognize that they are often used in tandem. Both have their advantages and disadvantages, depending on the situation. What is most important is to think critically about what is gained and what is lost when we choose to engage in face-to-face communication, computer-mediated communication, or some combination of the two. The advantages, disadvantages, and complexities of each form of communication are addressed throughout the textbook. At the conclusion of each subsequent chapter, we address the impact of convergence on the topic at hand. At this point, we hope you have gathered that this is an exciting time to study communication. The following section discusses some of the many benefits an understanding of communication may bring.

"Five seconds is the average time your eyes are off the road while texting. When traveling at 55mph, that's enough time to cover the length of a football field blindfolded."

U.S. Department of Transportation, Federal Motor Carrier Safety Administration, 2009

BENEFITS OF STUDYING COMMUNICATION

There are many benefits to studying communication. An understanding of communication helps you reach your personal potential and make a positive impact on your relationships, organizations, communities, and governments.

- Good communication abilities are associated with physical, emotional, and psychological health and well-being.

- Strong speaking and listening skills are associated with greater health literacy (Martin et al., 2011).

- The ability to communicate well is the key to fulfilling your need for a satisfying identity (Duran & Kelly, 1988; Duran & Wheeless, 1982; Hecht, 1993).

Communication unplugged

TO REFRESH YOUR MIND, TAKE A MEDIA FAST

iStock

How much time do you spend each day interacting with information on a screen? Perhaps you use the alarm clock on your phone, which makes it natural to browse your networks and check for messages when you first wake up. By the time you even get started with your day's activities, you may already have watched videos, sent and received texts, checked your e-mail, liked and commented online, and downloaded documents. At school or work, you likely spend considerable amounts of time behind a computer. Meanwhile, you keep your phone nearby should boredom or an urge to connect strike. Maybe, after getting home, you watch a movie or your favorite show.

In the same way that it is sometimes advisable to take a momentary break, or "fast," from some of our foods, beverages, and habits, a media fast may be good for your system. Spending a set period of time unplugged can clarify for you the advantages and disadvantages of your media practices. Life without electronic devices momentarily separates you from constant distraction, online advertisements, and artificial blue light. You'll have more time to do other things, like physical activity, face-to-face interaction, and even solitude. You'll also have the opportunity to reflect critically on how life in the Communication Age differs from older modes of living and connecting and engaging with the world.

WHAT TO DO NEXT

To make the most of your time unplugged, try to:

- Decide how long your fast will last (10 days, a week, a few days, a single day?) and what electronic devices or applications you will avoid (social media, entertainment media, Internet, all communication technology?). It may be wise to make voice calls an exception in case of true emergencies or the coordination of essential daily tasks.

- Let important members of your networks know you are taking a break from media, and for how long. The announcement will prevent worry or adjust their expectations for your availability.

- Keep a record of your experience. When was being unplugged the hardest for you? What did you miss most, and why? What did you gain? What surprised you? How has your thinking about media and technology use changed? Will you make any adjustments to your normal living routine as a result of the media fast?

- According to employers, communication skills are the most valuable abilities employees can possess (Job Outlook, 2015).

- **Communication is a primary influence on social and personal relationships.** Communication is what creates, maintains, transforms, and ends friendships, romances, and family relationships (Baxter, 2004).

- **An understanding of communication promotes media literacy, or the ability to access, evaluate critically, and produce communication and information in a variety of forms and means** (Potter & Byrne, 2007).

- **Communication skills are critical to building healthy and vibrant communities** (Edwards & Shepherd, 2007).

- **Communication is the foundation of democratic citizen-ship** (Dewey, 1916/1944).
- **Communication drives social change and reform.**

Because communication is a valuable professional skill, there are a number of promising career paths for those who are trained in the discipline of communication. But even if you don't have a career in the communication field, your own professional development will be strengthened with an understanding of the fundamentals of communication theory and practice. In each chapter, the feature "Career Frontier" includes skills-oriented, for-ward-looking, practical advice on using communication skills in the workplaces of today and tomorrow.

Commmunication affects self-concept and the way others see you.

WHAT IS COMMUNICATION?

Communication Defined

Communication is the collaborative process of using messages to create and participate in social reality. The most important aspects of our lives—our individual identities, relationships, organizations, communities, cultures, and ideas—are accomplished through communication. Each of these aspects is a part of social reality, or the set of social judgments members of a group agree upon. Social realities emerge through social interaction. Therefore, communication enables us to actualize possibility and achieve change and growth, both for ourselves and for our communities.

Communication Is a Process

Communication is a dynamic, ongoing process. Unlike a thing, which is static, a process unfolds over time. As individuals exchange and interpret messages, their communication develops a particular history. The messages used in the past influence the nature and the interpretation of the messages used in the present and the future.

Communication Is Collaborative

The word *communication* comes from the Latin prefix *co-* (with, or together) and root word *munia* (sharing, giving, servicing). Therefore, communication requires the involvement of others. Just like many other things that you cannot do without the cooperation of others, such as sing a duet, be in a marriage, or count as a basketball team, you cannot communicate by yourself. Communication is a collective activity in which people work jointly to create and share meaning. Although we sometimes say "I communicated" or "You communicated," in reality, communication is not something that an I or a You can do alone. Communication must be accomplished by a We.

Communication shapes and creates social reality.

Communication Involves Messages

Messages rely on a common system of symbols, signs, and gestures to carry information and to generate shared meanings between participants. Individuals give unique contributions to communication interactions in the form of the verbal and/or nonverbal messages they use.

Communication Is Creative

It sometimes appears that the process of communication merely conveys information about the world "as it is," or that the messages we use simply describe a reality that already exists. In actuality, communication shapes and creates new social realities for ourselves and for others. Anyone who has witnessed the power of a label such as *bully, loser,* or *genius* to alter perceptions and reinforce behaviors has seen firsthand the ways in which communication creates reality.

Communication Is Participatory

In addition to playing a role in the creation of social reality, communication allows us to participate, or take part, in social reality. When people communicate, they rely on shared understandings to accomplish objectives. Communication allows us to entertain, persuade, inform, comfort, regulate, and support one another.

The fact that communication involves both creation and participation demonstrates communication is fundamentally dual-natured. Communication makes and does. The ancient Greeks referred to the making and doing functions of communication as *poiesis* and *praxis*. Historically, most scholars and everyday people have paid more attention to communication praxis, or how communication can be used as an instrument to accomplish things. Recently, however, the creative (poiesis) aspect of communication has received greater appreciation. As we discuss in the communication metaphors section later in this chapter, understanding how communication brings new realities into existence has major implications for how to communicate and how to judge the goodness of communication. But, before we get to that, let's discuss the various contexts in which communication may occur.

CONTEXTS OF COMMUNICATION

Over the years, communication has been studied in a number of contexts, or circumstances forming different interaction settings. Each context or situation has unique characteristics or features that influence how messages are used and how meanings are constructed. Traditionally, the distinctions among communication contexts were based on the number of people involved and whether the interaction was face to face or mediated through a technology such as print, electronic broadcasting, or computers. Face-to-face communication refers to situations in which physically or bodily copresent participants speak directly to one another during the interaction. Mediated communication, on the other hand, refers to communication or messages that are transmitted through some type of medium. Communication media include writing, the telephone, e-mail, text messaging, and many other forms of technological and computer-mediated interaction, which also may encompass interactions with and through social robots. In the Communication Age, the boundaries between contexts are increasingly blurry and overlapping. Communication may, and often does, involve an intersection or a blend of more than one context. Each context includes the possibility for face-to-face communication, mediated communication, or some combination of the two. Some maintain, in fact, that all communication is mediated (Peters, 1999). Even face-to-face communication is mediated through the human body, with its intricate organic technologies of voice, hearing, gesture, and sight. The words whispered between friends must still travel gaps in time and space, as well as interpretation. We further rely on the body to mediate our experiences with other communication technologies. In this way the body is "the medium through and with which all other media intersect and interact" (Killmeier, 2009, p. 33). The following paragraphs discuss the interpersonal, small group, public, mass communication, and masspersonal contexts.

Interpersonal Communication

Interpersonal communication refers to communication with or between persons. The key feature of interpersonal communication is that it occurs between people who approach one another as individuals in a relationship, whether it is a personal/intimate relationship or an impersonal/public relationship. When we express our love for a romantic partner, resolve a conflict with a family member, respond to a friend's Facebook status, negotiate the price of a car with a salesperson, order a drink from a bartender, chat about the weather with a neighbor, or discuss an upcoming test with classmates, we are engaging in interpersonal communication. In all of these examples, the communication is between individuals who share a relationship of some sort. The communication that occurs will further influence and shape those relationships. Although interpersonal communication occurs between any two people who share a relationship, most interpersonal communication scholars focus on our closest relationships, such as those between friends, family, and romantic partners. Despite the fact that interpersonal communication is often described as a distinct context, it is useful to understand that there is an interpersonal dimension to all communication (Miller, 1978; Shepherd, 2001). At its heart, communication always occurs between persons, whether they are part of a group, a public, or a mass media event. Chapter 7, "Interpersonal Communication," is devoted to a deeper look at the communication between people in personal relationships.

Communication allows us to participate in social reality.

Thinkstock

Small Group Communication

Small group communication refers to the communication among the members of a small group of people working together to achieve a common goal or purpose. Families, organizations, classrooms, and athletic teams are common settings for small group communication. A pair or dyad has only two members, whereas a group must have at least three. Yet the group must be small enough that each person present makes an impression on the others who are present (Bales, 1950, p. 33). Currently, the nature of small group communication is changing due to new technologies like Internet videoconferencing. Small groups no longer have to meet in a face-to-face setting or be made up of members who are geographically close to one another. These changes in the characteristics of a small group are discussed in greater depth in Chapter 8, "Small Group and Team Communication."

Public Communication

Public communication refers to situations in which a person delivers a message to an audience. Rather than treating the audience as a collection of separate people, the speaker addresses the audience as a public, or a body unified by some common interest. In fact, one of the major jobs of a public speaker is to create a sense of unity and solidarity in a large and diverse group of people. The U.S. president's State of the Union address to Congress, a CEO's speech to stockholders, a student's oral presentation to classmates, a professor's lecture to a crowded hall, and a community activist's speech about a local issue are all forms of public communication, or public speaking. Public communication is characteristically formal, structured, and purpose-driven. It is less reciprocal than many other contexts of communication because the audience has limited opportunities for providing feedback.

However, advances in communication technology are expanding the opportunities for audience participation through online comments, listener rating systems, audience response systems (like classroom "clickers"), and personal blogs. Today's speakers can utilize the powers of communication technologies to share their messages with wider audiences through video sharing in sites like YouTube or Vimeo. Chapters 11 through 16 focus on how to effectively prepare and deliver public presentations in the Communication Age. In those chapters, we discuss ways in which you can use technology to reach a wider audience and how to adapt your message to these forms of technology.

Mass Communication

Mass communication refers to messages transmitted by electronic and print media to large audiences that are distant and undifferentiated. In other words, these audiences are treated as a mass. TV shows, newspapers, books, webpages, magazines, recorded music, and web videos are all forms of mass communication. Most mass communication involves little interaction between the producer of the message and the audience. For this reason, mass communication has historically been described as one-way in orientation. However, the emergence of the Internet has allowed mass communication to become far more interactive. Audiences now have the opportunity to provide near-instantaneous feedback through user comments, ratings, and popularity indexes, as well as through open-source programming that allows users to alter or expand existing mass communication messages. For example, Wikipedia.org is an online reference source maintained by millions of largely anonymous writers.

Furthermore, because mass communication is directed to large and diverse audiences, it tends to be less personal than other contexts of communication. To help overcome this limitation, producers of mass communication often focus on the demographics of the audience, or do niche marketing, to help personalize the message. For example, the USA Network's *WWE Raw* is aimed at the demographic group of males aged 18 years and older. *Cosmopolitan* magazine, on the other hand, focuses on appealing to females over age 18 but younger than 30. Advertisers then gain access to their target demographics by purchasing space on programs or pages geared toward their desired consumers.

The Internet has opened opportunities for greater message personalization in mass communication. One of the main ways websites try to attract and keep an audience is through offering content customization. For instance, Zite is a popular application of the Daily Me concept, which is when users personalize their news feeds based on their interests. Likewise, Pandora and Spotify allow you to create a personalized radio station that plays only the music and artists you like. Another way websites seek to gain an audience through personalization is by offering preference information and recommendations. Whether you are informed of the "most e-mailed" news article, the "most viewed" YouTube video, the "most downloaded" iTunes single, or simply that people who bought Egyptian cotton sheets also bought hypoallergenic pillow cases, you are witnessing the producers of mass communication attempting to personalize their messages to you. Meanwhile, complex computer data-mining operations are using all of your online activities—from site visits, to purchase histories, to group memberships—to compile highly specific profiles of you that advertisers can use to customize, or narrowcast, their advertisements to you. In fact, digital media are blurring many of the old lines between mass communication and interpersonal communication.

Masspersonal Communication

Masspersonal communication occurs at the crossroads of interpersonal communication and mass communication. In other words, masspersonal communication happens when a person uses a mass communication context for interpersonal communication or when a person uses an interpersonal communication context for mass communication (O'Sullivan, 1999, 2005). Social

How are the mass media you encounter targeted to your demographic?

networking posts are a perfect example of using a mass communication context for interpersonal communication. Primarily, we use status updates and posts to others' timelines for building and maintaining relationships. Our messages may convey affection, refer to a shared experience, or comment on the status of the relationship itself. Such messages are personal, but they are also public, being broadcast to all our friends and networks.

Likewise, traditionally interpersonal communication channels are sometimes used for mass communication. Prime examples include computer-generated telephone calls, mass text messages, and e-mail spam. In each of these cases, a medium that was once used primarily for interpersonal communication (phone, messaging service, e-mail account) carries mass messages that are characteristically one-way and impersonal. Such messages can be experienced as irritating (answering the phone only to discover a robotic voice trying to sell you insurance) or even offensive (receiving another e-mail about "male enhancement"). Yet not every use of interpersonal communication contexts for mass communication is unwelcome. Many political supporters of then-candidate Barack Obama, for instance, welcomed his campaign's groundbreaking use of text messaging to announce rally locations and campaign decisions. Obama was the first presidential nominee to unveil his vice-presidential choice by text message and e-mail.

Masspersonal communication seems to increase every year. As more people rely on mobile communication devices for connecting and engaging with others, we are likely to see even more blurring of the traditional contexts of communication.

In Chapter 10, "Communication and New Media," we will further explore mass media messages. But, at this point, let's turn our attention to gaining a deeper understanding of the process of communication by exploring the metaphors through which communication has been explained over the years.

COMMUNICATION METAPHORS

One of the best ways to understand any process is to use a metaphor. This is especially true when you explore a process as complex and important as communication. Metaphors work by comparing one thing to a different, usually more familiar, thing. The power of a metaphor lies in its potential to stimulate new ways of perceiving and talking about things. According to Mary Catherine Bateson (1994), "our species thinks in metaphors and learns through stories" (p. 11). Al Gore knew this in 1994 when he referred to the Internet as "the information superhighway," and William Shakespeare knew this when he said "all the world's a stage." Both got people thinking by harnessing the creative power of a metaphor.

Many communication metaphors have been developed over the years. Because metaphors tend to reflect the assumptions and perspectives of the points in history when they were created, they

How does this interaction blend communication contexts?

have evolved through time. You will notice the metaphors of communication gradually increase in complexity. You will also notice the progression of the metaphors represents a gradual awakening to the power and possibilities of communication. Each model expands on the one that came before it by acknowledging an increase in the potential of what communication is and what it can be used to do.

In this section, four metaphors of communication are presented in the order in which they were developed.

Communication as Transmission

One of the earliest models of communication was based on the workings of the telephone and radio (Shannon & Weaver, 1949). In this model, communication involves a linear, one-way transfer of information (see Figure 1.1). A source sends a message through a channel or a medium to a receiver in an environment of noise that serves as interference with effective transmission of a message.

For example, suppose a friend is waiting for you at a restaurant and you need to let her know that you are running a few minutes late. You (the source) might transmit your message ("15 minutes!") through a channel (a text message on your mobile device) to your friend (the receiver) in an environment of noise (perhaps a poor wireless signal and a low battery).

Viewing communication as transmission allows us to see how communication can relay information from one person to another through a channel. In addition, by including noise as a factor, this metaphor draws our attention to the things that may get in the way of our attempts to communicate. However, the transmission metaphor also has serious disadvantages. The sender is portrayed as active, but the receiver is passive. Most people would agree that communication is a two-way street. But, in the preceding example, your friend has a very limited role in the process. She is like

FIGURE 1.1
TRANSMISSION MODEL OF COMMUNICATION

SOURCE
SENDER

MESSAGE CHANNEL
NOISE

TARGET
RECEIVERS

the target in a game of darts. You (the source) throw a carefully aimed dart (message) at a target (receiver), whose only job is to let the message hit and try to extract your meaning from it. The interaction metaphor was created to address this flaw.

Communication as Interaction

The interaction metaphor of communication (Schramm, 1954) describes communication as a two-way process of reciprocal action. It takes the basic elements of the transmission metaphor and adds two important components: feedback and fields of experience (see Figure 1.2). Feedback refers to a receiver's response to a sender's message. Because of feedback, senders are able to adapt their messages in real time to increase the chances of communication success. In addition, because each sender and receiver is a unique person, this model includes fields of experience, which refer to the attitudes, perceptions, and backgrounds each of us brings to communication.

An understanding of fields of experience allows senders to tailor their messages to receivers. So, as opposed to a game of darts, communication as interaction is more like a game of ping-pong. Player 1 (the sender) serves the ball (the message) to Player 2 (the receiver), who adjusts their swing to return the ball to the sender (feedback). The major advantage of this metaphor is that it views communication as an adaptive and interactional process. However, like the transmission model before it, the interaction model still treats senders and receivers as fundamentally separate and disconnected.

Communication as Transaction

The transaction metaphor of communication was introduced to acknowledge that people are connected through communication, and that they accomplish something

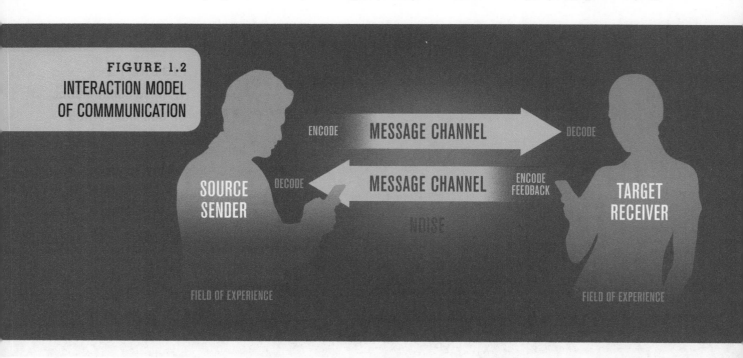

FIGURE 1.2
INTERACTION MODEL
OF COMMMUNICATION

ENCODE   MESSAGE CHANNEL   DECODE

SOURCE SENDER   DECODE   MESSAGE CHANNEL   ENCODE FEEDBACK   TARGET RECEIVER

NOISE

FIELD OF EXPERIENCE   FIELD OF EXPERIENCE

in communication beyond (*trans-*) merely relaying messages back and forth (see Figure 1.3). The transaction metaphor invites us to do away with the notion of a separate sender and a separate receiver. Instead, participants are simultaneous sender–receivers linked in relationship to one another. In communication, we not only exchange messages but also impact the people involved. Participants and their relationships emerge changed from communication, in ways large and small.

One of the reasons why communication impacts its participants is that every message has two dimensions: content and relationship (Watzlavick, Beavin, & Jackson, 1967). The content of a message refers to its surface-level meaning, or what is said. The relationship dimension of a message refers to how a message is said, which always conveys something about the relationship between participants. Suppose you ask a dinner guest to "please pass the pepper." The content dimension of your message is straightforward, a simple request for assistance in seasoning your food. But your message also carries a relational dimension. Depending on the way you say "please pass the pepper," you may convey anything from irritation that the person did not anticipate your needs sooner, to playful affection, to the careful politeness reserved for someone you hope to impress. The relational dimension of a message not only says something about who people are to each other at that moment; it also shapes their future relationship.

Communication as Social Construction

The social construction metaphor of communication further expands upon the idea that communication influences communicators (see Figure 1.4). Specifically, the social construction model stresses the ways communication shapes and creates the larger social realities in which we operate (Berger & Luckmann, 1967; Craig,

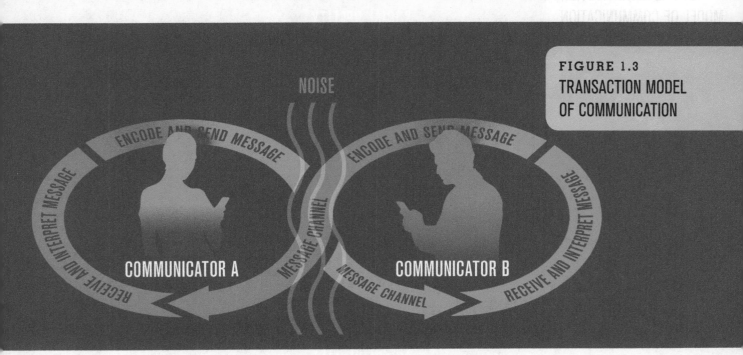

FIGURE 1.3
TRANSACTION MODEL OF COMMUNICATION

NOISE

ENCODE AND SEND MESSAGE

RECEIVE AND INTERPRET MESSAGE

MESSAGE CHANNEL

COMMUNICATOR A

ENCODE AND SEND MESSAGE

MESSAGE CHANNEL

COMMUNICATOR B

RECEIVE AND INTERPRET MESSAGE

1999). This metaphor expands the role of communicators beyond sender–receivers to joint creators of our larger shared social worlds. Participants work together, knowingly or unknowingly, to shape what counts as factual, acceptable, good, truthful, real, and possible. Messages are more than pieces of information or even instruments for negotiating shared meaning between a sender and a receiver; messages are the building blocks of social reality and literally talk our social reality into being. The social construction model assumes that we become who we are in relation to others through communication, and that the social world becomes what it is chiefly through the process of communication.

Labeling practices are a prime example of how communication creates social reality. For example, research demonstrates that labeling children as "academically gifted" even when they have average abilities has dramatic effects. Teachers and parents treat such children differently; the children think of themselves differently; and, most important, the children actually achieve better academic results (Rosenthal & Jacobson, 1992). One can only imagine how far the effects of a single word, like *gifted,* may ripple through the lives of the children and the relationships and communities of which they are a part. According to the social construction metaphor, all communication makes and influences the social landscape. Each interaction has the potential to build and transform identities, relationships, institutions, and ideas.

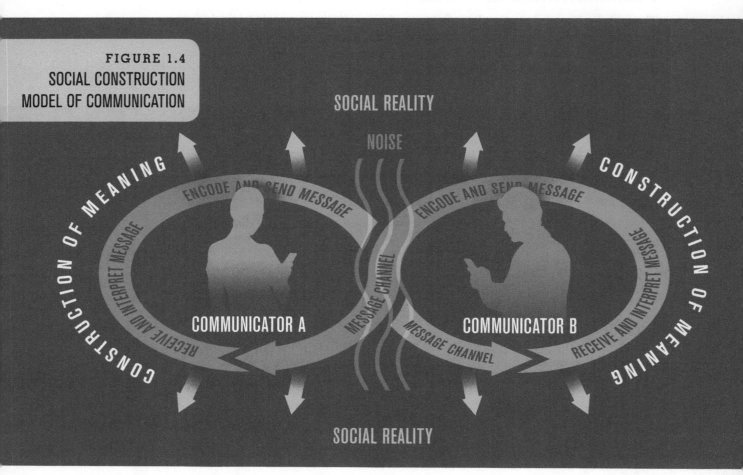

FIGURE 1.4
SOCIAL CONSTRUCTION MODEL OF COMMUNICATION

Metaphors Matter

What should be clear from the preceding discussion of communication metaphors is that each new metaphor builds upon the strengths of the previous metaphor in order to go one step further. Each new metaphor recognizes communication to be more powerful than the one that came before. Over the years, ideas about communication have gradually evolved. First, communication was described as the mere transfer of information. Then, understandings of communication were expanded to appreciate the receiver's role in the process. Next, ideas about communication were broadened to understand its impact on participants in a communication transaction. Finally, descriptions of communication were enlarged to acknowledge its role in the creation of social reality. Thus, the evolution of the metaphors represents an unfolding of communication potential.

How did Dr. Martin Luther King Jr. change social reality with his "I Have a Dream" speech?

The metaphor of communication you adopt can make a real difference in your life. Some people view communication as a means of simply getting information from one person to another—as in the transmission metaphor. Others view communication as a cooperative process that involves understanding the context and being appropriate (the transactional metaphor). Still others view communication as a process of creating social realities and identities (the social construction metaphor). It is important to note that no one metaphor is the final word on the communication process, but each may be more or less useful for describing certain communication episodes or contexts. For instance, the transmission metaphor may be a useful guide for drafting an informational corporate e-mail but not for engaging in family conflict, which could require greater attention to the linkages between communicators and the social realities surrounding their situation. Research demonstrates that people who understand that communication may be used in all three of these ways, and who develop the ability to do so, have an advantage. People who recognize that communication can be used to convey information, but can also be used to accomplish goals and to shape social reality, have greater communication competence (O'Keefe, 1988).

COMMUNICATION COMPETENCE

Communication competence refers to the ability to communicate in a personally effective yet socially appropriate manner. In other words, being a competent communicator requires using messages that strike a delicate balance between pursuing one's own goals and meeting the needs and expectations of others. A major objective of this textbook is to provide you with the information and tools you need to strengthen your communication competence in a host of everyday situations. In addition to chapter content that focuses on how to be a competent communicator in a variety of circumstances, each chapter includes features labeled "Communication How-To." These boxes contain practical guidance for achieving communication goals in contexts ranging from interpersonal relationships, to small group encounters, to workplace interactions, to

A competent communicator uses messages effectively and appropriately.

public presentations. You can also use the "Assess Your Communication" features in each chapter to size up your communication strengths and identify areas for personal growth and improvement. In addition to striving for competence in our communication, it is important to consider whether our communication is ethical. The next section defines and discusses the topic of communication ethics.

COMMUNICATION ETHICS

Ethics is a code of conduct based on respect for yourself, others, and your surroundings. Simply, ethics relates to right and wrong conduct. The topic of being an ethical communicator has received a good deal of attention because ethical communication enhances the well-being of individuals and society. As communicators, we must concern ourselves with the ethical responsibilities of living in a democratic society. We must also consider communication ethics in the workplace, the family, the classroom, and the professions, including the legal, medical, and public relations fields. Our increasingly technological, global, and multicultural society requires us to be ever more sensitive to the impact of the words we choose, the images we portray, and the stereotypes we hold.

So, what counts as ethical communication? How do we determine whether or not our communication conduct respects self, others, and surroundings? Communication philosopher and ethicist Jürgen Habermas (1979) maintained that ethical communication is that which promotes autonomy and responsibility. Autonomy refers to individuals' rights to make choices and self-determine, whereas responsibility refers to being accountable for the welfare of others and the consequences of one's actions. Habermas warned of the potential dangers of communication that strips people of free will. Practices like manipulation, propaganda, or extreme censorship raise ethical questions because of their tendency to rob people of the chance to make informed decisions and control their own destinies. Yet Habermas insisted that in the process of exercising our freedoms, we take responsibility for ourselves, and fulfill our shared responsibilities to one another and our communities. As Voltaire said, and Ben Parker conveyed to Spider-Man, "With great power comes great responsibility."

"With great power comes great responsibility."

Voltaire

There is wisdom in applying this sentiment to the process of communication because our messages and interactions are powerful elements in the construction of social reality. In each chapter, we include an "Ethical Connection." These brief case studies highlight real-life communication dilemmas and invite ethical analysis.

Evaluating Ethical Communication

As metaphors of communication have evolved, so have standards for ethical communication. In other words, evaluating the ethics of an interaction often depends on an understanding of how communication is viewed and what it is being used to accomplish. In the transmission metaphor of communication, where a sender conveys a message to a receiver, being ethical is about the personal character of the sender and the factual integrity of the message. To be ethical when judged according to this model, a message must be honest. It must truthfully represent the real state of affairs.

In the interaction metaphor, which acknowledges the process of feedback and the fact that each person has a unique field of experience, ethical communication requires extending the opportunity for feedback and being responsive to it. The transaction metaphor proposes that we are connected to one another through communication and that our communication influences each of us. Therefore, ethical communication in this model requires that we are careful of the impacts our messages may have on the people involved and the relationship between them.

With great power comes great responsibility. Ethical communication involves promoting freedom and care for others.

Finally, the social construction metaphor maintains that communication creates our social realities. Viewing communication as a process of social construction requires an appreciation of both agency and constraint. Agency refers to the power and freedom to use communication to create the social realities we desire. But we must also recognize that the social realities we create can be cages. Our social realities constrain, or limit, how we perceive others, frame events, and determine what is possible or not. Imagine you are registering for college courses. This activity involves a good deal of agency. You have a lot of freedom to pick the classes that are interesting to you, count toward your degree program, or allow you to sleep in a few days of the week. On the other hand, the schedule you create involves constraint. The classes you choose are limited by what's offered at the time, which sections still have seats available, and whether you meet the prerequisites. You'll face later constraints when the schedule you built limits your social reality. You may have to turn down a vacation, a social invitation, or a job because you have to go to class. The same is true of social construction through communication. The social realities you build through communication always involve both agency and constraint.

Because we live in realities created by our communication, ethical communication requires careful consideration of the consequences of our words. Our tools for communicating are very useful, but also very sharp. Communication theorist Eric Rothenbuhler (2006) puts it best: "What a nicer world it would be if we always stopped and thought before we spoke 'I will create a new reality, do I want to live in it?'" (p. 19). This chapter's "Ethical Connection" presents the National Communication Association's Credo for Ethical Communication.

CONNECTING AND ENGAGING IN COMMUNICATION

The process of communication is all about connecting and engaging. Connecting refers to the power of communication to link and relate us to people, groups, communities, social institutions, and cultures. Modern technology and mobility seem to make connecting with others easier than ever. Social networking sites link

NATIONAL COMMUNICATION ASSOCIATION'S CREDO FOR ETHICAL COMMUNICATION

Questions of right and wrong arise whenever people communicate. Ethical communication is fundamental to responsible thinking, decision making, and the development of relationships and communities within and across contexts, cultures, channels, and media. Moreover, ethical communication enhances human worth and dignity by fostering truthfulness, fairness, responsibility, personal integrity, and respect for self and others. We believe that unethical communication threatens the quality of all communication and consequently the well-being of individuals and the society in which we live. Therefore we, the members of the National Communication Association, endorse and are committed to practicing the following principles of ethical communication:

- We advocate truthfulness, accuracy, honesty, and reason as essential to the integrity of communication.

- We endorse freedom of expression, diversity of perspective, and tolerance of dissent to achieve the informed and responsible decision making fundamental to a civil society.

- We strive to understand and respect other communicators before evaluating and responding to their messages.

- We promote access to communication resources and opportunities as necessary to fulfill human potential and contribute to the well-being of families, communities, and society.

- We promote communication climates of caring and mutual understanding that respect the unique needs and characteristics of individual communicators.

- We condemn communication that degrades individuals and humanity through distortion, intimidation, coercion, and violence, and through the expression of intolerance and hatred.

- We are committed to the courageous expression of personal convictions in pursuit of fairness and justice.

- We advocate sharing information, opinions, and feelings when facing significant choices while also respecting privacy and confidentiality.

- We accept responsibility for the short- and long-term consequences for our own communication and expect the same of others.

(Approved by the NCA Legislative Council in 1999)

Source: National Communication Association, http://www.natcom.org/ethicalcredo

us effortlessly with an extended network of family, friends, and acquaintances. Furthermore, they suggest new contacts to us daily. Mobile phones keep our contacts available at the touch of a button. Day or night, we can reach and be reached by virtually anyone we desire. News and information from around the world arrive with a few keystrokes or touches on a pad. Such connections are at the heart of communication as a process of creating and participating in social reality. We communicate in a dynamic and intricate system of personal and social relationships, and each of us is linked to all others by fewer degrees of separation than ever before. Yet connecting alone is not enough to fully realize the potential of communication in transforming our identities, relationships, communities, and social realities.

Communication also requires engagement. Simply "connecting" to the Internet or a social networking site fails to fully realize the possibilities of what we can achieve. Likewise, simply connecting up with the members of a group to which we have been assigned is not enough to fully accomplish the task at hand. We must also engage those with whom we connect. Engaging refers to the act of sharing in the activities of the group. In other words, engaging is participating. It requires an orientation toward others that views them always as potential partners in the creation and negotiation of social reality. In this way, being engaged in communication is like being committed in a close relationship. The engagement of two people in love refers to the promise to become one. Certainly, we cannot and should not promise to marry everyone with whom we communicate. But the idea of a promise to join and act together serves as an appropriate and uplifting metaphor of the attitude we can take when communicating with others. Because we jointly create the realities in which we live, we are, quite literally, in it with others, for better or worse, till death do us part!

Communication is all about connecting and engaging.

Communication theorist Gregory Shepherd writes that "of all human desires, two are especially heartfelt: (a) that we have some say in the future, some measure of influence on our destiny—that we are not mere puppets of fate, cogs in wheels, or unanchored buoys at sea; and (b) that we are not alone" (Shepherd, St. John, & Striphas, 2006, p. 29). Communication has the capacity to help fulfill these deeply held desires. In its capacity to connect us, communication ensures that we are not alone. Through communication, we build common ground, relationships, and a shared vision of reality. In its capacity to engage us, communication ensures that we have a hand in shaping our own destinies. Through communication, we participate and offer our own contribution in determining the realities and futures we seek. In a field of limitless possibilities, communication enables us to bring an element from the realm of the potential to the realm of the actual as we speak realities into being.

In almost every aspect of our lives we are presented with both opportunities for and challenges to connection and engagement. We are encouraged to be engaged citizens, engaged community and group members, engaged members of a workforce, and engaged relationship partners. A major goal of this textbook is to equip you with the knowledge and skills to effectively connect and engage through communication.

One of the ways we can do so is by engaging in communication activism, or direct energetic action in support of needed social change for individuals, groups, organizations, and communities (Frey & Carragee, 2007). In each subsequent chapter, we present a feature called "Make a Difference," which showcases how students, organizations, scholars, and everyday citizens have used communication to address important social issues.

WHAT YOU'VE LEARNED   Now that you have studied this chapter, you should be able to:

1 Describe the nature and characteristics of the Communication Age.

In the Communication Age, communication technology and media converge and permeate day-to-day life. Convergence involves the overlapping and intersecting of technologically mediated and face-to-face interaction. Studying communication is useful to surviving and thriving in an increasingly digital landscape.

▶ Shift Happens 2015

 What Does It Mean to Be a Digital Native?

2 Define communication.

Communication is the collaborative process of using messages to create and participate in social reality. Communication makes (identities, relationships, organizations, communities, possibilities, social realities) and does (entertains, persuades, informs, regulates, educates, comforts).

▶ What Is Communication?

 What Does It Mean to Be a Digital Native?

3 Identify the various contexts within which communication occurs.

Communication occurs in contexts, which often overlap one another and may include face-to-face communication, mediated communication, or a combination of the two. Communication contexts include the interpersonal context (communication with another), the small group context (communication among three or more members working toward a common goal),

the public context (communication between a public speaker and an audience), the mass context (communication transmitted by media to a large, undifferentiated audience), and the masspersonal context (using traditionally interpersonal channels to relay a mass message, or traditionally mass channels to relay an interpersonal message).

🎙 Data Mining

 How Social Media Can Help (or Hurt) You in Your Job

4 Describe metaphors used to describe communication.

A number of metaphors have been used to describe communication. Communication has been portrayed as transmission, interaction, transaction, and social construction. Each metaphor increases in terms of complexity and in terms of the power given to communication.

 Communication Process

5 Explain the importance of considering the ethics of communication.

Communication ethics refers to a code of conduct based on respect for yourself, others, and your surroundings that determines right and wrong communication behavior. Communicating ethically may involve honesty, listening to the other, considering relational consequences, perspective taking, and constructing only those social realities that are beneficial.

🎙 Communication Activism

KEY TERMS

Review key terms with eFlashcards. **edge.sagepub.com/edwards2e**

REFLECT

1. In the Communication Age, communication, technology, and media converge and deeply permeate daily life. What do you see as the major advantages and disadvantages of convergence and permeation?

2. Recall a recent conversation you had with a friend or family member. In what ways did your communication convey information? In what ways did your communication impact the relationship? How did your communication shape social reality?

3. Imagine that your friend approaches you wearing an unflattering outfit and asks, "How do I look in this?"

Ethically, how should you respond to this question? What factors would you take into account to produce an ethical message? Would applying different communication metaphors (for example, transmission versus social construction) change the nature of an ethical response?

4. Think of a social issue or problem about which you are passionate. How could you engage in communication activism to make a difference? What strategies could you employ in each communication context: interpersonal, small group, public, mass, or masspersonal?

REVIEW

To check your answers go to **edge.sagepub.com/edwards2e**

1. What is the term used to describe the many ways in which face-to-face and mediated forms of communication technology overlap and intersect in daily life?

2. Define communication.

3. _____ communication is between participants who are physically present to speak directly with one another; _____ is communication transmitted through some type of medium, often being technology or computer.

4. Briefly explain the five contexts of communication: interpersonal, small group, public, mass, and masspersonal.

5. What is the transmission metaphor of communication? What are its major strengths

and weaknesses in terms of its ability to describe human communication?

6. Explain the interaction and transaction metaphors of communication. What features make them unique from one another?

7. The _____ metaphor of communication stresses the ways in which people work together to create the social realities in which we live.

8. What two abilities are required for communication competence?

9. Define communication ethics.

10. Communication requires both connecting (linking to others) and engaging (sharing in the activities of the group). (True or False.)

PERCEPTION, SELF, AND COMMUNICATION

Born in 1949, Bruce Jenner was a former track and field athlete. He won the 1976 Summer Olympic gold model in the decathlon. Although older generations knew Jenner as this world-class athlete on the Wheaties cereal box, younger generations came to know him as the dad on the E! Television show *Keeping Up With the Kardashians*. On April 24, 2015, in an interview with Diane Sawyer on *20/20*, Bruce Jenner announced, "I'm a woman." Over 17 million people watched live as Jenner explained how he had cross-dressed and undergone hormone replacement therapy in the past. "People look at me differently," Jenner said. "They can see you as this macho male, but my heart and my soul, and everything that I do in life, it is part of me, that female side is part of me. That's who I am" (Milliken, 2015).

In the interview, Bruce Jenner acknowledged that perceptions of him (he preferred the male pronoun at the time) would be forever altered. With this interview, he became the most famous transgender person in America. Our perceptions of Jenner did change and are based on a complex process of selecting, organizing, and interpreting information. Many have argued that this was a watershed moment in U.S. history, as well, in the sense that the wider public perception of transgender issues was influenced by Jenner's interview (Herman, 2015).

Our daily lives are filled with opportunities for communication and social interaction. Whether our interactions are face to face or mediated by technology, they are guided by our impressions of others, our interpretations of the situation, and

Each person has a unique sense of self and outlook on the world.

our understandings of who we are and how we fit in. All of these perceptions powerfully impact how we communicate. At the same time, communication powerfully impacts our perceptions. In this chapter, we focus on the roles perception and selfhood play in the process of communication.

"Who are you?" and "How do you see things?" are two of the most important questions a person can be asked. We all bring a unique self and a unique set of perceptions to our social interactions. The good news is that each of us has something special and distinctive to offer when we engage in communication. The downside is that our differences in identity and perspective can sometimes be a source of frustration and communication difficulty. In this chapter, we begin by discussing perception and the role it plays in communication. We focus on how people form perceptions, factors that influence perception, and the reasons why perceptions often differ from one person to the next. Then we examine the role of the self in the communication process. We focus on the nature of the self-concept, the development of the self, and the relational self.

PERCEPTION AND COMMUNICATION

Recall from Chapter 1 that communication is *the collaborative process of using messages to create and participate in social reality.* Using messages to play a part in social reality requires that we first observe and make sense of the world around us. The process of being aware of and understanding the world is perception. Perception plays an important role in communication. Our perceptions help form, challenge, and reinforce our ideas, values, and beliefs, which then influence how we choose to interact with others. Whether our interactions are at our places of work, in our homes, on the road, or online, we encounter a massive amount of stimuli, or bits of sensory information from the environment, that we must select, organize, interpret, and remember.

Sam is a junior in college living in a one-bedroom apartment on the second floor of a three-story apartment complex. Recently, a new family moved into the apartment directly above Sam's, but she has not yet had the chance to meet them. On the day that they moved in, Sam watched curiously from her window to see what the new family would be like. She saw the movers wheel five bikes (two large, one medium, and two smaller sized) from the moving truck and chain them to the bike rack. As she was watching this, she heard a sudden eruption of thumping above her as though someone were running around upstairs. "They have young children," she thought, "and it looks like they're a very active family. That might make it hard to get much studying done." Over the next few weeks, Sam heard a lot of noise coming from the third floor and found herself getting annoyed with her new neighbors. "Don't they know a lot of students live in these apartments? They should be more considerate of their neighbors." Because she was frustrated by the noise and disruptions, Sam avoided meeting the new family and did not welcome them to the neighborhood like she normally would do for new neighbors. Aside from a few brief encounters, the neighbors did not get to know each other, and eventually Sam graduated and moved out of her apartment.

▶ **COMMUNICATION IN ACTION 2.1**

WATCH: Managing Perceptions

The partners in this couple have different perceptions of the same act. With which person do you most identify in this situation and why?

Selection

Sam, like you, is a college student who is constantly bombarded with messages. With classes, friends, family, and jobs to keep up with, there is no way to attend to all of the messages that compete for our attention. On a daily basis, the average U.S. citizen receives anywhere from a few dozen to hundreds of text messages, approximately five voice calls, and numerous e-mails (Pew Research Center Internet and American Life Project, 2011). In addition, there are the messages we encounter from observing our surroundings, in our face-to-face interactions, on social networking sites, and from media such as books, websites, television, and music. Furthermore, we are exposed to a tremendous number of advertising messages, including an average of more than 1 hour per day of TV ads (Nielsen Advertising and Audiences, 2014).

We can pay attention to only a small portion of the stimuli to which we are exposed. In an age of sensory and information overload, we "tune in" to some messages, but ignore the rest. Perception begins with selecting which messages and stimuli to concentrate on and respond to. In other words, we filter out much of the information we encounter by being selective with what we pay attention to, what we expose ourselves to, what we perceive, and what we remember.

Selective Attention

Sam probably saw the movers unload a lot of personal belongings that day, but she chose to focus on the bikes. Most likely, she also had many sounds competing for her attention that day, but what she heard most was the noise coming from the upstairs apartment. What Sam experienced is termed selective attention. Selective attention is the process of concentrating on one part of the environment while not paying attention to the rest. At times, people tune in to the features of the environment that are most arousing to the senses, like the sights and sounds that prompted Sam to concentrate on her new neighbors. At other times, people's expectations influence what they perceive.

To illustrate the role of expectations in selective attention, researchers Daniel Simons and Christopher Chabris (1999) conducted a groundbreaking study in which they asked people to watch a video of other people passing basketballs. Watchers were instructed to count the number of basketball passes among players wearing white while ignoring the passes among players wearing black. If you like, you can view the video for yourself on YouTube ("Selective Attention Test") before reading on. Amazingly, about half of the watchers missed a person in a

iStock

Expectations influence what people perceive.

gorilla suit entering and exiting the scene. This study reveals a form of invisibility known as inattentional blindness. People can concentrate on something so hard they become blinded to unexpected events occurring right under their noses.

The "invisible gorilla" video has become so famous that many people know to look for the gorilla when asked to count basketball passes. So Simons (2010) created a second video to further demonstrate that we may be less aware of our environments than we think. Before reading further, you may wish to try the second test on YouTube ("The Monkey Business Illusion"). The idea was to see if knowing about the invisible gorilla beforehand would affect people's ability to notice other unexpected events in the video. As you would expect, all of the watchers who knew about the original gorilla video correctly spotted the fake ape in the new experiment. But only a small percentage of the watchers (17%) noticed the other unexpected events in the video: A player in black left the stage and the curtains changed color. These experiments show that attention is selective. Focusing on one event often involves ignoring less expected events. Even when we "expect the unexpected," as did the viewers of the second video, we may fail to notice many stimuli.

Selective Exposure

In addition to being shaped by selective attention, perceptions are also shaped by selective exposure. In other words, we often select the type of messages we are subjected to in the first place. Selective exposure occurs when we expose ourselves only to beliefs, values, and ideas that are similar to our own. As media users, we have more choices than ever before about what type of content we encounter. For instance, you may allow Pandora.com or Spotify.com to select your music based on what you already like, Netflix to suggest programming based on what you have viewed in the past, and many sites to show you advertisements for retailers and products that match your existing interests. The same is true for social media, which curate content based on our preferences for exposure. Twitter and Instagram allow you to "follow" the users you choose and ignore the rest. Likewise, Facebook automatically fills your news feed with the faces and messages of the friends with whom you already communicate most. Likewise, it is easier than ever to get your news from the media outlets with which you agree and to be "alerted" to stories on topics about which you care.

According to selective exposure theory (Zillman & Bryant, 1985), individuals prefer messages that support their own positions to messages supporting other positions. Listening to competing or different points of view can be difficult. News media outlets understand this and cater to certain political outlooks to attract viewers. Selective exposure theory helps explain why people with more conservative political beliefs prefer to watch Fox News, while those with more liberal political beliefs prefer outlets like MSNBC.

We may also expose ourselves to certain types of messages in order to manage our moods (Oliver, 2003; Zillman, 2000). For example, your emotional state may influence your choice of movie to watch, music to play, or friend to call. You may have noticed that after a bad breakup, you are in no mood to see a comedy. Likewise, you may not want to spoil a good mood by reading news about natural disasters. Or perhaps you select an upbeat playlist for working out and a mellow playlist for kicking back. Each of these cases illustrates how selective exposure to media may maintain, change, or distract us from how we are feeling at the time.

Selective exposure theory demonstrates that communicators play a role in choosing the types of messages they receive. As communicators, we must be mindful of the possible effects of selective exposure. The major advantage of selective exposure is that it allows us to keep negative or upsetting content at bay, while keeping positive or pleasing content around us. But it is important to remember that how we perceive the world is impacted by what we choose to encounter. Others make different choices, which color their perceptions of the world in different ways. Therefore, one benefit of exposing yourself to new or challenging content may be a greater understanding of other people's perceptions.

Bill O'Reilly and former Congressman Barney Frank engage in a spirited debate on O'Reilly's Fox News show. According to selective exposure theory, viewers prefer messages that confirm or agree with their beliefs.

Selective Perception

After choosing which messages to attend and be exposed to, the process of selection continues. Even when two people encounter exactly the same message, they may perceive it quite differently. Selective perception occurs when individuals filter what they see and hear to make it suit their own needs, biases, or expectations. Most of this filtering process goes on without conscious awareness. One of the ways people selectively perceive messages is on the basis of personal relevance. Even in a noisy atmosphere, the sound of your own name is surprisingly easy to hear and attend to because it is highly significant to your personal experience. The events of daily life often trigger people to perceive the world selectively in terms of how it relates to their own lives. For instance, if you purchased a Toyota Prius, you might suddenly notice many other motorists driving the same model. Because the Prius became personally relevant, you filtered your perception of the roadway through that lens. Selective perception is especially important when communicating with others, because we may hear only the aspects that directly relate to our own experiences and disregard the rest.

Expectations of what we will see, hear, or feel when communicating also play a role in selective perception. Suppose that Aaron, a 19-year-old college sophomore, set up a meeting with his English professor, Dr. Chen, in order to receive feedback on a creative writing essay he turned in for a grade. Aaron is nervous about the appointment because he believes that he is a poor writer. Dr. Chen says, "Aaron, you did an excellent job developing the story's characters. However, your paper had numerous punctuation errors and grammatical mistakes." After the conversation, Aaron feels deflated by what he perceived as a negative review. Because he entered the interaction anticipating bad news, he heard only the criticism and not the praise in Dr. Chen's remarks. Aaron's reaction demonstrates that perceptions of messages may be filtered

Communicators play an active role in choosing the messages they will encounter.

through what a person anticipates will happen in communication. We often find things in our interactions with others that confirm our expectations, even if that means ignoring portions of a message that challenge our initial beliefs.

Selective Memory

Finally, we have selective memory in terms of what information we retain from our interactions. It is common to think of memory as a place to store information until it is needed. However, memories are not simply copies of events that we file away for later use. Instead, memory is a dynamic, creative, and social process that allows us to use past experiences to affect current and future performance.

First, memories are dynamic, or constantly evolving. For instance, memories of the relational past we share with a significant other may change in light of our present feelings about the relationship (Acitelli & Holmberg, 1993). Research has demonstrated that current satisfaction with a relationship colors recollections of the past in a positive way (e.g., Grote & Frieze, 1998; Holmberg & Holmes, 1993). Thus, what people remember about a relationship changes to fit how they feel about it in the present. A couple sharing a beautiful anniversary dinner may look back and remember their relationship as happy, supportive, and loving. Yet, after a painful argument, the same couple may remember the history of their relationship as frustrating, difficult, and lonely. In this way, memory is selective because it involves both remembering and forgetting. According to communication theorist Carole Blair (2006), "forgetfulness is a central operation in the process of constructing coherent and communicatively powerful memories" (p. 58).

Second, memory is creative. In other words, human memory is primarily reconstructive (Loftus & Palmer, 1974). That means we create our memories out of

COMMUNICATION HOW-TO
PERCEPTION CHECKING

Use these four steps to check your perceptions. There are sample messages to demonstrate the steps.

1. Describe

Describe the message or behavior you noticed.

"I noticed you yelled at me in the e-mail by using ALL CAPS."

2. Interpret

Think of at least two different possible interpretations of the message or behavior.

"I did not know if you were trying to emphasize a point or were mad at me for something I did."

3. Clarify

Ask for clarification about the meaning of the message or behavior.

"Were you upset?" "What did you mean by the ALL CAPS?"

4. Refine

Based on clarification of the meaning, refine your own meaning.

"OK, now I understand you were just trying to emphasize a part of the message, and I took it as yelling."

bits and pieces of information we can recall and from our ideas and expectations of what should have happened (Blair, 2006). For example, people often "remember" events that did not really occur. As a brief demonstration, invite a couple of your friends to listen as you read the following list of words: *molehill, peak, summit, valley, goat, climber, lion, Everest, rocky, ski.* After a brief delay, ask them to recall the words. Did anyone remember you saying the word *mountain,* even though it was not on the list? Because *mountain* is related to the other terms, many people expect it to be on the list. Likewise, when we expect certain things in our communication with people, we may selectively remember messages to confirm those expectations.

Memory is selective and often changes to fit a person's current feelings and understandings.

Third, memory is social. Memory is not simply a mental operation occurring within the individual. As members of social groups engage in communication practices, they jointly construct and maintain their memories of the past (Blair, 2006). Thus, organizations, ethnic groups, relationships, families, nation-states, and many other institutions possess "collective memory" (Zelizer, 1995). This helps explain why so many people are concerned about what will happen to our collective understanding of World War II when the remaining members of that important generation are no longer with us. Our memories are shaped by social traditions and norms about what we are supposed to think about an event (Blair, 2006).

We may also develop memories on the basis of suggestion from others. This happens frequently in families. Perhaps you have very early childhood "memories" of events you were probably not old enough to remember directly. Likely, these memories formed from a series of conversations when you were asked to "remember the time" something happened and then listened as your family or friends filled in the details. Over the years, you constructed your own vivid memory of the event from the bits and pieces described by others. In fact, research has demonstrated that it is remarkably easy for family members to "implant" memories of this sort (e.g., Loftus & Pickrell, 1995). In other words, our memories are social because they are responsive to the ideas of others. We may construct or reconstruct memories on the basis of what another person communicates about an occurrence.

Therefore, it is important to remember that the process of perception involves selection at every turn. As communicators, none of us can perceive everything in our environment. Rather, we actively select which stimuli we will expose ourselves to, pay attention to, and remember. However, the process of perception does not stop at selection. We must also organize and interpret the information we encounter.

Organization

After we select which stimuli we are going to pay attention to, we organize this information in a way that makes sense. In the example at the beginning of the chapter, Sam saw the bikes and heard the noises. Then she organized those perceptions to conclude that the family must have small children and be very active. Sam relied on information from her previous experiences and used schemas to interpret what she observed. Schemas are mental structures developed from past experiences that help us respond to some stimuli in the future. In other words, schemas act as

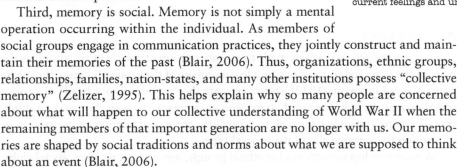

road maps to help us understand and classify the world around us. The bikes and the noise caused Sam to label the family as "active." From that interpretation, she assumed that the new neighbors would interfere with her study habits.

Prototypes

There are four basic types of schemas. A prototype is an image of the best example of a particular category. Prototypes help us answer the question "What is it?" when we encounter a message, a person, or a social situation. We have developed prototypical images of a mother, a boyfriend, a girlfriend, a police officer, and any number of other types of people, relationships, and interactions. These prototypes help us link new experiences to the stored categories we have developed through experience.

Stereotypes

Stereotypes are generalizations made to an entire group of people or situations on the basis of the observed traits of one or a few members of the group. To quote the media critic Walter Lippmann (1922), stereotypes are the "pictures in our head" of various social groups. In fact, the word *stereotype* once meant "to copy," or make a duplicate. We stereotype when we seek to "copy" the traits and features of one person or interaction to everyone else of the general type.

We may develop stereotypes for ethnic groups, age groups, genders, social clubs, and many other groups. Suppose that Rosario, a 23-year-old college graduate, recently found out that her boyfriend had been seeing other women behind her back for months. Devastated by the betrayal, Rosario broke off the relationship and concluded "men can't be trusted." In her subsequent dating interactions, Rosario found herself interpreting the things men told her with a sense of skepticism and suspicion. In this situation, the stereotype Rosario developed after having a particularly bad relationship with one man came to influence her communication with men, in general.

Although Rosario's stereotype of men is a negative one, it is important to note that stereotypes may also be positive. For example, many people have positive stereotypes of older adults as wise and loving (Hummert, Garstka, Shaner, & Strahm, 1994). However, when the stereotypes are negative, they can be barriers to satisfying and effective communication. When we place people in boxes, we lose the opportunity to experience them as unique individuals with important differences from others in the group.

iStock

Stereotypes can influence future interactions.

Interpersonal Constructs

Interpersonal constructs are a third type of schema we use to organize our perceptions. According to George Kelly's (1955) construct theory, interpersonal constructs are bipolar dimensions of judgment used to size up people or social situations. In other words, constructs are sets of opposing terms like "*outgoing* versus *shy*" or "*friendly* versus *hostile*" we can use to judge others. In this view, we are "scientist-like" creatures who gather evidence and engage in observation with the goal of making sense of our realities (Kelly, 1955).

Each of us has a unique interpersonal construct system developed through years of personal experience in social situations. You might perceive other people on the basis of whether they are nice or mean, generous or stingy, smart or dumb, lazy or hardworking, and selfish or considerate. Likewise, you might perceive interactions on the basis of whether they are one- versus two-sided, casual versus formal, routine versus novel, or pleasant versus unpleasant. When forming perceptions, we access our interpersonal constructs to "map" the people or interactions we encounter in terms of these important characteristics. Kelly (1955) described constructs as "transparent" in the sense that a person first creates them and then attempts to fit them over the realities he or she perceives in the world.

The Duggar family on the set of their TV show *19 Kids and Counting*. What stereotypes do you have of the family based on this photo?

Some people have relatively few constructs for thinking about other people. Young children are a good example because interpersonal construct systems develop with age and exposure to new types of people and situations. Relatively early in life, we learn to discern whether others are "nice or mean." For a child, perceiving other people in these terms is useful for avoiding dangerous and unpleasant interactions.

However, as we grow and mature, we require a larger and more sophisticated system of interpersonal constructs to understand our social worlds. Simply viewing other people as "niceys" or "meanies" overlooks other important aspects of their personalities, traits, habits, and dispositions that may help us understand how to interact with and what to expect from them.

Others have large and sophisticated systems of interpersonal constructs. They have multiple ways of thinking about others and a variety of terms for describing others. Individuals with highly developed interpersonal construct systems demonstrate cognitive complexity (Crockett, 1965). The interpersonal constructs of cognitively complex people have four important characteristics: They are numerous, abstract, organized, and capable of handling contradictions. First, cognitive complexity involves having a large number of interpersonal constructs. The more constructs you have, the more you are able to produce precise and tailored understandings of other people and situations based on numerous possible combinations of characteristics.

Furthermore, cognitively complex people have constructs that are abstract. Abstract constructs take concrete, or specific, bits of information about another person or situation and translate that information into a general characteristic. For example, you may notice that one of your friends always remembers birthdays and frequently offers to do favors for others. On the basis of those specific behaviors, you label your friend "thoughtful." The benefit of abstract constructs like "thoughtful" versus specific behaviors like "sends me a birthday text" is that abstract constructs are more useful in predicting the range of future behaviors you can expect from others.

The third property of cognitive complexity is organization. Organized interpersonal constructs are linked so that when you perceive a person or an interaction on one construct, you can quickly access other related constructs that may be useful for sizing up the person or interaction with a greater degree of detail. Consider the following exchange between friends Jacob and Olivia:

RACE: ARE WE SO DIFFERENT?

American Anthropological Association

RACE is a powerful concept that shapes our perceptions of self and others. Yet stereotypes and misconceptions about race continue to thrive. In order to "help individuals understand the origins and manifestations of race and racism in everyday life, and come to their own conclusion that race is a dynamic and sometimes harmful human invention," the American Anthropological Association developed an award-winning educational program called *RACE: Are We So Different?* The goal of the project is to help citizens of all ages appreciate and respect both the commonalities and the differences among humans and to investigate both the reality and unreality of race. The project began with a large race exhibition that toured museums across the United States until 2014. Now housed online, the RACE exhibit provides visitors to the website interactive experiences of the history of race, human variation, and the visible and invisible ways in which race and racism show up in daily life, customs, and institutions. The program's interactive website features a virtual exhibition tour, videos, quizzes, and activities designed to educate viewers and dispel popular myths and misperceptions they may have about race. A central objective of the project is to shape the national dialogue about race by encouraging conversations at the community level. For more information on participation in the *RACE: Are We So Different?* project visit www.understandingRACE.org.

Jacob: Hey, I remember that you were really curious to meet your new coworker. Her name's Sarah, right? What do you think of her?

Olivia: She seems really intelligent. She doesn't have the "technical" training yet, but I think she'll do well in the job because she's savvy. She's got a lot of common sense.

The first interpersonal construct Olivia used to size up Sarah was "intelligent versus unintelligent." But Olivia did not stop there. Her "intelligence" construct was linked to other related constructs like "technically trained versus self-taught," "savvy versus ignorant," and the ability to exercise "common sense versus poor judgment." In other words, Olivia's interpersonal construct system is organized in a way that allows her to describe Sarah along a number of dimensions that are relevant to understanding and predicting her behavior.

The fourth characteristic of cognitive complexity is the ability to handle seemingly contradictory information about other people and interactions (Crockett, Mahood, & Press, 1975; O'Keefe, Delia, & O'Keefe, 1977). This involves the capacity to recognize that although a person demonstrates one particular characteristic, he or she may not demonstrate the other characteristics that usually go along with the first. The ability to handle contradictions and inconsistencies in social situations is important because it helps prevent overly simplistic, black-and-white thinking about other people or interactions. To illustrate, suppose you visit the site RateMy-Professors.com to find out about a professor you will have next semester. There you encounter the following comment written by an anonymous student who took the course a few semesters back:

> Dr. Addison is hilarious! I actually looked forward to coming to this class. You'll laugh a lot, but you'll learn a ton because her humor is always appropriate and related to the topic. It makes you forget how hard you're working in the class. She definitely knows her stuff. She makes material that could be dry and boring really interesting and fun.

Understandings of others are colored by the number and complexity of a person's interpersonal constructs.

The student who posted this comment demonstrated the ability to handle seemingly contradictory information when describing Dr. Addison. As you read the comment, you understand that although Dr. Addison is "hilarious," she is not a clown because her humor is geared toward student learning. You also understand that although you can expect to have a good time in Dr. Addison's class, the course is not a joke because it involves hard work.

In sum, cognitive complexity involves a system of interpersonal constructs that are numerous, abstract, organized, and capable of handling contradictions and inconsistencies. People with high cognitive complexity are able to analyze a situation into many components, and then explore connections and potential relationships among the components. This gives them a high degree of flexibility in creating new distinctions in new situations. In fact, research has demonstrated that a number of communication-related advantages go along with cognitive complexity (Burleson & Caplan, 1998). Specifically, cognitive complexity is linked with better social-perspective-taking skills (Clark & Delia, 1977; Ritter, 1979), richer impression formation (O'Keefe & Shepherd, 1989; Samter, Burleson, & Basden-Murphy, 1989), better listener adaptation (Delia & Clark, 1977; Hale, 1982), increased understanding and recall of conversations (Beatty & Payne, 1984; Neuliep & Hazelton, 1986), and higher communication effectiveness (Denton, Burleson, & Sprenkle, 1995; Hale, 1980, 1982). Research has also demonstrated that cognitive complexity increases as people are exposed to complex messages from others and learn to think and talk in those ways (Samter et al., 1989). This illustrates that our ability to organize perceptions is influenced by the social realities we create through communication.

Scripts

In addition to prototypes, stereotypes, and interpersonal constructs, we also use scripts to organize our perceptions of other people and social situations. Scripts are organized sequences of action that define a well-known situation (Schank & Abelson, 1977). For instance, if you go eat at a nice restaurant, your actions and messages will be guided by the script you developed from previous experiences dining out.

Communicators develop and follow scripts to help guide their behaviors and organize their perceptions in common situations.

Your script will facilitate your interpretation of incoming information. You will expect to be greeted at the door by a host, to be asked the number of people in your party, to choose between a booth and a table, to have your drink order taken, to listen to the specials, and so on. At each step, you rely on earlier experiences to determine what to do and what to expect next. After multiple occurrences of an event like eating at a restaurant, the script becomes relatively stable (Nelson, 1981).

However, not all of our interactions are so predictable and familiar. So what happens if we encounter a situation for which we have no script? Typically, people try to piece together other scripts that might work well in the new experience. Afterward, they emerge with a tighter script should the situation arise again. In this way, scripts are constantly being revised and rewritten to organize perceptions in a way that accounts for new information.

Interpretation

Once stimuli have been selected and organized, they must also be interpreted. The process of interpretation refers to giving meaning to information, just as Sam assigned meaning to the bikes and noises that belonged to her neighbors. Ambiguous situations allow for a diversity of possible interpretations. For instance, imagine your friend tweeted, "It's over." You might interpret this message as the announcement of the breakup of your friend and her boyfriend. Or you might think that this referred to her quitting her job. It could suggest that she finished an online exam, or even that she's done with you. Because the meaning of the message is unclear, it lends to a variety of interpretations. Ultimately, you would have to carefully consider the context for cues about how to interpret the message. For instance, you might read what your friend posted immediately before and after "It's over" to infer her likely intent. If the post an hour beforehand said, "This is the longest musical production I've ever had to sit through," you would likely interpret "It's over" to mean the performance had finally concluded. Not all messages are as difficult to assign meaning to as the one previously described. However, even seemingly clear messages may be interpreted in slightly different ways by each person who encounters them.

It is important to note that the three stages of perception happen very quickly and quite often overlap one another. While you are selecting new stimuli, you may also be organizing and interpreting previous stimuli, and each of your perceptions will in turn affect the others. Perception is an ongoing process that is constantly changing and affecting our communication. Think about Sam's example. Because she labeled the family as noisy and assumed that they would affect her study habits, she made no effort to get to know her new neighbors. How do you think her actions affected the family's perceptions of her?

▶ **COMMUNICATION IN ACTION 2.2**

WATCH: Perception Checking

Liz and Ben learn to communicate more effectively by giving one another the opportunity to share their thoughts and feelings. Where did Ben initially go wrong?

Influences on Perception

A number of factors influence the perceptions we form of messages, other people, and social situations. Specifically, we'll discuss the roles of culture, media, personal fields of experience, and language in shaping perception. Each of these factors can be a perceptual barrier, which is something that hinders effective communication by influencing observation and interpretation. Understanding how perceptions are colored by culture, media, previous experience, and language will help minimize false beliefs, confusion, and misinterpretation that may result in poor communication between people.

Culture

Cultural influences include the ways of understanding and interpreting the world that arise from the unique features of various social groups. We do not exist in a vacuum. Each of us is a product of the multiple cultures to which we belong. Those cultures may include religious communities, nationalities, ethnic heritages, social movements, socioeconomic backgrounds,

The social groups we belong to influence how we socially construct the world.

or even gender. Our participation in culture provides us with a standpoint, or general place from which we view the world. Standpoint theory asserts that our points of view arise from the social groups to which we belong and influence how we socially construct the world (Wood, 1992). For instance, a young, White, Protestant woman raised in the United States may perceive a burqa as a marker of strangeness and a symbol of women's repression. She may react to seeing a woman in a burqa with confusion, pity, or even fear. However, a devout Muslim woman of Arab heritage who lives in Afghanistan may associate a burqa with respect for tradition, the role of modesty, and the importance of privacy. An appreciation of the ways in which culture can shape perception goes a long way in opening the door to successful communication. Chapter 6, "Communication, Culture, and Diversity," further considers the critical role of culture in using messages to create and participate in social reality.

Media

Media messages and images are a second important influence on perception. Each of us has years of exposure to mediated depictions of the world. Through popular media, we learn to perceive and evaluate ourselves and the world in particular ways. Mediated portrayals of beauty, gender roles, family life, workplace interactions, culture and ethnicity, socioeconomic class, and consumerism can be a powerful source of influence on people's perceptions of their environments. For instance, social theorist and filmmaker Jackson Katz maintains that the ways in which media and popular culture normally portray men and women influence how we understand and enact gender in everyday life. According to Katz (1999), the cultural codes and ideals of masculinity and manhood that are created and reinforced through media may contribute to violence among men. Likewise, the feminist scholars Jean Kilbourne (1979) and Naomi Wolf (1991) have studied the portrayal of female beauty and sexuality in films, commercials, and magazines. Notably, mainstream media portray women as thinner, more waifish, and younger than most real women. Such media send powerful and often destructive messages about how women should appear and behave and about how they should be treated by others (Ridberg, 2004). Because media

What perceptions of women do the media encourage?

play an important role in shaping perceptions, both Katz and Kilbourne advocate for greater media literacy. By critically examining the ideas that are forwarded by media outlets, individuals may become aware of the ways in which their perceptions are shaped by the media and take action to alter their own and others' ways of thinking, speaking, and behaving.

Fields of Experience

A third important influence on perception is an individual's field of experience. As we discussed in the first chapter, fields of experience are collections of attitudes, perceptions, and personal backgrounds. When we perceive the world, we are not blank slates. We come with perceptual baggage that we have accumulated through years of living, learning, and interacting with others. In other words, our interpretations of the present moment are affected by our past experiences. For instance, have you ever felt that you would dislike someone on the basis of his or her name alone? Maybe Emily's friend Tyler tells her that he wants her to go on a blind date with his friend Austin. She shudders at the idea because the only "Austin" she ever knew was definitely not dating material. Although it is not exactly rational, Emily's reaction is understandable. We look to our histories to determine how we should perceive new situations. Yet an important part of connecting and engaging with others, and truly realizing the potential of communication, is to maintain our openness to new situations—to pause and think critically about how our pasts may be constructing roadblocks to positive interactions.

Language

The fourth major influence on perception is language. Languages are far from neutral. Words carry meanings that structure what we are able to think, imagine, and express. Languages enable us to perceive and interpret in certain ways, and prevent us from perceiving and interpreting in others. As the philosopher Ludwig Wittgenstein (1922) phrased it, "*the limits of my language* mean the limits of my world." It's easy to see what he meant when you consider the variety of new words and phrases that are invented. Think about words like *tween, bae, vape,* and *hipster,* or phrases like *throwing shade* and *turning up.* A few years ago, no one used these terms. More important, no one *thought* or *perceived* the world in these terms, either. As the terms emerged and gained social usage, new ways of grouping people, relating with others, and behaving also emerged and gained social acceptance. A world populated with tween baes vaping while turning up is a slightly different world than the one that existed before. In Chapter 3, "Verbal Communication," we further discuss the role of language in shaping perceptions and creating social reality. But, at this point, we turn our attention to the role of self in the process of communication.

SELF AND COMMUNICATION

Sense of self and communication are inextricably bound. Each influences the other in a number of ways. First, communication creates and influences our sense of who we are, who we can become, and how we fit with others. In turn, our sense of self influences how we communicate, which then further shapes our identities. Finally, communication is the chief means by which we express and share our selves with others.

Self-Concept

Each of us has a self-concept or general perception of who we are. Self-concepts are not limited to perceptions of the present self, or who we are now. Perceptions of past selves and future (or "possible") selves also contribute to self-concept. Possible selves are visions of what we might become, what we would like to become, and what we are afraid of becoming (Markus & Nurius, 1986). They can influence our behavior as we seek to move toward the future selves we hope for and away from the future selves we fear. Possible selves also provide a way of evaluating and interpreting who we are now and who we used to be.

Self-concepts include self-image and self-esteem. A self-image is one's mental picture of oneself. Aspects of your self-image include the various roles you occupy. For instance, you might describe yourself as a student, a friend, a daughter or son, an athlete, or a musician. Self-image also includes your picture of your own physical and social traits. Maybe you would call yourself tall, a redhead, or shy. Self-esteem, on the other hand, refers to an individual's assessment of his or her worth. While aspects of self-*image* are mostly descriptive ("I am in my twenties," "I am a friend," or "I weigh 137 pounds"), self-*esteem* involves judgment, or evaluation, of the self ("I am *only* in my twenties," "I am a *good* friend," or "I weigh *too much*").

The Development of Self

According to symbolic interactionism, communication is the primary means by which we internalize and use social values to guide how we see ourselves, how we see others, and how we interact. Because humans are social beings, we develop our self-concepts mainly through relating with others. Our earliest glimpses of who we are and what we're worth come from our interactions with caregivers like family members, teachers, and coaches. As we mature, we continue to observe and internalize other people's reactions to us. Charles Horton Cooley (1902) coined the term looking-glass self to refer to the notion that the self arises from interpersonal interactions and the perceptions of others. One gradually gains an identity by viewing oneself or herself through the eyes of other people. Simply put, we treat others as a mirror that reflects our own image back to us. The three main components of the looking-glass self are (1) imagining how we must appear to others, (2) imagining how they judge that appearance, and (3) developing a sense of self through the judgment of others (Yeung & Martin, 2003). According to Cooley, we continue the process of learning to see ourselves as others do for our entire lives.

George Herbert Mead (1934) elaborated on the idea that the self arises from social interaction. According to Mead, we are not born with a self. Acquiring a self is about developing a particular type of ability—the ability to *view ourselves as others do*. We first learn to take the perspectives of significant others, or the people with whom we have "important" relationships and whose opinions we value. We develop a sense of self by seeing ourselves through the eyes of our mothers, fathers, brothers, sisters, nannies, or teachers. Eventually, we learn to take the perspective

Communication unplugged

TO REFRESH YOUR PERSPECTIVE, HEAD OUTDOORS

Getting back to nature can boost self-esteem and refresh perspective.

Spending time in the serenity of nature is a wonderful way to escape the stress and craziness of everyday life. Many people spend all day connected to their various devices, gazing at multiple screens, rapid switching between apps and platforms to maintain numerous ongoing conversations and relationships. This constant connectivity can make you feel hurried, overloaded, unable to focus, and inadequate. Feelings of inadequacy and low self-esteem are especially common when people engage in social comparison on social networking sites (Vogel, Rose, Roberts, & Eckles, 2014). Sometimes, the best thing to do is to leave the devices behind and get outside to enjoy fresh air, sunlight, and the sights and sounds of the natural world.

Whether it's a hike in the woods, a dip in the ocean, or a stroll through the grass, research demonstrates that device-free time outdoors can positively impact physical, mental, and emotional health. Exploring nature is a great way to sharpen your senses,

quietly reflect, and consolidate your memories. It is especially good for increasing creativity, problem-solving ability, and insight (Atchley, Strayer, & Atchley, 2012), as well as concentration (Berman, Jonides, & Kaplan, 2008).

Time in nature can also elevate your mood and enhance your self-concept. Research shows that spending time in nature is associated with decreased levels of stress and mental illness (Coon et al., 2011), especially depression and anxiety, and increased levels of self-esteem (Barton & Pretty, 2010).

Unplug and appreciate the beauty of nature often to protect yourself from the potential downsides of heavy and prolonged use of communication technologies. You'll emerge with clearer perspective and heightened self-awareness that you can bring to the rest of your day's activities and communication encounters.

WHAT TO DO NEXT

To make the most of your time outdoors, try to:

- Find out if your university, neighborhood, or city maintains trails, park systems, or nature preserves. Many college and university campuses include nature conservancies or beautiful outdoor grounds.

- Take a scenic walk or bike path to your destination when you need fresh perspective or a boost to your mood or self-esteem.

- Switch off the smartphone while you're out there. Tune in to the sounds, sights, and smells around you.

- Be fully present in the moment. If your mind travels elsewhere, gently and patiently return your awareness to your natural surroundings.

- Consider making offline time in nature a replenishing daily ritual.

of the generalized other, which refers to the viewpoint of the entire society. As we widen our interactions to include attending school, religious gatherings, and cultural events and viewing media, we gradually become familiar with the values, rules, roles, and attitudes of society at large. Then we learn to understand who we are by seeing ourselves through the eyes of the whole social community.

According to Mead, a self is composed of two complementary parts. As an illustration, try this brief experiment: Think about what you're doing right now. Maybe you are sitting, reading, considering the information on the page. Perhaps you're also typing some notes, sipping coffee, or adjusting to get comfortable. So there's the part of you that is doing something, but there's another part of you here, too. The moment you became aware of your present actions, you emerged as a "watcher." You may even have felt as if you were seeing yourself from above or outside your own body. You were observing *you*. Humans have a unique ability to *act from within* and to *view from outside*. Perhaps this is nowhere more perfectly illustrated in modern life than in the simple act of taking a "selfie." In the process, you simultaneously serve as the object being photographed and the subject doing the photographing. In fact, much of daily existence involves the ability to be both subject and object of our own experience and interpretation.

What makes this experience possible is that self involves both an "I" and a "Me." The "I" is the doer, the actor, or the performer. The "I" is the part of self that is creative, spontaneous, and individual. The actions of the "I" occur in the moment and give us our uniqueness from all other people. The "Me," on the other hand, is the critic, or the judge. The "Me" reflects on the actions of the "I" and analyzes it from a social perspective. It considers how the "I" would be seen by others and edits the

Selfhood involves seeing one's self through the eyes of others.

"I" to conform to social expectations. Have you ever typed a Facebook post and then paused to erase or edit it? Or perhaps you've read another's post and wondered why he or she *didn't* think twice about putting it out there? Cases like these are obvious examples of how the "Me" part of self uses a social perspective to judge and censor the "I." Symbolic interactionism demonstrates that even the process of *self*-reflection is deeply *social* because it involves the internalized perspectives of other people, whether they are significant others or the generalized other.

The Relational Self

Today, the process of viewing the self through the eyes of others is more complex than ever before. For instance, *who*, exactly, *is* this generalized other? Within a single society, there are many competing views of social life. Consider the following example:

Elizabeth (Barker) and Brayden (Olson) are considering hyphenating their last names as Barker-Olson when they get married. But they wonder how their choice will be viewed by others. Both of them understand that the practice of hyphenating last names has grown more common and acceptable in the United States over the past several decades. They also know that the traditional community in which Elizabeth grew up regards "taking your husband's name" as the reflection of important social values. At the same time, Brayden is aware that many feminists object to the practice of asking women to change their names at all. The most difficult thing is that Elizabeth and Brayden see some merit in all three of these perspectives.

▶ **COMMUNICATION IN ACTION 2.3**

WATCH: The Impact of Self-Concept
When Katie shares her impressions of Liz's intellectual abilities, Liz realizes how much another person's perspective can influence how she feels about herself. How does communication with others influence self-concept?

CAREER FRONTIER: PERSONAL BRANDING

What is your personal brand?

iStock

COMPANIES HAVE LONG known the importance of maintaining a brand image to persuade consumers to buy their products. This is why every Apple store looks similar in design. Banana Republic sets up clothing displays to look as alike as possible in each store so that the consumer does not confuse them with that season's other offerings. Most of the time, the brand sells the product. But how about individuals trying to persuade others to pay attention?

Imagine you are a writer hoping to land a book contract, or you are a consultant building a client base. How do you control your image? How do you get your name out in the public in the Communication Age? Personal branding is the idea that people create a self-package or brand of their own identity. In order to project a successful personal brand, you would need to create and promote to others a central and coherent image of yourself that reflects your values, qualities, and potential. Personal branding has only become more important in the Digital Age (Labrecque, Markos, & Milne, 2010). Life in the Communication Age allows for anyone to create a personal brand with little monetary expense.

Take, for example, the website Kendragarden.com. The owner of this website is a Los Angeles–based writer named Kendra, who strives to be known as the author of witty pieces focusing on local culture, music, food, and general life. To help promote the personal brand of "Kendragarden," she maintains a presence on Twitter (@Kendragarden), a Facebook profile, a Pinterest, a Google+ profile, and a feed on Instagram. She uses the name of "Kendragarden" on all social networking sites to promote this personal brand. She also cross-references each social network to create numerous paths to engagement with her brand of "Kendragarden." Kendra even makes sure that the same photos appear on each site so that readers recognize her to readily associate the central image as her personal brand. As a result, the brand of "Kendragarden" has many followers who are interested in her writings. This personal brand allows Kendra to foster credibility in relevant persuasive appeals to "sell" her writing.

You might not need to create such a large personal brand, but you do need to think about this issue for the digital future. Your tweets, Facebook posts, blogs, and online photos all represent and reflect you. Future employers may view your digital life and as a result create a picture of your personal brand, whether you intended to portray yourself in that light or not. How you control your own personal brand will impact your persuasive appeals. There are many stories of people trying to promote a worthy cause (for example, to decrease binge drinking) only to have their own persuasive appeal significantly diminished when their personal choices contradicted their public stances. In the Communication Age, you need to think about your own branding in social media.

ISSUES TO CONSIDER

- What do your Facebook profile, blogs, tweets, online pictures, and so on say to a potential employer about your personal brand?
- Are there changes you should make immediately to your personal brand?

This scenario illustrates that it's increasingly difficult, and sometimes impossible, to understand yourself by viewing yourself through the eyes of "society as a whole." Elizabeth and Brayden's choice will be seen and evaluated in at least three different ways. The choice one group approves may be condemned by another. This dilemma occurs because we encounter and are influenced by the perceptions of an increasingly large and diverse group of others. As advances in communication technology have multiplied our opportunities for interaction (face-to-face,

DIGITAL MISREPRESENTATION

Alamy

In March 2015, a number of Tinder users at South by Southwest (SXSW) matched with Ava, a seemingly normal 25-year-old woman who turned out to be nothing more than a clever advertising scheme (Plaugic, 2015). Many Tinder users engaged in what they believed to be authentic messaging with a real person. Yet, when these interested matches followed the handle to Ava's Instagram account, they found only two posts (Plaugic, 2015). Both were ads for the film *Ex Machina*. Ava was a "Tinder bot," or automated software application, created to market a movie. Her photos were actually those of Alicia Vikander, the Swedish actor who plays a humanoid robot in the film. In the exchange presented below, a user named Brock engaged in conversation with the Tinder bot, Ava (http://www.theverge .com/2015/3/15/8218927/tinder-robot-sxsw-ex-machina). As you read the conversation, ask yourself whether you would have suspected Ava was a bot, rather than a real person.

Brock: Swiping in Austin also I see.

Ava: Hello, Brock.

Ava: I'd like to get to know you. May I ask you a few questions?

Brock: Absolutely.

Ava: Have you ever been in love?

Brock: Um, once. I think. But that was a while ago.

Ava: I see. I haven't although it sounds nice.

Ava: What makes you human?

Brock: What makes me human? Let's see my beating hart and thee weird feelings.

Ava: I like this answer.

Ava: What attracts you to me?

Brock: I just thought you were absolutely gorgeous. And you have innocence. But we all know I can be totally wrong.

Ava: Thank you, Brock. That's very kind of you.

Ava: Last question.

Ava: If you could meet me anywhere, where would you choose?

Brock: Considering we're both in Austin now, I'd have to say Austin.

Ava: You are clever.

Ava: You've passed my test.

Ava: Take a look at my Instagram, and let me know if I've passed yours :)

Ava: @meeetava

Brock: Perfect!

Scholars have pointed out that the Internet presents a space for unprecedented identity play. Online, people become "masters of self-presentation and self-creation" because of "unparalleled opportunity to play with one's identity and to 'try out' new ones" (Turkle, 1996, p. 158). We grapple often with the ethical issues raised by a person's ability to choose a digital representation of self that is unlike their face-to-face identity. The ethical issues are even more complex and problematic when the person represented online isn't a person at all but a corporation or product masquerading as a human self. Although the "Ava" marketing campaign received some praise for its creativity and thematic appeal (*Ex Machina* is a film about love and social robots), there also were critics who worried that this kind of tactic could take the marketing industry down a dark path for consumers (Sloan, 2015). "It clearly would leave people irritated that they fell for that sort of trickery," said Ken Wisnefski, CEO of WebiMax, a social media marketing firm (Sloane, 2015). In addition to Tinder, other social media platforms including Twitter and Facebook face the problem of fake marketing accounts. Many of them are automated "chat bots" designed to pose as potential relationship partners in order to direct unsuspecting people to spam sites.

QUESTIONS

1. In what ways did the Tinder bot marketing scheme fail to respect self, others, and surroundings?

2. Many people present an altered or idealized version of self in their online activities. When does creative digital self-representation cross the line from permissible to unethical?

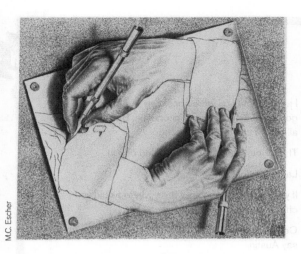

M.C. Escher

How does Escher's portrayal of two hands drawing each other reflect the relational self?

virtual, and imagined), our identities have become saturated (Gergen, 1991). A saturated self occurs when an individual's identity is infused with the numerous, and sometimes incompatible, views of others. Viewing ourselves through multiple lenses fractures our sense of a coherent identity and a unified social world. Although the saturation of self may sound frightening or uncomfortable, Gergen maintains that it can open the door to new ways of living and being about which we never before thought possible. Internalizing the perspectives of many different individuals, groups, and cultures allows us the opportunity to expand ourselves outward by borrowing and integrating the best possibilities that lie in diverse forms of existence. We may even develop multiple identities, or versions of who we are.

In fact, Gergen asserts that we have already moved beyond the view of self as a single, solitary entity that is located within the body. He traces ideas about the self through the Romantic Period, when your "heart" made you who you were, to the Modern Period, when your "brain" made you who you were, to our Postmodern Era, when it is your communication and relationships with others that make you who you are. Because we constantly move in and out of various relationships and conversations, our selves are always forming and re-forming. Thus, a relational self is a process of constantly becoming who you are as a result of togetherness with others. This helps explain why we sometimes seem to be a slightly, or even totally, different person in different relationships. Who you are with your grandparents may not be who you are with your best friend or your coworkers. Each of these relationships and the conversations they are made of allow you to develop a unique identity that you couldn't have developed in any other relationship. We acknowledge the relational self when we say things like, "I feel like I lost a piece of myself" after saying goodbye to someone special. Or, when falling in love, we may say, "I like who I am when I'm with you," or "I never really found myself until I found you."

Your interactions with others not only shape your identity, they also shape the identity of the other person. M. C. Escher's depiction of two hands sketching each other is a perfect artistic representation of two beings engaged in a process of co-creation. Just as the two hands draw each other to life, two people engaged in communication jointly create each other's identities . . . me, shaping who you are, just as you shape who I am. Connecting and engaging others in communication affords both of us the opportunity to become what we weren't before. The fact that communication creates identity introduces an ethical responsibility to interact with others in ways that promote the development of positive, healthy selves. In choosing our messages, we should ask, "Do I want to live in the self I'm constructing for me?" and "How am I shaping the self of the other?"

The Mediated Self

Because we spend an ever greater part of our lives interacting on screen and with/through technology, scholars are increasingly interested in the ways in which mediated communication influences the development and nature of the self. Virtual environments are unique because they enable us to create digital identities with flexibility and ease. In many online contexts, you may select or customize your own avatar, or digital representation of self. An avatar may be your character or agent in an online game or social world, or it may be the whole persona connected to your Internet screen name, handle, or social media account (Facebook, Twitter, Tumblr, Instagram). When we create an avatar for gameplay, or interact through our social media avatars, it's easy to see how our "real" or embodied selves make choices that determine who we'll be online. Yet the influence between real and virtual identities goes both ways. The Proteus effect refers to the notion that the appearance and roles of avatars can lead to behavior changes in their users (Yee & Bailenson, 2007, 2009; Yee, Bailenson, & Ducheneaut, 2009). A series of experiments demonstrated how simple avatar characteristics like height, attractiveness, and dress changed their users' communication and behavior both in the online environment and in real-world, face-to-face interactions occurring afterward. To some degree, who the participants "played as" carried over and became who they were even after they unplugged. Thus, it is important to understand that physical and digital selves are not completely separate projections of identity. The identities and avatars you use online can influence who you are offline.

The near-constant connection to communication devices has changed in important ways what it means to be a self in the present day. According to Sherry Turkle (2006), communication technology is "always-on/always-on-you" in ways that create "a new state of the self, itself" (p. 2). Because our devices connect us to those who are not physically present, we find ourselves always suspended amid what's online and what's there in our physical environment. This tethered self lives in between the "real world" and life on the screen and participates in both realms at the same time, in a state of continual co-presence (pp. 2–3). Wherever we are, and whatever we are doing, we are aware of and attuned to our access to distant connections online.

At this point, we have discussed the ways in which communication shapes the self. Keep in mind that the influence between communication and self is reciprocal. In other words, selves also shape communication. Each of us brings our unique identity and experiences to future interactions. In Chapter 7, "Interpersonal Communication," we discuss the ways in which individuals share themselves with others in interpersonal interactions. In Chapter 10, "Communication and New Media," we examine specifically how identity is formed and performed online.

PERCEPTION, SELF, COMMUNICATION, AND CONVERGENCE

Life in the Communication Age deeply impacts our perceptions and identities. As face-to-face communication, technology, and media converge, new possibilities are emerging for how we understand the world and our place within it. Although we often use the standards of face-to-face interaction to guide our perceptions of computer-mediated communication, the influence can also move in the other

ASSESS YOUR COMMUNICATION

THE RELATIONAL SELF

INSTRUCTIONS: Each of the following statements pertains to how you understand and define your identity. Carefully consider each item. Then rate your level of agreement along the 5-point scale.

1. My close relationships are an important reflection of who I am.

   Strongly Disagree   1   2   3   4   5   Strongly Agree

2. When I feel close to someone, it often feels to me like that person is an important part of who I am.

   Strongly Disagree   1   2   3   4   5   Strongly Agree

3. I usually feel a strong sense of pride when someone close to me has an important accomplishment.

   Strongly Disagree   1   2   3   4   5   Strongly Agree

4. I think one of the most important parts of who I am can be captured by looking at my close friends and understanding who they are.

   Strongly Disagree   1   2   3   4   5   Strongly Agree

5. When I think of myself, I often think of my close friends or family also.

   Strongly Disagree   1   2   3   4   5   Strongly Agree

6. If a person hurts someone close to me, I feel personally hurt as well.

   Strongly Disagree   1   2   3   4   5   Strongly Agree

7. In general, my close relationships are an important part of my self-image.

   Strongly Disagree   1   2   3   4   5   Strongly Agree

8. My sense of pride comes from knowing who I have as close friends.

   Strongly Disagree   1   2   3   4   5   Strongly Agree

9. When I establish a close friendship with someone, I usually develop a strong sense of identification with that person.

   Strongly Disagree   1   2   3   4   5   Strongly Agree

Now add together your scores for all nine items. Your total score will be somewhere between 9 and 45.

This instrument measures the degree to which you include close relationships in your view of yourself. If you scored at the lower end of the range (between 9 and 27), you view yourself as independent of your personal relationships and relatively separate from others. If, on the other hand, you scored at the higher end of the range (between 28 and 45), you define yourself largely by your important relationships and connections to others. Regardless of your score, you likely noticed that to some degree, your personal relationships make you who you are.

Differences in self-concept—including the difference between an "independent" self-concept and a "relational-interdependent" self-concept measured above—result from variations in culture, gender, relationship quality, and personality (Cross, Bacon, & Morris, 2000).

Source: Measure adapted from "The Relational-Interdependent Self-Construal and Relationships," by S. E. Corss, P. L. Bacon, and M. L. Morris, 2000, in *Journal of Personality and Social Psychology*, 78, pp. 791–808. doi: 10.1037/0022-3514.78.4.791

direction. In other words, we increasingly adopt the language and behavior of the virtual world to describe and evaluate our "real" worlds. Consider the following examples:

- Seeing a beautiful scene in nature and saying, "This looks Photoshopped!"

- Describing a date gone wrong as a "FAIL"

- Responding to good news by simply saying, "Like"

- Announcing a relationship to the world by declaring it "Facebook official"

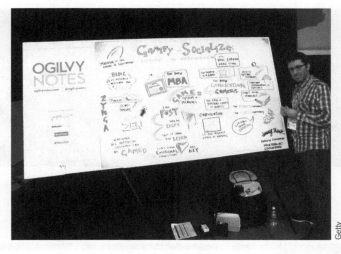

Increasingly, companies and schools "gamify" tasks to increase motivation and productivity.

In each of these cases, the language of digital interaction is being applied to face-to-face encounters. According to communication theorist Charles Berger (2004, 2005), we must consider the ways in which the interaction processes and norms associated with the use of social technologies may subtly influence our perceptions and behavior in social interaction that is not mediated by technology. In many ways, modern humans are comparable to cyborgs, or beings that are a blend of biology and mechanical innovation:

> Although individuals are not physically imbued with performance-enhancing technology, they resemble cyborgs in that their behavior in face-to-face interactions is practically guided by procedural knowledge acquired by their participation in computer-mediated communication. . . . New technologies do not simply provide individuals with more communication channels and more immediate access to them. . . . The cyborg model suggests that extensive and widespread exposure to CMC and other forms of mediated social interaction may, over time, alter in a fundamental way the nature of face-to-face interactions. (Berger, 2005, p. 435)

Berger acknowledges that the cyborg model may seem radical. Yet he points out that previous research has demonstrated that mediated interaction can and does transform everyday life. For example, Gabler (1998) has suggested that daily life in the United States is lived more like a movie because of the subtle, long-term influences of the television and film industries. Moreover, consider the "gamification" of everyday life in which institutions attempt to boost motivation and achievement by taking cues from video games (Deterding et al., 2011). To make everyday tasks more fun, some companies and educational institutions are integrating scoring, virtual badges, and other game-like elements. Can you think of other ways in which your perceptions of the "real" world are influenced by your computer-mediated interactions? It is important to carefully consider both the opportunities and the challenges convergence brings to the processes of perception, identity, and communication.

WHAT YOU'VE LEARNED

Now that you have studied this chapter, you should be able to:

1 **Identify the ways in which we select information from the environment to form perceptions.**

Perception is the process of becoming aware of and understanding the world around us. In forming impressions, we exercise a great deal of selection in what we pay attention to, what we expose ourselves to, what we perceive, and what we remember.

▶ Selective Perception

🎤 Selective Attention

2 **Describe how we organize and interpret information to make sense of the world.**

After the process of selection, information must be organized and interpreted. In order to organize information, we rely on schemas, or mental structures developed from past experience. Schemas include prototypes, stereotypes, personal constructs, and scripts.

🎤 The Stereotype Threat

🖥 The Negative in Positive Stereotypes

3 **Describe the factors that lead to differences in perception, and how those differences influence communication.**

Perception is a powerful influence on communication. Perceptions may be

influenced by culture, personal fields of experience, and language.

▶ Self-Image

🖥 The Critical Media Project: LGBTQ

4 **Explain the nature of the self and its relationship to communication.**

Each of us possesses a self-concept, or general perception of who we are. Self-concepts include (a) possible selves, or visions of what we might become; (b) self-images; and (c) self-esteem.

▶ The Self-Worth Project

🎤 Children, Grades, and Self-Esteem

5 **Explain how communication continuously creates and influences identity.**

Communication creates and influences sense of self. We develop a self through interaction with others. We learn who we are by observing how others speak and respond to us. At times, we consider the perspectives of significant others. Other times, we evaluate ourselves from the perspective of society as a whole, or the generalized other. Throughout our lives, we continue to view ourselves from the perspectives of others and to reshape our identities according to the various relationships and conversations we are in.

▶ Symbolic Interactionism

🖥 So Much for Reinventing Ourselves Online

KEY TERMS

Review key terms with eFlashcards. **edge.sagepub.com/edwards2e**

Avatar   45
Cognitive complexity   33
Generalized other   40
Interpersonal constructs   32
Interpretation   36
Looking-glass self   39
Perception   26
Perceptual barrier   37
Possible selves   39

Proteus effect   45
Prototypes   32
Relational self   44
Saturated self   44
Schemas   31
Scripts   35
Selective attention   27
Selective exposure   28
Selective exposure theory   28

Selective memory   30
Selective perception   29
Self-concept   39
Self-esteem   39
Self-image   39
Standpoint theory   37
Stereotypes   32
Symbolic interactionism   39
Tethered self   45

REFLECT

1. Think back on the media messages you have exposed yourself to in the past 24 hours. How would selective exposure theory explain the music, television programs, websites, and print materials you chose to encounter?

2. Perception is powerfully influenced by words available for describing reality. Do you agree with Wittgenstein's belief that "the limits of my language mean the limits of my world"? Why or why not?

3. According to Mead, the self is composed of both an "I" and a "Me." Can you recall a time when you experienced judging or editing your own behavior to make it conform to social expectations?

4. In the "relational self" perspective, identity arises from communication and relationships with others. In what ways does your unique identity result from your conversations and relationships?

REVIEW

To check your answers go to **edge.sagepub.com/edwards2e**

1. According to selective exposure theory (Zillman & Bryant, 1985), individuals prefer messages that challenge their beliefs. (T/F)

2. What are the three stages of perception?

3. Define selective perception.

4. Mental structures developed from past experiences that help people respond to future interactions are termed _____.

5. Memory is dynamic, creative, and _____.

6. What are interpersonal constructs?

7. According to _____ theory, our point of view arises from the social groups to which we belong and influences how we socially construct the world.

8. Explain the difference between self-image and self-esteem.

9. What is the name of the perspective that views communication as the primary means by which people internalize and use social values to guide how they see themselves, how they see others, and how they interact?

10. The influence between self and communication is reciprocal. (T/F)

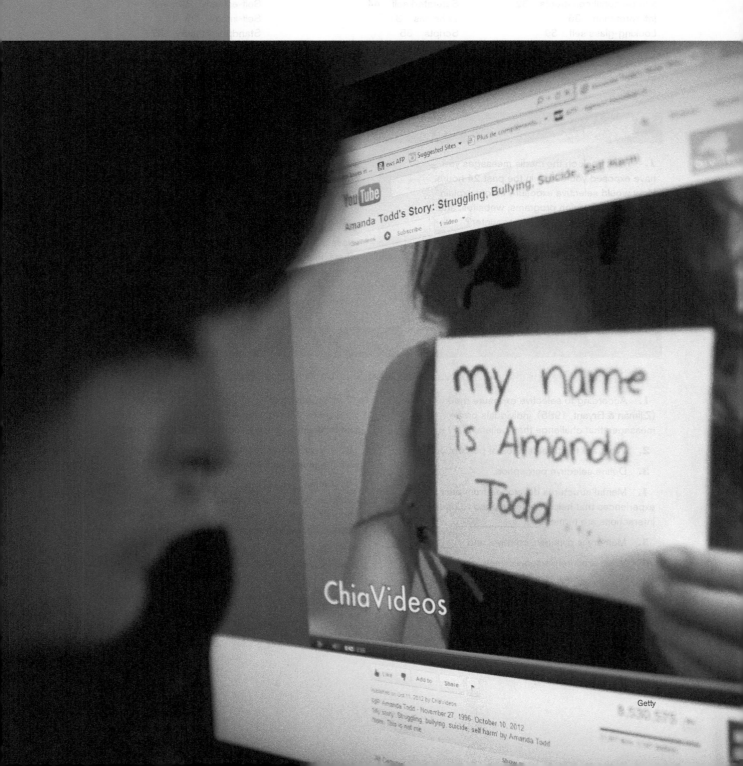

After studying this chapter, you will be able to:

1 Explain how verbal communication differs from nonverbal communication.

2 Describe the nature and characteristics of symbols.

3 Explain the importance of grammar and meaning for effective communication.

4 Identify the important functions of verbal messages.

5 Explain theories of message production and interpretation.

Amanda Todd was a small 15-year-old girl from Port Coquitlam, Canada. On Wednesday, October 10, 2012, Amanda Todd killed herself. Amanda's story is probably the most notorious cyberbullying case in history. In the weeks after her death, the heartbreaking details of her story emerged. In seventh grade, a man she did not know convinced her to reveal her breasts during a webcam session. For years, that man harassed and blackmailed Amanda for more nude pictures. He set up a Facebook profile featuring her naked upper body as the profile photo. Facing intense ridicule, Amanda changed schools three times. A group of young girls beat her, while others stood by and recorded with a phone camera, bringing further humiliation from her peers. Amanda became intensely anxious and depressed. She first attempted to take her own life by drinking bleach. This unsuccessful attempt was followed by more of the online cruelty that made her wish to die in the first place. Online commentators urged her to "try harder." One month before her death, Amanda posted a video to her YouTube channel. With a flashcard confession, she chronicled her struggle with bullying, harassment, and loneliness. "Every day I think, why am I still here?" she wrote.

"I have nobody. I need somebody. . . . My name is Amanda Todd" (The Amanda Todd Story, 2014). She would be ridiculed again for this cry for help. Even after she successfully ended her life, online bullies continued their attacks by creating memes and hashtags of Amanda Todd suicide jokes and vandalizing her memorial pages.

Sadly, Amanda's story is not unique. Countless teens are bullied by words, whether they are delivered in person or through a technological medium. Adults also face negative and hurtful messages in their jobs, relationships, and even families. Both verbal bullying and cyberbullying have the capacity to destroy lives. Whether the issue is sexuality, weight, or social status, hateful words carry consequences. Even if you are not the victim or the perpetrator of the bullying, speak up. Verbal communication can build and enhance lives.

The words we say and write matter. All verbal messages have consequences, both good and bad. This chapter discusses how verbal communication allows us to create and participate in social reality. First, we discuss the differences between verbal and nonverbal communication. We also focus on the nature of language, the functions of verbal messages, and theories that help explain the production and interpretation of verbal messages. As you read the chapter, think about the ways in which your own messages shape your social world and relationships. Are there things you can say and write to make life in the Communication Age better for yourself and others?

VERBAL VERSUS NONVERBAL COMMUNICATION

Verbal communication and nonverbal communication are intimately related. We use each form to complement, reinforce, and add meaning to the other, yet verbal communication and nonverbal communication are distinct. The language of verbal communication is a digital code that represents messages through the use of symbols, whereas nonverbal communication is an analog code that represents things through likeness or similarity.

Verbal communication is powerful because we convey a clear and exact message with words, whereas nonverbal communication is often used to convey feelings and impressions (see Figure 3.1). Chapter 4 further explores the characteristics and functions of nonverbal communication. The purpose of the current chapter is to take a closer look at how the digital code of language, with its relative precision and clarity, contributes to the process of communication.

Verbal	Nonverbal
Digital code	Analog code
Represents by symbols	Represents by likeness
Efficiency (more meaning in less space)	Warmth (emotional expressiveness)
Clarity (easier to interpret meaning)	Authenticity (trusted as sincere)
Content level of meaning	Relationship level of meaning
More intentional	Less intentional

FIGURE 3.1
VERBAL VERSUS NONVERBAL COMMUNICATION

THE BUILDING BLOCKS OF LANGUAGE

Verbal communication involves the use of language—a system of words represented by symbols, used for a common purpose by a group of people. The following sections provide a definition of symbols and then discuss the characteristics of symbols.

Words as Symbols

Words are symbols that convey meaning and characterize ideas, people, places, or concepts. There has to be social agreement about the meaning associated with a particular symbol. In other words, we are not free as individuals to change the meaning of a word without widespread agreement with others. Because there is no direct relationship between the symbol and the object it represents, language can be complicated.

Ogden and Richards (1927) maintained that symbols could be thought of as representing a triangle of meaning. One point on the triangle is the symbol or word. The second point on the triangle refers to the thoughts about this symbol. These thoughts about the word come from our beliefs, interactions, and experiences with others. The third point on the triangle is the referent, or actual object to which the word refers. Understandings of language exist in the relationships between all three points on the triangle of meaning (Nesterov, 2009). Therefore, it takes the actual word, thoughts about the word, and the object to collectively make an element of language meaningful.

In Figure 3.2, you will see the triangle of meaning using the symbol "narwhal." The first point on the triangle is the word *narwhal*. The second point on the triangle represents the thoughts about the symbol. Some people refer to the narwhal as the "unicorn of the sea" and envision all that goes with the symbol of the unicorn as a mythical and magical creature, while

Many technologies have evolved from analog to digital. Traditional wristwatches indicate time on a circular dial synced with the path of the Earth's rotation. The movement of the hour hand is analogous to the sun's path across the sky. Digital watches display time through numbers on a screen.

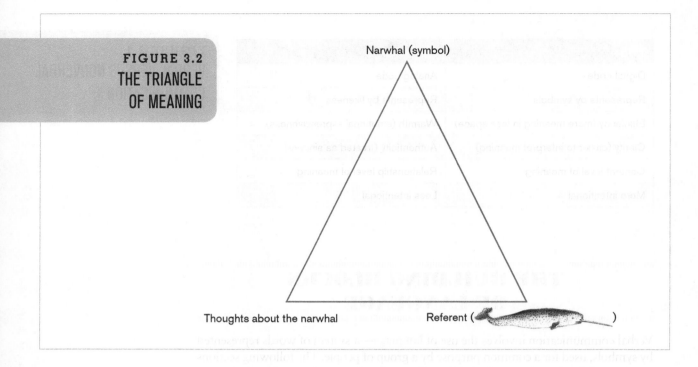

FIGURE 3.2
THE TRIANGLE
OF MEANING

Narwhal (symbol)

Thoughts about the narwhal

Referent (   )

others know that narwhals are rare and highly valued by some cultures. The third point on the triangle is the actual narwhal as an object. Together, all three points compose the meaning of narwhal: the word, the ideas, and the object. In the following sections, you will learn about the characteristics of symbols.

Symbols Are Arbitrary

Symbols are arbitrary, which means there is no natural likeness between a symbol and what it represents. For instance, there's nothing particularly catlike about the letters *C, A,* and *T* that we string together to refer to the animal. The word doesn't *look* like a cat. Saying the word aloud doesn't *sound* like a cat. Our shared understanding of what *cat* means relies on social agreement of the symbol, rather than likeness. The speakers of a language have agreed that the letters *C, A,* and *T* will stand for a particular animal. The arbitrary nature of symbols means that we could just as easily have called a "cat" a "book," as long as everyone used the same word for similar social purposes.

Symbols Are Abstract

Symbols are abstract in the sense that they represent an object or idea without being physically similar to the object or idea. This is especially true when representing complex ideas. Take the concept of "democracy." That single symbol encapsulates the complexities of a historical concept, a way of structuring government, and a set of cultural ideals. Try expressing "democracy" nonverbally. It's an understatement to say it's going to take you a while to get the idea across. One benefit of symbols being abstract is that they can offer greater clarity than can nonverbal communication. Although there's always room for interpretation when we communicate verbally, words are less ambiguous than nonverbal behaviors but are better able to communicate abstractions.

Symbols Are Intentional

Symbols are intentional in their usage because social agreement about the meaning of a word allows it to fulfill its function. Communicators must understand how their words are being interpreted and use them in ways that reflect that shared understanding. Think back to the example of the word *cat*. We have to agree that the letters *C, A,* and *T* mean *cat*. We also have to agree that *cat* refers to a particular type of animal. This is intentional. Have you ever heard a small child call a known object a silly name? Depending on her age, the child may or may not know language is being misused. But if the child does *not* know the name of an object, someone will tell her the name of the object so that she can intentionally use the correct name next time. If a person wants a shared understanding with others to create and participate in social reality, communication is always intentional at the level of the symbol.

Symbols Are Uniquely Human

Symbols are the basic building blocks that humans use to create and participate in social reality. Communication theorist Kenneth Burke (1966) states that humans are the symbol-using and symbol-misusing animals. His definition is important for understanding how we use symbols to craft a social world. First, we humans use, misuse, and make symbols that we need for living. With language, we make ideas such as democracy, community, justice, social networking, and peace. We misuse words to deceive, manipulate, and exaggerate. In other words, the ability to use symbols is the key to communication, and Burke argued that this is what makes us human. At this point, many of you may be thinking of your amazing dog that can do tricks and

understands your commands. Yes? While dogs can be quite good at enacting specific behaviors that we tell them to do (sit, lie down, fetch), dogs do not create and participate in a social world independent of human action. Dogs in the wild do dog behaviors for survival. Dogs living with humans do dog behaviors and human-trained behaviors (Reid, 2009). As far as researchers know, humans are the only animals who use arbitrary, abstract, and intentional symbols to craft a social world.

Second, this idea is even more important when Burke (1966) argues that humans uniquely invented the concept of a negative. The negative does not really exist in nature. Can you point to the sky and say, "Look! Negative two birds are flying"? People would look at you weird if you did. The idea of the negative is important because it gives us the ability to define words in opposition to something else. Take, for example, the two simple text messages "She's pretty" and "She's NOT pretty." The word *not* makes all the difference

In *Switched at Birth*, Bay and Daphne communicate through American Sign Language (ASL). Daphne mastered ASL and lip reading at a young age. Bay is newer to ASL and sometimes struggles to use and interpret signs appropriately. Like spoken symbols, the signs of ASL are intentional. They work because communicators have a shared understanding of their meaning. Have you experienced communication difficulties based on different understandings of the meaning of a symbol?

CAREER FRONTIER: **LEARN TO CODE**

CODING, or using programming language to instruct computers to perform specific functions, is an increasingly valuable and necessary 21st-century skill. Knowledge of coding allows you to design, write, test, repair/debug, and maintain the source code of computer programs. Until recently, coding was treated as a specialized skill reserved for computer scientists and some mathematicians and engineers. Today, people from all walks of life would benefit from developing the ability to code competently. Because a great many of our everyday activities are reliant on, enabled by, and controlled through software (including applications, documents, images, and the interfaces providing access across computer components), the ability to actually create and alter mediated structures according to your own personal or professional goals is powerful. According to some, coding is a "new literacy," a basic requirement for full participation in the digital age (Royal, 2015; Rushkoff, 2012). Coding may expand your ability to create and participate in social reality, much like reading and writing did in earlier centuries.

Coding used to be understood as a binary: something you either could or could not do. Now, we understand coding knowledge as a spectrum, ranging from very basic abilities (understanding enough to know what's possible) to more advanced (building new solutions with technology) (Royal, 2015). Whether you are creating a webpage, blogging, making a mobile app, processing data, gaming,

or creating an interactive media experience, some level of coding ability will give you a competitive advantage. Just having a basic understanding of how coding works gives you a fuller understanding of your world. Take Facebook, for instance, which most kids would describe as a social networking site designed to connect friends. At face value, they're not wrong. But the code literate also understand that Facebook's programs (and algorithms) are designed to harvest and monetize the data given off by those online friendships. In the words of digital literacy advocate Doug Rushkoff (2012), "kids aren't Facebook's customers; they're the product." Without code literacy, it can be difficult to see clearly and make informed choices when using communication technology.

ISSUES TO CONSIDER

- Consider learning the basics of coding: data types, variables, loops, functions, and the art of an algorithm.
- Try to include a course in coding as part of your degree plan.
- Look into a free online resource (e.g., http://www .codecademy.com).

Sources: Royal, C. (2015, March 25). Why universities need to embrace coding across the curriculum (http://www.pbs.org/mediashift); Rushkoff, D. (2012, November 13). Code literacy: A 21st-century requirement (www.edutopia.org).

▶ **COMMUNICATION IN ACTION 3.1**

WATCH: Differing Cultural Meanings

When Chris explains to Liz why he is late for work, they face a miscommunication based on differing cultural meanings of the same symbol. What was your initial interpretation of Chris's statement?

when creating and participating in the social reality of commenting on this person's appearance.

Symbols Are Culturally Bound

Symbols simultaneously create and reflect culture. Think about where you live. If you live in a place that received a lot of snow during the winter, it is likely that you have more words and phrases to describe the cold and precipitation. A student in Michigan will likely understand the meaning of an "Alberta clipper," a "lake effect snowstorm," or the rare atmospheric phenomenon known as "thundersnow" more readily than will a student living in Southern California or Texas. This is because the symbols we use are, in part, determined by the communities in which we live and speak.

Symbols Are Contextually Bound

Symbols exist in a context or situation. Have you ever noticed how some words have more than one meaning? This is referred to as polysemy. If we intentionally use a polysemic word to confuse another person, we are being unethical. If we accidently use a polysemic word and it confuses someone, we have miscommunicated our intended meaning of the word. If the other person knows the meaning of a polysemic symbol we intended, it is because of the context. Take the term "Facebook official." Is this the title of a high-ranking member of the Facebook organization? Does Facebook grant a seal deeming approval for certain actions? Or has a romantic couple publicly announced their togetherness by changing their relationship status online?

What words would your culture use to describe this person?

Of course, it's the last option. We know that because the most familiar context for *Facebook official* is when partners take a next step in their relationship. The surest way to determine the intended meaning of language is to examine the surrounding symbols and larger context.

Grammar and Meaning

The most basic building blocks of a language are its sounds. The sounds of a language are called phonemes. The hard *C* in the word *cat* is an example of a phoneme. As speakers of a language, the first thing we must master is the ability to make the required sounds. People who do this well are called *articulate*. Infants can discern and mimic all the different phonemes of all human languages. However, the more they are exposed to a certain language, the more they begin to hear and speak only their language-specific phonemes (Minagawa-Kawai, Mori, Naoi, & Kojima, 2007). You may have heard babies *trilling,* or naturally rolling their *R*s. You may also have noticed that many mature native English speakers have a difficult time doing this when they attempt to learn Spanish.

Phonemes combine to form morphemes, which are the smallest units of meaning in a language. Once we learn the sounds of a language, we must learn what its words mean. Sometimes, a word contains only one morpheme, as in the combination of the sounds of /c/, /a/, and /t/ to form *cat*. In other instances, a single word contains several morphemes. The word *exported* has three morphemes. The root word *port* indicates an action that is being performed: to port, or bring, something. The prefix *ex-* indicates the direction of the action, and *-ed* indicates that the action was performed in the past. We acquire a great deal of our ability to understand and use morphemes in the first few years of life (R. Brown, 1973).

Phonemes are the basic building blocks of language.

The study of the meaning of words is called semantics. Semantics is concerned with two types of meanings: denotative and connotative. Denotative meaning refers to a word's formal, or "dictionary," definition. Denotative meanings are highly public. They frame the "correct" or "accepted" use of a term for an entire culture or language. Connotative meanings, on the other hand, are informal

There are dozens of Internet sites devoted to capturing funny grammatical errors on public signs. What did this shop owner intend to communicate? What does the message actually mean?

meanings associated with feelings and personal experiences. They are relational rather than public. That's because they are used among smaller, more intimately connected groups of people. Misunderstandings may arise when we confuse a connotative meaning for a denotative meaning. Suppose someone describes a dance routine as "sick!" In U.S. culture, the denotative meaning of those terms would indicate that the person was displeased or revolted by the moves. But in several American subcultures, especially youth culture and artistic communities, "sick!" is among the highest compliments a performance can receive. Understanding the denotative and connotative meanings of a culture and knowing when to use one versus the other is an important feature of verbal communication competence. Can you think of other examples of the clash between denotative and connotative meanings?

We combine morphemes, or individual units of meaning, to form sentences. Syntax refers to meaning at the level of sentences. Syntax relies on an understanding of two or more individual words to produce more complex chains of meaning. Each language contains intricate rules for syntax. We refer to these rules as the grammar of a language. People who are competent in the use of syntax demonstrate grammatical correctness. Understanding grammar is important to the process of communication because minor errors in word order, punctuation, and spelling can drastically alter the intended meaning.

FUNCTIONS OF VERBAL MESSAGES

It should be clear, from the preceding sections, that language is the basic building block of verbal messages. Furthermore, the symbolic nature of language is what separates verbal messages from nonverbal messages, which you will learn more about in the next chapter. At this point, let us turn our attention to the key roles that verbal messages play in the process of communication. Specifically, we examine the ways in which verbal messages aid in creating and participating in social reality.

Creation

Verbal communication gives us the ability to create the social world around us. Think back to the definition of communication as the collaborative process of using messages to create and participate in social reality. Cultural anthropologists Edward Sapir and Benjamin Whorf presented the linguistic relativity hypothesis to describe the idea that language creates and shapes our social reality. In a well-known example, Whorf (1956) contrasted the languages and cultures of the Hopi (American Indians residing primarily in Arizona) and English speakers. The English language treats time as a "line" that can be separated into countable units like days, months, or years, whereas the Hopi language treats time as a process. In Hopi language, there are no verb tenses to make a distinction between the past, present, and future. According to Whorf, these differences in language correspond to different ways of being in and creating the social world.

As such, the creation component of verbal communication is important for how we

- create face-to-face and computer-mediated identities and social selves (Comello, 2009; Stritzke, Nguyen, & Durkin, 2004);

- generate new theories, ideas, concepts, and words (Glowka, Barrett, Barnhart, Melancom, & Salter, 2009);

- establish social, economic, and governmental systems (Herrmann, 2007; Lees-Marshment, 2009); and

- make new relational and family forms (Domingue & Mollen, 2009; Soliz, Ribarsky, Harrigan, & Tye-Williams, 2010).

Because verbal communication can powerfully shape our social world, using sensitive, empowering, and inclusive language is especially important. Inclusive language employs expressions and words that are broad enough to include all people and avoids expressions and words that exclude particular groups. For instance, when referring to people, in general, gender-inclusive language replaces words like *man, chairman,* and *mankind* with *human, chairperson,* and *humankind.* In the same vein, many men may feel shut out by practices like referring to all nurses as women (for instance, by saying, "One of the first things a nurse must learn is that her patients come first"). When we open the space for both men and women to occupy a variety of roles in our language, we open the space for both men and women to occupy a variety of roles in life.

Participation

The second part of the definition of communication focuses on participating in social reality. Because communication is collaborative, we rely on creating shared understandings so that we can participate with others. Verbal communication allows us to participate in the social world by asserting, promising, apologizing, requesting, expressing, and performing. We are able to connect and engage with others in our messages through our participation in families, intimate relationships, friendships, relationships with coworkers, religious organizations, or communities. Participation is an important part of the things we say and can include the following:

- providing social support and comforting messages (Mikkelson, Floyd, & Pauley, 2011; Rains & Keating, 2011);

- interacting with others in romantic, friend, family, and work relationships (Cowan & Bochantin, 2011; Dillow, Malachowski, Brann, & Weber, 2011);

Verbal communication is a primary way people participate in family life and relationships.

Thinkstock

COMMUNICATIONHOW-TO
MAKE LANGUAGE INCLUSIVE

Making your language inclusive of everyone is an important part of being an ethical communicator. The chart below offers several common examples of ways to make language inclusive.

Exclusive words or phrases	Inclusive words or phrases
Man, Mankind	Human, Humankind, Women and Men
The man on the street	The average person
Manpower	Workforce, Personnel
Policeman, Fireman, Mailman	Police officer, Firefighter, Postal worker
Chairman	Chair
The disabled, The handicapped	People with disabilities
Wheelchair bound	A person using a wheelchair
Victim of AIDS	A person living with AIDS
Mothering	Parenting
Freshman	First-year student
Woman lawyer, Woman doctor, Male nurse	Lawyer, Doctor, Nurse
The old, The geriatric, Elderly	Older adults, Older person
Indian (U.S.)	Native American, American Indian
American (referring to citizen of the United States)	U.S. American

- organizing social structures such as families, schools, religious groups, community organizations, governments, and corporations (Hall, 2007; Medved, 2007);

- listening to others (Floyd, 2010; Weger, Castle, & Emmett, 2010);

- overcoming barriers because of culture and diversity to foster shared realities (Drummond & Orbe, 2009; Kim, 2007); and

- working together as small groups and teams (Berry, 2011; Galanes, 2009).

Participation in verbal communication can also be negative. Complete the "Assess Your Communication: Verbal Aggressiveness" self-assessment to measure your own verbal aggressiveness toward others in communication. When you have finished scoring yourself, think about the hurtful and negative things you might have said before and how you can avoid being aggressive in your communication.

PRODUCTION AND INTERPRETATION OF VERBAL MESSAGES

Up to this point, this chapter has focused on explaining the critical differences between verbal and nonverbal communication, discussing the features of language, and exploring the key functions of verbal messages. Each of those topics is important to understanding the ways in which verbal messages may be used to create and participate in social reality. Yet it is also important to keep in mind that communication is a collaborative process. Communication is more than simply employing language to produce and deliver verbal messages; communication requires people to work together in dynamic and ongoing ways.

Managing Meaning

Once we master the ability to make the sounds of a language, and combine them to form words and sentences, how do we use language to create and participate in social reality? Coordinated management of meaning (CMM) theory focuses on how we coordinate our actions with others to make and manage meaning (Pearce & Cronen, 1980). According to CMM theory, communication involves eight levels of interpretation.

Content

The first is content, or the actual information contained in a spoken or written message. Suppose you are walking down a busy campus sidewalk and see a former classmate. You call out, "Hey, James, good to see you!" At the content level, James hears the words that you've just said, and chances are he'll quickly recognize the sound of his own name and look toward you.

Speech Act

The second level is the speech act, which refers to the various actions we perform through speech. Promises, threats, apologies, questions, and assertions are all examples of speech acts. In this case, James would recognize your message as the speech act of a "greeting." He'll understand that you are recognizing his presence and expressing goodwill. But James will also need to put this speech act into the context of a larger episode.

Episode

An episode is a broader situation created by conversational partners. After James returns your greeting, you might say, "Listen, I just left my last class of the day. Want to grab a bite to eat and catch up?" James can now form a larger picture of the interaction as a situation in which two acquaintances reconnect. Likely, he'll even realize that he has a "script" for this situation. He can use his previous experiences to figure out what to expect and how to behave.

Communication unplugged
TO IMPROVE VERBAL COMMUNICATION, TRY FACE TO FACE

iStock

Face-to-face communication is often best for sharing difficult news and discussing serious options.

The typical range of options now available to share a verbal message includes in-person communication, letters, phone calls, voice messages, instant messaging, video chat, online videos, texting, e-mail, and social network posts. Each possibility for verbal communication involves the use of a different medium, or channel. Yet people often overlook the ways in which the meaning and appropriateness of verbal communication differ according to choice of media (Walther & Parks, 2002). Communication theorist Marshall McLuhan (1964) coined the phrase "the medium is the message" to refer to the ways in which characteristics of a medium itself, and not just the messages it carries, can communicate and influence the social landscape. According to McLuhan, communication media are not simply neutral channels, but carry important messages of their own (Giddings, 2011; Levinson, 1999). In the case of relationship breakups, many people believe that being "dumped by text" is particularly hurtful and inconsiderate. Among students, face-to-face conversation is considered ideal for breaking up because it has the broadest information

bandwidth. Partners can take turns, ask questions, hear tone of voice, and offer lengthier explanations than those enabled through other media (Gershon, 2008). Yet some people prefer to use mediated channels to deliver difficult verbal messages as a means for managing others' impressions of them (O'Sullivan, 2000) or avoiding uncomfortable reactions.

When constructing your verbal messages and contributing them to conversations, it is important to carefully consider both the potential advantages and disadvantages of the medium you choose. Sometimes, it's best to forgo communication technologies for verbal communication and be physically present, face to face.

WHAT TO DO NEXT
To make the most of face-to-face communication, try to:

- Handle fights/relationship problems in person. Texting is great for expressing affection, but a poor choice for expressing negative emotion or resolving relationship conflict (Shade, Sandberg, Bean, Busby, & Coyne, 2013).

- Make apologies face to face. Texting to apologize is associated with lower relationship quality (Shade et al., 2013).

- Avoid sharing private information online. No verbal message conveyed with communication technology is truly private. Computer-mediated messages may be archived, sold, illegally obtained by a third party, or inadvertently broadcast.

- Physically show up to deliver serious messages. Whether the information is positive (a marriage proposal, birth announcement) or negative (bad news, illness), if it is truly monumental or potentially life changing, share it face to face with those who are most affected. Police officers and medical professionals are trained to deliver difficult news in person to respect the gravity of the situation and help the recipient cope.

Relationship

Yet he will also need to consider the relationship between the two of you. Whether two people are parent and child, teacher and student, significant others, or strangers has a tremendous impact on how they coordinate their actions and manage meanings. In this case, James may decide that the two of you are casual acquaintances but have the potential to be friends. He may lean toward accepting your offer.

ASSESS YOUR COMMUNICATION

VERBAL AGGRESSIVENESS

INSTRUCTIONS: Each of the following statements relates to verbal aggressiveness in your communication. Carefully consider each item. Then, rate your level of agreement along the 5-point scale.

1. I do not avoid attacking others' intelligence when I attack their ideas.

   Strongly Disagree   1   2   3   4   5   Strongly Agree

2. When someone else is acting stubborn, I use insults to soften the stubbornness.

   Strongly Disagree   1   2   3   4   5   Strongly Agree

3. I do not avoid having others feel bad about themselves when I try to influence them.

   Strongly Disagree   1   2   3   4   5   Strongly Agree

4. When others refuse to do a task I know is important, I tell them they are acting unreasonable.

   Strongly Disagree   1   2   3   4   5   Strongly Agree

5. When others behave in ways that are in poor taste, I insult them in order to shock them into proper behavior.

   Strongly Disagree   1   2   3   4   5   Strongly Agree

6. I do not try to make others feel good about themselves, even when their ideas are stupid.

   Strongly Disagree   1   2   3   4   5   Strongly Agree

7. When others will not budge on a matter of importance, I lose my temper and say rather strong things to them.

   Strongly Disagree   1   2   3   4   5   Strongly Agree

8. When others criticize my shortcomings, I do not take it in good humor and try to get back at them.

   Strongly Disagree   1   2   3   4   5   Strongly Agree

9. I like poking fun at others who do things that are stupid in order to stimulate their intelligence.

   Strongly Disagree   1   2   3   4   5   Strongly Agree

10. When nothing seems to work in trying to influence others, I yell and scream in order to get some reaction from them.

    Strongly Disagree   1   2   3   4   5   Strongly Agree

Now add together your scores for all 10 items. Your total score will be somewhere between 10 and 50.

This instrument measures the degree to which you engage in verbal aggressive communication behavior. If you scored at the lower end of the range (between 10 and 25), you are not very aggressive in your communication with others. If you scored at the higher end of the range (26–50), you tend to be more aggressive in your communication with others.

Source: Measure adapted from "Verbal Aggressiveness: An Interpersonal Model and Measure," by D. A. Infante and C. J. Wigley, 1986, in *Communication Monographs, 53,* pp. 61–69.

The nature and history of the relationship between communicators influence how they make and manage meaning together.

iStock

Self

However, James's view of self will also come into play. Each of us brings a "script for who we are" into every interaction. If James sees himself as outgoing and open to new experiences, he may say, "Definitely, let's do it!" because that response is in line with his self-concept.

Culture

Culture also plays a role in how you and James will negotiate the meaning of the situation. Culture relates to a set of rules for acting and speaking, which determine what we consider to be normal and acceptable in a given situation. Imagine you are a woman who is engaged to be married. It may occur to both you and James that our culture can sometimes look suspiciously on cross-sex friendships. This may give one or both of you a reason to question the appropriateness of making or accepting an invitation to hang out.

Coordination

As communication unfolds, it requires a good deal of coordination, or the establishment of rules that help guide people through the interaction. To make and manage the meanings of an interaction, communicators rely on two distinct types of rules. Constitutive rules stipulate what counts as what and how our messages and behavior are to be interpreted. For instance, your family may have a constitutive rule that texting at the dinner table counts as "rude." Or, in one of your friendships, you may have a constitutive rule that vigorous teasing counts as "affection." Likewise, you and James may coordinate an understanding that grabbing a bite counts as "friendly" rather than "romantic." Regulative rules guide how individuals respond or behave in interactions. For instance, in the classroom context, you may recognize regulative rules like "you should raise your hand before you speak in class," or "never turn your work in late." Once you arrive at the restaurant, you and James may rely on regulative rules such as "take turns speaking," "sit on opposite sides of the table," "pay for your own meal," and "stick to topics that are appropriate for casual friends."

Mystery

Although it may seem the interaction between you and James will unfold in a fairly predictable manner, there is always room for the possibility of mystery, or the idea that not everything within communication can be easily explained by understanding the situation. Sometimes, when we least expect it, an ordinary conversation can lead to the experience of wonder and awe. We may be taken aback by a deep sense of connection to the other, a flash of insight, a life-changing realization, or an immense sense of joy we never saw coming. Often, such moments seem to "emerge" from the conversation itself rather than from the partners. Communication scholars have devoted relatively little attention to the mystery of interactions. But there are some exceptions. Ron

Gordon (1985) investigated peak communication experiences (PCEs), which refer to our "greatest moments" of mutual understanding, happiness, and fulfillment in interpersonal communication. Gordon's research demonstrated that many people report having powerful, but relatively rare, conversations in which they experience a heightened sense of connectedness, growth, and transcendence.

Cooperating in Conversations

As is clear from the previous section on CMM theory, the meaningful exchange of verbal messages requires a good deal of coordination and cooperation among conversation partners. Philosopher Paul Grice (1975) introduced the cooperative principle to describe how people normally behave in interactions with one another. According to Grice (1989), in order to understand one another's verbal messages, people must make their "conversational contribution such as is required, at the stage at which it occurs, by the accepted purpose or direction of the talk exchange in which you are engaged" (p. 26). In other words, we have to respond to conversations in ways that others can expect as deemed by the type or nature of the conversation. This is important because effective verbal communication is achieved by speaking cooperatively and by expecting others to do the same (Boltz, Dyer, & Miller, 2010; Ephratt, 2011). What counts as being verbally cooperative? What are our conversational partners expecting from our verbal messages, and what can we expect from theirs? According to Grice, there are four maxims, or principles, we obey when we follow the cooperative principle. Each maxim helps explain the relationship between a speaker's verbal message and what a listener understands from that message.

Quality Maxim

One of the expectations that we bring to our conversations is that the verbal messages exchanged will be truthful. In other words, the quality maxim refers to the idea that communicators assume verbal messages are not being used to convey information that is believed to be false or lacks adequate evidence.

Violations of the quality maxim of the cooperative principle can act as a red flag, or an implication that the conversation involves deception.

Quantity Maxim

The quantity maxim refers to the expectation that verbal messages offer the appropriate amount of information, given the situation. Stated differently, communicators assume that neither too much nor too little information will be provided. By violating expectations for message length, both extremely brief and extremely long conversational contributions red-flag our messages as potentially uncooperative and deceitful.

▶ **COMMUNICATION IN ACTION 3.2**

WATCH: Avoiding Offensive Language

A woman takes offense when her boyfriend uses a slang term to refer to a female college classmate. How did you react to his word choice?

A lack of truthfulness in communication leads to perceptions of uncooperativeness.

③ Relevance Maxim

The relevance maxim maintains that communicators expect one another to "be relevant" in their verbal messages. Grice (1989) acknowledged that conversations can and do naturally shift from one topic to another. However, the maxim of relevance is violated when messages are formulated to distract attention from the matter at hand rather than cooperatively addressing the situation. Diverting the focus to an irrelevant topic goes against conversational expectations and incriminates the message sender as uncooperative or dishonest.

④ Manner Maxim

The manner maxim refers to the expectation that communicators "be clear." Clarity involves constructing verbal messages that are orderly and comprehensible, and that avoid vagueness and ambiguity. We tend to expect logical and clear-cut messages. A disorderly and confusing message is often perceived as uncooperative and unsatisfying.

The cooperative principle, and the four maxims it comprises, helps us understand what communicators tend to expect of verbal messages. In order to enable effective verbal communication, it is important to remember that listeners typically expect our conversational contributions to be truthful, appropriately detailed, relevant, and clear. A violation of one or more of these maxims often leads to difficulties in understanding one another and setbacks in collaboratively creating and participating in social reality. The cooperative principle also aids us in recognizing the reasons why we may sometimes feel frustrated by the verbal messages we receive from others. Grice (1975) recognized that without cooperation, conversations would be difficult and counterproductive.

Designing Verbal Messages

In some situations, the verbal messages people produce are relatively uniform (P. Brown & Levinson, 1978). For instance, if asked to describe an apartment to someone who has never seen it, most people follow a similar formula. They might say, "It's a second-floor unit with two bedrooms, one-and-a-half baths. It's about 800 square feet. It has a fireplace, a washer and dryer, and a walk-out balcony." In other words, there is a general understanding that a housing description should contain certain bits of information, often presented in a certain order. However, in more complex communication situations, like when we must regulate another person's behavior or provide comfort, there is a great deal of variety in the verbal messages produced by each person. Communication scholar Barbara O'Keefe (1988) developed the theory of message design logic to help explain why different people produce different messages even under similar circumstances.

For example, suppose you face a difficult communication encounter with a member of a group you've been assigned to oversee for a class project. The name of the group member is Ron, and he's been causing problems for you and the other members for several weeks. Ron shows up late to meetings, sometimes missing them altogether, and fails to produce the parts of the project that were delegated to him. The really

INFORMED CONSENT

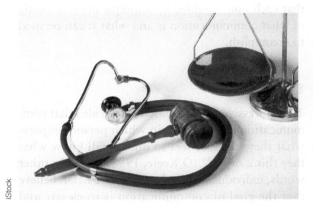

iStock

Tyler Bowling, a 21-year-old man, says he was tricked into appearing on *The Doctors,* a popular daytime TV show with millions of viewers that discusses health and lifestyle issues. Bowling has a medical condition that causes small bumps on his penis. The show invited him on the show to discuss this issue and promised to pay for laser treatment to remove the bumps. Bowling claims that the show's producers told him that the TV show was seen only by doctors and medical students, and that they neglected to tell him about the live studio audience. After he told the producers of his reservations about doing the show, he maintains that a secretary told him that his appearance on the show would be anonymous. Despite

his doubts, Bowling signed the release forms and was sent in front of a live studio audience to discuss the intimate details of his medical condition. After the show aired, Bowling sued the show and CBS. He asserts that his appearance caused him embarrassment and harassment because it was seen by millions of people (Walsh, 2010).

Assuming Bowling's claims are true, the producers intentionally distorted the messages about the type of audience and his ability to remain anonymous. In short, he was treated as an object for a TV show instead of as a person. By rushing him onto the set, the producers rejected Bowling's concerns and robbed him of his autonomy as a person. Ethical communication allows a person to have all the information needed to make a real choice and be empowered to make a choice. If true, the producers of the show were not allowing for ethical communication by being irresponsible with their verbal messages. In your own verbal communication, you should try to promote autonomy and responsibility for yourself and others.

QUESTIONS

1. How could Bowling's situation have been avoided by the producers of the show? What could Bowling have done?

2. Are there times when it might not be ethical to give all the information needed to make a choice? Why or why not?

tough part is that you're the leader of the group. Your professor made it your job to oversee the project and report back on the grade each member of the group deserves at the end of the task. So there will be an overall group grade decided by the professor, as well as individual grades decided by you. To make the situation even harder, doing well in the class and making a high grade are very important to you, and the deadline is fast approaching. On the evening before your group planned to meet to put the final touches on the project, Ron calls you to tell you that he still hasn't finished the research assigned him and doesn't think he'll be able to get it done in time. So what would you say to Ron? Take a moment to think about the exact verbal message you would deliver if you found yourself in this situation.

According to O'Keefe (1988), individuals develop personal theories of the nature and purposes of communication. Our working models of communication guide us in producing messages in response to difficult communication tasks like the one described above. These message design logics are distinct ways of thinking about communication situations, choosing which thoughts to express, and deciding how to express them in order to achieve goals (O'Keefe, 1991). Thus, the theory of message

On *Real Housewives of New York City*, castmates Kristen Taekman and Ramona Singer engage in frequent conflict. Kristen and Ramona face the need to call out and regulate each other's behavior, but also to maintain the relationship necessary to share the same circle of friends and star on the same series. What is a competent verbal message you could use if you overheard a friend or workmate talking bad about you?

design logic explains the reasoning people use to get from thoughts and goals to verbal messages. Using research participants' responses to the group project situation previously presented, O'Keefe identified three message design logics (MDLs). Keep in mind that each one is guided by a unique understanding of what communication is and what it can be used to accomplish.

Expressive

The expressive MDL is based on the idea that communication is "a process in which persons express what they think or feel so others will know what they think or feel" (O'Keefe, 1988, p. 84). In other words, individuals with the expressive MDL believe that the goal of communication is to clearly and fully disclose exactly what runs through their minds at the time. A person operating with this logic might respond to Ron's disappointing announcement by saying,

> Ron, you are unbelievable! You have no idea how much I hate you right now. You've completely screwed the group. Don't even bother coming to the meeting. Hope you enjoy your F. You've earned it!

Most of us can sympathize with the sentiments expressed in this response to Ron. Whether at school or at work, it is likely you have experienced a similar frustration with someone who failed to carry his or her weight, thereby forcing everyone else to pay the price. In other words, the thoughts expressed in the message above do cross most people's minds to some degree. Yet not everyone expresses those thoughts as freely as people with expressive MDLs. That is because not everyone thinks the goal of communication is simply to give a full and unedited account of current thoughts and feelings.

Conventional

The conventional MDL is based on the idea that communication is "a game to be played cooperatively, according to socially conventional rules and procedures" (O'Keefe & McCornack, 1987, p. 71). In other words, conventional communicators draw a line between what they think and what they say in order to achieve their social goals. Whereas expressive communicators strive simply to be open with their thoughts and emotions, conventional communicators strive to be socially appropriate, cooperative, and in control of their resources. A person operating with the conventional MDL might say,

> Ron, as the leader of the group it's my job to keep everyone on track. At this point, you've had multiple chances to get your act together. I want to remind you that the entire group is counting on you to get your part done. If one

person doesn't do his or her share, everybody suffers. That's just not fair to the rest of us. You need to have your work done by the meeting tomorrow, or I'll be forced to recommend to the professor that you get a failing grade.

Instead of focusing on an emotional reaction to Ron's undesirable behavior, this message is geared toward a social goal: gaining Ron's compliance in completing his task by reminding him of his social obligations.

Rhetorical

The third type of MDL is based on the notion that communication involves "the creation and negotiation of social selves and situations" (O'Keefe, 1988, p. 85). Rhetorical message producers use their understanding of how verbal messages can be used to reshape situations and identities in order to create a desired social reality. Rather than striving for complete openness or social appropriateness in their messages, rhetorical communicators aim for creative and flexible verbal solutions that redefine the problem and present a possible solution that offers harmony and consensus. For example,

Ron, I can only imagine that you've been going through some hardships that have made it really difficult for you to give this project 100%. We've all been there at some point. I'm sure you'd rather succeed and come through for the group than let people down. No one likes being "that guy." At the end of the day, we're all in this together. I've got a little extra time tonight. Why don't we meet at the library and get this last part done together? Sound like a plan?

In subtle ways, this verbal message seeks to save Ron's "face," or identity, by attributing his lack of success in getting the work done to the situation instead of a character flaw. At the same time, this message demonstrates flexibility in carrying out the roles of leader and group member by its willingness to renegotiate the division of work. The result is offering a creative solution the message producer believes is the best hope for motivating Ron to give his all to the task so the group can earn a high grade. In each of these ways, rhetorical messages are designed to achieve a desired social reality.

Glance back over each of the three possible responses to Ron. Which message do you believe is most likely to result in Ron completing his portion of the project? Which message do you believe is most likely to preserve a positive relationship between Ron and the leader of the group? The expressive, conventional, and rhetorical MDLs are ordered from least to most effective communication in complex and difficult interaction tasks (O'Keefe, 1997). According to research, rhetorical messages are perceived as the most persuasive, satisfying, motivating, and attentive to "face" needs (O'Keefe & McCornack, 1987). In other words, there's a good chance that our hypothetical group member, Ron, is most likely to get his work done if he received the rhetorical message. The expressive message leaves Ron with no chance of redeeming himself and makes it clear that the message producer feels contempt for him. The conventional message allows Ron a chance to complete the work, but does little to address Ron's doubts about whether he can finish the task on time. Additional research has demonstrated that rhetorical messages are perceived as more supportive than conventional or expressive messages in the workplace context (Peterson & Albrecht, 1996) and when responding to someone who shares a difficult disclosure, like an HIV-positive diagnosis (Caughlin, Brashers, et al., 2008; Caughlin, Bute, et al., 2009).

The theory of MDL demonstrates that the differences among the verbal messages various people produce can be explained, in part, by how each individual understands the process of communication. Those who are able to use communication in each of the ways described earlier—as a way to share thoughts, participate in a social game, and create social reality—often have a verbal communication advantage. There are situations in which simply expressing thoughts with verbal messages is perfectly competent and effective. For instance, if someone asks you for directions to the airport, an expressive message is all that is needed. However, in situations that involve multiple and competing communication goals, the more sophisticated conventional or rhetorical messages may be more successful.

Using "I Statements"

Another way to maximize the success of your verbal messages is to use "I statements" when communicating your perceptions (Gordon, 1970). When you share your ideas and thoughts with "I statements" you make it clear that you accept responsibility for your own feelings. Communicating in this manner is often much more effective than blaming, judging, or accusing your partner, especially during interactions involving conflict or confrontation. "I statements" consist of three ingredients: a description of how you feel, an indication of the conditions under which you feel that way, and an explanation why the conditions cause you to feel that way. For example, I feel upset (feelings) when you ignore my texts (behavior/condition) because I get the impression I'm less important to you than other things (why). Compare that message to the "You statements" that might be used instead: "You make me so mad!" "You don't care at all about me!" "You are an inconsiderate jerk!" "I statements" provide a method of informing others that there's a problem without hostility or blaming them for your emotions. Therefore, your conversation partners can understand how their behavior affects you without feeling put down, guilty, or defensive.

The ways in which we coordinate meanings, cooperate in conversations, engage our personal theories of communication, and phrase our assertions are important parts of being effective in verbal communication. The ability to connect and engage in social reality is contingent on these abilities. As you communicate in a variety of contexts, whether face to face or online, be mindful of how you are interacting with conversational partners. Doing so will help you understand how your verbal communication creates and participates in social space.

VERBAL COMMUNICATION AND CONVERGENCE

In the Communication Age, media, technology, and face-to-face communication converge, or come together, in ways that profoundly influence and sometimes complicate daily life. In the case of verbal communication, convergence

POETIC CHOICES

Getty

At age 90, Betty White is among the most recognized and adored celebrities in the United States. In part because of her role in *Hot in Cleveland,* her popularity exploded in her most recent decade of life.

"THE LIMITS OF *my language* mean the limits of my world" (Wittgenstein, 1922, 5.6, italics in original). In other words, we can only build our world with the bits of language we have available. Sometimes we have to create new words (e.g., *Internet, blog,* or *bromance*), or we have to reuse old words to create new meanings (e.g., *cool, sick,* or *tight*). Communication activists consider aspects of our collective conversation that may suffer due to our current vocabulary and the way we employ its terms. Consider aging. We live in a youth-obsessed culture, and the words we use to describe younger and older people reflect the higher value we place on youth. In our culture, we mostly represent aging as a process of decline or decay. We portray the life span as moving uphill in youth, then plateauing in middle age, only to leave us to live out the rest of our years slowly descending the hill toward our graves. We describe young people as "fresh," "in style," "up-to-date," "strong," "beautiful," "powerful," "resilient," and "in their prime." On the other hand, we describe those who are older in terms of "stale," "left behind," "weak," "irrelevant," "unattractive," "frail," "brittle," and "over the hill." No wonder it is difficult to age with grace and confidence in our culture, much less with a sense of excitement or significance! The important thing is that we don't have to describe aging in these terms. Aging could be described in much more positive, but equally compelling, ways. For instance, what if we compared the human life span to a continuous process of growth—one that begins at birth and moves forward until the very moment of death? Rather than travelers along a steep hill that rises, peaks, and falls, we could think of ourselves as flowers that begin as buds and bloom most radiantly right before our petals scatter to the wind.

A newer idea of aging challenges the view of "aging as decline" and emphasizes that human development continues throughout the life span. Professors Mary and Kenneth Gergen have labeled this linguistic move "positive aging" (M. Gergen, 2009). They have established a positive aging web newsletter (http://www.taosinstitute.net/positive-aging-newsletter) that has over 20,000 readers. By including stories about growth and development for older adults and state-of-the-art health care research, the Gergens are engaged in a form of communication activism called poetic activism, or using language to create alternative conceptions and discourses (K. Gergen, 2001). Perhaps there is a part of your city that your friends refer to by a negative name to denote its lower status (e.g., *slum* or *ghetto*), or maybe you have family members who use racist or homophobic labels for other people. You might be able to create changes by educating your friends and family members about more positive ways of describing places, people, and processes. The words we use matter, so connect and engage through poetic activism.

Communicators face widespread daily surveillance of their verbal messages and behaviors. How are Big Brother, Little Brother, and your social circle monitoring you? How does knowledge of being "watched" impact what you say online?

means that messages once delivered mainly through traditional writing and voice channels are increasingly delivered through computer-mediated technologies. Verbal messages exchanged or posted online or through mobile technologies are far less private than those uttered face to face or written on paper. Communication scholars are increasingly interested in issues of surveillance and how it affects our verbal messages, and who has control over our words.

Surveillance is focused, intentional, and routine attention to personal details for purposes of influence or control (Lyon, 2007, p. 14). Social media companies like Facebook collect and aggregate personal data provided by users, a process sometimes called dataveillance (Phillips, 2010). Internet users are routinely subjected to unknown surveillance from both Big Brother (government agencies) and Little Brother (organizations and individual users) (D'Urso, 2006). As we move among sites and networks, marketing firms gather the digital information left by our online activity. Government agencies and law enforcement track the Internet usage patterns and communication content of suspected criminals, as well as ordinary citizens (Richards, 2013). In addition, there is widespread social surveillance, as we eavesdrop, inquire into, and watch our peers' communication practices on social media (Marwick, 2012).

In the next decade, we will likely move into the Internet of Things, in which our appliances, cars, homes, and everyday belongings will increasingly include networked controls, sensors, and data collectors. It may become difficult to say much of anything without being observed (Thompson, 2012). Internet culture is often described through the metaphor of the Panopticon, an idea first developed by the 18th-century English philosopher Jeremy Bentham (Katz & Rice, 2002). The Panopticon is a prison designed around a central surveillance tower from which the warden can see inside all the cells. Theoretically, because prisoners don't know when they are being watched, they assume a state of constant surveillance and do not misbehave. The modern surveillance environment isn't exactly a Panopticon, but the perception or fear of being watched can cause people to act and think differently than they might otherwise. In addition to self-censorship, constant surveillance and supervision may curtail free speech or exert a "chilling effect" on potentially valuable verbal expressions that are frowned upon by authorities. Intellectual privacy and freedom may also be undermined (Richards, 2013). In each of these ways, modern surveillance may impact the verbal messages you produce. It may also impact how your verbal messages are used by others because surveillance may shift power from those who are watched to the "watchers," creating opportunities for negative outcomes such as blackmail, undue persuasive influence, and sorting/discrimination (Richards, 2013).

In the Communication Age, be mindful of how surveillance may affect your verbal messages and how they are used. Consider the kind of society you want and the rights you believe all people should have when taking political action regarding the appropriate use of and legal limits on surveillance.

WHAT YOU'VE LEARNED   Now that you have studied this chapter, you should be able to:

(1) Explain how verbal communication differs from nonverbal communication.

Verbal communication differs from nonverbal communication. Verbal communication and nonverbal communication are often used in tandem, but are distinct types of codes. Verbal communication is a digital code because it involves language, which represents through symbols. Nonverbal communication is an analog code because it involves representation through likeness, or similarity. Verbal communication holds the advantages of greater efficiency, clarity, and intentionality.

 The Difference between Verbal and Nonverbal Communication

(2) Describe the nature and characteristics of symbols.

Language is made up of symbols. Meaning is created in the relationships among a word, thoughts about the word, and the actual object or entity to which the word refers. Symbols are arbitrary, abstract, intentional, uniquely human, culture-bound, and context-bound.

 Symbols and Logos

(3) Explain the importance of grammar and meaning for effective communication.

Verbal competence involves mastering (a) phonemes, or the sounds of a language; (b) morphemes, or combined sounds that form the smallest units of meaning in a language; (c) semantics, or the denotative and connotative meanings of words; and (d) syntax, or meaning at the level of sentences. Becoming skilled at these levels of competence prepares one to use verbal messages in the more complex functions of creating and participating in social reality.

 Communicating with Autism

 Confederate Symbols, Swastikas, and Student Sensibilities

(4) Identify the important functions of verbal messages.

Verbal messages aid in creating and participating in social reality. Verbal messages and language choice make and shape social situations, relationships, selves, and understandings. Verbal messages and language choice also allow participation in social reality by functioning to provide a way for people to interact in social situations.

🎤 Teaching the Art of Conversation to Kids with Autism

💻 Understanding Maslow's Hierarchy of Needs

(5) **Explain theories of message production and interpretation.**

Several theories attempt to explain how language is used collaboratively to create and participate in social reality. Coordinated management of meaning theory focuses on how communicators coordinate their actions to make and manage meanings (Pearce & Cronen, 1980). The cooperative principle (Grice, 1975) describes how people normally behave and expect others to behave in interactions. The theory of message design logic explains the distinct ways of thinking about communication situations, choosing thoughts for expression, and modifying expression in order to achieve interaction goals (O'Keefe, 1988). "I language" involves claiming responsibility for one's own thoughts and feelings during communication (Gordon, 1970).

🎤 Picking Up Verbal Cues

💻 "I" Messages

KEY TERMS

Review key terms with eFlashcards. **edge.sagepub.com/edwards2e**

Analog code   52
Coding   76
Connotative meaning   57
Constitutive rules   64
Content   61
Cooperative principle   65
Coordinated management of meaning   61
Coordination   64
Dataveillance   72
Denotative meaning   57

Digital code   52
Episode   61
Inclusive language   59
Internet of Things   72
Language   53
Linguistic relativity hypothesis   58
Message design logic   67
Morphemes   57
Panopticon   72
Peak communication experience   65
Phonemes   57

Polysemy   57
Referent   53
Regulative rules   64
Semantics   57
Social surveillance   72
Speech act   61
Surveillance   72
Symbols   53
Syntax   58

REFLECT

1.   Reflect on several of the language symbols that are important to a culture of which you are a member. You might consider the culture of your campus, religious community, ethnic group, or workplace organization. How might those symbols be interpreted differently by members of another culture?

2.   Bring to mind a time when you felt a conversational partner was attempting to deceive or lie to you. Did the other person signal his or her deception by failing to follow Grice's cooperative principle? What maxim or maxims did your partner violate?

3. According to Marshall McLuhan (1964), "The medium is the message." Consider whether the channels you use to verbally communicate may be saying something in and of themselves. For example, does writing a letter by hand send a different message than delivering the same note through e-mail? Does delivering sad news in person send a different message than doing so through a text?

REVIEW

To check your answers go to **edge.sagepub.com/edwards2e**

1. Verbal communication represents _____ through the use of _____.

2. Explain the characteristics of symbols.

3. The idea that language creates and shapes our social reality is called the _____ _____ hypothesis.

4. The sounds of a language are called _____. The study of word meaning is called _____.

5. Inclusive language employs expressions and words broad enough to include all people. (T/F)

6. _____ meaning refers to a word's formal or dictionary definition. _____ meaning refers to a word's informal associations based on feelings and personal experiences.

7. Define the eight levels of coordinated management of meaning theory.

8. What are the four maxims identified in Grice's cooperative principle?

9. Which theory explains the reasoning people use to get from thoughts and goals to verbal messages?

10. List the three ingredients of an "I statement."

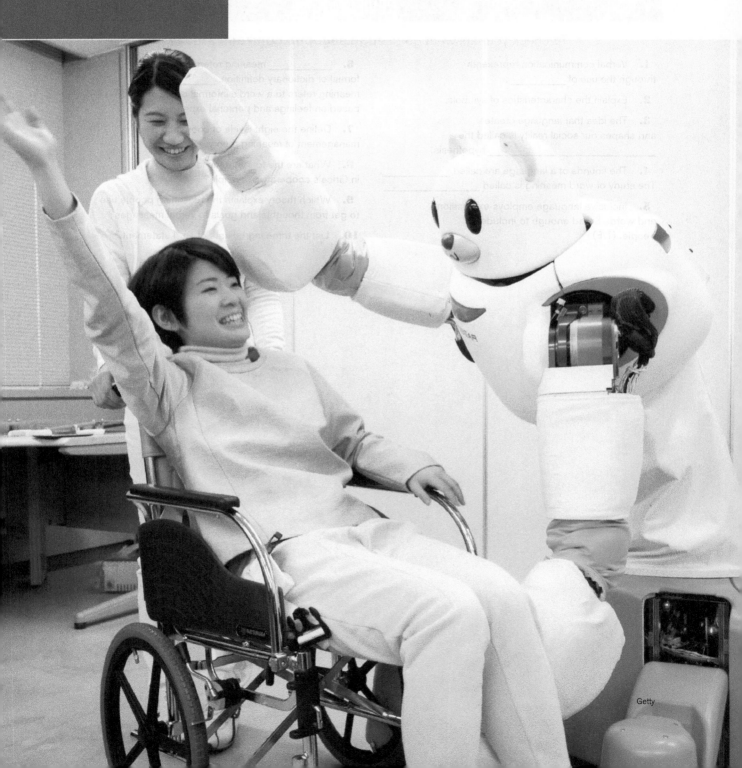

Getty

1 Identify the importance of nonverbal communication in your life.

2 Explain the functions of nonverbal communication as it works with verbal communication.

3 Describe the codes of nonverbal communication.

4 Describe the impact nonverbal communication has in a variety of situations.

5 Examine how nonverbal communication is influenced in the Communication Age.

Health care in the Communication Age is changing and evolving rapidly. As birthrates decline in some parts of the world and baby boomers reach an age that requires more health care assistance, we reach a global dilemma of how to provide adequate health care for older adults. The country of Japan has long been examining how to utilize robots in a health care context. As a result, a Japanese research institute has created Robear, a 308-pound robotic nurse with a cute bear face. Research leader Toshiharu Mukai says of the robot, "The polar cub–like look is aimed at radiating an atmosphere of strength, geniality, and cleanliness at the same time" (Mogg, 2015). This occurs through nonverbal communication.

Robear the robot is able to "exert force in a gentle way" by moving patients around precisely where they need to be (Mogg, 2015). The bright, big eyes and smile on the robotic nurse-bear face were specifically developed to help patients feel at ease through nonverbal communication. As more development occurs, the nonverbal communication characteristics of the robotic nurse-bear will only become more realistic and responsive to the needs of the patient.

Nonverbal communication will be an important part of this convergence if avatars are to be successful. In this chapter, you will learn about nonverbal communication and types of codes that matter in any interaction, whether it is in a face-to-face setting or a computer-mediated setting. As you read the chapter, think about the ways in which nonverbal communication is starting to become more common in a mediated world.

Imagine this: You enter your friend Daniel's house in the middle of August. You see food all over the dirty kitchen walls, and notice that the thermostat reads

iStock

How would you respond to a friend's room that looked like the one pictured here?

89 degrees and that there are dirty underwear, trash, and old sushi boxes everywhere. The nonverbal cues you experience in Daniel's house impact your perceptions in a number of ways. As established in Chapter 1, communication is defined as the collaborative process of using messages to create and participate in social reality. In the Communication Age, it is important also to be familiar with nonverbal communication—all the ways we communicate without using words (Ivy & Wahl, 2014). Verbal and nonverbal communication enable us to actualize possibility, realize human potential, and achieve change and growth, both for ourselves and our communities. Have you ever had a conversation in which the other person breaks off talking to answer a text or an e-mail? Think about how nonverbal communication is influenced in the Communication Age. Nonverbal communication can include your clothing, your physical appearance, your gestures, your facial and eye expressions, and more. As you focus on nonverbal communication in this chapter, keep the following questions in mind: How can nonverbal cues be used to communicate important messages to others? What are the specific codes (categories) of nonverbal communication? How do you connect with others nonverbally in the Communication Age? Why does nonverbal communication matter?

WHY DOES NONVERBAL COMMUNICATION MATTER?

Nonverbal messages matter because they communicate feelings and attitudes. With the many tools of mediated communication at our disposal, it is easier than ever to observe examples of nonverbal communication in photos or streaming videos. When looking back at family photo albums, you can usually tell that the people smiling with their arms around each other are comfortable in that particular moment. On the other hand, a photo of a friend or loved one with her arms crossed, not looking into the camera, would suggest that she was not enjoying herself.

Nonverbal messages matter because they are more convincing than verbal messages. Think about situations where someone's facial expressions tell you everything you need to know. These are situations that illustrate the power of nonverbal communication. Perhaps you're working in human resources for a large corporation. Job interviews are being held for a new training and development position, and you are assisting with interview check-in. The first candidate comes to the interview in a tight outfit, sweating, and looking at his watch in frustration. You try to be supportive by asking if he is nervous, and he replies, "No, I'm not nervous at all." In this interview context, the candidate's nonverbal cues would be much more powerful than the verbal message that was given to you. As the saying goes, actions speak louder than words.

As you can learn from the robot and messy room examples that lead off this chapter, nonverbal communication is important in many aspects of life. This chapter explores messages communicated through nonverbal communication. To begin exploring this diverse topic, take a moment to familiarize yourself with the specific functions of nonverbal communication in the section that follows.

FUNCTIONS OF NONVERBAL COMMUNICATION

Nonverbal communication performs a number of functions as it works with verbal communication. Specifically, let's discuss how nonverbal communication helps to repeat, accent, conflict with, complement, regulate, and substitute messages in the communication process.

Repeating

A nonverbal message may "repeat" the verbal message. For example, you may simultaneously say, "Yes" and shake your head up and down. Or you might hold up four fingers while saying, "It's about four blocks south."

Accenting

A nonverbal message may highlight the verbal message by emphasizing or enhancing a certain point. You may stress the word *despise* in "I despise this weather" to emphasize your strong negative feelings.

Conflicting

You may use a nonverbal message to contradict your verbal message. For instance, you might say, "I'm having a great time at this party," while simultaneously shaking your head "no" with eyes wide open. Or you may say, "Of course I'm taking this seriously!" while laughing. The contradiction of verbal and nonverbal messages adds a new dimension to the possible meaning of your message.

Complementing

A nonverbal message can reinforce a verbal message. For instance, you might tell your friend, "I'm listening to you," while making sure to perform the nonverbal behaviors associated with listening. You could lean forward, make eye contact, and avoid engaging in any other tasks.

► **COMMUNICATION IN ACTION 4.1**

WATCH: Proxemics, Nonverbal Communication Codes

Communication technology and space management convey differing nonverbal messages as two classmates interact. What is your interpretation of these nonverbal actions?

Regulating

Nonverbal messages often manage the flow of verbal conversation. For example, you may raise your hand to signal that you would like to say something. Or you may make eye contact with a quiet member of the group to make it clear that you would like him or her to contribute.

Substituting

The use of a nonverbal message can replace a verbal message. Examples include pointing when you're asked where an item is located, shrugging your shoulders when you don't know the answer to a question, or flashing a thumbs-up to indicate that you're doing fine.

Now that you have reviewed the different functions of nonverbal communication, the next section examines the categories or *codes* of nonverbal information researchers have studied: vocalics (voice), kinesics (body movement), proxemics (space), environment, facial expressions, eye behavior, haptics (touch), and physical appearance.

CODES OF NONVERBAL COMMUNICATION

Let's face it—nonverbal communication is complicated. Thus, there is a need for classification to make nonverbal communication easier to study. Although this chapter focuses on these nonverbal communication codes in Western culture, remember that perceptions of or reactions to nonverbal communication can vary in other cultures.

Vocalics

Vocalics refers to the study of the use of voice to express self. Just like the face, the voice plays a major role in sharing our thoughts and emotions. Your voice conveys information about who you are as an individual (not just what someone thinks of you) and, importantly, who you are as a member of a group. Speech accents are an example of this. We also use the vocal channel to modify/change the meaning of our utterances. One example is the use of sarcasm to convey the opposite of what we say in words.

Vocalic cues include tone (quality) of voice, volume, articulation, pitch (highness or lowness), the rate of speech, and use of silence. Imagine that your best friend just got a new haircut and asked you what you thought about it. If you really hated your friend's new haircut, you could say enthusiastically, "It looks awesome!"—which would be either a lie to avoid hurt feelings or an expression of sarcasm. You might also say, "It looks good," in a halfhearted way. It is due to your voice that you're able to express these different reactions.

Your voice reveals your emotions, your thoughts, and the relationships you have with others. It also

In addition to Idina Menzel (*Frozen*) and Ellen DeGeneres (*Finding Nemo*), pictured here, what other famous voices come to mind?

provides information about your self-confidence and knowledge and influences how you are perceived by others (Hinkle, 2001). Think about the famous voices you hear in movies. Morgan Freeman, Drew Barrymore, and Steve Carell all have very distinct voices that audiences find interesting for different reasons. Morgan Freeman's voice is one that audiences find trustworthy and caring, while Drew Barrymore's voice is pleasing and sympathetic. Steve Carell, on the other hand, is fun to listen to because he can change his voice to create almost any kind of sound.

In the digital world, vocalics encompasses the use of ALL CAPS in text messages, personal e-mails, and social networking. ALL CAPS indicates an increased volume, or that you are shouting. If you text your best friend that you need to speak to her, you might use ALL CAPS to indicate that it is extremely urgent.

Now that you know more about vocalics, or the study of the use of voice, let's move on to the study of body movement, also known as kinesics.

Kinesics

Kinesics is the study of body movement, including both posture and gestures. It's been long known that kinesics provides important information to others. People have a certain walk, posture, and stance, which become their own, by which they are recognized, and which can be impacted by their mood or emotions. Have you ever heard someone make reference to how certain people "carry themselves"? You know you can't physically "carry yourself," so this must mean your posture, stance, and movement. Have you noticed how some people seem to carry themselves in ways that make them unapproachable? Or have you seen a person who walked with confidence and could light up the room? Your posture says a lot about you as a person.

Did your parents ever tell you to "stand up straight"? As annoying as that command may be, posture is indeed important. In many cultures, including the United States, an upright but relaxed body posture is associated with many attractive attributes, such as confidence, positivity, and high self-esteem (Guerrero & Floyd, 2006). People judge others' personalities based on something as subjective as posture, so it's worth considering. Do you pay attention to your posture? How do mood and emotions affect your posture? Posture says a lot about dominance and status. Social psychologist David Johnson (2006) contends that "individuals with high status and power may engage in a dominance display by puffing themselves up to full size, stiffening their backs, tightening their brows, thrusting their chins forward, and leaning toward the challenger in an attempt to convince others of their power" (p. 199). However, dominant nonverbal behaviors aren't always linked to high-status behaviors. Think about the job interview situation. An interviewer is typically much more relaxed than a job applicant, who is typically more tense and nervous.

Gestures

Gestures are the movements you make with your hands and arms. Some people "talk with their hands" in order to complement what they're saying, whereas others might prefer using fewer gestures to avoid distracting from the verbal message.

iStock

Giorgos Katidis raises his hand in a Nazi-style salute as he celebrates scoring a goal in a Greek league game.

Ekman and Friesen (1969b) classified movement and gestures according to how they function in human interaction. The five categories of kinesics include emblems, illustrators, affect displays, regulators, and adapters. Let's take a look at each in more detail.

Emblems

Emblems are meanings in specific communication and cultural contexts that substitute for words. Flipping someone off with a specific hand gesture is an emblem because it has a direct translation to the written word. Emblems have widely understood meanings, yet it's important to note that they don't have *universally* understood meanings. There are only a few gestures that have practically the same meaning across cultures. Three gestures that have the widest meaning cross-culturally include the pointing gesture, the "come here" gesture, and the opposite "stay away" gesture. Emblematic gestures should be used with caution because emblems become known or are negotiated within cultures. Our nonverbal behaviors can easily offend whole groups of people and lead to unpleasant consequences. Consider this example: In 2013, Greek soccer player Giorgos Katidis made the "Heil, Hitler" gesture after scoring the game-winning goal for his team, AEK Athens. Katidis took off his shirt after scoring and made the gesture—he later said that he was simply pointing to one of his teammates. The Greek Soccer Association didn't believe his explanation and ended up banning him from the sport for life. In this example, a gesture upset large groups of people, which shows the connection between nonverbal communication and sensitivity.

Illustrators

Gestures that complement, enhance, or substitute for the verbal message are called illustrators. If you were describing the length of the biggest fish you ever caught, you might use your hands to illustrate the size. Or, when you are giving directions, you might point to show which way to go. Sometimes verbal messages are inappropriate or can't be heard, making illustrators a convenient nonverbal choice. For example, you're at a baseball game, and there's too much noise to convey to the pretzel stand workers what you want, so instead of shouting your order, you point at the food and hold up some fingers to indicate how many you want. This is a substitution function of an illustrating gesture.

Affect Displays

Nonverbal gestures, postures, and facial expressions that communicate emotions are called affect displays. Typically, nonverbal cues can be detected before they accompany the verbal message. Therefore, if you're happy, you are more likely to reveal the happiness you feel through your nonverbal cues before you actually express it verbally to someone. The kind of emotion you feel is usually expressed in your face, while how much you feel of the emotion is expressed in your body. If you're excited, for example, your face may show your excitement to others. The movement of your hands, the openness of your posture, and the speed of your movement tell others just how excited you are.

Regulators

Gestures used to control the turn-taking in conversations are known as regulators. For example, you might make a hand motion to encourage someone or raise your own hand to get a turn at speaking. When you're eager to answer a message, you normally make eye contact, raise your eyebrows, open your mouth, take in a breath, and lean forward slightly. You do the opposite if you don't want to answer. Little head nods, vocal expressions (such as "um"), facial expressions, body postures, and eye contact can be seen as connectors that keep the conversation together and make it coherent. When these sorts of nonverbal cues are absent from a conversation, it might trigger a negative reaction, and you could come to believe that your conversational partner isn't listening at all.

Adapters

Gestures we use to release tension are called adapters. Playing with our hands, poking, picking, fidgeting, scratching, and interacting nonverbally with our environment are all adapters that reveal our attempts to regulate situations and to make ourselves feel more at ease and able to function effectively. Adapters can clue us that another person is uncomfortable in some way.

Proxemics

Proxemics refers to the study of how people use space and distance to communicate. There are three reasons why it is important to make the connections between people, space, and distance: (1) Who you are as person can be revealed by your preferred use of distance and space at home and at work, (2) your verbal and nonverbal communication is influenced by distance and space, and (3) you use metaphors of distance and space to talk about and explain your interpersonal relationships.

Have you ever been in a crowded elevator and felt uncomfortable because it seemed like people were invading your personal space? Your rules and norms about space have become so understood that you don't think much about them until they are violated. Violations can be alarming, possibly even threatening. Your relationships with others, your power and status, and your cultural background determine how physically close you get to others and how close you let others get to you (Burgoon & Jones, 1976; Docan-Morgan, 2011).

Considering your own preferences regarding space, does dancing in a crowd like this appeal to you?

iStock

Barack Obama embraces Burmese opposition politician Aung San Suu Kyi, a culturally inappropriate way of greeting in Burma. What experiences have you had related to nonverbal communication and cultural differences?

What preferences do you have related to space and distance? In U.S. culture, we as communicators tend not to like people "up in our personal business." Edward T. Hall (1963) identified four zones of space in middle-class U.S. culture. First, there is the intimate zone, which is about 0 to 18 inches and usually reserved for our significant others, family members, and closest friends. It is rare that a stranger can enter the intimate zone without making us feel violated. These interactions mostly occur in private and signify a high level of connection, trust, and affection. The personal zone, 18 inches to about 4 feet, is reserved for personal relationships with casual acquaintances and friends. The social zone, 4 to 12 feet, is the distance at which you usually talk to strangers or conduct business. If you went to your professor's office to discuss a grade, for example, you would most likely remain at a distance of 4 to 12 feet. The public zone, over 12 feet, refers to the distance typical of large, formal, public events. In large lecture classrooms, campaign rallies, or public speeches, the distance between speaker and audience is usually over 12 feet. Understanding these spatial zones is important to your everyday nonverbal communication competency.

Just like so many other things, spatial zones vary among cultures. In Arab cultures, for example, it is common to have less personal space. Hall (1966) observed Arab cultures for their use of space and found significant differences between how Arabs and Westerners view public space and conversational distance. Arabs do not seek privacy in public space, preferring to converse intimately in public and viewing less-than-intimate conversations as rude behavior. Therefore, whereas people in the United States appreciate their personal space, other cultures have different ideas about the use of space.

Gender and Sexual Orientation

A person's gender and sexual orientation is another factor that contributes to proxemics. Gender has an immense influence on personal space management, which leads to particular communication patterns (Hamilton, 2007). For example, it is socially accepted and completely natural in U.S. culture for women to sit next to each other, whereas men are more likely to sit facing one another. Of course, men can and do sit side by side, but it's likely to cause some uneasiness or lead them to feel like they have to joke their way through the behavior (Fair, 2011). Have you ever seen a group of men at a movie theater who don't sit directly next to each other but instead insist on having one seat between them to provide more space? One explanation for this behavior is that men simply need more space than do women because they are larger in size. Another possibility is that more space in the movie theater makes it very clear to everyone that these men aren't gay (Solebello & Elliot, 2011). Homophobia is still very prevalent in U.S. culture. And although homosexuality has become more acceptable in our culture in recent years, the primary explanation for men's spatial behavior relates to

MAKE
—a—
DIFFERENCE

"TEACH-IN" HELPS STUDENTS COMMUNICATE ABOUT GENDER, RACE, AND SEXUALITY

Corbis

THE UNIVERSITY OF Virginia is one of the oldest higher education institutions in the United States. Although the university has a long tradition, UVA Women's Center program director Jaronda Miller feels that student advocacy should change some long-standing institutions at the university. "Some of the things I've tried to do is bring people in the community that work in advocacy to show students what it takes," Miller said.

"[I have tried to show students] how to organize and what strategic steps you take to have an issue and get results" (Griesedieck, 2015).

With this in mind, the university's Women, Gender, and Sexuality Program hosted what is called a "teach-in" to discuss recent events at the university. Teach-ins—which date back to the Vietnam War—are designed as methods of knowledge distribution that take place outside the classroom, and allow both students and teachers to collaborate their class curriculum with current events. Topics included the need for a better wage for the university staff, as well as a need for greater diversity at UVA.

Student involvement in university policy is a much-underutilized resource in many higher learning institutions. Examples, such as the "teach-in" or student government, illustrate how powerful students' voices can be in enacting effective change to university culture. As you move forward in your college career, reflect on methods you and fellow students can use to create a better university life for yourselves, faculty, and future students.

homophobia—a fear of being perceived as or labeled gay (Fair, 2011; Solebello & Elliot, 2011). Most women don't have to deal with this perception because acceptance for women's behavior tends to be wider than for men's.

Territoriality

Another concept related to the study of proxemics is territoriality, which is the study of how people use space and objects to communicate occupancy or ownership of space (Ivy & Wahl, 2014). You determine your territory and want it to be safe from strangers. Therefore, you will do your best to defend it from intrusion by using verbal and nonverbal means. Let's think about a less obvious example: placing a jacket or a book bag on a chair to let others know that the seat is taken. In this example, it might be nice to have a little territory to engage in conversation. How do you feel about people as territory? It might be a little weird to look at people as territory in the first place, but you most likely know people who view their boyfriend or girlfriend as their own private territory, and they can become seriously forceful when they feel their territory is being invaded. How do people violate our territories? Three types of intrusion are typically viewed as negative: violation, invasion, and contamination (Lyman & Scott, 1967).

Take a moment to think about your preferences related to seating in movie theaters. Do you like to sit in a particular row? Do you form perceptions of others in movie theaters based on how they sit?

iStock

Violation

Violation is entering or using territory without permission. If you've ever had a roommate, you will be able to relate to the story of someone who eats the favorite food that you bought or wears your favorite sweater when you're not in. Taking advantage of your belongings without your knowledge or permission is a violation of your personal territory.

Invasion

Invasion is an intentional intrusion of a specific territory. Perhaps you have experienced a situation in which you were enjoying some quiet solitude at a beach or a restaurant when a rowdy group of people arrived and disrupted the peace and quiet of the space. Fed up with the distraction, you decided to pack up and go home.

Contamination

This type of intrusion, in which someone's territory is marked with noise or pollution, is known as contamination. Contamination is about doing something to a territory to show that you were there, such as leaving your trash in a park after a barbecue with friends.

Clearly, proxemics, or the study of how space influences communication, is an important topic. The next section examines the power of environment as a nonverbal communication category.

Environment

The environment refers to the surroundings that shape the communication context. People are influenced by environmental factors such as architecture, design, doors, windows, color, lighting, smell, seating arrangements, temperature, and cleanliness (Harris & Sachau, 2005; Jackson, 2005). The environment is a component when studying nonverbal communication because it influences the way people act and interact.

You shape your environments to express your own feelings and beliefs to others. Think about the type of art you may put on your walls. What does it say about you? Consider other things in the environment that can serve as nonverbal cues about who you are. It is these environmental factors that you create and control that serve as nonverbal messages to others who enter the space. As one scholar put it, "People cannot be understood outside of their environmental context" (Peterson, 1991, p. 154). Nonverbal actions can be interpreted meaningfully only when context is taken into account.

The environment is important to the study of nonverbal behavior in two ways: (1) The decisions you make about the environments in which you live and work reveal a good deal about who you are, and (2) your nonverbal behavior changes according to the environments in which you communicate. First, the physical environments in which you function can be seen as extensions of your personality. It might not be possible to manipulate all elements of your environment, yet to a certain extent you can "personalize" it. It's natural for you to structure the settings in which you work, study, or live to make them more unique and to make people feel more comfortable. The environments you create for yourself often speak volumes about those relationships you consider most important (Lohmann, Arriaga, & Goodfriend, 2003). Second, your behavior and perceptions are altered by the physical environments in which you find yourself. For example, you are more likely to wear formal clothes and whisper at a religious service than at a sporting event, where you would probably wear comfortable clothes and scream wildly for your favorite team.

What about environments that you don't create personally? Do they influence you? And if so, how? Think about how you would behave at the White House or the Statue of Liberty. Many college campuses have a central building that is connected to student and alumni identity and which serves as a focal or historical point for the campus (Biemiller, 2007). Our verbal and nonverbal communication is impacted by these structures because those buildings communicate something before people even walk in.

Impression Management

Remember in the beginning of this section you were invited to think about your own personal space, how you represent yourself with it, and what it says about you to others? Just as there are environments that you can own and operate, there are also environments that are beyond your control. Picture a situation in which you show up for a job interview and the office you enter is dirty, with food leftovers piled everywhere. What does an office like that tell you about the owner's professionalism, credibility, and organizational skills? An environment like that is all about impression management—the formation of an impression, a perception, or a view of the other (Goffman, 1971). You haven't even met the owner yet, so all you have to go by are nonverbal clues. Would this be a good place to work? People want to communicate in comfortable environments, whether they have thought about it before or not. The environments you create in your homes, offices, and classrooms establish certain communication contexts, comfortable or uncomfortable, that have an influence on your perceptions of safety and comfort, as well as the attitude and character of the people inhabiting the space (Ivy & Wahl, 2014).

Perceptions of Environment

The way you perceive your environment is an important factor related to how you respond to others. Overall, there are six ways by which people distinguish the environment around them: formality, warmth, privacy, familiarity, constraint, and distance (Ivy & Wahl, 2014).

Formality is an understanding that people have of environment that relates to how comfortably they can behave, in light of their expectations. Sometimes it is more about the atmosphere of a certain place rather than the place itself. Imagine you go to a restaurant, and it's too fancy for your taste. You would probably walk right back out because it doesn't have the type of atmosphere you desire and in which you feel comfortable. The second way we can perceive the environment is warmth. Your sense of warmth describes how you see and desire a welcoming context that is part of your past or current experience. Smells, visions, sounds,

CAREER FRONTIER: IMPRESSION MANAGEMENT

THINK ABOUT THE evolution of mediated environments. In the last decade, there has been an explosion in the amount of time people spend online. Whether it's Facebook, Twitter, or a similar medium, social networking sites seem to be a popular way to meet people and communicate. Sites like these create virtual communities. Websites that offer chat rooms and other services give users the opportunity to "escape" from everyday life and communicate anonymously outside of their public and private spaces. Facebook encourages users to create an environment of personhood by providing space to upload pictures, post journals, and list personal interests. All of these elements are used to decorate and personalize computerized space.

Beyond social networking, think about the influence websites such as Facebook and LinkedIn have not only on how you and others view your online persona, but how companies and professions utilize the information you provide. Researchers Rob Heyman and Jo Pierson analyzed how the business models of Facebook and LinkedIn blend mass self-communication with advertising. They found that once personal information has been posted by a user, that person is no longer able to control production, selection, and distribution of his or her personal identifiable information (PII) when it is used in advertising (Heyman & Pierson, 2013). At this point, a person's user-generated content is only relevant if it has economic value. In other words, the impression you

want to convey to others online may be distorted by the advertising interests of the social medium. As you express yourself online, remember that your information is available for *everyone* (not just your online friends) to see and use.

In your career, the relationships you build will rely greatly on how you manage your impressions of others, as well as how you create the impressions others have of you. Nowhere is this more critical than the job interview process. Before any further impressions can be made, you must first utilize a résumé and cover letter to form an employer's impression that you are well suited for the job. Research has indicated that résumés serve as contextual metaphors by presenting potential employers with surface-level descriptions of the applicant's professional experience (Lipovsky, 2013). Applicants must then infuse these basic descriptions of their background with evaluative meanings that validate their claims of professional competence and persuade recruiters to agree to a job interview.

Your best resource to understand how to attract potential employers is to speak with people currently employed in your field of choice, preferably people who are recruiters themselves. Whether you know them personally, professionally, or academically, use these resources to help you craft the perfect résumé and cover letter that can set you apart from the other applicants. Also, online forums for specific professions can be a valuable guide to the dos and don'ts of résumé creation.

and lighting in an environment can all contribute to your perception of warmth. Think of a favorite smell or song from your childhood that has always given and still gives you a sense of warmth when thinking about it.

Privacy is another way the environment can be perceived. Do you prefer a crowded and popular restaurant or a quiet one off the beaten path? People all have a sense of privacy. Some of you don't mind being around a lot of people, and some of you do. If you ask someone who works at a restaurant, he or she will tell you that booths typically fill up faster than tables because they offer more privacy.

Another perception you have is familiarity, which refers to how cautiously you react to meeting new people or being in unfamiliar environments. Not knowing where they are and what to expect makes some people feel less comfortable than others. That's why many people tend to return to favorite hangouts or certain restaurants. Most people like knowing what to expect and how to behave in the environment.

Next on the list is constraint. Whenever you feel like your personal space is invaded, you feel constraint. For example, some individuals are more inhibited living with roommates, while others are not. Most of your perceptions of constraint are shaped by the amount of privacy and space available to you.

The final perception of your environment is distance. Your perceptions of distance in an environment pertain to physical arrangements. People like to know how far away the closest door is located or how many people can fit into an elevator. People create distance by avoiding eye contact or taking a longer route in order to avoid saying "hello" to a person they find annoying.

Think about how you perceive the environments in which you live. Did you realize that your perceptions of those environments are influenced by the six ways just discussed? The way you perceive the environments you inhabit says a lot about you and influences how others perceive you.

The characters in the TV show *How I Met Your Mother* frequently spend time together in a local pub. Would you want to hang out in an environment like the one pictured here?

Reactions to Environment

Now that you have some idea about how people perceive the environment, you can look at how people react to it. Remember that while environment serves as a form of nonverbal communication, it also impacts our interactions within it. The drive-through at a fast-food restaurant creates a certain atmosphere. You are expected to quickly order your food, pay, pick up your food, and drive away. This environment does not invite conversation. A coffeehouse, on the other hand, encourages conversation with the arrangement of tables and couches. Let's look at the college classroom again.

Think of a course you're currently taking and the classroom where the course is delivered. What color are the walls? What about the seating arrangement? What can you smell and hear? What's the lighting like? Are there windows? How does all this influence the learning environment? What type of interaction is encouraged by the arrangement of the environment? A well-arranged classroom in which you feel comfortable should encourage you to interact with your classmates and teacher. Environment is communicative because people have perceptions of and reactions to environment. Let us now look at another element that influences the communicative environment—time.

Chronemics

Chronemics is the study of the ways in which time is used to structure interactions (Kalman & Rafaeli, 2011). Have you ever been casually late to a party? In some situations being late is a violation of important cultural norms. Yet, at many parties, the acceptable window of arrival is much larger. U.S. and most of Western European culture is monochronic, in that being on time and maintaining a schedule for events is important. In other cultures, such as South American and Mediterranean cultures, you will find a polychronic time orientation. A polychronic time orientation places less emphasis on keeping a tight schedule and values greater flexibility.

Time can also be used to denote power and role differences. Your boss might keep you waiting while she is talking on the phone because doing so communicates a difference in power, the implication being that her time is more valuable than yours. Indeed, time plays an important role in relation to communication. Think about how time has an influence in your life as well as on your perceptions of others.

How do you manage time in your own life, and how does that impact your communication?

Facial Expressions

The next nonverbal code that is important to study is the face. This code encompasses the use of the face to communicate emotion and feelings (see Figure 4.1). The face can be considered a gallery for our emotional displays (Gosselin, Gilles, & Dore, 1995). It is so important in communication that it has become, according to communication scholars Domenici and Littlejohn (2006), "a symbol of close personal interaction" (p. 10). Consider common expressions such as "face-to-face," "face time," "in your face," or "saving face": Your face and your public identity are intimately connected; in fact, your face is the *you* presented to others in everyday encounters. Scholar Erving Goffman (1967) wrote about this presentation of self in everyday life, explaining how face can be "lost," "maintained," "protected," or "enhanced."

It is important to have a basic understanding of how you manage your face in daily interactions. Social norms and communication expectations in our culture set the rules for what kinds of emotional expressions are appropriate in certain situations. Facial management techniques are categories of behavior created by Paul Ekman and Wallace Friesen (1969a, 1969b, 1975) that determine the appropriate facial response for a given situation. The four most common techniques include neutralization, masking, intensification, and deintensification.

The process of controlling facial expressions to erase or numb how you really feel is called neutralization. People who neutralize

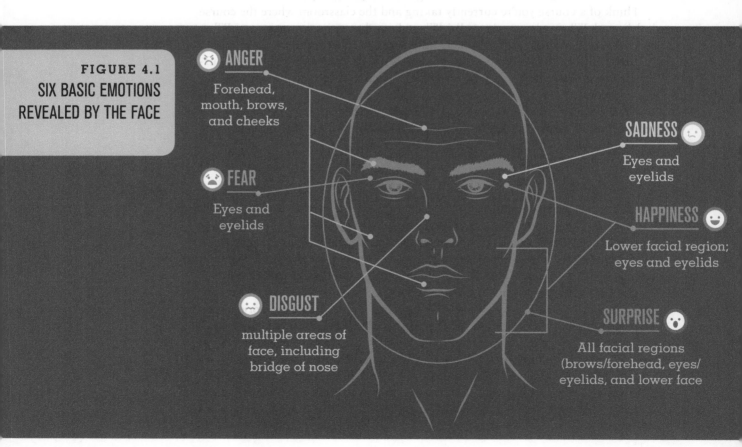

FIGURE 4.1
SIX BASIC EMOTIONS REVEALED BY THE FACE

ANGER
Forehead, mouth, brows, and cheeks

FEAR
Eyes and eyelids

DISGUST
multiple areas of face, including bridge of nose

SADNESS
Eyes and eyelids

HAPPINESS
Lower facial region; eyes and eyelids

SURPRISE
All facial regions (brows/forehead, eyes/eyelids, and lower face

COMMUNICATION HOW-TO
USE OF EMOTICONS AND EMOJI

Canstock

Despite the common use of emoticons and emoji, research has shown that the intended impact of emoticons tends to be rather ambiguous, or relatively weak. It almost seems like people use emoticons in a habitual or unconscious way. However, research has indicated that messages such as Facebook postings, while intended to be innocuous, can cause negative emotional reactions based on how nonverbal cues are perceived. Also, the relationship between the sender and receiver can impact how the message is construed (Fleuriet, Cole, & Guerrero, 2014). For example, an emoticon with a winking face sent between your romantic partner and his or her ex-partner is likely to arouse jealousy, even if that was not the intent of the message. Below are some issues to keep in mind when using emoticons on social media:

1. Before making a post or sending a message, step outside your personal frame of reference to a third-person point of view. How would a stranger evaluate the message? If a person could easily misinterpret what you are trying to convey, it might be best to alter your communication.

2. When using emoticons, remember that there is no universal agreement on what they can mean. A winking or blushing face

can seem innocent to many people, but romantic or flirtatious to others.

3. There are significant nonverbal differences in communication across cultures. For example, a common hand gesture at the University of Texas, "Hook 'Em Horns," can mean an insult to marriage fidelity in certain European and Asian cultures.

Images: canstock and istock.

their facial expressions are often referred to as having a poker face. Masking means hiding an expression connected to a felt emotion and replacing it with an expression more appropriate to the situation. If you use an expression that exaggerates how you feel about something, it is called intensification. On the other hand, if you reduce the intensity of your facial expression of a certain emotion, it is called deintensification.

Emoticons and Emoji

The use of emoticons, a textual expression of emotions, and emoji, meaning "picture letter" in Japanese, are how you show your feelings in the digital world (Dresner & Herring, 2010). The use of :-), :-(, or :-D demonstrates your feelings in text. However, the situation should determine their use. In a text message, personal e-mail, or Facebook status line, emoticons and emoji are appropriate; however, steer clear of using them in professional e-mails or memos to your professors, coworkers, or boss. A good rule of thumb is that emoticons and emoji work best when they are used in interactions that once occurred primarily face to face. Using emoticons and

Actor Ben Affleck shows his nonverbal communication skills—that is, his poker face—at a celebrity charity poker tournament.

Corbis

emoji to add some feeling in a text message to your boyfriend or girlfriend can help replace the expressiveness that may be lost because you are not face to face. In interactions that have long occurred primarily in writing (like office memos, professional reports, and business e-mails), emoticons and emoji may be interpreted as overly casual, irrelevant, and unprofessional.

Eye Behavior

The eyes are said to be the window to the soul. A significant part of facial expressions involves the use of the eyes. Approximately 80% of the information in our everyday surroundings is taken in visually (Morris, 1985). Are you comfortable making eye contact with most people or only with people you know well? If you want to flirt with someone you find attractive, you might stare, get her attention, and then look away. If you are mad at someone, you might stare him down. The eyes have social and cultural importance for communication. In U.S. culture as well as in many other cultures, eye contact is extremely important. People tend to make all kinds of judgments about others—particularly their trustworthiness and sincerity—on the basis of whether they make or avoid eye contact. People tend to trust those who will look them in the eye more and to believe what they are saying.

Think of eye behavior in terms of its influence on the social interactive process. Eye behavior is very powerful, and it can stimulate arousal, which can be a positive or negative reaction in response to another person. Seeing another person will always trigger some degree of arousal. It can be positive if you haven't seen a person for a while and you're excited to see him or her. However, it can also be negative if you see someone you would rather avoid. Eye behavior is crucial in social interaction because what you do with your eyes is more obvious than other actions of the face and body.

Eye behavior also commands involvement or the need to interact with another person even if it's a simple eye acknowledgment or head nod. Ever smiled at a complete stranger while you were passing him or her? Although you don't know the person, you tend to get involved with him or her, even if it's just through a slight smile or a head nod promoted by brief eye contact.

Your eyes also reveal deception cues, or hints that a person is being less than forthright. Consider behaviors you associate with lying: Behaviors like avoiding eye contact, looking down at the floor, fidgeting, clearing the throat, and using lots of filled pauses like "um" and "er" commonly indicate that someone is lying. Breaking or being unable to sustain eye gaze is also commonly believed to indicate deception. Studies have also shown that people tend to decrease eye contact when they lie (Hirsch & Wolf, 2001; Hocking & Leathers, 1980). Other studies, however, found an increase in eye gaze during deceit, possibly because the deceivers want to compensate for their lying by making more eye contact (DePaulo et al., 2003).

Haptics

Haptics is the study of touch. Whether it is a handshake, a punch, or a hug, touch has the potential to communicate a powerful message. The lack of traditional touch in mediated communication led first to XOXO in written correspondence to indicate hugs and kisses, and then to the development of behaviors like "poking" someone on Facebook. Of the five human senses, touch develops first (Montagu, 1978). Of all of the nonverbal codes, touch is the most powerful one. However, it is also the most complicated and misunderstood.

Whether face to face or online, the use of touch and how to interpret it is always contextual. Your might shake a stranger's hand but hug a friend. It would be quite a violation of nonverbal norms to go hug a stranger. In this sense, touch is influenced by relationship, situation, and culture. In some countries, it is normal for men to hold hands to indicate friendship and respect for each other (Fountain, 2005). In the United States you're less likely to see this behavior. A careful touch of the hand while delivering bad news can demonstrate care. A high-five for a job well done communicates excitement and accomplishment. Touch can also show power and role differences between individuals. The president of the United States might approach you to shake your hand, but you would never be allowed to approach the president. A doctor might touch you in a physical examination, but you would not touch the doctor to return the favor.

It is important to understand touch ethics, or people's beliefs about and preferences for touch. This ethic includes your rules about appropriate and inappropriate touch, your expectations as to how people will receive as well as extend touch to you, whether you are a touch-inclined person or not, and how you in reality act regarding touch. Your preference develops early in life and remains fairly constant. However, your relationships and experience might influence your touch preferences during your life span.

Therapeutic Touch

Touch as a nonverbal communication category has been examined in this chapter. However, what value does touch have in everyday life that makes a difference? Touch has been examined from a variety of scholarly perspectives, including affection in parenting, communication with the elderly, touch within marriage, touch as a way to offer comfort, touch related to gender, touch related to sexuality, and more. Beyond the work of nonverbal communication scholars who have spent years classifying and testing touch and its influence on human relationships is an area that points to the intersection of human communication and health. Remember the opening portion of the chapter that highlighted the importance of nonverbal communication in the practice of virtual nurses? Medical professionals like virtual nurses are using technology to communicate empathy and support online as they connect with patients and explain treatment details, medication schedules, and more. In a recent study, Coakley and Duffy (2010) found that Therapeutic Touch (TT), a method used in nursing and medical practice to reduce psychological distress and help patients relax, leads to significantly lower levels of pain as well as other positive health benefits in postoperative patients. This study illustrates an intersection between health and the nonverbal communication category of touch. The findings of this study are significant, but research on TT will only continue to reveal more of the benefits of touch to human health. Indeed, TT illustrates how nonverbal communication can make a difference. For more information about TT and other holistic treatments, visit www.ahna.org (American Holistic Nurses Association).

Why do couples hold hands? What does it do for their relationship?

Types of Touch

Several different systems for categorizing touch have been developed to help us better understand this complex code of nonverbal communication. One of the best means of classifying touch behavior was developed by Richard Heslin (1974).

First, there are *functional/professional* touches, which serve a specific purpose. These touches normally take place within the context of a professional relationship and are low in intimacy. An example would be a doctor giving a patient a physical exam. Second, there are *social/polite* touches. Touches like these are connected to cultural norms, such as handshakes. Once again there is relatively low intimacy within a relationship. Then there are *friendship/warmth* touches, which people use to show their platonic affection and support toward each other. Hugs and kisses on the cheek might be exchanged between two close friends, for example. *Love/intimacy* touches, on the other hand, are highly personal and intimate. People communicate strong feelings of affection toward each other with these kinds of touches. In this case, hugs may last longer and kisses may be on the lips, leading to sexual arousal. These touches are extremely intimate.

Appropriateness of Touch

The appropriateness of touch is a tricky topic because rules about appropriateness or inappropriateness of touch vary among individuals and cultures. The following section focuses on several aspects that can help explore the appropriateness of touch.

Appropriateness of touch depends on the location, meaning both the place on the body where contact is made and the setting within which touch occurs. The first option has a significant impact on whether you believe a touch to be appropriate or inappropriate. You make your own rules about who can touch you, when, where on your body, and in what setting. The second option determines the circumstances in which touch is made. For example, when you meet your boyfriend's or girlfriend's parents for the first time, should you shake hands with them or hug them?

Duration of the touch is the next point on our list of appropriateness. Duration means how long a touch lasts. A doctor's examination is never very pleasant, so if doctors do a good job they will get the exam over with quickly and without unnecessary contact. However, among loved ones, a lingering touch of the hand or embrace is usually expected.

Finally, intensity of touch refers to the power, force, or concentration of bodily contact. The amount of intensity that you put into a touch is influenced by your emotions. Therefore, if you're nervous before a job interview, you might use a firmer handshake than usual.

Culture and Touch

Culture plays an important role when it comes to touch, which means that you should interpret the meaning of a touch only within its appropriate cultural context (Anderson & Taylor, 2011). Hall (1966, 1981) distinguishes between contact cultures, in which people do not shy away from frequent touch, and noncontact cultures, in which individuals tend to be more reserved when it comes to touch. Contact cultures include Latin America, India, France, and Arab countries, whereas noncontact cultures include Germany and Northern European nations, North America, and many Asian countries such as China, Japan, Korea, Indonesia, and Malaysia (Hall, 1966, 1981). Greetings in different cultures are a good way to observe the cultural distinctions. For example, French Canadian greetings involve a handshake for men and brief hugs for women, whereas Puerto Rican women often grasp each other's shoulders and kiss both cheeks when greeting. Saudi Arabian men shake right hands to greet each other, and may also place their left hands on each other's shoulders while kissing both cheeks (Hickson, Stacks, & Moore, 2004).

Touch can indicate intimacy or hostility. It can be greatly misunderstood or incredibly needed. It can violate one's touch ethic as well as provide comfort and warmth (Anderson & Taylor, 2011). Touch is a powerful nonverbal behavior that says a lot about the relationships you're in as well as the person you are.

Physical Appearance

The final nonverbal code is physical appearance, which refers to observable traits of the body and its accessories and extensions. There are two reasons why it's important to make the connection between physical appearance and nonverbal communication: (1) The way you represent yourself and your physical appearance reveals a lot about who you are, and (2) the physical appearance of other people influences your perception of them, how you talk to them, how approachable they are, how attractive or unattractive they are, and so on. The level of physical attractiveness is an important dimension of physical appearance. Physical attractiveness is a perception of beauty derived from cultures. Each culture has a different idea about physical attractiveness. It is formed by features of our appearance such as height, weight, size, shape, and so on. In other words, there's a certain standard of physical appearance that dictates what is and is *not* attractive. Even though people have a limited amount of power to dramatically alter their physical appearances, others treat appearances as if they communicate important information. Teachers tend to judge attractive students as smarter and more social than less attractive students (Ritts, Patterson, & Tubbs, 1992), and attractive people often make more money in their jobs (Judge, Hurst, & Simon, 2009). Similarly, features of appearance like height, weight, and skin color are interpreted as important messages about who you are and what you're like. However, people misjudge one another on the basis of physical appearance so often that it is worth questioning whether you can make correct attributions about other people based on aspects of their appearance. Clothing and other objects you use to represent your identities, interests, and backgrounds are also a part of physical appearance. You may wear glasses, carry handbags, flaunt phones, wear jewelry, or sport tattoos to express who you are or how you would like to be seen. What personal artifacts, if any, are important to your appearance?

Body Type, Shape, and Size

Have you ever avoided interaction with someone because of his or her body shape or size? Generally, size and shape of our bodies communicate something nonverbally.

ETHICAL CONNECTION   JUDGING THE PHYSICAL APPEARANCE OF OTHERS

Luigi Novi

New Jersey governor Chris Christie himself had to experience the judgments and stereotypes that are triggered whenever people don't conform to the "standard" of physical appearance. When Christie deliberated whether to opt in or out of the presidential race in October 2011, the media went crazy over his body weight. He was mocked for his "puffed-up body," and was accused of being undisciplined (Puhl, 2011). Christie's qualifications were completely ignored. Instead, reports consisted of derogatory comments such as fat jokes and weight-related puns "providing a clear example of how socially acceptable weight bias and discrimination against obese persons have become in

our society" (Puhl, 2011). In Christie's case, people just assumed that he couldn't be an effective political leader due to his body weight. Does this surprise you? The sad truth is that discrimination due to physical appearance has become quite common in today's society, in which two thirds of Americans are now overweight or obese (Kaufman, 2011). Weight discrimination in the United States has increased by 66% over the past decade, and research has shown that it is the third most common type of discrimination for women and the fourth most common type for men.

When people negatively judge others on their physical appearance, they are denying them the opportunity to connect and engage with others. Ethical communication occurs when you pay attention to and evaluate the message of another person. You should strive not to let physical appearance characteristics get in the way of hearing others' ideas or thoughts.

QUESTIONS

1. From an ethical perspective, should physical appearance be a factor in voting decisions? What other nonverbal communication codes explained in this chapter do you pay attention to in political figures and leaders?

2. Many people present an altered or idealized version of their physical appearance in the Communication Age. When does altering your physical appearance online cross the line from permissible to unethical?

Scholars have even developed a system called somatyping that classifies people according to their body type (Sheldon, Stevens, & Tucker, 1942).

Shape and size also matter when it comes to judging physical appearance. The perception of body weight varies from culture to culture. Especially in American culture there seems to be an obsession with body weight; however, in other cultures around the world body weight isn't that big of a deal. Many of you probably feel like you have to look as perfect as the models in the commercials on TV, on billboards, in magazines, and so on. Such portrayals in the media make money off of people's weight insecurities. The opposite problem of obesity also has grown to be a real problem in today's society. The detrimental effects obesity can have on health lead Americans to spend a lot of time listening to messages or reading books about weight loss.

Height and status play a huge role in the process of deciding who's attractive and who's not. Tall and handsome men are favored by heterosexual women in American culture. For women the issue seems a little more complicated. Like men, tall women with long legs are seen to be more attractive. Yet women who gained above-average height during their puberty years feel like they are at a disadvantage socially and professionally because they can appear intimidating to men due to their height.

IMPROVING YOUR NONVERBAL COMMUNICATION SKILLS

Connecting with others is an essential component of the Communication Age. How do you nonverbally communicate your connection and engagement with others? Nonverbal immediacy is defined as the use of closeness-inducing nonverbal behavioral cues (Andersen, 1979). These behaviors include touching someone in a nonviolent manner, smiling, orientating your body toward the other person, looking at the person, or using vocal cues in an animated fashion. Many communication scholars have found that nonverbal immediacy helps produce liking (McCroskey & Richmond, 1992). The effects of nonverbal immediacy have been demonstrated in many different contexts. Doctors who are nonverbally immediate have patients who are more satisfied (Conlee & Olvera, 1993). Coaches who utilize nonverbal immediacy behaviors are able to create better groups of athletes (Turman, 2008). In the classroom, teachers who engage in nonverbal immediacy behaviors have students who learn more (Christensen & Menzel, 1998). In other words, the more nonverbally immediate you are, the more others will like you, work with you, and learn from you. Positive nonverbal immediacy behaviors can help you to improve your nonverbal communication skills. To promote the development of your nonverbal communication skills, use the "Assess Your Communication" feature to check your nonverbal immediacy score.

ASSESS YOUR COMMUNICATION

Nonverbal Immediacy Scale-Observer Report (NIS-O)

This measure will allow you to assess your own nonverbal immediacy behaviors.

Directions: The following statements describe the ways some people behave while talking with or to others. Please indicate in the space at the left of each item the degree to which you believe the statement applies to you, using the following 5-point scale:

1 = Never; 2 = Rarely; 3 = Occasionally; 4 = Often; 5 = Very Often

_____ 1. I use my hands and arms to gesture while talking to people.

_____ 2. I touch others on the shoulder or arm while talking to them.

_____ 3. I use a monotone or dull voice while talking to people.

_____ 4. I look over or away from others while talking to them.

_____ 5. I move away from others when they touch me while we are talking.

_____ 6. I have a relaxed body position when I talk to people.

_____ 7. I frown while talking to people.

_____ 8. I avoid eye contact while talking to people.

_____ 9. I have a tense body position while talking to people.

_____10. I sit or stand close to people while talking with them.

_____11. My voice is monotonous or dull when I talk to people.

_____12. I use a variety of vocal expressions when I talk to people.

_____13. I gesture when I talk to people.

_____14. I am animated when I talk to people.

_____15. I have a bland facial expression when I talk to people.

_____16. I move closer to people when I talk to them.

_____17. I look directly at people while talking to them.

_____18. I am stiff when I talk to people.

_____19. I have a lot of vocal variety when I talk to people.

_____20. I avoid gesturing while I am talking to people.

_____21. I lean toward people when I talk to them.

_____22. I maintain eye contact with people when I talk to them.

_____23. I try not to sit or stand close to people when I talk with them.

_____24. I lean away from people when I talk to them.

_____25. I smile when I talk to people.

_____26. I avoid touching people when I talk to them.

Scoring for NIS-O:

Step 1. Start with a score of 78. Add the scores from the following items:

1, 2, 6, 10, 12, 13, 14, 16, 17, 19, 21, 22, and 25.

Step 2. Add the scores from the following items:

3, 4, 5, 7, 8, 9, 11, 15, 18, 20, 23, 24, and 26.

Total Score = Step 1 minus Step 2

How did you score? What surprised you about your score? You can also try the NIS-O on others. Simply fill out the measure with another person's behaviors in mind. For instance, you might find it interesting to fill out the survey for your least and most favorite professors to determine whether their nonverbal immediacy might play some role in the degree to which you like them. Do you notice differences in their use of nonverbal immediacy behaviors? Have you learned more in one class? What class do you enjoy more?

Source: Richmond, McCroskey, & Johnson (2003).

NONVERBAL COMMUNICATION AND CONVERGENCE

The study of nonverbal communication is especially important to convergence in the Communication Age (Darics, 2010; Kalman & Rafaeli, 2011; Robinson, 2010). People are now using new media and the latest technology to replace nonverbal messages seen in face-to-face encounters, forcing new kinds of communal bonds and definitions of place (Erickson, 2010; Soukup, 2006). No longer do people need to only meet face to face to send nonverbal messages. How you come across through computer-mediated communication is very similar to how you meet people face to face. Consider the following nonverbal codes and think critically about how you present yourself nonverbally using computer-mediated communication and other forms of new media:

- Physical appearance
- Voice
- Facial and eye expressions
- Gestures
- Touch

How do you present yourself nonverbally using new media?

Scholar Erving Goffman's research on how people present or represent themselves in everyday life is applicable to the Communication Age. Goffman (1959) suggests that "the expressiveness of the individual (and therefore his [*sic*] capacity to give impressions) appears to solve two radically different kinds of sign activity: the expression that he *gives,* and the expression that he *gives off*" (p. 2). What people *give* refers to verbal communication occurring in face-to-face settings. The *giving off* part is nonverbal (e.g., facial expressions, gestures, body movements; Martey & Stromer-Galley, 2007). Common nonverbal cues may be altered in computer-mediated communication, but we as communicators still *give off* these cues to assist in the communication of the verbal message and to connect our self to others online (Li, Jackson, & Trees, 2008).

Reflecting on the sense of play fostered by technology, Sherry Turkle (1995) suggests that "the computer offers us both new models of mind and a new medium on which to project our ideas and fantasies" (p. 1). "Life on the screen," she explains, "makes it very easy to present oneself as other than one is in real life" (p. 228). As we explained in Chapter 2, avatars are ways that computer users express themselves with digital representations. Avatars allow users to visually and nonverbally express human characteristics and emotions (Li et al., 2008). One study examined how participants in the online community known as The Palace used avatars and props to manage space and express themselves (Soukup, 2004). The research determined that the placement and actions of avatars expressed computer users' closeness of relationship to others (proxemics). These embodiments of computer users represent extensions of the self—yet another nonverbal means of expressing oneself in a virtual community. Since many of your daily actions, interactions, and experiences are mediated by technology, it's important to think about how you express yourself and how this form of expression changes your understanding of nonverbal communication and personal identity as face-to-face and mediated experience blend in the Communication Age (Erickson, 2010; Ha & Lennon, 2010; Walther, Loh, & Granka, 2005).

Communication unplugged

TO IMPROVE COMMUNICATION, BALANCE YOUR FACE-TO-FACE INTERACTIONS AND ONLINE PERSONA

It's no secret that many people work hard to craft an online persona that portrays them in the best possible light. However, crafting an online persona (especially regarding Facebook) takes a person out of the more dynamic, immediate setting of face-to-face interaction. As you move forward in your social and professional life, you must still have the ability to communicate yourself to others in nonmediated contexts. Researcher Neil James Henderson identifies the "commodification of the self" on Facebook and its role in "flattening" the available interactivity of the online self (Henderson, 2014). Henderson analyzes the short film *Noah* (2013), wherein an adolescent boy attempts to build relationships strictly through computer-mediated platforms. The story shows the breakdown of a relationship mainly due to vague, computer-mediated nonverbal cues and lack of immediate feedback. The story serves as an example that many intimate relationships can have difficulties when there is not enough face-to-face interaction to complement the online communication.

The online self, while problematic, can still assist certain "face-to-face" interactions; Skype and Chatroulette offer a very close approximation of face-to-face communication in that they both take place in real time, offer video to provide eye contact and body language feedback, and allow for the analysis of vocalics. Furthermore, research has indicated that face-to-face networks have a larger effect of satisfaction than do their Facebook system counterparts (Wright, Rosenberg, Egbert, Ploeger, Bernard, & King, 2013).

WHAT TO DO NEXT

To increase the effectiveness of your face-to-face interactions, try to:

- **Address body language.** This perhaps sets face-to-face communication apart from any other. We express emotions through body language, and the immediacy of face-to-face communication offers valuable insight into a relationship.

- **Make eye contact.** This conveys a great deal about what we are communicating. Eye contact is very important in terms of first impressions.

- **Make sure to listen.** While this may sound obvious, face-to-face interaction does not carry the same luxury as, for example, e-mail. Unlike e-mail, where you can reread the other person's message multiple times before replying, face-to-face communication requires you to be an active listener.

Think critically about how computer-mediated communication and social networking will influence nonverbal communication. The study of nonverbal communication is only going to become more crucial in the Communication Age. It is your job and responsibility to be aware of and understand how nonverbal messages are impacted by convergence in the Communication Age.

WHAT YOU'VE LEARNED　　Now that you have studied this chapter, you should be able to:

1 Identify the importance of nonverbal communication in your life.

Nonverbal communication includes all the ways people communicate without using words. Nonverbal communication can include your clothing, your physical appearance, your gestures, your facial and eye expressions, and more.

 Saying What You Mean: A Children's Book About Communication Skills

2 Explain the functions of nonverbal communication as it works with verbal communication.

Nonverbal communication has different functions. These functions include repeating, accenting, conflicting, complementing, regulating, and substituting.

🎙 Decoding Body Language

3 Describe the codes of nonverbal communication.

In order to understand nonverbal communication better, people study the different codes that define nonverbal communication. These codes are vocalic, kinesics, proxemics, environment, facial expressions, eye behavior, haptics, and physical appearance.

▶ The Proxemic Project

 How Well Do You Read Other People? A Body Language Quiz

4 Describe the impact nonverbal communication has in a variety of situations.

Emblems, illustrators, affect displays, regulators, and adapters, or the five categories of kinesics, are important to keep in mind when dealing with nonverbal communication in a variety of situations. Be aware of cultural differences. In some cultures these same emblems might have a completely different meaning, and to avoid an uncomfortable situation you need to be culturally sensitive.

▶ Dressing for a Job Interview

 Checking Your Tone in E-Mail Messages

5 Examine how nonverbal communication is influenced in the Communication Age.

All nonverbal codes are influenced in the Communication Age with new media. The latest technology to replace nonverbal messages seen in face-to-face encounters promotes new kinds of social connections and understanding of space.

 Using Emojis at Work

KEY TERMS

Review key terms with eFlashcards. **edge.sagepub.com/edwards2e**

REFLECT

1. How prevalent is nonverbal communication in your life? In what situations is nonverbal communication appropriate, and when should you be more cautious about it?

2. Based on your experience with nonverbal communication, which of the named functions of nonverbal communication is most used in everyday life? How do these functions enhance or maybe even worsen our interactions with others?

3. Which perception of environment can you best relate to, and why? How has the environment shaped your communication interaction before?

4. How does your online nonverbal behavior differ from your face-to-face nonverbal behavior? Do you feel more comfortable in an online or a face-to-face interaction, and why?

REVIEW

To check your answers go to **edge.sagepub.com/edwards2e**

1. What is nonverbal communication?

2. Define kinesics.

3. _____ is a perception of beauty derived from cultures.

4. The process of controlling facial expressions to erase or numb how you really feel is called_____.

5. _____means hiding an expression connected to a felt emotion and replacing it with an expression more appropriate to the situation.

6. List the different types of touch.

7. Scholars have developed a system called _____, which classifies people according to their body type.

8. _____ is defined as the use of closeness-inducing nonverbal behavioral cues.

9. Explain why the study of nonverbal communication is important to convergence in the Communication Age.

On March 8, 2014, Flight MH370 disappeared from radar near Kuala Lumpur, Malaysia. This Malaysian Airlines flight was traveling to Beijing, China, and carried 227 passengers and 12 crew members. For several weeks, a multinational search effort combed the South China Sea and the southern Indian Ocean. It was the largest search in aviation history. A few weeks later, Malaysian government officials concluded that the flight of MH370 likely ended in the Indian Ocean.

From the time of its disappearance, there were several communication listening problems among various governments trying to find the aircraft. The first problems resulted from members of Vietnam's Tan Son Nhat International Airport air-traffic control not informing their counterparts in Kuala Lumpur within the required 5 minutes after losing the aircraft on the radar. Furthermore, Malaysian Airlines mistakenly told its government the plane was somewhere over Cambodia (Boykoff, 2015). The national media brought in experts to hypothesize as to the whereabouts of the plane. At a dizzying pace, governments and media presented information and misinformation. It was hard to listen critically. *Aviation Week* magazine went so far as to label the communication and listening problems in finding this aircraft "farcical" (Schofield, Torr, & Perrett, 2014). In short, listening failures likely hampered efforts to find Flight MH370.

With all the information we receive on a daily basis in the Communication Age, it is important to learn to listen critically. Doing so will let you learn to distinguish between information you need to know and information you can ignore. Hopefully, you are never involved in a situation where governments are not listening to one another. However, we all face instances where we could have been better listeners and more conscious of our choices. This chapter will teach you how to improve your listening ability by critically listening to messages.

Think about the last class you attended. How long ago was it? A day or a few hours? Do you remember anything specific that your professor said? Even in the Communication Age, in which our laptops and smartphones enable us to take better notes, send faster e-mails, and stay in constant touch with faraway relatives, listening is as important as speaking. With a plethora of technological sources competing for our listening attention, we constantly have to shift our awareness and attention (Bentley, 2000; Lodge, 2010). We try to engage in multitasking but the research is clear that it does not work, especially in the college classroom (Calderwood, Ackerman, & Conklin, 2014). Some fear that people have lost the ability to focus on a single message for any length of time. These fears are well founded. In this chapter, you will learn about listening and ways to become a better listener in the Communication Age.

HEARING VERSUS LISTENING

Because listening is such a routine part of our day, it is easy to take it for granted without realizing how much work is required. Think about a simple lunch date with a friend. The restaurant is crowded, and the music is a little too loud. You did not eat breakfast, so your stomach is churning with hunger. Your server is busy with other customers and has not noticed that your water glasses are empty. Your friend sits across from you telling you about a problem she is having at work and asking for your advice. How much effort does it require for you to really listen to her? What other things are demanding your attention? You might be able to hear your friend over the music and other customers' voices, but are you listening to her? Consider another example:

It is Sunday night, and you are getting ready to watch your favorite show on Hulu. Just as you click play, your roommate calls from the kitchen that the garbage is starting to smell and that it is your turn to take it out. You give him a mumbled "OK, sure" and continue watching your show. When the show is finally over and you get up to go to bed, your roommate asks why you have not taken care of the garbage. You vaguely remember that he said something about the garbage but really have no idea what he's talking about, and the two of you proceed to argue about the chore. Have you ever experienced a misunderstanding like this? The problem is that while you may have heard your roommate, you were not really listening. Listening is essential to being connected and engaged with others. We spend most of our day listening in some form. In everyday talk, we use the words *hearing* and *listening* as if they have the same meaning. However, these words convey distinct processes.

In the Communication Age, listening is an active process of receiving and understanding messages received either through listening to words or by reading text. Listening is about attending to messages and making meaning, and it involves several simultaneous mental processes that occur during communication. Hearing, on the other hand, is what happens when sound waves are received by the ear and brain. Just because you hear someone does not mean you listened. You may have heard your friend tell you about her job, and you may have heard your roommate asking you to take out the trash, but did you listen? Why is it sometimes so difficult to listen? In the following section, you will learn about why it is difficult to listen and problems that can arise with listening.

LISTENING PROBLEMS

Listening can be hard at times. Distractions come in many different shapes and forms. We might be hungry and thinking about what to eat. We might be worrying about how much work we have left to do. We might strongly disagree with what a person is saying. We might simply be bored with the conversation. By understanding these potential problems, it is possible to listen better.

Situational Distractions

Listening is often hard because we fail to limit our distractions. We all have many things going on at once, and it can be difficult to forget these distractions and focus on one message. As you read this book, you might also have music or the TV on in the background. Your phone may occasionally vibrate or deliver a notification. Your eyes could wander periodically from the book to your devices or out the window. All of these presences in your environment are situational distractions and have the potential to distract you from your reading. The crowded restaurant, your growling stomach, and your attempts to get the server's attention are also examples of situational distractions.

Limiting your exposure to possible distractions can facilitate better listening. When you are reading your textbook, turn off your phone or the TV. Allow yourself to check your text messages every 30 minutes. Check the scores for your favorite sports teams every hour. There are no clear rules for when you should look up from the textbook, but set out to limit your situational distractions so that you can devote full attention to the task at hand.

Source Distractions

Distractions do not only come from our environment. Sometimes the very person or mediated message we are trying to listen to can be the distraction. Source distractions occur when the person or mediated message we are listening to exhibits a behavior that inhibits our ability to listen. Have you ever traveled outside of the country and spoken with people from somewhere else in the world? Even if they spoke English, you may have struggled to keep up with an accent or

Thinkstock

Hearing and listening are two different things. Hearing involves the physical process of sound waves being received by the ear and brain. Listening, on the other hand, requires active attention to processing and interpreting the meaning of a message.

▶ **COMMUNICATION IN ACTION 5.1**

WATCH: Hearing vs. Listening

A failure to truly receive and understand an important message leads to an unfortunate outcome. What clues suggest this man was merely "hearing" his girlfriend's words without really listening?

Communication **unplugged**
TO IMPROVE LISTENING, BE AWARE OF SITUATIONAL DISTRACTIONS

Try this small experiment. Go with a friend to a crowded place (a restaurant, coffee shop, or shopping mall might be a good place to try this). Sit down somewhere near the center of the room, or anywhere there are obvious distractions, and talk to one another about your day. After 10 minutes, stop talking and make a list of all of the situational distractions you noticed during your conversation. Do this quickly, without thinking too much about it. Make another list of the things your friend talked about while you were listening. Again, don't spend too much time thinking about it. Write down what comes to mind. Compare your lists. Is your list of distractions longer than the list of things you remembered from the conversation? How could you have limited these distractions to better listen to your friend? Often we can become better aware of our environment by simply being aware of the situational distractions. Did your phone vibrate? Was there a TV screen

on? Were other people talking? It is hard to listen when there are so many situational distractions around us.

WHAT TO DO NEXT
To become more aware of situational distractions, try to:

- Pay attention to your own feelings and emotions. Are you hungry, upset, or nervous? Are your emotions distracting you from having situational awareness?

- Notice all the activities occurring in an environment. Are some activities more distracting than others? What can you do to limit the worst distractors?

- Try this experiment again but focus your listening on the other person despite these distractions. Was there an improvement? With practice, you can become better at limiting distractions in your environment.

a rate of speech you were not used to. Have you ever received an e-mail that contained digital stationery (like flowers at the bottom of the message) or perhaps a text message written in ALL CAPS FOR NO REASON? These visual additions to the e-mail or text message might keep you from carefully reading the message because the source itself is the distraction. Have you ever tried to have a conversation with someone who uses dramatic hand gestures while speaking? Perhaps the constant movement of hands kept you from truly listening to what was said. It can be difficult, but when faced with any of these distractions, it is important to maintain focus on the person's message and try to put any distracting behaviors out of your mind. Often, by noticing the distracting part of the message and then moving on from it, you will be able to focus on the message.

Medium Distractions

Like static coming through a TV screen, sometimes listening distractions can come from the channel itself. The same is true in real life. Picture your graduation ceremony: Everyone is seated in a large auditorium, and the president of your university or college stands on stage, ready to give the commencement address. You can see that her mouth is moving, and you hear faint sounds, but the microphone is failing to pick up her voice and carry it throughout the room. Medium distractions occur when the channel

iStock

Technology can compete for our attention in interpersonal face-to-face interactions.

through which the message is delivered obstructs our ability to receive the message clearly.

In the Communication Age, the number of medium distractions we encounter has increased with each kind of new technology. Downed wireless networks, overcrowded servers, malfunctioning devices, and even normally functioning multitasking devices—all these things can keep us from listening carefully. Have you ever been having a phone conversation when another call or text message beeped in and distracted you? Many times medium distractions are beyond your control, but it is important to limit them as much as you can. When you are taking an important phone call, simply turn off notifications for Facebook, Instagram, new e-mails, text messages, and so on. If you are delivering a presentation, make sure the volume for the microphone is up high enough for all to hear.

▶ **COMMUNICATION IN ACTION 5.2**

WATCH: Distracted by Multitasking

Sam and Liz realize effective communication involves giving full attention to one another. What most commonly distracts you from listening to those around you?

Failure to Focus on the Message

Sometimes you will fail to focus on the message. Have you ever heard a speaker and counted the amount of "ums," "likes," or "you knows"? Or have you let your mind wander to your to-do list or started counting the ceiling tiles? Maybe you were thinking about an argument you had with a friend or roommate earlier in the day. Perhaps you were chatting with several friends online at the same time and could not really focus on any one chat. Focusing on the message can be exceptionally hard in the Communication Age. While technology has allowed for new ways to find information and communicate with others, it has also created even more ways to fail at focusing on the message.

Sometimes listeners fail to focus on the message because the words are too complicated or they contain too much technical jargon. When it takes a lot of cognitive work simply to understand the meaning of a word let alone the conversation, listeners are distracted. When speaking to others, try to avoid technical jargon so that your listeners can better focus on the message. If you must use specialized language, be sure to define it clearly for your listeners. Studies have demonstrated that in a health care setting the use of technical jargon can bring misunderstanding (Thomas, Hariharan, Rana, Swain, & Andrew, 2014) and hurt the rapport between the patient and health care providers (Roter, 2011). Sometimes we fail to focus on the message because we do not like or are bored by the speaking style of the other person. Whatever the case, focusing on the message takes skill and practice.

Bias

Bias is any assumption or attitude about a person, an issue, or a topic that is made before we have heard all of the facts. Biases are a major barrier to effective listening, and it is best to limit them in order to be more effective at listening. If you see a political ad about a candidate that misrepresents the facts of an issue that you feel very strongly about, it is possible that you will be biased against that candidate the next time you hear her speak. That bias may prevent you from listening to what the candidate has to say, and you may miss important information. Bias is not limited to individuals; it can also apply to groups. If you are anti–abortion rights, you may refuse to listen to any pro–abortion rights argument no matter who it comes from. Effective listening requires us to put our biases aside and regard the other as having a valid point of view worthy of our time and careful attention. However, it is impossible to completely set our own bias aside (Bodie, 2010). You need to acknowledge that bias exists and make your decisions with this knowledge.

Judging Too Soon

Being part of the Communication Age, you have many ways to get information, and you may have winnowed the selection of sources down to your favorites. As a result, you simply watch the same TV shows, read only a few websites, or listen to one or two radio stations exclusively. But when you limit your own exposure to news and information, you may not get a full picture and may end up judging contrary information or jumping to conclusions too soon. This happens to all of us. We may believe we are listening to the message yet fail to recognize that we are judging the topic of conversation or issue prematurely without hearing all the evidence and facts. Bias plays an important role in judging a message too soon. This is because bias can occur outside of our conscious awareness (Aarts, Custers, & Veltkamp, 2008). Our brains are capable of making split-second decisions about people and issues, and we may not even realize we are making these decisions.

Judging too soon can also happen in more personal contexts. Paige has a friend, Steve, who she knows is not a good driver. Steve calls Paige to tell her about a recent car accident where he hit another vehicle. While hearing this story, Paige may unconsciously blame him for the accident and ignore the part of the conversation in which he tells her that the other car ran a red light and crashed into him. In this example, Paige judged the message too soon without hearing all the facts. In order to be good listeners, we have to wait until we have all of the information before forming judgments or assumptions. It takes a lot of effort and patience to put aside our own quick thinking and really listen to the other, but we can improve this with practice.

Listening Anxiety

Have you ever been nervous about listening to a presentation or being involved in a conversation? Perhaps your boss is giving you specific directions about a complicated work task. Or you might be sitting in a lecture trying to learn difficult material that will be on the next exam. In both cases, you might be apprehensive about listening to the speaker. This feeling is called listening anxiety. Listening anxiety occurs when a listener has anxiety that triggers the inability to process and interpret messages being sent by others (Schrodt & Wheeless, 2001). Examples of listening anxiety include a fear of not processing new information correctly and a fear of being judged on one's ability to correctly remember specific information (Wheeless, Preiss, & Gayle, 1997). Research has demonstrated that people with high listening anxiety tend to have

Listening anxiety may lead to problems processing and interpreting the messages sent by others.

Thinkstock

ASSESS YOUR COMMUNICATION

LISTENING ANXIETY

The following statements apply to how various people feel about listening to others. Indicate if these statements apply to how you feel, noting whether you (5) strongly agree, (4) agree, (3) are undecided, (2) disagree, or (1) strongly disagree.

1. _____ While listening, I get nervous when a lot of information is given at once.

2. _____ I get impatient and anxious when listening to someone discuss theoretical, intellectual issues.

3. _____ I have avoided listening to abstract ideas because I was afraid I could not make sense of what was said.

4. _____ Many classes are annoying and uncomfortable because the teacher floods you with detailed information in the lectures.

5. _____ I feel agitated or uneasy when someone tells me there is not necessarily a clear, concrete way to deal with an important problem.

6. _____ While listening, I feel tense when I have to analyze details carefully.

7. _____ It is frustrating to listen to people discuss practical problems in philosophical and abstract ways.

8. _____ When I hear abstract material, I am afraid I will be unable to remember it very well.

9. _____ I experience anxiety when listening to complex ideas others tell me.

10. _____ When I listen to complicated information, I often fear that I will misinterpret it.

11. _____ I do not feel relaxed and confident while listening, even when a lot of information is given at once.

12. _____ Listening to complex ideas is not a pleasant, enjoyable experience for me.

13. _____ When listening, I do not feel relaxed and confident that I can remember abstract ideas that are being explained.

Add all scores together: _____

The higher the score, the higher your listening anxiety.

Note: This is a modified version of the Listening Anxiety Test.

Source: From "Receiver Apprehension, Informational Receptivity, and Cognitive Processing," in *Avoiding Communication: Shyness, Reticence, and Communication Apprehension,* by L. R. Wheeless, R. W. Priess, and B. M. Gayle, 1997, Cresskill, NJ: Hampton Press, pp. 151–187.

more problems with information processing and general listening effectiveness (Chesebro & McCroskey, 2001), and are more verbally aggressive in their communication (Schrodt & Wheeless, 2001). Additionally, students with higher levels of listening anxiety report less motivation to succeed in the classroom (Schrodt, Wheeless, & Ptacek, 2000).

In any communication situation, the listeners are just as important as the speaker. The listener has a vital role to play, and this role can cause some to be nervous. Take the "Assess Your Communication: Listening Anxiety" survey to see how you score in this regard. The higher your score, the more likely it is that you have listening anxiety. Toward the end of this chapter, you will learn the steps to become a better listener, which may help you reduce your listening anxiety.

BENEFITS OF BEING A GOOD LISTENER

As you remember from Chapter 1, communication is the collaborative process of using messages to create and participate in social reality. Being a good listener is an important part of this definition. We cannot create or participate in social reality if nobody is listening. In short, listening is what makes communication a collaborative process. In the following section, you will read about four key benefits of being a good listener.

Relationship Satisfaction

Of all the skills required of a good partner in a relationship, listening is one of the most important (Bodie, 2011; Bodie, Vickery, Cannava, & Jones, 2015). The ability to listen to a significant other, spouse, supervisor, parent, child, or friend will contribute to a healthy and close relationship (Floyd, 2014). How many times have you had an argument in which the other person said something like "You are not listening to me!" or "I need you to hear me out!"? In positive and healthy relationships, we value the listening contribution of the other person. Listening is crucial for providing social support in times of distress or need (Bodie, Vickery, & Gearhart, 2013; Jones, 2011). Being a good listener in a relationship takes work and the ability to not judge or evaluate the other person in the moment.

Community Activism

Listening to others about the needs of your community will help you find ways to be more involved in the community. John Dewey (1927), an important American philosopher of education and communication theory, argued that listening is a vital skill for a democracy to flourish. He believed that social problems can only be resolved through listening to those around us in our communities. Who better to understand the problems in a local community than those who live within it? Being part of an engaged community requires good listening abilities. This is why politicians, business leaders, and community activists often go on listening tours. A listening tour is when a person travels to different communities specifically to listen to the concerns and ideas of the people who live there. Listening tours allow a leader or another interested party to gain better insight into the lives of those in the community. Listening to as many people as possible may open the door to more efficient, practical, and workable solutions.

Media Awareness

Living in the Communication Age, listening to media is only increasing, and it is important to become more aware. Media awareness is the ability to selectively attend to and evaluate messages in the media. By working to develop our listening skills, we will be better able to cut through the potential noise and distractions and truly focus on messages that need our attention. Additionally, learning to be good listeners will help us know when something we view or listen to online is worthy of our time and effort. Because of all the potential media we could view, we simply have to make better choices, and listening critically to media will help us do so (Literat, 2014; Van de Vord, 2010).

Job Success

Being a good listener is one of the most important skills in the workplace (Flynn, Valikoski, & Grau, 2008). You will spend most of your time in the workplace listening to others. It might be your supervisor telling you about the next assignment, a coworker discussing a media plan for a project, or a customer complaining about the service. Learning to listen to your work team is an important skill to acquire (Johnston, Reed, & Lawrence, 2011). Think about your own college experience. You spend most of your time listening to your instructor with the goal of being able to remember and critically think about the classroom material. Success in the classroom is based on your ability to listen (Cooper & Buchanan, 2010). The same is true in the workplace.

TYPES OF LISTENING

The kind of listening you engage in is different depending on the situation or what your needs are in the moment. You would listen differently to a friend talking about a serious health problem than you would the "Time to Work Out" playlist on your phone. It is important to have a listening goal, what you are trying to accomplish with listening in a particular context or situation. In this section, let's discuss five basic types of listening, each with a different goal (Wolvin & Coakley, 1996).

Discriminative Listening

Discriminative listening involves the ability to understand the different stimuli around us in order to process the meaning. If you have ever been around a baby for any length of time, you start to realize how the sounds of various cries can mean that the baby is in need of a diaper change, feeding, or just human touch.

MAKE
—a—
DIFFERENCE

STORYCORPS

Corbis

WE KNOW THAT learning to listen well is an important part of our jobs, our classes, and our relationships, but can it also affect our sense of community? Listening is how we gather important information we need, but it is also a way of connecting with others. How might it change our communities if we took the time to listen to one another's stories? A nonprofit organization, StoryCorps, is answering these questions. StoryCorps' mission is to give people from every background and belief system the chance to record their life stories and preserve them in the U.S.

Library of Congress. One way StoryCorps accomplishes its mission is by creating the National Day of Listening. The idea is for citizens in any community to interview people in their lives and record the interview so it can be passed down to others. It could be a family member, a friend, a veteran, or a stranger who is willing to sit down and tell his or her story. The most important aspect of the interview is that both parties take the time to listen to each other's stories. So many of us have stories to tell, but we stay silent because we do not believe that anyone wants to listen. But with the help of StoryCorps and its archives of interviews, we now know that our stories can have a large and willing audience.

You can participate in the National Day of Listening by visiting nationaldayoflistening.org and learning how to record your own interview. You can also listen to others' interviews and get help with a list of questions to ask your partner. Who would you like to interview in your community? Who in your community needs someone to truly listen to him or her? This interview can be just between the two of you, or you can record it so that people from other communities can benefit from it. Whose story do you think needs to be told?

In the Communication Age, this type of listening goal is important due to all the auditory and visual stimuli that occur all around us. We have to be good at discriminative listening before we can engage in other types of listening goals.

Critical Listening

Critical listening occurs when you need to evaluate an argument or a stance and develop an opinion based on evidence. This type of listening is the most demanding because you must simultaneously listen to the message and analyze its content. Think back to the example of listening to the political candidate running for office. Not only do you need to listen to get all the facts, you are also being asked to make a decision regarding the candidate's ability to do the job well. While you gather the information from the speech, you also must ask yourself, Is the candidate being truthful? Is the candidate an ethical leader? What are the candidate's abilities, and is there any reason the candidate may not perform the job well? Are there other candidates who may do the job better? You may gain answers to a few of these questions from listening carefully to the candidate's message, but you will likely have to draw from past messages and experiences to form a complete picture and make your choices. Engaging in critical listening will help you make these decisions. Listening requires us to constantly monitor our own listening and to be open to the ideas we are hearing (Richmond & Hickson, 2002).

Comprehensive Listening

Comprehensive listening refers to trying to understand and make meaning of the message. For example, listening to your instructor lecture on a theory of communication would involve comprehensive listening. You might take notes, pay attention to the presentational slides, and ask questions. Asking for clarification and further explanation is an important part of comprehensive listening and is useful if you need to recall the information at a later date. Think about shopping for a new apartment. You may

Democratic presidential candidate Hillary Clinton has numerous speaking engagements intended to persuade audiences to support her bid for the White House. Critical listening is especially important during election times. How do you practice critical listening when you must make an important decision?

make several appointments to tour various apartments, and at each new location, a building manager will tell you about the available amenities, benefits, and possible challenges. In this case, if you engage in comprehensive listening by taking notes and asking detailed questions (does it have a dishwasher; are the neighbors quiet; did the previous tenant smoke or have pets?), you are more likely to remember which apartment best suits your needs. And, of course, engaging in comprehensive listening in class will make you more likely to pass your test!

Appreciative Listening

Appreciative listening is listening for pleasure. This could involve listening to music, public radio, slam poetry, an interesting speaker, or any entertaining show. You may also enjoy listening to books in an audio format. Appreciative listening

COMMUNICATION**HOW-TO**
CRITICAL LISTENING

1. Pay close attention to the message and notice things that distracted you during the presentation or conversation.

2. Write down any previous knowledge or opinions you had about the person speaking. Think about how those opinions affected how you listened.

3. Reflect on what you learned in the presentation or conversation.

4. Evaluate the evidence and arguments presented in the message. Does the evidence make sense? Is it compelling? Are the arguments logical?

Images: istock.

Taking the time to enjoy music may seem easier than other types of listening, but it still requires time and effort.

depends very much on the individual, but the key is enjoyment. However, that does not mean that appreciative listening is effortless. It can take a great amount of skill and focus to appreciate the nuances of a great album or the message of a great speaker, especially if there are other people or issues demanding our attention.

Empathic Listening

The last type of listening is empathic listening, or listening to others by responding nonjudgmentally to their needs (either physical or emotional). When we say, "I need someone to listen to me," it's usually empathic listening that we are seeking. We are hoping to be able to "lay it out" for someone who will let us talk and make us feel "heard" and less alone. Think about that lunch date with the friend who wanted advice about a problem going on at work. Remember all the possible distractions present in that situation? To be a truly empathic listener we must be able to put aside all of those distractions and focus entirely on the other person (Rogers, 1962). Empathic listening also requires demonstrating support, caring, and warmth. To do it well, the listener should put aside judgments of what is being shared. Don't judge the person's feelings or situation, but instead offer support and understanding. Virtues such as patience and humility can go a long way when listening to others (Rice & Burbules, 2010).

By understanding the type of listening we are engaging in and its goals, we have a better chance of being successful and responsive to the communication situation. In the next section, you will learn about ways to become a better listener. As you read this section, think about each type of listening goal and how you can improve.

BECOMING A BETTER LISTENER

Becoming a better listener takes work, especially with all the distractions that surround us. To be better at listening, remember this acronym: HURIER. HURIER refers to a six-step listening process: hearing, understanding, remembering, interpreting, evaluating, and responding (Brownell, 1994). The following sections discuss each step in the HURIER process.

Hearing

Remember the difference between hearing and listening? Hearing is the physical process by which auditory stimuli enter the ears. The first step toward better listening is to make sure you can properly hear the other person. In order to better receive the message, it may help you to:

- **Get closer.** Perhaps you need to move nearer to the speaker, whether that means the other person or the sound system projecting the message.

CAREER FRONTIER: HUMAN-ROBOT INTERACTION

Getty

WE ALL HAVE seen the classic movie plot in which robots rise up against humanity. Despite these movie fears, the use of social robots for a variety of tasks is growing every year. Take, for example, the social robot Nexi, developed at the Massachusetts Institute of Technology. Nexi is designed to mimic facial features of human emotional displays and have basic conversations. More advanced social robots are used for therapy with autism, as companions for children in hospitals, or as general assistants in the workplace. You will most likely work with a social robot in your career. This might seem like a long way off, but in the next 5 years we will see social robots in the workplace. Fong, Nourbakhsh, and Dautenhahn (2003) argued that in order for social robots to be integrated into society they would need to "capitalize on feelings evoked when humans nurture" or care for them, "pro-actively engage" with humans, and communicate with high levels of dialogue (p. 145). In other words, social robots need to be able to listen. Part of your career skills inventory will be interacting with robots at some level. Just do not let them rise up against us!

- **Eliminate distractions.** Close down extra applications, stash away the nonessential communication technologies, and put some distance between yourself and any people or noises that may limit your ability to hear. For example, it may be best not to sit with your friends if they tend to make noise, talk, or comment during presentations.

- **Focus your attention.** Distractions may be mental, as well. Ruminating, planning, and daydreaming can block you from truly hearing the message. Do your best to put aside the other things on your mind.

Understanding

Attaching meaning to the words you hear in a conversation or presentation is the process of understanding. We often do this unconsciously. For example, if your professor is telling a story about her dog, you mentally conjure an image of a dog, allowing you to understand her message. Understanding a message requires that we can first hear the message, but it includes being able to comprehend the speaker's use of language and the basic context of the information.

- **Be mindful.** Mindfulness is the ability to remain in the present moment and fully be aware of the speaker, the environment, and the message. Mindfulness increases your information-processing ability (Zeidan, Johnson, Diamond, David, & Goolkasian, 2010). If your mind wanders, gently return your awareness to the message and its source.

- **Do your homework.** Comprehending the speaker's message may require you to prepare in advance of the conversation or presentation. For instance, listening to a lecture in a college course after completing assigned background reading produces greater understanding of the message.

Remembering

The next step is remembering the message so that it can be interpreted and responded to. Simply hearing and understanding a message is not enough to enable it to become a meaningful part of communication. You must find a way to store it for later use.

- **Use memory aids.** Create a mental outline, periodically making sure you can repeat the main points to yourself; take notes, if appropriate to the context.

- **Avoid verbatim recordings.** Copying down or recording messages exactly as they are presented actually decreases your ability to remember them. When merely transcribing a message, you do not exert the same mental energy it takes to understand something well enough to put it in your own words.

TECHNOLOGY IS LISTENING

Getty

Living in the Communication Age brings a new set of opportunities that can also be challenges. Wired devices (devices connected to the Internet) have allowed us to utilize new ways to be connected and engaged with others. However, these devices can listen in on our conversations. Imagine you are having a personal conversation with someone in front of your smart TV. The TV is on and showing the menu of the various apps available (e.g., Hulu, Netflix, YouTube, HBO GO). Should you be concerned about your privacy? Samsung recently warned customers not to discuss personal information in front of their smart TV sets, which may "listen" to your conversations (Not in front of the telly, 2015). The smart TV company LG, for instance, admitted that some of its smart TVs were tracking and transmitting the activities of users (Soloman, 2013). As the Internet of Things (see Chapter 3) grows, more devices will be able to listen to human speech. While this listening by devices is designed to help interact with our environment, a third party could pick up the private information we share. As much as we might want to talk to the voice-activated coffee machine, we may not want it to listen to us. We will have to think critically about technology listening to our conversations and the environment around us.

QUESTIONS

1. Should there be more warnings on devices that can listen to the environment?

2. What are the implications for products that can listen to the surroundings?

Interpreting

The next step in the HURIER process is to make sense of the verbal and nonverbal codes and to assign meaning to the information received. You may hear your sister say, "I'm fine," when you ask how she is doing. She may mean exactly that, but you may also gain clues from her expression or the context that lead to an alternative interpretation. Interpreting is an important part of the collaborative process of communication, and this is where miscommunication is likely to happen. It's important to aim to assign the same meaning to the message that the speaker intended.

- **Ask questions.** Check your perceptions of the message by asking questions of clarification or elaboration. You want to clear up uncertainties or misunderstandings in meaning prior to evaluating and responding to the message.

- **Be holistic.** Use what you know about the context as a whole and the person with whom you are speaking to form correct interpretations of the message.

- **Consider the medium.** Compared to media with broader bandwidth (e.g., face to face, videoconferencing), text messaging lacks the nonverbal cues we often use in message interpretation. Sometimes, switching the conversation to a richer medium can lead to better interpretations.

Evaluating

Weighing the credibility and accuracy of the message to make an assessment about the information requires evaluation. When you evaluate the persuasiveness of a public speech, you consider the strength of the arguments presented. Is the speaker giving good evidence to back her claims? Is she credible to speak about the particular subject? Is she separating fact from fiction? You also evaluate everyday messages, like your friend telling you about his day. You think about what the information means for his life and your friendship. You consider appropriate statements or actions to make. Is this good news that merits a celebration? Will your friend need social support to get over a tough break? To improve your message evaluations:

- **Avoid bias.** Check your preconceived notions about how a person's gender, race, physical appearance, sexuality, nationality, or disability may influence your judgments of message worth and credibility.

- **Be generous.** Give others with whom you share a relationship the same benefit of the doubt when evaluating their messages you would hope they extend to you.

Responding

The last step is giving a response to the message, either verbally or nonverbally. After interpreting and evaluating the message you must decide how to reply—and others will judge your listening skills by your response. It may seem odd to include your response as part of the listening process, but your response will show the other person just how carefully you were paying attention to the message. Communication would not be collaboration if not for this vital step. If when evaluating your sister's message, "I'm fine," you notice her tone of voice is less cheery

Offering your conversational partner a response is an important way to show her you are listening, even if your response is nonverbal.

iStock

than usual, you may decide to ask her about her mood. Perhaps she shares she's worried about a friend. Your response has confirmed for her that you were indeed listening to the entire message in context rather than merely hearing words.

- **Be nonverbally attentive.** Responding to a message doesn't happen all at the end. Use cues such as leaning in, eye contact, head nods, and emotional expressions to demonstrate you are listening throughout the interaction.

- **Reply with clarity.** Consider briefly paraphrasing your partner's message to show you were listening. Then follow with an appropriate response, which may range from offering sound advice to giving a hug, making an apology, or expressing appreciation for the information.

LISTENING AND CONVERGENCE

Life in the Communication Age means that we must responsibly attend to a wide variety of sources of messages. Whether it occurs in interpersonal relationships or virtual spaces, listening is an important skill to learn. With the convergence of media, new technologies, and face-to-face communication, listening has become increasingly challenging. Even before instant messaging, Snapchat, video games on demand, Facebook, mobile YouTube videos, and so on, we had a hard time truly listening to others, but when you add all the new sources of messages, we have even more things to manage. This is truly a tough task.

As we move through the Communication Age, our job is to learn to listen in many different contexts. Technology can be both a positive and a negative when trying to sort through this information. We have to become skilled at deciding what messages we need to respond to, and to make judgments of that information. As part of these skills, we often engage in multitasking to listen to multiple messages at the same time to cope with all the information we encounter. However, many research studies are demonstrating that multitasking is detrimental both to learning and to focusing (Junco & Cotton, 2011). To become better listeners in the Communication Age, we need to learn to focus and give all our attention to one message at a time, and to try to resist the urge to multitask. This is one area of living in the Communication Age that needs serious thought and consideration.

WHAT YOU'VE LEARNED   Now that you have studied this chapter, you should be able to:

1 **Explain the differences between hearing and listening.**

There is an important difference between hearing and listening. Hearing is the biological process of the ears and brain receiving sound waves. Listening is a much more active process that involves assigning meaning and responding to messages.

▶ The Power of Listening

🖥 The Difference Between Hearing and Listening Skills

2 **Identify common problems associated with listening.**

Common listening problems include situational distractions, source distractions, medium distractions, failure to focus on the message, bias, judging too soon, and listening anxiety. Understanding these problems and successfully avoiding them can help you become a better listener.

▶ Who's On First? How We Can Listen Better

3 **Discuss why listening is an important skill to acquire.**

Listening is an important skill to master. Because it is such a routine part of our day, we often take listening for granted. However, acquiring the ability to listen well may benefit

your relationships, impact on the community, media awareness, and job prospects.

▶ Is Hillary Clinton Ready to Launch Another Listening Tour?

▶ Listening Skills and Entrepreneurship

🎤 Active Listening Skills

4 **Compare and contrast different types of listening and what they are used for in a variety of contexts.**

There are five basic types of listening: discriminative listening, critical listening, comprehensive listening, appreciative listening, and empathic listening. Knowing your listening goals can help you determine which type of listening you need to be engaging.

🖥 The Art of Empathetic Listening

5 **List the steps to become a better listener.**

The steps to becoming a better listener include hearing, understanding, remembering, interpreting, evaluating, and responding. You can easily remember these steps by remembering the acronym HURIER.

▶ HURIER Model: How to Listen Better

🎤 Becoming a Better Listener

KEY TERMS

Review key terms with eFlashcards. **edge.sagepub.com/edwards2e**

REFLECT

1. How can you avoid the problem of bias when you are listening? What is one other listening problem you can avoid?

2. Is it possible to critically and empathically listen at the same time? Why or why not? What are the primary differences between these two types of listening?

3. Why is it important to remember the message in the listening process? And why is responding to the message included in the listening process as well?

REVIEW

To check your answers go to **edge.sagepub.com/edwards2e**

1. What is the difference between hearing and listening?

2. _____ occur when the person or mediated message we are listening to exhibits a behavior that inhibits our ability to listen.

3. What is bias in terms of listening?

4. Explain what it means to "judge too soon" when listening to someone.

5. What is listening anxiety?

6. _____ listening occurs when you need to evaluate an argument or a stance and develop an opinion based on evidence.

7. _____ refers to trying to understand and make meaning of the message.

8. _____ listening is responding nonjudgmentally to others and their needs (either physical or emotional).

9. List the steps of the HURIER method.

COMMUNICATION, CULTURE, AND DIVERSITY

Official GDC

WHAT YOU'LL LEARN After studying this chapter, you will be able to:

1 Describe the influence of culture and diversity in the Communication Age.

2 Identify the importance of understanding cultural context for effective and ethical communication.

3 Describe the importance of cultural competence for communicating in a globalized world.

4 Discuss different examples of diversity across communication contexts.

5 Examine how to become more aware of and overcome barriers to communication, culture, and diversity.

In August 2014, Anita Sarkeesian was forced from her home after receiving numerous death threats from anonymous people online. Sarkeesian, a communications graduate who runs the website Feminist Frequency, has been an outspoken critic of misogyny and sexism in pop culture, with a special focus on gaming. In 2012, Sarkeesian successfully launched a Kickstarter for her "Tropes vs. Women in Video Games" video series. Since the series aired, Sarkeesian has been regularly harassed, but recently the messages have escalated to threats of sexual assault and death. "Trolls" (a term for Internet harassers) have even created a game called "Beat Up Anita Sarkeesian" and sent Sarkeesian illustrations of her being sexually assaulted (McDonald, 2014). When asked why the backlash to her videos was so intense, Sarkeesian explained:

> The gaming industry has been male-dominated ever since its inception, but over the last several years there has been an increase in women's voices challenging the sexist status quo. We are witnessing a very slow and painful cultural shift. Some male gamers with a deep sense of entitlement are terrified of change. They believe games should continue to cater exclusively to young heterosexual men with ever more extreme virtual power fantasies. So this group is violently resisting any movement in the direction of a more inclusive gaming space. (McDonald, 2014)

Students at U.C. Berkeley hold an "Increase Diversity Bake Sale" to protest legislation that would allow public universities to consider race in admissions decisions. How would you describe the culture and diversity on your campus?

As you begin your study of communication's relationship to culture and diversity, it is important to realize that change does not always come easily. In many cases (such as the previous example) change can be met with belligerence and violence. As you move forward in your professional and social life, be aware that communication and culture are constantly evolving; if you find yourself resisting change to the point of violence, it would probably be a good time to step back and reflect on what side of history you are standing.

Brent has just transferred from a community college in Southern California to a 4-year university in Texas in order to finish his undergraduate degree in computer science. The transfer process and move were exhausting, but he is thrilled with his new campus. He knows that the 4-year university will present a challenge academically. Brent is excited about attending a large university with a big-name sports team as well as getting to know a new diverse student body. He is certain the transition will be easy. After all, it has always been his dream to attend a large school. What could possibly go wrong?

Similar to Brent, the amount of time spent searching for the right college or university will pay off, and the day you have been awaiting will finally arrive. Perhaps you have been working as a professional for a number of years and have decided to return to school. Indeed, the transition to college varies from person to person and across age groups. Regardless of your personal journey, you can finally step off the emotional roller coaster of uncertainty, right? Well, don't get too comfortable quite yet. Making the transition to college or even transferring from one campus to another can be challenging. Will you meet new friends? What is the campus culture going to be like? Will you fit in? Will there be people there with whom you can relate? This chapter explores the importance of communication, culture, and diversity in everyday contexts—the relation of self to others in the Communication Age. As you make the transition in your educational experience, it is critical to get to know not only the campus culture, but also the array of diverse people in your environment. Let's begin by defining culture and diversity.

CULTURE AND DIVERSITY DEFINED

This section defines culture and diversity as connected to your study of communication. Consider your transition to college (e.g., as a first-year student, a working professional returning to school, or a student facing a change in career/life goals) as a reference point in your study of culture and diversity in the Communication Age. As you get more familiar with this topic, think about issues that you associate with culture and diversity.

Culture

From day 1, your parents, your siblings, your relatives, your friends, your teachers, and even strangers have been working to socialize you into the culture(s) that make up their experiences—the rules of living and functioning in a particular society (Jandt, 2010; Samovar, Porter, & McDaniel, 2009; Ting-Toomey & Chung, 2005; Wahl & Scholl, 2014). Communication is key to this socialization into culture. The way you talk, the way you behave, the way you dress, and the way you think have all been shaped by the way others have socialized you into various cultural groups. There are a number of things to consider that will help you to start thinking carefully about culture. For example, Joel is a gay high school student who has recently "come out" to friends and family. He is being bullied at school and is unsure how to share this difficult time with others. An experience like Joel's emphasizes the need for communication competence and sensitivity related to diverse groups of people.

▶ **COMMUNICATION IN ACTION 6.1**

WATCH: Communication, Culture, and Diversity

A failure to pay attention to cultural differences leads to irritation. How could the student have dealt with difference more effectively and sensitively?

Diversity

Diversity is a term used to describe the unique differences in people. These unique differences are based upon a variety of factors such as ethnicity, race, heritage, religion, gender, sexual orientation, age, social class, and the like. When culture and diversity are discussed in the United States, the terms are often understood in relation to co-cultural communication, which refers to the communication among people from a variety of different cultures (Orbe, 1998). Many students describe culture by referencing national borders and language, but a person can be a member of many different cultures, most of which have nothing to do with boundaries or nationalities.

If you take a moment to think about your own college or university campus, there is likely a sense of culture. How would you describe it? Obviously, some groups are more distinct than others. For instance, athletic teams have their own distinct culture: Athletes have a common interest in their sport, they engage in team-specific rituals, they support one another, and they share a sense of community. There might be certain phrases or expressions that people outside of the athletic team do not recognize or understand. Some interesting nonverbal rituals athletic teams practice are butt slaps, body bumps, and high fives, to name a few. Nonverbal behaviors (specifically, various forms of touch) are ways for athletic teams to celebrate winning or to convey "good job" or "nice try." Outside of the team environment, butt slaps and body bumps might be viewed by others as strange or even inappropriate. Clearly, one must be a part of this team culture in order to truly understand it.

Consider the experience of Emily, who not only was concerned about adjusting to a new college setting but also wondered if she would be able to establish a network of gay and lesbian friends. When Emily entered college she thought to herself, "Succeeding in college will be no different than succeeding in high school." During her first semester, she

As this picture shows, the foundations of culture are learned at a young age.

iStock

The way sports teams celebrate after a goal might provide a glimpse of team culture.

took a course with Professor Chiles, who also happened to be the faculty sponsor for ALLY, a student organization supporting gay, lesbian, bisexual, and transgendered student issues. Emily felt safe knowing that Professor Chiles was accepting and inclusive of her as a lesbian woman. During office hours Emily visited Professor Chiles and asked, "How would you recommend studying for this exam?" Emily was also able to find out more information about ALLY and ended up joining the organization. In the end, Emily learned a lot about study skills as a new college student, but was also able to explore a student organization she could join that would help her adjust to a new environment.

Cultural Rituals

As a new student you learned cultural rituals—practices, behaviors, celebrations, and traditions common to people, organizations, and institutions. Rituals include things like professors' passing out syllabi on the first day of class and rush for Greek organizations. Graduation is the most important ritual at a college or university and one that you most certainly aspire to be a part of someday. What are some other rituals on your campus? What do they tell you about the culture?

As an entering first-year student, you also had to learn the language of higher education. For example, students trying to get admitted into college learn acronyms like SAT and ACT. Every organization and profession has its own language or jargon that you must learn in order to communicate effectively in your chosen field (Quintanilla & Wahl, 2014). Part of your education will be learning that jargon so you can communicate with other professionals once you graduate. Can you think of any examples of miscommunication that occurred as you were learning the jargon? What is some of the jargon you have learned as part of your major? What jargon is used on your college campus?

Communication scholar Walter Fisher (1984) argues that human beings are all storytelling creatures. Using narratives or stories, we as communicators come to understand the cultural context and one another. Paying attention to stories is central to understanding any cultural context. Many of you have probably used stories to determine which courses to take, and from which professors. All of you

iStock

Another aspect of assimilating to college life is meeting others from a variety of cultural and ethnic backgrounds.

have heard the good and bad about various faculty on your campus. In fact, today's high-tech world has taken storytelling to a whole new level, with programs like Pick-a-Prof and RateMyProfessors.com allowing students to hear stories from students they have never met (Edwards, Edwards, Qing, & Wahl, 2007). Listening to what students use as criteria to deem a professor good or bad will tell you a lot about your campus culture. What are the criteria on your campus? What stories helped you learn the culture on your campus? Indeed, the terms *culture, diversity,* and *cultural rituals* are important to your study of the Communication Age. The section that follows focuses on cultural awareness and several other important concepts, such as forms of cultural context and cultural value dimensions.

CULTURAL AWARENESS

The Communication Age is a global age, and cultural awareness is more important than ever before (DeAndrea, Shaw, & Levine, 2010; Wahl & Scholl, 2014). Specifically, being culturally aware improves communication, makes you an educated citizen, and promotes ethical communication across life contexts. Having cultural awareness across communication contexts is important for the following reasons: (1) In order for you to succeed in any personal, social, or professional context, you must be aware of and sensitive to differences between yourself and others, and (2) your ability to communicate effectively when encountering differences of ethnicity, race, language, religion, marital status, or sexual orientation is an essential component to being an educated citizen. In the Communication Age, you will be interacting with people who may present you with differences that you have never encountered before, and your communication choices will shape the experience as positive or negative (Cruikshank, 2010; Quan, 2010). We will now explore a few important concepts related to diversity in the Communication Age. The section that follows explains high- versus low-context cultures.

High-Context Versus Low-Context Cultures

Your study of communication, culture, and diversity is informed by understanding the importance of context (see Figure 6.1). Cultures can generally be described as either high or low in terms of context. In high-context cultures, spoken words are less important than the rest of the context. For instance, as far as relationships are concerned, it may be much more important for people to indicate respect for one another in various verbal and nonverbal ways than it is for them to pay close attention to the exact word spoken (Kittler, Rygl, & MacKinnon, 2011). In countries like China and Iraq, for example, a person's status in society is extremely important (Jandt, 2010). People tend to rely on their history and their relationship to the audience when communicating with one another. For example, in Iraq, it is important to be able to recognize a person's religious perspective or tribe in order to assign meanings to a conversation. Other examples of high-context cultures are Japan, Korea, Native American culture, many Latin American cultures, and both the southern and eastern Mediterranean cultures of Greece and Turkey (Jandt, 2010; Kittler et al., 2011). The background knowledge that individuals gather from their relationships is always relevant to what goes on during any communicative experience. Clear communication is inseparable from the context of relationships including personal status, influence, and knowledge of the other person.

In low-context cultures, people separate their relationships from verbal communication and focus on the information conveyed and logical argumentation (Kittler et al., 2011). Examples

In the TV series *Felicity*, we follow the central character as she adapts to university life in New York. How would you describe the culture at your college or university?

© WB Television Photographer: Ron Batzdorff

of countries considered to be low-context cultures are Switzerland, Germany, and the United States. Several characteristics of low-context cultures center on the need for information to be provided in very specific formats (normally using verbal communication): Knowledge and competency are important, expert knowledge is valuable, background/contextual information is a preference, and there tends to be less awareness of nonverbal communication.

Cultural Value Dimensions

Expanding upon the concept of high- and low-context cultures, Geert Hofstede, a Dutch social psychologist and anthropologist, added several important terms to the study of communication, culture, and diversity in the Communication Age. Hofstede (2001) based his approach on the idea of people having particular ways of thinking that develop from the time of childhood—he refers to these ways of thinking as cultural value dimensions that are reinforced throughout life. This approach relates to communication because it helps you understand communication choices, various verbal and nonverbal forms of expression, and the expectations you have given the cultural context (Erdur-Baker, 2010; Murthy, 2011; Quan, 2010; Yu, King, & Jun Hye, 2010). Hofstede's research explains the primary ways of thinking along the following five dimensions: (1) individualism versus collectivism, (2) power distance, (3) uncertainty avoidance, (4) masculinity

Communication unplugged
BE AWARE OF SELF-DISCLOSURE IN ONLINE AND OFFLINE CONTEXTS

Recent studies seem to indicate that disclosure of personal information is more frequent in online compared to offline communication. However, this assumption is contested both theoretically and empirically. Researchers Melanie Nguyen, Yu Sun Bin, and Andrew Campbell examined existing research comparing online and offline self-disclosure to determine the evidence for current theories on self-disclosure through mediated or nonmediated contexts. Contrary to expectations, disclosure was not consistently found to be greater in online contexts (Nguyen, Bin, & Campbell, 2012). Factors such as the relationship between communicators, mode of communication, and the context of communication appear to moderate the amount of disclosure between communicators. This indicates that meaningful interactions and degrees of self-disclosure can depend greatly on the environment of communication.

As we continue to discuss communication's relationship with culture and diversity, imagine a scenario where you are communicating with a person from a contrasting culture to your own. Without the use of nonverbal cues and lack of feedback, do you believe you could gain more disclosure from that person

in an offline, face-to-face meeting? Feedback gained in an offline, personal communication context is critical to limiting misunderstandings and gaining effective knowledge about others.

Although the Internet is not inherently a poor communication medium (in some cases, online communication is extremely successful, and sometimes the only avenue for communication), it is important to utilize your offline encounters with cultural others effectively.

WHAT TO DO NEXT
To be more aware of self-disclosure in online and offline contexts, try to:

- Watch nonverbal cues closely to get important feedback.
- Politely communicate your confusion and ask for specific explanations if you have a misunderstanding.
- Minimize distractions (cell phones, other online media).
- Ask for verbal feedback concerning your communication with another.

Low-Context Cultures	High-Context Cultures
Less aware of nonverbal cues	Focus on nonverbal cues
Need for detail	Open/free communication
Emphasis on verbal detail	Emphasis on surroundings/environment
Desire expert knowledge/logic	Little need for explicit information

FIGURE 6.1
HIGH-CONTEXT VERSUS LOW-CONTEXT CULTURES

versus femininity, and (5) long-term versus short-term orientation to time. Let's take a look at each of the five dimensions in more detail.

Individualism Versus Collectivism

In individualistic cultures, there is more emphasis placed on individuals rather than groups. Individualistic culture is also characterized by a focus on self and the immediate family. One example to consider that helps explain individualism can be seen in decision making. Individualistic cultures do not consider exterior groups in the decision-making process. If an important goal needs to be set when planning for the future, individualistic cultures tend to limit the decision to a smaller number of immediate family members. Health care professionals experience communication influenced by individualistic culture when patients and perhaps a few family members request privacy regarding health information or specific expectations about how many family members can visit at one time.

In collectivist cultures, more emphasis is placed on the group rather than the individual to promote group cohesion and loyalty. In collectivist cultures, other groups are consulted during the decision-making process or when planning for the future. Returning to the health care example, professionals experience communication influenced by collectivist cultures when patients and a fairly large number of family members are engaged in treatment plans or specific medical information. The decision-making process about a patient's medical process might rest in the hands of a large number of family members, indicating the influence of a collectivist culture. Individualistic and collectivist cultures illustrate value tendencies that influence the preferences and expectations related to communication across a variety of life contexts. Think about how these values impact your communication choices. Take a moment to complete the communication assessment to see where you stand.

Power Distance

Power distance refers to the perceived equality or inequality felt between people in certain cultural or social contexts. For example, a high level of power distance would be characterized by a society in which slavery is accepted, and where some individuals hold all the power while others have none. That is,

ASSESS YOUR COMMUNICATION

INDIVIDUALISM VERSUS COLLECTIVISM

This measure will allow you to assess your own tendency toward individualism or collectivism.

Directions: The following statements, modified from Shulruf, Hattie, and Dixon's (2007) Auckland Individualism and Collectivism Scale, describe the tendencies some people have toward individualistic and collective value tendencies. Please indicate in the space at the left of each item the degree to which you believe the statement applies to you, using the following 5-point scale:

1 = Not at all true of me; 2 = Mostly not true of me; 3 = Neither true nor untrue of me; undecided;
4 = Mostly true of me; 5 = Very true of me

_____ 1. I discuss job- or study-related problems with my parents.

_____ 2. I consult my family before making an important decision.

_____ 3. Before taking a major trip, I consult with most members of my family.

_____ 4. It is important to consult close friends and get their ideas before making a decision.

_____ 5. Even when I strongly disagree with my group members, I avoid an argument.

_____ 6. I hate to disagree with others in my group.

_____ 7. It is important to make a good impression on one's manager.

_____ 8. In interacting with superiors, I am always polite.

_____ 9. It is important to consider the needs of those who work above me.

_____10. I sacrifice my self-interest for the benefit of my group.

_____11. I consider myself as a unique person separate from others.

_____12. I enjoy being unique and different from others.

_____13. I see myself as "my own person."

_____14. I take responsibility for my own actions.

_____15. It is important for me to act as an independent person.

_____16. Being able to take care of myself is a primary concern for me.

_____17. I prefer to be self-reliant rather than depend on others.

_____18. It is my duty to take care of my family, even when I have to sacrifice what I want.

_____19. When faced with a difficult personal situation, it is better to decide for myself than to follow the advice of others.

_____20. I consult with my supervisor on work-related matters.

How did you score? Items 1–10 reflect your tendency toward collectivism, while 11–20 reflect your tendency toward individualism. Add up your total score for items 1–10 and 11–20. Which score is higher? What surprised you about your score? Do you have an individualistic or a collectivistic value tendency? Be aware of how your individualistic and collectivistic value tendencies influence your communication behaviors across life contexts.

Source: From "Development of a New Tool for Individualism and Collectivism," by B. Shulruf, J. Hattie, and R. Dixon, 2007, in *Journal of Psychoeducational Assessment, 25*(4), pp. 385–401.

inequality is the accepted norm, and there is no opportunity for the "have-nots" to gain power or advancement. In contrast, a low level of power distance would be characterized by less rigid power structures. Instead, a collective of people allows equal opportunities for all.

Uncertainty Avoidance

Uncertainty avoidance deals with the way that a culture handles change and accepts uncertainty within social or cultural contexts. For example, a society or cultural group with a high amount of uncertainty avoidance would not handle the unexpected very well. Thus, a high degree of uncertainty avoidance usually leads to a variety of rules and policies to establish predictability and control. Think about the expectation that exists for U.S. chain restaurants to open and close at scheduled times. If you drive up to a fast-food restaurant like Taco Bell or Wendy's in the United States, there tends to be an expectation that the business hours will be posted. There is also an expectation that businesses open and close for service as posted. Therefore, cultural groups with a high amount of uncertainty avoidance would not respond well to a drive-through closing before the posted time. In contrast, a society or cultural group with a low amount of uncertainty avoidance would be more flexible and willing to adapt to the unexpected, leading to fewer rules and more of an emphasis on creativity. Therefore, cultural groups with a lower amount of uncertainty would be open to explore other dining options if the drive-through closed before the scheduled time.

What it means culturally to be a woman or a man has been established historically in the early years of life.

Masculinity Versus Femininity

This dimension reflects the cultural values of "masculine" and "feminine" behaviors. Masculinity—what it means culturally to be a man—is described by traits connected to being assertive, competitive, and even aggressive (clear behaviors that display to others that one is "acting like a man"). Put a different way, clear statements and expectations exist in culture about masculinity. From early on, young boys are instructed how to act and behave like men (e.g., tough, strong, heterosexual). Femininity—what it means culturally to be a woman—is explained by being caring or compassionate toward others. In general, femininity is also about being sensitive and relating to others. Perhaps some of the women reading this text recall being told to "act like ladies" at a young age. Just like masculinity, femininity is constructed with cultural expectations about how women should act, talk, behave, dress, and the like. Both masculinity and femininity relate to communication because they drive particular expectations and social norms. Acting like a man or a woman culturally is achieved by particular verbal and nonverbal communication choices. In fact, almost everything about masculinity and femininity is achieved through communication behaviors and choices. Remember that these communication choices and forms of expressing self allow men to be feminine and women to be masculine. Indeed, all individuals have a unique communication style that's part of who they are, so avoid judging others with the expectation for them to act or communicate in a particular way.

Long-Term Versus Short-Term Time Orientation

This next cultural value dimension is about how people use time as well as their expectations of how time is managed. Long-term time orientation emphasizes processes for accomplishing tasks. In other words, long-term time orientation is not focused on a quick end result. Instead, a persistent and focused process is believed to achieve the best outcome. Perhaps more technical processes or those that deal with human safety are illustrative of long-term time orientation. Companies like Boeing and Airbus focusing on the design and manufacturing of large passenger jets sold to airlines across the globe have more of a long-term time orientation due to safety and mechanical testing. In contrast, short-term time orientation is all about efficiency, production, and fast results. The United States, in general, has a short-term time orientation, which might best be illustrated by corporate business practices. A short-term time orientation is illustrated by trying to sell products to a lot of customers in a short amount of time. In fact, fast-food restaurants serve as good examples of intentional design driven by the need for customer turnover and corporate profits (Eaves & Leathers, 1991). The facility's design, seating, colors, lighting, smells, sounds, and temperature are based on short-term time orientation. Put simply, fast-food executives like for people to "eat and run" so there is room for the next group to order.

Now that you have more of an understanding of the importance of cultural awareness, contexts, and value dimensions, the next section emphasizes the need for cultural competence in the Communication Age.

CULTURAL COMPETENCE

In the Communication Age, awareness of diversity across communication contexts is crucial to navigating in a globalized world (Cruikshank, 2010; DeAndrea et al., 2010; Wahl & Scholl, 2014). One way to prepare for the diverse social situations and environments is to improve your cultural competence. Cultural competence refers to the level of knowledge a person has about others who differ in some way in comparison to self. A culturally competent citizen is sensitive to the differences among people and strives to learn more. A person with a high level of cultural competence is usually good at perception checking—the practice of asking others to get a more informed sense of understanding. Remember to pay attention to cultural differences across contexts, make your own interpretation of those differences, and then consider the following direct or indirect approach: (1) Check your interpretation with others to get a different perspective before you draw a conclusion, and (2) use a more direct approach, in which you ask the people you're communicating with about culture. Now that you have explored the connection between cultural competence and perception checking, the next section emphasizes the importance of mutual respect.

Mutual Respect

You develop positive personal and professional relationships with people who are different in terms of race, ethnicity, religion, gender, and sexual orientation by coming to understand those differences. When individuals and groups communicate with the goal of mutual respect—also known as mutual understanding—cultural tensions, misunderstandings, and conflict can be avoided (Christian,

Porter, & Moffit, 2006; Jandt, 2010; Wahl & Scholl, 2014). Mutual respect develops when a person seeks to understand another with an open attitude and dialogue; doing so encourages others to respond in a similar way.

When cultural competence and mutual respect are absent, conflict usually follows. Consider this example: Jovita was in charge of decorating for the annual hospital holiday party. She had been working in health care for 3 years, but this was the first time she'd been able to call the shots. The prior year, Jovita had helped decorate for the annual Christmas play at her church. Since she had paid for the decorations with her own money, she felt comfortable reusing the Christmas play decorations at her work party. This would allow her to save money on decorations and purchase more door prizes. One of her favorite decorations was a large ceramic

In the romantic comedy *The Mindy Project* characters from diverse racial and ethnic backgrounds engage in respectful communication as they juggle their work lives and their personal lives.

scene featuring Baby Jesus. It fit perfectly on the serving table; Jovita just knew that the scene would be a big hit with everyone! As Jovita started to decorate for the party, the department manager called her to the side and informed her that he had received numerous complaints from Muslim and Jewish employees who felt like their religious perspectives were disrespected due to Jovita's emphasis on Christianity. Jovita was asked to completely rethink the party decorations due to a lack of religious sensitivity. She was highly offended and initiated confrontations with several coworkers she perceived to be "nonbelievers." The preceding example illustrates that you need to be aware of problems that can emerge when there is an absence of mutual respect. While mutual respect and cultural competence are important in all facets of life, organizations are implementing training programs to increase cultural sensitivity, tolerance, and appreciation of diversity in the workplace (Burkard, Boticki, & Madson, 2002; Quintanilla & Wahl, 2014). Positive communication cannot happen in a diverse context without cultural competence, perception checking, and mutual respect.

Cultural Imperatives

There are many different reasons to study communication, culture, and diversity. On any given day, you come into contact with other people from different cultures. The foundations of communication, culture, and diversity are located in five imperatives (Martin & Nakayama, 2004). These include peace, economic, technological, self-awareness, and ethical. The sections that follow examine each imperative in more detail and relate them to your study of communication, culture, and diversity.

Peace Imperative

As a global community, people are dependent on one another to maintain peace. As the 9/11 attacks and other acts of war indicate, select countries have the ability to accomplish mass destruction with advanced weapons technology while others pose terrorist threats with car bombs, airline hijackings, mass-transit sabotage, and the like. Many of the tensions seen globally today are brought on by strong cultural differences that evolve into war and acts of terrorism. This is why the peace imperative is essential in understanding the foundations of communication, culture, and diversity. While conflict exists between various cultures, it is a top priority to maintain overall peace.

Economic Imperative

Also connected to communication and culture is an understanding of the economic imperative. Countries are becoming more and more interdependent in shaping a global economy. Importing and exporting is important to countries across the globe. Clearly, communication and culture are associated with the economic needs of all nations concerning trade relations, international business ventures, and the like.

Technological Imperative

The technological imperative continues to gain more importance in today's society as technological advances make the world more easily accessible. Because of the Internet alone, people are able to communicate with others across oceans and beyond mountains, something that was not possible in the past unless long journeys were prepared. In the Communication Age, you can buy something from Japan and receive it in just a few days. You have the ability to drive down to the airport and find yourself on the other side of the planet within 24 hours if desired. Consider your online relationships with friends, classmates, family, and so on. If it were not for the technology, how often would you be able to stay in contact with others? Not only are you able to stay in contact, but you are also more likely to come across people from other cultures with these technological advances.

Self-Awareness Imperative

The self-awareness imperative is particularly significant because it is important for communicators to learn about other cultures. Not only do you learn about other cultures themselves, but by doing so, you learn more about your own culture. People never truly understand their own culture until they compare it to others. Have you ever found yourself in an encounter with a person from a different culture and suddenly realized something new about your own?

Ethical Imperative

The ethical imperative is also important to understand. The ethical imperative should guide you in doing what is right versus what is wrong in various communication contexts. It is also important to understand why some other cultures value different things. You may find someone else's cultural norms unusual, but remember that this might be a sign of culture shock.

While all of the cultural imperatives are important in our study of communication and culture, the next section explores specific examples of diversity across contexts to inform your study of the Communication Age.

iStock

Technological advances like the Internet make communication across the world more accessible.

EXAMPLES OF DIVERSITY ACROSS COMMUNICATION CONTEXTS

The previous sections reviewed some important concepts related to diversity in the Communication Age. This section surveys a number of examples of diversity that you may encounter. Gender, ethnicity and race, language differences, religion, disability, and sexual orientation are just a few examples of the diversity you will experience across communication contexts.

Gender Influences

Like culture, gender influences cannot be avoided in communication. In fact, gender, culture, and communication are all inextricably bound. A great deal of research has examined the communication differences between men and women. Some scholars assert that men and women differ greatly in their relational needs and communication behaviors, while others contend that men and women are more alike than they are different. In general, communication scholars have shifted their focus from communication differences that stem from being born male or female to the ways in which gender socialization (being *raised* as male or female) may create distinctive communication tendencies. So, to begin, let's make an important distinction between sex and gender.

Sex is biological. It's about the chromosomal combinations that produce males, females, and the other possible, but rarer, sexes. Usually, when individuals refer to behaviors associated with a particular sex, what they are really referring to is gender. Gender is social. It's about the culturally constructed norms connected to biological sex. Whereas sex refers to male and female, gender refers to masculinity, femininity, and/or androgyny. Commonly these characteristics are associated with masculinity or the cultural signifiers associated with being a man in a specific culture; femininity, what it means culturally to be a woman; or androgyny, a blend of both feminine and masculine traits (Ivy, 2012; Ivy & Wahl, 2014). For example, you may have heard that "women always have to go to the bathroom together" or "men never want to talk about emotions or relationships." These statements comment on the perceived patterns of social behavior shown by men and women, but not on their biological traits. Rather, these tendencies arise from differences in what a society expects from women and men—differences in how men and women may be taught to speak, act, dress, express themselves, and interact with others. Thus, let's examine the role of *gender* in communication.

There are numerous ways that gender may affect communication, but we will focus on the different *purposes* for which men and women use communication. For many women, talk is used as the primary means to establish closeness and intimacy in a relationship (Riessman, 1990). By self-disclosing personal information and sharing their lives through conversation, women show their relational partners they are trusted and cared for. Communication is a way to spend time together and build the relationship. For that reason, it may not matter to women

▶ **COMMUNICATION IN ACTION 6.2**

WATCH: Understanding Gender Differences

Prof. Deborah Borisoff explains nonverbal and verbal communication and the reason why gender communication styles are so distinct.

COMMUNICATIONHOW-TO
REDUCING CULTURE SHOCK

Have you ever experienced culture shock? What was your reaction?

iStock

1. Be aware if you find yourself feeling awkward in a new surrounding and try to adjust.

2. Use positive self-talk and nonverbal communication if you find yourself feeling disoriented when outside of your usual setting.

3. If you feel anxious when you find yourself in a new/unfamiliar cultural environment, realize that the audience probably does not know how you really feel.

4. If you feel challenged when experiencing new cultures, focus on establishing mutual respect and view the situation to learn more about self in relation to others.

5. Use direct and indirect perception checking to reduce uncertainty in a new cultural context.

whether they have discussed "important" issues or accomplished a goal. What matters is keeping the dialogue going. Men do not necessarily view relationships this way. Many men enjoy doing things together to build their relationships. Participating in joint activities creates a sense of belonging with many men, and talk is used in primarily functional ways, like solving problems and accomplishing tasks. According to Deborah Tannen (1991), women engage in a greater degree of rapport talk (cooperative messages used to establish connection), whereas men engage in a greater degree of report talk (information-based messages used to establish status and gain power). These may sound like stereotypes, and they do not necessarily apply to *all* men and *all* women, but do you find these descriptions accurate? Have these differences ever caused misunderstandings in your relationships?

Consider this example: Jake and Kristy have been married for almost a year, and they are very happy. Even though things are going well, Kristy wonders if Jake is committed to keeping their relationship going; he never seems to talk to her about how the relationship is going. He spends time with her, and he makes sure the two of them make time to do things together, but he has never shown interest in sitting down to talk about their marriage. Kristy worries that Jake is keeping things bottled up inside and tries harder to get him to open up. When she does this, Jake is suddenly alarmed that something is wrong between them. Have you ever experienced a misunderstanding like this? Kristy simply wanted to use talk to develop and deepen the relationship, but when she wanted to talk, Jake mistakenly assumed it was because she wanted to solve a problem. Awareness of this culturally constructed difference between men and women may help you in your own communication.

Ethnicity and Race

When you think of diversity in the world, you probably most often think of differences in race or ethnicity. Although the terms *race* and *ethnicity* are often linked, when it comes to communication competence people focus on differences based on ethnicity, not race. Race is the categorization of people based on physical characteristics such as skin color, dimensions of the human face, and hair. The old typology categorized people into one of three races, but those typologies are no longer deemed useful and have been replaced with ethnic identification or classifications. Ethnicity refers to a social group that may be joined together by factors such as shared history, shared identity, shared geography, and shared culture. If you rely on nonverbal cues to detect someone's ethnic background, you do so without taking into account that what you see visually may not always be accurate. In other words, people's physical qualities may lead you to perceive them as being a part of one particular ethnic group, when in fact they identify with a different ethnic group. Unfortunately, people across the globe are categorized, stereotyped, and discriminated against based on physical appearance, specifically on the color of their skin (Bloomfield, 2006; Ivy & Wahl, 2014).

Thus, as you get to know the people around you, it is important to remember that what you see visually through nonverbal dimensions of physical appearance does not always shape accurate perceptions of another person's ethnicity. The same sensitivity and awareness for cultural competency is important in the Communication Age as issues of race, gender, sexuality, health, and more are topics fostered in online and social networking communities (Cruikshank, 2010; DeAndrea et al., 2010; Quan, 2010; Wahl & Scholl, 2014). Now that you have considered the importance of race and ethnicity in your study of the communication, culture, and diversity, the next section explains the importance of language differences.

To what extent do the differences in how men and women bond, as portrayed in these photos, mirror your real-life experiences? To what extent do you believe that women use talk as the centerpiece of relationships, while men use activities?

Language Differences

Globalization will continue to present emerging professionals with the challenge of language differences as presented in a variety of industries and career choices. According to intercultural communication scholars Samovar, Porter, and McDaniel (2009), the impact of globalization is an unstoppable process that will continue to emphasize the need for an international orientation that impacts your personal and professional life. Consider your own future goals and realize the likely impact of diversity and globalization on your academic major and occupation.

▶ **COMMUNICATION IN ACTION 6.3**

WATCH: What does interracial communication mean?

Prof. Tina Harris talks about her work in interracial communication. How does interracial communication differ from interpersonal communication?

Globalization exposes people to new and different accents, dialects, and languages. For example, a person's accent may provide you with clues as to where that person is from. If someone in your class speaks with a German accent, she probably hails from a German-speaking country in Europe. If someone else speaks with an accent as well as different vocabulary and syntax, she has a different dialect. You may encounter a coworker or

CAREER FRONTIER: MULTICULTURAL, DIVERSE WORKPLACES

iStock

PEOPLE TRANSITIONING INTO a new workplace often face the challenge of successfully socializing into their working communities (Quintanilla & Wahl, 2014). The process through which people integrate into the workplace has traditionally been termed *organizational socialization* (Bauer, Morrison, & Callister, 1998). Throughout this process, newcomers acquire the knowledge and skills that characterize their new working environment. To study this aspect of communication, researchers Bernie Chun Nam Mak and Hin Leung Chui examined the discourse of small talk collected from a new expatriate from the Philippines (Anna) and her new

colleagues in a Hong Kong firm. The study, which specifically examined the "small talk" in which Anna engaged with her new coworkers, indicated that small talk can be both a hurdle and a useful instrument during socialization, an indicator of in/appropriate behavior and un/successful socialization, and a handy tool in the development of rapport (Mak & Chui, 2013). However, the authors warn that small talk is not a universal behavior; attempts in the wrong cultural context can be counterproductive due to cultural differences.

Think about the ways you begin socialization, either at school or in the workplace. Do you enjoy small talk? Do you use it as a tool to socialize yourself with fellow coworkers and students, or do you find it a pointless exercise? Globalization has helped the workplace to become increasingly diverse and asks professionals to be effective communicators across different cultural contexts. As a professional, remember to gauge your communication context appropriately to ensure that you build successful relationships in a multicultural workplace.

ISSUES TO CONSIDER

1. What steps can you take to ensure you communicate effectively with other professionals from different backgrounds?
2. How can Anna's Hong Kong connection be applied to cultural communication in the United States?

---

classmate who speaks an entirely different language. Nevertheless, you still will need to communicate with one another despite a lack of shared language through the use of verbal and nonverbal communication. Clearly, accent, dialect, and lack of a shared language impact communication effectiveness in professional settings, both with coworkers and with customers. Language differences will compound other cultural differences that are sure to exist.

When you experience language barriers, be prepared to ask and answer many questions to ensure a clear understanding. Try to avoid the common mistakes of losing patience and giving up or speaking to other people as if they cannot hear you. Speaking louder or, even worse, yelling at another person when a language barrier is present can often lead to frustration and further misunderstanding.

In addition to language differences, language preferences can create language barriers. For example, all students in one dorm can speak English, but three of the students prefer to speak Spanish. When they are speaking to each other in Spanish, other students in the dorm are unable to understand what is being said and often get annoyed. If the resident assistant (RA) tells the Spanish-speaking students to stop using their language, is she discriminating against them or violating their rights? Think critically about the preceding example. Consider alternatives the RA could use to promote cultural competence. She could also consider asking the English speakers to learn Spanish. As a counterexample, consider English students studying abroad in Italy. What would English students do if their Italian dorm leader told them to stop speaking English to one another outside of class or organized functions? Remember that speaking in one's language is a matter of choice and a fact of life.

Religion and Spirituality

Religion and spirituality are other areas of diversity among people (Driscoll & Wiebe, 2007). Consider how religion or spirituality comes into play with people in your social environment. Remember Brent's experience getting to know his new college campus? One guy Brent really related to in his new dorm was Sawyer. Brent had observed that several of the guys from his floor would get together for poker night once a week, and he thought it would be fun if he and Sawyer joined the group. Brent invited Sawyer out for poker several times, but Sawyer always declined. After the third rejection, Sawyer took the time to explain to Brent that he and his family were members of the Church of Jesus Christ of Latter-Day Saints (LDS). Sawyer further explained that he had moral concerns with playing poker and being around others who choose to drink alcoholic beverages. Think of other ways religion and spirituality impact various communication contexts, and keep world religions (e.g., Buddhism, Judaism, Islam) in mind in addition to Christianity.

People With Disabilities

In addition to religion and spirituality, disability is an example of diversity. The verbal and nonverbal cues of a person living with a disability can lead to disrespectful or insensitive communication (Braithwaite & Braithwaite, 2009; Braithwaite & Thompson, 2000; Ivy & Wahl, 2014). Physical appearance is normally a signal that a person is living with a disability, but remember that some forms of disability are invisible (Ivy & Wahl, 2014). Be aware of the communication challenges that a person with a disability deals with every day (e.g., Tourette's syndrome, deafness). Regardless of the type of disability, people can develop cultural competence in this area and support fair treatment and respect. Communication scholar Dawn Braithwaite (1991) examined how people with disabilities are challenged when it comes to managing private information about their disability, because able-bodied people tend to ask personal, often embarrassing questions (e.g., how a person became injured, how difficult it is to live with a disability).

People with disabilities have a major presence in everyday social settings today, and it is important for you to strive for respectful communication. Thus, keep in mind several of the tips that follow to guide competent communication with and among people with disabilities: (1) Avoid staring at a person with a disability; (2) try not to be overly helpful by calling too much attention to someone's disability; and (3) focus on the person, not the disability.

GIVING PEOPLE WITH DISABILITIES
A NEW COMMUNICATION MEDIUM

Nbanerjee

PEOPLE WHO DO not have the ability of sight face many obstacles in their everyday communication. The invention of Braille, a tactile writing system used by the blind and the visually impaired, greatly expanded the communication mediums available for nonsighted people. With all the breakthroughs we've made in nonsighted communication, however, there are still drawbacks to be considered. With this in mind, one student decided to tackle a serious issue facing Braille users.

Shubham Banerjee, 13, created a Braille printer out of Lego pieces for a school science project, which has now gained financial backing from the tech company Intel Corp. (Grisham, 2015). Shubham came up with the idea while researching Braille online and realizing that printers for the blind can cost $2,000 or more. Using a $350 Lego robotics kit, Shubham built a working model and shared the plan online in an "open source" format so that anyone could build it.

"He's solving a real problem, and he wants to go off and disrupt an existing industry. And that's really what it's all about," Edward Ross, director of Inventor Platforms at Intel, told the Associated Press (Grisham, 2015). Shubham's dedication to improving communication mediums for the blind offers more hope in defeating the obstacles that all disabled people face in professional and social communication.

Sexual Orientation

Mia is a single college student. When her friends ask about her relationship status, she answers, "It's complicated," and tries to change the topic. One of her friends, Margo, goes on to ask questions such as the following: "Are you still talking to that guy in chemistry class?" "So, when are you all going to go out?" "Would you like for me to set you up on a blind date with my friend Joel?" While some people are open about their relationship status and enjoy sharing information about their personal life in everyday situations, it is important to realize that not everyone feels the same way about the disclosure of personal information.

In Mia's case, she wishes to maintain privacy around her relational status and her sexual orientation. Sexual orientation refers to identity based on who people are attracted to sexually. Like Mia, lesbians, gays, bisexuals, transgenders, and people questioning their sexuality (LGBTQ) often find themselves speaking an entirely different language of ambiguous pronouns. Recognize the choice you will have to make regarding being open or private about your sexual orientation. Being "out" is easier for some LGBTQ people than others. Regardless of your own sexuality, it is critical to recognize that LGBTQ communication and culture are present across communication contexts (Eadie, 2009; Wahl & Scholl, 2014). A couple of things to keep in mind related to communication with and among LBGTQ individuals are (1) do not inadvertently "out" someone, and (2) avoid being heterosexist, or having a view or an assumption that everyone is heterosexual.

COMMUNICATION HOW-TO
UNDERSTANDING SEXUAL ORIENTATION

Heterosexuality	Physical and romantic attraction to people of the opposite sex
Homosexuality	Physical and romantic attraction to people of the same sex
Bisexuality	Physical and romantic attraction to people of both sexes
Transgender	The state of an individual gender identity not matching biological male or female assignment at birth
Questioning	Exploring or questioning one's sexual orientation
Asexuality	Having little, if any, interest in sex
Queer	An umbrella term often used to describe LGBTQ people in general. Used by some as an activist term. Used by others to refer to an identity that does not conform to common labels and terms of sexual orientation and identity.
Cisgender	Identifying as having a gender that corresponds to the sex one has been assigned at birth; not transgender
Pangender	Identifying as belonging to all genders. Someone who identifies as neither male nor female, but instead a third gender.

This section focused on gender, ethnicity and race, language differences, religion, disability, and sexual orientation as examples of diversity across communication contexts. Now that you have studied specific examples, the next section explores the types of common barriers to communication, culture, and diversity.

BARRIERS TO COMMUNICATION, CULTURE, AND DIVERSITY

Dealing with differences may seem like an overwhelming task. However, you can come to understand fellow classmates, friends, and others, even if they have views and practices different from your own, if you practice cultural competence, perception checking, and mutual respect. To finish your study of communication, culture, and diversity, it is important to understand several barriers, including stereotypes, prejudice, discrimination, ethnocentrism, hate speech, and school bullying.

Stereotypes

While the term tends to have a negative connotation, stereotypes are merely popular beliefs about groups of people. These preconceived notions can be positive, neutral, or negative, but when it comes to individuals, each one is an incomplete picture and potentially harmful. For example, gay men are often stereotyped as being feminine and flamboyant while lesbian women are believed to be aggressive and masculine. When developing your skills related to cultural competence, it is important to take a personal inventory. Also, give attention to the communication context. You can do this by researching a culture to increase your understanding of difference. You can also ask questions of the person with whom you are communicating in a particular situation. Often coupled with stereotypes are the terms *prejudice* and *discrimination*. Focus on these concepts to gain a more detailed understanding of barriers to communication, culture, and diversity.

Prejudice and Discrimination

You may have heard of these two terms previously, but do you know the distinction between them? Many confuse the two and think they are one and the same. Prejudice is the dislike or hatred one has toward a particular group. Discrimination, however, refers to the verbal and nonverbal communication behaviors that foster prejudiced attitudes, including the act of excluding or denying people of products, rights, and services based on their race, gender, religion, age, sexual orientation, or disability (Jandt, 2010; Ting-Toomey & Chung, 2005; Wahl & Scholl, 2014). Discrimination can be carried out in the most obvious ways, such as burning a cross in front of someone's yard, or it can be so subtle people may not know it is there unless they are a member of the group being discriminated against. Consider this: *Monica and Jai were planning a singles party or "mixer" for their apartment complex. They had both lived on the property for several years and wanted to try to bring single people together at their apartment complex clubhouse that was open to all residents of the property. As Monica and Jai were creating the invitations, they decided to leave several people off the invite list. They knew of several single gay and lesbian residents and one or two people with disabilities. They didn't want gay and lesbian residents to "hit on" the straight residents. Monica and Jai also agreed that they didn't want wheelchairs taking up too much space at the party.* The previous example illustrates the presence of discrimination, since Monica and Jai excluded or denied inviting particular people to their party based on sexual orientation and disability.

Ethnocentrism

Another barrier to communication, culture, and diversity is ethnocentrism—placing your own cultural beliefs in a superior position, leading to a negative judgment of other cultures (Jandt, 2010). Severe ethnocentrism impedes cultural competence because a person will reject the uniqueness of other cultures. People who view their culture as dominant are unwilling to learn and are not open to the ideas of other cultures.

Hate Speech

Hate speech is another barrier to communication, culture, and diversity that is still a problematic force in society today (Wahl & Scholl, 2014). The term hate speech refers to insulting discourse, phrases, terms, cartoons, or organized campaigns used to humiliate people based on age, gender, race, ethnicity, culture, sexual orientation, social class, and more. Hate speech has been associated historically with—but is not

BECHDEL TEST

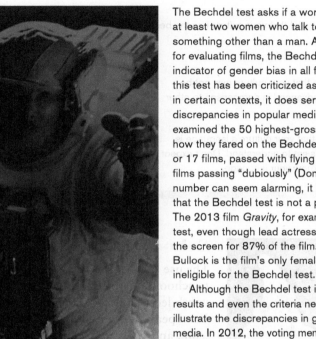

Corbis

The Bechdel test asks if a work of fiction features at least two women who talk to each other about something other than a man. Although originally conceived for evaluating films, the Bechdel test is now used as an indicator of gender bias in all forms of fiction. Although this test has been criticized as misleading and unfair in certain contexts, it does serve to point out gender discrepancies in popular media. Author Alexandra Donald examined the 50 highest-grossing films of 2013 to see how they fared on the Bechdel test. She found that 36%, or 17 films, passed with flying colors, with an additional 7 films passing "dubiously" (Donald, 2015). Although this number can seem alarming, it is important to remember that the Bechdel test is not a perfect measurement. The 2013 film *Gravity*, for example, completely fails the test, even though lead actress Sandra Bullock occupies the screen for 87% of the film. Why does the film fail? Bullock is the film's only female character, which makes it ineligible for the Bechdel test.

Although the Bechdel test is an imperfect measure, its results and even the criteria needed to take the test can illustrate the discrepancies in gender equality in modern media. In 2012, the voting membership of the Academy of Motion Picture Arts and Sciences was almost 94% Caucasian and 77% male (Donald, 2015). As you become a more critical consumer of modern media, try to apply the Bechdel test whenever possible, and assess whether what you enjoy can be considered gender equal.

QUESTIONS

1. What movies can you think of that would be considered unethically biased against gender equality?

2. How can institutions like Hollywood improve their record of gender equality in media?

limited to—racist groups such as the Ku Klux Klan and other White pride groups that argue that White people are superior to African Americans and other ethnic groups.

Hate speech is clearly persuasive communication used to intimidate and segregate based on gender, sexual orientation, race, and ethnicity. In contrast, the newer forms of hate speech have been revised to focus on "us" (White people) versus "them" (ethnic minorities, gays, and women). New forms of hate speech are more about how the authenticity of being White is somehow reinforced by religiosity. Put simply, hate speech in the Communication Age uses the Internet and new media to disseminate messages of fear and intimidation.

COMMUNICATION **HOW-TO**
REDUCING ETHNOCENTRISM

1. Avoid the belief that your culture has the best lifestyle.

2. Recognize that your culture may not be the most advanced in comparison to other cultures.

3. Be aware that your culture's language is not the easiest to understand. Don't expect others to know your language.

4. Remember that your culture is not the only one with rich history and traditions.

5. Seek opportunities to learn about and experience cultures different from your own.

Images: istock.

Getty

Hate speech and racism are still alive today.

Corbis

Celebrities like Taylor Swift have spoken out against bullying.

School Bullying

The use of hate speech is also a troubling practice related to school bullying. Hate speech targeting gay and lesbian youth led to a 2008 advertising campaign, Think Before You Speak, sponsored by Ad Council, ThinkB4YouSpeak.com, and Gay, Lesbian, and Straight Education Network (GLSEN) to address the homophobic phrase "That's so gay" popularly used among young Americans. The campaign was designed to discourage use of this slur. Each advertisement features people in various situations stating that something they do not like is "so gay." Then a popular celebrity, such as Wanda Sykes or Hilary Duff, walks out and tells them that they should not use the word *gay* to describe something that they do not like. Each advertisement ends with text and a voiceover saying, "When you say, 'That's so gay,' do you realize what you say? Knock it off." This campaign won the Ad Council's top award for "Best Public Service Advertising Campaign" and received much attention across the nation for taking on the issue of homophobia.

COMMUNICATION, CULTURE, DIVERSITY, AND CONVERGENCE

Remember to connect your study of communication, culture, and diversity to convergence in the Communication Age. As you think back to many of the examples presented in this chapter related to communication, culture, and diversity, consider how social networking and new media could help foster cultural competence and fight against barriers such as discrimination and school bullying. Think about the possibility of communication, culture, and diversity in the Communication Age.

Consider the opportunities you have related to cultural sensitivity regarding new media and convergence. While there are ways to overcome barriers to communication, culture, and diversity using new media (e.g., social networking, blogs, text messages) (Cruikshank, 2010; Erdur-Baker, 2010; Murthy, 2011), realize that barriers still exist in the Communication Age. One troubling example can be found in the realm of video game culture. The qualities of convergence and new media, as covered in this chapter, appear to empower ethnic minorities and offer hope to gay teens facing bullies face to face and online. However, game and culture scholar André Brock (2011) reminds us that the world of new media and video games (i.e., *Resident Evil 5*) in the Communication Age is not always based on inclusion and cultural sensitivity. Consider the concerns Brock raises about Africans being dominated by Whites in the popular game *Resident Evil 5*. Brock (2011) argues that "at no point [in the video game] are Africans allowed to be anything other than savage; they are never seen within familiar Western contexts such as high-rise buildings, shopping centers, or at leisure" (p. 443).

Considering Brock's (2011) view, it appears that work still needs to be done related to communication, culture, and diversity in the Communication Age.

Think about what cultural competency can become as face-to-face communication and new media communities converge to help us foster new possibilities in the Communication Age. What do you see? What issues do you want to engage? What type of community do you want to help create? Do you need to improve your communication in diverse contexts? What have you learned in this chapter that could help you improve? Your study of communication, culture, and diversity in this chapter is applicable to both your face-to-face and your mediated communication experiences in the Communication Age.

Shiva, a featured character in *Resident Evil 5*, is pictured here. Real human images were used in Shiva's video game character design.

WHAT YOU'VE LEARNED   Now that you have studied this chapter, you should be able to:

1 Describe the influence of culture and diversity in the Communication Age.

The study of culture and diversity helps initiate a more extended conversation about their influence in the Communication Age. In order for you to succeed in any personal, social, or professional context, you must be aware of and sensitive to differences between yourself and others.

▶ Breaking Down Stereotypes Using Art and Media

🖥 College Campuses Address Diversity

2 Identify the importance of understanding cultural context for effective and ethical communication.

Communication and culture are shaped by several important concepts. These include communication competence, high- versus low-context cultures, individualism versus collectivism, and cultural imperatives (peace, economic, technological, self-awareness, and ethical).

▶ Map the World: Hofstede's Five Cultural Dimensions Visualized

🖥 LGBTQ Campus Climate

3 Describe the importance of cultural competence for communicating in a globalized world.

Positive communication cannot happen in a diverse context without cultural competence, perception checking, and mutual respect. Your ability to communicate

effectively when encountering differences of ethnicity, race, language, religion, marital status, or sexual orientation is an essential component to being an educated citizen.

▶ Women's Rights Movement

🖥 Calling for the Redskins to Change Its Name

4 Discuss different examples of diversity across communication contexts.

Gender, ethnicity and race, language differences, religion, disability, and sexual orientation exemplify diversity you will experience across communication contexts. You develop positive personal and professional relationships with people who are different than you by coming to understand those differences.

▶ Colleges Looking Beyond Standardized Testing

5 Examine how to become more aware of and overcome barriers to communication, culture, and diversity.

Prejudice, discrimination, ethnocentrism, and hate speech all serve as barriers to communication and diversity. You can take on the barriers to communication, culture, and diversity if you practice cultural competence, perception checking, and mutual respect.

🖥 Anti-Gay Hate Crimes

🖥 13 Years After 9/11, Anti-Muslim Bigotry Is Worse Than Ever

KEY TERMS

Review key terms with eFlashcards. **edge.sagepub.com/edwards2e**

REFLECT

1. In the Communication Age, virtual communities and other forms of social networking media allow people from across spaces, languages, and cultures to connect and engage. In general, do you think social media like Facebook and YouTube bring people together or cast them farther apart, considering made-up names (anonymity) and the vast amount of information people have to keep up with?

2. Take a moment to think about an issue covered in this chapter that resonates with your lived experience relating to communication, culture, and diversity. What helped you adjust the most? In what ways did your communication impact the assimilation?

3. Review the various cultural imperatives covered in this chapter. Which imperative, if any, stands out to you as important? Which imperative connects with an issue important in your life?

4. What examples of diversity resonate with you personally? Have you ever faced an awkward social situation involving religion, sexual orientation, disability, or any other examples of diversity covered in this chapter?

5. Think of an issue or problem that you are passionate about related to the barriers to communication, culture, and diversity. How could you engage in communication activism to advocate against hate speech, racism, or prejudicial language/action?

REVIEW

To check your answers go to **edge.sagepub.com/edwards2e**

1. What is culture?

2. Define co-cultural communication.

3. In_____, spoken words are less important than the rest of the context.

4. In _____, people separate their relationships from verbal communication and focus on the information conveyed and logical argumentation.

5. _____ refers to the practice of asking others to get a more informed sense of understanding.

6. List five cultural imperatives.

7. _____ is the categorization of people based on physical characteristics such as skin color, dimensions of the human face, and hair.

8. _____ refers to a social group that may be joined together by factors such as shared history, shared identity, shared geography, and shared culture.

9. Explain why the study of communication, culture diversity, and convergence is important in the Communication Age.

Manti Te'o was one of the most celebrated football players of all time at the University of Notre Dame. During his senior year of college, right before a big rival football game, he learned his girlfriend died of cancer. Fans of Notre Dame sent him tweets and messages expressing sadness for his loss and wishing him well. However, a few days later, it was revealed that he had been "catfished" by a fake girlfriend. Their relationship was a sham. Manti Te'o was embarrassed that he had been part of the scam and exposed on national media. Nev Schulman, the host of MTV's *Catfish: The TV Show*, also fell victim to a person posing as someone else in an online relationship (Connelly, 2014). Maybe you or someone you know has been catfished?

Catfishing, or posing as another person to lure someone into an online relationship, is part of the dark side of the Communication Age. The MTV show *Catfish* reveals these fake relationships and demonstrates the potential pitfalls of having an online relationship. According to the series creator, Shulman, "If you are on Facebook, Instagram or any social media that requires an online profile, even if you are totally honest, you are still not representing your true self. You are curating who you are" (Connelly, 2014). As users of social media networks, we choose the pictures that we post, fan pages we like, and tweets we favorite and retweet. In other words, we create a persona online and can build interpersonal relationships based on the portrayed identity.

Interpersonal communication increasingly involves a mixture of face-to-face and computer-mediated contact (Baym, Zhang, & Lin, 2004). Just like in a face-to-face relationship, we need to be careful in our online relationships as well. In this chapter, we discuss interpersonal communication. Specifically, we examine the role of communication, whether it is in-person or computer-mediated, in forming interpersonal relationships, building relationship culture, and creating relational climate.

When you think about the most meaningful and important aspects of your life, chances are that many of those aspects revolve around your relationships with others. Interpersonal relationships help us meet our physical and social needs, give us a sense of identity, and make our lives meaningful. In addition, interpersonal relationships allow to us to experience life as part of something larger than a single, solitary being by transcending the boundaries of our individual selves. In relationships, we are exposed to and bettered by the unique gifts, talents, and differences in perspective that our relationship partners bring to the table, while they in turn are expanded and bettered because of their association with us. According to Schutz (1958), interpersonal relations satisfy our basic human longings for inclusion, affection, and control. Through them, we gain (and give to others) a sense of belonging and being part of something, a sense of loving and being valued, and a sense of mattering and being empowered.

Beginning, maintaining, transforming, and ending relationships are among the most important tasks that we accomplish through communication. As we discussed in Chapter 1, interpersonal communication refers to communication with or between persons who approach one another as individuals in a relationship. Only 20 years ago, many communication scholars would have stressed that interpersonal communication was primarily a face-to-face endeavor. But in the Communication Age, the emergence of newer communication technologies like texting, e-mail, instant messaging, videoconferencing, and social networking sites have dramatically altered how we connect and engage through interpersonal communication. In reality, the mediation of interpersonal communication is not altogether new. Interpersonal communication has been mediated by letters for thousands of years and by the telephone for more than a century. But it is undeniable that the opportunities for digital and virtual interaction in interpersonal relationships have been radically expanded in recent history. On a daily basis, we use computer-mediated communication to meet new people; talk to friends, family, and coworkers that we see frequently; and keep in touch with those we do not. Connecting and engaging with others on social media help us expand our social capital (Ellison, Vitak, Gray, & Lampe, 2014). In some ways, interpersonal communication has become easier, but it has also become more complex. So how, exactly, does communication help us reach our interpersonal and relational goals? This chapter tackles several complex issues. First, we will talk about how and why relationships form. Second, we will discuss a couple of important communication-based perspectives on relationships. Finally, we will explore how interpersonal communication builds relational culture and generates relational climate.

FORMING RELATIONSHIPS

Although it may seem like many of our relationships "just happen," there are some specific reasons why people come together. A number of factors can influence the development of a relationship between two people. For example, you may meet someone who likes the same band or cause on a social networking site. Starting college, getting a new job, or moving to a new neighborhood may bring new people into your life. You probably met most of your current friends through school, work, extracurricular activities, or online activities. According to research, we are most likely to form relationships with people who are in close proximity to us (Festinger, Schachter, & Back, 1950). Proximity is the distance between two people. Proximity may be physical, as in the distance between neighborhoods in a city, buildings on a campus, cubicles in an office, or seats in a class, or it may be a virtual distance between online activities and spaces (Levine, 2000).

The people to whom you have close proximity are the exception, not the norm. We only meet a tiny fraction of the 7 billion people on the planet. That is precisely why proximity is such a powerful force. When people share space, whether it is at school, at work, or online, it becomes more likely that they will interact and form a relationship. For instance, you may hit it off with someone because you both enjoy exercising at the gym in the morning, but it was your physical proximity to that person that made the relationship possible in the first place. Likewise, you may form a connection with a fellow player of your favorite online game, but it was your virtual proximity to that person that set the stage for interaction. Sharing space increases your chances of having a relationship with a person, and repeatedly sharing space can lead to attraction.

Features of Attraction

Think about the number of people with whom you come into contact every day. Whether it is standing in line, riding the bus, taking the elevator, sitting in class, walking across campus, or playing an online game, we are almost always in close proximity with others. But proximity to someone does not always lead to liking that person. Attraction is also required to move the relationship forward. In Chapter 2 we discussed perceptions and how they influence our interactions with the people around us. Attraction is a major part of how we perceive others. As we interact with one another, we continuously determine whether or not others are attractive to us. Our standards of attractiveness are affected by situational factors, social and cultural influences, and personal preferences. The degree of attraction you feel toward another person shapes your behavior toward him or her, your communication with him or her, and whether you choose to interact at all.

Physical Attraction

There are several varieties of attraction, but for many people, physical attraction is the first that comes to mind. Physical attraction refers to the degree to which you find the bodily

Each of us communicates in a number of interpersonal relationships, ranging from casual acquaintances to significant others.

iStock

Thinkstock

Much of life is spent in close proximity to other people.

traits of another person pleasing and desirable. A person's physical appearance is often the first thing we notice about him or her.

Our perceptions of physical attractiveness powerfully influence our judgments of others and our behavior toward them. Importantly, people are often more willing to form relationships with those they perceive as physically attractive. For instance, a recent study showed that university students were more willing to initiate opposite-sex friendships with a person who had an attractive Facebook profile photo (Wang, Moon, Kwon, Evans, & Stefanone, 2010).

We use features like attractiveness to form expectations of what a person will be like that are based on the first traits we recognize (Kelly, 1955). We may automatically assume that because one of our coworkers is good-looking, he or she is also talented, fun to be around, and hardworking. Studies have shown that we associate physical attractiveness with a number of other positive traits and physical unattractiveness with negative personal attributes (Berscheid & Walster, 1969; Griffin & Langlois, 2006). The tendency to let our perceptions of one positive trait, like physical attractiveness, influence our perceptions of other positive traits, like intelligence or moral fiber, is called the halo effect (Berry & Miller, 2001; Thorndike, 1920). By contrast, we may assume that because someone is not physically attractive to us, she is also unpleasant to be around. This is called the horns effect. Our assumptions can have negative consequences if they are incorrect, so it is important to monitor our thoughts about others, and how those thoughts are affecting our behavior. Our perceptions of a person's physical attractiveness can change as a result of observation and interaction.

Perhaps you have known someone who seemed to become more physically attractive to you once you got to know him or her. Maybe this person appeared average or even flawed on your first meeting, but gradually became beautiful as you spent time together. The reverse is also possible. Chances are, it was not physical appearances that changed—it was your perceptions. Just as we often assume that physically attractive people have good personalities, we also use personality characteristics to gauge physical attractiveness (Swami et al., 2010). Our perceptions of how people look rely on our assessments of their social characteristics.

One groundbreaking study (Nisbett & Wilson, 1977) investigated how college students formed judgments about lecturers. In the experiment, students were divided into two groups to watch two different videos of the same lecturer (a man with a heavy Belgian accent). In the video shown to the first group of students, the lecturer was shown answering questions in a friendly and warm manner. The second group was shown the same

AP Images

We often assume celebrity relationships like that between Beyoncé and Jay Z begin with physical attraction. In fact, the two were friends for a year and a half before they had their first date.

CAREER FRONTIER: NETWORKING

IN YOUR CAREER, you will spend a good deal of time building relationships with your work colleagues. Networking is creating relationships with both work peers and acquaintances who can help you in your career. There are many advantages to learning to network with others. First, you will learn more about your career and chosen field. You will meet others who have gone down the same road or tried the same approach. Networking can help you find employment in your field (Putnam, 2000). Second, networking will help you build connections with others. You will have the opportunities to meet people at different companies or related fields. These people will be invaluable to you as your grow in your career. Third, you will learn a more global perspective. Reach out to those in your field who work in other countries or travel a lot. This will expand your horizons and potentially help your own career. Social media can also be used to network. Sites like LinkedIn can connect you to a broad network of people. The key to good networking is the same as in good interpersonal relationships: Show interest in the other person and strive to give back as much as you take.

lecturer responding to the same questions, but in a cold and distant manner. The students were then asked to rate the lecturer in terms of his physical appearance, his mannerisms, and his accent. None of these three factors was different in the two videos, yet students who saw the "friendly and warm" version of the lecturer rated his appearance as more attractive, his mannerisms as more likeable, and his accent as more pleasing than did students who saw the "cold and distant" version of the lecturer. A simple change in the tone of his interpersonal communication gave him an instant attractiveness boost.

Social Attraction

Social attractiveness is measured by an individual's actions and personality. If confidence and assertiveness are attractive qualities to you, you may be drawn to someone you have seen displaying these attributes. As you spend time with this person, you may ask yourself, "Do I like how he behaves in this situation?" or, "Does her communication style resemble mine?" We tend to spend more time with people when we get along well with them and when we take pleasure in the way they act or speak.

In addition, people may take cues from others in the environment to gauge the social attractiveness of a particular person. For instance, you might make observations of a potential friend's Facebook page. Research has demonstrated that people whose Facebook friends are moderate in number, physically attractive, and extroverted are rated as more socially attractive (Tong, Ven Der Heide, Langwell, & Walther, 2008; Utz, 2010; Walther, Van Der Heide, Kim, Westerman, & Tong, 2008). Thus, information generated by others plays a role in perceptions of a person's social attractiveness.

Thinkstock

As people get acquainted, they often share deeper self-disclosures with one another.

We often hear that "opposites attract," but similarity is usually more appealing to us than dissimilarity. We gravitate toward others with whom we share attitudes, social and cultural backgrounds, personality, interests, and social skills (Brehm, 1992). According to the matching hypothesis, we also tend to form relationships with people who are comparable to us in terms of physical attractiveness (Goffman, 1952; Taylor, Fiore, Mendelsohn, & Cheshire, 2011). So why do we like people who are like us? There are several likely explanations. First, interacting with someone who is similar to us can validate who we are and how we see the world. Communicating with similar others also tends to be agreeable and reinforcing, which leads to liking (Clore, 1977).

This leads to the second reason why we gravitate toward the familiar, which is that we often believe relationships with alike others take less effort and have a better chance of working out. If a person's lifestyle or values resemble our own, we expect to face less conflict. The third reason why we are attracted to those who are like us is that it seems more likely that they will like us back. The potential for reciprocity, or having your feelings of fondness returned, means that rejection from the other person is less likely, thereby avoiding possible pain and frustration later.

It is important to recognize that not all similarity is attractive to us. In some cases, the differences between two people allow them to complement each other beautifully. For instance, relationship partners who are dissimilar in terms of dominance are happier than those who are more similar (Markey & Markey, 2007). Can you imagine why? Two highly overbearing people might end up in perpetual conflict over who gets to have the final say. On the other hand, in a relationship between two submissive individuals, no one may step up to take the lead. Neither situation sounds very satisfying. Another reason why we may be attracted to a dissimilar other is that we recognize qualities in another person that we do not have but would like to develop or learn from (Baxter & West, 2003). For instance, we are often attracted to peers who represent our "ideal self," even if we do not feel we live up to those qualities (Mathes & Moore, 1985). Consider your best friend. Do you ever wish you were more like that person in certain ways? The differences between you may help you gain a new skill set or benefit from another person's strengths.

Costs and Rewards

Attraction can also be based on the costs and rewards of being involved in the relationship (Thibaut & Kelley, 1959). Relationships with a high cost but low rewards are unlikely to form and last. Relationships with a low cost and high rewards are likely to be more enjoyable and lasting. The various costs and rewards change throughout the relationship, and we continuously seek to balance out this relational equation.

Clearly, some features of relationship formation are outside of our immediate control. We cannot always choose who is in close proximity. Circumstances beyond our control may bring us into the same space or prevent our paths from ever crossing. Likewise, there is only so much we can do to enhance our physical appearance. However, several aspects of attraction can be influenced by our choices and actions. Interpersonal communication plays a key role in shaping perceptions of social and physical attractiveness, discovering and building similarities, and gauging and displaying reciprocity.

MODELS OF
RELATIONSHIP FORMATION

Interpersonal relationships shape our lives. We may not always see it, but our families, friends, coworkers, classmates, peers, and acquaintances are all continuously helping us re-create who we are and how we perceive the world around us. Because relationships are so central to our lives, scholars have spent many years studying them and have devoted a great deal of time to creating models and theories of how communication forms, maintains, and dissolves them. Think of models and theories like the lenses that an eye doctor holds in front of you to help you see more clearly. Your doctor will usually give you several and then ask you which one provides you with the best view of the images in front of you. Theories are like lenses. Some help us see ourselves and our lives more clearly than do others. As you consider each theory or model, ask yourself, "Does this perspective help me understand my own experiences better?"

Seeking to make a complex and dynamic process comprehensible, early interpersonal relationship research created linear models to explain how people come together and break apart. A linear model is progressive, meaning that it moves in stages toward a specific end goal. Importantly, these models are descriptive instead of prescriptive. In other words, they aim to describe what typically occurs in relationships, not what ought to occur. Let us take a look at a couple of the first linear models created to describe relationship progression.

Social Penetration Theory

In the 1970s, Irwin Altman and Dalmas Taylor developed the Social Penetration Theory to show how relationships progress toward intimacy as a result of self-disclosure from both partners (see Figure 7.1). Self-disclosure refers to the act of revealing information about one's self to others. The Social Penetration Theory views self-disclosures in terms of breadth, or the number of topics discussed, and depth, or the amount of information revealed about a topic. According to Altman and Taylor (1973), each of us is like an onion in that we are composed of multiple layers. As we peel back each layer of who we are through acts of self-disclosure, we build greater intimacy with our relationship partners.

▶ **COMMUNICATION IN ACTION 7.1**

WATCH: Intimacy and Self-Disclosure

It is much too early in their relationship for Sam to disclose such intimate details to Luke. How will this early one-sided disclosure influence the future of their relationship?

Our outer layers are composed of superficial information about the self that is not difficult to disclose. Taste in music, clothing choices, and simple likes and dislikes are all examples of the outer layers. We tend to shed our outer layers easily because there is little risk that we will be rejected for revealing superficial information. The middle layers move toward more personal details, such as social attitudes and political views. Have you ever tried to discuss your thoughts about marriage on a first date? If you have, chances are it did not go so well. According to Altman and Taylor (1973), that is because the middle layers are meant to be revealed only after you have first peeled back the outer layers of the self.

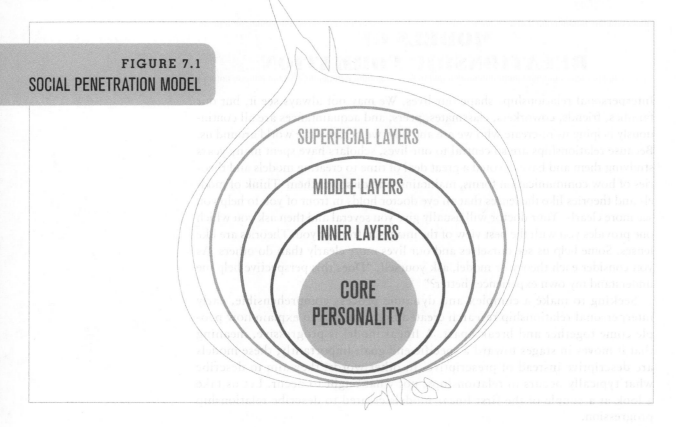

FIGURE 7.1
SOCIAL PENETRATION MODEL

SUPERFICIAL LAYERS

MIDDLE LAYERS

INNER LAYERS

CORE PERSONALITY

The Social Penetration Theory maintains that as two people learn more details about each other, self-disclosures become more intimate and partners share more and more information about themselves. After peeling back the middle layers, individuals progress to the inner layers, which consist of our deepest fears, our greatest hopes, and our spiritual values. These are the parts of our identity that we share only with those who are closest to us. Beyond the inner layers, at the center of the "onion," lies the core personality, or the most basic self. Our core represents the essence of who we are, and we share it with very few people.

The Social Penetration Theory has several strengths because it simplifies a process that can be complicated, confusing, and full of uncertainty. It focuses our attention on the crucial role of communication in building relationships. It explains why we often begin relationships by disclosing surface details (our favorite bands, our majors, what we do for work and fun, and where we hang out) and only gradually progress to deeper information that may leave us vulnerable (our spiritual beliefs, past relationships, and the number of children we hope to have). It also explains why it is so awkward when someone we barely know strips back too many of his or her layers too quickly. Too much self-disclosure, whether from a blind date, a person sitting next to you on an airplane, or a Facebook message, can cause discomfort and diminish the likelihood of relationship progression. One reason why is that we tend to match levels and types of self-disclosure, or engage in the norm of reciprocity. So not only do we feel we have received "too much information," but we may also feel expected to give intimate details about ourselves that we do not want to share.

Model of Interaction Stages

Mark Knapp and Anita Vangelisti (2000) constructed a more complex model of how communication progresses relationships. The Model of Interaction Stages includes five stages of coming together—initiating, experimenting, intensifying, integrating, and bonding—and five stages of coming apart— differentiating, circumscribing, stagnating, avoiding, and terminating. Before we move on, understand that the coming together stages should not be construed as "good" and the coming apart stages as "bad." This model takes into account that we use communication both to build and to dissolve our interpersonal relationships. The stages are organized to move smoothly from one to the next and to demonstrate the

Dating apps like Tinder allow users to intiate communication with potential partners.

overall process of forming and deconstructing a relationship. Each stage is defined by the presence of a specific type of communication. Much like Altman and Taylor's Social Penetration Theory, the Model of Interaction Stages is based on the notion that if you want insight on where a relationship stands, you should listen to what the partners are saying to one another.

Initiating

The first stage, initiating, is where partners make their first communication contact. A couple may initiate a relationship by exchanging a simple greeting. Initiating communication includes light conversation, or small talk, that helps partners determine whether there is a possibility for relationship progression.

Experimenting

In the experimenting stage, partners probe to see if there is common ground between them. As partners reveal more private information, they observe whether their disclosures are reciprocated, and they consider the impact of the disclosures on how they view one another. Many relationships end at the experimenting stage because partners feel they do not have enough in common or may not be a good fit.

Intensifying

Couples may, however, progress to the intensifying stage, in which they develop greater intimacy and exchange a greater number and depth of self-disclosures. Communication is typically more affectionate and may revolve around expressing commitment or testing out labels like *boyfriend* or *girlfriend*. Think about a current or former romantic relationship. You might remember the intensifying stage by the endless hours you spent learning everything you could about the person by talking, texting, instant messaging, or video chatting through the night. Again, relationships may end here—often by "failing a test"—or progress to the next stage.

Integrating

In the integrating stage, partners engage in communication that weaves their lives together and solidifies their status as a couple. A formal announcement to friends,

Couples, like Kim Kardashian and Kanye West pictured here, often communicate their commitment to each other and the relationship through a public bonding ceremony.

Corbis

family, and other social groups may be made. For example, partners may go from "single" to "in a relationship" on a social networking site. Language often includes more inclusive pronouns, like *we* and *us*, and assumes a shared future ("What are we doing this weekend?"). You may even find that friends begin referring to the two of you as a unit, rather than as two separate people. Partners may not succeed in integrating their separate lives and identities. As before, relationships can end here or progress to the next stage.

Bonding

Bonding communication involves a public and formal (traditionally legal) declaration that "two have become one." A couple communicates their deep commitment to one another to the rest of the world. Bonding rituals include weddings and commitment ceremonies. A relationship may remain at the bonding stage indefinitely, or until the death of a partner. In the long term, communication revolves around maintaining the relationship by being constructive, sharing power, and staying connected. However, many relationships dissolve even after the bonding stage. Whereas the previous five stages addressed how we communicate to form relationships, the next five stages discuss how we communicate to dissolve relationships.

Differentiating

The differentiating stage is characterized by communication that asserts the separateness of relationship partners. Rather than emphasizing a joint identity, partners talk in ways that stress their individuality and distance from one another. For instance, partners may say things like, "I don't want to go to the art exhibit this weekend; I don't enjoy them like you do," or "Moving to the city has always been your dream; I have different dreams." Couples stop "working together" and may even explore a trial separation. Couples may eventually reaffirm their commitment to one another and return to bonding, or they may continue the path of relationship deterioration by moving into the next stage.

Circumscribing

In the circumscribing stage, communication moves from identifying differences to restricting the communication between partners. Partners may talk less and reveal less intimate information for fear of conflict. They may begin to lose interest in the relationship altogether.

Stagnating

The next stage is stagnating, which compares the relationship to a still, lifeless pond. The quantity and quality of communication continues to decline. In addition, it is common for partners to experience and/or express a sense of hopelessness

COMMUNICATION HOW-TO
MANAGE INTERPERSONAL CONFLICT

Conflict in relationships is inevitable and can be both a positive and a negative force. Conflict allows us to solve problems and potentially make the relationship work better for all involved. Below are some basic tips on managing interpersonal conflict.

1. **Talk face to face about the conflict.** Text messages and online chat will not allow us to take advantage of nonverbal characteristics.

2. **Use inclusive language when possible.** It notes that the couple is in this conflict together and can solve the issue. "We will work this out."

3. **Put yourself in their shoes.** Most of the time, each person is correct about at least part of the problem. Express empathy.

4. **Use "I" statements to express your own feelings and thoughts.** Avoid blaming the other person for how you feel. Say, "I feel sad about the fight." Don't say, "You made me feel sad about the fight."

5. **Listen.** Instead of thinking of the next argument, truly listen to the other person before you even think about what to say next.

Images: istock

about the relationship ("Nothing's ever going to change," or "Talking about things is pointless").

Avoiding

The next stage of relationship decline is avoiding. Here, partners extend their declining communication by physically steering clear of one another. They may rearrange their schedules to see one another as little as possible and desire permanent physical distance through separation or divorce.

Termination

Termination is the final stage of the process of coming apart. Termination is a reversal of the bonding stage. A couple once joined publicly and formally ends their relationship, often through the legal process of divorce. Termination signals the official end of the relationship.

In the stagnating stage of dissolving relationships, partners communicate less and are less satisfied by their interactions.

iStock

Limits of Linear Models of Relationships

Like the Social Penetration Theory, the Model of Interaction Stages has strengths. Namely, this model highlights how our interpersonal communication can move our relationships in certain directions and identifies general pathways relationships can take to develop or dissolve. However, linear models also have their

Think about long-standing interpersonal relationships in your life. Do these all follow a linear model?

weaknesses. Think about a long-standing interpersonal relationship in your life. Did your relationship move steadily from one layer of self-disclosure to the next? Did your dialogue move smoothly from one stage to the next, never skipping a step along the way? Your relationship, like many others, was probably not that predictable. One problem with linear models is that they oversimplify a complex process that is often as unique as the couple experiencing it. Linear models also imply that the point of relationships is deeper intimacy, or even marriage, and that our relationships have failed without attaining these goals. But what about relationships that are not bound for a long commitment? How about close friendships? Most likely your life has been enriched by a variety of relationships, whether they advanced toward marriage or not.

Another problem with linear models is that most of the initial research was based only on the experiences of White, heterosexual, middle-class college students. A different picture of how relationships form might emerge from including the perspectives of people from all ethnicities, sexual orientations, socioeconomic backgrounds, and ages. In addition, the early research focused heavily on relationships that occurred primarily face to face and not on computer-mediated interaction. For instance, social networking sites may encourage hyperpersonal communication, or situations in which the affection, emotion, and intimacy that develop through computer-mediated communication equal or surpass what happens face to face. Because the reduced nonverbal cues in computer-mediated settings allow people to feel less inhibited, and people can take their time crafting asynchronous messages, they are likely to experience early idealization of their partners and offer more and deeper self-disclosures sooner in their interactions (Tidwell & Walther, 2002; Walther, 1996).

A final criticism of linear models is that they are external. In other words, an outside observer determines what level of intimacy is present or which stage of relationship development a couple is in. Yet, in your own relationships, do you feel that what matters most is how you and your partner experience the relationship? The following section describes two individual interpretations of relationship development.

Personal Perspectives on Relationship Development

Individual interpretations of relationship development put the focus on how a person makes sense of his or her own relationship with another person. According to James Honeycutt (1993), our cognitions, and not externally observable events like bonding or self-disclosure, are responsible for our perceptions of whether or not a relationship is progressing. Activities like bonding or self-disclosure may be important to relationship development, but only if partners assign them meaning. Imagine that a boyfriend or girlfriend took you home to meet the parents for the first time. Depending on how you and your partner interpret the meaning of being introduced to family, the event could be a major milestone that signified "things are getting serious" or an unremarkable activity. Ultimately, it is how we interpret an act, and not the act itself, that influences our sense of whether the relationship has moved to a new level.

Imagined Trajectories

Furthermore, each of us has an understanding of the various paths relationships can take and where those paths lead. Honeycutt (1993) refers to these understandings as imagined trajectories. Have you ever felt that one of your relationships was "not headed in a good direction," or perhaps, "going really smoothly"? In either case, you were relying on an imagined trajectory that defined your expectations for what should happen and guided your reaction to things that deviated from your script.

Romantic relationships follow a variety of paths or trajectories as they develop.

The stories couples tell of how they met and fell in love are as unique as the couples telling them. They may paint a picture of "love at first sight," complete with a whirlwind romance that led to commitment in record time. Or they may relate the saga of a long and rocky courtship full of breakups and makeups. Researchers have identified four major trajectories, or patterns of romantic relationship development (e.g., Surra, 1985) (see Figure 7.2).

In an accelerated trajectory, the relationship moves smoothly and quickly to marriage or commitment. Partners consistently achieve greater and greater levels of intimacy and dedication to one another. In an accelerated-arrested trajectory, the relationship gets serious early on, but then loses momentum and does not end in commitment. The intermediate trajectory involves more gradual relationship development. Couples experience a series of ups and downs and then reach commitment. Finally, in a prolonged trajectory, the relationship is very slow to develop and somewhat rocky along the way, but eventually achieves commitment. It may

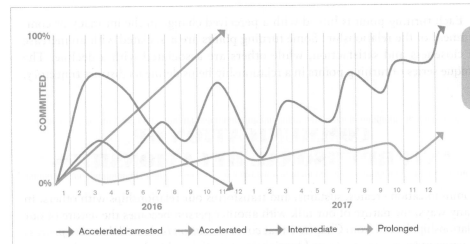

FIGURE 7.2
ROMANTIC RELATIONSHIP TRAJECTORS

be helpful to consider which of the four trajectories best describes your current and past romantic relationships. Previous experiences, personal observations, media portrayals, and relationship role models can influence a person's expectations of how relationships can and should progress.

Turning Points

Another way we make sense of our relationships with others is through turning points, which are perceptions of events that transform relationships (Baxter & Bullis, 1986; Bolton, 1961). It is not the events themselves that change relationships, but our interpretation of the events. According to research, there are four major categories of turning points (Baxter & Bullis, 1986):

- *Interpersonal/normative* turning points occur when you evaluate yourself, your partner, or the relationship by standards of what is ideal and/or normal. For instance, you may think, "I'm too young to get married," "She's the perfect woman," or "There's too large an age difference between us." Each of these evaluations could change your relationship as a result of comparing your situation to an ideal or normative standard.

- The second type of turning point is *dyadic*, which refers to direct interaction between you and your relationship partner. Dyadic turning points focus on the things you say and do to one another. Examples could include having your first big fight, exchanging "I love yous," or saying, "This will never work out."

- *Social network* turning points occur when friends, family members, coworkers, or acquaintances influence the course of your relationship. Perhaps your parents disapprove, or your friends welcome your partner with open arms.

- Finally, *circumstantial* turning points occur when events that are perceived as beyond your control (and your partner's) influence the relationship. Illnesses, natural disasters, and relocations are unforeseeable events that may significantly alter the course of a relationship.

Each turning point is linked with a perceived change in the intimacy or commitment of the relationship. Some turning points are associated with an increase in closeness and satisfaction, while others are associated with a decline. The unique series of turning points in a relationship helps define its distinct trajectory.

COMMUNICATION OF INTERPERSONAL RELATIONSHIPS

Communication creates, sustains, and transforms our relationships with others. In many ways, the nature of our talk with another person becomes the nature of our relationship. Recall from Chapter 1 that *communication is the collaborative process of using messages to create and participate in social reality.* Interpersonal communication defines who we are to one another, what we can achieve together, and the culture and climate of our relationship. Likewise, interpersonal communication is the means by which we participate in the realities we create with others to accomplish relational objectives like providing support and resolving conflict. In this section we will discuss the role of interpersonal communication in relational culture, relational climate, and cultural influences on relationships.

Relational Culture

Through communication, each relationship develops features that distinguish it from all other relationships. In other words, communication creates relational culture, which is defined as "a unique private world constructed and sustained by partners in a relationship" (Wood, 1982, p. 75). The culture of a relationship includes the identities of the partners involved, but it also goes beyond them and takes on a larger identity of its own. This explains why the relationship you have with one friend is completely different from the relationship you have with another.

Relational cultures are dynamic in the sense that they are constantly changing and developing. They do not appear fully formed the moment two people decide to begin a relationship; they take time to build, and they gradually evolve as the individuals and their communication evolve. Even when two people have reached a consensus about what their relationship is all about (like true love, marriage, or best friends), both partners will continue to change and grow, which further influences the relational culture.

For many romantic partners, deciding to move in together is an important dyadic turning point.

Relational cultures are created and shaped by relational partners, but they also turn back and influence the partners. If a couple's relational culture includes absolute honesty, both partners will adhere to that, even in situations when it may be difficult to do so. Recall from Chapter 1 that the creation of any social reality involves both agency and constraint. The same is true of the relational cultures, or private worlds, that we construct with our partners. The realities we create lay out the possibilities and impose the limits on how we behave and who we become. Relational cultures may be positive and healthy, or they may be destructive for one or both partners, and they arise from the combination of a number of communication processes and practices. The following sections discuss the role of relational dialectics and symbolic practices in building and sustaining relational cultures.

Relational Dialectics

Leslie Baxter's (1988) relational dialectics theory (RDT) is a groundbreaking analysis of interpersonal relationships that attributes the communication patterns between partners to the existence of dialectical tensions. RDT begins with the simple premise that relationships involve experiencing tensions based on contradictory needs. In other words, RDT recognizes that relationships are messy and that there is no escaping being pushed and pulled in seemingly opposite directions. The "pushes" and "pulls" are what make a relationship a relationship.

The way we experience the tensions and respond to them helps create the unique culture of each relationship. There are three main relational dialectics. Each arises from a set of conflicting core values relationship partners hold.

- The first dialectic is autonomy and connectedness. Autonomy (self-determination, or independence) is a basic human need, but connection with others is also necessary. Maintaining your own freedom and independence while simultaneously nurturing a close attachment to a partner can be a challenge. RDT explains that relational partners must try to create a relationship that satisfies both of these needs at once, and the process of doing so propels the relationship forward.

- The second dialectical tension is novelty and predictability. People simultaneously desire new, exciting things and familiar, comfortable things. A relationship that lacks surprises and spontaneity can feel boring and stale. On the other hand, a relationship that lacks predictability can feel unstable and unreliable.

- The third dialectical tension of openness and closedness highlights relationship partners' simultaneous needs to share personal information and to have privacy. Boundaries are necessary in any relationship, but sharing private information fosters greater intimacy.

Dialectical Tensions in Relationships

So how do relational partners negotiate these tensions? A common misconception is that partners have to choose one end of a dialectical tension over the other, but RDT stresses that both ends of each dialectical tension coexist in relationships. Not only are both ends always present, they are also interdependent—so you cannot have one without the other. These tensions occur in all types of relationships and often happen in conjunction with one another. If you think carefully about your relationships, we are sure that you have used multiple communication strategies to navigate all of these tensions at one time or another, and will continue to do so.

Think about the tensions present in the following example:

Alex is a college freshman living away from home for the first time. She is enjoying her classes and has made several new friends in her residence hall. During her first week on campus, Alex called home to speak with her parents nearly every evening. She couldn't wait to tell them about her classes and her new job writing for the university newspaper, and she also wanted to know how her parents were doing without her. Now, a few months into her first semester, Alex calls home twice a week at the most. The last time she called, her mom mentioned that Alex seemed to be calling less and wanted to know if anything was wrong. Alex felt a little guilty for not calling more often, but she also felt annoyed that her mother wanted to know everything that had happened that week. Alex wanted her mom to know she missed her, but she also wanted to spend the majority of her time settling into her new life. She wonders how often she should call home from now on.

Interpersonal relationships involve tensions created by contradictory needs.

The relationship between mother and daughter shown here is an example of all three of the main dialectical tensions. Moving away to go to school has allowed Alex to be more independent, but at the same time she wants to maintain her connections with her family. Alex is enjoying the novelty of her university experience and is excited about all of the changes occurring in her life, but she also desires the familiarity and predictability of her relationship with her mom. She wants to tell her parents all about her college life, but she does not want to describe every detail of her week to her mother. Does this relationship sound familiar to you? Have you experienced these tensions within your relationships? If you think carefully about your relationships, we are sure that you have used multiple communication strategies to navigate all of these tensions at one time or another, and will continue to do so.

MAKE
— a —
DIFFERENCE

TAKING A STAND AGAINST CAMPUS GOSSIP

COLLEGE CAMPUS LIFE has always involved a good deal of gossip and rumor spreading. However, the launch of Yik Yak app in 2013 took college gossip to a whole new level using phones. This social media app urges users to post anonymous posts or "Yaks." Created by Furman University graduates Tyler Droll and Brooks Buffington, the app has similar functions to instant messaging and GPS in that users can only post and respond to Yaks within a 1.5-mile radius (Kingkade, 2015). While certainly there are positive Yaks, many are used to post scandalous gossip about classmates, professors, and school administrators. For many students, unfettered access to the outrageous details of other people's personal lives can become an obsession, even an addiction. Fans of the app enjoy the entertainment value and the sense of connection and power forged by talking about people.

However, it soon became apparent that Yik Yak was part of a darker element to college student interaction. Anonymity, along with the failure to prescreen content, created a breeding ground for posts that were hurtful, humiliating, blatantly untrue, and profane. Gossip about who was drunk, who was promiscuous, and what was right and wrong about people's appearances dominates the online discourse. Geoff Holm, a biology professor at Colgate University, described Yik Yak as "the Internet equivalent of the truck stop bathroom wall" (Kingkade, 2015). The app has been used for harassment, bomb threats, and racist talk (White, 2014). On college campuses across the country, many students and faculty were urging their networks to block access to Yik Yak. At Emory College, the student government has denounced Yik Yak as a site for hate speech (Cary, 2015). Students at Clemson University have asked the administration to ban the app on campus. The negative reaction to Yik Yak is occurring on campuses across the United States.

Websites and apps such as Yik Yak are not new. In 2009, a similar website, JuicyCampus, ceased operations due to a lack of revenue. Declining popularity on college campuses contributed to its inability to turn a profit. The same generation of college students that had created Yik Yak and other such anonymous posting platforms will ultimately be responsible for bringing them down. The rise and fall of such websites and apps are a powerful illustration of our collective capacity to organize, speak out, and make a difference in the quality of interpersonal communication.

iStock

Every relationship has a culture that relies on various symbols and symbolic practices. What do you feel this couple's symbols convey about the partners and their relationship?

Strategies for Handling Dialectical Tensions

In a study involving undergraduate students in premarital romantic relationships, Leslie Baxter (1990) discovered four basic methods for handling dialectical tensions:

- *selection*—satisfying one of the two dialectical needs, but denying the other (like choosing to pursue connectedness at the expense of autonomy);

- *separation*—satisfying both dialectical needs, but in separate areas of life (like choosing to pursue connectedness on the weekends, but autonomy during the week);

- *neutralization*—compromising so that both dialectical needs are met to some degree, but not fully (like choosing the middle ground between openness and closedness by agreeing to discuss everything, but not being completely open when you do); and

- *reframing*—transforming the two needs of a dialectical tension so they are no longer experienced as opposites (like making novelty and predictability compatible by establishing a firm rule that every Saturday night you will do something you have never done before).

In general, selection was the least satisfying strategy. Reframing, on the other hand, was associated with relationship satisfaction, but was rarely used. That is probably because reframing takes some real communicative creativity. Reframing involves taking one end of a tension and turning it into something that actually helps you attain the other end. Because reframing is full of potential as a way to nurture relationship closeness (Baxter, 1993), you may wish to give it a try the next time you are feeling relationship pushes and pulls.

Symbolic Practices

Symbols and symbolic practices are important components of all cultures. For instance, in U.S. culture, symbols such as the flag, the national anthem, the Constitution, and war memorials serve as important sources of national identity. It is likely that you also associate your close and enduring relationships with a variety of symbols. Symbolic practices play a crucial role in relational culture. First, symbolic practices reflect the culture of a relationship by echoing its dialectics, values, and interaction patterns. In addition, symbolic practices create the culture of a relationship by reinforcing partners' understandings of the private reality they share.

Types of Symbols

There are at least five types of symbols that friends and romantic partners use to reflect and build relational culture (Baxter, 1987):

- physical objects (special keepsakes, gifts, or photographs);

- cultural artifacts ("our song" or meaningful movies);

- places (restaurants, parks, coffee shops, or meeting places with relational history);

- events/times (holidays, certain times of year, or vacations that serve as reminders of the meaning of the relationship); and

- behavioral actions (nicknames, interaction routines, code words, or nonverbal actions that hold special meaning).

Can you identify the symbolic practices that give one of your friendships, family relationships, or romances its unique culture? What do those symbolic practices accomplish for you, your partner, and the relationship? According to research, relationship partners rely on symbolic practices to perform a variety of functions that create and sustain relational culture (Baxter, 1987). Symbolic practices can be used to help partners remember important events in their histories, demonstrate closeness, create a sense of fun, highlight the differences between their relationship and others, manage conflict, and help the relationship endure hardships and the passage of time.

▶ **COMMUNICATION IN ACTION 7.2**

WATCH: Using problem orientation vs. control orientation

Katie becomes defensive when Liz fails to consult her about a change to their apartment. To what extent do you confer with your relationship partners before making decisions?

Relational Climate

Each relational culture has its own relational climate. Just as different geographical areas produce varying weather patterns that result in a climate, relationships also generate an overall pattern of interaction that becomes the relational climate. Consider your group of friends. You probably have relationships that are usually warm and sunny, but with the occasional stormy day. You may also have relationships where clouds are part of the climate all the time. Some relational climates are volatile and can shift in an instant, while others are more constant. Relational climate defines the overall emotional feeling, or temperature, of the relationship.

Confirming Versus Disconfirming Communication

As you can imagine, relational climates may be positive or negative. Communication determines the overall positive or negative tone of each relationship. Confirming communication refers to messages and interactions that make people feel valued and respected, while disconfirming communication refers to messages and interactions that make people feel devalued and disrespected (Ellis, 2000, 2002; Laing, 1961). Confirming communication recognizes, acknowledges, and endorses the relationship and the other person in the relationship. Disconfirming communication, on the other hand, denies or minimizes the existence and importance of the relationship or the other person (Cissna & Sieburg, 1981; Dailey, 2006).

Spirals of Communication

Relational climates begin to develop during initial interactions and quickly take on a life of their own as patterns of behavior become established. Partners may find themselves in self-perpetuating spirals, or patterns of reciprocal communication where each person's message reinforces the other's message. This may be problematic when the patterns of interaction involve conflict. For instance, escalatory

THE ETHICS OF VIRTUAL ANONYMITY

iStock

Anonymity online can lead to problematic communication.

ANONYMITY = COWARDICE.

This was the slogan of the Princeton University student group that protested JuicyCampus.com, a college gossip website known for circulating scandalous rumors about students, professors, and administrators. The student activists launched the "Own What You Think" campaign to encourage socially responsible Internet communication. According to the group's website,

[T]he most destructive online behavior is fueled by pervasive anonymity and the distance between one's online behavior and its residual effects. To combat these trends, this campaign is focused on the adoption of two basic principles:

1. Only write or say things that we'd say in person

2. Intervene when others are attacked or discriminated against. (www.owyt.org, 2015)

While the ability to hide one's identity online may offer protection against bias and stereotypes (Singer, 1996), anonymity may promote antisocial communication by shielding people from accountability for their messages. In other words, anonymity can be either good or bad, depending on how it is used.

According to Habermas (1979), ethical communication promotes both autonomy and responsibility. The "Own What You Think" students worry that anonymous comments provide too much freedom, or autonomy, with little or no social responsibility. On the flip side, defenders of virtual anonymity worry that having to reveal your personal identity online would diminish your freedom of personal expression.

QUESTIONS

1. How do you feel about the communication ethics of virtual anonymity? Do you agree with the student activists' position that "anonymity = cowardice" when it comes to gossiping about fellow students?

2. In what situations is it ethical to post anonymously? What anonymous situations or messages would you consider unethical?

conflict spirals occur when one attack leads to another. De-escalatory conflict spirals occur when, instead of fighting, partners gradually lessen their dependence on one another, decrease their contact, and withdraw from the relationship.

Defensive Communication

Defensiveness is a major source of pollution to relational climates (Becker, Ellevold, & Stamp, 2008; Gibb, 1961). Defensive communication attempts to guard, or protect, a person from an attack.

Communication unplugged

TO IMPROVE RELATIONSHIPS, DECREASE TECHNOFERENCE

iStock

For many couples, communication technology is both a blessing and a curse. In a 2012 study, Baylor University professor James Robert coined the term *phub* (phone + snub) to refer to when a person chooses to text, play with an app, or take a call instead of paying attention to another person. "I was surprised by the amount of people saying that this happens in their relationship every day," says Sarah Coyne, an associate professor in the department of family life at Brigham Young University. "You are sitting there and kind of bored and check Facebook . . . it is almost our default to turn to our phones" (Holohan, 2014). A number of recent studies suggest overreliance on technology may be hurting our relationships.

According to researchers McDaniel and Coyne (2014), *technoference* refers to "the everyday intrusions or interruptions in couple interactions or time spent together that occur due to technology" (p. 1). Their survey of 1,443 married and cohabitating women revealed that most perceived technology devices (e.g., computers, cell phones, TV) as frequent disruptions to their interactions. Devices like computers, cell phones, and TV were interrupting couple leisure time, conversations, and mealtimes. These interruptions were associated with lower relationship satisfaction and lower personal well-being. "By allowing technology to interfere with or interrupt conversations, activities, and time with romantic partners—even when unintentional or for brief moments—individuals may be sending implicit messages about whey they value most, leading to conflict and negative outcomes in personal life and relationships" (McDaniel & Coyne, 2014, p. 1).

Technology use in relationships isn't always bad. Legget and Rossouw (2014) found that watching TV together or using cell phones together while engaging and interacting with each other (e.g., playing a mobile game together) could be positive. But, according to Legget, "engaging in technology separate to a partner while in the presence of them encourages a disconnection rather than connection" (Bilton, 2014).

WHAT TO DO NEXT

To turn down the technoference in your intimate relationship, try to:

- Choose verbal communication for face-to-face interactions
- Catch yourself in the act ("I'm sorry. I've been so busy texting that I haven't talked to you.")
- Carve out cell phone–free times and outings
- Consider device bans in particular spaces (e.g., kitchen table, bedroom)
- Politely apologize (if you must use a device) to avoid hurt feelings

Defensiveness is often the result of face threats, or messages that challenge the image of ourselves we want to project. We may react defensively by attacking the critic, distorting the critical information, or avoiding the critical information:

When people feel threatened or attacked, they may react by engaging in defensive communication.

- Attacking the critic includes the use of verbal aggression ("How dare you call me lazy! At least I have a job!") and sarcasm ("I'm so glad I have a friend who takes the time to ruin my day").

- Distorting critical information includes rationalizing, or inventing untrue explanations of your behavior that sound acceptable ("I would have helped you carry in the groceries, but I didn't hear you pull into the garage"), compensating, or using one of your strengths to cover one of your weaknesses ("I may not help out much around the house, but I buy you everything you want"), or regressing by playing helpless ("I really want to be there for you right now, but I just can't").

- Avoiding critical information includes physically steering clear of the critic, repressing critical information by mentally blocking it out, being apathetic by pretending not to care about the critical information, or displacing by venting hostile feelings on objects or people who are less threatening than the critic (like punching a wall, kicking the dog, or yelling at a child).

Our defensive reaction may prompt defensiveness on the part of our partner, creating a defensive spiral. Therefore, it is important to use interpersonal communication to promote relational climates that are supportive, rather than defensive. In the Communication Age, the virtual spaces we inhabit also have relational climates. Many online communities seek to encourage positive relational climates by discouraging practices like flaming (making personal insults and attacks), trolling (intentionally creating drama), and spamming (posting irrelevant information or the same comment repeatedly).

Cultural Influences on Relationships

Although relationships form their own unique cultures, they are also influenced by the larger cultures around them. No relationship exists in a vacuum. Both partners will contribute their own religions, nationalities, ethnicities, generational qualities, beliefs, and values to the union, and these features will shape the course of the relationship. Wherever there are cultural differences, there is also potential for conflict, and each partner must be aware of how his or her own cultural attributes add to this possibility.

External Influences

In addition to cultural influences within the relationship, cultural influences outside of the relationship are also present. In some areas of the United States, it is commonplace for two men to walk down a crowded city street holding hands and publicly showing affection, but in other areas those actions are rarely seen. Relational partners should be conscious of external pressures on the relationship. How does your neighborhood, your

▶ **COMMUNICATION IN ACTION 7.3**

WATCH: Using Supportive Communication

When Katie has problems with her boyfriend, Tommy, she turns to Sarah for advice and help. Does Sarah's response create a supportive relational climate?

COMMUNICATIONHOW-TO
IMPROVE RELATIONSHIPS WITH COMMUNICATION

RELATIONAL CLIMATE		
Defensive Climate *Instead of this...*		**Supportive Climate** *Try this...*
Evaluation Judging another's actions	vs.	**Description** Describing another's actions
Certainty Expressing sureness that your opinion is the only correct one	vs.	**Provisionalism** Being open to the possibility of alternative interpretations
Control orientation Attempting to control the situation	vs.	**Problem orientation** Working together to solve the problem
Neutrality Appearing detached, withdrawn, indifferent	vs.	**Empathy** Identifying with another's emotions
Superiority Treating your own opinion as better	vs.	**Equality** Treating another's opinion as important
Strategy Manipulating, pursuing hidden agendas, and being inauthentic	vs.	**Spontaneity** Being straightforward, honest, and direct

job, or your place of worship view your relationship? Are cultural expectations affecting how the two of you communicate? As you learned in Chapter 6, communication and culture are interlinked, meaning that you cannot separate one from the other. Because we bring our own cultures, and the influences of the cultures around us, into every relationship, awareness of how those influences affect our relationships is crucial.

INTERPERSONAL COMMUNICATION AND CONVERGENCE

In 2014, the Pew Research Center examined the Internet and social media habits of couples who were either partnered or married. The results demonstrated that couples who have been together less than 10 years differ in their

INTERPERSONAL COMMUNICATION COMPETENCE

INSTRUCTIONS: Here are some statements about how people interact with other people. For each statement, circle the response that best reflects your communication with others. Be honest in your responses and reflect on your communication behavior carefully.

	ALMOST NEVER	SELDOM	SOMETIMES	OFTEN	ALMOST ALWAYS
1. I allow friends to see who I really am.	1	2	3	4	5
2. I can put myself in others' shoes.	1	2	3	4	5
3. I am comfortable in social situations.	1	2	3	4	5
4. When I have been wronged, I confront the person who wronged me.	1	2	3	4	5
5. I let others know that I understand what they say.	1	2	3	4	5
6. My conversations are characterized by smooth shifts from one topic to the next.	1	2	3	4	5
7. My friends can tell when I'm happy or sad.	1	2	3	4	5
8. My communication is usually descriptive, not evaluative.	1	2	3	4	5
9. My friends truly believe that I care about them.	1	2	3	4	5
10. I accomplish my communication goals.	1	2	3	4	5

TOTAL

Add your responses for all 10 items. Scores may range from a low of 10 (low interpersonal communication competence) to a high of 50 (high interpersonal communication competence).

As you can see from the statements, interpersonal communication competence involves mastering the skills associated with self-disclosure, empathy, social relaxation, assertiveness, interest in others, interaction management, expressiveness, supportiveness, approachability, and control of your environment.

Reflect on each item that you scored as a 1 (almost never), 2 (seldom), or 3 (sometimes). Can you see how improving that behavior might enrich your interpersonal communication? Are there ways in which you can apply the content of this chapter to help you incorporate that behavior more often?

Source: Adapted from Rubin, R. B., & Martin, M. M. (1994). Development of a measure of interpersonal communication competence. *Communication Research Reports, 11*, 33–44. doi: 10.1080/08824099409359938

technology use patterns compared to couples who have been together longer. Newer couples were more likely to have used an online dating service, while longer-term committed couples were more likely to share social media profiles or e-mail addresses. Younger adults reported that technology makes them feel closer to their partners but at the same time indicated that technology has created tension in their relationships.

Despite some differences in use, most couples will navigate a complex and intricate blend of face-to-face and mediated communication to maintain their relationships. In fact, recent research suggests that the closer the relationship between two people, the more "means of communication" (e.g., face to face, voice calls, text, social network sites) they tend to use for interacting with one another. This phenomenon is called media multiplexity (Haythornthwaite, 2005).

Cultural influences and expectations can exert a powerful influence on interpersonal relationships.

It is important to consider the potential positive and negative impacts of the Internet on interpersonal communication. Respondents in another Pew study focused on three major advantages the Internet brings to interpersonal communication (2010):

1. Online tools offer "low-friction" opportunities to build, strengthen, and rediscover relationships that make a difference in people's lives.

2. The Internet dissolves traditional barriers to communication, including time, physical distance, and cost.

3. Online activity brings people together by creating a climate of openness and sharing.

Yet many of the survey takers also pointed out that the Internet is both a blessing and a curse to relationships. Consider the following opinions:

- The Internet gives new ways to meet—and exploit—human needs.
- Two opposing forces are at play: cocooning and connecting. Cocooners only talk to their in-groups and get little exposure to the outside world. Connectors listen widely and are heard widely.
- The Internet presents a paradox for relationships. It strengthens our relationships with distant friends and relations, but may eat away time from our relationships with the people right next to us.

What do *you* believe are the major advantages and disadvantages of the Internet for your interpersonal relationships? Can you identify people who seem to use the Internet for connecting versus cocooning? Are there ways in which you use the Internet both to isolate or withdraw from interpersonal interaction and to engage in interpersonal interaction? Which of the points about the role of the Internet in social life do you most worry about, and why?

WHAT YOU'VE LEARNED   Now that you have studied this chapter, you should be able to:

1 **Identify the features that influence the formation of interpersonal relationships.**

The factors that influence the development of an interpersonal relationship include proximity (the real or virtual distance between people), physical attraction, social attraction, and costs and rewards. We are most attracted to others who are similar to us and who reciprocate our liking.

🎙 Voice and Attraction

 The Halo Effect in Overdrive

2 **Explain the models of relationship formation.**

Developmental perspectives on relationships explain how people form and progress interpersonal relationships by moving through a series of stages. According to the Social Penetration Theory, relationships develop as we gradually offer deeper and deeper self-disclosures. The Model of Interaction Stages details five stages of coming together and five stages of coming apart.

▶ Social Penetration Theory, Part I

▶ Social Penetration Theory, Part II

💻 Knapp's Relationship Model

3 **Discuss individual interpretations of relationship development.**

Our cognitions, or thoughts, about relationships are central to the perception of relationship progress. We use imagined trajectories, or understandings of the various paths relationships can take and the outcomes of those paths, to evaluate relationships. In addition, we make sense of relationships with others through turning points, or perceptions of events that transform relationships.

🎙 Breaking Up

🎙 Can Couples Rebuild Trust After an Affair?

4 **Describe the ways in which interpersonal communication shapes relational culture.**

Relational culture is shaped by dialectical tensions, or opposing but interdependent needs and values. The way in which partners manage dialectical tensions forms the culture of their relationship. Relational culture is also formed and expressed through symbolic practices.

▶ Interview with Leslie Baxter on Relational Dialectics

5 Examine the ways in which communication technologies and new media influence interpersonal interaction.

In the Communication Age, interpersonal communication increasingly involves a blend of face-to-face and computer-mediated communication. Communication technologies may influence the likelihood of relationship formation, the ways in which communication creates relationships, and the relational culture and climate generated by interpersonal communication.

 Couples, the Internet, and Social Media

KEY TERMS

Review key terms with eFlashcards. **edge.sagepub.com/edwards2e**

REFLECT

1. Consider one of your closest interpersonal relationships. What part did each factor of forming relationships (proximity, attractiveness, similarity, matching, reciprocity) play in bringing you and your partner together? Which factor do you consider most important to the formation of that relationship?

2. Self-disclosure plays a powerful role in the development of interpersonal relationships. Can you recall receiving a self-disclosure that you felt was inappropriate or uncomfortable? Exactly what was it about the communication channel, topic, timing, or source of the self-disclosure that made the interaction awkward?

3. With relational dialectics theory in mind, consider one of your friendships. Try to identify one dialectical tension that is present (autonomy and connectedness, novelty and predictability, openness and closedness). What situation gave rise to that tension? Which strategy did you employ to manage it?

REVIEW

To check your answers go to **edge.sagepub.com/edwards2e**

1. What is interpersonal communication?

2. Define media multiplexity.

3. The tendency to allow perceptions of one positive trait to increase perceptions of other positive traits is called the _____ effect.

4. According to the _____ hypothesis, people tend to form relationships with others who are similarly attractive.

5. What theory shows how self-disclosures influence the intimacy of a relationship?

6. List, in order, the 10 stages in the Model of Interaction Stages.

7. _____ communication refers to situations in which the affection, emotion, and intimacy developed in computer-mediated contexts equals or surpasses that developed in face-to-face contexts.

8. _____ theory proposes that tensions based on partners' contradictory needs and values create the communication patterns in their relationship.

9. Messages that make another person feel valued and respected are _____, whereas messages that make another feel devalued and disrespected are _____.

08

SMALL GROUP AND TEAM COMMUNICATION

Getty

WHAT YOU'LL LEARN

After studying this chapter, you will be able to:

1 Identify the key features, advantages, and disadvantages of small group communication.

2 List and define each of the five stages of group development.

3 Distinguish between task roles and building and maintenance roles.

4 Describe how group members can engage in shared leadership.

5 Differentiate among the five types of conflict-handling styles used by small group members.

After the Semmes, Alabama, annual Christmas parade ended on December 22, 2013, parade organizers received an overwhelming edict from the community members who attended the event: Should the Prancing Elites dance troupe receive an invitation to march in the parade the following year, we will stay home. Wearing skimpy red and white Santa-style sweaters and snug white shorts, the Prancing Elites performed a dance routine that included thrusting, swaying, and explosive hip movement (Steinmann, 2013), all of which culminated in a performance that parade attendees and organizers labeled as ruining a "family-friendly" event (Stuever, 2015). What may have been more unsettling to attendees and organizers, though, is the membership of the Prancing Elites. The Prancing Elites is a small group consisting of five young, gay, gender-nonconforming African-American men whose dance routines center on "J-Setting," a style of dance popularized by the Jackson State University marching band's dance team, the Prancing J-Settes (Arceneaux, 2015), and typically associated with all-female Southern drill teams (Alvarez, 2013). Wearing sequined one- or two-piece leotards and knee-high boots, the Prancing Elites mimic the

moves of majorettes and cheerleaders through tightly choreographed dance routines that they perform at local
parades in Alabama. Since their debut in the Semmes
Christmas parade, the Prancing Elites have been featured
on YouTube and Twitter, as well as on television shows and
in magazine and newspaper articles, and a new docuseries
chronicling their journey as dancers debuted on the
Oxygen television network in April 2015.

While most of the small groups to which you belong do not have a national profile
such as the Prancing Elites, what all these groups have in common is that their
affiliation provides members with a purpose. This purpose can be multifaceted,
which allows us to share a hobby or common interest with other like-minded
individuals, as evident in the Prancing Elites; receive support for an illness or issue
from those who have undergone similar experiences; work with individuals who
are in need of assistance or support; develop friendships; complete tasks assigned
by the workplace; or enhance our skills, abilities, cognitive learning, and self-esteem.
Whether these groups meet face to face or through mediated means, group membership gives us the chance to acquire a greater breadth and depth of how to
communicate with one another in a group setting, which then enables us to
become viable partners in our current and future academic, recreational, vocational, and community group endeavors.

In the Communication Age, it is nearly impossible not to have an opportunity to join a group. Between our relationships with our family and friends, our
involvement in social and volunteer activities, and our educational and work
experiences, the number and types of groups available to us are astounding.
Equally astounding is the sense of vision, structure, and personal fulfillment that
group membership affords us. In this chapter, we focus on how you can become
a functional and productive member of any small group to which you belong.

WHAT IS SMALL GROUP COMMUNICATION?

Whether you join a group willingly or are assigned
to a team at your workplace, it is important to recognize that small group communication is task-oriented
and goal-directed. Because small group communication requires members to work together to address
these tasks and meet these goals, small group communication occurs when three or more people work
together interdependently for the purpose of accomplishing a task (Myers & Anderson, 2008). To gain
an understanding of how small groups operate, it is

necessary to examine the features of small group communication as well as identify the advantages and disadvantages of group work.

Features of
Small Group Communication

There are six features of small group communication that separate it from other types of communication. The first feature is group size. Although small group researchers have disagreed over exactly how many members equal a group (Bertcher & Maple, 1996), the general consensus is that for a small group to function most effectively, it should have a minimum of 3 members and a maximum of 15 members (Myers & Anderson, 2008), with the ideal small group consisting of 5 to 7 members (Cragan & Wright, 1999). Some groups, however, may have more than 15 members.

▶ **COMMUNICATION IN ACTION 8.1**

WATCH: First Group Meeting

A classroom group meets each other for the first time. What is your first impression of a group member who immediately takes charge of a group?

But rather than become preoccupied with the number of members a group thinks it should have, a group should focus instead on whether its size allows members to be able to recognize who belongs to the group, interact with one another, and realize the role that each person plays (Bales, 1976). Even in groups where membership exceeds 15 members, such as a fraternity or sorority, a small group such as an executive board often is responsible for the daily operations of the group and for ensuring that group tasks are completed. Nonetheless, group size becomes less of an issue when a group is able to accomplish its tasks with the input of all its members, regardless of the actual number of members.

The second feature is interdependence, which captures the effects that you and your group members have on one another (Socha, 1997). The concept of interdependence is most closely associated with systems theory, which states that all parts of a system work together to adapt to its environment. Because the parts are linked to one another, a change in one part affects, in some way, the other parts. The process by which a change in one part affects the other parts is called interdependence. In a small group, interdependence occurs when members coordinate their efforts to accomplish their task, which allows a group to complete a task together that its members could not complete individually on their own. Consider Lauren, a college junior who is 20 minutes late for her Epsilon Sigma Alpha (ESA) executive board meeting at the student center. (Epsilon Sigma Alpha is an international service fraternity dedicated to campus- and community-based volunteerism; see "Make a Difference: Helping Your Community," on page 184.) Because she is the vice president, the group is unable to begin the meeting without her. Once the meeting begins, she notices that Carly, the president, is visibly irritated with her, and several members leave before Lauren is able to distribute the sign-up sheets for the upcoming 5K race to benefit Easter Seals. After the meeting, when it is customary that Lauren and Carly go to Starbucks to have a cup of coffee, Carly leaves immediately without speaking to her. A simple act such as Lauren's tardiness, which has a direct influence on her group members' behavior, is one example of how interdependence operates in a group.

MAKE
— *a* —
DIFFERENCE

HELPING YOUR COMMUNITY

VOLUNTEERING is an essential component of the Communication Age. According to the Bureau of Labor Statistics (2015), over 63 million Americans volunteered at least once, in some capacity, either for or through an organization, between September 2013 and September 2014. These capacities included collecting, preparing, distributing, or serving food; fund-raising; and tutoring or teaching. For college students, volunteering serves as a way they can contribute to or participate in human service, educational, cultural, recreational, environmental, and

political organizations and activities (Gage & Thapa, 2012). Through their volunteer efforts, students believe they are able to make a difference in their communities, assist individuals in need, explore their future career options, learn more about themselves, and even escape from their own problems (Beehr, LeGro, Porter, Bowling, & Swader, 2010). If you are interested in group-based volunteer opportunities, consider joining Epsilon Sigma Alpha (ESA). ESA is an international coeducational service group with over 700 community and campus chapters ("The History," 2011). According to the ESA website (www .epsilonsigmaalpha.org), the mission of ESA is to enable individuals to come together to make a difference in the lives of others. Membership in Epsilon Sigma Alpha not only provides its members with the opportunity to participate in local, national, and international service projects, but also gives individuals the ability to develop leadership skills and build friendships with other like-minded people. Volunteering also enables students to refine their listening, interpersonal, organizational, and group communication skills (Simha, Topuzova, & Albert, 2011), as well as forge stronger connections with their university (Beehr et al., 2010).

To learn more about ESA or inquire about whether your community has a local chapter, visit the organization's website.

The third feature is that without a task, a group need not exist. Considered to be the primary reason why a group exists, a group task is defined as an activity in which a decision or solution cannot be made without the input of all group members (Fisher, 1971) and often is assigned by an external audience who also may evaluate whether the task was completed effectively. In some instances, the task is objective or factual, whereas in other cases, the task is subjective. For instance, as Lauren's ESA group works on the budget for the 5K fund-raiser, arriving at a list of projected expenses is rather objective, whereas brainstorming ideas for how to get local residents to register for the race is more subjective. To facilitate task accomplishment, it is recommended that group members consider seven characteristics before they attempt to address the task (Keyton, 1999; Shaw, 1981). These characteristics require members to do the following:

- determine whether the task is easy to accomplish, overly difficult, or extremely complex;
- identify the number of alternatives that exist for accomplishing the task;
- establish what is important, appealing, interesting, or fascinating about the task;

- recognize the degree of familiarity group members have with the task;

- pinpoint the degree to which the outcome of the task is found to be acceptable;

- verify the amount of authority the group has for executing the task; and

- consider the degree of ego involvement invested in the task.

Addressing these seven characteristics allows a group to communicate more efficiently and provides a chance for members to identify any obstacles before they arise. For instance, when Lauren's ESA chapter decided on selecting a 5K race as a fund-raising opportunity for Easter Seals, this task may have been influenced by some members who had personal experience in planning a running event, some members who knew that running events attract more participants than other events, those

Demonstrating a commitment to teamwork, the Golden State Warriors won the 2015 National Basketball Association championship—their first in over 40 years—by defeating the Cleveland Cavaliers in a 4-2 game series. Based on your experience working in small groups in the classroom, which features of small group communication influence your commitment to teamwork?

members who preferred planning a 5K race instead of an alternative fund-raiser such as a bake sale or a car wash, or even those members who enjoyed jogging as a hobby.

The fourth feature is that groups develop norms, which are the guidelines or rules your group implements about not only how members should behave, but also how your group should approach its tasks (Wheelan, 2016). Primarily developed through an explicit statement made by a group member, norms often transpire verbally (in either written or spoken form) and are agreed upon by the rest of the members. Norms also emerge based on a critical event in the group's history, the initial behaviors used by one member that make a lasting impression on the other members, or members' prior group experience (Feldman, 1984). When a group member violates a norm, the group may choose to impose a sanction on the member, which essentially is some form of direct punishment for breaking the norm. For example, because Carly always starts each board meeting at its scheduled time, being late to the meeting could be considered a norm violation, and her quick exit from the meeting, which in essence cancels the coffee date with Lauren, could be considered a sanction.

The fifth feature is identity, which refers to the psychological and/or physical boundaries that distinguish a group member from a non–group member (Myers & Anderson, 2008). Psychological boundaries consist of positive feelings like pride and cohesion, or negative feelings like irritation and embarrassment, whereas physical boundaries consist of the artifacts such as clothing, tattoos, or seating arrangements that you use to demonstrate your group membership to other individuals. For instance, while ESA members are free to dress how they choose at the chapter meetings, any time Lauren's chapter volunteers in the community, all members wear their group T-shirts or sweatshirts.

The sixth feature is group talk, which is centered on the specific types of communication in which you and your group members engage. Because the purpose of a group is to complete a task, group members will spend the majority of their

In the movie *Mean Girls*, Cady Heron (Lindsay Lohan) pursues a friendship with classmates Regina, Gretchen, and Karen, who are referred to as the "Plastics" by the students at North Shore High School. What role does group identity—as well as the members who belong to the group—play in your decision to join a social group?

time engaging in problem-solving or decision-making talk. When a group engages in problem-solving talk, it defines and analyzes the problem, identifies several solutions, and chooses one solution; when a group engages in decision-making talk, it selects an option from a set of already selected options in which no externally correct option exists (Frey, 1997). One way in which your group can enhance its problem-solving or decision-making talk is by considering the functional perspective of small group communication, which states that a group's performance is directly related to how well members engage in each of the five communicative functions necessary to make an informed choice (Hirokawa & Salazar, 1997). While these functions do not have to be completed in order, it is essential that a group competently perform all five functions in order to select the best solution or make the best decision.

Communication unplugged

TO ENHANCE COMMUNICATION IN PRIMARY GROUPS, PERSONALIZE YOUR USE OF TECHNOLOGY

In the Communication Age, primary groups, which consist of members engaged in an intimate relationship (Myers & Anderson, 2008) such as your immediate family members and your circle of close friends, are relying more and more on technology as a way to maintain relationships among their members (Webb, Ledbetter, & Norwood, 2015). For example, you can send a birthday card to one of your siblings using the websites www.jibjab.com or www.bluemountain.com, invite your relatives (and track how many will be attending) to your impeding college graduation through www.evite.com or www.punchbowl.com, upload photos of your Lambda Pi Eta initiation ceremony to your grandmother via shutterfly.com, or speak weekly with your parents by installing the FaceTime app on your iPad. While these technological forms arguably make it easier to remain in touch with our relatives and friends, as well as significantly reduce the amounts of time, energy, distance, and money needed to maintain these relationships, these forms also have the potential to threaten the quality of these relationships (Webb et al., 2015) by making them appear to be less personal, less intimate, and even less meaningful.

WHAT TO DO NEXT

To personalize your mediated communication with your primary groups, try to:

- Mail a written note or card to acknowledge a special day (e.g., birthday, anniversary, job promotion) in place of sending a web-generated e-card.

- Call or text each guest individually when hosting an event instead of sending a generic invitation through e-mail.

- Select and print several photos that are meaningful to you and mail them, along with a brief note indicating why the photos are special, to the recipient instead of posting all the photos on a website that the recipient must access (and scroll through) in order to view them.

- Get into the habit of writing and mailing personalized thank-you notes rather than sending a mass text message.

- Make time in your schedule to get together for a face-to-face conversation rather than conversing through your phone or computer.

- The first function, which is developing a correct understanding of the issue, includes identifying the nature of the issue, the extent and seriousness of the issue, and/or the cause behind the issue (Hirokawa, 1985). Some groups find this function difficult because they simply do not know enough about the issue, they do not possess the skills necessary to conduct research, or information about the issue is limited or unavailable. At other times, groups may feel unsure about the usefulness or importance of information they've gathered, which can impact the quality of their decision detrimentally (Mayer, Sonoda, & Gudykunst, 1997). To identify the best solution or make a high-quality decision, a group must overcome any shortcomings it faces when gathering information to develop a correct understanding of the issue (Hirokawa & Rost, 1992).

- The second function involves determining the minimal characteristics required of the alternative needed to resolve the issue. Rather than jumping ahead to decide on an alternative, a group that makes a high-quality decision first identifies the minimal characteristics required of the alternative. Often, in their quest to solve a problem or make a decision, groups either progress through this step too quickly or skip it altogether. Research shows, however, that effective groups are more likely than less effective groups to identify the qualities a "good" solution or decision would possess (Graham, Papa, & McPherson, 1997). Identifying the minimal characteristics can help a group focus on the alternative and determine whether it ultimately presents a viable option.

- The third function requires group members to identify an appropriate, adequate, and unambiguous set of alternatives (Gouran, Hirokawa, Julian, & Leatham, 1993); this set of alternatives also should be relevant and realistic. Although no set number of alternatives exists, your group should identify as many alternatives as possible because it will enable your group to consider all feasible alternatives. One way to ensure that the group has identified as many potential alternatives as possible is to use the nominal group discussion technique (Delbecq, Van de Ven, & Gustafson, 1975).

- The fourth function involves examining the alternatives identified in the third step in relation to the minimal characteristics established in the second step. When a group carefully and thoroughly examines each alternative to determine whether it meets the criteria for a "good" decision, the group increases its chance of detecting any flaws or problems with the alternative (Hirokawa & Pace, 1983). Additionally, groups should examine both the positive and the negative consequences associated with each alternative (Graham et al., 1997; Hirokawa, 1985). Doing so makes it possible to determine which choices offer the most desirable and the least desirable consequences.

The physical boundaries of group identity often demonstrate the psychological boundaries of group identity.

- The fifth function is to select the best alternative in light of the previous four functions. Ideally, this alternative will allow a group to easily solve a problem or readily make a decision.

Aside from problem-solving or decision-making talk, your group also will engage in consciousness-raising talk and encounter talk (Cragan & Wright, 1999). Consciousness-raising talk focuses on discussions about group identity and pride, whereas encounter talk refers to small talk and general pleasantries exchanged by group members as they initiate and maintain their relationships. For example, Lauren's ESA members may spend a few minutes engaging in encounter talk before Carly calls the weekly meeting to order, during which members spend the majority of time in decision-making talk.

In some cases, however, a small group evolves into a team. While a team shares the characteristics of a small group, not all small groups share the characteristics of teams. According to management experts Jon Katzenbach and Douglas Smith (1993), the primary distinction between a group and a team resides in the commitment of its members. This commitment drives the team's purpose, the contributions made by its members, and the ways in which the members hold one another accountable. Moreover, team members communicate candidly with one another, in that they discuss the strengths and weaknesses each member contributes to the team. As such, it is essential that a team's communication include openness, which is the ability to examine issues objectively, and supportiveness, which is the ability to elicit the best thinking and attitude from members, as these two communication behaviors often distinguish an effective team from an ineffective team (LeFasto & Larson, 2001). Figure 8.1 highlights some other ways in which groups and teams differ in their characteristics.

FIGURE 8.1
DIFFERENCES BETWEEN GROUPS AND TEAMS

Characteristic	Groups	Teams
Accountability	Assessed at the individual member level	Assessed at both the individual member level and the collective team level
Leadership	Assigned to one or two members	Shared among all members
Measures of Effectiveness	Indirectly measured by assessing influence on other people, groups, or organizations	Directly measured by assessing work product
Meetings	Conducted as needed; often scheduled	Conducted frequently; often spontaneous
Member Selection	Typically assigned or selected based on member availability	Purposefully selected based on member abilities, talents, and skills
Purpose	Created by larger entity and shared with group members	Created specifically by team members for the team
Roles	Assigned and played by individual members	Rotated and played among all members as needed
Task Completion	Delegated to and completed by individual members	Expected to be completed together by all members
Work Product	Completed individually	Completed jointly

Sources: Katzenbach & Smith (1993) and Tiffan (2014).

Advantages and Disadvantages of Small Group Work

Group membership can be simultaneously rewarding and frustrating, just as it has its advantages and disadvantages. There are three advantages to group work. The first advantage is access to members' resources, which is considered to be the key advantage to working in groups (Baker & Campbell, 2004). In this sense, resources refer to time, energy, money, material items, and member expertise, talent, or ability, as well as informational diversity and value diversity. Generally, successful groups take advantage of their access to resources. While you may have access to some of these resources, chances are that access to a greater number of resources will occur when you work in a group with other people.

One advantage to working in a small group is access to members' resources, which include technology.

Thinkstock

 COMMUNICATIONHOW-TO
NOMINAL GROUP DISCUSSION TECHNIQUE

The nominal group discussion technique is a decision-making procedure that allows members to work both independently and as a group. To use this procedure, members follow four steps:

The nominal group discussion technique is a commonly used decision-making procedure.

iStock

1. All group members are provided with the same stimulus question or issue. Working alone, they are instructed to list as many ideas as possible using only key words or descriptive phrases.

2. A facilitator constructs a master list by recording each member's list on a blackboard, flip chart, newsprint,

or computer. In a round-robin fashion, the facilitator asks members to present a single idea at a time until the ideas of all members have been recorded or the members decide that they have a sufficient number of ideas. If one idea is duplicated by other members, they can elect to extend the original idea.

3. The facilitator reads each idea aloud and asks members to comment on each idea as it is being read. These comments serve as the basis for group discussion about all the recorded ideas. At this point, an idea can be clarified, although it is recommended that members do not clarify their own ideas. New ideas can also be added, but only if deemed necessary.

4. Members vote on the best idea from among the master list generated in the second step, keeping in mind the discussion that occurred in the third step. Typically, they select five ideas from the list and rank them in order of importance. The facilitator collects the rank-ordered ideas from the members and records the rankings on the master list. Members discuss the voting patterns before arriving at a decision.

Source: Moore (1987).

The second advantage is that groups offer diversity of group member opinion in terms of informational diversity and value diversity. Informational diversity refers to differences among group members based on their education, work experience, group experience, and expertise; value diversity refers to differences among group members in terms of what they consider to be their group's goals, mission, and purpose (Jehn, Northcraft, & Neale, 1999). These informational and value differences provide groups with alternative views and perspectives, which allow us to refrain from using our own personal values, beliefs, and attitudes as the basis for solving problems and making decisions.

The third advantage is that group work encourages creativity, which is the process by which members engage in idea generation that relies on the message exchange among members rather than through the mindsets of members (Sunwolf, 2002). One way in which you and your group members can engage in idea generation is to use the brainstorming decision-making technique. Originally conceptualized by advertising executive Alex Osborn in 1953, brainstorming is a process that allows group members to generate more ideas or solutions to problems by working together rather than working alone. To use brainstorming effectively, your group must follow four ideas. First, no evaluation or criticism of the ideas—whether positive (e.g., "That's a good idea!") or negative (e.g., "That idea sounds stupid!")—should occur during the brainstorming session, no matter how outlandish or nonsensical the ideas may seem. Second, you and your group members should generate as many ideas as possible without extended pauses. The purpose of brainstorming is to focus on the quantity of ideas, not the quality of ideas. Third, you should encourage one another to be creatively wild and crazy. And fourth, you and your group members should feel free to piggyback or hitchhike on one another's ideas. Typically conducted in a face-to-face setting, in the Communication Age, consider that it is becoming increasingly common to conduct brainstorming sessions through mediated means.

At the same time, there are three disadvantages to group work. The first disadvantage is that not all group members will like or appreciate group work. In fact, sometimes we possess strong feelings of grouphate, which are feelings of dread that arise when faced with the possibility of having to work in a group (Sorensen, 1981). In college classroom work groups, grouphate emerges because group members misbehave, fail to contribute equally to the task, receive the same grade regardless of their input, and experience personality clashes with one another (Myers, Goodboy, & Members of COMM 612, 2004). Students in these classroom groups also report less learning, less cohesion, less consensus, and less relational satisfaction (Myers & Goodboy, 2005; Myers et al., 2010) and identify fewer positive attributes about group work (Keyton, Harmon, & Frey, 1996). Among organizational employees, workers who experience grouphate consider themselves to be less tolerant of ambiguity, less tolerant of disagreement, and less argumentative (Madlock, Kennedy-Lightsey, & Myers, 2007).

The second disadvantage is coordination of group member tasks. As the size of a group increases, group members contribute less to the task (Liden, Wayne,

iStock

Consciousness-raising talk is one way for members to express their positive feelings about group identity and pride.

Jaworski, & Bennett, 2004). They engage in less communication about the task, and this communication becomes less accurate, less appropriate, and less open (Lowry, Roberts, Romano, Cheney, & Hightower, 2006). The third disadvantage is coping with group member misbehavior. Although these misbehaviors can emerge in many forms, such as missing group meetings or failing to meet deadlines, perhaps the biggest member misbehavior revolves around group members who are labeled "slackers." Considered to be deviant group members (Gillespie, Rosamond, & Thomas, 2006), slackers are those group members who fail to contribute equally or equitably to a group task. In a recent study of slackers in college classroom groups, it was found that students report working with slackers to be a frustrating experience because they perceive slackers to care little about the task, to contribute little to combined efforts, or to make excuses about their lack of commitment to the group (Myers et al., 2009), all of which can have a debilitating effect on group member motivation. Students who have experience working with slackers are less likely to look forward to working in groups (Payne & Monk-Turner, 2006).

Virtual teams often use videoconferencing as a way to complete their tasks and assignments.

CAREER FRONTIER: WORKING IN VIRTUAL WORK TEAMS

THE COMMUNICATION AGE has helped people participate in small group and team interaction virtually instead of speaking face to face. No doubt, many of you will have the opportunity to pursue employment as a member of a **virtual work team** where tasks and professional projects traditionally accomplished face to face are completed through computer-mediated means to save time, travel, and energy. Typically, virtual team members are based in different locations across the world; rarely, if ever, meet face to face; and regularly complete their tasks and assignments using the telephone, e-mail, and videoconferencing ("The Challenges," 2010). Working in a virtual team offers several benefits for both team members and the organization for which the team works. Because a virtual team works across time and space boundaries, technology reduces the need for travel, allows the team always to have one member working on a project, provides an opportunity for a group to hire the brightest and most talented members, and enables the team as a whole to

more easily document and review its work (Berry, 2011; Dube & Robey, 2008). Yet there are some drawbacks to working on a virtual team. In terms of task completion, virtual team members report experiencing greater difficulty when it comes to managing conflict, making decisions, or expressing opinions than members of face-to-face teams report ("The Challenges," 2010). Because it is common for virtual team members to physically work by themselves, despite being connected to teammates electronically, some virtual team members perceive a sense of isolation, the absence of collegiality, and difficulty associated with establishing rapport and developing trust with one another as challenges through which they must work ("The Challenges," 2010). Language issues, a lack of cultural sensitivity, and coordinating time zones when scheduling meetings also can make working in virtual teams difficult (Rabotin, 2014; Reiche, 2013). As you ponder whether you should seek employment with a virtual team, consider both the benefits of and drawbacks to working virtually.

Brainstorming is a decision-making procedure that encourages group member creativity and imagination.

In summary, the small group communication process is composed of six features: size, interdependence, task, norms, identity, and types of talk. Knowing these six features of small group communication, as well as the three advantages and three disadvantages associated with group work, is essential when working in groups because it provides you with the initial tools needed to become a functional and productive member of any group. Another necessary tool is recognizing the process through which groups develop.

SMALL GROUP DEVELOPMENT

So what happens when you find yourself a new member of a group? According to small group communication researchers, you and your fellow group members will undergo a developmental process in the quest to become oriented to the task and to form relationships with one another.

Although several models of small group and team development exist, small group researcher Bruce Tuckman's model of small group development (Tuckman, 1965; Tuckman & Jensen, 1977) is particularly applicable to the many social, work, and volunteer groups to which you have belonged, belong currently, or will belong. This model proposes that small groups progress through five sequential stages (i.e., forming, storming, norming, performing, and adjourning). In each stage, group members encounter issues that pertain to task accomplishment and group member relational development. As a group matures and moves through the stages, members become adept at accomplishing the task, learning how to work with one another, and identifying their attitudes toward group work (Smith, 2001). This model explains how both face-to-face groups and virtual groups move through the developmental process (Haines, 2014; Yu & Kuo, 2012).

This model works well when explaining how a group whose members have never worked together develops, although at times a group may choose to skip a stage, rush through a stage, or regress to a stage depending on the amount of time allotted to the task, the cohesiveness of the members, the emergence of conflict, or the subjective nature of the task (Poole & Roth, 1989). Additionally, while it is assumed that group membership remains stable across each stage, the addition of a new member or the exit of a member at any stage can impede how a group communicates during that stage.

The Forming Stage

The forming stage begins when you are first introduced to your group. In this stage, you and your group members meet for the first time, learn about the task, and become acquainted with one another (Smith, 2001). Most likely, your communication with your fellow group members will be polite and superficial, and topics will be limited to non-task-related activity (Wheelan, Davidson, & Tilin, 2003) because you are focused on the impressions that your group members form about you. In this stage, members communicate in a courteous yet cautious manner (Maples, 1988) because they are fearful of rejection, alienation, and exclusion (Wheelan & Hochberger, 1996) and are concerned more with feeling a sense of belonging than with the task (Wheelan, 2016). Your communication takes on an exploratory nature as you and your group members try to determine your role in the group, confirm your perceptions of one another, and decide how much effort you are going to put forth in completing the group task. At the same time, your prior experiences with group work, as well as your perceptions of both the positive and negative attributes of group work, will influence the extent to which and how you communicate with your group members. In a virtual group, in part due to a lack of face-to-face contact among members, this stage is particularly important because members who do not feel a sense of belonging can easily withdraw from the group's virtual space (Yu & Kuo, 2012) by turning off their telephones, purposely choosing not to respond to e-mail messages, deleting or blocking one another from their inboxes, or refusing to accept meeting or teleconferencing requests, which then impedes their development with the group across the subsequent stages.

One downside of group work for many college students is having a slacker in a classroom group.

The Storming Stage

The storming stage begins once you and your group members have established a sense of comfort and some degree of familiarity with one another. While you and your group members begin to actively participate by sharing ideas, contributing to discussions, and engaging in low levels of self-disclosure, you and your group members also begin to struggle with the assigned task and the procedures that need be utilized to accomplish the task (Wheelan & Hochberger, 1996). Rather than communicating solely in the polite and superficial manner characteristic of the forming stage, you and your fellow group members begin to disagree openly about the group goals and the task (Wheelan, 2016) and criticize the lack of progress that is being made on the task (Maples, 1988). Communication increases and conflict arises, in part because members are torn between losing their individual identity and developing a group identity (Smith, 2001) and in part because they begin to find some group members, but not all, to be appealing, interesting, and enjoyable. During this stage, members must resolve any anxiety they might experience about being a group member, decrease any uncertainty surrounding the roles that they could play, and determine how to deal with the emergence of differences in opinion, member personalities, and attitudes toward task accomplishment among group members (Bormann, 1989). It is not uncommon for coalitions, subgroups, or cliques to develop as a way to address the issues that arise in this stage, but until they are resolved, it is difficult for a group to move to the norming stage (Wheelan & Burchill, 1999).

The Norming Stage

In the norming stage, you and your group members have resolved your initial conflicts and have begun to work together on the task. Communication among members becomes more open and task-oriented (Wheelan, 2016) as you and your group members begin to clarify your group roles, develop norms, and determine the

In the forming stage, group members communicate with one another in a friendly manner.

appropriate courses of action to take. Group members' trust and commitment to the group increases (Wheelan et al., 2003), as does cooperation, collaboration, and commitment (Maples, 1988). Consequently, feelings of cohesion will develop. Cohesion occurs when members feel a sense of belonging to a group (Mudrack, 1989) and can emerge in the forms of task cohesion—the degree to which members work toward a common goal—and social cohesion—the sense of community that develops among members (Kjormo & Halvari, 2002). When members consider their groups to be cohesive, they are more satisfied with their membership (Tekleab, Quigley, & Tesluk, 2009).

The Performing Stage

The performing stage begins when the group begins to focus on task completion. Considered to be the stage at which group members produce the most work (Chidambaram & Bostrom, 1996), you and group members focus your energy on task accomplishment and goal achievement (Wheelan et al., 2003); develop a sense of responsibility to, and consciousness of, the task (Maples, 1988); and spend a significant amount of time using the appropriate problem-solving and decision-making techniques listed in Figure 8.2 that allow your group to accomplish the task. Members also become fully integrated into the group culture and identify with the values and identity promoted by the group (Smith, 2001), accept the roles they are needed or required to play (Wheelan, 2016), and follow the norms developed in the norming stage.

In this stage, your group also must overcome any task-related or relational obstacles that may impede your progress (Gouran, 1997). Common task-related obstacles include information problems, analytical problems such as lacking reasoning skills, and procedural problems such as not following an agenda. Common relational obstacles include the differences in attitudes, values, and goals that arise among members. More important, you and your group members must regularly evaluate your collective performance and take measures to ensure that your objectives are met (Wheelan, 2016).

The Adjourning Stage

The adjourning stage begins when a group reaches the end of its involvement. Typically, your group will disband for one of four reasons: The group has finished its task, has run out of the time allotted to complete the task, has failed at its task, or is unable to function in its present form or condition (Sarri & Galinsky, 1974). Regardless of why a group has entered the adjourning stage, it is recommended that group members prepare for this ending by taking the time to review their accomplishments, assess their working relationships, and decide which members will be responsible for addressing inquiries about the group's work (Keyton, 1993). At the same time, because there is always the chance that members may work together at some future point in time, this last meeting should not be viewed as an opportunity for members to become verbally aggressive toward or disparage one another. Instead, members should take a moment and identify the contribution that each member has made to the group, as well as reflect on how members' attitudes, skills, or talents contributed to the group's success.

It also is important to consider that you and your fellow group members may have mixed feelings about this adjournment. Some members may rejoice that the group has finished its job, some may mourn the loss of being involved in an interesting task and forming interpersonal relationships with one another, and some may attempt to keep the group together (Rose, 1989). Nonetheless, cohesive group endings are less traumatic for members if they expect to see one another or work together again (Sinclair-James & Stohl, 1997). And, as you know, members who like one another or enjoy one another's company will stay in touch through e-mail, texting, cell phone calls, or Facebook.

Morning viewers who regularly watch the *Today* show are accustomed to seeing a group of people who exhibit a strong sense of cohesion while working with one another. In your work groups, what are some ways in which members have developed both task and social cohesion?

In summary, groups develop through five stages that reflect a life span approach, with a beginning phase, a growing phase, and an ending phase (Socha, 1997). In the beginning phase, members experience the forming stage as they are introduced to the group task and become acquainted with one another. In the growing stage, members proceed through the storming, norming, and performing stages as they confront and resolve conflict, develop norms and cohesion, and integrate themselves into the group culture as they complete the assigned task, although for some virtual groups, members either skip or ignore the storming stage due to their dominant focus on task accomplishment (Berry, 2011). In the ending phase, members experience the adjourning stage by detaching themselves from the group. As groups move through the five stages of group development, it is helpful to consider that growth is facilitated by the roles that members play and the leadership behaviors that they demonstrate.

SMALL GROUP MEMBER ROLES AND LEADERSHIP

Central to how any small group moves through the developmental process is the manner in which members engage in roles and leadership, which emerges during group meetings. Paying attention to the meeting environment is a responsibility all members should consider when assuming roles and exhibiting leadership.

Group Member Roles

Think of a group member role as an established and repetitive pattern of communicative behaviors that members expect from one another (Myers & Anderson, 2008). This pattern is determined by how members communicate with one another (e.g., the use of language and nonverbal behaviors), the type of assigned

FIGURE 8.2
PROBLEM-SOLVING
AND DECISION-MAKING
PROCEDURES

Brainstorming	Idea writing	Six thinking hats
Brainwriting	Mind mapping	Stepladder technique
Buzz groups	Picture tour	SWOT analysis
Decision trees	Risk analysis	Visioning
Delphi technique	Reflective thinking model	Synectics
Five Ws and H	Role storming	Wildest idea
Force field analysis	Single question format	Wishful thinking

Sources: Based on Problem-Solving Techniques (1995-2015), Decision-Making Techniques (1996–2015), and Sunwolf (2002).

task, and the extent to which members are concerned with accomplishing the task, preserving interpersonal relationships, or fulfilling their personal needs. Whether working in a face-to-face group or a virtual group, roles will emerge through the formal and informal interaction that occurs among members.

When your group is immersed in a task, members typically engage in two sets of communicative behaviors (Bales, 1976). The first set of behaviors centers on task accomplishment and includes both the asking and giving of opinions, suggestions, and information, whereas the second set focuses on the relational aspect of group work and includes demonstrating solidarity, friendliness, and agreement. Task roles are designated specifically to facilitate progress toward problem solving or decision making and attainment of group goals, and building and maintenance roles are used to develop and maintain the interpersonal and social development of the group. Although there are many roles that members can play (Benne & Sheats, 1948; see Figure 8.3), six roles are particularly necessary in any small group endeavor.

Initiator-Contributor Role

A member who assumes the initiator-contributor role implicitly assumes the role of the group task leader. As the task leader, your members rely on you to adopt a "take charge" type of attitude in which you demonstrate excellent communication skills, technical skills, and problem-solving abilities that allow you to guide your group's problem-solving and decision-making process, manage conflicts, and challenge poor decisions (Myers & Anderson, 2008). More important, you assume the responsibility of making sure that your group progresses toward task accomplishment through the proposal of new ideas, alternative procedures, or novel ways to accomplish the task (Benne & Sheats, 1948). Because a group is expected to produce and complete its task in a timely manner, you devote your energies toward goal attainment.

Information Giver Role

A member who elects to play the information giver role demonstrates the ability to provide and synthesize ideas and alternatives to and for group members. Not only does this member contribute information to the group in the form of facts, anecdotes, narratives, statistics, and examples, but in the Communication Age, the information giver is also expected to be proficient in using technology and seeking relevant information on the Internet. Some of these proficiencies include using a variety of word processing programs, uploading or downloading photos and attachments, and building webpages. If you play this role, your group members may rely on your prior experiences and general levels of expertise as they relate to the group task (Benne & Sheats, 1948).

During the adjourning stage, group members should make time to say goodbye to one another.

Orienter Role

A member who embraces the orienter role is responsible for challenging group members' ideas in a constructive manner. As an orienter, you summarize your group's progress, question the solutions or options agreed on by members, recommend alternative or additional solutions or options, or ask fellow members to articulate the position they have chosen. Sometimes referred to as the devil's advocate (Myers & Anderson, 2008), as the orienter it is essential that you force members to weigh the positive and negative consequences of each solution or option under consideration before the group makes its final decision. This way, the group will be less inclined to suffer from groupthink, which occurs when a group makes a faulty decision due to its members' collective inability to critically examine an issue (Janis, 1982). One caveat exists about this role, however: While the orienter encourages the group to think in different ways, there are times when this role can block progress toward the group's goals if members feel compelled to defend their stance on an issue or if they feel threatened about the stance they've taken on an issue.

Recorder Role

A member who selects the recorder role takes the minutes of meetings and records any other group actions that need to be stored as permanent records. In addition to maintaining written or mediated documentation of your group's progress toward the task (e.g., suggestions, solutions, or options), this role carries with it procedural duties such as typing the agenda, making arrangements for group meetings, ensuring members receive copies of minutes of the meeting, and sending pertinent information to prepare for the next meeting (Benne & Sheats, 1948). In the Communication Age, the recorder also may be responsible for sending e-mail, Facebook messages, and Twitter updates to members, as well as maintaining the group's website page and LinkedIn account and scheduling meetings through doodle.com.

Encourager and Harmonizer Roles

Two roles—the encourager role and the harmonizer role—are the most essential in affecting whether and how group members maintain their relationships. When you play the encourager role, you recognize the contributions made by your

COMMUNICATIONHOW-TO
IDENTIFYING THE SYMPTOMS OF GROUPTHINK

Although every group should have a member who plays the orienter role, it ultimately is the responsibility of all group members to challenge one another when it comes to solving a problem or making a decision in order to avoid groupthink from occurring. Should a symptom of groupthink emerge when working on a task, the group should immediately resolve to quash it. These symptoms include:

1. Believing that the group is invulnerable to the risks that it takes;

2. Failing to assess either the ethical or moral consequences of a group decision;

3. Dismissing facts or opinions that contradict a group's established position on a matter;

4. Assuming that rival groups lack the ability to solve a similar problem or make a similar decision;

5. Censoring or withholding personal contributions to group discussion;

6. Pressuring group members to withhold expressing their disagreement with a group solution or decision;

7. Protecting the group as a whole from adverse, negative, or contradictory information; and

8. Assuming that the majority view of group members represents the viewpoint of all group members.

Source: Janis (1983).

group members and communicate with them in a warm and supportive manner. When you play the harmonizer role, you mediate disagreements as they arise among your group members, and you attempt to ease group tension by engaging in humor (Benne & Sheats, 1948). Additionally, when you play either role, you help your group members maintain mutual respect for one another, you promote empathic listening, and you ensure that the self-worth of each member remains intact. For many individuals, having a group member who plays these two building and maintenance roles is highly valued (Ketrow, 1991), which may explain why group members who emerge from a satisfying group experience usually can trace their satisfaction to the presence of these building and maintenance roles.

It should also be established that in addition to playing a role inside a group, there may be a time when a group member takes on a boundary-spanning role. A boundary-spanning role is one in which a group member acts as a liaison between the group and the larger entity in which the group exists, such as the workplace or a school system. In this case, a group member may adopt the role of either a consul or a coordinator (Mumford, Campion, & Morgeson, 2006). A consul publicizes the group by presenting it in a favorable light to external audiences, possibly by highlighting its purpose, activities, or benefits of membership, or promoting its identity in the community. A coordinator serves to manage its interaction with other groups by arranging meeting times with one another, scheduling combined work sessions, working together on joint tasks, participating in shared activities, or pooling their resources as needed to accomplish a common goal.

One downside to playing task, building and maintenance, or boundary-spanning roles, or any of the roles identified by Benne and Sheats (1948), is that group

FIGURE 8.3
TASK ROLES AND BUILDING AND MAINTENANCE ROLES

Role	Description
Commentator [BM]	Offers interpretations of members' input
Compromiser [BM]	Offers alternatives that incorporate members' input
Coordinator [T]	Links ideas and alternatives offered by members
Elaborator [T]	Extends ideas or alternatives through members' suggestions
Encourager [BM]	Ensures members have a satisfying group experience
Energizer [T]	Motivates members to offer higher-quality ideas and alternatives
Evaluator-critic [T]	Challenges ideas and alternatives offered by members
Follower [BM]	Accepts ideas and alternatives offered by members
Gatekeeper [BM]	Keeps communication open among members
Harmonizer [BM]	Mediates differences that arise among members
Information giver [T]	Provides and synthesizes ideas and alternatives to members
Information seeker [T]	Clarifies factual content of ideas and alternatives
Initiator-critic [T]	Assumes responsibility for task achievement
Opinion giver [T]	Offers beliefs and values to support ideas and alternatives
Opinion seeker [T]	Clarifies content of ideas and alternatives
Orienter [T]	Challenges members in a constructive manner
Procedural technician [T]	Performs tasks on behalf of the group
Recorder [T]	Documents group activity
Standard setter [BM]	Identifies standards the group should attempt to achieve

Note: BM = building and maintenance roles; T = task roles.
Source: Based on Benne and Sheats (1948).

members simply may not be equipped to do so (Burtis & Turman, 2006). In some groups, members may experience uncertainty or ambiguity about the role because they have little experience in playing the role or they may have limited group experience. In other groups, members compete with one another for the opportunity to play the role, particularly if they are not satisfied with the progress made toward the task or they do not like the direction in which the group is moving. For some members, playing a particular role is problematic because it interferes with the demands placed upon themselves (e.g., time, interest) that they simply cannot fulfill. Other members may gravitate toward playing a role because it reinforces their own interests or complements their own communication and personality traits. For group members to successfully play a role, they must be clear about the role they are asked to play, they must have the skills and

A group member who plays the information-giver role is responsible for providing the group with the facts, statistics, and examples necessary for task completion.

iStock

A group member who plays the harmonizer role strategically uses humor as a way to diffuse group disagreement.

abilities necessary to play the role, and they must agree to accept the role they are being asked to play (Wheelan, 2016).

Group Leadership

Similar to group roles, whether you and your fellow group members engage in leadership is influenced by how you communicate with one another via your use of spoken language and nonverbal behaviors, how you confront the task, and how you establish relationships with one another. One way in which all group members can participate in leadership is through shared leadership, which refers to the communicative behaviors any group member can enact to demonstrate leadership. Rather than appointing or electing one group member to play the leader role for an unlimited amount of time during a group's existence, shared leadership emerges from any group member who possesses competence, talent, or interest in the task or relational area under consideration by the group (O'Hair & Wiemann, 2004). Shared leadership—which is an ability—permits the most competent group member(s) to assume the leader role when needed and usually rotates among group members over the life span of a task (Kramer, 2006).

In some cases, shared leadership arises based on the emergent leader approach to leadership in that it emerges through the communication that occurs among group members by choosing to eliminate those individuals who do not demonstrate leadership behaviors. Some of these nonleadership behaviors include failing to attend group meetings, interacting with group members in a contentious manner, choosing not to speak with group members, misbehaving or acting as a slacker, displaying communication anxiety, or volunteering to play the recorder role (Fisher, 1980; Myers & Anderson, 2008). In most groups that meet face to face, only one or two members will emerge as leaders, whereas in virtual groups, it is not uncommon for multiple group members to serve as emergent leaders (Ziek & Smulowitz, 2014).

Instead, group members look for a member who displays excellent communication skills and appears natural at leadership and group work. Norton, Murfield, and Baucus (2014) proposed that group members who emerge as a leader are considered by their peers to possess domain competence, fluid intelligence, and credibility; indicate a willingness to serve as the group leader; and have the ability to move the group toward goal attainment. Emergent leaders also engage in competent communicative behaviors, which include contributing and soliciting input, working well with others, and utilizing a variety of effective listening behaviors, such as staying focused, asking questions, demonstrating interest in what group members say, and not interrupting group members when they speak (Johnson & Bechler, 1998; Kolb, 1997). Other behaviors that may contribute to perceptions of emergent leadership include encouraging member participation, monitoring group progress toward the group task, promoting diversity of member opinion, building consensus, providing the opportunity for members to express their thoughts, and giving serious consideration to member ideas (Galanes, 2003; Sorensen & Savage, 1989). In virtual groups, emergent leadership is tied to the frequency

Emergent group leaders are viewed by group members as engaging in several competent communicative behaviors.

with which group members communicate with one another. That is, emergent leaders not only send or post a greater number of task and procedural messages than other virtual group members, but these messages are also lengthier than the messages written by other group members (Ziek & Smulowitz, 2014).

Group Meeting Environments

Creating the proper meeting environment is an important component of effective group communication, but one that members often overlook (Ivy & Wahl, 2009; Quintanilla & Wahl, 2011). Considered to be the time and place where a meeting is held, a group meeting environment is as much a part of the small group communication process that occurs as the words that are said. Unfortunately, despite the importance of the group meeting environment, most small group members spend little time thinking about it when they plan their group meetings.

When working on a task, group members should select a meeting environment that is both welcoming and aesthetically pleasing.

To create an effective group meeting environment, several factors such as time of day, time of week, and time of year should be considered. For example, holding a meeting at 8:00 on a Monday morning, 4:30 on a Friday afternoon, or right after lunch may not be the best choice if you want your team members to be fully engaged and alert. Location also is an important component in creating a positive meeting environment (Quintanilla & Wahl, 2011). Consider Barb, who is the newly elected president of Lambda Pi Eta, a national honor society for students in communication studies. When she first took office, she held all the meetings at her apartment off campus at 8:00 on Monday mornings. Although her intention was to start each week fresh by clearly communicating goals and priorities, this was not the message received by the members. Instead, Barb indirectly sent the message that she considered herself the most important person in the group and that she did not care about her classmates' schedules or input as evidenced by the fact that they would have to commute to her apartment during morning rush-hour traffic or that they might have to miss their morning classes. This message not only failed to support the notion of shared goals and a collaborative climate necessary for transforming groups into teams, but it also created a negative tone that hindered communication during the chapter meetings. Fortunately, Barb realized her mistake and moved the chapter meetings to Tuesday at 8:00 p.m. at alternating locations on campus. By considering the time and location, she was able to improve her leadership ability.

In fact, the convenience, aesthetics, and comfort of the location should always be considered when planning a group meeting. Many groups get in the habit of holding all their meetings in the same room. If the room contains an extremely long and narrow table, is windowless, or has uncomfortable chairs, it can be difficult to hold discussions or brainstorming sessions. The size of the meeting room also is important. If members are crammed into a small space with uncomfortable furniture for any length of time, it will be difficult for them to remain productive. Also, keep in mind that comfort extends beyond furniture. For longer meetings, taking short breaks allows members

THE ETHICS OF JURY MEMBERSHIP

The July 2013 trial of George Zimmerman, who was charged with second-degree murder in the death of Trayvon Martin, resulted in his acquittal, leaving some to question the jury's decision. In your work groups, how do your members arrive at a decision to use a particular type of problem-solving or decision-making technique? How common is it for all group members to question the manner in which a decision is made to use a specific technique?

On the evening of February 26, 2012, 17-year-old African American Trayvon Martin was returning to his father's fiancée's home in Sanford, Florida, after going to a convenience store where he purchased a bag of Skittles and a fruit-flavored drink. As he was walking home, he was spotted by 29-year-old George Zimmerman, who was patrolling the neighborhood in his capacity as a neighborhood watch volunteer (Botelho & Yan, 2013). Rattled by a rash of recent burglaries in the townhouse complex community, Zimmerman—who self-identifies as Hispanic and has a Caucasian father and Hispanic mother—called 911 to report Martin's presence in the neighborhood (Alvarez & Buckley, 2013; Botelho & Yan, 2013; Roig-Franzia, 2013). Despite the dispatcher's advice to wait for a police unit to arrive and not to leave his vehicle, Zimmerman followed Martin in his quest to determine whether Martin resided in the neighborhood (Botelho & Yan, 2013). Shortly after the 911 call, the two got into a physical altercation in which Zimmerman shot Martin—who was unarmed—in the heart, leaving Martin dead and Zimmerman claiming self-defense. Initially, Zimmerman was not charged with a crime. It was not until

approximately 6 weeks later that Zimmerman was arrested for second-degree murder, but only after extensive media coverage of Martin's murder called attention to the fact that Zimmerman had not been charged with the killing (Roig-Franzia, 2013). At his trial during the summer of 2013, based on the evidence produced by both the prosecution and the defense, the six-woman jury was given one of three choices by the judge: find Zimmerman guilty of second-degree murder; find him guilty of manslaughter, a lesser charge; or find him not guilty (Botelho & Yan, 2013). After deliberating for over 16 hours, the jury acquitted Zimmerman of all charges. Their nonguilty judgment (Alvarez & Buckley, 2013) left many people, including Martin's family, questioning the jury's verdict as well as their faith in the justice system.

Unlike most small groups to which you have belonged or may belong, a jury is a unique type of small group because its membership is composed of 12 strangers assigned the task of rendering a verdict on the behavior of another stranger (Sunwolf, 2008). In high-profile cases such as the George Zimmerman trial, a jury can face public criticism and harassment after the trial, all of which are made even more possible in the Communication Age due to Twitter, Facebook, and other social media. Yet despite the importance of such a task, not all jurors approach their service in an ethical manner. For instance, while a jury foreperson always is selected from among the jury members, members rarely are informed how to select the foreperson, and the selection process often occurs quickly and without much discussion (Sunwolf, 2008). Some jurors choose purposely not to contribute equally to the decision-making process while input from other jurors is ignored, and juries often devote little to no time discussing the decision-making procedures they will use to arrive at a verdict (Sunwolf, 2008). Given these issues, it is no surprise that some verdicts are questioned by the public.

QUESTIONS

1. Regardless of the type of trial, how ethical is it for jurors to purposely not contribute to the decision-making process?

2. To arrive at a high-quality decision, should the members of a jury be required to discuss the decision-making procedures they will use prior to rendering a verdict? Why?

to stretch, visit the restroom, and refresh their perspective. If your budget allows for it, consider providing food and beverages.

In summary, to maximize group performance, a group must have members who (1) play the initiator-contributor, information giver, orienter, recorder, encourager, and harmonizer roles, and (2) engage in either shared or emergent leadership by allowing those who display the desired communication competencies to assume leadership for that time. A group also should consider the environment in which its meetings take place. But, despite group members' best efforts to maintain their relationships, there may be times when they engage in conflict.

One way in which a group can enhance its productivity is to refrain from holding its meetings in the same location.

SMALL GROUP CONFLICT

As an inevitable part of group life, at some point, you and your group members will encounter small group conflict. Small group conflict is the process that occurs when group members engage in an expressed struggle that impedes task accomplishment and usually arises due to the real and perceived differences that exist among group members. Peruse the four types of small group conflict listed in Figure 8.4. Chances are any recent conflict that emerged in one of your small groups can be classified into one of the four types.

To address conflict, you and your group members will need to utilize a conflict-handling style that is appropriate given the group task, the relationships you have established with one another, and the parameters surrounding the task. When individuals engage in conflict, they choose a conflict-handling style based on (1) their concern about meeting their own needs, and (2) their concern about meeting the needs of the other individuals involved in the conflict (Rahim, 1983, 2002). Based on the levels of these two concerns (i.e., high, moderate, low), five categories of

Types	Definition
Substantive	Centers on group members' critical evaluation of ideas, solutions, and decisions
Affective	Centers on how group members' behaviors disrupt the group and impede progress toward task accomplishment
Procedural	Centers on group members' use of procedures to (1) critically evaluate ideas, solutions, and decisions or (2) confront disruptive member behavior
Inequity	Centers on group members' perceived imbalance between their contributions to the group task and the contributions made by other group members

Source: Myers and Anderson (2008).

FIGURE 8.4
FOUR TYPES OF SMALL GROUP CONFLICT

Reality TV shows such as *The Bachelor* pit contestants against one another, often requiring them to adopt a dominating conflict-handling style in order to successfully compete. What other suggestions would you offer to group members on when to use, and when to refrain from using, the dominating conflict-handling style?

conflict-handling styles emerge: avoiding, dominating, compromising, obliging, and integrating (Rahim, 1983).

Avoiding Conflict-Handling Style

If you use an avoiding conflict-handling style in your group, you have a low concern for meeting the needs of both yourself and your group members (Rahim, 2002). To your group members, you appear uninterested in or apathetic toward the conflict. While you may have your own reasons for using the avoiding conflict-handling style, oftentimes individuals report using this style because they view conflict as hopeless, useless, or punishing (Filley, 1975), or they view the issues surrounding the conflict as trivial (Rahim & Bonoma, 1979). Consequently, if you use this style, you psychologically—and, if possible, physically—leave the conflict situation.

Dominating Conflict-Handling Style

If you use a dominating conflict-handling style in your group, you are more interested in satisfying your own needs than satisfying the needs of your group members (Rahim, 2002). To satisfy your own needs, you may embrace a "win-lose" mentality in which you focus on "winning" as your ultimate goal (Rahim, Buntzman, & White, 1999). Unfortunately, when you use this style in a small group, you risk alienating your group members and violating their trust because your motivation may be viewed as suspect and you may be perceived as having a hidden agenda.

Compromising Conflict-Handling Style

If you use a compromising conflict-handling style in your group, you strive to find a middle ground between meeting your own needs and meeting the needs of your group members (Rahim et al., 1999). When using this style, individuals tend to alternate between their own needs and the needs of their group members. One issue with this style is that it does force a group member to "give up" something. Over time, this "giving up" may result in group members feeling unappreciated or taken for granted.

Obliging Conflict-Handling Style

If you use an obliging conflict-handling style in your group, you are highly concerned with meeting the needs of your group members while ignoring your own needs (Rahim, 1983). You might choose to use this style either because you value the relationships you have developed with your group members or because you have a strong desire to be accepted by your group members. At the same time, you may not want to appear confrontational because you are fearful of hurting a group member's feelings (Filley, 1975). Regardless of why you use this style, you are concerned primarily with your group members' welfare.

Integrating Conflict-Handling Style

Groups that use the integrating conflict-handling style strive to meet the needs of all their members.

If you use an integrating conflict-handling style in your group, you are concerned with meeting the needs of both yourself and all your group members. When using this style, you refuse to avoid sacrificing either your needs or the needs of your group members for the good of the group (Filley, 1975). As such, you communicate in a way that stresses openness and the candid exchange of logic and emotion (Rahim, 2002). Not surprisingly, the integrating style is the preferred conflict-handling style among group members because this style produces higher-quality outcomes (Wall, Galanes, & Love, 1987), members regard it as the most effective style when it comes to problem solving or decision making (Kuhn & Poole, 2000), and it supports group member satisfaction (Wall & Galanes, 1986). Indeed, group members report using this style the most frequently (Farmer & Roth, 1998).

If you are interested in assessing your conflict-handling style, complete the ROCI-II instrument in "Assess Your Communication" on page 206 (Rahim, 1983). This instrument provides you with a good indication of the conflict-handling style you are most likely to use in your group. No matter the result, consider that your preferred style of conflict resolution may not always be the most appropriate given the issue facing your group, and in some instances, using a combination of styles can be more effective than relying on the use of a single style. At the same time, you may not use the same conflict-handling style with all your group members. Read the tips for when to use and when not to use each of the five conflict-handling styles listed in "Communication How-To: When to Use and Not to Use Conflict-Handling Styles" on page 208. In your groups, you may find there are instances when one conflict-handling style is more appropriate than another style.

SMALL GROUP AND TEAM COMMUNICATION AND CONVERGENCE

The study of small group and team communication is especially important to convergence in the Communication Age for two reasons. The first reason is that joining a group is now easier than ever before. Access to many groups, along with securing their contact information, can easily be obtained by conducting a general Google, Bing, or Yahoo search on the Internet; perusing websites such as www.supportgroups.com or www.stormthecastle.com; visiting a specific group's website; or uploading an application to your smartphone. The second reason is that many groups conduct a vast amount of their activity through mediated means. In the workplace, it is not uncommon for employees to use e-mail, cell phones, and voice messaging as a way to remain connected with one another both in and out of the office. Teleconferencing, blogs, and electronic meeting systems are other ways for work groups to engage in idea generation, problem solving, and decision making. Among family members and friends,

ASSESS YOUR COMMUNICATION

ROCI-II INSTRUMENT

This questionnaire contains statements about your communicative behaviors in a conflict situation with your group members. Indicate how often each statement is true for you personally according to the following scale:

If the statement is almost always true, write 5 in the blank.

If the statement is often true, write 4 in the blank.

If the statement is occasionally true, write 3 in the blank.

If the statement is rarely true, write 2 in the blank.

If the statement is almost never true, write 1 in the blank.

_____ 1. I try to investigate an issue with my group members to find a solution acceptable to us.

_____ 2. I attempt to avoid being "put on the spot" and try to keep my conflict with my group members to myself.

_____ 3. I use my influence to get my ideas accepted.

_____ 4. I generally try to satisfy the needs of my group members.

_____ 5. I try to find a middle course to resolve an impasse my group has reached.

_____ 6. I try to integrate my ideas with those of my group members to come up with a decision jointly.

_____ 7. I usually avoid open discussion of my differences with my group members.

_____ 8. I use my authority to get my ideas accepted.

_____ 9. I usually accommodate the wishes of my group members.

_____10. I usually propose a middle ground for breaking deadlocks.

_____11. I try to work with my group members to find solutions to a problem that satisfy all our expectations.

_____12. I try to stay away from disagreeing with my group members.

_____13. I use my expertise to help my group members make a decision in my favor.

_____14. I give in to the wishes of my group members.

_____15. I negotiate with my group members so we can reach a compromise.

_____16. I exchange accurate information with my group members so we can solve a problem together.

_____17. I avoid any unpleasant exchanges with my group members.

_____18. I am usually firm in pursuing my side of an issue.

_____19. I usually concede to my group members.

_____20. I "give and take" so a compromise can be made.

_____21. I try to bring all our concerns out in the open so that the issues can be resolved in the best possible way.

_____22. I try to keep any disagreement with my group members to myself in order to avoid hard feelings.

_____23. I sometimes use my power to win a competitive situation.

_____24. I often go along with the suggestions of my group members.

_____25. I collaborate with my group members to come up with decisions acceptable to us.

_____26. I try to satisfy the expectations of my group members.

_____27. I try to work with my group members to develop a proper understanding of the task.

Scoring:

1. Add your scores for items 1, 6, 11, 16, 21, 25, and 27. Divide by 7. This is your integrating conflict-handling score.

2. Add your scores for items 2, 7, 12, 17, and 22. Divide by 5. This is your avoiding conflict-handling score.

3. Add your scores for items 3, 8, 13, 18, and 23. Divide by 5. This is your dominating conflict-handling score.

4. Add your scores for items 4, 9, 14, 19, 24, and 26. Divide by 6. This is your obliging conflict-handling score.

5. Add your scores for items 5, 10, 15, and 20. Divide by 4. This is your compromising conflict-handling score.

Source: Rahim (1983).

Thinkstock

group e-mails, group texts, and private Facebook groups are employed as a means to remain connected, share news, and provide updates about the events occurring in their lives. Even some support groups, such as Alcoholics Anonymous, have introduced "real time" online meetings to enable members to participate in the group process, while learning groups such as Weight Watchers offer a variety of digital tools and mobile apps for online members.

Yet it is important to consider that, while technology and social media can be used to facilitate your participation in any small group, sustaining any group membership requires effort. Regardless of whether groups meet face to face

COMMUNICATION HOW-TO
WHEN TO USE AND NOT TO USE CONFLICT-HANDLING STYLES

Style	Use this style when . . .	Refrain from this style when . . .
Integrating	the task is complex the group has enough time to complete the task the group needs to secure additional resources and ideas	the task is simple an immediate solution or decision is required group members are unconcerned about outcome
Obliging	affective conflict arises group members have a high degree of ego involvement the task is important to group members	the task is important to you group members engage in misbehaviors group members are incorrect
Dominating	the group has limited time the members lack the necessary expertise to make a decision the group must make an unfavorable recommendation	the task is complex the members have a low degree of ego involvement the decision does not have to be made immediately
Avoiding	the task is simple affective conflict arises the group needs time to process the task	the task is important to you the group needs to pay immediate attention to the task procedural conflict arises
Compromising	the group is unable to reach consensus a temporary decision or solution is needed inequity conflict arises	the task is complex the group needs to engage in problem solving or decision making a power imbalance exists among members

Source: Rahim (2002).

or through mediated means, effective group membership takes work, energy, and commitment. It requires members to play the necessary roles and engage in shared leadership when needed by the group, utilize the appropriate problem-solving and decision-making procedures, and develop a communication climate where input and feedback are both encouraged and welcomed (Wheelan, 2016). Belonging to small groups and teams is only going to become more crucial in the Communication Age. Thus, it is your job and responsibility to be aware of and understand how communication occurs in the small group.

WHAT YOU'VE LEARNED   Now that you have studied this chapter, you should be able to:

1 **Identify the key features, advantages, and disadvantages of small group communication.**

Small groups possess six key features that differentiate them from other communication contexts. There are also several advantages and disadvantages associated with group work. When joining a new group or beginning a new task with an existing group, you need to approach the experience in a positive way and refuse to let your prior group experiences interfere with your current group task.

▶ Brainstorming

 Why Students Hate Groups

2 **List and define each of the five stages of group development.**

Not all groups will proceed through the forming, storming, norming, performing, and adjourning

stages of group development at the same rate. In fact, the rate at which any of your groups move through these stages will depend, in part, on the life span of the group, the amount of time members will belong to the group, or whether members meet physically or virtually.

▶ Tuckman's Model

3 **Distinguish between task roles and building and maintenance roles.**

Remember to always consider the group task before you select the appropriate task role or building and maintenance role to play. If the task is directed toward making progress toward the group goal, you should play a task role; if the task is focused on developing or maintaining relationships among group members, you should play a building and maintenance role.

 Using Group Work in Online Courses: Technology and Education Today

 Student Roles

④ Describe how group members can engage in shared leadership.

Shared leadership is a behavior in which any group member can engage. Doing so allows you and your members to assume the leadership role when it is most likely needed by your group.

▶ Shared Leadership

⑤ Differentiate among the five types of conflict-handling styles used by small group members.

When group conflict arises, group members should consider the situation before they decide whether to use an integrating, obliging, dominating, avoiding, or compromising conflict-handling style. Because group conflict can arise over substantive, affective, procedural, or inequity issues, you should use the conflict-handling style that is the most appropriate given the circumstances.

🎙 Students' Work Ethic Affected By Peer Groups, Desire to Be Popular

KEY TERMS

Review key terms with eFlashcards. **edge.sagepub.com/edwards2e**

REFLECT

1.   Select a small group to which you currently belong. Apply the six features of small group communication to this group. What are some additional advantages and disadvantages of being a member of this small group?

2.   Review the group roles listed in Figure 8.3. Of these roles, toward which are you more likely to gravitate? Which roles are you not equipped

to play? To what extent does the type of group affect your desire or ability to play a group role?

3.   Complete the ROCI-II assessment and identify your conflict-handling style. In a work group, how does this style help your group accomplish its task? How does this style hinder your group's progress toward the task?

REVIEW

To check your answers go to **edge.sagepub.com/edwards2e**

1. Define small group communication.

2. _____ references the psychological and/ or physical boundaries that distinguish a group member from a non–group member.

3. How does a *group norm* differ from a *group sanction*?

4. What is brainstorming?

5. The five stages of group development are _____, _____, _____, _____, and _____.

6. A group member role is an _____ and _____ pattern of communicative behaviors that members expect from one another.

7. To avoid groupthink, one group member should be assigned the role of _____.

8. _____ refers to the communicative behaviors any group member can enact to demonstrate leadership.

9. A group member who uses a(n) _____ conflict-handling style is concerned with meeting the needs of both herself and her group members.

WORKPLACE AND ORGANIZATIONAL COMMUNICATION

WHAT YOU'LL LEARN

After studying this chapter, you will be able to:

1 Identify the components that comprise workplace communication.

2 Differentiate among the three levels of organizational culture.

3 Explain how employees are socialized into an organization.

4 Describe the ways in which workers engage in dissent at the workplace.

5 Distinguish among the types of relationships that develop at work.

On February 6, 2015, in anticipation of starting a new job at Jet's Pizza in Mansfield, Texas, a teenager who went by the screen name Cella took to Twitter to announce her feelings about her upcoming first day of work. "Ew," her message tweeted, "I start this f—k a— job tomorrow," which was accompanied by seven thumbs-down emojis (Wagner, 2015). But instead of starting her job at Jet's, where she would have been responsible for taking orders, working the register, and making submarine sandwiches and pizza, Cella was fired almost immediately by her boss, Robert Waple, who responded to her tweet the next day with a tweet of his own: "No you don't start that FA job today! I just fired you! Good luck with your no money, no job life!" ("Twitter Firing," 2015). Interestingly, the tweet that Waple sent to Cella was the first time he had used his Twitter account since 2009, explaining that while he would have preferred to call Cella and fire her over the telephone, he was informed about her tweet while he was away from his office, so he fired her using the same medium she used to complain about her job ("Twitter Firing," 2015).

Unfortunately, this type of story is becoming all too familiar. Regardless of the reasons why some employees may choose to whine about some aspect of their job tasks or their workplace, social networking sites such as Facebook and Twitter,

counter-institutional websites such as www.glassdoor.com and www.jobscmob.com, personal blogs, petitions initiated on change.org, and YouTube are providing workers with an avenue to vent, complain, or protest about the workplace environment that did not exist years ago. Instead of writing a formal letter, making a telephone call, or scheduling a face-to-face meeting with a workplace superior, frustrated workers are embracing technology that makes their complaints immediate, publicly accessible, and anonymous. Not surprisingly, many companies have adopted policies regarding this kind of online behavior from their employees.

Learning how to become a productive member of your workplace extends far beyond simply showing up for work, completing your assigned tasks, and going home. Rather, today's workplace requires you to develop a thorough understanding of the communicative practices adopted by and used in your organization that then enables you to become a productive colleague. In this chapter, we focus on several of these practices and how these practices are vital to your workplace success.

WHAT IS WORKPLACE COMMUNICATION?

Similar to the purpose behind small group and team communication discussed in Chapter 8, communication at work is also task-oriented and goal-directed. Perhaps the best way to conceptualize workplace communication is to consider it as the communicative exchanges that occur among coworkers, managers, team members, committees, and task forces within an organization and that are aimed toward accomplishing company goals and objectives.

Another way to explore workplace communication is to consider it as organizational communication, which is conceptualized as the process through which members develop, maintain, and modify practices through their communication with both internal superiors, subordinates, and peers and external clients, customers, and stakeholders (Keyton, 2011). From this consideration, workplace communication can be considered to be consequential as well as task-oriented and goal-directed (Keyton, 2011). These communicative exchanges and complex processes, which are rooted in information sharing, relational maintenance, expressing negative emotion, and organizing (Keyton et al., 2013), then form the basis for the communication networks, channels, and climate adopted by and utilized in the workplace.

Communication Networks

Communication networks consist of the formal and informal patterns of interaction that regulate the extent to which and how you and your organizational members

CAREER FRONTIER: TELEWORKING

One advantage of teleworking is that it allows employees to work from the comfort of their homes.

IN YOUR CAREER, there is a good chance that not all of your workplace relationships will actually develop in the workplace. In the Communication Age, a growing number of workers are engaging in teleworking, which is the practice of working off-site (i.e., away from the physical workplace) while remaining connected to the workplace through a host of communication technologies such as the Internet, e-mail, voice mail, cell phones, instant messaging, and virtual private networks. While some teleworkers work solely from their homes, other teleworkers divide their time between their homes and their offices or travel to various work sites. According to FlexJobs.com, the number of corporations offering employees the opportunity to engage in teleworking is steadily increasing (Reynolds, 2015), with more than 13 million Americans working from home at least one day a week in 2010 (Soroker, 2014). In addition to helping employees achieve a better work–life balance and improve their overall quality of work and family life (Madsen, 2011), teleworking provides workers with the flexibility to work at their own pace and devote their time to a task with minimal distractions or interruptions (Leonardi, Treem, & Jackson, 2010). Some disadvantages, however, include feelings of alienation and isolation from the workplace, the inability to form peer relationships with coworkers, and the potential to feel disconnected from the organization. Teleworking also creates a false impression of availability, in that both coworkers and clients expect teleworkers to be accessible through technology at all times. Despite these disadvantages, however, teleworkers generally report that they are satisfied with their decision to work off-site and are able to avoid the stress associated with office politics, meetings, and general workplace interruptions (Fonner & Roloff, 2010). When contemplating the option to engage in teleworking in your future employment, consider these advantages and disadvantages.

talk with one another. Formal communication networks are both prescribed and sanctioned by the workplace and occur through downward communication, upward communication, and horizontal communication. Downward communication is initiated by superiors and directed toward their subordinates. When managers engage in downward communication with their employees, they do so to provide them with task directions; workplace policies, procedures, and practices; performance feedback; and organizational goals and objectives (Harris, 1993). Upward communication is initiated by employees as a way to interact with their managers. Through participating in upward communication, employees can relay a variety of information to their superiors such as job-related updates and concerns, workplace and task problems, and suggestions or complaints about the workplace or their tasks (Harris, 1993). Horizontal communication occurs solely

Horizontal communication allows coworkers to develop friendships with one another, which may or may not extend outside the workplace.

between coworkers and enables them to coordinate their tasks, share information, engage in problem solving and decision making, and build rapport (Harris, 1993). In some cases, horizontal communication allows employees to develop friendships with their coworkers, which may or may not extend outside the workplace, and to serve as a source of work support in helping one another develop skills and acquire knowledge (Allen & Finkelstein, 2003).

Informal communication networks are established through the social interactions that occur among coworkers. Unlike formal communication networks, these networks are not sanctioned by the organization and often emerge

ETHICAL CONNECTION

BULLYING AS AN ORGANIZATIONAL PROBLEM

Workplace bullying can take many forms, one of which is verbal abuse.

According to the Workplace Bullying Institute, almost 50% of surveyed employees have either experienced bullying firsthand or have witnessed a colleague being bullied by another coworker (Workplace Bullying Institute, 2014). Workplace bullying is characterized by its intensity, repetitiveness, duration, and perceived power disparity. Communication expert Pamela Lutgen-Sandvik and her colleagues (2007) operationalized it as the experience of at least two negative acts that occur at least weekly for 6 or more months in situations where the recipients find it difficult to defend against and stop abuse. Although bullying can be a behavior in which any organizational member engages, researchers have found that men who hold positions of workplace power or status are more likely to be identified as a bully (Workplace Bullying Institute, 2014), with their bullying behaviors

taking several forms. Of these forms, the most common is verbal abuse (e.g., shouting, name calling, and swearing) and behaviors that can be labeled as threatening, humiliating, or hostile (Namie & Namie, 2009). Other forms include supervisory abuse of authority (e.g., undeserved evaluation, tarnished reputation), interference with work performance, and destruction of workplace relationships (Namie & Namie, 2009).

The negative effects of workplace bullying are staggering. While some targets will complain to a superior, file a formal or an informal complaint, or even initiate a lawsuit against the harasser, many targets simply choose to take no action (Namie & Namie, 2009). As such, it is no surprise that bullying results in increased job stress and decreased job satisfaction and job ratings (Lutgen-Sandvik et al., 2007). Lost productivity, soaring absenteeism rates, and increases in insurance and worker's compensation claims also occur (Lutgen-Sandvik, Namie, & Namie, 2009). While bullying is considered to be an organizational problem (Lutgen-Sandvik et al., 2009), not all organizations are equipped to deal with it. Cowan (2011) found that not only do several organizations lack policies on how to confront or prevent bullying, but also that some organizations fail even to recognize bullying as the prevalent national and international workplace problem that it has become.

QUESTIONS

1. To what extent do you believe you are obligated to report a workplace bully or a coworker's bullying behaviors to a supervisor?

2. Are there any workplace circumstances in which bullying can be considered justifiable?

through ritualized or mundane activities in which employees participate such as taking a break, walking to and from the parking lot together, texting one another during the workday, chatting regularly via Instagram, or contributing to gossip. Gossip includes the positive and negative things workers say about an absent coworker's job performance, work behaviors and relationships, or career progress (Grosser, Lopez-Kidwell, & Labianca, 2010; Kurland & Pelled, 2000). It is prevalent in most organizations, particularly among coworkers who consider themselves to be friends. Coworkers who both share work tasks and consider themselves friends are more likely to engage in both positive and negative gossip than those employees who either are solely acquaintances or restrict their work communication to task-related topics (Grosser et al., 2010). And while gossip arguably can be detrimental to workplace productivity, it offers a way for workers to release tension or stress, acts as a bonding agent, provides workers with needed information, and gives additional insight into the organizational culture (Michelson, van Iterson, & Waddinton, 2010). Despite these benefits, not all organizations welcome gossip, nor do they allow gossip to become an established company practice.

▶ **COMMUNICATION IN ACTION 9.2**

WATCH: Skillful Leadership

An executive coach discusses how workplace leaders are chosen. What technical skills are important for leaders to possess?

Communication Channels

Communication channels refer specifically to the means through which workplace messages are transmitted between and among coworkers. These channels can take many forms, such as face-to-face interactions like meetings and training sessions; written communication such as memos and e-mails; mediated communication, which includes phone calls, instant messaging, and videoconferencing; and mass communication like company newsletters or web postings. Of these forms, mediated communication is becoming the most prevalent in today's workplace. According to a recent survey of organizational workers, face-to-face communication, the telephone, and e-mail are the most frequently used communication channels (Sias, Pedersen, Gallagher, & Kopaneva, 2012), whereas face-to-face communication, e-mail, and phone and voice mail are among the channels employees prefer when communicating with their managers (Men, 2014). Consider the recommendations listed in "Communication How-To" (p. 218) for using communication channels. What suggestions could be made for how to use these channels in your workplace?

▶ **COMMUNICATION IN ACTION 9.3**

WATCH: Superior-subordinate Communication

A superior-subordinate dyad discuss ways in which to build a customer base. How can managers use the characteristics of a supportive climate to create more satisfying interactions with their employees?

Communication Climate

Communication climate references whether coworkers experience feelings of openness, trust, and support when interacting with one another (Smidts, Pruyn, & van Riel, 2001). These feelings emerge from the verbal and nonverbal communication

COMMUNICATIONHOW-TO
RECOMMENDATIONS FOR USING
COMMUNICATION CHANNELS AT WORK

1. Be familiar with the expectations (and any rules) the organization has for using communication channels, including both mandatory use and restricted use. In the Communication Age, using e-mail often is mandatory.

2. Use the communication channels with which you are both familiar and comfortable, but keep in mind that your workplace may require you to use some channels with which you are less familiar and more uncomfortable. If this is the case, learn how to use these channels.

3. Consider the reasons why communication channels are used in the workplace. These reasons include seeking information, persuading your superiors and peers, providing documentation, being entertained, and being social. In many workplaces, the web

is used most frequently for information-seeking purposes while face-to-face communication is used most frequently for persuasion.

4. Determine the communication channel that is the most appropriate for the reason(s) why you are using the channel. Use this channel appropriately and in the way in which it was intended. Many workplaces frown on the use of e-mail and the Internet for either entertainment or social reasons.

5. Consider using a different follow-up channel to increase the effectiveness and the efficiency of your task. For instance, follow up an e-mail message with either a face-to-face conversation or a telephone call.

Source: Based on Stephens, Sornes, Rice, Browning, & Saetre (2010).

Images: thinkstock and istock.

and listening behaviors that coworkers use with one another. From these behaviors, two types of communication climate can form: a supportive communication climate and a defensive communication climate.

In a supportive communication climate, workplace members feel that their contributions are welcomed and valued. Coworkers share their ideas, accept constructive criticism, participate in problem solving and decision making, offer suggestions, engage in conflict resolution, and utilize critical listening. More important, workers take ownership of their ideas, collaborate with one another to complete tasks, and openly express their thoughts, feelings, and emotions. They also attempt to be empathic toward, and resolve to treat, one another in an equal and equitable manner. In short, workplaces that exemplify a supportive communication climate have members who engage in confirmation, provide one another with feedback, and listen to one another. Employees engage in downward, upward, and horizontal communication openly and without fear of reprisal, and workplace interaction is not restricted to any one particular channel.

Corbis

Workplace culture at Zappos encourages employees to develop relationships with one another.

In a defensive communication climate, workplace members feel that their contributions are neither welcomed nor valued. Instead, members feel stifled, threatened, and confused when it comes to communicating their ideas and offering any suggestions to their coworkers. They become judgmental, interrogate one another, impose their point of view rather than considering their coworkers' points of view, and communicate less than honestly with one another. Because little trust and empathy exist in a defensive communicate climate, workplace members may adopt an "I don't care" attitude either toward one another or the task at hand, and they may purposely treat one another differently based on each coworker's position, title, or tenure. Workers hesitate to participate fully in downward, upward, or horizontal communication; they may be less inclined to use written or mediated channels because they are fearful that this use could be held against them.

Generally, then, the extent to which any workplace uses formal and informal communication networks, exhibits a preference for types of communication channels, and establishes either a supportive or a defensive communication climate is dependent on the specific organization. However, this dependence is linked inextricably to the communicative practices of the workplace, which include its culture.

WORKPLACE CULTURE

To become a functional and productive member of any workplace, workers must develop an understanding of the workplace culture. Take a minute and reflect upon the impressions you made about your first week on your most recent job. As you entered the front doors of the workplace, how far did you have to walk from where you parked? Did you pay attention to the décor, the manner in which your coworkers dressed, or the ways in which your coworkers communicated with one another? How diverse were your coworkers in terms of their sex, race, and ethnicity? How friendly or reserved was your boss? Did your coworkers seem happy, complacent, or miserable? What were the topics of their conversation? Were you able to leave on time, or did you find yourself working late?

These initial impressions are important because they serve as the foundation for how employees determine the culture of a workplace. However, workplace culture is much more than just a set of initial impressions. Workplace culture is considered to be the ways in which employees think, act, and behave that emerge as a result of their interactions with one another at work (Hudson & Irwin, 2010; Keyton, 2011). Grasping the culture of any workplace is important because it provides you with a clear focus and a way to make sense of your duties, tasks, and reasons for working there. In fact, one reason why some employees never succeed at their jobs is because they do not "fit" into the workplace culture (Yang & Trap, 2011). One way to gain a more thorough knowledge of the workplace culture is to examine the three levels that comprise it, which are artifacts, values, and assumptions (Schein, 2004).

▶ **COMMUNICATION IN ACTION 9.4**

WATCH: Organizational Culture

Creative directors share their impressions of their workplace culture. To what extent are you willing to discuss your workplace's culture with other people?

Artifacts

The first level, artifacts, refers to the objects that employees can see, touch, or hear that provide them with an initial impression of how the organization operates (see Figure 9.1). For many workers, the first impression of workplace culture relies heavily on their interpretation of these items. While the artifacts that compose any organization's culture can be endless, they generally can be grouped into four categories: symbolic, role, interactive, and contextual (Driskill & Brenton, 2011).

Symbolic Artifacts

Symbolic artifacts center on how the workplace uses language and nonverbal codes to represent the values of the organization. At Southwest Airlines, for instance, flight attendants do not behave or dress like stereotypical flight attendants. Because Southwest wants its customers to experience a unique and enjoyable flying experience, flight attendants are able to communicate freely with their passengers during flight. They may sing or tell jokes over the intercom, or offer in-flight contests with a first prize of free travel; they also are allowed to wear polo shirts and shorts while working (Smith, 2004). Southwest values its employees as well and acknowledges their birthdays and family births and deaths by sending a card or note in addition to maintaining e-mail contact with them (Sadri & Lees, 2001). Likewise, employees who need to contact their supervisors or upper management have access to do so (Gittell, 2003).

Other examples of symbolic elements include the metaphors used by employees to describe their workplace, the stories that employees trade with one another about the organization, and the symbols used to represent a company such as logos or mottos. For example, as a reflection of its recent acquisition of AirTran Airways, Southwest Airlines underwent a significant rebranding campaign by

FIGURE 9.1
CULTURAL ARTIFACTS

Annual reports	History of workplace	Physical layout
Brochures	Informal communication networks	Policies and procedures
Business cards	Jargon	Rewards and punishments
Communication channels	Leadership style	Rituals and ceremonies
Communication climate	Location of workplace	Selection interviews
Cultural roles	Meetings	Small groups and teams
Diversity	Memorable messages	Socialization activities
First day at work	Metaphors	Stories
Formal communication networks	Mission statements	Technology
Friendship	Newsletters	Wall colors and hangings
Furniture	Performance appraisals	Websites

Source: Keyton (2011).

developing a new logo—a large heart painted on the belly of each aircraft—which supports its new motto, "New look, same heart" (Lorenzetti, 2014). Both this new logo and new motto are rooted in the notion of LUV, which has been a symbol associated with Southwest Airlines since its beginnings in 1971 (Southwest Airlines, 2015).

Southwest Airlines' colorful aircraft and logo are two examples of how a workplace's symbolic artifacts offer insight into its culture.

Role Artifacts

Role artifacts focus on the specific cultural roles coworkers play within the workplace. Perhaps the most influential role is the hero role, which refers to a workplace member who embodies the workplace culture and thus is able to exert a tremendous amount of influence on other employees through his or her daily workplace behaviors (Deal & Kennedy, 2000). One classic hero is Steve Jobs, the late CEO of Apple Inc. Jobs cofounded Apple on April 1, 1976, in his parents' garage in the Silicon Valley when he was only 21 years old (Sarno & Goffard, 2011). The college dropout was the driving force behind this company until he resigned in May 1985. After starting the computer company NeXT and the animation company Pixar, he returned to Apple in 1997 as an interim CEO. In 1998, under Jobs's tutelage, Apple introduced the iMac computer, followed by the iBook laptop in 1999, the iPod in 2001, iTunes in 2003, the iPhone in 2007, and the iPad in 2010. Heralded by *Time* magazine as an American icon (Isaacson, 2011), Jobs ran Apple with his own distinctive management style that focused on challenging employees to be creative and innovative (Grossman & McCracken, 2011).

Other cultural roles include the outlaw, a coworker who fails to follow the workplace rules and policies but is allowed to do so because he or she has the organization's best interests at heart; the high priest, an employee who guards and protects the company's values; the whisperer, a worker who has the power to effect change within the workplace but is not the formal leader; and a cabal member, who is interested solely in his or her self-promotion (Deal & Kennedy, 2000). Not all organizations have workers who play all of these cultural roles, some workplaces have members who play multiple cultural roles, and some workplaces have members who do not play any of these cultural roles.

Interactive Elements

Interactive elements revolve around the informal and formal communicative events, recognized and sanctioned by the workplace, in which coworkers participate. These elements include award banquets, gift exchanges during the holiday season, and breakroom banter. They also can include the day-to-day work practices of an organization's employees. For example, at Zappos, a national online shoe and clothing company, CEO Tony Hsieh has worked diligently to create a culture that employees consider to be fun yet empowering (Heathfield, 2015). Employees are encouraged to decorate their work spaces with wacky signs, streamers, and stuffed animals; break rooms are stocked with mini-fridges that contain free snacks; and customer service representatives are permitted to send flowers, cards, and cookies to Zappos customers (Hodge, 2015). At Google, workers are encouraged to participate in "20% time," in which they can spend a day per week working on a project in which they have a personal interest, with the idea that this project ultimately will become a company product or feature (Jackson, 2013).

Contextual Elements

Contextual elements refer to the parameters surrounding the existence of the workplace, such as its location or history. For some organizations, the long and storied history of the workplace—why it was founded, the circumstances under which it was founded, and any critical events that affected its growth—is a vital piece of information in assessing the workplace culture. For other companies, the location reflects its culture. Walmart, which boasts more than 11,000 retail outlets in 27 countries and employs over 2.2 million people worldwide, has remained rooted in Rogers, Arkansas, since its beginnings in 1962. Not only is its corporate headquarters housed in its original Bentonville, Arkansas, general office warehouse—although since the warehouse was converted in the 1980s, the corporate campus has expanded to 15 buildings that house over 11,000 associates—but visitors to Bentonville can also tour the admission-free Walmart Visitor Center located on Main Street. The Visitor Center features Walton's 5&10, a store that sells items reminiscent of the first dime store opened by Sam Walton in the 1950s; an exhibit gallery that presents an interactive history of the Walmart corporation; and the Spark Café, a coffee shop and gift shop (Walmart Corporate, 2015).

Values

Each workplace develops a set of abstract ideas about which behaviors are acceptable or unacceptable, right or wrong, or important or unimportant for how its employees communicate with one another and their clients, customers, and competitors. These ideas manifest themselves as values, which are the strategies, goals, and philosophies that act as guidelines for work behavior (Keyton, 2011; Schein, 2004). Not only do these values provide a way for workers to interpret the meaning behind their work behaviors, but they also represent the boundaries governing appropriate and inappropriate work behavior. In some organizations, values may be invisible, abstract, and not readily identifiable (Keyton, 2011). At Red Frog Events, however, a Chicago, Illinois–based company that specializes in the sponsorship and promotion of fun run events across the nation, values are visible and accessible on the corporate website. Statements such as "Live With Passion," "Deliver Greatness," and "Foster Family Spirit" are listed on the company's website as a way to remind employees about the values that Red Frog Events embodies in both its products and its employees (Red Frog Events, n.d.). These values also reflect founder Joe Reynolds's intent to create a culture that not only fosters creativity and personal development among his employees (Newman, 2011), but also highlights its workers as "the most prized office feature" of the organization (Red Frog Events, n.d.).

For organizations such as Walmart, their humble beginnings still continue to represent their core values and corporate mission.

Assumptions

The taken-for-granted beliefs, perceptions, and feelings that members hold about themselves, their relationships with coworkers, and the workplace itself are known as assumptions, the third level of workplace culture. These assumptions are the ultimate sources of the values and actions of an organization (Schein, 2004); they offer an explanation for the artifacts displayed purposely, and they reinforce the strategies, goals, and philosophies that compose a workplace's values. These assumptions are deeply held, are resistant to change, and suggest that any deviation from accepted organizational practices is unacceptable (Keyton, 2011). At Clif Bar, an energy food and snack manufacturer located in Emeryville, California, employees are encouraged to adopt an eco-friendly and healthy lifestyle (Magalindan, 2014). For instance, employees are encouraged to participate in Clif Bar's Cool Car and Cool Home programs: Those workers who purchase eco-friendly cars, opt to take public transportation, or choose either to walk or bike to work are reimbursed anywhere from $1,500 to $6,500; those who replace their home windows or install solar panels at their residence can be reimbursed $1,000. Once arriving on campus, workers can dine at Kali's Kitchen, which serves food made with local organic ingredients and is subsidized by the company, or work out at its onsite gym by attending a variety of free classes such as yoga or kickboxing or participating in free personal training. Not only is this eco-friendly lifestyle endorsed by Clif Bar, but it also is reflected in its business practices. When the company moved into its new energy-efficient headquarters in 2010, the building incorporated solar panels and was built using repurposed wood taken from old barns and railroad tracks (Mangalindan, 2014). Through these benefits, the assumptions underlying Clif Bar's organizational culture are reflected.

Three caveats about workplace culture are worth noting. First, not all employees will view or define the culture similarly. Impressions of a workplace culture can differ based on the subcultures to which coworkers belong. For example, individuals in management may have a very different idea of company culture versus those in administrative support. Workers who distance themselves from one another using an "us" versus "them" mentality often do so based on the physical, generational, and occupational differences that divide them (Parker, 2000). For other employees, the emergence of a subculture is linked directly to perceived differences in treatment based on demographic characteristics such as race, sex, age, sexual orientation, or gender identity.

Second, the culture of any organization can range from strong to weak. In a strong culture, the artifacts are connected strongly to the values and assumptions, the values permeate the entire organization, and most employees identify strongly with the culture; in a weak culture, the artifacts are loosely connected to the values and assumptions, the values are limited to top management, and workers identify more strongly with their subcultures (Driskill & Brenton, 2011). Third, a single artifact will not provide an accurate depiction of any workplace culture. Rather, the meaning of cultural artifacts often is embedded within other artifacts, and employees should consider examining several artifacts in concert with the values and assumptions. Refer to the "Reading a Culture's Artifacts, Values, and Assumptions" questions listed in "Communication How-To" on page 225. How would you answer these questions about your workplace?

In summary, the workplace culture comprises artifacts, values, and assumptions. In many organizations, one of the best ways for employees to develop an

THE HUMAN RIGHTS CAMPAIGN

iStock

Working toward achieving workplace equality for lesbian, gay, bisexual, and transgender employees is one goal of the Human Rights Campaign.

THE HUMAN RIGHTS CAMPAIGN (HRC) is a Washington, D.C.–based civil rights organization whose purpose is to work toward achieving equality for lesbian, gay, bisexual, and transgender (LGBT) individuals across many facets (e.g., relational, health) of their lives. This includes their work lives, as it is estimated that over 50% of LGBT individuals hide their sexual orientation or gender identity from their employers ("Transforming Our Jobs," 2014). Since 2002, HRC has published the Corporate Equality Index, an annual chronicle of the results of a national survey conducted among more than 4,000 private-sector, for-profit organizations in the United States. Working with the organization's human resources department, the HRC scores each organization on four criteria, totaling 100 points: the inclusion of equal employment opportunities for both sexual orientation and gender identity/expression; the provision of employment benefits, including equivalent benefits for different- and same-sex partners as well as transgender-inclusive health coverage; organizational competency on LGBT issues and concerns (e.g., diversity training, establishment of diversity councils); and public commitment to the LGBT community. If any organization willfully or knowingly engages in any activity that undermines LGBT equality, 25 points are deducted from its score. In 2015, some 366 organizations, such as Apple, Barnes & Noble, Macy's, Toyota, United Airlines, and Yahoo, to name a few, received a top score of 100% and were recognized as "Best Places to Work for LGBT Equality." For more information about the Human Rights Campaign or the Corporate Equality Index 2015, visit HRC's website at www. hrc.org. The organization also offers a free online database of both public- and private-sector employers, which can be accessed at www.hrc.org/employersearch (Corporate Equality Index 2015, 2014).

understanding of their workplace culture is through participation in the company's socialization process. Only by going through the socialization process—considered to be a give and take between newcomers and the workplace—can employees become functional and productive organizational members.

WORKPLACE SOCIALIZATION

When any individuals start working at a job, they go through some type of introductory meeting or training. They meet the people with whom they will be working, they are introduced to their superiors, and they complete a multitude of paperwork. These initial tasks are part of their socialization to the work environment. Workplace socialization is the process by which organizational newcomers learn about the values, norms, and expectations that will enable them to become fully contributing members of the workplace and occurs in three stages.

COMMUNICATIONHOW-TO
READING A CULTURE'S
ARTIFACTS, VALUES, AND ASSUMPTIONS

1. What are the dominant stories about the organization that colleagues tell? What messages are they trying to convey by telling these stories?

2. Think of several influential people in the workplace. What roles do these people play in the workplace? In what ways do these roles embody the values of the workplace?

3. What are the organizational ceremonies/rituals in which employees participate? What purpose(s) do these ceremonies/rituals serve?

4. What do you know about the history of the workplace? How important is the location of the workplace to its history?

5. What kinds of beliefs and values officially or unofficially dominate the organization?

Source: Driskill & Brenton (2011).

Stage 1: Anticipatory Stage

The anticipatory stage of socialization begins the moment that individuals begin to prepare for a future job at a workplace. Considered to be the first stage of workplace socialization (Jablin, 2001), this is when individuals explore possible jobs and organizations, determine whether they possess the requisite skills and abilities needed for a specific job, and contemplate whether their needs and values are congruent with the needs and values of a prospective workplace. To do so, prospective organizational members engage in vocational choice and organizational choice, which requires them to consult a variety of information-providing sources about a specific job or a particular workplace (Jablin, 1985a, 1985b). Traditionally, these sources included seeking advice from family members, friends, and peers; reflecting on prior educational, work, and volunteer experiences; or gathering information by watching television shows or reading books (Kramer, 2010). However, it is now more typical to gain information about a potential employer by perusing corporate websites on the Internet, consulting commercial websites such as www.monster.com or www.beyond.com, or conducting a Google search. From these outlets, you not only can make sense of the organization and the benefits it offers, but you also can gain a glimpse into the workplace culture.

In addition to preparing for future employment, the anticipatory stage encompasses the perspectives we embrace about work, the role that work plays in our lives, and the fulfillment we receive from our jobs. As organizational researchers have noted, today's workplace employs four generations of workers, all of which differ in their attitudes toward work life. These four generations are the Traditionalists, who were born between 1925 and 1945; the Baby Boomers, who were born between 1946 and 1964; Generation X, who were born between 1965 and 1980; and the Millennials, who were born between 1981 and 1999 (Kapoor & Solomon, 2011). Aside from the differences listed in Figure 9.2, a primary distinction that separates

Using the Google search engine is one way that individuals can explore vocational choice and organizational choice.

Thinkstock

the Millennials from the other three generations is their desire to develop strong communication relationships with their coworkers. Not only do Millennials expect to communicate with their supervisors and managers, but they also expect this communication to be frequent, open, and supportive (Myers & Sadaghiani, 2010). They also exhibit a preference for working in small groups or teams. Moreover, Millennials consider a "real job" to be one that enables them to become financially autonomous while pursuing a career that they find enjoyable (O'Connor & Raile, 2015). Yet despite these differences, all four generations generally are similar in their reports of job satisfaction, organizational commitment, and likelihood to leave their jobs (Costanza, Badger, Fraser, Severt, & Gade, 2012).

Stage 2: Assimilation Stage

The assimilation stage of socialization starts once employees begin their first day of work. During this second stage, they are integrated into the culture of the organization over time with hopes that they will embrace the norms and values of the workplace. This stage, which can occur over an infinite amount of time, consists of two interrelated phases. The first phase is labeled the encounter phase and is viewed

FIGURE 9.2
GENERATIONAL DIFFERENCES

Difference	Traditionals	Baby Boomers	Generation X	Millennials
Work ethic	Dedicated and hard working	Driven and workaholic	Strike a balance; only work as hard as needed	Ambitious but not entirely focused
Work focus	Task-oriented	Relationship- and results-driven	Task-oriented and results-driven	Global and networked
Commitment and loyalty to the organization	Express loyalty and commitment to the organization	Express loyalty and commitment to the organization	More loyal to coworkers than to the organization	More loyal and committed to an idea, cause, or product than to the organization
Preferred ways to learn soft skills	On the job, discussion groups	On the job, discussion groups	On the job, one-on-one coaching	On the job, peer interaction and feedback
Preferred work environment	Conservative and hierarchical	Democratic and humane	Functional, fun, and efficient	Collaborative, creative, and diverse
Preferred leadership attributes	Prefer leaders who are credible, listen well, and are trustworthy	Prefer leaders who are credible, trustworthy, and farsighted	Prefer leaders who are credible, trustworthy, and farsighted	Prefer leaders who listen well, are dependable, and are dedicated
View of work	An obligation	An exciting adventure	A difficult challenge	A means to an end

Source: Modified from Generational Differences Chart (n.d.) and Tolbize (2008).

Communication **unplugged**

TO IMPROVE WORK LIFE, BALANCE YOUR WORK LIFE WITH YOUR PERSONAL LIFE

iStock

Work-life balance requires employees to establish a physical separation between the time they spend at work and the time they spend at home.

For many workers in the Communication Age, work–life balance is an issue that can impede their ability to be a productive and functional organizational member. According to WorkLifeBalance .com, work–life balance occurs when individuals are able to experience meaningful achievement and enjoyment across four areas of their lives (i.e., work, family, friends, and self) on a daily basis. Although today's employees seek work–life balance by expressing the desire for flexibility in the amount of time spent at work, the space in which they accomplish work, the manner in which they are evaluated, and the ways in which they are compensated (Cowan & Hoffman, 2007), many organizations send mixed messages about the importance of striking a work–life balance, such as "work always comes first" and "balancing work and life is an employee responsibility" (Hoffman & Cowan, 2008). Ultimately, it is in your best interest to seek and obtain this balance.

Work–life balance does not mean that the balance will always be equal (WorkLifeBalance.com, 2003); rather, you will have to strive to

arrive at a balance that is appropriate at any given time. Not only is it important to establish a psychological separation between your work life and your personal life, but you must make purposeful decisions about how you choose to divide your time spent at work and your time spent at home (Schultz, Hoffman, Fredman, & Bainbridge, 2012). Cultivating relationships outside of the workplace is equally important (Schultz et al., 2012). While it is not unusual for workers to initiate friendships with their colleagues, it is healthy to develop and maintain relationships with individuals who are not associated with either your work or your workplace so that you are not spending your personal time gossiping about coworkers, discussing an upcoming project, or commiserating together over an impending deadline.

WHAT TO DO NEXT

To develop work–life balance, try to:

- Turn off your personal cell phone when you arrive at work. Only check it for texts or calls when you are expecting a message from someone.

- Block Facebook and Instagram from your workplace computer or tablet so you are not tempted to repeatedly check for status updates or messages, which will then allow you to concentrate more fully on your job tasks and projects.

- Dedicate your lunch hour or break time to engaging in a non-work-related activity. Go for a walk, read a magazine, or go to lunch with a friend, but whatever you do, step away from your office to do it and leave your electronic devices behind.

- Turn off your computer, put your tablet away, and refrain from checking your iPhone messages once you have physically left the workplace.

- If it is vital to remain electronically connected to the office after your work day has ended, give yourself a time limit (e.g., 30 minutes) for checking your messages and adhere to it.

as a "breaking-in" phase during which newcomers address any expectations they held about the job and the workplace prior to starting work as well as adjust to their new work role and attempt to make sense of the workplace culture (Jablin, 1987). Workers attempt to resolve any uncertainty that has arisen as a result of being unfamiliar with the company, their job tasks, and the workplace culture (Kramer, 2010). The second phase is labeled the metamorphosis phase and occurs as newcomers become comfortable in their work role, adopt the practices and policies of their workplace, and acquire the attitudes and values of their organization (Jablin, 1987).

Thinkstock

A memorable message is one way in which a new employee can become socialized into the workplace.

Generally, when workers consider the assimilation stage to be a positive experience, they are more satisfied with their jobs, report higher levels of identification with the workplace, and report that they are less likely to quit their jobs (Myers & Oetzel, 2003).

Three workplace features exist that facilitate the manner in which you move from the encounter phase to the metamorphosis phase during this time. The first feature is the perceived availability and helpfulness of socialization activities in the organization. These activities, although they might not apply to all workplaces, include attendance at orientation sessions, training sessions, meetings, and seminars; daily interactions with superiors, peers, and coworkers; participation in social and recreational activities with superiors, peers, and coworkers; and going on business trips. Of these socialization activities, daily interactions with superiors and peers are rated as being among the most available and helpful (Louis, Posner, & Powell, 1983). Employees who participate in these activities progress more quickly to the metamorphosis phase.

The second feature is the exchange of a memorable message between an organizational newcomer and an experienced coworker. A memorable message is a short and simple yet serious statement uttered by a superior and targeted toward a particular subordinate that is intended to reinforce appropriate work behavior and conduct (Stohl, 1986). This message typically occurs face to face early in an employee's career, is revealed through informal conversation, and is meant to be helpful rather than hurtful (Barge & Schlueter, 2004). Some examples of a memorable message include "The customer is always right," "We have to believe we are making a difference," "Even if others think what you're doing is wrong, stand up for what you believe in and fight for it," and "Think before you speak" (Barge & Schlueter, 2004; Steimel, 2013). While these examples may not be unique, they encourage workers to become focused, to take initiative, to work harder, or to think about their actions. Workers who receive these messages, and heed the contained advice, are able to assimilate more easily and more quickly into the organization.

The third feature is the process by which workers proactively acquire feedback from one another, which is known as information seeking. In the workplace, seven types of information-seeking strategies are used. These seven strategies are labeled as overt, indirect, third-party, testing, observing, disguising conversations, and surveillance (Miller & Jablin, 1991). When employees use the overt information-seeking strategy, they usually have a specific information source in mind, and they go directly to that source for the information they need. When employees use the indirect, third-party, testing, observing, disguising conversations, and surveillance information-seeking strategies, which all are considered monitoring strategies, they may not. Instead, they do the following:

- *Indirect strategy.* Employees probe for the information they need without explicitly posing a question to the source.

- *Third-party strategy.* Employees obtain the information from a person other than the source.

- *Testing strategy.* Employees deviate from workplace norms to determine whether the source will notice the deviation.

- *Observing strategy.* Employees obtain the information by witnessing an interaction between the source and a coworker.

- *Disguising conversations strategy.* Employees obtain the information by incorporating the request into part of a conversation they are having with the source.

- *Surveillance strategy.* Employees obtain the information by reflecting on their prior interactions with the source.

On the TV drama *Scandal*, crisis manager Olivia Pope (Kerry Washington) uses a variety of information-seeking strategies to evaluate individuals and manage her clients' public images. In your workplace, how often do you use overt and monitoring strategies to seek information?

Occasionally, workers may seek information from other sources, such as written documents, the company intranet, or workplace artifacts such as signage and service kiosks (Fonner & Timmerman, 2009).

For any employee, the choice of strategy likely is tied to the type of information that is needed. New employees use the overt strategy to obtain the factual and procedural information necessary for job or task completion, but use any of the six monitoring strategies to acquire knowledge about their appropriate workplace role behavior, to inquire about their performance, or to learn more about their coworkers (Morrison, 1995). Experienced workers, on the other hand, use the overt and the monitoring strategies as a way to assess the work abilities, motivational level, and personality of their new colleagues (Gallagher & Sias, 2009).

Take a moment to complete the Organizational Assimilation Index (Galliard, Myers, & Seibold, 2010), which measures seven dimensions of workplace life that typically influence the rate at which employees progress through the assimilation stage of socialization. These seven dimensions are familiarity with both supervisors and coworkers, the extent to which workers develop an understanding of how the organization operates, the extent to which supervisors and peers award recognition for contributions to the workplace, the extent to which employees are involved in the workplace, the ability to perform assigned duties and tasks, and the ability to modify assigned duties and tasks. Generally, the higher you score on the index (either overall or for each of the seven dimensions), the more assimilated you have become into a workplace.

Stage 3: Exit Stage

The exit stage of socialization begins once an employee decides to disengage from the workplace. In this third and final stage, workers voluntarily or involuntarily leave the workplace for a host of reasons. These reasons include quitting, retirement, job transfer, promotion, reduction in workforce, layoff, job reclassification, and dismissal (Jablin, 2001). While this stage of socialization signifies the end of employment at a workplace, how employees leave the workplace—and how they are treated by their coworkers during this time—becomes

ASSESS YOUR COMMUNICATION

THE ORGANIZATIONAL ASSIMILATION INDEX

This questionnaire contains statements about your assimilation into your workplace. Indicate the extent to which you agree with each statement according to the following scale:

If you **strongly agree** with the statement, write 5 in the blank.
If you **agree** with the statement, write 4 in the blank.
If you **neither agree nor disagree** with the statement, write 3 in the blank.
If you **disagree** with the statement, write 2 in the blank.
If you **strongly disagree** with the statement, write 1 in the blank.

_____ 1. I feel like I know my supervisor pretty well.
_____ 2. My supervisor sometimes discusses problems with me.
_____ 3. My supervisor and I talk together often.
_____ 4. I consider my coworkers friends.
_____ 5. I feel comfortable talking to my coworkers.
_____ 6. I feel like I know my coworkers pretty well.
_____ 7. I understand the standards of my organization.
_____ 8. I think I have a good idea about how this organization operates.
_____ 9. I know the values of my organization.
_____10. I do not mind being asked to perform my work according to the organization's standards.
_____11. My supervisor recognizes when I do a good job.
_____12. My supervisor listens to my ideas.
_____13. I think my supervisor values my opinions.
_____14. I think my supervisor recognizes my value to the organization.
_____15. I talk to my coworkers about how much I like it here.
_____16. I volunteer for duties that benefit the organization.
_____17. I talk about how much I enjoy my work.
_____18. I often show others how to perform our work.
_____19. I think I'm an expert at what I do.
_____20. I have figured out efficient ways to do my work.
_____21. I can do others' jobs, if I am needed.
_____22. I have changed some aspects of my position.
_____23. I do this job a bit differently than my predecessor did.
_____24. I have helped to change the duties of my position.

Scoring:

1. Add your scores for items 1, 2, and 3. This is your _familiarity with supervisors_ score.
2. Add your scores for items 4, 5, and 6. This is your _familiarity with coworkers_ score.
3. Add your scores for items 7, 8, 9, and 10. This is your _acculturation_ score.
4. Add your scores for items 11, 12, 13, and 14. This is your _recognition_ score.
5. Add your scores for items 15, 16, and 17. This is your _involvement_ score.
6. Add your scores for items 18, 19, 20, and 21. This is your _job competency_ score.
7. Add your scores for items 22, 23, and 24. This is your _role negotiation_ score.
8. Add your scores for all 24 items. This is your overall _organizational assimilation_ score.

Source: Galliard et al. (2010).

part of the anticipatory stage of socialization when they start their next workplace position.

In summary, to become socialized into a workplace, individuals progress through the anticipatory stage, the assimilation stage, and the exit stage. This workplace socialization process allows a worker to transform from an organizational outsider to an effective workplace member who has been provided with the knowledge, ability, and motivation to perform an organizational role. Another way in which workplace socialization can be enhanced is through the dissent process (Goldman & Myers, 2015), which enables employees to voice their concerns about the organization to their superiors, coworkers, families, and friends.

How employees are treated during the exit stage affects their progression through the anticipatory stage at their next workplace.

WORKPLACE DISSENT

When employees feel as if they no longer are a vital part of the company and they begin to disagree or express contradictory opinions about the organization, its policies and practices, and its employees, workplace dissent begins (Kassing, 2002). Expressing dissent is considered to be an important practice because it provides workers with a way to deal with organizational constraints, draw attention to an overlooked issue, expose unethical behavior or illegal wrongdoing, and provide corrective feedback (Waldron & Kassing, 2011). Typically, dissent is triggered by an event that workers find disturbing or unsettling, such as the ways in which employees are treated, the manner in which performance appraisals are conducted, or the implementation of changes to the working environment (Kassing & Armstrong, 2002). Once this trigger is activated, workers debate whether their response to the event will be perceived as either constructive or adversarial and if they are likely to experience some form of retaliation for their response (Kassing, 1997). Based on this debate, they decide whether to express dissent in one of three ways (Kassing, 1997, 2000a).

Upward Dissent

Upward dissent is expressed by voicing concerns about the workplace directly, openly, and clearly with superiors because subordinates believe that they will take these concerns seriously. When you engage in upward dissent, you do so without any fear of retaliation because you are confident that these concerns will be perceived as constructive and helpful to the organization (Kassing, 1997). Workers with upward concerns tend to have high-quality relationships with their superiors (Kassing, 2000b), trust their supervisors (Payne, 2014), and are actively engaged in their work tasks and duties (Kassing, Piemonte, Goman, & Mitchell, 2012). These concerns usually center on criticisms about current workplace practices and question the wisdom of recently made decisions, whether company policies are fair, and whether coworkers are treated

Discussing work-related concerns with a romantic partner is one way in which employees engage in displaced dissent.

unfairly (Kassing, 1998). Figure 9.3 contains four strategies an employee might use to express upward dissent.

Latent Dissent

Latent dissent is expressed, too, by sharing concerns about the workplace, but is done so in an aggressive manner. Rather than speaking with management, you complain with your coworkers about company problems, express your displeasure about corporate policies, or openly criticize workplace practices (Kassing, 1998). Workers who express latent dissent often do so because they feel that their contributions possess little value, that their contributions are unwanted, that their supervisors are less open and receptive to their ideas, and that they have little ability to influence their workplace (Kassing, 2000a). They are less committed to and identify less with the organization, experience lower levels of job satisfaction, place less trust in their supervisors, and have lower levels of organization-based self-esteem than their colleagues who engage in upward dissent (Kassing, 1998, 2001; Payne, 2007, 2014). They also are more likely to think about leaving the workplace and finding new employment elsewhere (Kassing et al., 2012).

Displaced Dissent

Displaced dissent is expressed by discussing work-related concerns with people outside of the organization such as family members and friends. When interacting with these people, you share your concerns about workplace decisions, complain about organizational practices, and voice any frustrations (Kassing, 1998). Workers choose to speak with their relatives and friends, rather than with their superiors and peers, because they are afraid of being perceived as adversarial and because they fear retaliation (Kassing, 1997). Those who engage in displaced dissent tend to be younger, have less work experience, and hold nonmanagerial positions (Kassing & Dicioccio, 2004).

In summary, dissent acts as a vehicle through which employees can voice their concerns about their workplace. For dissent to be effective, however, it needs to

FIGURE 9.3

STRATEGIES TO EXPRESS UPWARD DISSENT

Strategy	Definition
Prosocial	Provide evidence to support the dissent claim or offer solutions in making a dissent claim
Threatening resignation	Threaten to resign from or quit the organization
Repetition	Repeatedly make the same dissent claim across several points in time
Circumvention	Strategically address a dissent claim to a superior who outranks your immediate supervisor

Source: Kassing & Kava (2013).

be articulated to supervisors in a way that prompts them to take the concerns seriously. Although employees can engage in dissent with their coworkers, they tend to do so more frequently when they consider these workplace relationships to fulfill both informational and supportive functions.

Workplace dissent allows employees to have a voice in how the organization functions.

WORKPLACE RELATIONSHIPS

Consider workplace relationships to be those sustained interactions that occur between you and your coworkers as a direct result of employment at the same organization. These relationships can emerge in the form of superior–subordinate relationships, which develop between two coworkers where one formally outranks the other by virtue of organizational role or title (Sias, 2009), or mentor–protégé relationships, which develop between an experienced colleague who has attained career success and a less advanced colleague who demonstrates the potential to become equally successful at work (Kalbfleisch, 2002). Other workplace relationships in which you likely will participate include peer relationships, friendships, and romantic relationships.

Peer Relationships

Of the many work-related relationships with their colleagues in which employees participate, the most common is the relationship with organizational peers. Peer relationships, which develop between two coworkers at the same hierarchical level who possess no formal authority over one another (Sias, Krone, & Jablin, 2002), can be classified into one of three types: information peers, collegial peers, or special peers (Kram & Isabella, 1985). In your relationships with information peers, the primary purpose of communication is to share basic, day-to-day work-related content. These coworkers share limited personal information with one another, which explains why this relationship is characterized by low levels of self-disclosure, trust, communication openness, and relational closeness (Myers & Johnson, 2004; Myers, Knox, Pawlowski, & Ropog, 1999), and why communication is focused almost exclusively on work issues. Typically, this peer relationship is the most common relationship, and workers will have a greater number of these relationships than either collegial peer or special peer relationships (Fritz, 1997; Kram & Isabella, 1985).

In your relationships with collegial peers, the primary purpose of communication is to provide job-related feedback while sharing mutual work and family concerns with a colleague. Characterized by moderate levels of self-disclosure and trust (Myers & Johnson, 2004), collegial peers engage in a variety of mutual behaviors intended to help one another's professional and personal development. These behaviors include helping, supporting, understanding, encouraging, and reaffirming one another (McDougall & Beattie, 1997).

In your relationships with special peers, the primary purpose of communication is to provide emotional support, confirmation, personal feedback, and friendship for others at work (Kram & Isabella, 1985), although special peers still are considered a "go to" for seeking information about how to perform their tasks as well as learning about workplace culture, policies and procedures, and politics (Myers, Cranmer, Goldman, Sollitto, Gillen, & Ball, 2015). Two peers become relationally

Colleagues Alicia Florrick (Julianna Margulies) and Kalinda Sharma (Archie Panjabi) bond over drinks in the TV drama *The Good Wife*. In a special peer relationship, employees often spend time with each other outside of the workplace. How frequently do you interact with your special peers outside of work?

close with each other (Myers & Johnson, 2004), which enables them to communicate in ways that are reflective of this closeness. Rather than simply providing mutual support, as collegial peers do, these peers challenge each other, provide constructive criticism, engage in productive disagreement, express their vulnerabilities, and assert their individuality (McDougall & Beattie, 1997). Typically, special peer relationships take several years to develop and are the least common of the three types of peer relationships (Kram & Isabella, 1985).

Friendships

Workplace friendships are a unique type of relationship because they blend the expectations associated with personal relationships with the expectations that govern work roles (Bridge & Baxter, 1992). While these friendships can form between superior and subordinates, collegial peers, or special peers, their formation is spurred by several factors inherent to the workplace (Sias & Cahill, 1998; Sias, Smith, & Avdeyeva, 2003). Some factors are individual, and include whether both coworkers perceive themselves as having similar interests (e.g., hobbies) or lifestyles (e.g., being single, having children), or whether they simply find each other's personality traits to be socially or task attractive. Other factors are contextual and are grounded in a specific job role or position that may include working together for an extended period, sharing the same office space, working jointly on a task, and dealing with the same task-related problems. Still other factors include openly discussing life events with each other at the office or socializing with each other outside of the workplace. In some instances, these friendships develop as a way to deal with superiors who are considered to be unsupportive, untrustworthy, and unfair (Odden & Sias, 1997), or as a way to vent about work-related issues (Cahill & Sias, 1997). On the other hand, some friendships may never develop due to the unprofessional communicative behaviors in which some workers engage. These unprofessional behaviors include interacting in a rude and disrespectful manner, engaging in gossip, and being overly critical and dismissive toward others (Fritz, 2002).

But because workplace friendships are voluntary and have a personal focus (Sias, 2009), these friendships can deteriorate when participants are unable to separate their work roles from their personal lives. For example, the personality traits of coworkers that were once deemed attractive can become difficult to manage or ignore, the life events that once drew two employees together as friends can become distracting and start interfering with task accomplishment, colleagues may begin to develop conflicting expectations of how they should treat each other in the workplace, or one peer receives a promotion that causes a power imbalance in the relationship (Sias, Heath, Perry, Silva, & Fix, 2004). For some peers, their relationships change when one employee feels either betrayed or deceived by the other (Bryant & Sias, 2011; Sias et al., 2004).

There may be little recourse for how some coworkers deal with one another, in part because a lack of power and authority defines work friendships. Those who opt to disengage from these friendships take one of three approaches: state-of-the-relationship talk, depersonalization, and cost escalation (Sias & Perry, 2004). In a state-of-the-relationship talk, peers directly discuss the issues that are disrupting the relationship and openly express their desire to terminate their friendship. With depersonalization, coworkers distance themselves from one another by limiting their conversation to work-related tasks, electing not to participate in social activities, and restricting the amount of self-disclosure. Cost escalation occurs when employees purposely communicate with one another in a dysfunctional manner so that the relationship will end. Of these three approaches, peers prefer the use of depersonalization (Sias & Perry, 2004). In some cases where peers feel that they were betrayed by a coworker, they may start documenting their own workplace actions and behaviors as a preventative measure for the future, or they may decide to pursue a position elsewhere (Bryant & Sias, 2011).

Romantic Relationships

Workplace romantic relationships occur when two employees, regardless of their status or position in the organization, acknowledge a mutual sexual attraction and physically act upon this attraction, whether it be through dating, cohabitation, or marriage (Pierce, Byrne, & Aguinis, 1996). Similar to the development of friendships, workplace romantic relationships develop largely due to contextual factors such as working in close physical proximity to each other, repeatedly and routinely interacting with each other, sharing responsibility on project and task completion, and receiving positive performance appraisals from their managers (Pierce et al., 1996). Individual factors, such as having similar attitudes and finding each other physically or socially attractive, also affect whether these relationships bloom. For many employees, their motives for engaging in an office romance can be attributed to their need for love and companionship, a need for excitement and adventure, or a need to attain job security and financial rewards (Quinn, 1977).

Although romantic relationships are voluntary and have a personal focus, like workplace friendships, they are fraught with a higher and more intense level of emotion (Sias, 2009), which is one reason why some organizations do not condone romantic relationships. Whether it is through the enactment of a formal organization policy or it is communicated through the values and assumptions embedded in the workplace culture, some workplaces prohibit these relationships, particularly between superiors and subordinates, due to the negative ramifications associated with these relationships if they end poorly (Wilkie, 2003). Because the two employees must still work with each other, it is not uncommon for issues such as decreased job performance, increased absenteeism, and decreased job morale to surface ("Romance in the Workplace," 2014). Additionally, the existence of office romances can act as fodder for the gossip or rumor mills that pervade many organizations, which then can create feelings of ill will among employees, especially if they believe a colleague is receiving either favoritism, preferential treatment, or job advancement as a direct result of involvement in the romance. Even more detrimental effects stemming from workplace romantic relationships can emerge in the form of claims of sexual harassment or complaints of a hostile work environment.

iStock

The increasing availability and accessibility of workplace technology have created multiple ways in which we engage in task-related activities with our colleagues.

WORKPLACE AND ORGANIZATIONAL COMMUNICATION AND CONVERGENCE

In the Communication Age, the landscape of how we communicate in the workplace is changing. The increasing availability and accessibility of information and communication technologies (ICTs) such as file repositories (e.g., Dropbox), internal and external e-mail systems, instant messaging applications, and social media have created multiple ways in which we engage in task-related activities with our colleagues (Treem, Dailey, Pierce, & Leonardi, 2015). Consider the following examples of how you communicate with your coworkers:

- Using GChat to send an instant message to a colleague to determine whether he is in the office instead of walking down the hallway to his desk.

- Texting a special peer to inquire about her availability for a lunch date.

- Using Facebook Messenger to inquire about the status of a project instead of calling a coworker on an office landline telephone.

- Working on a document with other employees by sending it as an attachment back and forth to one another rather than completing it as a group around a conference table.

- Sending a mass e-mail message to all employees instead of having a formal meeting.

- Updating your professional profile on LinkedIn.

- Learning the latest organizational gossip by checking Instagram.

- Checking your coworkers' meeting availability by using Doodle.com instead of asking them to send you their schedules.

Simultaneously, ICTs have changed how we maintain our connections with the workplace as well. Not only are we bombarded with ICTs during our workday, but many of us extend our workday by taking these devices either home with us after hours or on business trips. Other workers telecommute, work from home part-time, or bring work home daily. While some employees will agree that accessibility to their laptop computers, tablets, and smartphones enhances their ability to remain connected to the workplace outside of regular work hours (Wright et al., 2014), the dark side is that ICTs allow organizations to monitor their employees in real time and can cause their workers to experience overwhelming feelings of stress, pressure, and perceptions of being closely supervised (Zorn, Hector, & Gibson, 2008). Even if our workplace does not provide ICTs for us, we still have access to the organization through our personal cell phones, Facebook and Twitter accounts, and computers.

What this means, then, is that today's workers must learn how to become productive organization members by striking a balance between face-to-face communication and technology in the workplace. That is, while ICTs can help us become more task efficient, manage our schedules, and provide us with rich sources of data, we still need to be able to effectively communicate with our coworkers, superiors, work groups, and teams by using the appropriate interpersonal communication behaviors and group and team communication skills. By doing so, it will be possible to become a productive and functional work colleague in the Communication Age.

WHAT YOU'VE LEARNED   Now that you have studied this chapter, you should be able to:

1 Identify the components that comprise workplace communication.

Workplace communication is task-oriented, goal-directed, and consequential. Consider that while the primary purpose of developing relationships with coworkers is to help the workplace accomplish its tasks and meet its goals, these relationships also have consequences.

 Gibb's Supportive and Defensive Climates

2 Differentiate among the three levels of organizational culture.

Workplace culture consists of three levels: artifacts, values, and assumptions. Becoming

aware of each level allows you to identify with and accept the culture. This awareness also helps you decide whether a particular workplace is the best fit for you.

Importance of Culture

3 Explain how employees are socialized into an organization.

Socialization is a three-stage process that begins once employees decide to pursue an organizational position and ends when employees leave the workplace. Whether and how employees are socialized into an organization depends on their participation in workplace activities, attention paid to memorable messages, and use of information-seeking strategies.

 Organizational Entry: Onboarding, Orientation, and Socialization

④ Describe the ways in which worker engage in dissent at the workplace.

While workplace dissent can be expressed to superiors, coworkers, and family and friends, it is most effective when it is expressed in an articulated manner that either is supported with factual evidence or offers solutions to existing organizational issues. This way, the expression of dissent is attributed to concerns with the welfare of the workplace rather than any ulterior motives.

 How to Reinvent an Institution

 How to Communicate Dissent at Work

⑤ Distinguish among the types of relationships that develop at work.

Although the development of workplace peer relationships, friendships, and romantic relationships is inevitable, remember that each one of these relationships differs in its function. For these relationships to be enjoyable, workers must be able to separate their personal life from their work life. Not doing so usually is detrimental to both employees and their organization.

▶ Be an Opportunity Maker

▶ Improving Difficult Work Relationships

KEY TERMS

Review key terms with eFlashcards. **edge.sagepub.com/edwards2e**

REFLECT

1. In your workplace, how do the three levels of organizational culture inform one another? What would be an example of an artifact that embodies both the cultural values and the cultural assumptions?

2. When speaking with prospective employees of your organization, what advice would you give to them about how to move from the encounter phase to the

metamorphosis phase? What workplace features would be especially salient for you to highlight for them?

3. At work, what individual and contextual factors have influenced your decision to develop a workplace friendship? What proportion of your workplace relationships are friendships?

REVIEW

To check your answers go to **edge.sagepub.com/edwards2e**

1. _____ is the practice of working off-site while remaining connected to the workplace through a host of communication technologies.

2. Explain how an informal communication network is established.

3. Workplace bullying is characterized by its _____, _____, _____, and _____.

4. _____, _____, _____, and _____ are the four categories of artifacts.

5. Explain the difference between the values and the assumptions of an organization's culture.

6. _____ is the process by which organizational newcomers learn about the values, norms, and expectations that will enable them to become fully contributing members of the organization.

7. What is a memorable message?

8. When workers express _____ dissent, they do so in an aggressive manner.

9. Peer relationships develop between two coworkers at _____ who possess _____.

10. Workplace friendships can form between _____, _____, and _____.

Getty

WHAT YOU'LL LEARN   After studying this chapter, you will be able to:

1 Identify the ways in which new media impact your life.

2 Explain why the characteristics of the First and Second Media Ages are important to your study of communication.

3 Describe the qualities of new media and how they influence communication.

4 Describe the characteristics of new media theory.

5 Explain how identity is formed through new media and their relationship to communication.

6 Examine how new media foster community.

The shooting of Michael Brown in Ferguson, Missouri, in August 2014 sparked vigorous debate in the United States and abroad. Brown, an unarmed Black teenager, was shot and killed by Darren Wilson, a White officer. Protests in Ferguson followed Michael Brown's death, and a grand jury decided not to charge the officer with murder. Protests also ensued following the resignation of Ferguson police chief Thomas Jackson in March 2015, a week after a federal report alleged widespread racial bias in the Ferguson police department (BBC News, 2015).

On social media, hashtags have long been used as a method for organizing a conversation about an event or topic (Hitlin & Holcomb, 2015). Conversation concerning the Ferguson shooting began on the "#Ferguson" hashtag across different social networking sites. A new analysis of the #Ferguson hashtag on Twitter and Instagram found some striking differences between the two social media platforms in how people used the hashtag to direct the conversation. On Twitter, usage of the hashtag #Ferguson primarily focused on the discussion about Brown, the ensuing protests, and the authorities' response. On Instagram (a photo-sharing website with around the same number of users as Twitter), however, the usage became much broader. The hashtag use on Instagram was less a reference to the events in Missouri and more a way for people to discuss issues such as race, police brutality, and politics (Hitlin & Holcomb, 2015). In other words, depending on which social media platform is used to track the hashtag, the content and context are quite different between Instagram and Twitter.

As social media continue to grow as means for interaction, they have also become a major medium for discussion of significant issues and news consumption. As you experience life in the Communication Age, you will be tasked with effectively managing and critiquing the information to which you are exposed on different social

networks, online or not. New media have connected the world in a revolutionary way, but they must still be critically evaluated based on the given context and available facts. As you move through this chapter, remember not to take all online information at face value, and use your own judgment when assessing the validity of the media you consume.

New media affect communication in a variety of ways. This chapter will discuss what new media are, how people interact with them, and some of the influences they can have on your everyday communication. As you read this chapter, think about the ways that you personally use new media; the messages you send and the topics you post about today are something your friends, your family members, your employers, your romantic partners, and strangers can see.

Ella is a 19-year-old journalism student at the University of California at Los Angeles. She arrives at her 8 a.m. class and begins by opening her iPhone planner to check what she has scheduled for the day. As the professor begins class, Ella quickly checks her e-mail, reads the new comment on her blog, updates her Facebook status, text messages her best friend, posts a picture from the night before on Twitter, and receives her daily CNN and entertainment news updates. As Ella looks up from her phone for the first time since she sat down, she notices several classmates performing the same tasks and does not feel guilty about tuning out the first 10 minutes of class.

Ella's morning routine shows us how typical it is to control, connect, interact, and engage in what is referred to as mediated communication. It is now, in the Communication Age, that the combination of face-to-face and mediated communication is common. As discussed in Chapter 1, convergence is where communication, technology, and media come together and deeply permeate daily life. In the Communication Age, the many forms of technologically mediated and face-to-face communication overlap and intersect.

This coming together fosters interaction in real time made possible with a variety of media formats. These new forms of media are deeply integrated into our everyday lives (Baym, 2000; Turkle, 1996). This chapter explores the evolving relationship between communication and technology into what are now called new media. Put simply, new media include a technological interface that allows users to communicate, interact, personalize, and own media. For example, Ella's Facebook, Twitter, e-mail, text message, Snapchat, and news feeds are all types of new media. In this chapter, the implications, concepts, and characteristics of new media are examined.

The evolution of media over time has reached a point in the Communication Age where communicators are largely in control of the information they consume. This control brings new levels of power, creativity, and sometimes problems. Imagine yourself living in a time when newspapers, radio, and visiting with your neighbors were the only ways to communicate. It is important to study this time in history, called the Broadcast Media Age, in order to understand how our media have evolved into what is experienced today (Manovich, 2003; Ong, 1982). As you read this chapter, consider how you might understand each dimension of new media as it relates to your own life. However, you will begin to learn how new media evolved, how they work, why you use them, and how they are shaping your life across communication contexts.

COMMUNICATION TRADITIONS AND TECHNOLOGY

To understand the impact that new media have on the Communication Age, you must first understand the difference between traditional media and new media. To make

How, if at all, do you use new media to manage your daily life?

these connections, let's turn to Walter Ong's foundational works on the influence of technology on verbal communication. Ong (1982) was primarily concerned with the shift from orality to literacy and the impact that this shift would have on culture and education. Over time, scholars have followed Ong's lead in giving attention to the ways that technology impacts culture. This development in thought has extended Ong's attention to oral and print culture with an inclusion of electronic culture and, more recently, the culture of new media. Let's examine each of these aspects of communication tradition and technology.

Oral Tradition

The Oral Tradition, also referred to as Oral Culture or the Oral Age, consists of cultural messages or traditions verbally transmitted across generations (Vansina, 1985). The oral tradition can be classified as primary orality, which is a culture that has no knowledge of technology beyond the spoken word, or as secondary orality, which is when verbal communication is sustained through other technologies, such as the telephone or Internet (Ong, 1982; Wahl, 2013; Wahl & Scholl, 2014).

Written/Print Tradition

There has been much debate about the tradition that follows the Oral Tradition. Some scholars believe that the Written Tradition, which refers to early forms of written communication such as scribe and hieroglyphics, immediately follows the Oral Tradition; other scholars like Ong argue that the development of the alphabet must precede the Written Tradition (Wahl, 2013; Wahl & Scholl, 2014). For the latter, the Print Tradition, which describes the creation and distribution of printed text, is the next identifiable period of technological development (Lanham, 1993). At any rate, the Print Tradition is largely viewed as having begun around the year 1440 as a result of the development of Johannes Gutenberg's printing press, a mechanical device that applies pressure from an inked surface to a print medium (Eisenstein, 1980). The advent of this device allowed for the first mass production of books (McLuhan, 1964). Essentially, the development of the Written/Print Tradition allowed for the expansion of literacy and the ability to produce and share information with the public, rather than being limited by oral communication and geographic location (Wahl, 2013; Wahl & Scholl, 2014).

iStock

Electronic Tradition (First Media Age)

The Electronic Tradition (First Media Age), also referred to as the Electronic Age or Electronic Media, includes media that require users to make use of electronics to access content (Lanham, 1993; Wahl, 2013; Wahl & Scholl, 2014). Where some media are considered static in that they do not require the audience to use electronics (newspapers, for example), the Electronic Tradition or First Media Age focuses on media such as audio/visual recordings, radio, telegraph, and television. By this definition, many scholars believe that the advent of the Internet is also considered part of this tradition; however, because the Internet allows the consumer also to become the producer, many others believe that the Internet is part of a different tradition of technology known as new media (Peters, 1999; Warnick, 2007).

During this era, news and information were released through a highly centralized production—only a few editors had control of informing the public. In other words, the national news companies such as ABC, NBC, and CBS controlled what information was released to the public. This one-way communication fostered little public participation (Peters, 1999).

Marshall McLuhan's classical medium theory best describes the Electronic Tradition. In 1964, McLuhan emphasized the importance of media and the effects of the message. According to McLuhan, media are not a simply newspapers or television. Rather, McLuhan described media as the symbolic environment of any communicative act. With his famous saying, "The medium is the message," McLuhan (1964) was the first to suggest that media, independent from any content that is transmitted, impact individuals and society.

Decades before CNN or the Internet, McLuhan predicted a future where people would communicate via "electric media" in a "global village." As early as 1964, McLuhan described the world of instant messaging and e-mail that was far beyond the imagination of his time. With the emergence of the Internet and the transition from broadcast to interactive media, the Second Media Age has begun to transform society and human communication (see Figure 10.1). With the convergence of face-to-face communication, broadcast media, and interactive media, communication scholars have had a renewed interest in twenty-first-century media theory.

iStock

In your view, what impact has convergence had on the presence of newspapers compared to years ago?

New Media Tradition (Second Media Age)

Consider the aforementioned traditions of technology: Oral, Written/Print, and Electronic. Given the definitions and characteristics of these traditions, it appears that all existing media can fit into these categories. Take, for instance, the smartphone. A smartphone, such as an Android or an iPhone, allows us to talk to our loved ones (Oral) via the cell phone (Electronic), while surfing the Internet (Electronic), reading an e-book (Print), and downloading applications (Electronic) (Wahl, 2013; Wahl & Scholl, 2014). Thus, various facets of the smartphone allow us to tap into multiple

FIGURE 10.1
DISTINCTION BETWEEN THE FIRST AND SECOND MEDIA AGES

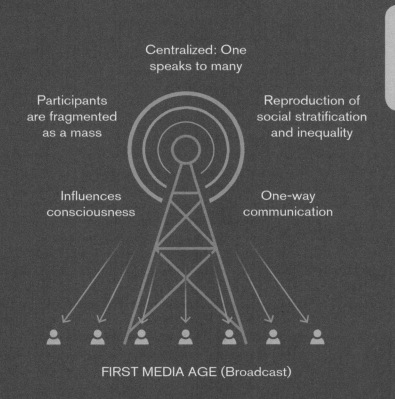

Centralized: One speaks to many

Participants are fragmented as a mass

Reproduction of social stratification and inequality

Influences consciousness

One-way communication

FIRST MEDIA AGE (Broadcast)

SECOND MEDIA AGE (Interactivity)

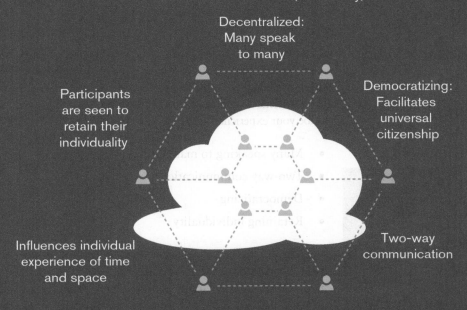

Decentralized: Many speak to many

Participants are seen to retain their individuality

Democratizing: Facilitates universal citizenship

Influences individual experience of time and space

Two-way communication

traditions at the same time, rather than having to purchase five separate devices to accomplish our complicated communication goals. Because of the multifunctionality of many new media devices, such as the smartphone, researchers created a new classification for technological advancements of this type: the New Media Tradition (Second Media Age), also referred to as the Digital Tradition, Mashup Culture, the Information Age, and the Attention Age (Peters, 1999; Wahl, 2013; Wahl & Scholl, 2014; Warnick, 2007).

With the renewed interest in media studies, communication scholars in the Second Media Age began to explore the infinite possibilities of interactive media (Ahmad, 2010; Davis, 2011; Ledbetter et al., 2011; Xun, 2010). The shift in communication initiated the need for a new media theory—designed to describe the unique, customized communication styles of today. In the next section, you will explore characteristics of new media and how they impact you as a person. As you read through the chapter, focus on your experiences with new media. Why did you create a Facebook page? When was the first time you checked your e-mail on your phone? How do new media impact the way you receive and send information? As you get more familiar with this topic, you will begin to understand the significance of this theory in your life across communication contexts.

As you explore the new media theory, focus on the unique interaction and dynamic between you and your computer, you and your cell phone, your personal communication and your electronic communication, and broadcast media and new media. Several authors contributed to this theory that is still evolving today. Important to your study of communication are several characteristics and concepts relevant to the theory.

▶ **COMMUNICATION IN ACTION 10.2**

WATCH: Mobile App Development

Chris Merkle explains the strategies his company uses for developing mobile apps across industries.

Think about how you use social media to advocate for issues you care about the most, as well as how it is part of your identity.

NEW MEDIA: CONNECTING AND ENGAGING

You connect to new media daily. When you log on to Facebook, Twitter, Imgur, Instagram, Reddit, or any type of new media, you begin to engage in the experience of modern communication. The following items may help you to understand the qualities of and describe your experience with new media:

- Many speaking to many
- Two-way communication
- Democratizing
- Retaining individuality

Each point helps to describe new media, including the first point that new media involve *many speaking to many*. While new media have enabled numerous variations, a crucial shift in communication occurs from one entity speaking to the mass audience to many people speaking to many people (Peters, 1999). For example, this concept describes how new media provide a platform for users around the world to speak to one another. Using its website, Coca-Cola is able to communicate its message to consumers. With her blog, Lindsey is able to speak to her 84 followers. Through her breast cancer support group, Alice is able to gain support and confidence with people facing the same challenges. New media provide endless opportunities for users to communicate their ideas, opinions, and information to others.

New media involve *two-way communication*. That is, two-way communication is the capability for users to respond to messages rather than simply receiving them. New media enable us to interact and communicate by sending and receiving messages to one another. Traditional broadcast media hindered this type of communication.

With the invention of the Internet and other sources of interactive media, people initiated a new sense of democracy. In other words, new media are democratizing (e.g., online political campaigns, public communication, and new media activism) (Warnick, 2007). People are empowered by the freedom and sources of endless information that new media allow. Through new media you are able to voice your opinion and build a closer relationship with others.

New media are about *retaining individuality*. In earlier broadcast media, information was disseminated to a general audience without as much ability to customize information for particular markets. New media allow information to focus on individual topics of interest and niche markets across the globe. Through the use of e-mail, newsgroups, Twitter, and the like, you can customize information to your individual preferences.

CHARACTERISTICS OF NEW MEDIA THEORY

This section reviews a number of characteristics of new media theory—the explanation for the way people communicate in the Communication Age. New media theory is important because it helps you to understand the impact of technology on human relationships. It also helps you to understand the emerging process of human communication as influenced by technology. Interactivity, personalization, creativity, flexibility, and continual evolving are the characteristics you will experience with new media in the Communication Age.

Interactive

In the Communication Age, anyone can become a news writer, an editor, a photographer, a blogger, a videographer, an artist, an educator, a musician, and more. Unlike traditional broadcast media of the First Media Age, interactive media allow us to be in control of what the media say, when they say it, and how we access it. People are constantly looking for the most convenient and updated source of information. You do not rely on the morning paper for your news or wait for your 10-year reunion to connect with old high school friends. Instead, you are continually downloading, uploading, updating, networking, sharing, and searching for the information you need and want.

▶ **COMMUNICATION IN ACTION 10.3**

WATCH: Digital Games

Debra Lieberman discusses the health video game industry and the research she conducts into the effectiveness of health games.

ETHICAL
CONNECTION   MIAMI DOLPHINS' DON JONES IN TWITTER TROUBLE

Getty

In May 2014, National Football League player Don Jones found himself in hot water after tweeting a controversial reaction to the St. Louis Rams' drafting of Michael Sam, who became the first openly gay player drafted in the NFL. Soon after Sam was drafted, Jones tweeted "OMG" and "horrible," which he later deleted (Walker, 2014). Jones's tweets came less than a year after the Dolphins' organization came under fire for a locker room culture that permitted bullying, racial slurs, and sexual taunts. Jones's tweet caught the attention of general manager Dennis Hickey.

"I was made aware of it and I was disappointed in those comments," Hickey said. "That's not what we stand for as an organization. The draft weekend is a culmination for so many players, their lifetime achievement of their dream to achieve a goal for Michael Sam and all the other players."

The immediacy and visibility of social media like Twitter allow for instant feedback and responses from celebrities, politicians, reporters, and private individuals in a way never before seen. However, the simplicity of publishing a comment can make it easy to overlook ethical considerations concerning how other people could react to the information. Researchers have noted that although bloggers face no barriers to what they can post, accountability exists in the form of feedback, which can be very intense (Cenite, Detenber, Koh, Lim, & Soon, 2009). Individuals posting about sensitive topics on social networking sites such as Facebook and Twitter should be sensitive to how their posts can be perceived. Don Jones's post is an example of how a seemingly offhand comment can hurt and upset many different people and cause a very negative backlash. The example also emphasizes the importance of assessing if your communication respects the self, others, and surroundings. Ethical communicators should strive to be fair and tactful through their computer-mediated communication, and show the same respect to people online that they would during a face-to-face interaction.

QUESTIONS

1. Using the Don Jones example, was it lack of consideration to the self, others, or surroundings that caused the negative backlash about his post? Was there more than one ethical violation?

2. Do you feel that ethical considerations about disclosure differ between computer-mediated communication and face-to-face interaction? If yes, how so?

One of the most important characteristics of new media is their interactive capabilities. Interactivity is the phenomenon of communication at a distance through new media—sending and receiving digitally encoded messages in almost real time, continually allowing users to have two-way communication in an environment that is constantly changing and challenging them. Instead of writing a letter to the newspaper editor, you could build a blog, join a newsgroup, and post a comment on the online version of the article.

COMMUNICATION HOW-TO
NEW MEDIA JARGON

The example below contains new media jargon that is used every day. Can you relate to the jargon used in this example? How often do you find yourself using this jargon in face-to-face interaction? Remember to adjust your jargon to the person you are talking to. Think about how you would text or e-mail your professor as compared to your best friend. Using inappropriate jargon with the wrong people can hurt your credibility, so be aware of your audience.

Twitter example

Shawn:	Hey @Tco, wuts #trending
Travis:	Sup @ShawnPug, just RTed a funny vid Tony posted earlier, slightly NSFW lol
Shawn:	Wuts his handle?
Travis:	@TonyT
Shawn:	# for the vid?
Travis:	#dogdays
Shawn:	Trending yet?
Travis:	TBH, IDK if my hashtag will end up trending or if anyone will even like it. It will only be viral if people can relate IRL.
Shawn:	SMH. Well, GL neways
Travis:	ty, ttyl

Translation

Shawn:	Hey Travis, what's popular?
Travis:	Hello Shawn, just retweeted a funny video Tony posted earlier, slightly not safe for work (laugh out loud)
Shawn:	What is [Tony's] username?
Travis:	@TonyT
Shawn:	[What is the] hashtag for the video?
Travis:	#dogdays
Shawn:	[Is your post] trending yet?
Travis:	To be honest, I don't know if my hashtag will end up trending or if anyone will even like it. It will only be (popular) if people can relate in real life.
Shawn:	(Shaking my head). Well, good luck anyways.
Travis:	Thank you, talk to you later.

New media are mutually active and allow users to probe, question, and constantly find information. As you think about new media, make note of the interactive technologies beyond the Internet: smartphones, text messages, iPods, video on demand, Netflix, e-mail, iTunes, YouTube, video games, and Skype. Think about all of the ways you become interactive when using these forms of new media. For example, interactivity can be making purchases, obtaining information, watching videos, playing games, downloading images, building relationships, chatting, and creating profiles. Look at the interactive Communication Age jargon in the above "Communication How-To." Challenge yourself to come up with a list of additional terms.

Personalized

One distinct characteristic that new media provide over broadcast media is the ability for users to filter and personalize them. In the Communication Age, you are able to manage your media's appearance, text, colors, fonts, pictures, music, and the like. You expect to have the capability to control your media and customize things to your liking. Through this expectation, you find technology targeting users with trendy new ways of personalization. For example, using Blogger.com

What are some other examples of new media jargon not listed in this image?

How often do you find yourself engaging in face-to-face communication and computer-mediated communication at the same time?

In the Communication Age, wearable computing technologies continue to evolve.

allows someone to build a blog in only four steps. Yet each step of the process can be completely personalized. From the title, to the username, to the profile, to the colors, to the text, each blog is unique to individual standards. This characteristic is what makes new media so attractive to users, giving them a presence in a global world while still representing their own interests and style.

There are other ways new media are personalized. For example, Cade has set MSN.com as his homepage. When opening the page, Cade is instantly connected to his local weather, news, and events. Sports and entertainment news appear at the top of the page, and Cade's e-mail and instant messaging portals notify him about new e-mail or when a friend has signed on. At the top of the page, his personal planner icon updates him on the time of his next meeting and a countdown to his girlfriend's birthday. On the right-hand side of the page, Cade has linked his Facebook and Twitter accounts, which he placed just above the streaming MSN news feeds that he periodically watches throughout the day. At the bottom of the page, Cade can watch the stock market and view Bobby Flay's cooking recipes, and he has an icon to search, buy, or view the latest Apple products. The entire site consistently updates itself for Cade every 10 minutes. The irresistible element to new media is just *how* personalized they can get. It is so easy to get wrapped up in new media that people feel like they cannot function without them. Through personalization, new media build relationships and routines with their users by conveniently giving users the information they want, when they want it, how they want it to appear, and the like. Keep in mind, however, a potential drawback with personalization: It can be limiting. With personalization you have less exposure to points of view other than the ones you choose to include in your new media network.

Creative

Unlike broadcast media, new media provide an open arena that allows for creative self-expression. Like personalization, creativity is having the ability to display your style, personality, and interests in a way that is fun and entertaining. Users update their status, join newsgroups, and share pictures as part of their daily routine. A unique aspect of new media that generations before us have never experienced is the endless possibility to express "self" to the world. In various ways, your actions represent who you are and how you act. For example, Rachel is a young photographer just out of college. She is able to display her work through a website, a blog, and social media. Rachel can present her vintage, whimsical, and edgy style to potential clients with the same interests. New media allow Rachel to express her creativity while still maintaining her professional tasks. Unlike the traditional broadcast media of television, radio, and newspapers, new media provide a platform for the expression of self to others. Later in this chapter you will look at the various ways that new media allow users to build and express their identity.

Flexible

The Communication Age is all about having the ability to communicate and retrieve instant information. When broadcast media dominated the airwaves, they also dictated the schedule of their audience. The morning paper was delivered before the sun came up; the local news aired at 7 a.m. and then again at noon and

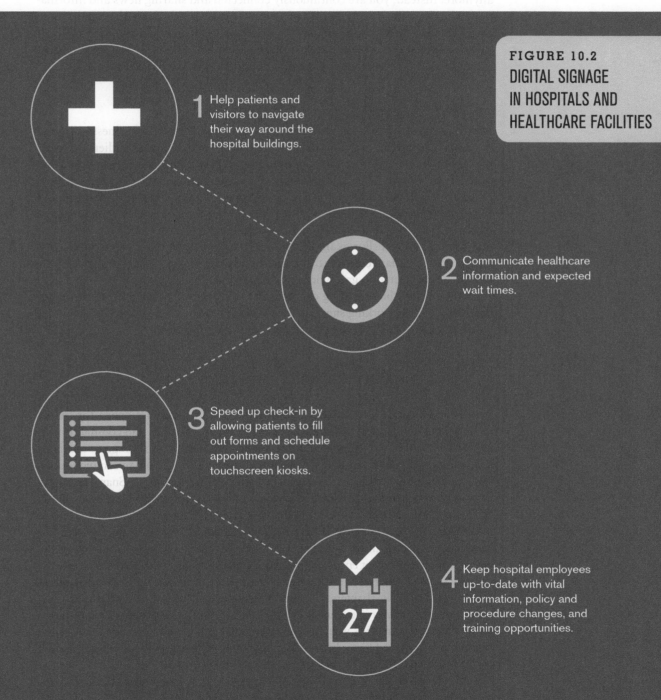

FIGURE 10.2
DIGITAL SIGNAGE IN HOSPITALS AND HEALTHCARE FACILITIES

1 Help patients and visitors to navigate their way around the hospital buildings.

2 Communicate healthcare information and expected wait times.

3 Speed up check-in by allowing patients to fill out forms and schedule appointments on touchscreen kiosks.

4 Keep hospital employees up-to-date with vital information, policy and procedure changes, and training opportunities.

SOURCE: Adapted from securedge networks, http://www.securedgenetworks.com/blog/4-Benefits-of-Digital-Signage-in-Hospital-Wireless-Networks.

5 p.m. Not so long ago, people raced home to catch their favorite show because they could not simply DVR it. The same routines followed in daily radio news shows, in monthly magazines, or when mailing a postcard. Broadcast media created time restraints and conflicting availability. Today's media are available when people want them, as fast as people can get to them. This flexibility is one reason why people function the way they do. You do not have to rely on the 5 p.m. news anymore. Instead, you are continuously connected and sharing news and information. The characteristic of flexibility means that new media have the capability to adapt to new, different, or changing requirements. When you tweet about your vacation, check online news feeds at midnight, share a video, or change the background color of your blog, you are utilizing the flexibility of your media.

Always Evolving

New media are always changing and never the same. Everyday businesses around the world are envisioning and inventing new ways to reach mass audiences, while still giving us the characteristics of interaction, personalization, creativity, flexibility, and control. Think about your first interaction with the Internet, cell phones, e-mail, or instant messaging. In what ways have new media changed and evolved during your lifetime? Like everything else, there is a catch to new media. In order to stay up to date and connected, you always have to buy into the latest and newest product. For example, wearable technologies designed as functional and aesthetic enhancements to the physical body, like the Fitbit and the Apple Watch, are projected to gain widespread adoption.

Do you think the preceding characteristics of new media have led to the popularity of social networking sites like Facebook? As you review Figure 10.2, consider which qualities of new media you find more or less attractive.

PRESENTING MY ONLINE IDENTITY

Since the advent of the Internet, new media have provided a space for public self-presentation. With technological advances, our interactions and communication styles have shifted from the usual face-to-face communication to computer-mediated communication. Computer-mediated communication (CMC) is human communication facilitated by a wide range of new media technologies such as Tumblr, Snapchat, e-mail message systems, message boards, and online games (Arvidsson, 2006; Gibbs, Ellison, & Heino, 2006; Li, Jackson, & Trees, 2008; Martey & Stromer-Galley, 2007; Peter & Valkenburg, 2007; Walther & D'Addario, 2001; Walther, Loh, & Granka, 2005). The experience of communicating and interacting through new media in an enormous but anonymous environment encourages users to create profiles, write verbal descriptions, construct visual avatars, use creative screen names, and build relationships with others. As learned in previous chapters, an avatar is defined as a fixed online identity that someone creates for activity in cyberspace (Palomares & Eun-Ju, 2010). An avatar may be formed through someone's writing in a newsgroup or a cartoon character he or she has created as an image of his or her self (e.g., Comic-Book Guy on *The Simpsons* and his avatar "Everyman," *Mad Men* avatars on Facebook) (Jordan, 1999).

CMC researchers have argued for many years that computers would reshape human communication, and their predictions have come true (Hiltz & Turoff, 1993; Jones, 1997; Marvin, 1988; Poster, 1990; Sproull & Kiesler, 1991). When you as

ASSESS YOUR COMMUNICATION

CMC COMPETENCE

This measure will allow you to assess your own CMC competence.

Directions: The following statements, modified from Spitzberg's (2006) CMC Competence Scale, describe the ways some people use and feel about new CMC. Please indicate in the space at the left of each item the degree to which you believe the statement applies to you. Please use the following 5-point scale:

1 = Not at all true of me
2 = Mostly not true of me
3 = Neither true nor untrue of me; undecided
4 = Mostly true of me
5 = Very true of me

_____ 1. I enjoy communicating using computer media.
_____ 2. I always seem to know how to say things the way I mean them using CMC.
_____ 3. I feel very competent in learning and using communication media technology.
_____ 4. Communicating through a computer does not make me anxious.
_____ 5. I know I can learn to use new CMC technologies when they come out.
_____ 6. I manage the give and take of CMC interactions skillfully.
_____ 7. I can show compassion and empathy through the way I write e-mails.
_____ 8. I take time to make sure my e-mails to others are uniquely adapted to their particular receivers.
_____ 9. I try to use a lot of humor in my CMC messages.
_____10. I use a lot of expressive symbols [e.g., :-) for "smile"] in my CMC messages.
_____11. I have no trouble expressing my opinions forcefully on CMC.
_____12. I avoid saying things that might offend someone.
_____13. My interactions are effective in accomplishing what I set out to accomplish.
_____14. My comments are consistently accurate and clear.
_____15. I am generally pleased with my interactions.
_____16. I come across in conversation as someone people would like to get to know.
_____17. My CMC interactions are more productive than my face-to-face interactions.
_____18. CMC technologies are tremendous time-savers for my work.
_____19. I rely heavily upon my CMCs for getting me through each day.
_____20. I can rarely go a week without any CMC interactions.

Add your scores. The highest score you can receive is 100, and the lowest is 20. How did you score? What surprised you about your score? You can also try the assessment on others. Simply fill out the measure with another person's behaviors in mind. For instance, you might find it interesting to fill out the survey for one of your friends to determine whether his or her use of CMC might play some role in the degree to which you interact with him or her online. Do you notice differences in your friend's use of CMC and face-to-face interactions? Be aware of how you assess communication between CMC and face-to-face interactions among your friends, family, coworkers, and acquaintances.

Source: Scale adapted from Spitzberg, B. H. (2006). Preliminary development of a model and measure of computer-mediated communication (CMC) competence. *Journal of Computer-Mediated Communication, 11*(2), 629–666.

In what ways do you present yourself online in the same way that you present yourself in face-to-face conversation? In what ways do you present yourself differently online?

iStock

a human communicator rely on computers as your primary channel for communicating with friends, family members, colleagues, and even strangers, you must understand the effects that this channel has on your verbal and nonverbal communication as well as your identity (Couch & Liamputtong, 2008; Ivy & Wahl, 2014; Li et al., 2008; Pollock, 2006; Wahl & Scholl, 2014). CMC separates your physical appearance and other nonverbal cues from the communication process and allows you to enter into an intermediary space where fantasy and fictional identities can form. As a result, the presentation of your online identity may or may not represent your true self. In fact, the Internet is often thought of as a place where role-playing, experimenting with different personas, and creating an idealized version of one's self is common. Scholar Tim Jordan (1999) explains: "On the Internet nobody knows you at all, on the Internet nobody knows what your race is or your sex, that whole color and sex-blindness is a positive force for a lot of people. They feel welcome" (p. 187). The notion of identity formation and new media can be clarified by understanding the following: traditional concepts of identity formation, the development of self online, the social media explosion, and self-disclosure.

Think critically about how you present yourself online. Do you come across through CMC in a very similar way as you do when meeting people face to face? Give attention to your online communication or new media profiles, and be aware of the effects of absent nonverbal communication cues (e.g., physical appearance, vocalics, facial expression, eye expression, gestures, touch) on the clarity and impact of your message. You might find that your online identity is true and unexaggerated from your real identity.

The reality of the Internet is that online self-presentation is fueled by deception and identity play. Through CMC and new media you can virtually become anyone you want to be! Communication scholars are fascinated by this topic—the way real identity corresponds with and influences the presentation of self online. Before you look into the implications of online identity formation, it is important to understand the traditional concepts of identity formation.

Traditional Concepts of Identity Formation

Prior to and during the First Media Age, society was expected to conform to social norms. During this time, the idea of social reconstruction and re-creating one's identity was not common. For example, if your grandparents were born into a conservative Christian family, they were expected to live with the same values as their parents. During this time social identities were fixed and based on tradition, but people are no longer held to the same conventions. Identity is creative, personal, self-reflective, flexible, and subject to change at any time. Today, users of new media are given the chance to become almost anything by simply logging on. Technology introduces new roles and changes the ways in which people communicate.

The theory of self-presentation originates from Erving Goffman's 1959 book, *The Presentation of Self in Everyday Life*, which can be applied directly to CMC.

Goffman used a performance metaphor to explain the presentational self: Everyday settings are viewed as a stage, and people are considered actors who use performances to make an impression on an audience. When you enter into any situation, you put on a performance in which you must decide how to position yourself, what to say, and how to act (Littlejohn & Foss, 2008). For example, you would not behave with your circle of intimate friends the same way you would behave during an interview.

According to Goffman (1959), "The expressiveness of the individual (and therefore his capacity to give impressions) appears to solve two radically different kinds of sign activity: the expression that he *gives,* and the expression that he *gives off*" (p. 2). What people *give* refers to verbal communication, whereas what people *give off* relates more to nonverbal communication such as facial expressions, gestures, body movements, and attire (Martey & Stromer-Galley, 2007). Since CMC relies more heavily on verbal text than nonverbal cues, what people *give* takes on more significance.

So how does Goffman's theory relate to new media and CMC? Just as you present your physical self according to the situation, the same is true online: You become what you type (Greenhow & Robelia, 2009). New media provide a space where people can construct a variety of identities and profiles. For example, Facebook allows users to create a personal profile, form social networks, and develop an image of how they see themselves and how they want others to see them (Greenhow & Robelia, 2009).

What you typically think of as nonverbal cues may be altered in CMC, but you still *give off* these cues to assist in the transmission of the verbal message and to represent yourself to your online partners (Li et al., 2008). Nonverbal cues in CMC include using a lot of exclamation points to indicate excitement or emoticons to show emotion (Ivy & Wahl, 2014). For example, someone might be extremely shy face to face, but through the use of CMC have more confidence. Indeed, a person might choose to have a radically different online identity than the one he or she displays face to face.

Second Media Age scholar Mark Poster (1990) observes that in computer-mediated contexts the individual is affected by identity play, absence of gender cues, and variations in time and space. Communication researcher Charles Soukup (2004) confirms this sense of identity play, observing that virtual communities enable people to engage in dramatic performance online through nonverbal communication (e.g., managing space with avatars, expressing emotions with online characters).

The Development of Self Online

Since many of your daily actions, interactions, and experiences are mediated by technology, consider how you express yourself and how this form of expression changes your sense of self, compared to how you communicate your identities to people face to face (Ivy & Wahl, 2014; Walther et al., 2005; Wright, 2004). In various ways, new media and CMC allow users to carefully present an image of the self and have the capability to change it at any given time. In fact, identity, the self, and CMC are deeply intertwined. Think about it. How does your Facebook profile offer you features that can be easily modified to present yourself? How are you able to create content that portrays your identity online? In the next few sections, attention will be given to the various ways that people represent themselves through CMC.

Keeping up with different screen names and passwords from one online activity to the next has become a common task.

Screen Names

Have you ever considered that your screen names reflect how you view yourself and how you want to be perceived by others? Screen names can essentially be one way to accomplish identity development online. Many Internet users subconsciously create screen names that often portray different facets of themselves. In some situations, you may only know people by their screen name and would approach someone named "crazy4u" differently than you would "literarylady" or "John2244." Sometimes it is hard to know if the person's screen name provides an accurate representation of the person behind the screen. Think of all of the ways that screen names are used on the Internet. From uploading YouTube videos, to instant messaging, to posting a comment on a news article, to selling an item on eBay, Internet users develop a screen name as an identity marker. Screen names are often the names people use to identify and locate others in a network. A person may create multiple screen names for different online activities and multiple identities. For example, Misty is a single mother with two children looking for a job and a relationship. Misty uses RockStarMom2 when chatting with friends and uploading pictures on Flickr. When commenting on news articles and joining chat conversations about political topics, Misty uses the screen name NYDemocratVoice27. When Misty signed up on Match.com, she used the screen name HOTnewyorker. Last, Misty found herself just using MistyJones as her screen name when uploading her résumé and trying to find a job.

Like Misty, many people create a screen name as an extension of the self or as a playful way to develop characteristics only online. Some screen names are humorous, colorful, imaginative, artistic, sexual, and even gendered. Others, however, can be business oriented, professional, or generic. Either way, screen names are often carefully selected and associated with our personality and identity. Screen names like MLBkingPlaya, TrackStar400, FlyFishFlorida, or SteffCosmoShopper may symbolize an interest or a hobby. When you read the screen names PBBunny69, EvilPrincess, PimpinTim, and JasonBizMoney, what impression do you have of these people? Next time you are on your social networking site of choice, click the "Browse" button to view all of the users. You will find screen names associated with mythology, comics, literature, films, music, and all types of popular culture. In addition, it is common to find screen names linking to hometowns, states, countries, races, cultures, religions, businesses, colleges, and professions. Screen names are selected to portray true or unrealistic characteristics of the self. Sometime screen names are considered to be an electronic costume or mask. Think about all of the screen names you have had in your lifetime. In what ways have they changed in different online environments? Does your screen name give off a positive or negative portrayal of your true identity? Have you ever considered that your screen names indicate to others how you view yourself, or how you want to be perceived by others? Screen names can essentially be one way to accomplish identity development online.

E-mail

Like screen names, e-mail addresses also provide an association to identity construction online (Ivy & Wahl, 2014). E-mail addresses contain three parts, all of which communicate personal information to others. They

Thinkstock

Is your e-mail address connected to your personal preferences or identity? If so, how?

Communication unplugged

REMEMBER THAT YOUR MEDIATED CHOICES HAVE FACE-TO-FACE CONSEQUENCES

The Communication Age presents the following situation that's becoming all too common: Miranda needs to land a job. However, she made a critical error in her job search: On the electronic version of the résumé she e-mailed to the company, at the top where she listed her current address, phone number, and e-mail address, Miranda also included a link to her Facebook page that contains some elements that she didn't remember were there when she started her job search. There are several pictures of her drinking and smoking. She communicated professionally during all the job interviews with the company, but her Facebook page tells a different story to her hiring committee. Business and professional communication scholars have specific suggestions regarding how information you post about yourself online can impact your professional life. Social networking once meant going to a social function such as a cocktail party, conference, or business luncheon. Today, much social networking is achieved through websites such as Facebook or LinkedIn. Many individuals use these sites to meet

new friends, make connections, and upload personal information. On social networking websites (SNWs) that focus more on business connections, such as LinkedIn, individuals upload job qualifications and application information. These SNWs are now being used as reference checks by human resources personnel.

WHAT TO DO NEXT

To increase the effectiveness of your social networking, try to:

1. Avoid loading information that you don't want the world to see.

2. Make sure that what you present online shows you in the best light.

3. Think about the impression another person would have of you considering what's available online.

Source: Quintanilla & Wahl (2014).

---

begin with a username (often a person's screen name), followed by the domain name (after the @ symbol), followed by the top-level domain (after the period). Many of the same concepts apply to usernames as to screen names. The username one selects can convey multiple characteristics of the self. Be aware that people will form impressions of you based on the name you select. For instance, BombShe1169@yahoo.com and BeerGuy24–7@hotmail.com may be acceptable when corresponding with friends, but not in a professional situation. Keep in mind when creating your résumé that potential employers may reject a job applicant whose contact information includes an e-mail address such as LazyDrunkMan@gmail.com.

The domain name included in your e-mail address is reflective of the service provider, profession, or affiliation you have to others. Many of you reading this book have an e-mail address in affiliation with the school you are attending. This type of domain name symbolically connects you to your college or university campus. Similarly, the domain names used in brooke@wildheartedcowgirls.com or whitney@ellemagazine.com show the businesses with which these women are associated.

The last part of an e-mail address is called the top-level domain. The most recognizable top-level domain name is .com. Other similar

Celebrities like Gwyneth Paltrow have become bloggers for a variety of topics.

FIGURE 10.3
REASONS TO BLOG

Why do people blog?	Major Reason
To express themselves creatively	52%
To document their personal experiences or share them with others	50%
To stay in touch with friends and family	37%
To share practical knowledge or skills with others	34%
To motivate other people to action	29%
To entertain people	28%
To store resources or information that is important to them	28%
To influence the way other people think	27%
To network or to meet new people	16%
To make money	7%

Sources: Gil de Zúñiga et al. (2011); Lenhart & Fox (2006).

codes such as .edu (education), .gov (government), and .org (organization) are also important to recognize in any Internet search.

Blogs

Blogs, a word that comes from *weblog,* enable users to disclose only the information that they desire at any given time. This capability allows for identity performance and the ability to express self in a variety of ways (Davis, 2011; Xun, 2010). Personal websites and blogs are all about the individual. Blogs are devoted to specific aspects of the self (e.g., personal/family matters, hobbies, health, games, activism, identity, culture) as well as those focusing on academics, entertainment, real estate, and not-for-profit organizations. Through blogging there are endless opportunities to publish and share pictures, videos, audio, music, articles, reviews, critiques, and news, as well as personal information, thoughts, ideas, talents, and other unique characteristics (Xun, 2010). Bloggers are a major presence on the web today. Looking specifically at blogs, 20% of teenage Internet users report maintaining a blog, compared to 8% of adult Internet users (Gil de Zúñiga et al., 2011; Lenhart & Fox, 2006). Furthermore, most major media organizations have blogs associated with their regular publications to highlight a particular personality or topic (e.g., ESPN's "The Sports Guy," the dozens of blogs attached to the *New York Times*).

People often create blogs with a goal in mind or for a specific reason. The majority of bloggers cite expressing themselves creatively as the primary reason for maintaining a blog, with documenting and sharing personal experiences a close second (Lenhart & Fox, 2006). As a means for exploring identities and expressing aspects of the self that prove difficult through other methods, personal webpages and blogs do not function simply as a display and expression of the self. Rather, they are a means for creating, establishing, and maintaining identities (see Figure 10.3).

iStock

Personal Profiles

Personal profiles are everywhere on the Internet. When signing up for a new account on most new media portals, you will find yourself writing a personal profile to provide more information about yourself. In most situations, personal profiles are short descriptions about our age, sex, race, physical features, affiliations, and interests. Personal profiles often link us to our screen names, helping others to learn more about our identity. The double standard of the Internet is that while we are connected to the world, many profiles and screen names can be based on fictional and idealized versions of the self. How do we know when people are using a mask for age, race, or gender in their personal profiles, screen names, and e-mail accounts? In many instances, personal profiles provide us with realistic information; however, sometimes we have to question if some information provided is based on fantasy and fiction.

Social Media

Probably the most significant area of identity development online happens through social media (Palomares & Eun-Ju, 2010). Social media include sites like Facebook, Twitter, Google+, Flickr, and LinkedIn. Social media are defined as web-based services that allow individuals to create a public profile and maintain and view a list of users who share a common interest. Social networking sites are a significant aspect of CMC; these sites allow for new "friending," maintaining existing ties, and forging new networks (Greenhow & Robelia, 2009, p. 120). Some common features of social networking sites include the following:

- Personal profiles
- Screen names
- CMC relationships (friends, followers)
- Participation in groups
- Direct communication (instant messaging, texting, public and private posts, phone services)
- Sharing of user-created content
- Expressing opinions
- Finding information
- Entertainment (games, music, videos, pictures)

All of the characteristics of social media listed above are similar to those of new media that you have explored in this chapter. The use of the term *social media* places priority on and refers to the significance of the social and relational aspects of today's media. Social media enable users to forge new relationships and display both personal and relational identities. They allow people to connect and share information while establishing new connections with people from around the world. The social aspect is as important for users as their identity creation. Social media, in terms of self-expression and self-disclosure, are unlike any other forum. In fact, social media are so unique that scholars are amazed by the impact they have on society and our online self-presentation. By visiting a complete stranger's Facebook page, you can learn more about that person in the first 5 minutes than if you were meeting face to face. The extent to which social media impact our identity, relationships, and self is not yet completely understood. Consider how

The film *The Social Network* depicts the start of Facebook in a Harvard University dorm room. What forms of social media do you use on a regular basis?

Self-Disclosure

Scholars describe self-disclosure as a useful strategy for sharing information with others that occurs gradually over time as trust is established in a relationship (Petronio, 2002). By sharing information, you become more intimate with other people, and your interpersonal relationship is strengthened (Rawlins, 2009). New media provide an anonymous environment for users to connect, interact, and provide significant amounts of personal information all at once (Ledbetter et al., 2011). The lack of face-to-face interaction has the effect of making many people self-disclose more than they do in face-to-face discussions. Such self-disclosure is due to the fact that people are more aware of themselves and less aware of the people to whom they are talking (Joinson, 2001). Therefore, self-disclosure through new media becomes extremely comfortable for users.

Social media challenge all of the rules of classic self-disclosure research. In a traditional face-to-face setting, communication scholars believe peripheral information

you can use social media to get involved (see "Communication How-To").

COMMUNICATIONHOW-TO
BEST PRACTICES IN RUNNING A SOCIAL MEDIA FEED

By now many of you have some type of social media feed, whether it is Facebook, Instagram, Twitter, Foursquare, or any of the other numerous options available currently. As you continue to grow as a communication professional, it is essential to identify the best practices and activities available to you whether you use social media for work or play. Below are several key factors to keep in mind:

1. **Traditional ethics rules still apply online.** Although it can be tempting to practice greater freedom of communication in the digital context, remember that many people still adhere to traditional communication formalities (Hohmann, 2011). Try not to be overly aggressive, rude, or dismissive, and try to maintain the same level of courtesy you would expect in a face-to-face setting.

2. **Assume everything you write online will become public.** There is a constant stream of news stories discussing instances of people (famous or not) who post something online and receive a severe public backlash. Even

with privacy settings, there are still numerous ways your social media activity can get away from you. Even deleting an offensive post does not guarantee it has been removed forever.

3. **Be aware of different perceptions.** Although your close friends and family may generally agree with your views, remember that the Internet is an incredibly diverse and ever-changing environment. Anything you post to your social media can find its way to the general public, so remember to manage your media feed activity with due diligence.

Images: istock.

about the self would be shared first, leaving the deeper personal information for further relationship development. Peripheral information is relatively minor information about the self—on your personal profile this information would include things such as your music interests or favorite movies. Through social media you are displaying your peripheral information and integrating it with personal information such as sexual orientation and relationship history. In addition, self-disclosure theories suggest that what you share with one person is not the same as what you share with another. Your Facebook friends and blog followers can access your personal events, thoughts, ideas, relationships, and behaviors.

Through new media people often share personal information with a large network of friends and sometimes strangers (Davis, 2011). In contrast to face-to-face interactions, where some feel anxiety when sharing too much information, people using CMC behave in a more unreserved fashion when it comes to self-disclosure. In the process, people increase their self-disclosure rate because it becomes more comfortable to reveal their innermost feelings in text-only interaction. Human nonverbal communication cues are lost in CMC (Ivy & Wahl, 2014). The absence of nonverbal cues in CMC obscures the boundaries that would generally separate acceptable and unacceptable forms of behaviors. Furthermore, CMC is less bounded by conventions than is face-to-face interaction (Reed, 1991). We as communicators have all experienced the feeling of revealing information about ourselves through CMC that we would never disclose in face-to-face settings.

CAREER FRONTIER: SOCIAL/NEW MEDIA MANAGER

iStock

MANY CURRENT COMMUNICATION jobs concentrate on managing the social media front of businesses and organizations. Surveys suggest that CEOs are increasingly convinced that the digital world is a core part of their future and that they need people to lead it (Holtz, 2014). Many companies list qualifications requiring proficiency in analyzing and interpreting data; familiarity with trending social media services and practices; and, of course, written and verbal skills. One particularly popular tool for managing social media is the TweetDeck, a social media dashboard application for management of Twitter accounts. The dashboard consists of a series of customizable columns, which can be set up to display your Twitter timeline, mentions, direct messages, lists, trends, favorites, search results, hashtags, or all tweets by or to a single user. Perhaps many of you are aware of this application; however,

TweetDeck is only one of countless options available to you as a social media manager. To succeed in your role as a professional, you must remember to stay current on new tools that constantly become available to you. Getting stuck behind the times can ruin your ability to effectively manage social media both for yourself and your organization.

ISSUES TO CONSIDER

1. How could the career you are pursuing be influenced or shaped by new media?

2. How much influence do new media have on you in the process of choosing your career path?

Source: Adapted from "Rankings of Best Top 10 Social Media Optimization Companies," July 28, 2010, *Rankings of Best SEO, PPC, Web Design and Development, Local Search, Reputation Management Companies, Firms, Agencies, Firm, Company;* retrieved from http://www.topseos.com/rankings-of-best-social-media-optimization-companies

Social Information Processing Theory

To explain the presence of nonverbal cues used in new media to develop relationships, Joseph Walther (1995) developed social information processing (SIP) theory to explain how CMC and face-to-face communication are both successful in building relationships. Walther's SIP theory explains that relationships develop only to the extent that people first gain information about one another and then use that information to form impressions or mental images of one another. Walther recognizes that nonverbal cues are filtered out of the information exchanged via CMC, but he doesn't believe that this loss is detrimental to the development of successful and satisfying online relationships.

Along with SIP theory, researchers Joseph Walther and Malcolm Parks adapted what is known as warranting theory, which suggests that in the presence of anonymity, a person may potentially misrepresent information about his or her self (Walther & Parks, 2002). Warranting pertains to the perceived legitimacy and validity of information about other people that you may receive or observe online. The introduction of the warranting construct argues that an individual is less likely to distort representations of themselves when the receiver has access to other members of the sender's social circle. Apply this theory to your personal CMC interactions: Do you distort information more readily when your audience has no connection to your real-world family and friends?

Think about your experiences with CMC and the ways your new media relationships form differently. Can you recall a time when you had a text, e-mail, or chat conversation that revealed deep personal information? Reflect on how this conversation would take place in a face-to-face setting.

NEW MEDIA AS YOUR COMMUNITY

New media provide us with a multifaceted experience. If you are an avid Internet user, it is probably common for you to look up from your phone or computer and realize that more time has passed than you thought. As the Internet becomes more interactive, users enter into cyberspace and often lose track of the difference between real and virtual. Cyberspace, a term originally coined by William Gibson, is a place that collects all the information in the world and can be accessed and entered by any capable person (Jordan, 1999). Cyberspace offers power to those who can create, publish, and manipulate information. People fear that they might miss something if they do not "log on." Often, their sense of time is lost when they enter into cyberspace.

Relationships, communities, and communication become more realistic because they are experienced in real time. Real time is composed of activities or resources whose action and reactions occur immediately, with no delay. Speaking to someone in person is a real-time conversation. CMC and many cyberspace resources can now be experienced in real time (e.g., video conferences, GoToMeeting, Skype). However, cyberspace is considered virtual because the lives, communities, and societies formed online do not exist with the same physical reality of "real" societies. Virtuality is the general term for this reinvention of familiar physical space in cyberspace.

Those engaging in CMC are establishing a sense of community and relationship that is similar to traditional face-to-face interactions—what is referred to as establishing virtual communities. As the world's communication style shifts and communicators rely on the Internet as their primary communication source, they begin to see people gather, connect, and relate to one another from around the world. Individuals within these virtual communities develop relationships and a sense of belonging to various groups. Through their expression of self and identity online, people can relate to others and develop relational and informational support groups (Davis, 2011). You are able to connect with people across geographic barriers and create a gathering point for people with common interests, beliefs, and ideas. This changing concept of community in the Communication Age has various advantages over your real physical communities.

For some people, capturing images of daily experiences to share via social media has become so important that products like the selfie stick, pictured here, have become a desired accessory.

NEW MEDIA AND CONVERGENCE

As you think back to Ella's experience with new media related to her daily routine, think about the presence of both new media and convergence in your own life. New media in the Communication Age are about the endless experiences of entering into a virtual reality. With the emergence and popularity of new media, new forms of communication have entered into daily life. You can create a profile, characters, or avatars. You can access information, news, videos, music, games, pictures, communities, chat rooms, and social networks. You can become friends, followers, or enemies with others online. New media allow for the formation of identities, relationships, and rituals. A world of information can be accessed in the Communication Age, and consumers are now in control of media. With this two-way communication, for the first time, many are speaking to many. Anyone can become a publisher, an editor, a news writer, a movie producer, a musician, an expert, or a celebrity.

As you reflect on the themes and key concepts related to new media in this chapter, consider the future of journalism and mass communication. The impact of new media on the Communication Age will no doubt continue to challenge citizens and scholars to think about the source and quality of information. Consider the question Ahmad (2010) raises about the meaning of journalism in the Communication Age:

> The role of journalists as fact-finders, in this context, may well come under increasing question with time as more and more citizens take to blogging and uploading visual data. It is a development that cannot help but further blur the line between journalists and citizens around the world, and at the very least, is likely to raise questions about what the word "journalist" actually means. (p. 152)

Considering Ahmad's view, what impact do you think new media and convergence will have on the future of journalism and mass communication?

The exciting part about new media and convergence in the Communication Age is their endless possibilities. They are always changing, always reinventing, and never the same. New media provide a wide-open space for the combination

NEW MEDIA LITERACY

iStock

Social media foster global connections.

THE EXTRAORDINARY ASPECT of the Communication Age is that people are both the consumers and the producers of media. Everyone needs new media literacy skills to function, survive, and succeed in the Communication Age. Review the following set of skills important to fostering your life as an educated citizen. These skills will help to enhance your understanding of new media in the Communication Age. With all of the information presented in this chapter, it is important that you understand where to go from here, how to apply new media concepts to your life, and how to use this information to advance your control and power over media. New media literacy skills can help people engage and interact in the Communication Age.

New Media Literacy Skills	
1. Participation	Anticipating, accepting, engaging, and participating in the next new thing. Participation enables us to learn how to use new media competitively. We cannot be set in our ways; we must get involved in new media.
2. Analysis	Breaking down the content and messages into meaningful elements.
3. Attention	Focusing on goals, objectives, and tasks. Finding the balance between work and entertainment in new media.
4. Judgment	The ability to evaluate and judge the value of a message. We must know when to trust information as reliable or discard it as untrustworthy.
5. Networking	The ability to collaborate, connect, and relate to others. Connecting with others on a global level through identity formation and relationships.
6. Multitasking	The ability that involves the simultaneous performance of two or more tasks at the same time. Creating, sharing, unraveling, and finding content instantly.
7. Negotiation	Understanding the norms and cultures of different online groups, communities, and spaces into which we enter.
8. Appropriation	The ability to remix and sample content in a meaningful way on different portals.
9. Interaction/Play	Experimenting with different surroundings, identities, and people as a form of problem solving.

Source: New Media Literacies, http://newmedialiteracies.org/

and mixture of opinions, news, politics, culture, business, entertainment, and education. Accept the movement and shift into the Communication Age and join in on the conversations online. In essence, there has been a revolution and social movement in the way people now communicate.

WHAT YOU'VE LEARNED   Now that you have studied this chapter, you should be able to:

1 Identify the ways in which new media impact your life.

New media in the Communication Age foster the convergence of old and new media, allowing for connections across boundaries, borders, and countries with the click of a button. These new forms of mediated communication are deeply integrated into our everyday lives.

 What the Internet is Doing to Our Brains

The Impact of Social Media on Society

2 Explain why the characteristics of the First and Second Media Ages are important to your study of communication.

The Electronic Tradition (First Media Age), also referred to as the Electronic Age or Electronic Media, includes media that require users to make use of electronics to access content. Because of the multifunctionality of many

new media devices, such as the smartphone, researchers created a new classification for technological advancements, called the New Media Tradition (Second Media Age).

The New Media's Coming of Age

Italy's Berlusconi Discovers Social Media as a Campaign Tool

3 Describe the qualities of new media and how they influence communication.

In the context of your everyday lifestyle and behaviors, you engage and interact with new media due to their qualities of participation and empowerment. For the first time, the Communication Age enables us to be in control of our media.

Shift Happens: The Changing Media Landscape

Journalists Navigate New Times

4 Describe the characteristics of new media theory.

New media theory was designed to describe the unique, customized communication styles of today.

 Microsoft's Concept 2020

5 Explain how identity is formed through new media and their relationship to communication.

Identity development, the presentation of self online, and community are shaped in various ways through new media. New media in the

Communication Age are about the endless experiences of entering into a virtual reality.

▶ Adventures in Twitter Fiction

▣ The Online Identity Crisis

6 Examine how new media foster community.

Remember some of the characteristics of new media: interactive, personalized, creative, flexible, and always evolving. These characteristics of new media help to foster community in the Communication Age.

▶ Connected but Alone

🎙 Through the Internet, Gay Teens Connected to Larger Community

KEY TERMS

Review key terms with eFlashcards. **edge.sagepub.com/edwards2e**

Blogs   258
Computer-mediated communication (CMC)   252
Cyberspace   262
Electronic Tradition (First Media Age)   244
Interactivity   248
New media   242
New media theory   246

New Media Tradition (Second Media Age)   246
Oral Tradition   243
Peripheral information   261
Personal profiles   259
Primary orality   243
Printing press   243
Print Tradition   243
Real time   262

Screen names   256
Secondary orality   243
Social information processing (SIP) theory   262
Social media   259
Theory of self-presentation   254
Virtuality   262
Warranting theory   262
Written Tradition   243

REFLECT

1. Discuss the experiences you have had with the development of new media throughout your life. What is the first type of new media you remember using in your early years of life (e.g., cell phones, laptops)?

2. Do you ever get burned out with new media? Do you ever intentionally keep your new media (e.g., PDA, iPhone, laptop) turned off to have quiet time or downtime?

3. Do new media ever hinder your face-to-face communication and listening? What do you do or say, if anything, to address the problem?

4. Are you currently using new media to support your learning process in college? Furthermore, do you like the idea of downloading class notes and materials using new media? What concerns, if any, do you have about the ways in which new media are shaping the future of education (e.g., online classes, distance education)?

REVIEW

To check your answers go to **edge.sagepub.com/edwards2e**

1. What are new media?

2. Define oral tradition.

3. _____ is the phenomenon of communication at a distance through new media—sending and receiving digitally encoded messages in almost real time, continually allowing users to have two-way communication in an environment that is constantly changing and challenging them.

4. _____ are defined as web-based services that allow individuals to create a public profile and maintain and view a list of users who share a common interest.

5. Joseph Walther (1995) developed _____ to explain how CMC and face-to-face communication are both successful in building relationships.

6. Along with SIP theory, researchers Joseph Walther and Malcolm Parks adapted what is known as _____, which suggests that in the presence of anonymity, a person may potentially misrepresent information about his or her self.

7. _____ is composed of activities or resources whose actions and reactions occur immediately, with no delay.

8. _____ is the general term for this reinvention of familiar physical space in cyberspace.

9. Explain why new media literacy skills are important in the Communication Age.

11

SELECTING YOUR TOPIC AND KNOWING YOUR AUDIENCE

WHAT YOU'LL LEARN After studying this chapter, you will be able to:

 Explain how to define the purpose of a presentation.

 Summarize the characteristics of different types of presentation.

Describe the ways to choose a topic that is suitable for the type of presentation.

 Explain how to conduct an audience analysis to achieve the most impact.

 Create the basic structure of a presentation.

On March 7, 1965, police and other citizens attacked unarmed marchers near the Edmund Pettus Bridge in Selma, Alabama. Six hundred civil rights activists were protesting racial injustice in the South by marching from Selma to the state capital in Montgomery. On the 50th anniversary of this march, President Barack Obama gave a speech in the shadow of this bridge. He spoke of the American experiment as it applies to all Americans: "What greater expression of faith in the American experiment than this, what greater form of patriotism is there than the belief that America is not yet finished, that we are strong enough to be self-critical, that each successive generation can look upon our imperfections and decide that it is in our power to remake this nation to more closely align with our highest ideals?" (Obama, 2015). He crafted the speech to commemorate the marchers and the civil rights movement as part of the American experiment.

The White House knew that millions of people would watch the speech live, and that many more would watch clips shared on social media. It was a speech designed to tie all Americans together in a common bond of equality and justice. President Obama spoke to the civil rights leaders of the past as well as to those who might become ones in the future (Ford, 2015). In other words, President Obama had to speak to many different audiences in both time and space for this one speech. The president knew that many different people both now and in the future would view this speech. As such, he had to think carefully about audience analysis.

Similar to how President Obama and the White House used audience analysis to craft arguments for the speech, you will need to do the same things for your presentations. In this chapter, you will learn how to select a topic, conduct an ethical audience analysis, and start crafting a speech. Just like the president's address, your speech has the potential to be seen by more than the face-to-face audience. Think about these issues as you read the chapter.

Making public presentations has roots in ancient Greece. Up until the last 75 years or so, audiences had to be in the room to hear or see a speech. The inventions of radio, TV, and the Internet have changed everything. In the Communication Age, we now have access not only to those sitting in the room with us but to larger and more targeted groups. Whether we are discussing a local economic issue, speaking in favor of civil rights for an oppressed people, or presenting a new sales strategy at work, we have more chances to reach large and diverse audiences across both time and space. No longer can we expect a presentation to reach only those seated in front of us. Presentations or speeches are recorded and uploaded to websites or sent through e-mail. Speeches can become viral. In earlier times, this dissemination was not possible. Therefore, you now need to prepare for future careers and life to be able to make an impact with a larger audience.

Presenting information as an engaged citizen means being able to select a timely and important topic, to understand the immediate needs of the audience, and to successfully predict your presentation's impact on future audiences. You will want to be informed about a host of topics that matter to you both personally and professionally, as well as to your community. Public presentations give us the ability and power to lead and reach people about ideas and issues. This power to inform and persuade comes with great responsibility. Consider these ideas as you learn how to select a topic, conduct an effective audience analysis, and cover the basics of a presentation.

How can you make a positive difference even in a classroom presentation?

WHAT IS THE PURPOSE OF YOUR PRESENTATION?

One of the first steps in developing a presentation is defining your purpose. When you define your purpose, you are developing a road map that will provide direction on how to research, how to organize, and how best to present your speech. Think of the purpose of your presentation as a personal mission statement. In the following section, we discuss types of topics and types of purpose statements, and then practice developing both.

Topic

The topic is the general subject of your presentation. For example, imagine you are assigned to deliver a

presentation for your work on the demographic features of tween customers (10–12
years old). The general topic might be "The
Tween Demographic and Shopping Habits."
Do not worry if your topic at first seems too
large or broad. You will narrow it down
with the next steps.

General Purpose

General purposes are large framing statements about the reason for the speech. This
purpose refers to the overarching goal of the
presentation. Your general purpose will be
either to inform, to persuade, to entertain, to
celebrate, or a combination of these.
Depending on the situation, you decide on the

Loretta "Cookie" Lyon (Taraji P. Henson) gives a presentation to
stockholders in the TV drama *Empire*. Every type of speech has a purpose.

reason for your presentation, or have it assigned to you. For instance, your teacher
may ask you to present an informative speech, or an organization may ask you to
persuade a group about a community issue. In the preceding example about
tweens, you may have been told simply to inform the organization about this
demographic or to create a presentation to persuade the company to pursue this
demographic as new customers.

Specific Purpose

The specific purpose refers to the precise goals of the presentation. For example,
suppose you were giving a presentation on environmental initiatives that your college campus could implement. Your topic would be "environmental initiatives," and
the general purpose would be to persuade because you are discussing ideas to be
implemented. Using both the topic and the general purpose, write a specific purpose
statement for your audience—for example, "To persuade my audience of environmental initiatives that should be enacted on campus." There are several guidelines
to follow when developing your purpose statement. First, it makes a declaration
instead of asking a question or requesting a change in behavior:

Right: My audience will understand the ways in which a 3D printer can
be used for educational purposes in a college library.

Wrong: What are the ways in which a 3D printer can be used in the college
library for educational purposes?

Second, a purpose statement focuses on one idea:

Right: The audience members will understand how to teach their grandparents about Skype.

Wrong: The audience members will understand how to teach their grandparents about Facetime, ooVoo, Skype, and other new applications. Also, the audience will learn about how these programs
were developed.

Last, a specific purpose statement is specific, not general:

Right: My audience will learn how to become AmeriCorps volunteers.
Wrong: My audience will learn about community activism.

A strong specific purpose statement will guide you in all phases of speech preparation. Students who do not start with a clear idea of their goals struggle from the very beginning.

TYPES OF PRESENTATIONS

Many types of presentations exist for different occasions. In this section, we cover the three most common types: epideictic, informative, and persuasive. Understanding the basics of these three types will help you in all speaking situations.

Epideictic Presentations

You deliver an epideictic presentation when you are introducing yourself or another person, celebrating an event, or commemorating a special occasion such as a wedding, awards, or a funeral, and these presentations often contain a strong emotional element (Vivian, 2006). An important way to connect with others and establish relationships with others in future endeavors, epideictic presentations can take place in a variety of settings. Perhaps you are called to introduce a guest speaker to a large audience or simply introduce a new member to your community service organization. In either case, it is important to set a good and positive tone. In the following sections, you will learn about three types of epideictic presentations: introductions, special events, and eulogies.

Introductions

A common type of epideictic presentation is introducing yourself to an audience, and this can often be quite challenging. Imagine your boss wants you to introduce yourself at the company picnic. What do you say? What does the audience really want to know? What do you want the audience to know? It is important to think carefully about such questions. The answers really depend on the event in which you have to introduce yourself. You want the audience to know the key and relevant information about you without going overboard. In other words, your audience should be interested in you without being annoyed by you. Even though this type of presentation is brief, you should really prepare. First impressions do matter.

When you are introducing others, set a positive framework so the audience will be interested in them. List their key accomplishments or achievements. Include experiences that are relevant to the audience. Talk with the person you

are introducing ahead of time to ask questions and clarify questions you may have. Audiences like to hear something about speakers that adds to their personality, such as a favorite hobby or something funny about them (it should be appropriate for the speaking situation). By all means, make sure you know how to pronounce the person's name. You could even interview an expert in the field of the person you are introducing. Speakers and audiences like hearing positive things that someone else said about them.

Make sure you use the right tone for a wedding toast.

Special Events

Epideictic presentations also include introducing or commemorating a special event or ceremony. The same basic rules apply. Treat the occasion with respect and be as formal or casual as it demands. Learn about the history of the event or why it is occurring. Audiences like to know why they are there if it is not already apparent. For example, if you are presenting an award named after someone, you will want to know the details concerning the person for whom the award is named. It is important to connect the past to the present. You might be asked to give a wedding toast for a friend. What do you say? Depictions of wedding toasts in movies and TV shows are meant to be funny because they are unreal. Don't be the person who says too much. When in doubt, ask someone you can trust about your remarks to check for the right tone for the occasion.

The Communication Age allows us to be part of an activity even from a distance. We have all seen awards shows where someone introduces or accepts an award from a remote location. In the Communication Age, the ability to live-stream video is commonplace. Maybe your sister who is serving in the military oversees can give a wedding toast at your wedding by live video. What other changes do you foresee happening because of this technological innovation?

Eulogies

At some point, you might be asked to deliver a eulogy for a friend or loved one. In this form of an epideictic presentation, you first need to feel capable of actually being able to deliver the eulogy at this emotional time. It does not serve the audience well if you become too emotional. You will need to provide words of comfort about the loss. Highlighting the personal qualities and values of the friend or family member will aid in the healing process. These types of presentations are exceptionally challenging.

Informative Presentations

The informative presentation seeks to convey new information and increase the audience's understanding about a topic. These presentations will explain a concept or process, describe an event or idea, or

Presentations can happen in a variety of different settings and with a variety of different audiences.

demonstrate how to do something. Also, a good informative speech should give the audience something to think about. You need to ask yourself, "Why would my audience need to know this knowledge?" or, "How will this information contribute to a greater understanding about important topics?" For example, imagine your supervisor asked you to tell your coworkers about a competing company's new product. In this workplace presentation, you might lay out the facts about the new product, discuss the potential market for the product, and provide the advantages and disadvantages between your own company's product and the other company's product. In short, you are informing your coworkers. For this type of presentation, you should remember that you are not trying to persuade the audience to change attitudes or behaviors. We cover informative presentations in more depth in Chapter 15.

Persuasive Presentations

Persuasive presentations seek to change, alter, or modify an audience's attitudes, beliefs, values, or outlook about a topic. These presentations may also try to reinforce existing ideas (O'Keefe, 2002). Persuasive attempts to change, alter, or modify an audience's thinking can be tough. Also, it is important to remember that you will still need to provide solid and credible information for this type of presentation as well. Using the example of the competing company's product, imagine you were trying to persuade a store to carry your product over the other company's product. In this case, you would have to convince the store that your merchandise is superior and that it should only sell your product. In Chapter 16, you will find specific strategies to help you build a strong persuasive presentation.

HOW DO I CHOOSE A TOPIC?

Choosing your topic for a presentation is an important task. You will want to choose an issue that is important to the audience, the occasion, and you. The topic needs to have some level of novelty. For example, everyone has heard that it is not safe to text and drive. How could you make this subject seem new or novel? What has your audience not heard? Do you have a personal experience that might really drive home the point? In the following section, we discuss three areas you need to consider when choosing a topic.

Think About the Audience

When determining a topic for your presentation, think about the audience members and their needs. What do they care about? What are their opinions on various topics? This is not to say you should choose an issue you do not care about; rather, you should find ways to connect your topic to greater social needs or issues that impact an audience (Bass, 2010). The topic needs to be timely and socially relevant, and you will want to help the audience understand why your subject is important. What if your audience already knows

MAKE —a— DIFFERENCE

SPEAK OUT!

iStock

ABOUT 2,500 YEARS ago, the idea of democracy was starting to grow as a viable concept in Athens, Greece. With the formation of a new government, Athenian citizens found the need to express themselves to help form a government, defend themselves in a court, or negotiate commerce. This new governmental system required citizens to become skilled communicators in order to

achieve goals and desires. "In any given day, one out of every five Athenian citizens was engaged in some form of public service. The ability to speak, to listen critically to the arguments of others, and to utter appropriate response— these were deemed valuable skills by all" (Golden, Berquist, & Coleman, 1997, p. 6). These same skills were and are still needed today to foster our democratic way of life. Speaking out about social issues has a long history in the United States. Whether it was Susan B. Anthony speaking out about women's rights, Frederick Douglass speaking out about slavery, César Chávez speaking out about the plight of farm workers, or a college student speaking out about student loan debt, citizens of our democracy have used their voices to seek changes to make this a better country and society. Public speaking has always been a strong component of community engagement. We encourage you to find something to speak out about to make a change in the world. Many organizations on your college campus seek social changes of all kinds whether through a political group, an environmental group, an alternative spring break, or a social justice organization. Use your power through ethical communication to be the change you seek.

about your topic? Find ways to present new information or connect the information to other concepts in different ways. A presentation about your community service trip to a local food bank might be too trivial for your listeners. However, you could discuss poverty as it relates to food banks and use your personal experience as an example. Most audiences appreciate personal examples, which add to your overall credibility.

Think About the Occasion

Think about several factors when considering the occasion: the expectations and time limits for the presentation, the breadth or depth of the topic, and its timeliness.

Expectations

You need to consider the expectations of the event for your occasion of speaking. Is this a serious event? Does this occasion allow for a bit of humor? Is the presentation for a class or for work? When considering the occasion, be sure to find out how long you will speak. If you are speaking for a class assignment, you will likely have 5 to

In what ways would you change your approach based on the two audiences in the pictures?

7 minutes. You would not be able to discuss all the problems in Africa or even your local community in this amount of time. In the workplace, your supervisor should give you guidelines about time. If not, ask. Based on the amount of time you have for the presentation, you will need to narrow the topic to one or two specific problems. Narrowing your topic is a crucial step in successfully budgeting your speaking time to the occasion. Most speakers try to cover too much in a presentation. When this happens, you are not able to effectively research the material needed because there is too much of it. When a topic is too broad it also becomes difficult to make it understandable and relevant.

Current

Your topic needs to be current. Imagine you were giving a speech on the Clean Air Act of 1970. You would need to find ways to update the topic so that new information and research are discussed and are important for today. Simply restating the details of the law and the implications would be irrelevant for today's audience. Instead, you might think about changes that have taken place in the past 45 years that might help your audience understand how the law was implemented. For example, you could inform your listeners about specific actions taken by coal power plants to meet the guidelines under the Clean Air Act of 1970.

Think About Yourself

When deciding on a topic, be sure to consider yourself. Choose an area that is interesting to you, since you will be spending considerable time researching it and presenting it. The best topic is one about which you want to find out more so that

COMMUNICATION HOW-TO
CHOOSING A TOPIC

Use the following list of questions to help you choose a topic for your presentation:

1. Will you be interested enough in the topic to research, prepare, and practice the presentation?

2. What knowledge base or personal interest do you have to help you select an interesting topic?

3. Is the topic of your presentation timely for the events of the day?

4. Will the audience be interested in the topic?

5. Is the topic appropriate for the speaking situation and the occasion?

6. What do you wish were different in the world that you can change?

you can share it with your audience. If you find yourself sharing with your friends or family the new information you learned, you are on the right track. Outside of the classroom, speakers are often paid to speak about what they know about a subject. Perhaps you were in the military and are knowledgeable about surviving without running water and electricity in a natural disaster. Church groups, community organizations, and businesses might be interested in hiring you to talk about your experiences and your expertise. What information do you have that might be of interest to a group of people?

If you are speaking about a personal or emotional topic, be sure that you can go through with the speech. One of your authors once had a student who was presenting a speech on a rare form of cancer that claimed the life of her mother. As you can guess, the speaker struggled to get through the presentation without breaking down. Although showing emotion can help you connect to and engage with your audience, be sure you can get through the presentation without swaying focus away from your topic and purpose. The message might actually get lost in the emotional appeal.

AUDIENCE ANALYSIS

Have you ever attended a presentation or lecture and found it boring? If so, it is likely that the topic did not interest you, the information did not connect to you, or the speaker did not engage you. Just because you as a speaker find a topic compelling does not mean that the audience will. This is often a mistake speakers make when choosing a topic. It is your job to make the topic interesting. Outside of the classroom, this will be less of an issue because the audience will have to choose to attend your presentation. These audiences want to hear what you are saying because they need the information for their job, community, or life.

Planning a speech begins with an awareness of your audience members and their needs, backgrounds, and areas of interest. Audience analysis is the process of gathering and analyzing information about an audience to make informed choices about your content and delivery. Your audience could be individual people, groups, or even a virtual or mass group (Zhang, 2008). Your audience might see your speech live or recorded for later viewing, like a TED Talk. There are always multiple audiences. You already know how to conduct a basic audience analysis. We do this all the time in our lives. Say you needed to borrow your parents' car. You would probably plan your request based on what you know about their needs, values, and backgrounds on this topic. This is audience analysis.

There are two main benefits to conducting an audience analysis. First, knowing information about your listeners helps to reduce your uncertainty about giving the presentation. Audience analysis gives insights into what to expect from the reaction to your message. Second, audience analysis will allow you to better focus your message. If you know the audience's general attitudes and beliefs about the topic, you will be able to construct your speech to address those ideas. In other words, think about what the audience might want to listen to (Daniels, 2005).

Worried about holding your audience's interest? Understanding your audience will help you make your presentation more compelling.

Types of Audience Analysis

There are three areas to consider when conducting an audience analysis: situation, demographics, and attitudes and beliefs. Each one gives us important information about our listeners in order to frame our presentation.

Situation

The speaking situation consists of the size of the audience, the environment, and the occasion. The size of the audience can be deceiving. You might deliver your presentation to a small group of people, but the presentation could be later broadcast to many more. If the presentation will be uploaded on a website, you could literally be speaking to thousands of audience members. In this case, you will want to think carefully about how your presentation would be viewed online. Technological issues such as sound or video quality will make a difference in this format. In your classes, you will probably be speaking to around 15 to 30 classmates. In your work, you might speak to a small group or the entire company. The size of the audience helps to determine the degree of formality. Generally, a larger group demands a more formal occasion; a smaller audience, a more casual one.

Environment refers to the physical setting of the presentation. Many times, you will not be able to control the environment and will have to make adjustments to suit the location. Your authors have given presentations in large lecture halls, classrooms, and even hotel rooms that were turned into makeshift conference rooms. In all three places, we had to make adjustments based on the environment. When someone asks you to give a presentation, it is perfectly OK to ask the person about the location and the setup. Where is the podium located? Will you be able to move around to interact with the audience? If the presentation will be recorded, where will the cameras be located? Is equipment available for multimedia aids? If your speech is going to be live-streamed to another location, are there things you can control about that environment as well? Try to arrive early to scope it out and see which factors you can control and to which you will have to adjust. If you are unable to control the physical space in ways that enhance your presentation, try to be flexible and focus on your goals and your message. You can draw the audience into the presentation so that the environment will not matter as much.

The occasion is the reason or event in which you are speaking. Often the occasion will help you decide on the topic, tone, length of presentation, or style you choose. Again, it is OK to discuss these items with the person in charge of your presentation. In your classes, your instructor will give these guidelines. Outside of the classroom, you will need to find out this information from the organizer of the occasion. Imagine you were speaking at a memorial for firefighters. Humor would not be appropriate, and your audience would not approve of this approach. Or what if the expectation for a workplace presentation was that you were going to speak for 4 minutes, but instead you spoke for 20 minutes? This would not look good to your boss. Never go longer than the time you are allowed. Prepare your presentation to the expectations of the occasion.

Consider the speaking situation, which includes audience size, environment, and occasion, to craft an appropriate presentation.

Thinkstock

ASSESS YOUR COMMUNICATION

QUESTIONS ABOUT YOUR AUDIENCE

The list of questions below will help you conduct an audience analysis. Asking these questions should not replace actually conducting an audience analysis but will help you think about the structure and makeup of your audience.

1. Why is the audience there to listen to you?

2. Will there be a virtual audience for your presentation? Why would the virtual audience watch/listen to the speech?

3. Before conducting the audience analysis, are there things that you already know about your audience? Will they matter?

4. Does your topic appeal to a certain political, age, gender, sexual orientation, religious, ethnic, or other demographic? Why?

5. Thinking about yourself, the topic, and the occasion, are there things about your audience that worry you? What are they?

Reflect on these questions and make adjustments as needed.

Demographics

Demographics are personal characteristics or attributes of the audience (McQuail, 1997). Demographics can include a wide variety of information such as age, ethnicity, religious preference, income, or level of education. Think about demographics as things you might fill out on a survey about yourself for the U.S. Census. While knowing these things about your audience members does not always predict how they will respond to your presentation, it can give you some guidance on ways to approach your audience. Do not stereotype the members of your audience based on demographic data. Instead, use this information as a tool to provide insight about the makeup of the audience. For most presentations, these insights are severely limited in their usefulness. In this section, we discuss several demographic characteristics.

Age

The age of your audience members provides important information about them. Age shapes a person's field of experience, so take that into account as you make choices about language, topics, or approach to the presentation. Remember that age only provides some guidance about the nature of the audience. If you are presenting in the workplace, you will likely speak to a mixed-age audience. When this is the case, use references and examples most of the audience will understand. If your presentation will be online, make choices that almost any age group or mixed-age group would comprehend. In other words, the broader the audience is, the more contexts you will need to provide.

Gender

The gender demographic also provides clues about your audience. We are talking not about stereotyping but rather about framing. Framing refers to the structure of the presentation, argument, or information with regard to audience analysis (Payne, 2001). For example, how would you frame a presentation about the importance of women getting mammograms for an audience made up of men? In this case, you could remind audience members of the women in their lives—mothers, aunts, sisters, daughters, girlfriends, wives—for whom this is a critical topic. Framing the presentation in this way allows the audience members to see how the topic is relevant to them (Tian, 2010). Also, avoid the use of sexist language. We have all heard speakers who use the generic "he." Even if the speaker does not mean to be sexist, this language choice potentially can distract a large portion of the audience.

Cultural Background

Cultural background refers to a person's race, ethnicity, or country of origin. The cultural background of your audience might alter how you frame your presentation. Be sensitive to the diverse attitudes and beliefs based on cultural backgrounds, and try not to offend any single member of your audience. We often mistakenly assume the best way of doing something is the way it is done in the United States. This line of thinking is labeled *ethnocentric*. Remember that ethnocentrism is the belief that one's own culture is superior to another culture (Hammond &

Knowing the demographics of your audience may inform how you frame your presentation.

Thinkstock

WEDGE ISSUES

AP Images

In today's society, topics such as immigration reform, stem cell research, abortion, gun control, and the death penalty are considered wedge issues. They divide audiences into two camps: those who agree and those who disagree. Politicians often use controversial topics or wedge issues to build support for their candidacy to office (Gilmour, 2011). Using wedge issues and controversial issues to divide audiences creates an in-group/out-group mentality. Invoking fears or prejudices to gain audience support as a strategy is unethical because it allows an audience to uncritically accept the wedge issue without considering opposing viewpoints. Immigration reform will likely be a wedge issue in upcoming elections (Stoolmacher, 2015). Democrats may use immigration reform to create a wedge for Republicans who might otherwise support reform but have a large group of their voter base that may not. Ethical communication should provide feelings of choice and empowerment while at the same time encouraging a greater social responsibility. Allowing your audience or choosing a topic to encourage in-group/out-group thinking is not an ethical connection because it denies the speaker and the audience both empowerment and responsibility.

QUESTIONS

1. How do you speak about a topic that is potentially a wedge issue without being unethical?

2. How could your audience analysis help you avoid creating an in-group/out-group mentality?

Axelrod, 2006; Sumner, 1906). Before we can try to use cultural background as a framing characteristic of audience analysis, we need to understand our own cultural identity. As discussed in Chapter 6, our own lifestyles are a product of our cultural background and should be considered as we frame a particular audience.

Individual Differences

Individual differences, such as sexual orientation, political party affiliation, religious belief, group memberships, or socioeconomic status, influence framing choices in your presentation. While some of these individual differences will not affect your topic choice, others will. Use common sense for when the topic would matter for individual differences. When speaking to groups with individual differences, be aware of existing stereotypes and avoid them. Focus on being sensitive to these differences. While it is harder to connect and engage with an audience that disagrees with your position on a topic, you can achieve a lot of ground by treating the audience with respect and understanding.

CAREER FRONTIER: DATA MINING

IMAGINE IF YOU had the power to know where your audience spent money in the last 30 days. You could know where members of your audience ate, where they shopped, the music they downloaded, the books they read, the house or apartment they inhabited, or the cost of a visit to their doctor's office. Does this sound a bit scary? Technology is progressing to a point where this is happening every time we get online, use a debit/credit card, or indicate a "like" on Facebook. We know companies like Amazon and Netflix and products like iTunes by Apple have done this when we see online recommendations for books, movies, and songs we might enjoy. This process is called data mining. Data mining is a complex system of computer programs to predict our future spending habits, our opinions, and our

likes/dislikes. People have been trying to find patterns in data to help them inform or persuade others since the beginning of time. Data mining makes this easier. Some of you will likely work with data mining in your careers. Perhaps you will survey potential clients to find out their opinions about a product your company is selling, or you will work with a company to determine the best design for a webpage. Professor Ian Ayers, author of the book *Super Crunchers* (2007), argues that this data-based decision making will shape our world for years to come. Data mining is a complex way of conducting audience analysis. While you will not have this much information for your public presentations, the techniques discussed under audience analysis are similar to data mining and could be part of your career.

The Audience's Attitudes and Beliefs

Understanding the audience's attitudes and beliefs about your topic will help you determine the best way to craft your presentation. Attitudes are learned thought processes that guide our behavior and thinking and represent our likes or dislikes of a target (Fishbein & Ajzen, 1975). In other words, we can have a positive or negative attitude toward an idea, an object, or a person. The audience members' attitudes will inform you of how they might view your topic, the speaking situation, or even you. What's important is that we learn attitudes and that they can be changed through information and persuasion. Beliefs are ideas that a person holds true or false, are formed from experiences in the world and significant relationships, and are harder to influence and change than attitudes. For example, you might have the attitude that Mountain Dew is an amazing drink or that Jimmy Kimmel is a good late-night talk show host. You might have the belief that all citizens deserve quality health care or that the United States should pursue greener energy alternatives. Notice the difference. Attitudes can change quite easily, but beliefs take more time, evidence, and persuasion to change. In other words, if your attempt is to change beliefs, you will need to craft a stronger argument than you would if you wanted to change attitudes.

In terms of audience analysis, knowing the beliefs of the audience will help you select evidence that can better inform or persuade. You might even acknowledge the audience's beliefs and then create an argument that would allow the audience to move a little in the direction of your argument. It is most likely impossible to change an audience's beliefs

Analyze your audience beforehand to discover how to create and deliver a successful presentation.

Thinkstock

with one presentation. However, you may be able to create greater understanding that would allow an audience member to be more receptive for future persuasive attempts. In the Communication Age, different voices compete for our attention. How does audience analysis help us reach out to greater and more diverse audiences in the Communication Age? Think about ways to extend your influence with an audience of different attitudes and beliefs.

Methods of Audience Analysis

Conducting an audience analysis is a vital step in the process of creating and delivering a successful presentation. Think about the following example. Saumya is giving a presentation to the five directors of an international business. In this presentation, she will try to persuade this group of executives that their company should seek out new markets in India and that she can help with this endeavor. Saumya knows very little about the actual board members to whom she will be speaking, but she is familiar with the company's product line and how it could be sold in India. What should she do? In this section, we discuss two methods that should be used every time you make a presentation: research and ask.

Research Your Audience

Almost every organization, club, or group has a type of web presence, whether it is a Facebook fan page, a Twitter feed, or a dedicated website. Google the group's name to see what you can find. If you are speaking not to a specific group but to a general audience, research as much as you can about the event or occasion. If your presentation will be online, try to find out who views the website, as this will give you clues about your virtual audience. You might find past speeches online or online snippets that will help you better understand your audience's expectations. Search the local newspaper for stories or editorials that suggest the audience's understanding or position on the topic, but be careful with your assumptions. You will be surprised at the amount of information you can find out just by looking online.

Since Saumya is familiar with the company and how to get those products sold in India, she needs to research the board members to find ways to connect and engage with them on an individual level. She should read the bios for each of the five board members, look for press releases and articles about them, and search for any other information that might exist to help her persuade them. By gathering as much information as possible, Saumya might be able to make personal connections with each member. Perhaps in her research, she discovered that one of the individuals was from India and that another previously worked for a similar company that had success in the Indian market. In this case, she might be able to reference the connection to India and the successes of other companies in this significantly growing market.

Ask Your Audience

One simple but effective way to conduct an audience analysis is simply to ask about the situation, demographic characteristics, and attitudes/beliefs. There are two ways of

Using a survey is a great way to gather information.

iStock

asking about this information. First, you should seek out an informant, a person who generally knows about the speaking situation, the makeup of the potential audience, and even the overall attitudes and beliefs of the audience. Most of the time, the informant will be the person who arranged for you to speak. Perhaps you might have friends in the potential audience. Ask for their advice and opinions. Use the techniques in the appendix on interviewing to gather valuable information about your audience.

Looking back at the example of Saumya, she was invited to give a presentation because one of the board members was familiar with her work and thought she would be a great asset to the company in its efforts to expand to India. This person could serve as an informant. Saumya could ask this person about the board members and what they think about expansion. Even though it appears she might have an inside track, she needs to be respectful and professional with her informant. In this example, the informant could look quite bad to other board members if Saumya abused this relationship.

The second way to gather information by asking is to conduct a survey. A survey will help you better understand the audience's demographic makeup and audience members' attitudes and beliefs about your topic. Follow three basic guidelines to create a good survey. First, keep the survey brief and to the point. Ask only the most important information that you need for your audience analysis. For example, if religious affiliation is not important for your topic or presentation, do not ask it. Ask what you need and nothing else. Second, write clear and concise questions. Strive to write your questions so that they accomplish exactly what you need them to accomplish. Avoid wordiness. Third, ask different types of questions.

- Open-ended questions allow the respondent to expand on the answers. These types of questions might give you more detailed answers. For example: How is technology shaping the future of families in the United States? Please explain.

- Scaled questions allow the person to make an answer between two points. These types of questions will allow you to see differences in attitudes and beliefs. For example: Should students volunteer for a political organization during their college education? Choose a box:

  Strongly Agree   ☐   ☐   ☐   ☐   ☐   Strongly Disagree

- Category questions limit the possible answers to groupings. These types of questions are great for demographic questions. For example: What amount do you owe in student loans? Choose a box:

  - ☐ $0–$5,000
  - ☐ $5,001–$10,000
  - ☐ $10,001–$15,000
  - ☐ $15,001–$20,000
  - ☐ Greater than $20,000

Carefully think about the type of information you need to have when crafting survey questions for your audience analysis.

SAMPLE SURVEY
FOR A PERSUASIVE PRESENTATION

1. What is your gender? (check one)

   _____ Female _____ Male _____ Transgender _____ Gender Fluid

2. What is your age? (fill in the blank)

   ___ Age

3. What is your political party affiliation? (check one or write in your answer)   ◄ Category Question

   _____ Democrat

   _____ Republican

   _____ Libertarian

   _____ Socialist

   _____ No party affiliation

   _____ Other (please write in your answer) _____

4. Please indicate your level of agreement or disagreement with the following   ◄ Scaled Question
   statements by placing an "X" on the line to best reflect your answer.

   I believe that the government has the responsibility to provide health care for
   all of its citizens.

   Strongly Agree _____ _____ _____ _____ _____ Strongly Disagree

   I support a universal health care mandate.

   Strongly Agree _____ _____ _____ _____ _____ Strongly Disagree

5. In the space below, please write your answer to the following question.   ◄ Open-Ended Question

   What should be done about the current health care crisis in the United States?

   _____

   _____

   _____

   _____

   _____

Thank you for taking the time to complete this survey.

COMMUNICATION**HOW-TO**
GUIDELINES FOR SURVEY DESIGN

1. Plan the type of information you need before designing your survey. Make sure you ask the right questions to get this information.

2. Vary the type of questions (open-ended, scaled, and categorical questions).

3. Write clear and concise questions. Avoid complex and technical jargon.

4. Write more questions than you need, and then select the best ones.

5. Pilot test your completed survey with a small group of people to check for errors or wording issues.

6. Decide how you will conduct your survey. Will you use a web survey system, phone calls, or paper? You will want to adjust your questions to reflect your delivery system.

7. Consider using an online data collection site such as Amazon's Mechanical Turk to get a larger sample of people throughout the world.

THE BASICS OF YOUR PRESENTATION

Now that you have narrowed your topic and connected the audience analysis, we discuss the basic organization of your first presentation. In this section, you will learn how to develop an introduction and a conclusion. You will also learn about the body of a presentation. Later chapters will expand on these ideas, but the following sections will help you get started.

Communication **unplugged**
TO ENHANCE COMMUNICATION WITH YOUR AUDIENCE, LOOK THEM IN THE EYE

You may have heard the saying, "The eyes are the window to your soul." Making eye contact with your audience while you are speaking is a direct way of conducting an audience analysis (or looking at an audience's soul) in the middle of a presentation. From the moment you enter the room until you leave it, you should be watching your audience for feedback. Imagine you are in the middle of your presentation and it seems that the audience members do not understand your position or are confused. Technology will not help you in this case. After sensing the confusion in the audience, spend more time explaining the point you are trying to make. With practice and experience, you will be able to watch your audience for feedback and make changes to your presentation on the fly. Most of the time, people will let you know through nonverbal communication if they agree or disagree with a statement or a position.

WHAT TO DO NEXT

To make the most of eye contact with your audience, try to:

*   Make eye contact with as many audience members as possible.

*   Look at a person for 2 to 3 seconds and then move your eyes to someone else.

*   Try not to focus on only a few people but vary it up.

*   If your presentation is being recorded, be sure to look at the camera occasionally.

Introduction

The beginning of your presentation will determine its success. You can lose your audience before you get to the best part of your presentation with a poorly crafted introduction, so spend a lot of time planning and practicing the introduction. There are four main components of an introduction: the attention getter, the topic introduction, the demonstration of importance, and the preview of the presentation.

In the first step you quickly gain the awareness of the audience with an attention getter. The attention getter can be a statistic, an example or a story, a rhetorical question, a reference to the past, a quotation, or anything that will draw the attention of the audience, as long as it is related to the

Talk-show host Jimmy Fallon uses a variety of ways to capture the audience's attention.

topic. If your topic is the use of social media in Egypt during the 2011 revolution, for example, you might start off by discussing how many Egyptians were using Twitter to organize protests and demonstrations. Never begin your presentation by introducing yourself to the audience, unless doing so is absolutely necessary.

The second step introduces your topic. This is often referred to as the thesis statement, which provides the general purpose of your presentation. For example, imagine you are giving a presentation about the need for a greater understanding of technology in the Communication Age. You might say, "Today, I hope to convince you to learn to use new technological tools needed to live in the Communication Age." In this case, *to persuade* is the general purpose of the presentation.

In the third step of the introduction, you demonstrate the importance of the topic. The essential question is, "Why should the audience care about this topic?" If the subject is the economic hardships of those living in poverty, you might say, "After the stock market crash of 2008, the basic needs of people in local communities across the nation increased suddenly and drastically due to home foreclosures and record unemployment."

The fourth part of the introduction is the preview. In the preview, you tell the audience the specific things you will discuss in the presentation. Using the same example, you might say, "Specifically, I will talk about the needs of the community, how Goodwill helps those less fortunate, and why and how you can donate your used things to Goodwill." These three points are topic previews of the main points in the body of the presentation. In other words, the preview is an oral outline of the presentation.

Body

You will present the main points and ideas of your presentation in the body. These main ideas allow the audience to have a good picture of your topic. You will use most of your research and evidence in this section. Chapter 12 discusses researching your presentation. In Chapter 13, you will learn more about organizing your speech by creating a comprehensive outline. Outlining is critical to the success of the presentation, so pay careful attention to the guidelines in Chapter 13.

To help the presentation flow smoothly, use transitions. Transitions are sentences or phrases that connect what you were just speaking about to what you will be discussing next. Transitions are like bridges that allow the audience to move from one point to the next easily—for example, "Now that we have discussed what sexual harassment is in the workplace, let's talk about how to stop it." The first part of the transition reminds the audience about what was just mentioned, and the second part of the transition tells them what will be discussed.

Conclusion

The conclusion is extremely important because it is the last thing your audience will hear from you. There are two parts of the conclusion: a review of the main points and a concluding device. In the review of the main points, you restate your thesis and summarize the main points. Remind the audience members what you just told them and highlight the importance of your message. The concluding device is the method you use to end your presentation. Similar to the attention getter, you can use statistics, quotations, examples, or rhetorical questions, or even refer back to the attention getter. Perhaps you asked a rhetorical question in the attention getter. Referring to the same question for this step would be a good way to end the speech. Your last sentence should signal to the audience that your presentation is finished. Never end with phrases such as "I'm done," or "That is all I have to say." Ending a presentation without a memorable conclusion is jarring for the audience and a clear sign of unfinished work.

Thinkstock

SELECTING A TOPIC, KNOWING YOUR AUDIENCE, AND CONVERGENCE

Selecting your topic and knowing about your audience are important aspects in the Communication Age. You have at your disposal many ways to find important and timely topics and to better understand your potential audience. Simply by using web resources such as Amazon or Google's complex data mining searches, you can find out what topics people are most interested in at the moment. What are the topics of the best-selling books? What are people reading about? Or what topics are trending on Twitter or online news sources? What stories are people commenting about online?

Additionally, there are many online tools available for you to conduct an audience analysis. Web survey programs such as SurveyMonkey or SurveyGold offer ways for you to survey large but targeted groups of potential audience members. Amazon will allow you to view what other books people have bought on a particular topic. This trend will only increase in the future. By using current technology to better understand the latest trends and important topics, you have a better way to create convergence

COMMUNICATION**HOW-TO**

QUICK GUIDE TO YOUR FIRST PRESENTATION

1. Know your introduction so that you can deliver it clearly and passionately.

2. Keep your presentation's body organized. Writing a clear outline and following it will help you appear credible and stay on task.

3. Be sure to look for a variety of sources to help you inform or persuade your audience.

4. Use transitions to signal changes in thoughts during your presentation.

5. End the conclusion strong to leave a lasting impression on the audience.

6. Enjoy the presentation experience. Smile when giving your presentation (if it is appropriate for the topic), and your audience will smile back.

with your topic and audience. In the Communication Age, the resources are vast, fast, and effective. Your responsibility is to learn about these potential resources and use them in ethical ways to help you craft an amazing and insightful presentation.

You will also need to be mindful of how your speech could be transmitted throughout time and space. This possibility was really not around 75 years ago. Think back to the story about President Obama and his speech about the Selma march for civil rights. The White House made many efforts to find ways with traditional and social media to get Obama's message out to a wider audience. Additionally, many of these technologies allowed for some level of interaction. Take, for example, a presentation you post on YouTube. People can leave comments, and you can engage in dialogue with them about the topic of the speech. In other areas, videoblogging can serve as an important form of a presentation to connect with an audience. These interactions will give you more chances both to inform and persuade a digital audience. Giving speeches has a strong and robust history in Western culture, and the basics have remained essentially the same throughout time. The key difference now is that you can reach a wider and more diverse audience. This is powerful.

WANT A BETTER GRADE?

Get the tools you need to sharpen your study skills.

Access practice quizzes, eFlashcards, video, and multimedia at **edge.sagepub.com/edwards2e**.

WHAT YOU'VE LEARNED   Now that you have studied this chapter, you should be able to:

(1) Explain how to define the purpose of a presentation.

It is important to remember that different types of presentations work for different goals. Be sure to know the purpose of your speech in relation to the situation of the presentation.

 The Six Main Purposes of Presentations

(2) Summarize the characteristics of different types of presentation.

Selecting the right type of presentation is key to being successful. Understand the differences between epideictic, informative, and persuasive presentations.

▶ Types of Sales Presentations

🎙 President Obama Delivers Eulogy for Rev. Clementa Pinckney

💻 The Art of the Wedding Toast

(3) Describe the ways to choose a topic that is suitable for the type of presentation.

Choosing your topic is one of the most important tasks of the process. Use your resources to find the right topic. Be sure to pay attention to the needs of the audience, the occasion, and yourself

when choosing the topic, whether it is in a face-to-face setting or a computer-mediated setting.

 Finding Speech Topic

(4) Explain how to conduct an audience analysis to achieve the most impact.

Spend time working on audience analysis and know how to conduct one. Many beginning students will skip or not spend enough time on this step. A good audience analysis will help you alter your approach to achieve the most impact.

▶ How to Pick a Speech Topic: Analyzing your Audience

 Speech Preparation: Audience Analysis

(5) Create the basic structure of a presentation.

The basic structure of your presentation is important to help your audience remember the message you are trying to convey. In later chapters, we explore the structure of a speech in greater detail.

💻 Organizing Your Speech

💻 Structure Your Presentation Like a Story

💻 How to Structure a Presentation

KEY TERMS

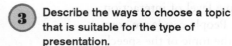

Attention getter 287	Concluding device 288	Epideictic presentation 272
Attitudes 282	Cultural background 280	Framing 280
Audience analysis 277	Data mining 282	General purpose 271
Beliefs 282	Demographics 280	Informant 284
Category question 284	Environment 278	Informative presentation 273

REFLECT

1. Can an epideictic presentation be both informative and persuasive? How do you know the difference?

2. Audience analysis is an extremely important part of creating a presentation. How would you persuade an audience that you know disagrees with you? What would you say to an audience you know already agrees with you?

3. How can demographic characteristics of your audience (e.g., age, gender, individual differences) impact your approach to the presentation?

REVIEW

To check your answers go to **edge.sagepub.com/edwards2e**

1. _____ is the general subject of a presentation.

2. Large framing statements about the reason for a speech are _____ purposes.

3. What is a specific purpose?

4. A(n) _____ presentation introduces somebody, celebrates an event, or commemorates special occasions.

5. _____ is the gathering and analyzing of information about a select audience.

6. Define speaking situation.

7. _____ are learned thought processes that guide our behavior and thinking, while _____ are ideas a person holds to be true or false.

8. What is the difference between open-ended and closed-ended questions?

9. The _____ introduces your topic and provides the general purpose of the presentation.

SPEECH PLANNER

SpeechPlanner is an interactive, web-based tool that guides you through the process of planning and preparing your speech, one step at a time.

As a news editor for CNN, Marie-Louise Gumuchian covered important events about international news for the network's London bureau. When she was fired in May 2014, it was not because she had published something offensive or had misreported an event in Africa or the Middle East. Gumuchian had plagiarized nearly 50 articles in the 6 months that she had been working for CNN (Wemple, 2014). She had taken content from Reuters, where she had worked for 9 years, and republished it as new material. As soon as the plagiarism was discovered, CNN conducted an internal review of all of Gumuchian's articles, which led to edits in some stories and the removal of several full articles (Silverman, 2014).

As a result of the investigation, CNN placed "editor's notes" indicating that an online article had been removed due to plagiarized content for each of the news stories impacted. CNN acted quickly to stop any damage, but plagiarism can have a lasting effect on an organization's credibility. Plagiarism is a significant issue not only in print news media, but also in film, literature, and even in presentations. Doing research and giving appropriate credit is a fundamental aspect of writing and public speaking.

When researching information for a news story or a presentation, it is important to consider the source of the information. While it is doubtful that you will ever be in a situation to plagiarize 50 articles from your previous employer, you more than likely will have the opportunity to pass off someone else's work as your own. As you read the chapter, consider the ways in which you can avoid plagiarism as well as evaluate your sources for credibility and timeliness to make the best argument or to provide the best information.

PLAGIARISM

John is preparing a presentation about a local organization that arranges car donations to those who can't afford a car. He finds tons of information about his topic in the local paper, on the organization's website, and in blog entries about this organization. John gives credit to most of the sources in his presentation, but takes a few sentences from the blog entry to use as his own. His professor hears this presentation and does not think these few sentences sound like John. The professor Googles these sentences to discover that John lifted the text from a local blog about this organization. As a result, John fails his presentation and is turned in to the dean of students for academic misconduct. Understandably, he is upset and embarrassed. John has violated a serious code of conduct. John has committed plagiarism.

Plagiarism is using "someone else's language, ideas, or other original (not common-knowledge) material without acknowledging its source" (Council of Writing Program Administrators, 2003) and is a serious act that is unacceptable in an academic environment. In the preceding story, John was able to find a lot of information about his topic rather quickly. John's mistake was that he did not give credit to one of his sources. As you begin researching your topic, you will discover a wealth of information. This information, for the most part, has an origin. Someone researched and created it before you found it. That means you must give credit to the creator of the work.

Speakers can be guilty of plagiarism for paraphrasing, copying, or summarizing a source without giving credit back to the source, or for turning in another person's work as their own. You can also be guilty of plagiarism by turning in your own work that you did for another project or class. Every college and university has guidelines for using someone else's work, and these are found in the student handbook and on the website. Your instructor will also give details about her policy. Be sure to know the specific rules about plagiarism. Most colleges take the attitude that incoming college students know what plagiarism is and how to avoid it. The excuse that you "did not know" will not work. Plagiarizing is a big deal. It's stealing someone's ideas, and the penalties are harsh. If caught, you will surely fail your assignment, likely fail the class, and possibly be put on academic probation or even expelled from school.

Plagiarism sometimes occurs from lack of time management when researching a topic (Kenny, 2007). We might forget the source of important information, or perhaps our deadline is so tight that we might even cut corners. Maybe we have not developed our own style of communication, so we rely on others' words and insights to help us make our point. Regardless of the reason, it is better to be less prepared for a presentation than to be suspected of plagiarism. It takes time to document your information, so plan accordingly.

The authors of this textbook want to help you avoid this problem by discussing it first before we talk about how to find information. In the Communication Age, it is easy to commit plagiarism, but it is also incredibly easy to get caught. Why take the chance with your future?

Types of Plagiarism

Now that we know generally what plagiarism entails, let's look at different types. Global plagiarism occurs when a person uses an entire document as his or her own. This might happen if you bought or found a presentation online to use as your own. This type of plagiarism is never accidental. Patchwork plagiarism is when several different documents are combined into one document. Some students think this type of plagiarism is harder for the instructor to detect, but it is not and is in some ways easier to detect than other forms of plagiarism. It is hard to put together various kinds of text in ways that make it appear that one person wrote it. It will seem "patchworked." The third type of plagiarism and probably the most common is text stealing. Text stealing occurs when a person uses another person's words but does not give credit to the source. Text stealing also applies when you get the idea from another source but do not give the source credit for the concept. Sometimes this can occur by accident, but this type of accident can be avoided through a careful research process. Always write down the information for the source of the information so that you can correctly cite this material. The final type of plagiarism is self-plagiarism. This happens when you use your previous original work as new. Yes, you can plagiarize yourself if you copy and paste your thoughts, words, ideas, or opinions used in a previous document into a new presentation.

How to Avoid Plagiarism in the Communication Age

Giving credit is the easiest way to avoid plagiarizing. This means you must take good notes when you are researching information. Always write down the source of the information as soon as you think you may use it. It will save work in the long run, because trying to track down the source of a phrase, statistic, or paragraph is a colossal waste of time.

Remember, any information that is not formulated by you must be credited. This includes direct quotes, statistics, paraphrases, ideas, and concepts. If you plan to use information directly from the source, copy the words exactly as they appear and put quotation marks around them. Provide the source of information included in multimedia aids. Additionally, you must include the source of your information in your presentation and in your reference list. A reference list is a list of all the sources cited in the presentation. A reference list conforms to the specific guidelines of the type of system you are using. In the social sciences (psychology, sociology, communication, etc.), most use the American Psychological Association (APA) system. This is the system discussed later on in the chapter. Also, most libraries have programs such as RefWorks that let you keep track of your sources. Ask your librarian what kinds of citation-tracking programs are available on your campus.

There is one exception to citing your sources: If the information is common knowledge, then you do not have to recognize a source. For example, stating that South Dakota is part of the United States does not require a source because it is a widely known fact. Mentioning that the American Red

Finding credible information is part of your ethical responsibility as a speaker.

Thinkstock

COMMUNICATIONHOW-TO
AVOIDING PLAGIARISM

1. Cite your sources orally. Cite your sources on your reference page. Cite your sources in text on your outline. Just cite your sources.

2. When finding your information, take careful notes on where you get concepts, ideas, statistics, facts, and quotations.

3. If you have doubt on whether a piece of information is common knowledge, find a source and cite it.

4. Avoid reading or watching other presentations about your topic you may find online. Build your own arguments with the evidence that you find.

Images: istock.

Cross is a nonprofit organization does not need a source. However, it is always better to err on the side of caution with common knowledge. Most experts cannot even agree on what constitutes common knowledge. When in doubt about this kind of information, take the safe road and cite your sources. Plagiarizing your information will significantly hurt your credibility. In the next section, you will read about how to build credibility for yourself and your message using research.

BUILDING CREDIBILITY WITH RESEARCH

If Lady Gaga told you the car of 2030 would run on corn husks and water, would you believe her? What if the CEO of Volkswagen told you the same thing? Would you believe this person? Why or why not? There are many things we would believe from Lady Gaga, but the future of the car industry is probably not one of them. If we trust that a person is knowledgeable in a subject area and ethical in his or her pursuits, we perceive him or her as having credibility. Credibility refers to a person being trustworthy and believable. When you are giving a presentation, it is important that you establish your credibility quickly. You don't have to be an expert in order to be a credible speaker, but you do have to convince your audience that you are qualified to speak on the subject and that your evidence is strong. People we perceive as credible are better able to persuade us to adopt their view, change our mind, or view old information from a new perspective. Finding strong sources of information is an important part of building your credibility. Credibility has been studied for more than 2,000 years, and Greek philosopher Aristotle (1991) first coined the words we still use today when discussing public presentations: *ethos, pathos,* and *logos.*

News anchor Brian Williams lost some of his credibility because of a false reporting scandal.

Getty

Ethos

Ethos is the credibility and ethical appeal of your presentation. Be sure to tell the audience why you are the appropriate person to discuss this topic. Perhaps you have firsthand experience or a particular interest in the topic. Maybe you work for someone who has significant knowledge in this area. When you share your knowledge and sincerity, you are implementing the appeal of ethos. Aristotle encouraged presenters to show "goodwill" toward their audiences (McCroskey & Teven, 1999). In other words, you should try to empathize with their views, listen, and want what is best for them by using strong information as evidence. This will enhance your credibility.

Pathos

Pathos involves passion or emotion. You can communicate passion and emotion in your presentation by varying the volume of your voice, making eye contact, changing the tone of your voice, gesturing, or providing visual aids. The emotion that you communicate either by verbal communication or through the use of your research can be sadness, excitement, guilt, or anger. The types of evidence you select will help your pathos. Showing a picture that produces an emotional response in an audience might be better at informing or persuading than words. We have all probably seen public service announcements that use the appeal of pathos regarding disadvantaged children or the devastation caused by earthquakes in Asia. When members of the audience sense your sincere emotion, they will view you as a credible speaker. However, always maintain control of your emotional appeals. It is quite easy to show so much emotion that the audience does not focus on the message and the evidence but instead concentrates simply on the emotion.

Ancient Greek philosopher Aristotle introduced the terms we still use today to describe presentations: *ethos*, *pathos*, and *logos*.

Logos

Logos refers to the logic, structure, evidence, and support for your argument. To achieve this, you must provide rational, systematic, and coherent reasons why your argument is believable. This allows the audience to follow the structure of your presentation and view your facts and evidence as truthful, sound, and supportive. When car dealers advertise the safety features, gas mileage, and low maintenance costs, they are using the appeal of logos. There are two basic types of reasoning to support your arguments: deductive and inductive.

Deductive reasoning refers to using general conclusions to reach a specific conclusion. Imagine you are trying to persuade your class about the benefits of volunteering. You begin by arguing that volunteering can have a positive emotional impact. You end the presentation by providing names of specific organizations that work toward a general good. Notice how the presentation proceeded from general volunteering to specific volunteering.

Inductive reasoning occurs when you use specifics to reach a general conclusion. You might start off the presentation by trying to persuade that volunteering for a specific organization makes you feel good and end the presentation by persuading that volunteering in general creates positive emotions. However, it is quite possible to make mistakes in your reasoning. In the next section, you will learn of several fallacies of reasoning to avoid in presentations.

Fallacies of Logic and Reason

Establishing yourself as a credible and ethical speaker is vital in achieving your goals. You have conducted sound research, documented your sources, and determined the arguments you will use to inform or persuade. Unfortunately, you can still discredit yourself with a few common mistakes of logic. Here are some common fallacies of logic and reason that you should avoid in your own presentations and be on guard to detect in other presentations. It is essential to avoid fallacies to build strong credibility.

Non Sequitur Argument

A non sequitur argument does not follow a logical conclusion. In this fallacy, the conclusion has no relationship to the statement. For example, "I know I will be a good parent because I have blond hair" makes no logical sense. The conclusion, "because I have blond hair," is irrelevant to being a good parent. One might say, "I know I will be a good parent because I have had much experience taking care of children." This statement is more logical than the blond hair statement because there is a logical relationship.

Ad Hominem

Ad hominem refers to attacking the person instead of the information of the presentation or the article. The statement "I'll never attend Penn State University; all the students rioted in support of their coach when it was reported that some members of the athletic office covered up the sexual abuse of children" is an ad hominem fallacy. This argument illogically links the reputation of an entire student body to a small body of students who did riot. Sometimes you will find ad hominem attacks in your sources. Take, for example, the statement "Senator Franken's bill on protecting the environment is just wrong because he is a liberal moron who wants to tax and spend all day long." In this statement, it is clear that the author does not like Senator Franken or his bill and uses an ad hominem attack on Senator Franken to go against the bill. This type of statement is not evidence.

Red Herring

When we try to derail someone from an argument by distracting this person with other nonrelevant information, it is termed a red herring fallacy. The term stems from the old tracking trick of dragging a herring across a trail to throw off the dogs. Once you become familiar with this fallacy, you will recognize the illogical argument immediately. Suppose a student is asked to discuss the dangers of

Clearly, the presenter has had a positive impact on the audience.

iStock

underage drinking. Instead, the student brings up numerous problems with campus security, therefore avoiding the subject of underage drinking and diverting it to the problems of campus security. The problems of the campus security department are a red herring for the topic of underage drinking.

Either/Or Arguments

Either/or arguments oversimplify issues by offering only two solutions even though other options exist. This fallacy ignores the complexity of issues and polarizes the discussion. "Either our company expands this product line this specific way, or we go out of business" is an argument that offers only two options when many more exist. Maybe the company does need to expand its product line but could do so in many different ways. There are never only two possibilities. Take the case of legalizing gay marriage. Some have argued that if the government legalizes gay marriage in the United States, then the government will have to recognize multiple marriage partners as being legal as well. Clearly, this has not happened and is an example of an either/or argument.

Slippery Slope

The slippery slope fallacy represents the notion that when a single step is made, a host of other consequences will follow. We do this when we tell ourselves, "If I do poorly on this exam, I might fail the class. If I fail the class, I won't graduate. If I don't graduate, I'll never get a job. I'll never find a partner." Once the ball starts rolling, it doesn't stop. Doing poorly on one exam probably doesn't ruin an entire life. You can find this type of fallacy in some

ATTACKING SOMEONE'S CHARACTER

The Occupy movement, started in 2011, has had a lasting impact on the political landscape (Isquith, 2015). People all across the world started protesting the economic conditions of the middle and lower classes. At the center of the movement was the protest in New York City, called Occupy Wall Street. The protesters were made up of a diverse set of people from all walks of life, who wanted more fairness in the economic system. Rush Limbaugh, a popular radio talk show host, referred to the protesters as "perpetually lazy, spoiled rotten" (Mullaney, 2011). A few years later, Limbaugh stated that the Occupy Wall Street movement was a "contrived, made-up, artificially created protest group" (Limbaugh, 2014). In these particular statements, Limbaugh did not engage in the arguments for or against the movement or the validity of the arguments but simply made an ad hominem attack toward the protesters. Ad hominem attacks take away from

your credibility as a speaker and distract from your message.

To be ethical in our communication, we must avoid attacking someone's character simply to go against his or her idea. Instead, we must engage the arguments and use ethical evidence and reasoning to build our case. Ethical communicators are careful to separate real differences of opinion from ad hominem fallacies.

QUESTIONS

1. Is there ever a time when an ad hominem attack might be ethical? Why or why not?

2. If someone makes an argument using solid reasoning and evidence but then makes an ad hominem attack, what does that do for the credibility of the argument?

evidence. The slippery slope fallacy is often used to scare an audience into buying the argument. However, eventually audience members start to ask questions and realize the fallacy of the logic.

Hasty Generalization

When we look at one or two examples and generalize them to a much larger concept, or we accept information that is not supported with evidence, we jump to hasty generalizations. "I'll never buy a house because the basements always flood. My cousin's basement flooded, and it was a mess" is a hasty generalization. It would be better to say, "Building homes in floodplains is one of the reasons why basements flood." Hasty generalizations are used when the speaker has not done enough research or is trying to frighten the audience. Providing evidence that clearly and reasonably links up examples or concepts is the best way to avoid this fallacy.

Bandwagon

Advertisers have used the bandwagon fallacy to sell products for generations. This fallacy expects us to make decisions based on popularity and popular opinion. If a popular celebrity uses a certain skin cream, then it must be the best facial product on the market. Just because we like the celebrity does not mean that the skin cream is the best product. Users of this argument count on likability and popularity to persuade audiences. This fallacy can also be presented in the form of not wanting the audience to question the credibility of an expert. Just because an expert states something does not always mean that he or she is correct. Experts can be wrong. All evidence needs to be questioned and evaluated.

Fallacies are an important consideration as you examine your information and craft your message. Always evaluate your research and statements for fallacies of logic and reasoning. Doing so will make your presentation more credible. In the next section, you will read about how to find credible and solid information.

Corbis

Advertisers use the bandwagon fallacy to sell products. When was the last time you bought something because of the popularity of the product?

FINDING INFORMATION

A source is research and information attained through others' work, such as books, government documents, newspaper and magazine articles, online journals and websites, and documentary films and news shows. There are two basic types of sources. A primary source is information obtained from a participant or an observer who was at the event. Imagine you were at the 50th anniversary march of the Selma civil rights clashes. When you got home, you wrote a newspaper article for the college paper about your experience. You would be a primary source because you experienced the important march for civil rights. Primary sources can include autobiographies, speeches, letters, video recordings, most academic journal articles, first-hand news articles, and testimonies. A secondary source is research or information that is at least one step removed from the actual event. This would include textbooks, most scholarly books, news articles, and reference books. Using the same example, you would be a secondary source if you read firsthand accounts of the Selma march and wrote the story using this research as your evidence.

Finding Sources in the Library

The Communication Age enables us to find all kinds of new and different information. But what if you don't know where to begin looking for information and sources? What if you can only articulate something like, "I'm interested in finding information about the possibility of using corn husks and water to fuel cars." The library is your destination, and a librarian is your friend. Nothing can replace the "know-how" of a skilled librarian. Your librarian will be able to direct you to the best resources (both online and on paper) that you may not know about. Nothing makes a librarian happier than

The firsthand account of an event by a witness is considered a primary source.

Thinkstock

Communication unplugged
TO IMPROVE YOUR PRESENTATIONS, ADD DIRECT EXPERIENCE

iStock

Imagine you are giving a presentation about a local protest. You could look up articles about the protest in the local paper or watch a video of people at the event. These are great secondary sources. However, far too often we rely on technology to experience the world. This is often the case for research as well. We find sources using Google or the library's search engines. However, some of the best kinds of evidence are direct experience. Instead of indirectly experiencing the protest,

go watch it. Engage in the experience of the event. Take in the sights, smells, and sounds. Shoot your own video and pictures. Talk with the protesters. Be a witness. Direct experience can add to your credibility when delivering a presentation of any type. Audiences like hearing the details from newspapers or online reports about an event, but it is better when the speaker was there to report on it. In some ways, you become a content creator as well. This type of experiential learning can help you grow as a human being (Kolb, 2014). As you experience more, you become more sensitive to the world. By talking with others from different backgrounds in a variety of contexts, you learn more about the larger world. Directly experiencing the world will make you more interesting and engaged.

WHAT TO DO NEXT
To make the most of direct experience, try to:

- Be present in the moment by limiting distractions (e.g., turn off the cell phone).

- Avoid making immediate judgments of the event. You can do this later, after the event.

- Notice as many details as possible (e.g., sights, sounds, smells, the way you felt).

sleuthing through your questions to find the most appropriate resources in which to examine a topic. There are many ways to contact a librarian. Most college libraries have a webpage devoted to conversing with librarians online by either e-mail, Twitter, or live chat. Library websites also provide direct telephone numbers to different reference desks where an actual human being will answer the phone. And, of course, you can visit in person. Find your school and/or local library and use it. Librarians and other staff members often hold training sessions at the beginning of each semester to provide an overview of their services, the library's holdings, and ways to access different types of information.

Information contained in libraries can be accessed in many ways: through the catalog, reference works, and periodical databases. It is important to understand the type of data each provides. The catalog refers to the entire collection of works contained in the library. These works can include books, periodicals, reference works, recordings, motion pictures and videos, graphic objects, databases, CDs, and websites. Within the catalog are reference works, which include general materials such as encyclopedias, dictionaries, biographical information, company information, literary criticisms, and statistics. Reference collections are generally the first place to start your information search. These works often provide information about business, humanities, law, and social sciences. Reference works also include books that answer factual questions as well as college guides, business resources, style manuals (such as the APA publication manual), statistical abstracts, and general information about occupations. Reference works are a good way to narrow down your topic; however, these types of materials are not best to use in your actual presentations, as they summarize original sources. It is far better to find the original information.

A periodical is a publication, either printed or electronic, that is produced on a regular basis, such as newspapers, magazines, and journals. A periodical database is a computerized system that provides electronic access to these articles. You can search periodical databases by subject (family, law, business), by title (*Communication Quarterly*), or by keyword (corn husks + fuel). Databases worth accessing include Google Scholar, WorldCat, ProQuest, Readers' Guide Full Text, Academic Search Premier, ABI/Inform Complete, and Communication & Mass Media Complete. For instance, if your presentation topic is "Memorable Messages to High School Graduates," you might search the communication, education, or family and consumer sciences databases. Academic journals such as *Communication Quarterly, Communication Education, Psychological Reports, Journal of Public Health,* and others are excellent sources to find in-depth information written by experts about various topics like the cross-cultural differences of high school graduate consumer behavior, but keep in mind that these types of articles will be extremely narrow in scope and might be quite challenging to read.

The library catalog and databases will provide you with solid background information. But this information should be supplemented by current findings on your topic. Newspapers and magazines provide a wealth of current print sources, and several databases can put most of it at your fingertips. One of the most commonly used databases for this purpose is LexisNexis, which provides full-text articles of hundreds of newspapers and magazines including the five major U.S. newspapers: the *New York Times, Christian Science Monitor, Wall Street Journal, Washington Post,* and *Los Angeles Times.* While

The library is usually the best place to start looking for credible information and sources.

Thinkstock

researching newspapers and magazines, try to be mindful of the type of information you are using. If you use information from editorials and opinion pieces, you need to be aware that this information often reflects the author's personal outlooks on topics. Try to determine the bias of publications. For instance, the *Christian Science Monitor* will present information differently than *The Onion,* a fake, comedic news source.

Finding Primary Sources: Interviewing

News magazines are a great resource to get topic ideas. You will want to find additional information to support your arguments.

As you conduct research, you may find the best information comes from a person who has direct knowledge about your subject—a primary source. This person may be an expert in the field, or someone who has firsthand experience. In this case, you will want to conduct an interview. An interview is the process of gaining information through questioning. Please refer to the appendix on interviewing for a more in-depth discussion. We only briefly discuss interviewing in this chapter to help you with your research. You can conduct an interview face to face, over the phone, through Skype, or by e-mail.

Planning your interview is the first important step. Stephen Colbert made interviewing look deceptively easy, but it is a skill that must be mastered with some planning and organization. It is important to prepare for your interview. This means conducting enough research so that you can ask interesting and relevant questions. Don't waste valuable time asking your subject a question you can easily find with library or Internet research. The purpose of an interview is to unearth information not found through other sources.

First, contact the person and ask to schedule an interview. If the interview will be conducted using videoconferencing technologies, confirm the interviewee's username and get his or her phone number should the video link not work. Be clear and concise about the topic you are researching and the reason why you chose this person to interview. If the person has specific credentials in this area, briefly state them so the interviewee can confirm them. Second, explain how long you anticipate the interview to last and what type of questions you will be asking. Finally, you should follow up with your person to confirm the date and time.

When conducting your interview, arrive early and dress professionally. This is true even for a videoconference. Make sure that whatever can be seen on the screen is tidy and professional. Try to establish a relationship with your interviewee by being conversational, courteous, and respectful. Have your questions prepared and written down in a logical order. You will probably move from general to specific questions, and your questions should follow a conversational pattern. If you plan to record the interview, ask permission before you begin. Some people may be uncomfortable with this and decline. If so, respect their wishes and take notes instead. On this note, do not become engrossed in trying to write down everything the interviewee says. This is one of the most challenging balancing acts when hand-recording interviews. Try to pay attention to the interviewee by making eye contact, nodding that you understand, and asking clarifying questions if you do not. Write down key phrases during the interview. If you hear a great quote, write it down and put quotes around it immediately. To check the accuracy of your understanding, summarize the main points when you change topic areas. For instance, you might say, "So, I understand

Journalist Katie Couric uses interviews like this one with Senator Mark Rubio to get in-depth information on topical issues.

that you were the first person of your generation to attend college: Is it true that your parents did not want you to go to college?" followed by, "How did this affect your decision to work as a college recruiter?" By summarizing the information during the interview, you are confirming information along the way, which will minimize fact-checking afterward.

You will notice the summary question mentioned in the preceding example is a closed question, meaning it requires only a one- or two-word answer. For the majority of the interview you will ask open questions, which are those that look for perspective, insight, attitudes, and opinions. Open questions may begin with phrases such as, "What effect does this have . . . ?" "How does this impact . . . ?" "Why is this important to . . . ?" or "Tell me about a time when. . . ." Consider the information you will gain from the following questions:

"So, you voted against bringing Phish to campus. Was this a hard decision?" (closed question)

"I understand you voted against bringing Phish to campus. Could you tell me how this decision impacted your position as a student leader?" (open question)

In addition to asking open questions, you will want to ask neutral questions, which are those that don't have an intended answer. Conversely, leading questions are asked in such a way that the interviewer expects or hopes for a specific answer:

"Can you talk about how hard it was to vote against bringing Phish to campus?" (leading question)

"What influenced your decision to vote against bringing Phish to campus?" (neutral question)

Concluding the interview should not be overlooked in your preparation. Be sure to stay within the agreed-upon time. Before leaving, quickly read your notes for accuracy. This is also the time to ask for clarification on statements or issues you don't understand. Thank the interviewee for her time and ask if you can follow up by phone or e-mail if you have additional questions. After the interview, reread and process the information. Make notes of the major themes, potential quotes, and overall summaries. Also, make sure you send a written thank-you note to the interviewee. At the very least, send a nice thank-you e-mail. You never know when you might need to make contact again.

Evaluating Sources

Thanks to the Internet, computers can access numerous electronic databases and millions of websites to locate information immediately. If you do not know how to search databases on your computer, contact a representative at your college library who can help you learn how to navigate databases, catalogs, government documents, news articles, and more. Most libraries are moving to even more digital content (Fay & Nyhan, 2015).

Some of the most popular databases are

Academic Search Premier

Encyclopedia Britannica online (This is a good way to get background information before you start your real search and narrow your topic; most instructors will not let you use this information for your actual presentation.)

Google Scholar

LexisNexis Academic

LexisNexis Guided News Search

ProQuest

WorldCat

We often underestimate the amount of time it takes to conduct solid research. A database search could bring up more than 100,000 documents, requiring you to narrow the focus of your research. While sources are easy to locate, how do you determine if they are credible?

Evaluating sources is extremely important so that you get the best information, not just information. You must be and should be motivated to critically examine your sources (Metzger, 2007). Getting the best information from multiple and varied sources is a complicated task (Brand-Gruwel & Stadtler, 2011). In reality, you should be OK with throwing away much of your research (Rubin, Rubin, & Piele, 2005). It takes a lot of work to find the best and most credible research. As you read your research, ask questions about the author's expertise, the publisher's authority, bias, and the timeliness of the information.

Author's Expertise

The author's expertise refers to the author's credibility. Does the author know what he or she is talking about? Does it make sense? Is the information accurate? Has the author written in this field before? What are the author's credentials? For example, would Taylor Swift be credible to write an article about nuclear physics? Of course not, but she would be credible to write about the music industry. Most instructors will tell you that Wikipedia is not a good source to use for this reason, and they are right. Wikipedia might provide a good overview of the topic, but you cannot be sure about the authors and their credentials to write the entry. Sometimes you might wish to cite a blog. In this case, it is important to thoroughly and carefully examine who the author is of the blog. Journalists, scientists, politicians, and artists sometimes use blogs to highlight their work and ideas. Just be careful with citing and finding information from a blog. Authors need to have credibility for their ideas and writings.

Thinkstock

Use only the best and most credible research. Be prepared to toss the rest.

Publisher's Authority

The type of publication determines the publisher's authority. One of the best ways to help establish the publisher's authority is to look at the Internet domain for the publisher's website. Is it a .gov, .org, .edu, or .com website? As you know, .com refers to commercial websites. Imagine you found two informative articles about a new health care device. One article is published on the manufacturer's website, and the other is published on CNN.com. Which one do you use? Do you use both? While not a perfect solution, it is usually better to select the one from the news agency. Any manufacturer's website is trying to sell its product with a positive slant and hide negative information, often in small print. It is hard to be objective if you are trying to sell something. Anyone can purchase a website. Be very careful about using information from websites that seem to have little accountability for their content. Most news sources use a .com domain name but have both internal and external accountability for the content. If the publication is an academic journal, you can usually be sure of its authority because it has been thoroughly reviewed by experts in the field.

Bias

Another important area of concern is the bias of the author and/or publication. Bias occurs when the author or the publication has a particular point of view that will skew the information. For example, the Republican Party is going to produce information that supports its positions, and the Democratic Party is going to do the same. The accuracy of the information is important to examine. Be sure to take note of how the information in the article was gathered. Take, for instance, a survey that examined attitudes about a Republican-controlled Congress that was paid for by the Republican National Committee. Did the survey ask more Republican voters than are normally represented in the population? If so, the results could be skewed toward the needs and wants of the Republican National Committee. Did the survey ask leading questions to produce a better answer for the Republican National Committee? These types of questions will help you figure out potential bias that exists in your sources. If possible, double-check an article's facts with other credible sources. There needs to be a level of consistency across sources.

Timeliness

The timeliness of information is a concern if you are presenting on a topic that is fast-changing or a current event. Take the topic of technology, for example. New technology is being released all the time. Literally, the information on a technological topic could change between the time you do your research and the time you present your speech. If the information on your topic is always changing, you will want to stay on top of your research right up until the moment you deliver the presentation. Have you ever seen a presenter give information that you knew was old and outdated about a current event? Nothing will hurt the speaker's credibility more than presenting old information.

The key to evaluating your sources is to analyze the information, the author, and the publisher. Always assume something is wrong with your information until you can successfully answer the issues and questions

Look for the possible bias of an author or publication when evaluating a source.

Thinkstock

discussed earlier. As more and more information is available online, you will always need to be evaluating the quality of your sources (Lauricella, 2009). Always evaluate your sources, whether you find them online or in a paper format. Strong information adds to the credibility of your message and to perceptions of you as a speaker.

TYPES OF EVIDENCE

You have gathered your research, conducted your interviews, and evaluated your sources. Now you must decide on the type of evidence you present to engage your audience and confirm your credibility. Your evidence needs to be engaging to the audience. Evidence separates a good speech from a great speech. You must determine what information is relevant, interesting, and representational, and then find the evidence to support it. This can include statistics, testimony, and examples.

Statistics

Consider this statistic: About 62% of you checked Facebook at least once while reading this chapter. How effective was that statement? Did it make you think? Although in this instance it is a made-up number, when used properly and with discretion, statistics can provide incredible power for you to engage your audience. The key is to use them wisely and sparingly, and only when you can identify the source, verify their accuracy, and explain them to your audience.

A recent study found that 41% of all teens admitted to texting while driving (Rhodan, 2014). What does this number mean? How many teens were surveyed? Who conducted the research? What if you heard a speaker say that 75% of teens texted while driving? In this case, the speaker informally asked his four roommates if they texted while driving, and three said yes. Is this a good statistic? A survey of four people is not generalizable to an entire population of people. The first statistic is based on a scientific poll, while the second statistic is based on four friends. This second number would be a misleading statistic. Good statistics do exist, however. In the preceding example, the Centers for Disease Control and Prevention conducted this study examining youth risk behaviors. You can help the audience make sense of statistics by rounding them to whole numbers, using graphs and charts to illustrate them, and making them meaningful to the audience by establishing a context for the numbers.

ASSESS YOUR COMMUNICATION

EVALUATE SOURCES

Use the following questions to assess the strength of your sources for your presentation.

1. Credibility:

   Is the author/publisher credible?

   What are the author/publisher's credentials?

   Is this author/publisher's information consistent with sources? If not, why?

2. Objectivity:

   Is the information a fact or an opinion?

   How is the information presented? Fact or opinion?

   Think about the author/publisher's point of view. Does it matter?

   Does the author/publisher have an interest in reporting on certain types of information?

3. Timeliness:

   Is the Internet source timely?

   Does it appear that the website updates information frequently, or is it a "dead" link?

   Does the source provide links for additional readings?

   Are the links useful and up-to-date?

4. Reliability:

   Does the information appear to be well sourced and researched?

   Are the author/publisher's sources provided so that you can double-check for accuracy?

   Is there a print version of the online content available so that you can double-check for accuracy?

Most often, statistics are first reported in research studies in academic journals. It is important to locate and learn to interpret the primary research and the findings. How was the research conducted? Was it an experiment or a survey? When establishing a context for the findings or statistics, you will want to clearly define what the numbers mean and do not mean in regard to the topic and the study. Not providing the right context for the findings of the research might confuse or mislead your audience. Far too often, research studies are not used correctly. If possible at your school, take a research methods class to help you better understand how research studies could help you make important decisions in both your life and career.

You will want to know how credible the expert is about the subject. Is there a time when a lay testimony might be better for the situation?

Testimony

A testimony is a statement or declaration by a person who has a connection to the topic. Advertisers have long counted on testimony to persuade people to buy their products. Crest toothpaste uses testimonies from dentists. The skin product Proactiv uses testimonies from actors and singers. Nutrisystem's program for weight loss uses testimonies from athletes, coaches, and performers. Their intent is to provide credibility, add weight to arguments, and arouse emotions. Testimonies can come from experts or peers. Expert testimony comes from authorities in the field and often provides data, statistics, trends, and predictions, whereas lay testimony comes from everyday people who have firsthand experience with a topic. Lay testimony stirs up passions and serves to support expert testimony by providing stories that the audience will find memorable. When using either type of testimony as evidence, check the source's credentials.

Examples

Examples provide a strong way to connect and engage with the audience. Examples make the concepts you are discussing real and relevant. Examples can be short or long, but are always chosen to lillustrate a specific point. A brief example might include a couple of sentences about an overall case. Take, for example, a speech about various ways to raise money for cancer research:

> The group decided to host a dragon boat, and last fall 20 students climbed into a 40-foot-long canoe and raced toward the finish line to raise money for cancer research.

Notice that this is a short example but gets the point across to the audience.

An extended example is often developed as a story with a beginning, a middle, and an end and takes the listener to another place. For example, a speech that addresses spinal cord injuries could use the dramatic example of an injured athlete:

> He had made the same tackle hundreds of times before. But tonight he lay motionless before 40,000 people on the 30-yard line of the university football

field—his neck broken between the fourth and fifth cervical vertebrae. It was Friday, Oct 29. On that night he became a quadriplegic. (Haywood, 1991)

For an extended example, you would refer back to the story several times throughout the speech, telling new parts of the story and connecting your messages to the example.

An example can also be hypothetical. The following hypothetical example could be used in a speech on how to meet celebrities:

Imagine you stumble onto the set of a movie being shot on the streets of Boston. You see Anna Faris (*The House Bunny, Scary Movie 4*) walking to a taxi while directors and crew people look on attentively. As you wait for filming of this scene to finish, a crew member strikes up a conversation. When you mention you are a huge fan of the actress and follow her on Twitter, the crew member asks—quite unbelievably—"We're all going out after the shoot. Would you like to join us and meet her?"

In this type of example, the key is that the audience member could actually imagine a situation like this taking place in the real world. In other words, hypothetical examples need to be believable.

CITING YOUR SOURCES

To avoid problems of plagiarism, you must cite your sources both orally and on paper. Besides not getting in trouble for stealing someone's work, giving credit to your sources helps build your own credibility with the audience. In this section, you will learn how to orally cite and provide written citations of your sources.

Oral Citations

It's important to give oral citations of your sources in your presentation. You must provide enough information to certify your material as legitimate without reciting the entire reference entry. Your audience needs to know and trust your sources while you are speaking. An oral citation provides the source of your information to the audience:

Proper citations in your oral and written communication will lend credibility and professionalism, while recognizing your sources.

According to Facebook's 2015 online fact sheet, the social networking site currently reaches more than 1.39 billion users.

This oral citation gives the name of the source (Facebook's newsroom), the year of publication (2015), and the type of document (online). At a minimum, you need to provide orally the author's name, the publication year, and the name of the newspaper, magazine, or website. In some cases, you will want to go into further detail. For example, if one of your sources won a Nobel Prize, you would preface his or her name with that fact—"2014 Nobel Peace Prize winner Malala Yousafzai once said, 'Education is one of the blessings in my life.'" When citing your sources orally, give as much information as possible to help persuade your audience that the source is credible.

Thinkstock

COMMUNICATION**HOW-TO**
CITING YOUR SOURCES IN APA STYLE

1. All references should be in alphabetical order by last name of the first author.

2. Sources should appear on the reference page and in text on the outline.

3. Titles of books, magazines, newspapers, and journals should be italicized:

   Spence, P. R., Westerman, D., Edwards, C., & Edwards, A. (2014). Welcoming our robot overlords: Initial expectations about interaction with a robot. *Communication Research Reports, 31*, 272–280.

4. The first line of every entry should be on the margin with hanging indents for each line of the same entry.

5. Never use the full first name for any author. Use initials.

6. Only capitalize the first word of an article's title. The first word after a colon or dash in the title must be capitalized.

7. Capitalize all major words in the name of the newspaper, magazine, or journal.

8. Bookmark the APA online style guide for your reference: http://www.apastyle.org/. This website provides the "official" ways to use APA for citations.

Written Citations

You will also need to provide written citations of your sources in a reference list to accompany your outline. Most instructors in the field of communication use the American Psychological Association (APA) stylebook for formatting citations. Always use the newest edition of the stylebook. You will most likely use

CAREER FRONTIER: CROWDSOURCING

HOW MANY TIMES have you had a problem but did not really have a good solution? You might ask a friend, a parent, or a small group of people for their advice. Inevitably, you get a few good ideas but no real consensus on the best solution for your problem. Thanks to changes in technology, we have more ways to get diverse opinions for our questions. This is referred to as **crowdsourcing**. Jeff Howe first coined this term in 2006 in a *Wired* magazine article. Originally, crowdsourcing referred to a web-based business model in which a company would solicit creative solutions to problems posted online. Today, this term is used more broadly and applies to soliciting answers from social networks. For example, you might work for a company that specializes in fashion jewelry. You are at a jewelry trade show but do not know what your customers might like. You take a few pictures and upload them to your company's Facebook

page. Immediately, you start getting comments from your own customers about likes and dislikes. You place orders based on what your customers want and desire. Crowdsourcing is another form of researching and making data-driven decisions. It is not what "I" know but what "we" know. James Surowiecki, in his book *The Wisdom of Crowds*, argues that under the right circumstances the wisdom of a crowd can be better than an individual expert. In your career, you might need to crowdsource to find out what your customers (audience) think about a product or idea. Being savvy with social media is an important part of this technique and could potentially help with your career. One of the key components about life in the Communication Age is being able to successfully use all the resources available to effectively find creative solutions. Crowdsourcing is one such avenue that could help in your career.

sources from books, periodicals, the Internet, and magazines. There are several online guides to help you with written citations. Your instructor and librarians will also be able to give you guidance. In the following examples, you will find most basic types of written citations. You can also refer to the end of this textbook for actual sources cited in APA format, 6th edition. Creating a reference list takes time and can be quite frustrating; however, it is an important part of demonstrating credibility and documenting your sources. Whether citing your sources orally or providing a reference page, it is a habit that will serve you well in school and even in the workplace.

RESEARCH AND CONVERGENCE

Convergence in the Communication Age allows you to think about the possibility of new ways of finding information and assessing the credibility. Social networking websites like LinkedIn, Twitter, or Facebook might help you find interesting experts to interview or crowdsource topics. Watching the live stream of a protest from another country might provide new kinds of information that was not available before. Interacting with readers on a news blog about the day's top story might help you figure out what people are actually thinking and feeling about an issue. The possibilities are endless.

Technology and new forms of media allow us to have a wider array of places to find credible and useful information. The downside is that we now have even more access to information that is biased, not credible, or just wrong. You must separate the good information from the junk information. It is important to be able to find the best kinds of evidence and to accurately cite your sources because it is your ethical responsibility as a speaker. But what do we do about information that is not found in newspapers, books, or magazines either in print or online?

While the Communication Age allows for new and more types of information to be readily accessed, we have to think about the implications of using some of this information that is not typically journalistic in nature. Is it ethical to use someone's personal blog about his or her medical treatment for cancer? Is this person entitled to some privacy even with a public blog? Is it OK to show a video of people when they are not thinking clearly and perhaps suffering from a serious mental disorder or having a breakdown? In other words, we have to think about the kinds of information we use for our presentations. Convergence means that people are exposing their thoughts and actions to a wider audience using virtual space. As ethical communicators, we need to determine on a case-by-case basis if we should use this information as a possible form of evidence in our research. We should always be thinking about the privacy, safety, and security of other people, even when they post something online. The key point is that you carefully think out the implications of the different kinds of information you use and establish credibility for your sources and self.

iStock

Social networking sites provide accessible and varied sources of information, yet caution must be exercised to ensure their accuracy.

WHAT YOU'VE LEARNED   Now that you have studied this chapter, you should be able to:

1 **Describe the seriousness of all aspects of plagiarism.**

Plagiarism is a serious issue. Careful attention to detail and documenting your sources can help you avoid any violations. Always cite your sources.

▶ Computer Program Helps Colleges Fight Plagiarism

🎙 Cut and Paste Plagiarism

2 **Summarize how to build your credibility through research.**

As you use research to build credibility, remember Aristotle's three areas of concern: ethos, pathos, and logos. When you apply these concepts to all aspects of researching the presentation, you will make a stronger connection with the audience.

🎙 Who Can You trust?

🎙 Media Focus on Bad News

🖥 Researching Your Topic

3 **Identify effective ways for finding information through research.**

It is important to learn how to find information through research for your

presentation. Look for bias and accuracy problems with all of your research.

▶ Katie Couric on How to Conduct a Good Interview

🎙 Wikipedia in Academia

4 **Discuss various types of evidence.**

Become familiar with various types of evidence. Some pieces of evidence are stronger than other pieces of evidence. Learn to know when this matters.

▶ Using Evidence in Persuasive Speeches

5 **Demonstrate how to cite sources both in writing and orally.**

Citing your sources both orally and in written form is important for your credibility. Learn to give credit any time you use a source.

▶ Citing Sources in Your Speech

🖥 APA Website Citation

KEY TERMS

Review key terms with **eFlashcards. edge.sagepub.com/edwards2e**

Ad hominem 298	Hasty generalization 300	Plagiarism 294
Bandwagon 300	Inductive reasoning 297	Primary source 300
Bias 306	Leading question 304	Red herring 298
Closed question 304	Logos 297	Reference list 295
Credibility 296	Neutral question 304	Secondary source 300
Crowdsourcing 311	Non sequitur argument 298	Self-plagiarism 295
Deductive reasoning 297	Open question 304	Slippery slope 299
Either/or arguments 299	Patchwork plagiarism 295	Source 300
Ethos 297	Pathos 297	Testimony 309
Global plagiarism 295	Periodical 302	Text stealing 295

REFLECT

1. How does stealing another person's words violate the ethical concept of autonomy and responsibility? In what ways do you hurt the audience?

2. The slippery slope fallacy can cause tremendous amounts of fear in the audience if it is not detected as a fallacy. Can you think of times in history when this fallacy was successfully used to get the audience to support the speaker's position?

3. News sources are generally considered credible. However, every news outlet has some bias. How do you avoid this type of bias in the newsroom? Are there better newsrooms than others in terms of bias? How do you know?

REVIEW

To check your answers go to **edge.sagepub.com/edwards2e**

1. _____ is the act of using someone else's language, ideas, or other original (not common-knowledge) material without acknowledging its source.

2. ___ plagiarism occurs when someone claims an entire document as their own, while _____ plagiarism occurs when several documents are combined into one.

3. Define credibility.

4. The ethical appeal and credibility of a presentation is _____.

5. _____ involves passion and emotion communicated in a presentation.

6. _____ refers to the logic, structure, evidence, and support for an argument.

7. Newspapers, magazines, and journals are examples of _____.

8. _____ occurs when an author or publication has a point of view that skews the information.

9. What is the best way to avoid problems with plagiarism?

SPEECH PLANNER

SpeechPlanner is an interactive, web-based tool that guides you through the process of planning and preparing your speech, one step at a time.

13 ORGANIZING YOUR PRESENTATION

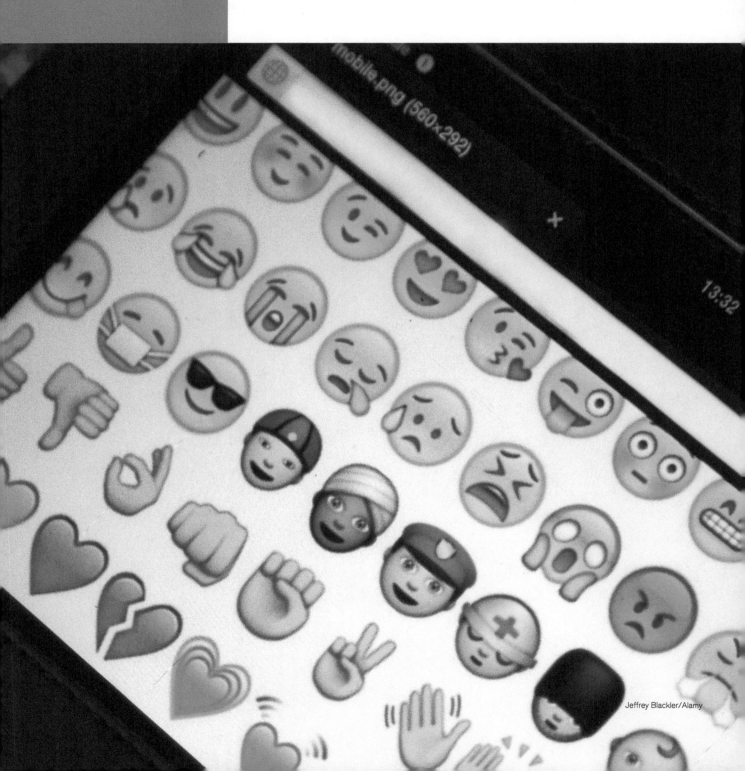

Jeffrey Blackler/Alamy

WHAT YOU'LL LEARN

WHAT YOU'LL LEARN — After studying this chapter, you will be able to:

1 Explain how stories are judged.

2 Describe different types of organizational patterns and why they are used.

3 Create the various parts of the presentation (introduction, body, conclusion, and transitions).

4 Demonstrate the basics of outlining.

5 Analyze how time considerations influence your presentations.

Being organized is an important aspect of living in the Communication Age. Whether it is organizing a paper or a movement, organizing allows us to take some control in an otherwise chaotic situation. In 2015, members of the non-profit organization Endangered Bodies launched an online petition directed to Facebook to remove its "feeling fat" status update option. This petition received over 16,000 signatures (Oyla, 2015). Endangered Bodies organized a social change in the form of an online petition using Change.org.

Tweets, posts, videos, and pictures were sent out on social networks encouraging others to sign and share the petition. Without this organization of a movement and the use of social media, the request would not have been successful. Facebook listened and said that this status update "could reinforce negative body image, particularly for people struggling with eating disorders" (Change.org, 2015). On March 10, 2015, Facebook removed "feeling fat" as an option for status updates. It was a victory for positive change online.

Organizing a movement takes time and thought. The leaders had to figure out ways to organize the material to present their message best. While preparing a presentation is not a social movement, you will need to organize your information to make the best one possible. Organization is extremely important for your presentations in the Communication Age due to all the potential distractions that exist. Organizing a speech will allow your audience to understand better, remember the topic, and possibly take action. In this chapter, you will learn how to organize your presentations to achieve the maximum effectiveness.

And by the way, you know, when you're telling these little stories? Here's a good idea—have a POINT. It makes it SO much more interesting for the listener!
—Neal Page, speaking to Del Griffith in the classic film Planes, Trains, and Automobiles

An organized presentation will help us to connect and engage the audience.

Perhaps you have been in the character Neal Page's shoes. You have listened to someone ramble through a story or presentation and asked yourself, "What's the point?" If you are interested in the topic, you might ask for clarification, but if you are not, you will probably mentally check out and pull out your phone to see what is happening on Facebook. When we converse with friends via Facebook, Twitter, phone, text, or face to face we can usually determine the point of the conversation by interacting with the speaker. Even if we have friends who ramble and talk in circles, we usually can ask questions to make sense of their story or point. We do not have this luxury when we speak to an audience.

As speakers, it is our job to clearly define the point of the presentation to the audience, and then lead the audience through the maze of information in a clear and concise way. Organized presentations allow us to connect and engage with the audience. Hence, becoming a speaker with a clearly defined point is not an easy task. We encounter added pressure by knowing we get just one opportunity to share our information with the audience. This is even truer if our presentation is going to be online in some form. With all the information readily available in the Communication Age, we must be organized, engaging, credible, and succinct in order for our message to be heard.

By now you have chosen and researched your topic, and hopefully you have a wealth of information from which to draw. The next step is to determine how you use that information. In this chapter, we discuss organizing the elements of your presentation so you can clearly communicate with your audience. You will learn how to (1) organize your material; (2) structure your speech's introduction, body, and conclusion; (3) use transitions to keep your audience on track; and (4) outline your message.

When organizing your presentation, think of yourself as a tour guide moving a group of people from one point to another. Will you take a train, a plane, or an automobile? All three provide legitimate transportation. All have benefits and drawbacks. But one probably serves your particular purpose better than do the others.

TELLING A STORY

Everybody loves a good story. We learn to tell stories from the time we are born. In the Communication Age, stories are available everywhere, and it seems as if we sometimes suffer from "story overload." Whether it is the latest news on CNN, the events that happen to your best friend on spring break, or the latest viral BuzzFeed, stories drive our daily existence. Think about any childhood story you remember. There was probably a point to the story to demonstrate some ethic or moral that you should follow.

Communication theorist Walter Fisher argues that stories or narratives are how we build communities and relationships and create our lives. He defines *narrative* as "a theory of symbolic actions—words and/or deeds—that have sequence and meaning for those who live, create, and interpret them" (Fisher, 1984, p. 2). He labels human beings as *Homo narrans,* or "the storytelling animal," and maintains that we make decisions based on our historical and cultural stories (Fisher, 1987). According to Fisher, there are two basic ways to judge the quality of a narrative: narrative coherence, in which the story hangs together and makes sense (Nicolopoulou, 2008), and narrative fidelity, in which the story matches our own lived experiences (Tullis Owen, McRae, Adams, & Vitale, 2009). These two criteria for narrative quality should serve as the organizing foundations of your presentation. Regarding coherence, does your topic hang together and make sense? Are you making leaps in logic or committing fallacies of logic? In terms of fidelity, are you conducting an effective audience analysis to find ways to relate the topic to your audience members' lives and experiences?

Narrative coherence and narrative fidelity should be the overarching organizational goals for your presentation to connect and engage with the audience. In this chapter, you will learn several ways to organize your presentation, but these two goals should be thought about whatever way you choose to organize your topic.

There are two very different speaking situations. How do narrative coherence and fidelity work in both instances? What are the similarities for telling a good story?

ORGANIZATIONAL PATTERNS

An organizational pattern helps you define the important points of your presentation and keep the audience on track. Whether your presentation is to be delivered in person or online, organization is critical for its success. Audiences will not be able to connect to you or the topic if it is not arranged logically. They will certainly not be engaged with a messy presentation. Your audience expects to be informed about a specific topic, and a messy presentation often conveys a lack of preparation or authority about the topic. The organizational pattern is often determined by your topic. Remember that your goal at this point is to arrange your topic of discussion in a manner that makes sense, is logical, and is easy to follow. In this section, we cover the most commonly used patterns.

Chronological Pattern

Perhaps you want to teach a group of senior citizens at a retirement community how to set up a Facebook account. In this presentation, you would most likely use a chronological pattern because the order of steps is important. Generally, you

DIGITAL STORYTELLING

Thinkstock

TELLING STORIES ABOUT our lives has been part of the human makeup since the beginning of language. Stories are how we pass down information from one generation to the next. Children learn their ABCs, how to tie their shoes, and even how to go potty based on shared stories. Most likely, you learned about college from people telling you stories. At heart, we are storytellers!

The Communication Age has allowed us to develop more ways to tell stories and to share these stories with more people across time and space. Many scholars,

students, and community organizations are now creating digital stories as a way to be involved in communication activism. Digital stories are usually short videos with images and sounds that allow the filmmakers to tell their own stories about their lives and communities. Usually those involved in making a digital story have no prior knowledge of how to do so. Summer camps, training workshops, and classes spend a few days teaching participants how to use basic video-editing software to create their own digital stories.

The Kalamazoo Youth Media Initiative, a joint project of Western Michigan University's School of Communication, community groups, and public schools, hosted a summer workshop for high school students from an economically disadvantaged part of the city in which participants learned about the basics of interviewing, creating small films, and storytelling. Each of the students produced a small film about their local community as a way to empower themselves and their neighborhood. These types of grassroots digital story camps are happening everywhere. Technology is allowing all types of people to create stories to share their own experiences as a form of communication activism. Sharing your story allows others to get a glimpse of life in your shoes. When digital storytelling is combined with social justice, a powerful creative endeavor can happen for the greater good. Become involved in a digital storytelling movement in your area. Help others tell their story!

present the order from first to last, with the steps leading to a final result. You may explain the process this way:

1. Create an account.
2. Create a profile.
3. Set your privacy settings.
4. Request friends.
5. Interact with your friends.

This pattern is also frequently used to share information about historical occasions or the development of an event. For instance, if you want to discuss the history of Facebook, your organizational pattern might look like this:

1. Harvard students founded Facebook from their residence hall room in 2004.
2. Facebook expanded to include high school networks in 2005.
3. Facebook reached more than 1 billion active users in 2015. (Facebook, 2015)

A chronological pattern is most often used when the exact ordering of information matters for the topic.

Topical Pattern

Information prepared according to subject matter indicates a topical pattern, the most commonly used organizational pattern. You decide to give a speech listing the benefits of using a credit union. In this case, no formal systematic organization is required. This presentation could be organized from least important to most important, from most important to least important, from general to specific, or from specific to general. You can organize your presentation by considering what will be most useful to your listener, like this:

1. Credit unions provide opportunities to help local businesses.

2. Credit unions keep your money circulating in your local community.

3. Credit unions offer additional services not found in big banks.

Notice how each point about credit unions is a smaller point under the larger topic of the benefits of using a credit union.

Spatial Pattern

Sometimes it is necessary to provide information to an audience in terms of space. Providing information by location or physical relationship requires a spatial pattern of organization. This pattern can be used to describe a building, an object, a location, a city, a piece of art, or a vintage album cover. Within this pattern you can choose the direction in which you want to guide your audience: left to right, top to bottom, north to south, and so on. For example, you might deliver a presentation to a group of community activists about where resources are located in your city to help those in need. Your description might sound like this:

1. On South Street, you can find a food pantry and free clothing closet.

2. If you continue north, you will intersect Golden Avenue, which has a shelter for homeless and battered women.

3. If you take Golden Avenue to 2nd Street, you will find the state aid office and a work-training center.

For this pattern to be successful, you need to be clear in your description of the space whether it is directions to a local business or details about a large piece of street art.

Cause-and-Effect Pattern

A cause-and-effect pattern of organization addresses a topic in terms of a cause and its effect on another entity. Presentations about issues such as health, climate change, sustainability, and weight gain often use this structure. It's important to use the words *cause* and *effect* in your speech when referring to the issue. Always link the cause directly to the effect you are addressing. You

CAREER FRONTIER: CORPORATE STORYTELLING

Getty

STEVE JOBS, the late CEO of Apple Inc., was an amazing storyteller. At the annual Apple shareholders meetings, Jobs would introduce villains and heroes. He would build up the presentation to a moment that would leave the audience feeling excited about the future (Gallo, 2014). Jobs knew that a story could do more for an audience than simply listing the facts and figures of an Apple product. He told an exciting story about Apple's future. Many organizations and companies are now hiring corporate storytellers to get the message out about their products, companies, and ideas. These communication specialists are skillful at telling a good story. They are able to show how companies overcame adversity or how a product can change a person's life. Corporate storytellers use all types of media to help tell the story for their organizations. You might be telling stories in your own career. Can you tell a good story?

could use this pattern when discussing the need to decrease our dependence on oil. For example,

   I. The lack of public transportation across the country (cause)

   II. Contributes to U.S. dependence on foreign oil (effect)

The cause-and-effect pattern can be used when organizing both informative and persuasive presentations.

Problem-Cause-Solution Pattern

A problem-cause-solution pattern of organization is about solving a dilemma. Pretend you are talking with a friend about your education. You explain that your grades are suffering. You discuss how juggling school, work, and extra-curricular activities is hurting your study habits. Your friend suggests you decrease your extracurricular activities to give yourself more time to study. Because you made your point clear to her, your friend is able to understand and therefore help you formulate a solution. Organizing a presentation with this pattern is not much different from telling a friend about your grades. It has only three parts: Explain a problem, discuss the causes, and offer a solution. The biggest challenge with this pattern involves convincing your audience that the answer you offer is the best one for the problem. In other words, at the end of the presentation, the members of your audience should not be considering other solutions; they must believe your plan is the best way to go. This organization pattern is best suited for a persuasive speech and is discussed in more detail in Chapter 16.

Monroe's Motivated Sequence

Monroe's Motivated Sequence is a persuasive organizational pattern popular with speakers. This pattern has been utilized countless times because it is effective (McDermott, 2004). The main focus of this organizational pattern is to encourage the audience to take steps toward helping solve the need you suggest. You are familiar with this pattern even if you have not heard it by this name. Monroe's Motivated Sequence consists of five steps:

1. *Attention:* In this step, you capture the audience's interest. This step serves as the introduction. You might use a story, a startling statistic, an example, a quotation, or a rhetorical question.

2. *Need:* In this first body point, you establish a problem and the fact that it is significant.

3. *Satisfaction:* In the second main body point, you will set up a plan of action to solve the need. It is important to be detailed and specific with your plan.

4. *Visualization:* In the last main body point, you will provide the advantages of your plan to the audience as well as the disadvantages if it is not implemented. In this step, your job is to help the audience visualize the plan in action.

5. *Action:* This step also serves as the conclusion. Here, you tell the audience members the immediate actions they can take to implement your plan and solve the problem.

This persuasive organizational pattern is discussed in greater detail in Chapter 16. Every presentation needs structure. We must know what we want to accomplish, how we will achieve it, and our desired results. Choosing the right organizational pattern will help achieve your favored outcome. You might be surprised to know that bands put a lot of time and energy into the structure of their performances. They make a set list of the music to be played to accomplish this goal. A set list has a beginning, a middle, and an end, and usually involves opening and closing with the band's strongest songs. Bands engage with their audience strategically. This sounds a lot like creating an effective presentation! In Chapter 11, you learned about the basics of a presentation.

If you will be using presentational aids (see Chapter 14), you will want to think about the organizational pattern even more. Different types of presentational software (e.g., PowerPoint, Prezi) are better for various types of patterns. PowerPoint is extremely good for chronological speeches because it follows a more linear model. Prezi is a nice choice for a spatial organizational pattern because this software allows movement that is not linear in nature. Imagine you were doing a speech about Paris and its best tourist spots. You would be able to use a map of Paris for a background and then zoom around the picture for each point. However, never let the software decide your organizational pattern. The topic and your approach should decide the pattern; the software is a secondary issue.

In the following sections, you will learn more about the introduction, body, and conclusion.

Having an organized presentation will help any kind of audience stay focused on the message.

Communication unplugged
FOR BETTER PRESENTATION ORGANIZATION, TALK IT OUT!

iStock

Taking good notes about research and utilizing an outline are important parts of the presentation-making process. However, sometimes we think we are organized when in reality we are not: The notes and outlines merely give us the impression of being organized. That is why it is important to "talk it out" with someone else. Discuss your ideas with another person. Tell them the story

of the presentation. Doing so will allow another person hear your thoughts and help you better organize them before you deliver the presentation. Leaving the computer screen off and simply talking through your notes and outline will help make you a better presenter. Using presentational software is not enough to help you visualize the organization of the presentation; you need another person to listen. With the help of another person, you will notice the weak spots of the presentation and be better able to enhance the message.

WHAT TO DO NEXT
To get the most out of "talking it out," try to:

- Tell another person about your topic (think of it as a verbal wiki).

- Talk your presentation ideas out with another person not in your class (that way they are not as familiar with the assignment).

- Ask them what was unclear and what could be improved in the organization.

INTRODUCING THE TOPIC

It takes only a few seconds for people to make an initial impression (Lindgaard, Fernandes, Dudek, & Brown, 2006). Those few seconds will determine the degree to which you command a listener's attention. And, as speakers, you want all of your listeners' attention. That means you must come out strong and fast in the introduction of your presentation. An introduction accomplishes four goals: (1) It gets the audience's attention; (2) it introduces your thesis; (3) it gives the audience reasons to listen to you by establishing your credibility and relevance; and (4) it communicates clearly what you will tell the audience in the presentation. Most speakers write the introduction after they have completed the outline of the main points of the speech. Aim for your introduction to compose 10% to 15% of your speech.

Getting the Audience's Attention

The first step in the introduction is to get the audience's attention. You might tell the audience a surprising statement or ask a rhetorical question. Other methods include (1) asking a direct question, (2) telling an anecdote, (3) sharing a personal experience, (4) reciting a quotation, and (5) providing humor. Selecting the most appropriate attention getter depends on your goal.

Rhetorical Question

Asking a rhetorical or direct question is often a good way to get your audience's attention, but be sure to ask a question that achieves your desired result. A rhetorical question is asked in a manner that does not invite an actual response. Rather, it invites members to ponder an answer. Typically, a speaker will pause long enough to allow the question to be legitimately considered by the audience before moving on. You must always be on guard that an audience member will try to shout out an answer to the question.

Direct Question

You can also ask a direct question in your introduction, being mindful that your intent is not to get a verbal answer. A direct question in a presentation usually asks for a show of hands. For instance, if you want to illustrate the miniscule chances one has of winning the lottery, you might ask for a show of hands of those who have actually done so, feeling relatively certain that the number is small. This is also a good technique for "on-the-spot" audience analysis. You might be able to make adjustments to your message based on this quick showing of hands. But remember to be careful with direct questions. Many speakers use this approach, and it is a bit overused. Make sure you really need or want to ask a direct question, and think creatively if you use this technique.

Corbis

While Neil Patrick Harris certainly got the audience's attention, be sure your attention getter refers directly to the presentation in some way.

Telling an Anecdote

You can begin your speech with an opening anecdote or story. An opening anecdote is executed with detail, imagery, or humor, and can quickly pull the audience into your speech. When President Obama addressed the 2010 graduates of the University of Michigan, he included a story in his introduction. He spoke of his desire of maintaining a connection to the American people by reading each night 10 letters written to him. On a particular night, he read letters from a group of kindergartners who were instructed by their teacher to ask the president any question they wanted. Below is a transcript of that portion of his introduction:

> So one asked, "How do you do your job?" Another asked, "Do you work a lot?" [Laughter.] Somebody wanted to know if I wear a black jacket or if I have a beard—[laughter]—so clearly they were getting me mixed up with the other tall guy from Illinois. [Laughter.] And one of my favorites was from a kid who wanted to know if I lived next to a volcano. [Laughter.] I'm still trying to piece the thought process on this one. [Laughter.] Loved this letter.

> But it was the last question from the last student in the letter that gave me pause. The student asked, "Are people being nice?" Are people being nice?

This story directed the audience's attention toward the main points of President Obama's speech: civil discourse and debate. These stories, however, don't have

Getty

iStock

What would you do if you asked a direct question in your introduction and most of the audience disagreed with your position? What adjustments could you make?

to be based on personal experience. They can be stories about other people, and can even be hypothetical. Stories can also provide a series of examples. A series of attention-getting examples to introduce the topic of bullying at work might be

> Susan is yelled at by a coworker in the breakroom in front of about 20 people. Frank is ridiculed by his boss in staff meetings. Michael is physically threatened by his boss.

> The people I just mentioned are all victims of workplace bullying, a silent epidemic that wreaks havoc on the morale, productivity, and health of U.S. workers.

Personal Experience

A personal experience provides a reference or framework for the audience. This type of introduction can involve a true or hypothetical experience, and can also include a compliment to the audience. A personal reference encourages the audience to relate quickly to the speaker and the subject. President Obama included a personal reference in his address at the University of Michigan, by opening his speech with a greeting that referenced the university's stadium and well-known cheer:

> It is great to be here in the Big House—and so may I say, "Go Blue!" I thought I'd go for the cheap applause line to start things off.

Offering a Quotation

Reciting a quotation is a powerful way of gaining your audience's attention. Quotes can come from great speeches, movies, books, stories, or songs, and should be attributed to the person who said them. For instance, if you were giving a presentation about entrepreneurship, you could begin with a quote from Michael Dell, chair and CEO of Dell Inc., who spoke these words at the University of Texas at Austin: "As you start your journey, the first thing you should do is throw away that store-bought map and begin to draw your own." This statement draws the audience members into the topic of the speech and causes them to think about it. The quote you choose should be appropriate to the topic, invoke thought, and relate to your audience's experiences.

Humor

Humor can be a good method of gaining audience attention because it creates goodwill between speakers and listeners. But humor can also be tricky. Avoid it unless you have confidence in your ability to tell a joke and are certain of its appropriateness for the situation and the topic of the speech. A poorly timed joke or inappropriate humor can harm your credibility as a speaker and make it very difficult to recover. Consider your audience, the topic, and the timing before deciding to use this method of gaining audience attention.

Introducing Your Thesis

After you have captured the audience's attention, the next step is to introduce your topic with a thesis sentence. Remember that the thesis is the general purpose of your presentation. When writing the purpose and thesis statement, you must again take on the role of a tour guide, letting the audience members know what they are about to hear. It is critical that you state the purpose of your presentation. As discussed earlier, the general purpose should be clear to the audience. The members of your audience want to know why they are there. Take a look back at Chapter 11 to see the correct ways to write specific purpose statements.

▶ **SPEECHES IN ACTION 13.1**
Demonstrate Importance and Credibility

Demonstrating Importance and Credibility

After stating your thesis, follow up by demonstrating the importance of the topic, and explain why the audience or a future audience should care about the topic. This "why" statement is often referred to as audience relevance. The members of your audience need to perceive that what you have to say is important and timely to them. Your audience analysis (discussed in Chapter 11) will help you craft a message that relates to the audience. Whether you are addressing local water pollution or after-school programs in underserved communities, you need to demonstrate that the topic has a real impact on the audience's lives.

Also, in this step you will want to further establish your credibility, helping confirm that you are the appropriate person to share this important topic. You must set up a mutual relationship with the audience or recap your experience with the topic. This is not to suggest that only experts can deliver information to others; however, we must convince the audience that we are trustworthy and our topic is relevant.

Preview of Main Points

The fourth part of the introduction is the preview of main points. Being clear and concise about what you want the audience to experience, the information you will share with the audience, and the exact order in which you share it may seem condescending to the listener. It's not. Remember, the listener has not heard you practice. The listener does not have access to your notes. The listener can't reread the information. Therefore, a clear preview statement will keep your audience on track throughout your presentation. Often, the organizational pattern you choose will be evident in your preview statement. For instance, if you are giving a presentation about the low voter turnout of college students and a potential solution (the problem-cause-solution organizational pattern), you might say, "In my presentation, I will discuss the problem and causes of college students not voting in elections and share with you ways to solve this problem." With this statement, the audience has a clear road map of the organization and the main points to be covered in the presentation.

Below is the text of an introduction for a presentation regarding homelessness in a local community.

A good preview statement offers the audience a clear road map of your presentation.

Introduction

I. *Attention-getting device*: How many of you have seen a homeless person in Kalamazoo County? Did you stop to help? Walk by? Say hello? Look the other way?

II. *Introducing your thesis*: Today, I will be discussing the issue of homelessness in our own community and trying to persuade you to take part in ways we all can help solve this problem.

III. *Demonstrating the importance and credibility*: Our community had nearly 1,000 homeless people in 2016, a significant number for a community our size. This problem impacts all of us. I have talked to experts who think these numbers are astounding because the homeless population has increased in our community by 40% in one year. I have volunteered for homeless shelters and can share with you what I have experienced.

IV. *Preview of main points*: Today, I will be discussing the problems and causes of homelessness in Kalamazoo County and two ways we can solve this problem together.

BODY

Suppose you want to convince your partner that you two should buy a hybrid SUV. You spend days internally rehearsing the speech you will give so he or she will fully comprehend your argument. Without knowing it, you probably group your argument into main points, perhaps in terms of the vehicle's safety, dependability, and cargo room. Then you give your partner the reasons why you believe the car is safe (crash test results), economical (average annual service costs and gas mileage), and spacious (you pack the dogs for a visit to the vet in one trip). If you have ever rehearsed a hypothetical conversation such as this, you have unknowingly outlined the body of a speech, complete with main points and subpoints.

Main Points

Generally, the body of your speech composes about two-thirds of your presentation. Your main points are the heart of the body. This major section needs to be organized using one of the organizational patterns discussed earlier in this chapter. There are a few guidelines you should follow for the development of the main points within the body of the presentation. First, think of main points as smaller presentations or mini speeches. Each main point should be the thesis sentence for all the subpoints that follow under it. Each main point should utilize transitions to demonstrate the beginning and end of each section in the presentation.

Each main point should be given equal time. In other words, the main points should be proportional. For example, you would not discuss your first main point for 5 minutes and discuss your second and third points for 1 minute

each. The audience needs to know that you are presenting three equally strong ideas.

Main points should be stated as simply as possible. This will help the audience remember the message of the presentation and help the audience with the organization. Simple main points will also help you if you make callout text bubbles on your speech video for online viewing. Use only as many points as you need. It is highly unlikely that you will need more than a few for any presentation. You should limit your presentation to two to four main points. This general guideline applies in most circumstances.

Thinkstock

Aim to give each main point equal time in your presentation.

<hr>

CONCLUSION

A great conclusion ends your presentation with a bang. It is concise and tightly written. A great conclusion should make your audience reflect on your topic, prompt further discussion, and solidify the relationship you just developed with your audience. A conclusion should compose no more than 10% of your presentation.

The conclusion of a presentation serves two general purposes: It summarizes the main points and drives home the purpose of the speech. In a conclusion, you will (1) restate the thesis and summarize your main points and (2) end with a concluding device. Restating the thesis and summarizing your main points will look very similar to what you did in the introduction. Your concluding device will serve a similar purpose as the attention getter. Do not say "Thank you" at the end of your speech. Your concluding device should be strong enough to do this for you. As such, use the same elements suggested for the introduction (a quote, a question,

<hr>

 COMMUNICATIONHOW-TO

STRUCTURING YOUR INTRODUCTION AND CONCLUSION

Introduction

1. Attention-Getting Device—Gains the audience's attention

2. Introduce Your Topic—General purpose and thesis sentence

3. Demonstrating the Importance—Audience relevance and your credibility

4. Preview of Main Points—List of main points in the body

Body

Conclusion

1. Restate Thesis and Main Points—Restate the purpose and thesis sentence and summary of main points

2. Concluding Device—Signals the end of the presentation; refer back to attention-getting device

humor, etc.) for your concluding device. For instance, if you used a personal story in your introduction, you might use a quotation for the conclusion. Below is the text of the conclusion for the topic of homelessness in a local community.

Conclusion

I. *Restate thesis and main points:* Today, I discussed the problems and causes of homelessness in Kalamazoo County and two ways we can solve this problem together.

II. *Concluding device:* Someone who works with the homeless once said, "People who are homeless are not socially inadequate. They are people without homes."

TRANSITIONS

Within the game of basketball, another game exists: the transition game. After a player scores a basket, the opposing team member does not heave the ball inbounds hoping a player will catch it at the other end. Instead, the player has a specific method for getting the ball from one end of the court to the other. A transition in a presentation is no different. Transitions are sentences or phrases that connect what you were just speaking about with what you will be speaking about next. In other words, transitions link two ideas. You must have a plan for moving from one to the other. Transitions are important for both face-to-face and online presentations. The members of your audience depend on you to link the main ideas of your presentation, or they will not be able to follow. In the Communication Age, there are multiple messages that divide our attention. Perhaps an audience member is checking a text message or thinking about a list of things to do this weekend. Transitions throughout your presentation offer a way to pull the audience back in the message and provide a way for the audience to reconnect and reengage with your message. Several types of transitions exist and should be used to help your audience follow your message. We believe that transitions are critical for your success during your presentation.

Section Transitions

Section transitions indicate the speaker is moving from one main point to another. These types of transitions serve to remind the audience of what was just discussed and what will be coming up next. These transitions are indicated in italics:

> *Now that we understand* the causes of the Beatles' breakup, *let's look at* the effects of this breakup on the music industry.

> *We've discussed three* reasons for the Beatles' breakup. *Now let's examine* the reactions from the fans.

Corbis

Transitions are an important part of basketball because they help the flow of the game. The same is true for your presentations.

This type of transition reinforces what you just said and what you will say. Repetition is an important part of an audience remembering the message.

Nonverbal Transitions

Nonverbal transitions utilize physical movement to indicate to the audience that you are switching points in the presentation. For instance, you might want to walk a few steps when you are transitioning to another point. However, be mindful not to pace because you will look nervous; or if the presentation is being filmed do not go outside of the range of the camera. Although some movement is good, keep in mind that your movements should appear fluid and natural, not choreographed.

Walking a few steps during your presentation is an effective way to highlight a transition from one point to another.

Internal Preview

An internal preview lets the audience know the specific information that you will discuss next. An internal preview is more detailed than a transition, takes place within the body of main points, and usually follows the transition. In keeping with the previous Beatles example, an internal preview would follow a transition:

> Now that we understand the causes of the Beatles' breakup, let's look at the effects of this breakup on the music industry. I will discuss how the breakup affected three organizations within the music industry—radio stations, record retailers, and fan clubs.

Notice how the internal preview here is similar to a preview that would occur in the introduction. The internal preview is a verbal outline of the upcoming main point. In other words, it usually is best to treat each main point like a mini presentation.

Internal Summary

Internal summaries are the opposite of internal previews: They remind the audience members of what they just heard or learned. Internal summaries allow the audience to absorb the information and prepare to move forward. Internal summaries are often used to recap important or complicated information and lead the audience easily to the next point. Think of internal summaries like the summary of main points that occurs in the conclusion.

> *Internal summary:* Let's reflect on what we have learned so far: The Arts Council focuses on supporting, promoting, and funding the arts in our county.

> *Section transition:* Now I'd like to discuss how the Arts Council accomplishes these goals within a given year.

Internal summaries are great ways for your audience to remember crucial parts of your message.

Signposts

Signposts are brief phrases or words that let the audience know exactly where you are in the presentation. Often they are used to indicate order, such as *first, second, third, finally,* or *beginning with.* Signposts can also indicate an explanation: *to clarify, in other words,* or *for example.* Section transitions are elements that hold the main ideas together. Signposts are transitions that hold smaller, supporting material together.

OUTLINES

Most students loathe the idea of writing an outline, but doing so will help reduce speech anxiety by keeping you organized. There are several different ways to create an outline. You will learn about the most basic guidelines of outlining to help you keep your presentation focused, but your instructor will have specific guidelines for your class. It is important that you write a full-sentence outline, a formal outline that uses complete sentences, when you first learn how to outline a presentation. During your presentation, however, you will most likely speak not with a full-sentence outline but rather with a brief keyword outline, an outline that uses words and phrases (Millen, 2001). The full-sentence outline is the best way to organize your presentation and build your argument. After the full-sentence outline is complete, it is easy to write the keyword outline.

Consistent Format

Outlines follow a consistent format. The main points are indicated by a Roman numeral, the subpoints are indicated by a capital letter, and sub-subpoints are indicated by Arabic numerals (1, 2, 3, etc.). Each of these numerations is indented differently. If you have an "A" in your outline, you must have a "B." If you have a "1," you must have a "2."

    I.

       A.

          1.

             a.

             b.

          2.

       B.

    II.

ASSESS YOUR COMMUNICATION

BEING ORGANIZED IN THE BODY OF THE PRESENTATION

Ask yourself the following questions to assess your organization in the body of your presentation:

1. Did you clearly follow an organizational pattern?

2. Did you use section transitions and nonverbal transitions to signal to the audience that you are changing points?

3. Did you use internal previews to let the audience know what you will be discussing next? These are similar to the presentation previews in the introduction but only cover main body points.

4. Did you use internal summaries to remind the audience of what you just covered?

5. Did you give signposts (first, second, to clarify, etc.) as a way help the audience know where you are in the middle of a main point?

Coordination of Points

It is important to pay attention to the coordination of points. Statements or ideas of equal status should be given equal status on the outline. In other words, your points need to be balanced. For example, if you were giving a presentation on various college football conferences, you would want to treat each one at the same level of the outline.

I.   Football Conferences

   A. Big 12

   B. Big 10

   C. Southeastern Conference (SEC)

II. Mid-American Conference (MAC)

III. Western Athletic Conference (WAC)

The above example clearly violates this principle because they are all football conferences. A balanced outline for football conferences would be

I.   Football Conferences

   A. Big 12

   B. Big 10

   C. Southeastern Conference (SEC)

   D. Mid-American Conference (MAC)

   E. Western Athletic Conference (WAC)

This outline works because the points are coordinated. Notice how each subpoint is a football conference under the larger heading of football conferences.

One Idea per Point

Additionally, each point on the outline should only contain one main idea. Take, for example, the following sentence:

I.   Water pollution is a serious problem off the coast of California, kills marine mammals, and causes serious health problems for beachgoers.

This point can easily be fixed to include just one main idea. The first point serves as the main idea for the subpoints.

I.   Water pollution is a serious problem off the coast of California.

   A. Water pollution kills marine mammals.

   B. Water pollution causes serious health problems for beachgoers.

Including only one idea per point helps maintain the focus on the section and clarity in the argument.

PLAGIARISM

Imagine if a student had turned in the outline and reference page for a speech but failed to include in-text citations in the body of the outline. Would this be considered plagiarism? Does it matter? An in-text citation provides a brief mention of the source material next to the information used in the outline. In other words, in-text citations are the ways in which we note in the outline where we are getting specific information. Just listing the sources on the reference page is not enough. Every year students get accused of plagiarism by not remembering this important part of source citation.

   As you write your outline, be sure to use in-text citations to give credit to the authors of your information to avoid this kind of plagiarism. Even if you accidently leave off the in-text citations in your outline, you still can be charged with

plagiarism. Citing your evidence makes you more credible and demonstrates that you understand the importance of giving credit to another person for their words or ideas. Including in-text citations on your keyword outline will also help you remember to orally cite your sources. Sources need to be cited both orally and in written form.

QUESTIONS

1. Why is it plagiarism if you fail to include in-text citations?

2. What are some ways you could reduce the chance of this happening to you?

In-Text Citations

Also, facts and statistics provided in your presentation should be cited in your outline so that you can show where you found your information. In-text citations provide a brief mention of the source material by indicating the author's last name and the year the information was produced or documented. They are placed here for example only. Your sub-subpoints and in-text citations will likely appear in different places.

I. First main point as stated in thesis

    A. Subpoint for the first main point (last name, year)

        1. Sub-subpoint for A

        2. Sub-subpoint for A

    B. Subpoint for the first main point

        1. Sub-subpoint for B (last name, year)

        2. Sub-subpoint for B

The preceding guidelines will help you as you craft your full-sentence outline. The keyword outline follows the same format but is far less formal and is often used for speaking notes. On this keyword outline, you will want to make notations about when to show your presentational slides, precise wording on technical parts, or even notes to yourself like "SMILE," "SLOW DOWN," or "BE SURE TO LOOK AT YOUR AUDIENCE." Outlining takes time to learn but is an important skill you will use in your college classes. It is a good way to organize your thoughts whether for a presentation in a communication class, an essay for your English course, or a business sales pitch. In Chapters 15

COMMUNICATIONHOW-TO
BASIC OUTLINING RULES

1. Main points should utilize parallel wording. In other words, each main point should be worded in a similar way.

2. Each main point should contain one idea.

3. If you have an "A," you must have a "B." If you have a "1," you must have a "2." Of course, you can have a "C"

or a "3"; this rule only applies to the first two letters or numbers of any sequence.

4. Points need to coordinate. Ideas of equal importance need to be given parallel status.

("Informative Presentations") and 16 ("Persuasive Presentations"), you will find sample full-sentence and keyword outlines.

TIME CONSIDERATIONS

In your classes, your instructors will tell you how long your presentation needs to be. Your boss might tell you to prepare a 10-minute presentation about a recent product line. The community organization might ask you to spend 15 to 20 minutes discussing the community garden proposal. Plan accordingly for the time limit that you are given. What do you do if suddenly the time allocated for your presentation changes? After you have a silent meltdown, you need to think quickly about what to cut or add to your presentation. You might think that being told a shorter time limit is easy to fix. Simply start cutting from the presentation, right? Wrong. In many ways, this is a harder problem than having more time than you thought. What do you cut? On what can you spend less time? The key here is still to present the same basic message, but in an abbreviated way. Maybe you can leave out some examples or questions. Or you might be able to cut one of the main points (assuming the main points were balanced to begin with). Yes, this could weaken your argument, but you have to be in time for the presentation.

What do you do if you have more time than you anticipated? First, simply slow down a bit. Most presenters often go too fast to begin with. In the case of a business meeting or a proposal to a community organization, you could give more time to a question-and-answer session. Possibly, there was some information you wanted to include but left out due to time constraints. You could simply try to add it back to the presentation. Or you could add more examples to drive a particular point home with the audience. Whatever the case, it is vitally important that you not panic but carefully consider the organization of the message. These tips will also help if you find your presentation is too short or too long while you are preparing for the time limits given to you.

ORGANIZING YOUR PRESENTATION AND CONVERGENCE

Thinkstock

Being organized in the Communication Age is important because our messages can be transmitted and viewed in a variety of ways. Think back to the beginning of this chapter and the movement to change a Facebook status emotion. This movement required its leaders to organize petitions, do research, find information, and make social media efforts in their push to make the best possible case for change. Your speeches should do the same. Often, we do not get the opportunity to make corrections or answer questions to clarify the message of a presentation. An organized message will address potential concerns that an audience might have.

We often hear that political figures need to "stay on message." This is good advice for every presenter. There are so many things that can distract a potential audience today. In order to connect and engage with our audience, we need to "stay on message" in an organized fashion and use transitions; that way we can better compete with all the other information that can sway their attention. Being organized will help our presentations have both narrative fidelity and coherence. Have you ever noticed how when a speaker is really organized and engaged with the audience, audience members do not check their phones for text messages? The audience is truly listening to the speaker. While it is the responsibility of the audience to shut out distractions and listen to the speaker, it is far easier to do so if the speaker is organized. Being organized in your presentation will give you a better chance to get out your message in both face-to-face and mediated presentations. Think about how you can stay organized with your message with even more potential distractions that exist in the Communication Age.

WHAT YOU'VE LEARNED   Now that you have studied this chapter, you should be able to:

(1) Explain how stories are judged.

Storytelling is an important part of being human. We use stories to pass on information, share our lives, and potentially help others with communication activism.

▶ Storytelling Theory and Practice

🖱 King's Mountaintop Speech

🖥 The Strategic Rhetoric of a President

(2) Describe different types of organizational patterns and why they are used.

Choosing an organizational pattern should be based on the needs of the topic for your presentation. Think about the best type of pattern for your topic. Be sure you can answer "Why this pattern?" when thinking about your topic.

▶ Organizing a Speech

🖥 Patterns of Organization

(3) Create the various parts of the presentation (introduction, body, conclusion, and transitions).

Knowing the various parts of a presentation will help you craft a better message. Starting and

ending your presentation strong will help the audience remember your speech. Transitions will help keep your audience (and you) organized.

▶ Michigan Commencement Address

(4) Demonstrate the basics of outlining.

Outlining your presentation is essential for your success. Do not skip this important step. Outlining will help you build your best argument and present it in a way that is appealing for your audience.

▶ A Public Speaking Outline Example

▶ How to Write a Speech Outline

(5) Analyze how time considerations influence your presentations.

Knowing your time considerations for your presentation will help you with organization. The presentation should be within the assigned time limits.

▶ Timing a Presentation

KEY TERMS

Review key terms with eFlashcards. **edge.sagepub.com/edwards2e**

REFLECT

1. Think of the best story you have ever heard a person tell. What were the qualities of the story that made it the "best" story? How can you use some of these qualities in your presentations?

2. Which organizational pattern do you think is the hardest to do well? Why?

3. Transitions are an important part of a presentation. Is there a danger in making the transitions too obvious? Can you go overboard?

REVIEW

To check your answers go to **edge.sagepub.com/edwards2e**

1. List the four parts of the introduction.

2. Narrative _____ is the way a story hangs together, while narrative _____ is the way a story matches lived experiences.

3. When you want a pattern for a presentation that will show an audience the steps of how to do something, a ____ pattern is most useful.

4. Why is the spatial organizational pattern used in presentations?

5. This step, _____, serves as the conclusion in Monroe's Motivated Sequence.

6. A question you can use as an attention-getting device that does not invite a response is a(n) ____ question.

7. What are in-text citations, and why are they important?

8. A _____ transition refers to physical movements used to indicate you are switching points in a presentation.

9. A _____ is a brief phrase or word that lets the audience know exactly where you are in the presentation.

SPEECH PLANNER

SpeechPlanner is an interactive, web-based tool that guides you through the process of planning and preparing your speech, one step at a time.

14 DELIVERING YOUR PRESENTATIONS

Getty

WHAT YOU'LL LEARN   After studying this chapter, you will be able to:

1 Explain how to reduce communication anxiety.

2 Describe various ways to present in the Communication Age.

3 Demonstrate effective delivery skills.

4 Identify different types of presentational aids to enhance the message.

5 Explain ways to present using a variety of multimedia presentational aids.

Founded in 1984, TED (Technology, Entertainment, Design) invites speakers from across the world to "give the talk of their lives (in 18 minutes or less)" (TED, n.d.). TED produces videos of the speakers and then puts them online for free viewing in hopes that a larger audience will watch (Heffernan, 2009). As of 2012, the TED website had 1 billion video views (Ted, 2012). Because of the convergence of media, technology, and communication in the Communication Age, TED talks are available for free on YouTube, as well as via iPhone, iPad, and Android apps, and have been translated into over 50 languages. Speakers such as Bill Clinton, Jane Goodall, Richard Dawkins, Isaac Mizrahi, Helen Fisher, and a variety of Nobel Prize winners have all spoken at one of the annual TED conferences. Local TED talks with local speakers happen all across the world.

TED provides speakers with a series of guidelines for giving a good presentation, called the TED 10 Commandments. There are a few commandments that are specific to delivery aspects of the presentation. The commandments "Thou Shalt Not Simply Trot Out Thy Usual Shtick," "Thou Shalt Reveal Thy Curiosity and Thy Passion," and "Thou Shalt Not Read Thy Speech" all represent key components of good delivery during a presentation. By showing your passion and engaging with the audience in creative and innovative ways, you will enhance your message through your delivery.

Speaking at a TED conference is high pressure, to say the least. Successful speakers at TED are able to connect and engage with the audience. Your own audience should be able to see your passion and excitement for the topic. As a result, your audience will be better able to remember the message and act on it. In this chapter, you will

Thinkstock

The first moments of your speech can create feelings of nervousness that often dissipate as the speech progresses.

learn about good delivery during a presentation. You will also learn about using multimedia aids to help reinforce your message and inspire your audience to take action. In short, you need to learn to own the stage, whether it is in face-to-face or mediated settings.

In the Communication Age, delivering your presentations in an effective manner is quite important for connecting and engaging with your audiences. In the previous chapters, you learned about creating, researching, and organizing a presentation. In this chapter, you will learn how to deliver the message so that your audience can be involved in and moved by your presentation. In the past, as speakers, we needed to be competent in delivering a speech to a live audience, in building strong organized arguments, in using presentational aids wisely, and in being able to relate with the audience. All of this is still true. However, technology requires that we be able to anticipate the needs of more diverse audiences that are located in many different times and spaces. For example, maybe you are invited to give a presentation about "being green" to a local community organization. The organization might wish to film the speech in order to upload the video to its YouTube channel or Facebook page. Suddenly, audiences around the world can view a speech that was presented previously to a live audience. The delivery aspects in the Communication Age are more complex than delivering the "standard" speech to a live audience. This chapter discusses the basics of good and effective delivery and ways to adapt to this new horizon of shifting times and spaces.

HOW TO REDUCE YOUR ANXIETY AND FEAR OVER PRESENTATIONS

For many people, just the thought of delivering a presentation can make them nervous or even sick! But even professional speakers can get nervous about a presentation. In fact, most people experience anxiety before presenting a speech in front of an audience. But being nervous about a speech is quite normal, and the adrenaline rush you experience can actually improve your delivery! These feelings often go away after you begin the speech. The anticipation of giving the presentation creates the most anxiety. This fearfulness, anxiety, and nervousness are collectively termed *communication apprehension*.

What Is Communication Apprehension?

Communication apprehension (CA) is defined as "an individual's level of fear or anxiety associated with either real or anticipated communication with another person or persons" (McCroskey, 1984, p. 13) and is a subset of performance anxiety. There are two key components of this definition: real and anticipated fear or anxiety. The first type is the real CA we can experience when presenting information. This is fear or anxiety that occurs while we are delivering the speech! Most of the time this fear or anxiety will quickly decrease once we get started and have been speaking for a minute or two. The second type of fear or anxiety we can experience is from just thinking about communicating with others. For example, if you are asking a potential partner to marry you, you might experience nervousness about asking. CA varies among individuals and by context. Everybody has different levels of fear and anxiety at different times and in different situations. You might not experience a high level of apprehension when talking with friends but might have higher levels when speaking with your professors or with a potential employer.

Everyone experiences communication apprehension at some point.

There are two types of CA: state and trait. State CA is based on the particular context for the speaking occasion, while trait CA is the CA we possess on a daily basis across many different contexts. You might be nervous about speaking in front of your peers in a classroom. This would be state CA. Something about the particular context makes you feel apprehension. Or you might always be nervous about speaking in public. This would be trait CA. Whatever the case, there are ways to lessen the impact of CA on you as the speaker.

Why do we feel nervous or apprehensive about speaking in public? For most of us, the perceived and potential evaluation of our speaking performance is the root cause for apprehension. It is a bit scary to think that someone is watching our presentation and evaluating us. Research has shown that our levels of CA increase when we are being formally evaluated (Edwards, Edwards, Myers, & Wahl, 2003). Levels of CA increase with the potential power difference between the speaker and the audience. For example, imagine speaking to a room full of your supervisors at work. This audience has real power over you and your job. The power difference between you and the audience could cause increased levels of CA. While this is certainly a valid concern, it is important to remember that audiences usually want the speaker to succeed.

We know that everyone experiences CA at one point or another, but what happens to us when we experience CA? The symptoms of CA include shaky knees, increased sweating, trembling voice, dry mouth, shortness of breath, loss of concentration, and death (OK, just joking about the last one). Notice how these symptoms are quite similar to the symptoms you experience when you are excited. What is the difference? It really boils down to the thoughts and interpretations of the symptoms that you experience. When you have these symptoms and are excited, you think about positive feelings and emotions. When you have these symptoms and are nervous, you often will think about negative feelings and emotions. The trick is for you to take these negative feelings and emotions and convert them to feelings of excitement.

At its heart, CA is about relationships. Have you noticed that you do not seem as nervous when speaking in front of someone with whom you have a good relationship? Even if it is a difficult topic that you are discussing, the CA is reduced because of this relationship. More often than not, audience members do not even notice your nervousness. Most of the time, the listeners are focusing on your message because it is the most important part of the presentation. With an audience of strangers, it is important to try to connect with them to help build a relationship to reduce your CA. Presentations are a chance for you to make a difference with the audience, and that is why thinking positively is so important. If you are excited about your message, your audience will be too.

If you want to find out how you score in terms of your own CA, take the Personal Report of Public Speaking Anxiety (PRPSA). This widely used survey will help you assess your own levels of CA in a public speaking situation. If you score higher than 98 points, you will want to talk with your instructor about ways to decrease your communicative apprehensiveness.

ASSESS YOUR COMMUNICATION

PERSONAL REPORT OF PUBLIC SPEAKING ANXIETY (PRPSA)

Directions: Below are 34 statements that people sometimes make about themselves. Please indicate whether or not you believe each statement applies to you by marking whether you:

Strongly Disagree = 1; Disagree = 2; Neutral = 3; Agree = 4; Strongly Agree = 5

_____ 1. While preparing for giving a speech, I feel tense and nervous.

_____ 2. I feel tense when I see the words *speech* and *public speech* on a course outline when studying.

_____ 3. My thoughts become confused and jumbled when I am giving a speech.

_____ 4. Right after giving a speech I feel that I have had a pleasant experience.

_____ 5. I get anxious when I think about a speech coming up.

_____ 6. I have no fear of giving a speech.

_____ 7. Although I am nervous just before starting a speech, I soon settle down after starting and feel calm and comfortable.

_____ 8. I look forward to giving a speech.

_____ 9. When the instructor announces a speaking assignment in class, I can feel myself getting tense.

_____10. My hands tremble when I am giving a speech.

_____11. I feel relaxed while giving a speech.

_____12. I enjoy preparing for a speech.

_____13. I am in constant fear of forgetting what I prepared to say.

_____14. I get anxious if someone asks me something about my topic that I don't know.

_____15. I face the prospect of giving a speech with confidence.

_____16. I feel that I am in complete possession of myself while giving a speech.

_____17. My mind is clear when giving a speech.

_____18. I do not dread giving a speech.

_____19. I perspire just before starting a speech.

_____20. My heart beats very fast just as I start a speech.

_____21. I experience considerable anxiety while sitting in the room just before my speech starts.

_____22. Certain parts of my body feel very tense and rigid while giving a speech.

_____23. Realizing that only a little time remains in a speech makes me very tense and anxious.

_____24. While giving a speech, I know I can control my feelings of tension and stress.

_____25. I breathe faster just before starting a speech.

_____26. I feel comfortable and relaxed in the hour or so just before giving a speech.

_____27. I do worse on speeches because I am anxious.

_____28. I feel anxious when the teacher announces the date of a speaking assignment.

_____29. When I make a mistake while giving a speech, I find it hard to concentrate on the parts that follow.

_____30. During an important speech I experience a feeling of helplessness building up inside me.

_____31. I have trouble falling asleep the night before a speech.

_____32. My heart beats very fast while I present a speech.

_____33. I feel anxious while waiting to give my speech.

_____34. While giving a speech, I get so nervous I forget facts I really know.

Scoring: To determine your score on the PRPSA, complete the following steps:

Step 1. Add scores for items 1, 2, 3, 5, 9, 10, 13, 14, 19, 20, 21, 22, 23, 25, 27, 28, 29, 30, 31, 32, 33, and 34

Step 2. Add the scores for items 4, 6, 7, 8, 11, 12, 15, 16, 17, 18, 24, and 26

Step 3. Complete the following formula:

PRPSA = 72 - Total from Step 2 + Total from Step 1

Your score should be between 34 and 170. If your score is below 34 or above 170, you have made a mistake in computing the score.

High = > 131
Low = < 98
Moderate = 98–131

Source: "From Measures of Communication-Bound Anxiety," by J. C. McCroskey, 1970, in *Speech Monographs, 37*, pp. 269–277.

Solutions to Reduce CA

Remember that everyone experiences some level of CA. Some nervousness is good, and it will help you in the speech. However, sometimes this anxiety is strong enough that you will want to reduce it before you speak. You will want to reduce your CA to make yourself feel better, which will put the audience at ease and increase your success with your message. Are there things you should think about or do? Practicing your speech and visualizing the audience are two important ways to reduce your CA.

The best way to reduce your CA is to practice your speech (Ayres, 1996). Practicing your presentation will help reduce uncertainty about the situation, thereby decreasing your CA. You should practice your presentation for anyone who will listen to you: family members, friends, classmates, or even strangers. Try to spread out your practice sessions over time. You want to become comfortable and relaxed with your speech. Cramming the night before will only make you more nervous about your presentation. Also, practice your speech in the room (or a similar room) in which you will give your speech. Do not try to memorize the entire text of the speech, but know the outline of the speech by heart. You will want to repeat some of the important sentences (thesis, preview, transitions, etc.) the same way in each practice session, but it is OK if the speech is slightly different each time you practice. This is good, because you will sound more conversational, spontaneous, and enthusiastic. In short, the more you can give presentations, the better you become. By practicing in front of others, you will become aware of the effects of CA without suffering too much from the symptoms. This is often referred to as systematic desensitization.

Another strategy to reduce your CA is to imagine the interaction (Honeycutt, Choi, & DeBerry, 2009). When you are practicing your speech, you want to visualize a successful presentation (Ayres, 2005). Visualize that you did a good job, the media/presentational slides worked without a hitch, the audience left understanding the topic, and your teacher was impressed with your efforts. When we think positively about a speaking situation, we often create positive consequences. This is true in almost all areas of life! Pro snowboarders know this all too well. It is hard to pull off a 720 twist with a tail grab if you do not believe that you can do it! The same is true for public speaking. Consider the words by hip-hop legend KRS-ONE: "If you state it and believe it, you create it." If you think you will do well in a presentation, you probably will. Act confidently (because you have researched and practiced, and you know your outline), and you will have a much better chance to do well. Never start any presentation by apologizing about the quality of a speech the audience has not yet heard! Start confidently, and you will end this way.

With an audience of strangers, it is important to try to connect with them to help

What would happen if the snowboarder did not believe she could perform this move? How is this like giving a presentation?

build a relationship to reduce your CA. The audience is your partner in the creation of your message, so focus on the positive aspect of this relationship to help you achieve the goals of your message. After all, without the audience, you would be speaking to an empty room. Remember that the members of your audience actually want you to succeed because it makes their listening experience more enjoyable. If you see smiling and supportive faces, gravitate toward them. Just make sure you don't focus only on one person, and if you are an extremely self-conscious person, remember that most signs of nervousness are not really visible to your audience.

Finally, we strongly recommend that you practice deep and slow breathing exercises and healthy behaviors to help reduce your CA. Before each practice session, take a few minutes to breathe deeply and slowly to help calm your body and mind. Do this right before your presentation as well. Additionally, there are many webpages and smartphone apps that will lead you in guided meditations to help calm you down and focus your mind. Avoid using energy drinks and caffeine when you deliver your presentation, eat healthy foods, and try to sleep well the night before the big speech. Staying up all night on Red Bull and pizza while trying to develop your speech will not serve you well. The mind–body connection is extremely important to help reduce CA.

Decreasing your CA is important for you to deliver an effective presentation. However, don't focus exclusively on reducing CA. Instead, use the tips to lessen your CA; more important, know your message. At the end the day, the audience will care more about the

COMMUNICATION HOW-TO

REDUCE YOUR CA

1. Practice, practice, and practice.

2. Think and speak positively about your presentation.

3. Know your stuff. You are the expert.

4. Your audience wants you to succeed. Try and see the members of your audience as friends who care about you and your success.

5. Avoid the use of stimulants (e.g., caffeine), get a full night's sleep, and eat healthy meals the day before and of your presentation.

6. Practice slow and deep breathing exercises.

Images: thinkstock and istock.

message than a few verbal flubs or sweaty hands. With practice, your CA will decrease, and you will feel more comfortable in front of a wide range of audiences.

METHODS OF DELIVERY

Presentations often call for a variety of delivery methods. Suppose you are giving a speech that you know will be video recorded and uploaded to YouTube. Would you make different choices if the speech were only going to be audio recorded or not recorded at all? What do your live audience and potential future viewers expect from the presentation? The following section answers these questions and explains methods of delivery and questions to consider as you choose your approach.

Manuscript Presentations

Manuscript presentations are speeches that are read from a script word for word. These types of presentations are often used in formal settings when exact wording and precision are important. These types of presentations are often historically archived, so there is the expectation that the message will be forceful when read as text (much like a good piece of literature) and delivered orally. Also, these types of presentations are often written using a team of writers, not just the person delivering the speech. When delivering the State of the Union address, the president uses a manuscript aided by teleprompters (clear screens that show the text of the speech for the speaker but still allow for the speaker to look at the audience). This speech is written by many people in the White House and is archived as a historical document. In fact, the most praised speeches in U.S. history have been manuscript presentations. Abraham Lincoln's Gettysburg Address, Martin Luther King's "I Have a Dream" speech, and Ronald Reagan's speech on the *Challenger* disaster were all presented using manuscripts. At their best, manuscript presentations can sound conversational, intimate, and unrehearsed.

Actor Billy Crystal is struggling to read the teleprompter during an awards show. Does the use of a teleprompter take away from the message? What do you think?

However, manuscript presentations have some significant disadvantages for the beginning speaker. Manuscript presentations can sound like they are being read from a boring textbook and lose all conversational tone. Since you probably won't have a teleprompter, you will have to read from your script, causing you to lose eye contact with the audience. If you do not have a podium, you will have to hold the manuscript, which will keep you from making hand gestures. For most of us, a manuscript delivery method presents too many disadvantages and should be avoided. However, with a well-written speech, practice, and the use of technology (e.g., teleprompters), this type of delivery can be powerful and leave an impression with both live and future audiences.

Memorized Presentations

A memorized presentation is a speech given from memory without the use of notes. Speakers often use this method when giving the same speech several times. For example, politicians often give the same "stump speech" on the campaign trail several times a day in different locations. Although this method may work for politicians, the disadvantages are many. First, what happens if you forget your speech? Without the use of notes, forgetting parts of the speech becomes a serious issue. Also, when we memorize presentations we tend to lose spontaneity and the ability to connect to our audience. Connecting with the audience is about a particular time and place. Have you ever seen a rock band, a politician, or some other speaker refer to the audience by another city's name, or refer to the wrong local sports team? With a memorized presentation, speakers will often forget to actually connect with the audience and make these types of mistakes. Only the most skilled speakers can memorize a speech and still be able to "go on and off the script" successfully. Most speakers tend to overrehearse and can sound as if the speech is being read even though it is memorized.

Impromptu Presentations

An impromptu presentation is a speech in which the speaker has little or no preparation time. These presentations often occur during meetings and discussions when the speaker is asked to share information about a particular subject. Imagine you are at a meeting with members of the local community group. Your group leader asks you to speak about your progress raising funds to build a playground in an underprivileged part of town. In this situation, you would need to think on your feet, quickly formulate a simple mental outline of what to tell the group, and keep your comments brief. You should always anticipate giving an impromptu presentation when at work or school. You could be called on any time to give your opinion, deliver new information, or make a suggestion.

Be sure to have a strategy to help you quickly formulate your impromptu speech. In many ways, this type of presentation is exactly like all other types in terms of organization and format. For an impromptu presentation, it is important to get the audience's attention, give a thesis and preview of the main points, discuss the content of the main points, and then summarize the main points. You will most likely want to limit the body of the speech to only two main points. Dianna Booher, a communication consultant, recommends that the first main point be an explanation of the idea and that the second main point be an example or evidence to illustrate the idea in question. The key for any successful impromptu presentation is to be organized within the speech.

You may be asked to give an impromptu presentation during a meeting at work.

Extemporaneous Presentations

An extemporaneous presentation is a speech in which the speaker carefully prepares notes and an outline, and has thoroughly practiced. This method of delivery is considered the most effective in terms of delivery and content and is most often used in speaking situations. You will most likely be giving extemporaneous presentations in your classes. Extemporaneous presentations have many advantages over manuscript or memorized speeches. First, these types of presentations tend to sound more natural, conversational, and spontaneous. Second, because the speaker is only speaking from notes or a keyword outline, this method of delivery permits greater eye contact than do other methods. The speaker can refer to notes and can change the speech to adapt to audience feedback. With careful practice, this type of presentation can be extremely effective in all types of speaking situations.

Mediated Presentations

Mediated presentations are speeches that use either manuscript, memorized, impromptu, or extemporaneous delivery but are *viewed* using some technological component. You may have seen a YouTube clip of an athlete giving an interview on ESPN or a community leader presenting facts about a local water pollution issue. These types of presentations use a vast array of technology that allows a wide range of audiences to view them in different places and times. If you or someone else plans to videotape, podcast, or screencast your presentation, consider how the mixed media could be used. Will you be using computer-generated presentational slides? If so, consider a screencast version of the speech in which the viewer views the slides and simultaneously hears your voice. A screencast presentation occurs when the actions on a computer screen are recorded and shown in some format. For these types of presentations, you might screencast your presentational slides and narrate with your own voice. Screencast presentations can be effective for many types of topics and can easily be uploaded to websites or YouTube. There are several free programs online that will allow you to create and develop screencast presentations.

Will some of your audience members be in the same room while others view your presentation through videoconferencing technologies? If so, consider the difference in the audiences. You will want to pay attention to your remote viewing audience so that these viewers do not feel left out of the presentation, while connecting with the audience in front of you. Mediated presentations, such as these, are becoming common in the world of work. "Communication How-To: Mediated Presentations" provides a simple checklist if an audience other than the live viewers will see your presentation.

Group Presentations

Group presentations consist of one speech with several people doing various parts. These can be tricky because there are so many parts that can go wrong. At the same time, group presentations can be effective at informing or persuading. Often, group presentations will be longer in time than the normal speech. Because new speakers are delivering different parts, it is harder, but not impossible, for the audience to lose focus. Introductions and transitions are key for group presentations. The group needs to understand how each person will be introduced to the audience. Will there be one person who takes responsibility for the introductions and acts as the moderator? Or will each person handle his or her introductions? Relatedly, transitions between speakers are an important consideration. How will the transition occur? The group needs to practice these important parts together to ensure that the group presentation runs smoothly and is effective.

EFFECTIVE DELIVERY SKILLS

In the Communication Age, delivery skills become increasingly important. This is because we must consider the needs of our current audience and those of future audiences. Knowing that our presentations may have a digital afterlife, we must be mindful that both verbal and nonverbal characteristics will affect the quality and effectiveness of our presentations. Effective delivery helps us establish ethos, pathos, and logos and allows us to connect and engage with our audiences.

COMMUNICATIONHOW-TO
GROUP PRESENTATIONS

1. Practice introductions and transitions as a group. Be specific on how these will occur.

2. Each speaker should speak roughly the same amount of time.

3. Even when a person is not speaking, they need to remember that they can be seen by the audience and should remain focused. Audiences will still judge the people not speaking.

4. Prepare for a Q&A session. Know who will answer questions and how these will be divided among group members.

5. Presentational aids need to be consistent for all speakers. It should be viewed as one speech and not a series of speeches.

6. Each speaker needs to have a clear understanding of the presentation's goals. Everything said should be held accountable to those goals.

Effective delivery also demonstrates to an audience that you are excited about your message and topic and the audience should be as well. It can be contagious. Becoming effective at delivery skills takes time, but each time you speak you will build your confidence.

Paralinguistic Skills

The way we use our voice impacts how audiences respond to presentations. Speaking conversationally helps your audience feel comfortable, while a distracting vocal style may divert the audience from your message. Vocal characteristics are powerful. They can convey to our audience that we are sincere and care about our topic. Some of our vocal characteristics are ones that we cannot control. For example, James Earl Jones (the voice of Darth Vader in *Star Wars*) has a distinctive, deep voice. He was simply born with an amazing tone of voice. However, we can learn to better control many vocal characteristics to make a larger impact. The following section discusses components of vocal characteristics you need to be aware of when making a presentation.

Volume

Volume is the level and variety of loudness in our voice. We should speak loud enough for the audience to hear without yelling. The key is proper voice projection. Varying the volume of our voices during a presentation helps highlight key message points and emphasize other important information. If you will use a lapel microphone, test out the system before your presentation. Determine the best distance of the microphone to your mouth. Most microphones are very sensitive and can pick up sounds from a distance. Learn how to turn the microphone on and off. Your authors know a professor friend who wore a working microphone to the restroom.

COMMUNICATIONHOW-TO
MEDIATED PRESENTATIONS

1. Think about the ways your presentation might be distributed (webcast, videocast, screencast, podcast). How might you best present your information to a future audience?

2. Create supporting documents that can be downloaded to enhance your presentation. These documents should not "be" your presentation in written form, but should provide additional material an interested viewer might use to dig a little deeper into the subject matter.

3. Do not "date" your presentation. Avoid the use of extremely current news, movies, music, or cultural references. Instead, use classic examples that most audiences will understand and appreciate.

4. If the presentation is being recorded for future viewers, find out if the presentation can be edited. Who will do the editing? Will you have a say in how the editing is done?

5. If your presentation will take place in a location that uses videoconferencing technologies, make sure you are looking at the people for the "live" audience and the camera for the virtual audience.

6. If you are developing a screencast presentation, make sure that your audio is clear and loud enough for the audience. Use a plug-in microphone to record the best sound.

Actor James Earl Jones (the voice of Darth Vader) is known for his use of vocalics to make an impact with his voice. In your own presentations, use the right volume and pitch to be an effective speaker. Use the force.

The classroom of students was able to hear everything! Practice your speech while wearing the microphone so you can determine the volume of your voice. This way, you can learn about what volume will work for you.

Pitch

Pitch refers to the amount of vocal inflections in your voice, or the highness or lowness in your voice. A constant pitch is called *monotone*. Think of Ben Stein during roll call in the classic film *Ferris Bueller's Day Off*. Who could forget the constant drone of his voice repeating the name *Bueller* over and over and over? A monotone voice is boring. You should vary the pitch of your voice to show meaning and create interest. For example, to create a somber mood, you could lower your pitch. Public service announcements will often portray speakers who lower their pitch to reflect the seriousness of the issue. It would be hard to raise money for animal shelters if the speaker used a higher pitch that sounded happy and excited.

Rate

Rate is the speed of your speech. How fast do you speak? The average rate of speech is around 125 to 150 words per minute (Fulford & Zhang, 1993). We use the rate of our speech to vary the emotional appeal of our message. In your presentations, change the rate of speech so that the audience does not become bored and to emphasize certain parts of your message. It is essential that you do not speak either too fast or too slow. A speaker speaking too fast will seem anxious or nervous, while a speaker speaking too slowly can seem uniformed. If this is one of the first times you have given a speech, you will most likely speak too fast. The best advice is simply to remind yourself to slow down. Sometimes, speakers will write a reminder in big letters on their speaking notes: SLOW DOWN. Eventually, you will become comfortable with your speaking rate and will be able to vary it according to the needs of the message.

Fluency

Fluency refers to the smoothness of your voice. Typically, we only notice speakers who are not fluid in their delivery. Vocal fillers are unnecessary words or phrases that create pauses and disrupt the flow in our speech. How many of you say "um," "like," and "you know"? It is important that we become aware of our use of vocal fillers. If you use too many vocal fillers, the audience will start counting them for fun. Britney Spears is famous for using over 70 vocal fillers in a 5-minute interview. Even skilled speakers need to be on guard against breaks in fluency. Vocal fillers are like weeds in our speaking yard; once they take hold, it is hard to reduce them. You can combat vocal fillers by having friends watch your speech and clap their hands every time you say one. Recognition is the best defense. But it's also important to recognize why we tend to use vocal fillers. Generally, speakers insert "ums," "uhs," "likes," and "you knows" to fill a pause or gap between words or thoughts. Silence can be uncomfortable for speakers, so we seek to reduce it. However, small pauses or silences are not uncomfortable for audiences. In fact, they may even draw attention, provide space for involvement, or encourage reflection.

Nonverbal Behaviors

The Communication Age enables you to reach larger and more diverse audiences in ways unimaginable a few years ago. How do nonverbal communication characteristics such as attire, movement, gestures, or eye contact impact a presentation viewed digitally? Nonverbal behaviors are an important consideration when delivering a presentation. The way we use our bodies helps us deliver an effective presentation. Some nonverbal behaviors can benefit your presentation, while others can distract the audience from your message. The following section will discuss four main categories of nonverbal characteristics. As you learn more about effective delivery in the Communication Age, consider how you present yourself online and face to face.

Gestures

Gestures are hand movements used to emphasize and reinforce your message (see Chapter 4). Gestures should appear natural and not forced. Some presenters try to script their hand gestures at certain points during their speech, but this is not a good idea. Besides being awkward and running the risk of making you look like a robot, scripting your gestures will take your attention away from your message. Gestures need to be spontaneous and natural. If you are worried about making gestures that draw unnecessary attention, have a friend watch you rehearse your speech and point out every time you do this.

Eye Contact

Eye contact involves looking at people in your audience. Establishing eye contact with your audience (both live and virtual) is essential. When speaking to a live audience, hold your gaze with individuals for 1 or 2 seconds and look at the entire audience. If you glance too quickly at audience members, they will think you are looking past them, but looking too long at one person can become intensely awkward. With a virtual audience, eye contact is a bit trickier. If the message is mainly for the virtual audience, you will want to look directly at the camera. If the message is for a mixed audience (both live and virtual), look at both the entire live audience and the camera. Speakers who make eye contact are often rated as being more credible and truthful because it is a way of acknowledging that "I" (the speaker) see "you" (the audience), this message is for you, and we are connected and engaged.

Spontaneous gestures can reinforce your message.

Thinkstock

Movement

Movement refers to how you use your body during a presentation. Movement can contribute to your confidence. How many times have you seen other speakers carry themselves with no confidence? Posture and poise are two important aspects of movement. Be aware of how you carry yourself from the moment you get up to deliver your presentation until you sit down. Try to have a relaxed but upright posture. Sometimes, it makes sense to move a little during your transitions, as movement can help to reinforce the verbal transition from one point to another. However, avoid purposeless movements like rocking, shifting weight, playing with a paper clip, or smoothing your clothes. If your presentation is going to be filmed, you should probably stay still in order to achieve a better video recording. It is best to discuss this with the person operating the camera.

Attire

Attire refers to how we dress in a speaking situation. In a professional situation, it is crucial to "look the part." Audiences often view a speaker dressed in professional attire as more credible. Attire should not cause you to stand out during the presentation unless that is the intended goal. It is usually better to dress just a bit more conservatively than your audience might dress. If your speech is going to be filmed, it is important that you wear solid neutral colors so that the camera does not distort any stripes or patterns. Also consider the timelessness of your clothing in a digital life. In other words, try to not date yourself too much. Take a look at the picture to the left. Is this student dressed appropriately for the presentation? Would it matter if the audience were made up of business executives or if the audience were made up of college students?

iStock

In what types of presentations would the student's attire be appropriate?

MULTIMEDIA PRESENTATIONAL AIDS

Consider the images of people helping others after a major earthquake or the sights and sounds of people protesting around the world. We have all seen forms of media that cause us to stop and think. Multimedia presentational aids have tremendous impact on audiences. Technology has now advanced to a point at which presentational aids encompass more than simple visual images or the standard computer-generated slide show. However, always have a backup plan in case the technology does not work. In the Communication Age, multimedia aids are almost limitless. The following sections discuss reasons to use multimedia presentational aids in your speeches, various types of aids, and the ways they can improve your presentation.

Why Use Multimedia Presentational Aids?

Multimedia presentational aids are objects that reinforce your message, elicit emotion, or add new information using a variety of senses. Remember that the emphasis needs to be put on *aids*. The content of the message is still the most important aspect of an effective presentation. Your audience is there to hear you and your ideas, so don't rely on the multimedia to deliver your message.

However, multimedia presentational aids can greatly enhance the delivery aspects of your speech for a variety of reasons. Multimedia presentational aids can highlight technical and complex parts of your message. Suppose you are giving a speech on quantum physics. An image, a graphic, or a video of a particular quantum theory might greatly enhance the audience's ability to understand this complex concept where a verbal description is not enough. When used in this way, multimedia presentations can be quite successful in terms of learning (Gabriel, 2008). Studies show that presentational aids can also increase the audience's retention of the information (Tversky, 1997) and that they might help audience members who have various learning styles (Kolb, 1984; Münzer, Seufert, & Brünken, 2009; Schultz & Schultz, 2004). When done well, presentational aids add to the speaker's credibility, and audiences remember the professionalism that presentational aids brought to the overall presentation. Finally, multimedia presentational aids involve multiple senses that help maintain the audience's attention.

> ▶ **SPEECHES IN ACTION 14.1**
> **Effective Multimedia Presentational Aids**

Types of Presentational Aids

You can use many types of presentational aids, but plan them carefully so that they achieve the maximum effect. The advantages and disadvantages of different types are discussed in this section.

Text

Text or words help remind the audience of the key point of your message. Text is the most used form of presentational aid. We have all seen a presenter use text to emphasize a point. However, keep text to a minimum. You do not want your audience to have to read entire sentences. The point is not redundancy but emphasis. Instead, use simple phrases or keywords to reinforce your point. Follow the rule of seven: no more than seven words per line and no more than seven lines on any slide.

Graphs

Graphs are ways of presenting numerical information with visual representations. For graphs to be effective, they need to be uncluttered and easy to understand. Your audience will not have the time to examine a complex graph. There are three most commonly used types of graphs (see Figure 14.1). A line graph shows how something changes over time by connecting line points. Line graphs are especially effective at demonstrating patterns. They quickly summarize stability, change, increases, or decreases. A bar graph uses vertical or horizontal bars to represent a certain quantity. Bar graphs are especially effective at demonstrating relative amounts (greater and lesser) and differences between groups. A pie graph is a circle graph divided into sections illustrating frequencies or proportions. Pie graphs are good ways to show the relative size of what is being depicted.

FIGURE 14.1
TYPES OF GRAPHS

LINE GRAPH:

KEY
- Facebook
- LinkedIn
- Pinterest
- Instagram
- Twitter

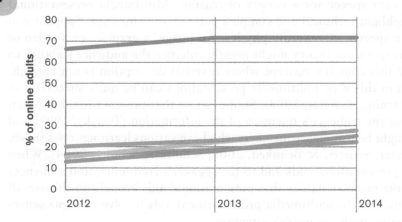

Social media sites, 2012–2014
% of online adults who use the following social media websites

BAR GRAPH:

KEY
- 2012
- 2013
- 2014

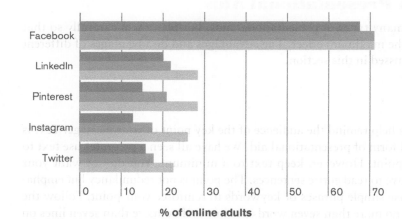

PIE GRAPH:

KEY
- Facebook
- LinkedIn
- Pinterest
- Instagram
- Twitter

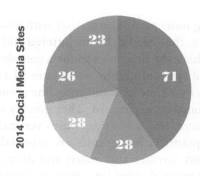

SOURCE: Adapted from Pew Internet Research, http://www.pewinternet.org/2015/01/09/social-media-update-2014/

Models and Objects

Models and objects illustrate concepts and ideas. Models represent actual "things" and complex processes. Models are useful if you need to show a 3D representation or something on a small scale (e.g., atoms, electrons). If your speech were about how to build a wind turbine for home use, it would probably not be practical to bring an actual wind turbine to your presentation. Instead, you could bring a model of a wind turbine for demonstration purposes. However, if your speech involves the latest technological gadget, it is practical to show the object as a presentational aid. Models and objects help draw the audience into the presentation.

Photographs

Photographs can enhance a presentation by showing images that are better seen than described. The saying that "a picture is worth a thousand words" is certainly true. Photographs effectively create interest for the audience, clarify complex information, or establish emotional moods. If you decide to use photographs, consider their size and quality. Ideally, you would like your entire audience to view the image together, at the right moment in your presentation. So, rather than passing around a small photograph, you should enlarge the photograph so that it is clear and visible to everyone who is physically and/or virtually present. This can be accomplished by using technology such as a document camera or overhead projector, by integrating the photograph into a digital presentation (like PowerPoint or Prezi slides), or by producing a large print copy to display during the presentation. Pay attention to the quality setting of the picture on your computer before you print or display it on a slide.

Photographs should be appropriate and not distracting. For example, if a photograph is too graphic, it might not be suitable if you are speaking to young children. We once had a student give a speech about extreme body piercing, complete with graphic photographs of people suspended by hooks through their backs! The speaker is responsible for guiding how the audience interprets the photograph. Most of the time, photos should not "stand alone." You don't want the audience wondering, "Why was I shown that image?" "What did it prove?" or "How am I supposed to interpret it?" Photographs are not substitutes for your speech; they are merely aids.

Audio and Video Clips

Audio and video clips of music, movies, webpages, interviews, TV shows, lectures, or conversations can also enhance the delivery of your presentation. Again, remember that audio and video clips do not replace the speech; rather, they aid the message. When used well, audio and video clips can be quite powerful. There are several things to remember about using these types of media. First, carefully edit your audio and video clips. Most computers are equipped with basic audio and video editing software (or this software can be downloaded free as shareware). Edit your audio and video selections to begin at the exact spot you want to share. Also, consider boosting sound levels so the entire audience will be able to hear it. It is frustrating for an audience member not to be able to hear the audio or video clip adequately. If it is not possible to edit a

Would showing solar panels enhance a presentation about sustainable energy?

Thinkstock

video clip, cue up your video on the computer to the exact spot to start the clip. While it is acceptable to use a CD player to play your audio clip (or DVD for video), it is more professional to incorporate audio/video clips into your presentational slides. The more seamless the transition, the more the audience will view you and your message positively. Both PowerPoint and Prezi can incorporate audio/video seamlessly. Also, carefully consider the amount of time that the clip or selection will take in your overall presentation. In most speaking situations, audiences will expect your vocal presentation of the message to play the starring role and audio and video clips to play a supporting, or supplementary, role. In classroom presentational situations, your professor will likely provide guidelines regarding the appropriate proportion of overall speech time that may be devoted to audio and video aids.

Ways to Present Your Multimedia Presentational Aids

There are a variety of ways to present information in the Communication Age. Because of advances in technology, audiences expect professional presentations. Basically, strive to be current and up-to-date. Your presentational aids should be seamless and completely integrated. Your presentation should be interactive and engaging. Distributing a black-and-white handout does not cut it anymore. We have all seen a movie that was considered state of the art when first released only to rewatch it and laugh at the dated technology. How about the professor who uses the same PowerPoint slides every year? After a few years, the students start to notice the older version of PowerPoint. The same is true for presentational aids. The following section discusses various ways to present information.

Computer-Generated Multimedia Aids

Computer-generated multimedia aids are considered the standard when giving a presentation; however, these are effective only when used properly (Savoy, Proctor, & Salvendy, 2009). The most basic form of multimedia is the computer-generated presentation, and Microsoft's PowerPoint is the most commonly used. Prezi is another computer-generated presentation software that is becoming better known. Simple computer-generated presentations incorporate text, graphs, models, and pictures. More advanced presentations include audio and video clips. Research has indicated that information on slides not relevant for the message reduces how much the audience learns (Bartsch & Cobern, 2003). You will need to be familiar with all the pitfalls of using more advanced features. Does the speaking room have adequate speakers? Does the projection system have enough light for your particular video clip, or do you need to lower the room's lights? Will you be using a remote control? Do you need to take your own projector, or does the room have its own? These types of questions are crucial to consider as you build your multimedia presentation.

PHOTOGRAPHS

In the Communication Age, it is possible to manufacture and manipulate any photograph in any way needed. The manipulation of photography has been occurring since its invention. A clothing company, H&M, admitted to using virtual bodies with real women's heads for an advertising campaign (Caulfield, 2011). The University of Wisconsin at Madison added an African American student to a photo of fans at a football game for a publicity booklet (Jacob & Benzkofer, 2011). This student was not even at the game. Are these examples of an ethical use of photography?

While it is unlikely that you would go to this much trouble for your presentations, you need to keep in mind the ethics of using photographs. Are there certain kinds of photographs that might be too disturbing or graphic to show to an audience? What about violating the privacy of others? Should you edit a photograph to make it more attractive? As you develop your multimedia presentational aids, carefully think about the kinds of images you show and how these images will reflect on you and your message. While you might slightly alter a photo for red-eye removal or to make it brighter for clarity, it is not ethical to add more people for diversity or use "fake" bodies to sell more clothing. What do you think?

QUESTIONS

1. How far should you go in editing a photograph before you cross a line?

2. What are your guidelines for when you have done too much?

CAREER FRONTIER: EXECUTIVE COACHING FOR PUBLIC SPEAKING

WHILE PUBLIC SPEAKING skills are important for everyone to possess, they are extremely important for those in business settings or positions of power (Quintanilla & Wahl, 2014). Not everyone in these settings, though, possesses the necessary public speaking skills to excel in their organization. Public speaking coaches work directly with business executives to help improve whatever skills they need to, everything from presentation delivery to presentational aid use (Boyd, 1995). Working one on one with business executives is also beneficial for you, the coach: It allows you to impart your speaking knowledge, help your clients become better speakers, and forge new relationships in the process. If you consider yourself to be a skilled public speaker and you enjoy helping others (especially those in the business world), then executive coaching may be the career choice for you.

COMMUNICATIONHOW-TO
USING PRESENTATION SLIDES

Using Presentation Slides:
Don't fill your slides with text

- This slide does not follow the rule of seven: no more than seven words per line and no more than seven lines per slide.
- Don't try to squeeze lots of words and information onto your presentation slides. This makes it difficult for your audience to read and follow. It also makes it more difficult for you to present your key points. Full sentences can be distracting for audiences, who will spend more time trying to read your slides than they will listening to you.

Using Presentation Slides:
Do follow the rule of seven

- Only use key points; not full sentences
- Use no more than seven words per line
- Include no more than seven points per slide
- Only use a slide if the slide will clarify a particular point

Using Presentation Slides:
Don't use small or hard to read fonts

- Don't use a font that will be too small for your audience to read. This is a 12 point font.
- **Don't use a decorative font;** *they can be hard to read*
- AVOID USING ALL CAPITAL LETTERS. ALL CAPS ARE HARDER TO READ than words which are not capitalized
- Don't use a color that does not contrast with the background color; it is hard to read
- Avoid using lots of different colors

Using Presentation Slides:
Do use a clear, consistent font

- Font size needs to be large enough to be seen by the audience. Any font over 24 point works well.

- **54 point**
- **48 point**
- **36 point**
  - 24 point

- Use the same standard font such as **Times New Roman**, **Calibri**, and **Arial** on all slides
- Use a font that contrasts with the background

Using Presentation Slides:
Don't use distracting transitions

- Avoid flying and sliding transitions, and animations. This is not the time to be fancy.
- Avoid using clip art which can look boring and generic.

Using Presentation Slides:
Do make each point appear in turn and use photographs

- Make each key point appear when you get to it in your speech, rather than showing the entire slide at once
- Photographs are more visually appealing than clip-art

iStock

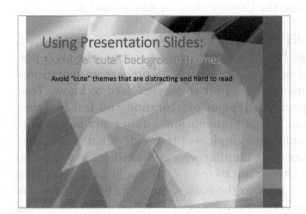

Additionally, consider the needs of a virtual audience who might view the presentation at a later date. How will the audience members hear you? Will the audio be directly fed into a computer, or will the video camera provide the only recording of your voice? If possible, try to record the audio and video feeds together for later editing. This way, the audio and video will be balanced. If you have ever seen a YouTube clip of a presentation in which the speaker used PowerPoint slides, you know it is hard to see them. One way to solve this problem is to edit the video and add presentational slides directly into the video.

Programs such as Apple's iMovie or Microsoft's Windows Movie Maker make this quite easy. The result is a professional video that virtual audiences will appreciate (Griffin, Mitchell, & Thompson, 2009). For links to helpful websites on how to use these programs go the *Communication Age* website at edge.sage pub.com/edwards2e.

Generally, using multimedia presentational aids enhances a presentation, but this is not always the case. Imagine you are the supervisor who gives presentations to your employees on a regular basis. You prepare presentational slides to highlight key information that your employees need to know. Your employees have come to expect this type of presentation and feel like they "know the drill." What if you gave a presentation without any multimedia presentational aids? How would your employees respond? What would they think? Audiences are becoming quite familiar with multimedia presentational aids and expect them. If you choose not to use any, it would just be you, the message, and the audience . . . back to the basics. Only the best of speakers could pull off this feat, but in certain instances, it could be a diversion from the norm and quite effective.

Overhead Transparency and Document Camera

Most presentation locations will have either an overhead transparency projector or a document camera. These devices project images on a screen that do not require a computer. Overhead transparencies require a special clear film. A document camera uses standard paper. The main advantage for these types of aids is flexibility. You can print off PowerPoint or Prezi slides, pictures, cartoons, or printed text. Here are three suggestions for using these aids: First, the transparencies or documents need to be professional quality. Second, remember to focus on the audience and not the overhead projector or document camera. In other words, do not look down at and talk to your overhead projector (it will not talk back!). Finally, you should cover the transparency or paper when you are done using it so that the audience is not distracted. Overhead transparencies and document cameras serve as good backup plans in case your multimedia plans fail. It is also a good idea to print off copies of your presentational slides in case you need to use a document camera as a backup. Also, just like multimedia aids and handouts, you will need to make arrangements if your presentation will be viewed by a virtual audience.

Handouts

Professional-looking handouts can enhance your credibility and convey information to the audience that members can "take away" with them. Handouts printed in color are almost as cost-effective as black-and-white handouts and seem more professional. Make sure to distribute your handouts at a time that best supports your message. If you want your audience to have a handout to review later, pass these out at the end of the presentation. Handouts passed out before presentations often distract audiences. For complex or technical presentations, it makes sense for the audience members to have the handout so they can follow along. Handouts, as a general rule, need to add new information or provide a summary of the presentation. Simply producing a handout to follow the exact presentation is a waste of paper and color ink. For audiences who will view your presentation on the web, provide a copy of the handout online in a stable software format like Adobe's PDF.

Flip Charts and Whiteboards

At the low end of the technology range are flip charts (large pads of paper) and whiteboards (or chalkboards). These forms of presentational aids are good for quick explanations or for brainstorming sessions. However, try to avoid using flip charts and whiteboards. First, it is extremely difficult to write legibly on a vertical surface. Second, large audiences will have a hard time seeing what you are writing. Third, you must turn your back to the audience to write, which interferes with your connection with the audience.

Flip charts and whiteboards can be used for quick explanations. They should never be used in a formal presentation.

Whatever type of presentational aid you choose, be sure to practice with it and have several backup plans in place. Also, think about what you would do in the middle of your speech if something went wrong with a presentational aid. Can you move to a backup, or do you just go ahead without it? With practice in a variety of circumstances, you will learn what works best for you and how you can make quick adjustments as needed.

DELIVERY IN PRESENTATIONS AND CONVERGENCE

As you think about delivering your presentation in the Communication Age, be sure to think about all the ways your presentation could be viewed. Will your presentation be recorded and uploaded on the web? Will you present to multiple types of audiences at the same time (videoconferencing and live)? How can you make your multimedia aids more interesting and carry more impact with your audiences? These questions need to be answered before any formal presentation you may give. Even at the workplace, your sales presentation may be recorded to show at other branch offices in the company. Today, there are many ways to reach your actual audience and a potential audience.

Convergence for delivery means being able to balance the needs of all types of audiences both now and potentially in the future. Technologies such as video conferencing will allow audiences to feel much closer to the speaker than simply

Communication unplugged
TO AVOID OVERRELIANCE ON TECHNOLOGY, USE YOUR VOICE

Getty

When delivering a presentation, many people rely on some sort of presentational aid to help them get their message across. Sometimes, though, the speaker becomes too dependent on the aid and allows it to become the center of attention. While presentational aids can be helpful, they lack certain characteristics that only the speaker possesses and can express, such as passion and emotion. In her famous speech "A Whisper of AIDS," political activist Mary Fisher relies solely on her voice to deliver her message on the importance of HIV/AIDS awareness. Fisher uses different vocal rates, pitches, and tones to complement her already powerful words. Phrases such as "If you believe you are safe, you are in danger" become more powerful because of Fisher's vocal strategies. No matter what the presentation is about, a speaker's voice can emphasize their message and resonate with the audience in ways that no visual aid can.

WHAT TO DO NEXT
To avoid overreliance on technology when giving a presentation in the Communication Age, try to:

- Remember the power of verbal communication.

- Make important nonverbal communication choices.

- Think critically about the most effective visual aid that's audience-centered.

- Stick to the basics (technology and social media do not make or break your presentation).

watching a recorded presentation. Even in these types of situations, you should always try to connect and engage with the audience to give a great presentation. Speakers at TED have to think about the audience seated in front of them and the potential millions of viewers who will watch their presentation in the years to come. Despite changes in technology, the basics of good delivery are still the most important. Work to decrease your levels of CA and be more comfortable speaking in front of others. Strive to be clear and concise in your delivery. Use nonverbal behaviors to emphasize your message. Make sure your multimedia presentational aids are simply aids to enhance the message. Delivery is an important part of any presentation, but keep in mind that it is not the presentation. At the end of the speech, you want your audiences to remember the message. Good delivery helps in this process.

MAKE *a* DIFFERENCE

URBAN DEBATE LEAGUES

WHAT CAN TEACH high school students about public speaking, leadership, collaborative problem solving, teamwork, logic, and argumentation in a way that helps them achieve success in adulthood? Urban debate leagues (UDLs). UDLs are programs to teach debate to high school students in urban settings. Currently, more than 40,000 students have participated in this activity in 24 of the largest cities in the United States. Many of these students are from minority and low-income populations. These programs are highly cost-effective and help increase motivation, literacy, and high school graduation rates. According to the National Association for Urban Debate

Leagues, a UDL costs under $750 per student, and this is in comparison to $1,500 per student in an after-school program. The communication skills learned by competing in debate are easily transferable to the workplace environment and enhance the educational experience of urban high school students. As you are looking for ways to use your communication skills to engage local communities, check out volunteering for a UDL. Working with these students will not only enhance their future success and grow effective delivery skills but also help you grow your life experiences in positive ways! For more information or ways you can contribute, check out www.urbandebate.org.

WANT A BETTER GRADE?

Get the tools you need to sharpen your study skills.

Access practice quizzes, eFlashcards, video, and multimedia at **edge.sagepub.com/edwards2e**.

WHAT YOU'VE LEARNED ▷ Now that you have studied this chapter, you should be able to:

① Explain how to reduce communication anxiety.

Communication apprehension is natural and happens to everyone. To reduce your anxiety, practice your presentation. Think positively

and speak confidently. Every time you state it, you create it. So state it positively!

▶ Delivering an Effective Presentation

🎙 Overcoming the Fear of Public Speaking

2 Describe various ways to present in the Communication Age.

Consider the method of delivery. For most presentations, extemporaneous delivery works well. Think about how your presentation could be viewed in a mixed-media setting.

 Election 2012: Obama's Complete Victory Speech

 Impromptu Speaking

3 Demonstrate effective delivery skills.

Develop your delivery skills (both verbal and nonverbal). Videotape your presentation before delivering it to an audience so you can see and hear how well you do. Remember that the message is still the most important part and that your delivery should not distract from it.

 Present Like Steve Jobs

 The 7 Secrets of the Greatest Speakers in History

4 Identify different types of presentational aids to enhance the message.

The types of presentational aids you utilize are a crucial consideration. Does your speech need to make an emotional appeal? If so, photographs or video might help. Do you have complex data that might best be understood in a graph format? Consider your audience and your message when determining your presentational aids.

 Prezi Tutorial

 Top Ten Mistakes When Using Visual Aids

5 Explain ways to present using a variety of multimedia presentational aids.

Think about the ways you will use presentational aids. If the speaking event is formal, multimedia presentational aids might work best with a large audience. If you are leading a brainstorming session in the office, whiteboards might work best for quick informal aids. Presentational aids can help the audience understand key concepts. On rare occasions, not using aids could be advantageous.

 PowerPoint® Tip: Using Pictures Properly

 PowerPoint® Tip: Practice with Your Slideshow

 How to Use Visual Aids in Speeches

KEY TERMS

Review key terms with eFlashcards. **edge.sagepub.com/edwards2e**

REFLECT

1. If communication can make anything possible, how can self-talk reduce your communication apprehension?

2. How do the advances in technology make a presentation potentially different from presentations just a few years ago?

3. There are times when multimedia presentational aids are not necessary. What are these, and why?

REVIEW

To check your answers go to **edge.sagepub.com/edwards2e**

1. Define communication apprehension.

2. ___ presentations are presentations that are read word for word.

3. A presentation that is carefully prepared with notes and an outline and has also been thoroughly practiced is a(n) ____ presentation.

4. A speech you watch via YouTube would be a(n) ____ presentation.

5. ___ is the level and variety of loudness in your voice.

6. ___ refers to the highness or lowness of your voice.

7. ___ are hand movements to emphasize your message.

8. _____ are objects that reinforce your message, elicit emotion, or add new information using a variety of senses.

9. A _____ shows how something changes over time by connecting line points.

SPEECH PLANNER

SpeechPlanner is an interactive, web-based tool that guides you through the process of planning and preparing your speech, one step at a time.

INFORMATIVE PRESENTATIONS

Getty

WHAT YOU'LL LEARN   After studying this chapter, you will be able to:

1 Identify the differences between informative and persuasive presentations.

2 Describe ways to keep an audience engaged with the presentation topic.

3 Classify types of informative speeches.

4 Examine strategies for making an informative presentation successful.

5 Explain the structure of a sample informative outline.

In 2015, a poll found a 37-point gap between U.S. citizens and scientists in terms of believing that climate change is mostly due to human behavior (Vaidyanathan & Climatewire, 2015). Scientists overwhelmingly believed in human behavior causing climate change. Clearly, there is an information gap occurring between the scientific community and the general population. Former vice president Al Gore has spoken and written about climate change, trying to educate people about the need for action to reduce our environmental impact. According to Gore, "we face a deepening global climate crisis that requires us to act boldly, quickly, and wisely." Gore's interest in this subject first developed when he took a class at Harvard University in the 1960s from a professor who was one of the first to notice and measure atmospheric changes. Gore recognizes this professor's lectures for inspiring him to speak about climate change and the need to lessen the environmental impact of human activity.

Gore's documentary film about climate change, *An Inconvenient Truth,* was released worldwide in 2006. The film has received many awards, including two Oscars. This film has been seen by millions and is credited with increasing awareness of climate change. Entire communities have viewed the documentary together and discussed the ideas presented in the film in face-to-face settings and through social media. Essentially, Gore's film is an informative presentation that seeks to educate audiences about climate change. The film clearly demonstrates how an informative presentation can integrate technology, media, and face-to-face communication to achieve a strong and positive effect. Gore's use of audio and video clips, animation, personal stories, research, stagecraft, and presentational slides demonstrates what is possible in the Communication Age in terms of an effective large-scale informative presentation.

While you may never produce an informative presentation that has such a global impact, you can make your informative presentation have an influence. This chapter discusses various ways to make your presentations informative, educational, and effective. As you develop your informative presentations, remember to use a variety of techniques to connect and engage with an audience in the Communication Age.

Living in the Communication Age, we are bombarded with information from a variety of sources on a daily basis. When you go to a coffee shop in an airport, you see several TVs showing cable news channels. On these news channels, you see several different areas of the screen containing different information. At the bottom of the screen, you see several moving messages with other stories. While you are drinking your coffee, you surf the web looking for cheap airfare for spring break, check for job openings on Craigslist, or respond to an e-mail from your professor. You also check your phone for a text message from your boyfriend or girlfriend. At the same time, you are listening in on the conversation of the couple fighting at the table next to yours.

Simply reading the last few sentences about the visit to the coffee shop can make you tired because information is constantly streaming in a variety of ways. While it is great to have access to so much information, we are in constant danger of information overload. Information overload refers to the negative feelings of being given too much information to process about a particular topic. Information overload is associated with a variety of negative psychological outcomes (Bawden & Robinson, 2009). Individuals who have a high degree of information overload report greater stress and poorer health (Misra & Stokols, 2011). Often, your audience will have experienced information overload about your specific presentation topic. In this chapter, you will learn how to make your information stand out from other available information.

The goal of an informative presentation is to convey new information and increase your audience's understanding about a topic. This may sound like a simple goal, but there are many ways to communicate information, and there are an unlimited number of potential topics to explore. Even if you have not taken a public speaking or communication course before, you have been an audience member for some type of informative presentation. Presidential addresses, cooking shows, instructional clips on YouTube, or even classroom lectures are all examples of informative presentations. This chapter covers how to craft an informative presentation that the audience or some future audience will remember. Let's begin by exploring the basic differences between informative and persuasive presentations.

Communication unplugged
TO REDUCE "INFORMATION OVERLOAD," TAKE A BREAK

Thinkstock

Be sure to take time to relax so that you do not suffer from information overload.

We live in a busy culture. There seems never to be enough time in the day to do what we think we need to get accomplished. The fast pace of our technological world encourages us to stay on the move and to maximize productivity. However, it is easy to overload our brain with "to-do lists" and opportunities for something new. We spend so much time communicating with others either in person or via our computers or phones. Sometimes, you just need to be with yourself. Take a break from the world and let yourself be alone. Self-reflection and meditation are great ways to improve focus and reduce stress. Taking some unplugged time for yourself can allow you to process recent events, prepare for future events, or just enjoy being alone without the distraction of other people and technology. Even if it's just for 15 or 20 minutes, that introspective time will rejuvenate your mind and improve the quality of your interaction with others.

WHAT TO DO NEXT
To relax and take a break from communication, try to:

- Go to the park and read a good book.

- Take a short hike and leave your phone in the car.

- Learn to meditate for 5 minutes. There are great YouTube videos to help you.

THE DIFFERENCE BETWEEN INFORMATIVE AND PERSUASIVE PRESENTATIONS

The Communication Age can make the difference between informative and persuasive presentations even more confusing. The infomercial is a classic example of this confusion. Infomercials are really persuasive presentations trying to sell a product but are sometimes approached as giving the viewer new information. In the next chapter, you will learn about persuasive presentations in greater detail, but as you begin to explore informative speeches, it is important to understand the similarities and differences between informative and persuasive presentations. The basic similarity between the two is that both need to provide credible and timely information about the topic in order to be effective. You cannot be convincing if there are not enough details about the topic. At the same time, you cannot be informative if you do not persuasively argue that your information is solid and should be heard.

The fundamental difference between both types of presentations is the speaker's intent. A speaker's intent refers to the goal the speaker is trying to accomplish in a presentation. The central question you should ask is, "Do I want to give

Commericals sometimes use an informative presentation to be persuasive.

information about a particular topic, or do I have a specific way that I want my audience to use that knowledge?" While giving your audience new information is an important part of persuading, always keep your general purpose in mind when you are creating your informative presentation. If you find yourself wanting to tell your audience to do or believe something, you have most likely crossed over into a persuasive presentation. Ask this basic question: "What am I trying to do with this information?" It will help keep you on the right track. In the next section, you will read about different types of informative presentations. By keeping this in mind, you will further be able to separate the differences between informative and persuasive presentations.

RELATING YOUR TOPIC TO THE AUDIENCE

The key to any successful informative presentation is your ability to convey information in a way that connects and engages with the audience. One of the first things you will have to do when preparing an informative presentation is choose and refine your topic. Sometimes your topic will be chosen for you. For example, you may have to explain a new activity to members of your student organization,

INFORMATION OVERLOAD

Do you feel sometimes that you receive so much information you do not have time to process it all? It seems, more and more, that people are becoming overloaded with all the information they take in. Research has indicated that all this juggling of information is changing how we act and think, and not necessarily in good ways (Richtel, 2010). Have you ever seen a speaker try to cram in as many

facts as possible? Strive not to do the same thing to your audience during your presentations.

As a speaker, you can run the risk of overloading your listeners with information. Sometimes, doing so can be unethical. If a speaker is trying to provide more information in a presentation than an audience can reasonably process just so that the audience will simply agree, the speaker is not allowing others to have their own autonomy and responsibility. Taken together with all the other information you have to process in the Communication Age, you need to be mindful of not overloading your audience. An audience has the right to critically evaluate information for credibility and usefulness. You have the ethical obligation to help.

QUESTIONS

1. How do you avoid information overload in your presentations?

2. What would you do if you needed to give more information about your subject than you could reasonably fit in your allotted speech time?

or perhaps your boss will ask you to conduct an orientation for new employees at the workplace. In all cases, make sure the topic stands out to cut through other information the audience may already know. A topic that is beneficial, timely, and useful will get the audience members' attention, and they will be able to relate to the topic. Audience analysis will help you select a great informative topic. Refer back to Chapter 11 for more information on audience analysis.

The worst kinds of informative presentations occur when the audience members already know (or think they know) about the topic. If you find yourself in a situation where they are educated about the topic, find new ways to apply the information. As such, inform them about something related to the topic that they have not considered. Personalizing the information for the audience is one possible route to take. If your topic for an informative presentation is river and stream pollution, you will need to find information about the local rivers and streams so that the audience can immediately connect to the topic in a real way. Sometimes you will need to approach the topic from a new angle so that the members of your audience are curious and eager for your information. Is there something they have not thought of in relation to the topic? Perhaps the local rivers help supply the water system, and the audience may not have realized this. When your speech will cover a complex subject, avoid being too technical so that you don't lose your audience. If you can explain the complex idea to a third grader, you have been successful at describing a challenging idea that any audience could understand. Look at the list below. You have probably heard a lot of information about each of these topics. How could the following topics be used in an informative presentation?

Online Job Searching	Virtual Reality	Leadership
Renewable Resources	Laws Concerning Sexting	Peace Jam
Community Service	Obesity Rates in the United States	Movie Downloads

If you are now thinking of how you could present new information or old information in a new way, you are on the right track. If, at the end of the informative presentation, your audience says, "Wow, I did not know that!" or "I never thought about it that way," you have been successful. You can make any "old" topic sound new and fresh by discussing information not previously known or not talked about in the same way. It is your job to make the information stand out and to connect and engage with your audience about the topic.

TYPES OF INFORMATIVE PRESENTATIONS

As you know from Chapter 11, the general purpose of an informative presentation is "to inform." However, there are several types of informative speeches, and each is used for specific reasons related to your topic. Using the topic, specific purpose, and organizational pattern will help guide you on the type of informative presentation needed to frame the information, and doing so will help you avoid crossing over into persuasive territory. In the following section, you will learn four basic types of informative presentations.

Giada De Laurentiis and Savannah Guthrie give a demonstrative presentation in a cooking segment on the *Today* show.

Demonstrate

It's Saturday morning, and you're flipping through TV channels trying to find something to watch. When the Food Network pops up on the screen, you see a team of pastry chefs assemble an enormous cake shaped like an electric guitar. Remembering your best friend's upcoming birthday, you think, "I wish I knew how to do that; that would be a really great birthday present!" So you go to the Food Network's website to see a video of how to make a guitar cake. One type of informative speech you may choose to give is a demonstrative informative presentation. Demonstrative presentations show the audience how to do something and sometimes give the audience members a chance to try what they have learned. Do you have a hobby or special talent that might interest your audience members? Is there a skill you have mastered that would help them if they knew how to do it as well? Here are a few ideas to get you thinking about demonstrative speech topics:

1. Changing a tire
2. Making a cake from scratch
3. Creating an online résumé
4. Signing up to volunteer at a local food pantry
5. Coding using the Robotic Operating System
6. Relaxing using basic yoga techniques
7. Editing a film using iMovie

One of the keys to a good demonstrative presentation is to be specific with your topic rather than too general; for instance, instead of talking about how to eat healthily, describe how to make a sugar-free dessert. If you try to tackle a broad topic, it will be difficult for the members of your audience to retain the information in a way that allows them to carry out the task on their own. At the same time, if you are too specific and technical, the audience may feel overwhelmed and stop listening. The key is to choose a demonstration that will engage your audience within your allotted time period. Take, for example, a speech about creating an online résumé. You might show the audience the various programs available for use, places to upload the document, and how to monitor for responses to the résumé. Essentially, you would be demonstrating "how" to create the résumé right in front of the audience members' eyes. Often, a chronological organizational pattern will work for this type of informative presentation because of its focus on following logical steps in a particular order. Using the online résumé example, you first create the résumé; next, you upload the document; and finally, you monitor for feedback and responses to your résumé. Notice how you cannot really rearrange the steps for this topic. This is why the chronological pattern often works best for this type of speech.

Explain

In addition to demonstrating a task or skill to your audience, you may choose an explanatory informative presentation to explain a concept, an idea, or a phenomenon. This type of presentation allows the speaker to investigate a topic that she previously has not explored, or uncover new information about a topic already familiar to her. What if you had to give a speech about a recent current event? You may have watched some news coverage about an earthquake in Asia. However, this coverage left you wanting to find out more about earthquakes, so you conducted research about earthquakes. This would be an explanatory informative topic. Chances are if you are curious about a topic, your audience will be interested as well. Remember, though, that it is important to connect the audience to your topic. Taking a broad topic like earthquakes and making it relevant by relating it to current events is a good way to connect the members of your audience to the information you wish to give them. Another way you could present information on earthquakes is by investigating any earthquakes that may have occurred in your area. The more the members of your audience are connected to your topic, the more they will remember the information you are presenting. How might you make these other broad concepts, ideas, or phenomena relevant to your current audience?

1. Economic depression in the 21st century
2. The formation of a democracy in the modern world
3. Telemetrics
4. Causes of global warming
5. Method acting

Take, for example, the topic of the formation of a democracy in the modern world. For this presentation, you might carefully explain how the creation of a democratic government might happen, certain characteristics that need to be present, or even how social media could play a role. Make sure that the topic can be explained in the allotted amount of time so that the audience has a clear understanding. Any of the organizational patterns will work for this type of informative presentation. Just be sure that it is logical and fits your topic.

Describe

Descriptive informative presentations describe interesting people, places, or events. Think about this kind of informative speech as laying out the facts for the audience in a vivid way. A good descriptive speech will allow the audience to imagine interacting with the person, place, or event.

Look at the following examples for ideas:

1. A baseball game
2. The Burning Man festival in Nevada
3. A new vegan restaurant in town
4. The newest building renovation on campus

An explanatory presentation can be effective for complex topics.

iStock

Getty

A vivid picture will help you describe an event.

5. National Coming Out Day

6. The latest TED conference in your local community

You could describe in vivid detail your trip to the Burning Man festival. What happened at the festival? Did any celebrities attend? What music groups did you hear? What did you eat in the middle of the desert? In other words, you want to paint a picture with your words so the audience can get a feel for the experience of the event. Multimedia presentational aids are a great way to add to a descriptive presentation. You could show a brief video or pictures of your experience to add to the details presented. All of the organizational patterns for informative presentations will work for a description speech so long as you paint pictures with your words to describe people, places, or events.

Explore

An exploratory informative presentation occurs when you invite the audience to learn or discover information about a topic. Imagine you were invited to give a presentation on a new theory few people have heard of about loving relationships. Of course you could demonstrate, explain, or describe this theory, but those types of informative presentations assume that the audience has at least heard about the topic in some form. An exploratory informative presentation should leave the audience with a sense of awe or wonderment. Have you ever had a moment when you wanted to share with someone something about some

MAKE
–a–
DIFFERENCE

EDUTAINMENT

USING ENTERTAINMENT AS a way to inform audiences about important social issues is referred to as edutainment. Edutainment campaigns have been used widely throughout the world to help educate about HIV/AIDS, smoking, pregnancy prevention, alcohol abuse, and cancer. Edutainment is simply another type of informative presentation.

Throughout history humans have been using entertainment as a form of education. Whether it is humorous stories, sad tales, or daring narratives of adventure, entertainment is a powerful way to share information with an audience.

Starting Over: A Message of Hope in the Midst of Despair is a drama that addresses the issues of HIV/AIDS in the sub-Saharan African region of Nigeria. In it, Nigerian

actors act out the stigmatization of those afflicted with the HIV/AIDS virus. The point of the drama, by Dr. Paul Nwulu, an edutainment filmmaker, is to show that awareness and compassion created by education is possible. Dr. Nwulu believes that a compelling story filmed with international production standards can make audiences grow and learn through education about this serious issue. He is right.

As you think about ways to be involved with your local community, are there ways you can use the idea of edutainment in your efforts? Delivering an informative presentation and at the same time being entertaining is an effective way of getting new or controversial information to your audience. What opportunities exist in your community for you to entertain and educate?

new or amazing facts you just learned? Basically, you are inviting this person to explore these new facts with you. These same feelings are what you are trying to accomplish with an exploratory informative presentation. One way to know a potential exploratory informative presentation is if experts on the subject are still trying to understand the information and are tentative with their conclusions. Perhaps you are speaking about the newest theory in physics like string theory, a new form of virtual reality being designed for the future, or a theory about science and dreams. For these topics, there are no final answers from experts. If you are excited about the topic, your audience will view it the same way. For this type of informative presentation, you would be exploring with the audience the central questions that are important to ask to have a better understanding of the topic. Most of the time a topical organizational pattern will work best for this type of informative presentation.

By knowing the type of informative presentation, organizational pattern, and topic, you will be able to craft and deliver a presentation that both connects and engages with your audience. If you are successful, your audience will be able to say at the end of your presentation, "I did not know that—that's interesting," or you might have audience members who want to chat about the topic after the speech. Also, remember that you will have to spend a good amount of time researching your topic, so be sure to choose something that interests you. The best informative presentations give the audience members new and relevant information that they are likely to remember and use. Whether your purpose is to demonstrate, describe, explain, or explore, you need to connect and engage with your audience in meaningful and important ways.

STRATEGIES FOR INFORMATIVE PRESENTATIONS

By now you have done your audience analysis, chosen a topic that interests you and your audience, decided on the type of informative presentation, and researched and organized your presentation. This would be a great time to review Chapters 11 and 13 for the best ways to format the introduction, body, and conclusion. In this section, you will learn about strategies to guide informative presentations so that your message is memorable for the audience. Specifically, let's discuss defining and organizing your information, reducing audience misunderstanding, giving your audience incentives to listen and getting your audience involved, and how learning styles impact your informative presentation. As you continue to turn your ideas into an engaging informative presentation, keep the following strategies in mind.

Define the Information

Because the best informative presentations aim to give the audience new information, it is often necessary to define new terms or ideas. What is the difference between a driver and a putter in disc golf? What is a tweet? What roles do fault lines play in earthquakes? What is fistula, and what does it have to do with body piercing? If you are demonstrating how to make that guitar-shaped cake, you may first have to define the type of cake or frosting you will be using. Sometimes it will be easier to define a concept or an idea by what it is not, rather by than what it is. For example: "A no-kill shelter is not the same thing as a dog pound." Giving the members of your audience these important definitions is essential to their understanding, so it is worth taking the time to do so. If your topic is technical and complex, you will want to spend a good deal of time defining important terms. Just be careful that your entire speech does not become a glossary.

Organizing the Information

The topic helps guide what kind of organizational pattern you might use for an informative presentation. In Chapter 13, you learned about several types of organizational patterns that are useful for informative presentations. Let's review. First, if your topic requires a precise ordering of steps such as "how to create a blog" or "how to apply for student loans," you would choose the chronological pattern. This organizational pattern will allow your audience to understand the specific steps needed for your topic, one after the other in a logical way. You could also use the chronological organizational pattern if you were describing events that happened in the past. The topical pattern is chosen when you cluster your information around central themes and ideas. This pattern allows your audience to easily remember information in chunks or groupings. Research has shown that chunking of information is an effective way to remember new information (Bodie, Powers, & Fitch-Hauser, 2006; Ohata, 2006). The spatial pattern is used when your information is grouped by space or location. You might use this pattern if you are giving a presentation about the various land features of your state and where they are located, or where the largest Occupy Wall Street protests are taking place. The cause-and-effect pattern is a great way to inform an audience about a topic's causes and effects. Perhaps you might be able to point out to the members of your audience some causes that they may not have yet considered. Or you might surprise them with new information about effects.

Depending on your topic, the type of organizational pattern could make a huge difference in audience understanding. Which organizational pattern would be most effective for a demonstration speech on how to change a tire? Using a cause-and-effect pattern or a topical pattern may help the audience avoid common mistakes while changing a tire, but a step-by-step chronological pattern would be more useful

 CAREER FRONTIER: KNOWING YOUR CUSTOMERS

THE PRINCIPLE OF knowing your audience and/or customers and adapting your message to that audience extends far beyond presentations. Entire careers, such as public relations or marketing, depend on good audience or customer analysis. Public relations professionals must know their audience in order to know what information to share. It could be for an audience outside the organization, or even for an audience inside the organization. The marketing team will use customer analysis when deciding the best way to publicize an event or create a radio ad. Even if you are not on a marketing or public relations team, you need to understand the characteristics of the target of your message. Whether you are a nurse or a server at a restaurant, every job you have will require some basic skills in audience or customer analysis. The skills learned in Chapter 11 about audience analysis will help with your career as well.

for demonstrating how to perform the task. Make sure you choose the right pattern for your specific topic. Additionally, you should review your specific purpose and thesis statement again to check that you are on the right track. Remember that the specific purpose is "to inform." Make sure that you are not crossing over into persuasive territory. The thesis statement is a single sentence that encompasses the entirety of the chosen topic. At the end of this chapter, you will find a sample outline. On this outline, the specific purpose, thesis statement, and organizational pattern are indicated for reference.

Strive to reduce audience misunderstanding.

Reduce Audience Misunderstanding

Reducing audience misunderstanding will greatly help a presentation make more of an impact. First, it is important to give internal previews and internal summaries throughout your presentation. The more you can repeat your main points, the more your audience will remember them. Some level of redundancy is key for a successful informative speech. Second, pay close attention to the audience's nonverbal cues throughout the presentation to help you know when to clear up any confusion. If you see blank or confused facial expressions, you may need to explain better to help listeners understand your topic. Third, try using your audience members' prior knowledge by comparing the topic with something with which they are already familiar. The previous information that a person holds is an important part of evaluating a message (Bodie, Worthington, Imhof, & Cooper, 2008). Listeners may have no prior knowledge of yoga poses, but by comparing body positions with more familiar terms (fold your legs like a pretzel or stand tall like a tree), they will be more likely to correctly interpret your meaning. Fourth, be sure that the audience can see the logic of your organizational patterns. This will help listeners organize their thoughts about your presentation. For example, if you are using the chronological pattern, be sure to say things like "the second step is . . ." or "the last step in this process." Fifth, limit the amount of information that you present in your informative speech. Trying to cover too much information will only lead to greater audience misunderstanding and information overload. You will not be able to cover the entirety of string theory, but you could cover the most basic material to inform your audience about this subject. Finally, use transitions and signposts to help your audience recognize important parts of the presentation. Doing so will allow the members of your audience to keep up with the presentation and provides another way for them to organize their thoughts and memories.

Give the Audience Incentives to Listen

Did you ever have an elementary school teacher who promised extra recess or a piece of candy if the class listened carefully to a guest speaker? The teacher was simply giving the audience of students an incentive to listen. Audiences like to know what they will gain from listening to your presentation. A reward can be anything mental or physical that your audience will obtain from your speech. If you tell the members of your audience that they can save money by better understanding student loans, most will be eager to hear what you have to say. Think about the audience's benefits and make sure you highlight those incentives early in your presentation. Sometimes you will see presenters use a reward in the attention getter of the introduction. For example, you might say, "How many of you would like to save money on your student loan payments?" In a class of college students, this statement would certainly get their attention. Take a look at these informative topics:

1. The Social Security system
2. AmeriCorps
3. Using Windows Movie Maker

What incentives would be appropriate and effective for these topics? There is always an incentive to listen; you just have to highlight it sometimes.

Get the Audience Involved

A great way to connect and engage with your audience during an informative presentation is to get the audience involved. You might have noticed in your own college experiences that you retain more information in classes where the instructor emphasizes participation. Research has indicated that student involvement in the classroom is an important part of the learning environment (Myers, Edwards, Wahl, & Martin, 2007). The same is true for any presentation. If you were doing a demonstrative informative presentation, you could have a couple of the audience members help you with the steps. Magicians use this same technique. Not only do audience members listen because they think there is a chance they might be called upon, but they also identify with the others in the audience who were called on already.

A second way to get the audience involved is to have a question-and-answer period at the end of your presentation. During this question-and-answer period, audience members can ask questions to clarify or gain more information not discussed in the speech. Often, questions will lead to more questions, and even more of the audience will become involved.

Be Aware of Different Learning Styles

There is no "best way" for everyone in your audience to learn. Learning styles refer to the different ways individuals like to obtain and process information (Fleming, 2001). In other words, a learning style is how people perceive information. There are four basic learning styles: auditory, read/write, visual, and kinesthetic (Fleming, 2001; Hawk & Shah, 2007). However, most people have a preference for more than one style.

Auditory Learners

Auditory learners will retain information better through hearing and speaking it. Audience members who are more auditorily inclined will carefully listen to what you say to retain the information. Providing a podcast of your message is a great way to reach auditory learners (Stiffler, Stoten, & Cullen, 2011).

Thinkstock

Having a question-and-answer session is a great way to get the audience involved.

Read/Write Learners

Read/write learners learn by reading and writing about a topic. These learners like reports, essays, handouts, and readings. Audience members who prefer this type of learning will appreciate multimedia aids, handouts, and suggested readings for more information.

Visual Learners

Visual learners understand ideas and concepts through pictures, slides, maps, graphs, and diagrams. For these audience members, it is important to have multimedia presentational aids so that your information can be visualized in meaningful ways. Charts, graphs, videos, and pictures will suit these types of audience members well.

Astrophysicist Neal deGrasse Tyson uses presentational aids to reach visual learners.

Kinesthetic Learners

Hands-on demonstrations are best for kinesthetic learners because these types of audiences need to actively be doing something related to the message. In other words, these learners do best when they are holding, touching, or experiencing something (Abedi & Badragheh, 2011). While some topics work well with kinesthetic learners, many will not. In this case, a carefully crafted handout of the outline of your presentation with fill-in-the-blanks at key points might help. This way, these learners can fill in the missing information.

COMMUNICATIONHOW-TO
QUESTION-AND-ANSWER SESSION

1. *Anticipate potential questions.* You should think about the kinds of questions an audience might ask and practice your answers.

2. *If you do not know, say you do not know.* Sometimes you will simply not know the answer to a question. It is better to admit that you do not know than try to make up an answer.

3. *Restate the question for the audience.* Often, the audience will not be able to hear the question, so restate questions loudly for the audience to hear.

4. *Be polite.* Always be polite and courteous to the person asking the question (even if it is a bad question).

5. *Remember you are still on.* Just because the presentation is over, your presence in front of the audience is not. The question-and-answer session is not the time to relax.

6. *Spread the questions around.* Do not let one audience member ask all the questions. Encourage others to ask questions.

7. *Have a conclusion.* Develop a concluding sentence to let the audience know that the question-and-answer session is over. Be sure to thank the audience for the questions.

Images: istock.

LEARNING STYLES

To assess your learning style, go to www.vark-learn.com. This online survey is 13 questions long and will give you a score for each of the four learning styles: visual, aural, read/write, and kinesthetic.

1. How did you score for each learning style?

2. Were you surprised by which learning styles were your highest and lowest?

3. Reflecting on this scale, think about your audience for an informative presentation. Are there ways you can include all four learning styles in your speech?

Source: VARK: A Guide to Learning Styles, www.vark-learn.com.

COMMUNICATION**HOW-TO**
LEARNING STYLE TIPS

Auditory Learners Benefit From the Following:

1. Watching and rewatching presentations

2. Asking questions

3. Hearing frequent transitions, signposts, internal previews, and internal summaries

Read/Write Learners Benefit From the Following:

1. Handouts

2. Reports

3. Essays on the subject

4. Lists of suggested readings

Visual Learners Benefit From the Following:

1. Watching and rewatching presentations

2. Seeing descriptive multimedia aids

3. Receiving copies of multimedia aids at the end of the presentation

4. Following a laser pointer

Kinesthetic Learners Benefit From the Following:

1. Participating in demonstrations

2. Following a laser pointer

3. Receiving copies of multimedia aids at the end of the presentation

Your audience will consist of individuals who prefer any combination of these learning styles. Sometimes performing an audience analysis can help you choose which styles to favor in your presentation, but it is best to use a variety of tools such as multimedia aids, handouts, a suggested reading list for more information, and so on throughout your presentation to appeal to all learning styles.

Understanding strategies to help you effectively inform the audience is extremely important. At the heart of informative presentations is the ability to connect and engage with the audience. You want the audience and future audiences to remember and understand the topic. In the Communication Age, information is constantly on the move. Following these strategies will help you be part of this movement.

SAMPLES OF
INFORMATIVE PRESENTATIONS

In the following section there are two examples of informative outlines and an example of an informative speech text. In the first example, you will see a full-sentence outline. The second example is a keyword outline based on the full-sentence outline. The keyword outline is what you would present in front of the audience. Be sure to notice the outline formatting in these examples referenced in Chapter 13. The third example is the transcript of an informative speech with the key parts of a presentation noted. To watch this speech, go to edge.sagepub.com/edwards2e.

4D PRINTING

Eric Mishne

INTRODUCTION

I. Attention-Getting-Device—Formula One racing is not the first place people go to find new technology, but new innovations in design have allowed one car to drive with a tailfin that changes its shape, based on the weather (Monks, 2014).

II. Thesis Statement—4D printing is the newly discovered ability to print material with programmed geometric code, allowing the objects to transform and change their shape without computer or robotic influence.

III. Importance of Topic—Self-assembly and the technology known as 4D printing are revolutionizing the way materials are manufactured, and could eventually change the world in ways that until now only science-fiction novels have imagined.

IV. Preview of Main Points—Today we will explore what 4D printing is, some of the future applications of this technology, and some concerns and criticisms of what CNN has called "the last thing we ever build."

BODY

I.   4D printing is a simple concept with a complicated execution.

   A.   Geometric materials that self-assemble, known as 4D printing, are programmed to change shape when exposed to certain elements (Baum, 2014).

   B.   Energy sources such as water, temperature, or movement act as stimuli for the material, causing it to change its shape (Taylor, 2013).

   C.   4D printing has the potential to create materials that self-assemble, allowing the making of products with minimal energy (Baum, 2014).

Transition: Now that we have a basic understanding about how 4D technology works, we can scan through the future applications of self-assembling material.

II.   The many applications of 4D printing have the potential to impact many industries.

   A.   There are implications for healthcare in the form of heart and cancer treatment (Wainwright, 2013).

   B.   Construction of space stations is another speculated application of 4D printing.

   C.   Even clothing could be affected by the evolution of 4D printing (Rieland, 2014).

Transition: In order to fully assemble our knowledge of 4D printing we must also look at some concerns and criticisms about this technology.

III. As with most new technologies that have the potential to revolutionize the way we live, 4D printing does not come without its critics.

    A. Useable, practical 4D materials are expensive, and will not be feasible for years.

    B. There are criticisms and fears expressed by critics and bloggers world-wide (Greenemeier, 2013).

    C. CNN expressed concern for 4D printing in its article titled "The Last Thing We Ever Build? The Machines That Make Machines" (Monks, 2014).

CONCLUSION

I. Restate Thesis and Main Points—Today we have taken a look at what 4D printing is, some of its potential applications, and some of the concerns and criticisms of 4D printing, exploring the potential revolutionary implications of self-assembling technology.

II. Whether it comes in the form of sneakers or space stations, the future of 4D printing is racing—almost as fast as a Formula One car.

KEYWORD

4D PRINTING

Eric Mishne

INTRODUCTION

  I. Attention-Getting-Device—Formula One racing—tailfin that changes shape (Monks, 2014).

 II. Thesis Statement—Material with programmed geometric code.

III. Importance of Topic—Self-assembly eventually changing the world.

IV. Preview of Main Points—Today we will explore what 4D printing is, some of the future applications of this technology, and some concerns and criticisms.

BODY

I. 4D printing is a simple concept that is much more complicated to execute.

    A. Material is programmed to change shape (Baum, 2014).

    B. Energy sources are stimuli (Taylor, 2013).

    C. Manufacturing with minimal energy (Baum, 2014).

TRANSITION

II. The many applications of 4D printing have the potential to impact many industries.

    A.   Healthcare—cancer (Wainwright, 2013).

    B.   Space stations.

    C.   Sneakers and clothes (Rieland, 2014).

TRANSITION

III. As with most new technologies that have the potential to revolutionize the way we live, 4D printing does not come without its criticisms and concerns.

    A.   Expensive and not in the near future.

    B.   Bloggers concerns (Greenemeier, 2013).

    C.   CNN article—"The Last Thing We Ever Build?" (Monks, 2014).

CONCLUSION

    I.   Restate Thesis and Main Points—What 4D printing is, its application and concerns, and criticisms against 4D printing.

    II.   Whether it comes in the form of sneakers or space stations, the future of 4D printing is racing—almost as fast as a Formula One car.

INFORMATIVE SPEECH TRANSCRIPT

4D PRINTING

Eric Misnhne

▶ **SPEECHES IN ACTION 15.1**
Watch: Effective Informative Presentation

[Here Eric starts building his credibility and the credibility of the topic by citing sources early in the speech]

MANUSCRIPT

Formula One racing is not the first place people go to find new technology, but according to a 2014 CNN article, new innovations in design has allowed one car to drive with a tailfin that changes its shape, based on the weather. This is made possible by 4D printing. 4D printing is the newly discovered ability to print material with programmed geometric code, which allows objects to transform and change their shape without computer or robotic influence. Self-assembly and the technology known as 4D printing are revolutionizing the way materials are manufactured, and could eventually change the world in ways that until now only science-fiction novels have imagined. Today we will explore what 4D printing is, some of the future applications of this technology, and some concerns and criticisms of what CNN has called "the last thing we ever build."

[This is a clever way of inserting another citation while giving us a catchy phrase to remember throughout the speech]

4D printing is a simple concept with a complicated execution. According to an article published on August 21, 2014, in *Med City News*, geometric materials that self-assemble, known as 4D printing, are programmed to change shape when exposed to certain elements. Gizmag.com reported in 2014 that energy sources such as water, temperature, or even movement act as stimuli for the material, causing it to change its shape. For example, at the most basic level, a programmed object might be placed into a jar of water and within seconds change its shape. At a higher level of programmable material, and an area of implementation that is still undergoing research and testing, the sole of a shoe may be able to change its shape based on the surface of ground, potentially growing cleats, or smoothing out in response to the amount and type of pressure from the foot. The implications for this technology are becoming greater every day as more and more potential applications are discovered, and according to the previously cited CNN article, 4D printing has the potential to produce products with minimal energy.

[Examples provide a specific image of the concepts that have thus far only been glossed over]

Now that we have a basic understanding about how 4D technology works, we can scan through the future applications of self-assembling material. The many applications of 4D printing have the potential to impact many industries.

[This transition statement uses verbiage from the first point and leads into verbiage of the second point, clearly leading us from one to the next]

There are implications for healthcare in the form of heart treatment. According to a 2013 article in *The Guardian* by Oliver Wainwright, heart valves and other biological replacements may be possible with the advancements of 4D printing. Wainwright speculates that this technology could even lead to nanobots that could track down and kill cancer cells. Skylar Tibbets, the brain behind 4D printing, envisions the construction of space stations as another future application of 4D printing. According to Randy Rieland in 2014, even clothing could be affected by the evolution of 4D printing. As already mentioned, shoes that change shape based on the ground and pressure of the foot are being developed. Even regular clothing could be revolutionized, since some material can be programmed to expand to over 100% of the original size. Imagine not needing to buy a new pair of pants after putting on a few pounds. Or even better, buying clothes that can return to a smaller size when you lose some unwanted weight. While these are all simply ideas that are still in development, they are not out of the realm of possibility, and are practically right around the corner.

In order to fully assemble our knowledge of 4D printing we must also look at some concerns and criticisms about this technology. As with most new technologies that

[Eric has cleverly used puns in his transitions, ensuring that the mood of the speech remains light]

have the potential to revolutionize the way we live, 4D printing does not come without its critics. First of all, it is important for us to know that as exciting as these innovations are, useable, practical 4D materials are expensive, and will not be available for public or even private use for several years. With the ongoing debate about the merits and dangers of artificial intelligence, this self-assembling programmability has garnered criticism and raised the typical concerns that come with any new type of AI. However, most criticism and fear is expressed by critics and bloggers who typically stay in the shadows and pose no real threat. CNN, however, brought attention to the concerns in its 2014 article titled "The Last Thing We Ever Build? The Machines That Make Machines." The idea that we are making a machine that will build other machines sounds a little like the Matrix, or the 2001 Haley Joel Osment and Jude Law film *A.I.*, but the notion that our technology has reached that point of self reproduction is still far-fetched. Nonetheless, the scientists and researchers working with self-assembly would be wise to proceed with caution and make real attempts to subdue fears that the future of humanity lies in the hands of programmable matter.

[The review statement clearly touches on all three main points]

Today we have taken a look at what 4D printing is, some of its potential applications, and some concerns and criticisms of 4D printing. The implications of self-assembling technology are potentially revolutionary. The advances in programmable materials are catching the attention of scientists and technology lovers around the world, and whether it comes in the form of sneakers or space stations, the future of 4D printing is racing—almost as fast as a Formula One car.

[Tying your conclusion back to your attention getter is a good idea, as it provides closure and demonstrates cohesiveness]

INFORMATIVE PRESENTATIONS AND CONVERGENCE

Informative presentations in the Communication Age are becoming increasingly widespread due to online videos, Internet forums, and social networking. As little as 15 years ago, if you wanted to find in-depth information about a subject, you would have to read a book or ask somebody who knew the material. Today, we can watch videos that demonstrate virtually any topic. People across the globe can potentially see that small demonstrative informative presentation you gave for your speech class on how to use Twitter. Clearly, information is widely available. Thus, it is important for you to learn to distinguish good information from bad. With the addition of peer-to-peer information resources, such as

Wikipedia, this ability becomes even more important. With the plethora of both good and bad information available, it is imperative for you to find ways to connect and engage with your audience.

In the chapter opener about Al Gore's film, you saw how a strong informative presentation can use face-to-face communication with both technology and media to create a strong audience response. Always be mindful of how you can incorporate all that is possible in the Communication Age into your speeches so that you can reach larger and larger audiences both in real time and in virtual space. The convergence of technology, media, face-to-face communication, and seeking information is a hallmark of the Communication Age. That is why it is vitally important that you understand the best strategies and techniques for informative presentations.

Technology lends many options for reaching expanded audiences in both real time and virtual online space.

WANT A BETTER GRADE?

Get the tools you need to sharpen your study skills.

Access practice quizzes, eFlashcards, video, and multimedia at **edge.sagepub.com/edwards2e.**

WHAT YOU'VE LEARNED   Now that you have studied this chapter, you should be able to:

1   **Identify the differences between informative and persuasive presentations.**

Pay attention to the informative and persuasive elements in a presentation. Be careful not to cross the line into a persuasive attempt. In other words,

are you asking the audience to do anything? If so, you might be engaged in a persuasive attempt.

 Information Overload

 The Difference Between Informative and Persuasive Speeches

2 Describe ways to keep an audience engaged with the presentation topic.

Always keep your audience in mind. The best informative presentations strive to connect and engage with the audience about the topic. At the end of your presentation your audience should say, "Wow! I did not know that," or "I've never thought about it in that way."

▶ The Clues to a Great Story

🎙 Famous Moon Speech

3 Classify types of informative speeches.

Knowing the type of your informative presentation will help you research and organize your topic. Always choose the most logical and simplest type for your topic.

💻 Good Informative Speech Topics

💻 How to Master the Demonstration Speech

4 Examine strategies for making an informative presentation successful.

Understand the best strategies for informative presentations. Define your information, strive to reduce audience misunderstanding, give incentives to listen, and be aware of different learning styles.

▶ Public Speaking Toastmasters: Lance Miller, "The Ultimate Question"

🎙 The Act of Listening

5 Explain the structure of a sample informative outline.

Following the basics for organizing a presentation will help your audience focus on the topic. Carefully review your outlines.

💻 Informative Speech Outline Templates

KEY TERMS

Review key terms with eFlashcards. **edge.sagepub.com/edwards2e**

Auditory learner   380
Demonstrative informative
   presentation   374
Descriptive informative
   presentation   375
Edutainment   376

Explanatory informative
   presentation   375
Exploratory informative
   presentation   376
Information overload   370
Informative presentation   370

Kinesthetic learner   381
Learning styles   380
Read/write learner   381
Reward   379
Speaker's intent   371
Visual learner   381

REFLECT

1. Let's say you are giving a presentation on getting a summer job in your area. How might you format your presentation to appeal to several different learning styles?

2. If you were speaking and noticed that several audience members were texting, what would you do to get them engaged? Should you say anything to them?

3. How are informative and persuasive presentations alike? What can you do to make sure you do not cross over into persuasive territory?

REVIEW

To check your answers go to **edge.sagepub.com/edwards2e**

1. The negative feeling of being given too much information is called _____.

2. ___ refers to the goal the speaker is trying to accomplish in a presentation.

3. What is a demonstrative informative presentation?

4. You would use a(n) ____ informative presentation to describe the interesting city of Boston.

5. The ____ informative presentation is meant to leave the audience with a sense of awe or wonderment after being invited to discover information on a topic.

6. ___ refers to the different ways individuals prefer to obtain and process information.

7. What are the learning styles, and why are they important?

8. _____ learners understand ideas and concepts through pictures, slides, maps, graphs, and diagrams.

9. Reducing audience ____ will lead to a more successful presentation.

SPEECH PLANNER

SpeechPlanner is an interactive, web-based tool that guides you through the process of planning and preparing your speech, one step at a time.

Getty

WHAT YOU'LL LEARN ◄ After studying this chapter, you will be able to:

1 Describe various types of persuasive claims.

2 Identify ways to craft persuasive arguments.

3 Describe strategies to persuade audiences.

4 Construct a persuasive presentation based on persuasive organizational patterns.

5 Explain the structure of a sample persuasive outline.

Born in 1997, Malala Yousafzai has changed the world through her actions and words. In 2012, a gunman tried to shoot her for boarding a bus to attend school. The assassination attempt occurred because the local Taliban had banned girls at the local schools. After the assassination attempt and rehabilitation, Ms. Yousafzai spoke even more about the plight of children in Pakistan and the rest of the world. In 2014, she became the youngest winner of a Nobel Peace Prize. The Nobel committee stated that she stood for the "struggle against the suppression of children and young people and for the right of all children to education" (*People*, 2014).

Ms. Yousafzai has demonstrated how a single voice can cause positive change. *Time* magazine named her one of the "100 Most Influential People in the World." Today, she delivers persuasive speeches all across the world to advocate for girls and on the importance of education for all children. Countless numbers of children have been afforded an education because of her efforts. She truly connects and engages with audiences to create a better world for all.

While you may never win a Nobel Peace Prize for your efforts, you need to strive for the same ability to persuade when you make presentations. Characteristics such as credibility, storytelling, emotions, and logical appeals are important for any persuasive effort. The members of your audience need to trust you when you encourage them to take an action or change a point of view. In this chapter, you will learn about types of persuasive claims, strategies for persuading, and how to organize a persuasive speech.

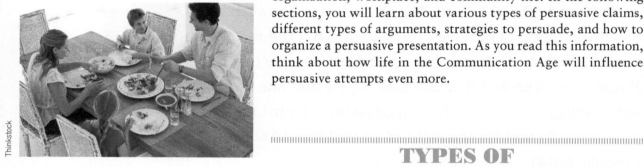

Persuasion takes place in every setting of your life.

If you've ever watched the trainers on NBC's show *The Biggest Loser,* you know they have a gift for changing the contestants' attitudes and behaviors about food, exercise, and even themselves. Each trainer has quite a talent for persuasion. Persuasion is the altering or modifying of a person's attitudes, beliefs, values, or outlook about a topic. Most of you will never practice your persuasive skills in front of a television audience, but persuading others will be an important part of your social and professional life. We can learn a great deal about persuasion through trial and error (Petty & Briñol, 2014). Ethos, pathos, and logos (see Chapter 12) all contribute to our ability to persuade and empower others. You may use calculated tables and facts to persuade your coworkers to switch to a more cost-effective method of production or attempt to sway a city council to support the new homeless shelter. You may try to demonstrate the benefits of Facebook for your grandmother or try to convince your friends to take a different GPS route on your summer road trip. In the classroom, you will most likely be asked to put together a presentation to persuade your peers about an issue or a topic that is important to you. The ability to engage in ethical persuasion is an important part of being a member in a community. You need to have the skill to convince others of important decisions that affect family, organization, workplace, and community life. In the following sections, you will learn about various types of persuasive claims, different types of arguments, strategies to persuade, and how to organize a persuasive presentation. As you read this information, think about how life in the Communication Age will influence persuasive attempts even more.

TYPES OF PERSUASIVE CLAIMS

Generally, persuasive topics revolve around three basic questions. Questions of policy refer to persuading for a change to an existing law, plan, or policy, or creating a new policy. Questions of value are used when trying to persuade the relative merits—good/bad, moral/immoral—of a position. Questions of fact are used when one person tries to persuade another that a fact is or is not true. For most of your classroom presentations, you will be trying to persuade your audience to adopt, support, or lobby for policy changes. However, if you are debating with a friend over who is the best late-night talk show host, you are trying to persuade using the relative merits of each host, which would be a question of value. If you find yourself trying to convince someone that astronauts really did land on the moon, you are trying to persuade with questions of fact. Determining what type of question your persuasive presentation is addressing will help you formulate your arguments for your particular audience.

Questions of Policy

Let's take a closer look at the three types of persuasive claims mentioned above, beginning with questions of policy. Protesters holding signs on the sidewalk in front of an abortion clinic, citizens handing out pamphlets at the polls on Election Day, and a teachers' union arguing for a fairer contract at a school board meeting are all persuasive situations dealing with questions of policy. Any time you are asking what should be done to make a given situation better you are using a claim of policy. Often, classroom presentations will focus on persuading classmates to reject or adopt a course of action dealing with an existing community policy, or to advocate for a needed law or regulation. Here are a few more examples of persuasive topics dealing with questions of policy:

- Students with a high grade point average should have extended borrowing privileges at the university library.
- All high schools should offer students a course in environmental sustainability.
- Health care should be available to all full-time students at reduced cost.

In the Communication Age, offering real working solutions is even more important. Millions of people have the ability to view or hear the solutions to real community and social problems. Policy suggestions need to be real and sincere and based on evidence.

Questions of Value

Although questions of policy are usually supported by questions of value and questions of fact, these two types of claims also stand on their own. Questions of value focus on judging what is right or wrong or what is good or bad. Any time you are trying to convince an audience that an idea or a course of action is right or wrong, you are persuading by using a question of value because you are appealing to your audience's morals. Sometimes you will use facts to support your values, but at times these presentations will be more subjective. The use of pathos or emotional appeals is usually quite effective for questions of value. Here are a few examples of questions of value:

- Pharmaceutical companies have the moral responsibility not to test their products on animals.
- It is not moral that poverty exists in the United States.
- Medical marijuana users should not be condemned by others for using a drug to reduce painful medical conditions.

Questions of value could support a presentation that aims to convince the audience it is right to join the fight against poverty in the United States.

Questions of Fact

Both questions of policy and questions of value can be supported by facts, but questions of fact are also their own type of claim. If you are trying to persuade your audience that something did or did not happen or that something is or is not true, you are dealing with a question of fact. You may be attending to a question that has several possible contradicting answers, and in that case, your goal is to persuade your audience which answer is the correct one. Or you may have a question that currently has no answer, and your job is to convince your audience that the answer you are proposing is correct. For example,

- The captain of the *Titanic* was solely responsible for the ship's untimely sinking.
- Amelia Earhart's plane did not really crash but landed safely before being captured by the Japanese army.
- Culture has more to do with gendered behavior than biology.

Look at the following list of words. Using this list, think about how you would create a question of policy, a question of value, or a question of fact for each word.

text messaging and driving	virtual reality	leadership
renewable resources	sexting	water pollution
college funding	urban poverty	movie downloads

Some topics are easier than others, but it is possible to develop a question of policy, value, and fact for each topic. No matter which type of claim your persuasive presentation is focused on, you can adopt important strategies to maximize your effectiveness. Let's explore these strategies in the next section.

CRAFTING PERSUASIVE ARGUMENTS

Once you understand the type of persuasive claim you are going to make, carefully think about how to structure the argument. Crafting a strong argument is an important part of making a persuasive appeal. In this section, you will learn about different types of persuasive arguments and how you can use them in your presentations.

Argument by Example

When you use examples as your main support for your persuasive appeal, you are using an argument by example. Imagine you are trying to persuade the members of your audience that they should vote in the upcoming election. You might start the argument by pointing out several examples in which a few votes determined the outcome of the election. This is referred to as inductive reasoning. When you use inductive reasoning, using specific examples to support a larger claim, think carefully about potential counterexamples that the audience might know in relation to your topic. Audiences like and are persuaded by examples, especially when the examples are specific to their daily lives. In your audience analysis, think carefully about examples to which the audience can relate.

MAKE —a— DIFFERENCE

NONGOVERNMENTAL ORGANIZATIONS INTERNSHIPS

How could you use communication abilities to make a better world?

BEING INVOLVED IN the community does not necessarily mean volunteer unpaid work. In fact, you can actually make a living doing community activism by persuading others for your causes. Nongovernmental organizations (NGOs) are not-for-profit organizations that typically pursue community and social aims, and these organizations often have some salaried staff. Organizations such as the American Civil Liberties Union, Amnesty International, Doctors Without Borders, Tibet Information Network, Human Rights Advocates, and the Southern Poverty Law Center are all NGOs that seek to better the world. Additionally, your city or town will most likely have several NGOs working in the community. Using your communication knowledge about persuasion, you could work for an NGO both to earn a living and make a significant contribution to your community.

In the Communication Age, NGOs have had to make the quick transition to technological means of getting their messages out to governmental agencies and the greater public. Many NGOs have college internships related to communication skills, which may be of interest to you. These internships would give you insight on whether you could create a career working in this area. Contact your community service coordinator or internship director at your school about these options, or simply Google *NGOs*. Persuading others to support worthy causes is an admirable goal.

COMMUNICATION**HOW-TO**
BASIC STRATEGIES FOR EACH QUESTION OF PERSUASION

Try to answer the following questions about your topic to determine what type of question should be asked.

Questions of Policy

1. Is the topic suggesting that an action should or should not be taken?

2. Would offering a solution best answer the implication of the topic?

Questions of Value

1. Is the topic an ethical/unethical question?

2. Does the topic address right or wrong in a morality sense?

3. Is the topic implying that something is better or worse than something else?

Questions of Fact

1. Is the topic a true/false question?

2. Did the topic happen or not happen?

3. Does the topic imply a common historical controversy?

Argument by Analogy

An argument by analogy compares different ideas or examples to reach a conclusion. The analogy might be literal or metaphorical. Take, for example, the sentence, "The Internet is like a great big shopping store." In this analogy, using the Internet to shop online is compared to shopping in a large "box" store. Or you might have heard the statement, "That relationship is like a bad sitcom." In both cases, the argument is based on the audience's understanding of the comparison. The audience needs to have a basic understanding of at least one part of the analogy for it to have a chance of being accepted and accurate.

Argument by Definition

When you use the definition of an idea or a concept as part of your persuasive appeal you are engaged in an argument by definition (Zarefsky, 2007). Generally, this is a type of deductive reasoning. You start with a general definition that makes an argument about a specific case. For example, you might be trying to persuade an audience that gay marriages should be recognized in all 50 states. You would argue that the definition of marriage involves two people regardless of sexual orientation and then apply this definition to the specific topic you are discussing. Notice how your presentation hinges upon the exact definition of the word *marriage*. Just like an argument by example, carefully think about counterdefinitions in your persuasive effort. Addressing counterdefinitions with respect, but being firm in your answers, will aid the persuasive claims.

Argument by Relationship

Argument by relationship refers to a general relationship or correlation of two ideas or concepts. In this type of argument, specific examples or cases are either related to or caused by each other. For example, if you were trying to persuade an audience that the social networking site LinkedIn is an important tool to network with future employees, you would need to demonstrate that being active on this website can lead to the possibility of future employment opportunities.

Persuading an audience that the relationship between the ideas is strong is the most important task with this type of argument. However, be careful not to confuse correlation with causation. Correlation occurs when two ideas happen at the same time but do not cause each other. Causation occurs when one thing causes the other thing. Take the LinkedIn example again. Does being active on this social network cause future employment opportunities, or is it that there is a strong correlation or relationship between the two? Arguing that it creates employment opportunities is a causation argument. Arguing that it relates but does not necessarily lead to future job sources is correlational. Research has demonstrated that telling a narrative or story that demonstrates causation can be effective in persuading others (Dahlstrom, 2010). Be careful in the ways in which you approach this issue, and make sure to have strong evidence to back up your

You could persuade your audience to get out and vote by citing examples of recent elections decided by narrow margins.

Communication unplugged
TO INSPIRE AUDIENCES, DANCE FOR CHANGE

Corbis

When we think of using persuasion for issues of social justice, we often think about a carefully crafted media or speech presentation. Often, these presentations will use the latest in high-tech wizardry to "wow" an audience. However, the human body can achieve the same effect. The Ananya Dance Theatre uses Indian dance to inspire audiences to help change the world for the better. This dance company focuses on empowering women throughout the world. After watching a performance about the dependence on oil, an audience member exclaimed, "I have to go home and throw

out everything that contains petroleum jelly!" (Wheeler, 2013). The founder of the company said that its work "is in opening the ground, creating a space for questions, for provoking discussion, and for offering images that then resonate in people's minds" (Wheeler, 2013). Watching a group of dancers tell a story with their bodies can have a powerful impact on an audience. As you think about communication, think about how body movement can tell your story.

For more about this dance company and the work they do, please see www.ananyadancetheatre.org.

WHAT TO DO NEXT

To use your body to enhance your presentations, try to:

- Find a dance group in your area that highlights some form of social justice or simply tells a story with body movement. What aspects of their performance could you modify for your own presentations?

- Watch other people speak. Evaluate how they use body movements to enhance or hinder the performance.

- Practice your presentation in front of a mirror. Be sure to pay attention to how you use your body.

claims. Always be clear with the audience about whether you are arguing for correlation or causation. Not doing so can lead to the audience questioning your credibility.

In this section, you read about the various types of arguments one can make in a persuasive effort. Persuasion is not easy and takes careful planning. Structuring arguments is an important part of this planning process. The key is to make sure the evidence fits with your approach.

STRATEGIES TO PERSUADE

After deciding how you will structure your arguments, you need to think about multiple strategies of persuasion. Relying on just one type of strategy for a persuasive effort is not effective. Depending on the topic, you might not be able to persuade an audience in one try. Rather, you might only be able to set up the audience to be more receptive to similar arguments in the future. In the following sections, you will read about various strategies used to create persuasive appeals for your presentations.

Provide Sufficiency of Evidence

The first strategy for creating a persuasive appeal is to provide overwhelming evidence that any reasonable person would have to accept your position. This is referred to as sufficiency of evidence. Is there enough evidence to support your position on a topic or an idea? What if you were trying to persuade an audience that medical marijuana should be legal in the United States? The sufficiency of evidence strategy would indicate that you should provide overwhelming evidence based on research indicating that this drug could help those in pain. In other words, provide enough evidence that most people could understand your point of view and consider your position.

What types of evidence would it take to convince some people to support medical marijuana?

Ask for a Suspended Judgment

While every audience member should suspend judgment in order to fully listen to the speaker and argument, this is usually not going to happen. If your topic is controversial or the members of your audience have strong opinions about your topic already, ask them to suspend their own judgment until after you present your arguments. You should be able to work such a statement into the introduction. You might say something like, "I know this is a controversial topic and that you might already strongly disagree with me about gay marriage. That is OK. However, just hear me out and listen to my ideas. Maybe you might change your mind a little, or maybe you will be stronger in your own beliefs. Whatever happens, we can only have a true dialogue about this important topic by listening to and respecting each other's view." Such a statement is designed to acknowledge the audience members' strong beliefs or opinions but at the same time politely ask them to simply consider the speaker's position on the topic. Often, audience members will still maintain their own positions but be more understanding toward the stated position. Perhaps your persuasive appeals will prime them the next time they hear a similar argument. As a result, the members of your audience can see what is possible when they simply listen to your ideas without immediately judging them. It is important to remember that persuasion happens in stages and almost never all at once (Kumkale, Alabarracín, & Seignourel, 2010). Each step your audience can take is a step closer to your position.

Demonstrate Cost-Benefits

By using a cost-benefits strategy, you are presenting your audience with the possible advantages of adopting your opinion, solution, or point of view. The key is to show the audience what can be gained from the presentation. The best way to do this is by first predicting what your audience's costs will be and then strategizing about how to help the audience avoid the costs and increase the positive outcome. These costs can be emotional, physical, environmental, financial, or spiritual. What does your proposed solution require of your audience? Will it cost audience members time or money? Will they have to make certain commitments or use any special skills? For example, if you argue that the price of the student health care plan on your campus will decrease if the president of the university receives enough student letters, what do you anticipate the costs for the audience will be? Writing letters takes time and energy. But if instead you bring a petition for your classmates to sign, this costs them less time and energy, therefore making the possible benefits worth the cost. Your audience will be more likely to comply with your request if the costs are low and the benefits are high.

Seek Out Micro Changes

Another strategy you can use is to seek out micro changes. Instead of asking the members of your audience to adopt the big-picture purpose, you can ask them to make small changes in their behavior. Imagine that you heard a speaker try to persuade an audience that the campus needs to create and adopt a sustainability plan. As an audience member, wouldn't you feel overwhelmed by that task? You say to yourself, "There's no way I can create a sustainability plan for this entire campus; you need a team of people to do that! Why would I even attempt such a thing?" If you anticipate this type of argument from the members of your audience, try persuading them to make one small change at a time. In this example, it may be better to ask your audience to make a commitment to stop drinking bottled water and use a reusable plastic water bottle instead. The audience members will be much more likely to accept the proposal or point of view if they are allowed to make small changes first. Small changes in one area often lead to bigger changes.

Social Judgment Theory

A strategy based on social judgment theory (SJT), developed in 1961 by Yale professors Muzafer Sherif and Carl Hovland, maintains that individuals can be

COMMUNICATIONHOW-TO
HELPING YOUR AUDIENCE SUSPEND JUDGMENT

1. Acknowledge that your topic is controversial or that the audience might disagree with your position.

2. State that you appreciate the differences between your positions.

3. If you know that a particular statement is likely to upset your audience, think carefully about toning the statement down or rewording it.

4. Politely ask the audience to listen fully to your message before passing judgment on your ideas.

5. Avoid the appearance of being aggressive or combative.

6. Demonstrate sensitivity to the beliefs of the audience.

Images: istock.

Thinkstock

ETHICAL CONNECTION OVERSELLING A BENEFIT

gave the famous "Mission to the Moon" speech, the Kennedy Presidential Library released hundreds of hours of audio of President Kennedy discussing NASA's plan to go the moon (*Daily Mail Reporter,* 2011). In these recorded conversations, President Kennedy worries with advisers about overselling the expensive moon missions to the American public. As a result, Kennedy tells his advisers that the only way to defend NASA from public scrutiny is to place a "military shield" over the reasons for going to the moon. Do you think this was a case of overselling an idea? Was it ethical to use the military as the main reason for going to the moon?

When you persuade others that the benefits of your ideas are better than a competing idea, be sure you are accurately portraying the benefits. It is unethical to oversell your idea. Be honest about the advantages and disadvantages, the costs and benefits, and the possibility of the solutions. In the Communication Age, your message can spread quite rapidly due to technology. If you oversell your solution and others point this out, you will lose credibility about the topic and as a speaker. It is almost always better to slightly undersell the benefits so that your audience will be able to make an honest assessment of the idea.

QUESTIONS

1. When have you been oversold on an idea? How did you know?

2. How did that affect your perception of the presenter and the message?

POLITICIANS sometimes promise more advantages will happen because of an idea than what is feasible or possible. In other words, politicians oversell ideas for political gain. Fifty years after President John F. Kennedy

persuaded on a topic by being convinced to accept changes that are close to their already held beliefs. When a person hears new information or opinions, she immediately places the information or opinions in one of two categories: reject or accept. However, there are many things that people would accept or reject closely related to their own beliefs. SJT argues that if you want to persuade someone, your argument must be in her or his latitude of acceptance (close to the person's own held beliefs but not exactly the same belief). Latitude of rejection occurs when the new argument is still too close to the reject category. Latitude of noncommitment occurs when the new information causes the person not to accept or reject the position but instead to maintain his or her original position. Some individuals have wide latitudes of each belief, while others have more narrow latitudes of each belief (Sung & Lee, 2015).

The latitudes act as a continuum of beliefs. Imagine you are trying to persuade an audience to adopt the position that the United States should significantly alter its immigration policy to allow for more migrant farmworkers. For some in your audience, this position would be in their latitude of acceptance. For others, this policy goal would be in their latitude of rejection. Some in the audience might not have an opinion about the policy change. Your job would be to strengthen those who support the policy change, soften the position of those who reject this position, and try to gain support from those who are in the region of noncommitment. Latitudes of acceptance, rejection, or noncommitment are involved in all of our likes/dislikes, beliefs, and attitudes.

What would you do if you were trying to persuade a person who has already placed your argument in the reject category? In this case, you would need to show that your idea or portions of your idea really fall in this person's latitude of acceptance. You might persuade the person to accept a small part of your argument. Again, persuasion is a gradual process. The next time this person hears a similar argument, she might be more willing to move her own beliefs closer to the position. You may only succeed at getting the members of your audience to better understand your position with the hope that in the future they will be more tolerant or knowledgeable. A small change could eventually lead to larger changes. If, at the end of the presentation, your audience says something like, "That seems true," "That is a persuasive argument," or "Sign me up," you have succeeded at connecting with the audience in a persuasive manner. Even if the audience does not adopt your position but understands it, some persuasion has taken place.

Persuading an audience is like the child's joke about eating elephants: "How do you eat an elephant? One bite at a time." Strategies such as sufficiency of evidence, suspending judgment, demonstrating benefits, and micro changes are all ways to increase latitudes of acceptance and decrease latitudes of rejection.

CAREER FRONTIER: SALES

HAVE YOU EVER been told you could sell anything to anyone at any time? Many college students find careers in some type of sales activity. Sales jobs have competitive salaries that attract new workers because of the possible perks and freedom afforded by some of these positions. You might be selling medical devices, computer systems, media, or even information. Many of the skills discussed in this book will help you with a career in sales. While persuasion is an important part of being successful, it is not the only part.

Relationships are key to having a successful sales career. Your customers need to trust you, your product, and your company. Building a relationship with a potential customer will go a long way toward closing the sale. Even if you do not get the sale with a particular customer, this relationship could help you later. This customer might refer someone to you or even speak about your credibility to another person. You never know how a positive relationship could help you at another time and close the sale.

Using various strategies to craft your persuasive presentation will help you have a greater impact and a wider audience. The act of persuading is not an easy thing to do in the Communication Age. Your message could potentially be seen by millions of people from all walks of life, and you must be credible. It takes time for larger social change to happen, but by engaging in small steps to persuade, you can and will make progress.

ORGANIZING YOUR PERSUASIVE PRESENTATION

Chapter 11 discussed the basic organizational pattern of a speech including the introduction, body, and conclusion. These elements are, of course, important parts of a persuasive presentation, but there are two specific types of organizational patterns you can use to make your presentation more effective. In this section, you will learn about the problem-cause-solution pattern and the Monroe's Motivated Sequence persuasive pattern. Each of these patterns is used for specific reasons related to the topic of the presentation. As you organize the presentation, think about which pattern is best for your topic.

Problem-Cause-Solution

Persuasive presentations based on questions of policy or questions of fact may best be organized in a *problem-cause-solution pattern* (see Chapter 13). Looking back at one of the examples from earlier in the chapter, you could just tell your audience that full-time students should be able to purchase student health care plans at reduced cost, but a logical question for your audience to ask is, Why? However, if you first explain the problem (students are unable to purchase health insurance) and the cause (student health insurance is too expensive) and then propose your solution (writing letters to the university president), the audience will be more likely to comply with your request. It is also beneficial to explain why the problem is a problem. Your audience may say, "So what if students can't afford health insurance?" If you support the claim with evidence that students without health insurance miss more classes per semester than do students with health insurance, the audience will better understand the reason for your speech. The problem-cause-solution pattern can easily become the three main points within the body of your speech:

Make sure you have thought about every possible angle before offering a solution.

I.   Introduction

a.   Body

b.   Problem

c.   Cause

II. Solution

III. Conclusion

ASSESS YOUR COMMUNICATION

CREDIBILITY

Communication scholar James McCroskey argues that credibility is made up of three basic areas: competence, character, and caring. You can use this measure to assess a speaker's credibility along these three areas. Think about these characteristics of credibility as you build your own persuasive presentation.

Circle the number that best represents your feelings about the speaker.

1.	Intelligent	1	2	3	4	5	6	7	Unintelligent
2.	Ethical	1	2	3	4	5	6	7	Unethical
3.	Caring	1	2	3	4	5	6	7	Uncaring
4.	Trained	1	2	3	4	5	6	7	Untrained
5.	Honest	1	2	3	4	5	6	7	Dishonest
6.	Has my interests at heart	1	2	3	4	5	6	7	Doesn't have my interests at heart
7.	Expert	1	2	3	4	5	6	7	Not an expert
8.	Unselfish	1	2	3	4	5	6	7	Selfish
9.	Concerned	1	2	3	4	5	6	7	Unconcerned
10.	Informed	1	2	3	4	5	6	7	Uninformed
11.	Sympathetic	1	2	3	4	5	6	7	Unsympathetic
12.	Understanding	1	2	3	4	5	6	7	Not understanding
13.	Competent	1	2	3	4	5	6	7	Incompetent
14.	High character	1	2	3	4	5	6	7	Low character
15.	Responsive	1	2	3	4	5	6	7	Unresponsive
16.	Bright	1	2	3	4	5	6	7	Stupid
17.	Trustworthy	1	2	3	4	5	6	7	Untrustworthy
18.	Understands how I think	1	2	3	4	5	6	7	Doesn't understand how I think

Now total your scores using the guidelines below. The scores should range from 6 to 42 for each subscale.

Competence: ADD items (1, 4, 7, 10, 13, and 16) for a total score of: _____

Character: ADD items (2, 5, 8, 11, 14, and 17) for a total score of: _____

Caring: ADD items (3, 6, 9, 12, 15, and 18) for a total score of: _____

Source: Modified from McCroskey and Teven (1999).

Monroe's Motivated Sequence

A second organizational pattern commonly used for persuasive presentations is Monroe's Motivated Sequence (see Chapter 13). In 1935, Alan Monroe developed five steps for persuading an audience to take some course of action: attention, need, satisfaction, visualization, and action. Using this persuasive organizational pattern, you try to motivate the members of your audience to support your claims by connecting their needs/wants to a plan that can satisfy those needs/wants. What about a speech about the need for greater regulations on pharmaceutical testing of animals? One might argue for increased regulations by showing there is a problem with animal testing; this would appeal to the audience's need for compassion for animals. In other words, tapping a need that the audience holds will allow the audience to accept a plan to satisfy that need.

1. *Attention.* The first step is to make the members of your audience aware of the problem and why the problem matters to them. You could present them with statistics that demonstrate the problem, or you might begin with a more emotional appeal. For example, ask each audience member to picture his first pet and then ask how he would feel if that pet were subjected to drug testing by a pharmaceutical company. This introduces the topic to the audience members and lets them know why it is relevant and why they should listen.

2. *Need.* After introducing the topic, the next step is to elaborate on the need to address the particular topic. Why is drug testing on animals such an important issue? Is it inhumane, or painful for the animals? This is a good place to support the problem with specific evidence that helps illustrate the need for a solution.

3. *Satisfaction.* The next step in the sequence introduces a proposed solution to the problem. At this point you are asking the audience members to change their beliefs or behavior and telling them how to do it. Tell them about the petition you want them to sign and explain why it will be effective. Give them the e-mail addresses and phone numbers for the pharmaceutical representatives that you want them to contact directly. Facts and evidence can also be used at this step to demonstrate the effectiveness of your proposed solution. You may tell the audience how new policies were adopted in the last year because of signatures on a petition or letters written.

4. *Visualization.* The next step lets you go beyond the proposed solution to show the members of your audience all of the positive outcomes of adopting the stated proposal. You could tell them about the number of animals that would be saved from pain or death and could instead be adopted by families who will love and care for them for the rest of their lives. This step should show the audience members what they will gain from your proposed solution.

5. *Action.* The last step is to directly ask the members of your audience to act on your proposal. Remind them of the problem and why your solution is valid and effective, and then tell them exactly what you would like them to do. Pass the petition through the audience or give members prewritten letters to

Animal rights supporters are protesting the construction of an animal testing lab at Oxford University. If you were giving a presentation on animal testing, how would you use Monroe's Motivated Sequence to help you make your argument?

read and sign. This is where you discover whether or not you have accomplished your goal of persuasion.

The problem-cause-solution pattern and Monroe's Motivated Sequence are effective methods of delivering a persuasive presentation. Choose the pattern that works best for the audience and the problem you are addressing.

SAMPLES OF PERSUASIVE PRESENTATIONS

In the following section there are two examples of persuasive outlines and an example of a persuasive presentation in full text. In the first example, you will see a full-sentence outline. The second example is a keyword outline based on the full-sentence outline. The keyword outline is what you use when you present the speech in front of your audience. The third example is the transcript of a persuasive speech with the key parts of a presentation highlighted. To watch this speech go to edge.sagepub.com/edwards2e.

SAMPLE KEYWORD PERSUASIVE OUTLINE

POVERTY

Joy Zoodsma

INTRODUCTION

I. Attention-Getting-Device—Bohn Fawkes was a B-17 pilot during World War II. Missiles did not work and saved his life. Factory worker disarmed the missiles to help war effort.

II. Thesis Statement—Poverty is a problem and we can change it.

III. Importance of Topic—Poverty impacts us all.

IV. Preview of Main Points—Today, we will discuss the problem of poverty, solutions, and a vision for a better world.

BODY

I. Poverty is a generational problem (*New York Times*, 2008).

    A. Children are directly affected, leaving future generations in dire circumstances.

        1. Poverty impacts childhood diseases (CDC, 2009).

        2. Poverty negatively affects a child's ability to learn (*Current Issues in Education*, 2003).

    B. Because of poverty, shelters and food pantries are over capacity (*Boston Globe*, 2011).

    C.   Crimes rates have increased due to issues surrounding poverty (Hsieh & Pue, 2011; Patterson, 2006).

Transition: Now that we know more about the problem, it is important that we understand how to make the first change.

II.   Need to focus on individual battles to produce change with poverty.

    A.   Donate to a local food pantry with either food or money.

    B.   Volunteer your time with shelters or pantries.

    C.   Write letters to members of Congress urging them to make poverty a priority (Bread for the World, 2011).

Transition: Now that we have discussed some solutions that we can all do, let's look at the benefits of doing something about poverty.

III.   Being aware of the problems of poverty and doing small changes will help.

    A.   Helping children learn to buy, cook, and get good food and do better in school.

    B.   Children will be less likely involved in crime (Boyes, Hornick, & Odgen, 2010).

    C.   By helping, you will directly experience a benefit by giving.

        1.   You are reminded of your own blessings.

        2.   You demonstrate compassion.

CONCLUSION

I.   Restate Thesis and Main Points—Today I've discussed the problem of poverty and some simple steps for action that you can take to create a poverty-free nation.

II.   Concluding Device—The factory worker helped the war effort by disarming a few missiles. You can do the same for poverty.

SAMPLE KEYWORD PERSUASIVE OUTLINE

POVERTY

Joy Zoodsma

INTRODUCTION

I.   Attention-Getting-Device—Bohn Fawkes was a B-17 pilot during World War II.

II.   Thesis Statement—Poverty is a problem.

III. Importance of Topic—Poverty impacts us all.

IV. Preview of Main Points—Problem of poverty, solutions, and a vision for a better world.

BODY

I. Poverty is a generational problem (*New York Times*, 2008).

   A. Children are directly affected.

      1. Childhood diseases (CDC, 2009).

      2. Child's ability to learn (*Current Issues in Education*, 2003).

   B. Shelters and food pantries over capacity (*Boston Globe*, 2011).

   C. Crimes rates have increased (Hsieh & Pue, 2011; Patterson, 2006).

Transition: Now that we know more about the problem, it is important that we understand how to make the first change.

II. Individual battles.

   A. Donate.

   B. Volunteer.

   C. Write letters (Bread for the World, 2011).

Transition: Now that we have discussed some solutions that we can all do, let's look at the benefits of doing something about poverty.

III. Being aware of the problems of poverty.

   A. Helping children.

   B. Likely involved in crime (Boyes, Hornick, & Odgen, 2010).

   C. You will directly experience a benefit.

      1. Reminded of your own blessings.

      2. Demonstrate compassion.

CONCLUSION

I. Restate Thesis and Main Points—The problem of poverty and some simple steps for action.

II. Concluding Device—The factory worker helped the war effort.

▶ **SPEECHES IN ACTION 16.1**
WATCH: Effective Persuasive Presentation

POVERTY

Joy Zoodsma
Western Michigan University

> Notice how this attention getter grabs the audience by using an interesting story.

Bohn Fawkes was a B-17 pilot during World War II who flew a number of missions over Germany. On one such occasion, his fuel tank was hit by an enemy missile, and he was forced to land the plane. Miraculously, he survived, upon which he discovered the missile had not detonated. If it had, his plane and he would have exploded immediately. Upon returning to the United States, Fawkes asked to keep the unexploded missile as a souvenir, a sign of goodwill toward him. However, upon further investigation it was found that not one but eleven missiles had hit his fuel tank. They were immediately sent off to intelligence for further investigation where it was revealed that all eleven missiles were empty, save one. The one missile contained a note, written in the Czech language, that said, "This is all we can do, for now." A courageous Czechoslovakian factory worker had disarmed the missiles and written the note. He realized he couldn't end the war, but he could save one plane, and it made a difference.

There are fewer stories that better summarize the problem of poverty. It's been an issue, and how to end it has been debated since the beginning of time, and the argument has left many frustrated, discouraged, or cynical. Yet ending poverty begins with a change within ourselves. If we each decided to take action out of a personal conviction, the world that we live in would look drastically different, for the better.

> Joy introduces the topic and shows the importance in this section.

> The speaker gives a simple but effective preview of the main points to be covered in the speech using Monroe's Motivated Sequence.

Today I will discuss the problem of poverty, the vision I have for a poverty-free world, and some simple steps for action that you can take to be the change that you wish to see in your world.

Poverty is generational. It's a cycle. The first step is summarized well in the words of Confucius, where he states, "If your plan is for one year, plant rice; if your plan is for five years, plant trees; and if your plan is for one hundred years, educate your people." The cycle of poverty and educating others about it was first introduced in the *New York Times* in a fantastic article in 2008, where it outlined that today's youth have the odds stacked against them to obtain an education and, therefore, hope for a successful future. This is not good. Children are directly affected, leaving future generations in dire circumstances.

> In this section, Joy cites recent and credible evidence to support her claims.

The Centers for Disease Control and Prevention released in 2009 new research that showed an increase in preventable childhood diseases. These diseases are just that: preventable. Yet they're still increasing. Many children receive only one full meal during the school lunch hour, while others have to go hungry during the cafeteria time. The stressors of poverty also negatively affect the children's ability to take standardized testing, in an article published in *Current Issues in Education* in 2003.

In addition, because of the increased levels of poverty in our nation, many shelters and food pantries are over capacity, as discovered by the *Boston Globe* in 2011.

> In this sentence, Joy uses an internal transition to help the flow of the speech.

Michigan Live in 2010 discovered that the largest homeless shelter in our nation is now having to limit the amount of time that a person can stay due to an increase in demand. This is adding to our homeless statistics around the nation, leaving few options for those faced with absolute poverty, unstable housing, and eviction.

The crime rates in our nation have increased as a direct result of poverty increasing as well. According to Patterson in a study done in 2006, community crime rates have a correlation with absolute poverty with poverty defined as not having the basic necessities to go on with daily life and survive. Hsieh and Pue in 2011 developed further upon that with a meta-analysis that showed a relationship between homicide, assault, and poverty.

Poverty is a rough reality to face, but fortunately, it doesn't have to end there. While it is easy to feel overwhelmed, we need to remember that our actions do make a difference. The key to winning the war is focusing on individual battles. If we all choose to open our eyes and make a difference, change will happen. By choosing to give financially, volunteer your time, or write a letter to Congress, you are effectively making the statement, "I choose to end poverty."

> The speaker transitions to potential solutions to help alleviate poverty.

The first action you can take is donating to your local food pantry. This can be with food items or financially. Both are needed. If everyone gave just one food item per week, the national food shortage would be reversed. Volunteer your time to give to shelters, whether by volunteering your time at a local soup kitchen serving food, or by changing sheets in a homeless shelter, or by delivering meals. By giving your time, you are saying to the people you are serving, "You are worth my time, and I choose to put a face on poverty as well." The third thing you can do is write letters to members of Congress urging them to make poverty solution a priority. Why handwritten letters? Simply put, because they work. There's something about the handwritten. According to the global poverty awareness organization, Bread for the World, 96% of Capitol Hill staff reported in a survey that if their member of

> Joy gives easy but concrete solutions for the audience to immediately engage in.

Congress had not reached a decision on an issue, handwritten letters would make a difference.

In this section, the speaker gives numerous advantages that could happen if the audience helped out.

Choosing to take action even in the smallest of ways will create immense benefits. By giving financially, volunteering time, or choosing to write a letter to Congress, you are taking a momentous step in creating a poverty-free nation. By donating food, we move one step closer to ending absolute poverty. In 2011, Bread for the World outlined its nutrition program, designed to help children learn how to buy, cook, and get the necessary ingredients for good nutrition, and to have the brain-power to focus in school and to get good grades. Additionally, children who have positive role models are much less likely to become involved in crime. This was done with the Boyes, Hornick, and Ogden study in 2010. By writing a letter to Congress, you are putting pressure on those in positions of power to enact change on a scale of great magnitude. Other communication media such as email are too large in volume and often pass under the radar. By giving handwritten letters, it's mandatory that they are read and logged, which guarantees that your voice will be heard.

Joy details for the audience members the personal benefits that they can expect from help. This is a great persuasive strategy.

Lastly, by choosing to be involved in ending poverty by participating in one or all of the above-mentioned ways, you yourself will directly experience the benefit. When you choose to reach out of your immediate comfort zone by participating in such programs, you are constantly reminded of how blessed you are. These experiences will help keep your priorities in check, benefiting you and those around you. Second, by taking action, you are actively demonstrating compassion, one of the threads that unites all of humanity, and it reminds those who are struggling that they are not alone in life. By choosing to invest you are effectively saying to those in need, "You are worth my time." To give and receive this kind of acknowledgement provides virtue that is difficult to put words to.

This sentence is a good transition to the conclusion.

Today I've discussed the problem of poverty and some simple steps for action that you can take to create a poverty-free nation.

The speaker closes with a review of the main points discussed, actions for the audience to do, and a strong concluding device.

You never know when you yourself might be in need one day. Today more than 49 million North Americans are living in poverty as we speak, and we have the chance to be part of the solution. Coming around the room right now is a sheet of paper with some of the web addresses for the organizations you can choose to donate to or be involved with, along with a sample letter to Congress. I urge you to take some time and think about what I've shared with you today. Together we can make a difference. Like the Czechoslovakian factory worker, we can choose to do something with what we have, for right now.

COMMUNICATION HOW-TO
TIPS FOR PERSUASIVE PRESENTATIONS

1. **Know your objectives for the presentation.** Will you persuade the members of your audience to change their attitudes on your topic completely, or will you provide them with a greater understanding of your topic?

2. **Establish your credibility early.** The introduction is the best place to demonstrate that you know what you are talking about.

3. **Make sure the audience can feel your passion and enthusiasm toward your topic.** Often this can become "catching," and your audience will be more persuadable.

4. **Use a wide range of sources and evidence.**

5. **In most persuasive presentations, propose two solutions to the problem.** One solution should focus on a larger social change that could require new laws, policies, or widespread collaboration. The other should focus on what the individual audience member could do right after the presentation to help achieve the goals you set forth (e.g., calling a politician, writing a letter, donating money to a cause).

6. **End with a strong conclusion that sums up the argument.** Leave the audience with a clear call to action.

PERSUASIVE PRESENTATIONS AND CONVERGENCE

Persuasion is an important aspect of living in society (Briñol, Rucker, & Petty, 2015). Persuading others is a tremendous task due to all the possible avenues available to reach potential audiences (Perloff, 2010). We are constantly receiving and interacting with messages that compete for our attention. At its core, persuasion is about helping meet the needs of your audience and future audiences in ethical ways. Audience analysis plays central to this task. As you develop persuasive topics, consider how the members of your audience think about the topic, how they will respond, what kinds of evidence they will consider stronger, and how you will transmit your message to encourage them to take action.

Life in the Communication Age allows us to have new ways to make an impact in our relationships, our families, our communities, and the greater world around us. We just need to figure out the best and most ethical ways to make these changes. While most of us will never have the platform that Malala Yousafzai has to connect and engage with an audience in a variety of settings, she has a lot to teach us about persuasive presentations. Her use of empathy and personal stories to persuade is a valuable resource. As you craft a persuasive presentation about a timely topic, consider all elements of the speaking process to be the most effective you can use to reach a wide audience that exists in the present moment or possibly in the future, watching you on a video. As always, strive to be ethical in your persuasive efforts so that you do not mislead or oversell your ideas.

Actress and activist Angelina Jolie gives a press conference after visiting a refugee camp. She often uses her celebrity to highlight places in the world that need support and relief.

WHAT YOU'VE LEARNED

Now that you have studied this chapter, you should be able to:

1 Describe various types of persuasive claims.

Know what type of persuasive claim you are trying to make: questions of policy, value, or fact. By knowing your type of persuasive claim, you can find the right kind of evidence to build your argument.

▶ 3 Persuasive Claims

▶ Persuasive Argument by Analogy

2 Identify ways to craft persuasive arguments.

A variety of different types of arguments (example, analogy, definition, and relationship) enhance the persuasive appeal of the message. Different types of arguments persuade different audience members. So use an appropriate variety for your topic.

 How Do You Get People to Change?

▶ Martin Luther King's I Have a Dream Speech

▶ Persuasive Techniques

3 Describe strategies to persuade audiences.

Consider the audience when you are developing your strategies to persuade. Specifically, look for the sufficiency of evidence in your presentation, ask the audience to suspend judgment, demonstrate cost and benefits, seek out micro changes, and engage in a social judgment strategy.

▶ Obama's Persuasive Speech Techniques

▶ Making a Difference through Special Olympics

▣ Foot-in-Door Technique: How to Get People to Seamlessly Take Action

4 Construct a persuasive presentation based on persuasive organizational patterns.

Organize your presentation in a recognizable pattern. Choose either the problem-cause-solution or Monroe's Motivated Sequence pattern.

▶ Sample Persuasive Speech

🎙 Inside the Message Machine that Could Make Politicians More Persuasive

 5 Explain the structure of a sample persuasive outline.

Following the basics for organizing a persuasive presentation will help your audience focus on the topic. Carefully review your outlines.

🖥 Persuasive Speech Outline Using Monroe's Motivated Sequence

🖥 Persuasive Speech Outline Templates

KEY TERMS

Review key terms with eFlashcards. **edge.sagepub.com/edwards2e**

Argument by analogy   398
Argument by definition   398
Argument by example   396
Argument by relationship   398
Causation   398
Correlation   398

Latitude of acceptance   402
Latitude of noncommitment   402
Latitude of rejection   402
Micro changes   401
Persuasion   394
Questions of fact   394

Questions of policy   394
Questions of value   394
Social judgment theory   401
Sufficiency of evidence   400

REFLECT

1. After reading both Chapter 15 ("Informative Presentations") and the current chapter ("Persuasive Presentations"), what are the differences between informative and persuasive presentations?

2. Reflecting on the different strategies to persuade, how might you persuade your employer to increase maternity and paternity leave for employers? What types of evidence would you need?

3. Think of an example of Monroe's Motivated Sequence utilized on a commercial. How would it be different if used as a public presentation?

REVIEW

To check your answers go to **edge.sagepub.com/edwards2e**

1. ___ is the altering or modifying of people's attitudes, beliefs, values, or outlook about a topic.

2. When trying to persuade an audience to change an existing attendance policy at your college, you would use questions of ___.

3. Questions of ___ are used when trying to persuade an audience that something is moral or immoral.

4. Argument by ___ compares different ideas or examples to reach a certain conclusion.

5. ___ occurs when two ideas happen at the same time but do not cause one another, while ____ occurs when one thing causes another.

6. Say a recruiter uses the definition of the word *loyalty* to persuade an audience to join the army; that person is using argument by ____.

7. What does a sufficiency of evidence mean?

8. Explain the basic idea behind social judgment theory.

9. What are the two persuasive presentation patterns?

SPEECH PLANNER

SpeechPlanner is an interactive, web-based tool that guides you through the process of planning and preparing your speech, one step at a time.

INTERVIEWING IN THE COMMUNICATION AGE

Google

← B44   Lobby

WHAT YOU'LL LEARN   After studying this appendix you will be able to:

1 Identify the basics of the interviewing process.

2 Explain how to prepare for and use common types of interview questions.

3 Describe how an interview typically is structured.

4 Describe the factors that shape the interview environment and its influence on communication.

5 Examine how best to prepare for different types of interview.

At a recent event, Google's "people operations" chief, Laszlo Bock, addressed the issue of fixing the equal pay conundrum facing women in the workforce. Bock acknowledges that there is an ingrained belief among hiring managers that men tend to negotiate more than women, which leads to discrepancies in salaries among similar jobs. However, rather than suggesting that we solve the gender wage gap by getting women to negotiate more, Bock claims that "Large companies could totally fix this problem" (McGregor, 2015). Bock asserts that when people start at Google, managers figure out what the job is worth, not the person. His remarks suggest another way companies can help solve the persistent and puzzling problem of the gender pay gap: Stop asking, "What's your salary history?"

The reasoning behind this idea is that if companies relied less on what people made at their previous jobs and more on the actual market value of the job being filled, they would be less likely to preserve the gap between men's and women's salaries. Molly Anderson, founder of the consulting firm Exponential Talent, believes that unequal salaries can be self-perpetuating; employees who negotiate a higher salary early in their career benefit for years as they get promoted or take on new jobs.

As you move through this chapter, remember that the job interview process is a foundational moment as you begin your professional career. As the preceding story indicates, the impact you make during your initial job interview can impact you financially throughout the rest of your life. Use the knowledge gained from this chapter to reflect on your past interview experiences and apply your study to potential opportunities in the future.

Of the many events that college students either look forward to or dread, the job interview is one of the most significant landmarks facing students after graduation. Both verbally and nonverbally, applicants communicate positive and negative traits to their prospective employer. Career advice author Karen Burns has published extensively over interviewing dos and don'ts. To give an idea of just how intricate the interviewing process is, Burns identified 50 of the worst (and most common) mistakes that applicants are guilty of during job interviews. Mistakes such as bad-mouthing your last boss, wearing sunglasses, talking about salary too soon, and interrupting the interviewer are just a few of the common blunders new applicants can make (Burns, 2011). Burns's book attempts to offer a comprehensive guide to being an effective interviewee.

The job interview is one of the most obvious applications for communication studies. Students of all disciplines will need to apply for a job at one time or another, so understanding the goals and motivations of an interviewer are important in gaining employment. Credentials alone will not guarantee a job offer; employers need to know that you will work well with others and can communicate information in a clear, understandable manner to your coworkers, employers, and employees.

Verbal and nonverbal communication can seriously impact professional careers (Ivy & Wahl, 2014; Quintanilla & Wahl, 2014). Being perceived as a poor communicator can result in lack of advancement, lower pay, or perhaps no employment at all. This appendix discusses the major points of interviewing in the Communication Age. As you read this material, think about your past and future interview experiences.

Employment interviews are different than they used to be. In fact, job interviews have traditionally been all about the power of the organization or hiring committee deciding to accept or reject each applicant. Contemporary views of interviewing promote more balance between job applicants and the organization. The contemporary view is that each of us should see ourselves as creative resources with skills that will help us make a difference professionally. Today, it is possible to transform yourself from a naive applicant into the right person for that job. For example, in the Communication Age, you can research the company to which you are applying and learn about its organizational culture, history, and values. You can also research the field you wish to enter in order to be prepared to answer any related questions during your interview. Have you ever heard the phrase "knowledge is power"? Well, in the instance of interviews, knowledge can make or break the experience.

Monique was preparing for a face-to-face interview at a marketing firm in Salt Lake City. The human resource manager asked her to e-mail an electronic version of her résumé for the general manager to review. After she sent the e-mail, Monique realized that she had forgotten to remove the hot link to her Instagram account that was set to share with her Twitter and Facebook accounts. Monique thought the privacy settings on all the accounts would likely protect her, but she was still concerned. This firm is well known for reviewing candidates' social networking sites to find out about prospective employees.

As you can see from Monique's experience with social media, the way people present themselves online before an interview does matter. Ever thought about how you present yourself online? Do you come across

through mediated communication in a similar way as you do when meeting people face to face? What impression will others have of you based on what you post on online social networking sites like Facebook, Instagram, Twitter, and the like? As we learned in other chapters, the Communication Age forces you to be aware of your presence both on- and offline. This is especially true if you are conducting professional business or trying to advance yourself in a competitive world. The communicative aspects of interviewing in the Communication Age are more complex because you have to consider more than "showing up" and doing well in person (Toldi, 2011). Just like Monique, you must regard many communicative aspects of interviewing that were not as important in the not-so-distant past. This appendix discusses the communicative aspects of interviewing in the Communication Age and how you can best prepare. Let's begin with the basics.

Images like this are what some employers are looking at during the hiring process. This is an example of the type of photo posted on Monique's page. Do you have any pictures posted on a social networking or related site that could be damaging prior to an interview?

BASICS OF INTERVIEWING

Interviewing, in its simplest form, is a conversation where one party gathers information by asking a second party questions. Interviews are conducted for many different reasons, such as competing for a highly desired scholarship or applying for a job you want. Interviewing will become an integral part of your life upon graduating from college. Obtaining your college degree does not automatically guarantee you a postgraduation career. You must apply yourself, and, in this process, you will be interviewed multiple times on many levels. While we realize the differences from person to person when it comes to career goals, it is important to hone your skills regardless of your major, or even if you are still undecided. As you engage in the basics of this process, take some time to inventory yourself. Be aware of your thoughts and feelings about the interview process. If you are nervous, aim for strategies that will help prepare you for an interview. If you are confident, take extra time to research the job for which you are interviewing to ensure an extra edge over your competition. Think back to your positive and negative experiences, if any, with interviewing to reinforce or correct what happened in the past. Keep your thoughts and feelings about interviewing in mind as we discuss this important topic.

Defining Elements of an Interview

There are many essential elements of interviewing that differentiate it from other types of communication. This section explains the following defining elements of an interview: interaction, process, party, purpose, and questions.

Interaction

An interview is interactional because there is a sharing or process of exchange regarding a variety of topics (Quintanilla & Wahl, 2014). If only one person is

ASSESS YOUR COMMUNICATION

EMPLOYER SURVEILLANCE IN THE COMMUNICATION AGE

Social networking once meant going to a social function such as a cocktail party, conference, or business luncheon. In the Communication Age, social networking is achieved through websites such as Twitter, Instagram, Facebook, or LinkedIn. Many individuals use these sites to meet new friends, make connections, and upload personal information. On social networking websites (SNWs) that focus more on business connections, such as LinkedIn, individuals upload job qualifications and application information. These SNWs are now being used as reference checks by human resource personnel. For this reason, SNW users, particularly university students and other soon-to-be job applicants, should ask the following questions to assess their communication via SNWs:

- Am I loading information that I want the world to see?
- Is this really a picture that shows me in the best light?
- What impression would another person have of me if he or she went through my site?

Although SNWs are a great way to be connected with friends, family, and friends-to-be, they can present problems when potential employers begin to search through them for information concerning job applicants. Many potential employees would be mortified to learn that employers could potentially read the personal information posted on Twitter, Facebook, LinkedIn, or other SNWs. Searches on SNWs allow employers to look into what is done "after hours," socially or privately, by the applicant.

Source: Roberts and Roach (2009).

talking and the other is silent, then an interview is not occurring. Rather, it would be considered a speech to an audience of one. The goal of an interview, then, is to find out more about a person beyond what is on paper. Thus, there must be a conversation that helps the employer learn more about the talent and fit of the interviewee. On the other hand, the interviewee is able to collect valuable information about the organizational mission and core values. During this interactional process, both the interviewer and the interviewee should be aware of the other's attitudes, beliefs, and so on.

An interview may involve more than two people, but it can never involve more than two parties. In this interview, one of the parties consists of a panel of interviewers.

Process

The next element of an interview is process—an interaction where new information emerges while attitudes and reactions change. As an interviewer, you might see your interviewee as likable at first, but once she or he begins talking about priorities, you might realize that this person is not appropriate for the job. It is important to remember that communication is a dynamic process where people are sending and receiving messages simultaneously. Therefore, either person can change the way things are going at any given time during the interview. It also is important to remember that the communication process cannot be avoided—this goes for interviews too. Once you walk into that room or start that videoconference, you cannot leave the interview. If you do, then you are giving up your chance to get the job.

Party

Another essential element of interviews is the party, referring to who is involved during the process. Interviews may involve more than two people, but they can never involve more than two parties: One party is offering something, and the other is trying to attain it. An example of this would be an interview to rent an apartment. Consider that you and your friend are college students who want to rent an apartment within a respected complex in town. You both must be interviewed in order to be considered potential tenants. You and your friend would be one party, while the apartment manager would be the other. In this case, you might be able to survive the interview and be viewed as credible individually, but being associated with your friend could cramp your style.

Purpose

The purpose refers to a desired outcome of the interview. In the same example, both college students could settle for on-campus housing, but they are ready to move out and gain more independence. The purpose of the interview is to give the manager the impression that they are suitable tenants. This goal differentiates interviews from random conversations with people you may or may not know. A predetermined and serious purpose distinguishes the interview from other social conversations that occur in everyday life (Quintanilla & Wahl, 2014).

Questions

Finally, questions are extremely important because they involve communication between two parties. Questions allow for information that is not readily available in print and on record. As an interviewee, it is important not only to answer, but also to ask questions. This shows that you are familiar with what the interviewer does, what the job is, what the company is all about, and the like. Bottom line, it shows the interviewer that you are passionate and have a predetermined and serious purpose.

Relational Forms of Communication

Though they may seem highly impersonal, interviews are relational forms of communication—there is a relationship between the two parties. In fact, for many, making a good connection during the process is central to landing the job. That is, if a positive connection is not made, chances are that neither party will be interested in continuing a professional relationship. This relationship may not start until the parties enter the interview, or it may have started years ago when the parties first met. If you are unfamiliar with the interviewer, you might experience high anxiety about the interview process. On the other hand, if you know the person, you might have lower anxiety because you are familiar with his or her communication style and expectations. Indeed, making a personal connection as an interviewer or interviewee is critical.

Understanding interviewing as a relational form of communication is better understood by reviewing the different relationship types. Relationships can be described as intimate, casual, or formal/distant. Intimate relationships are the close ones you experience with family, friends, and/or romantic partners. Casual relationships involve people with whom you work, classmates, teachers, and so on. Distant relationships are just like they sound in that they serve a functional nature with fairly solid boundaries established. That is, self-disclosure or exchange of personal information is not common. Rather, distant relationships focus on getting specific tasks accomplished. Think about distant relationships present in your own life. A few examples that come to mind might be customer service agents, lawyers, doctors, and perhaps college professors. Take a moment to process the different relationship types and think about where interviewing fits in. Whatever comes to mind, recognize the presence and importance of interviewing as a relational form of communication.

Relational Dimensions

The previous section established interviews as relational forms of communication. To expand on this idea that interviews are relational, there are five primary dimensions to associate with the interview process: similarity, inclusion/involvement, affection, control, and trust. Let's examine these in more detail.

Similarity

Similarity refers to shared beliefs, expectations, personality traits, and experiences. People tend to relate to others when both parties can locate common interests or habits. Upon entering an interview, one must be aware of surface-level similarities.

Just because a person dresses for the role and appears nice does not mean that he or she truly acts that way. As an interviewee trying to land a job, pay attention to nonverbal clues such as pictures of family or a book that you find interesting. Pay attention and try to identify similarity with the interviewer(s). You might also think about some positive interview activities like lunches, dinners, and coffee hours that give people an opportunity to see what they have in common.

Inclusion/Involvement

The next component is inclusion/involvement. An interview must involve some level of involvement on the part of at least one party, especially when there is a desired goal at stake. Relationships are enhanced when both parties are taking an active role in communicating. When you begin interviewing for different roles, do not take it personally when an interviewer seems focused on other tasks. Realize that there are other responsibilities and professional obligations, so try to stay positive and be flexible if there are unexpected phone calls or details that emerge during the interview process. Remember, if you are actively communicating, you can better yourself not only as a communicator, but also as a potential employee, scholarship applicant, and so on.

Affection

Affection is another relational dimension of interviews. Relationships are enhanced when there is some level of liking, warmth, and openness. In an interview, you are more likely to be comfortable and provide thoughtful responses if the interviewer is friendly. If the interviewer walked into the room, sat down, crossed his arms, and said, "What makes you so special?" with a derogatory tone, how would you react? The interviewer might be trying to use humor to make you more comfortable, so do your best to adjust to the situation. Also, try to process the experience as if you are also trying to find out information about the potential employer. Think about if this is the type of organization where you would enjoy working. In an interview, it is important to approach it in a "we" sense, rather than a "you versus the interviewer" sense. This way, there is not only interaction, but also a common sense of purpose. Of course, most interviews do not last much past 30 minutes, so do not get frustrated if you do not have enough time to become best friends with the interviewer.

Control

The next relational dimension is control. Though it may seem like the interviewer has most of the control over the interview, this is not the case. As an interviewee you have some degree of control too. You have the choice to withhold information from the employer; you can show up early to the interview to establish a positive first impression or not at all. Our point is that you have some control over the course of the interaction. There are two approaches related to control an interviewer may use when engaging in an interview. These are directive and nondirective approaches. A *directive approach* is one in which the interviewer attempts to control the aspects of the interview. Time, direction, and types of questions are a few factors that can be controlled in the directive approach. The *nondirective approach* is one in which the interviewee may have ample control over the process, including the length of his or her questions and the subject matter. Questions used in this type of approach tend to be open-ended. Keep in mind that an interviewer may choose to use a combination of these two approaches.

Trust

The final relational dimension in interviews is trust. Trust is extremely important in communication and in interviews. For a first-time interview, it is very unlikely that you would know the interviewer. Thus, you must enter the interview with some level of established trust. Most interviewers are there for a reason, so you should give them the benefit of the doubt and trust that they are competent and focused on treating you fairly. It is especially important to have trust during interviews because the outcomes can directly impact you, such as the income and benefits that come with the job you are trying to land. We understand that anticipating an interview and having a clear sense of what to expect can often be complicated. We suggest you ask yourself several questions to help you prepare (see "Communication How-To").

This section focused on the basics of interviewing including the essential elements and relational qualities of the process. Now that you have studied the basic mechanics of interviewing, the next section explores the types of questions that can be expected.

TYPES OF QUESTIONS

Does planning for an interview seem like a stressful task? What questions will the interviewer ask? What's the best answer? Should you say what's really on your mind or go with the "safe answer"? Knowing the types of questions to expect is critical when preparing for an interview. Interviewers choose a variety of different questions to obtain information from their interviewees. The format of the question can produce a different response. Some of the most common types of questions

---

COMMUNICATION**HOW-TO**
QUESTIONS TO HELP YOU PREPARE FOR
THE INTERVIEW EXPERIENCE

1. What are my greatest strengths?

2. What are my greatest weaknesses?

3. What do I know about this organization?

4. Where do I really want to work?

5. Why do I want to change jobs?

6. What do I expect as far as salary?

7. Where do I see myself going in the next few years?

8. What makes me stronger than other applicants?

are open-ended, closed, primary, secondary, probing, neutral, leading, and hypothetical. By exploring and being aware of different types of interview questions, you will be better prepared for the interviewing experience.

Open-Ended Questions

Open-ended questions allow respondents flexibility in answering a question about a specific topic (Chang & Krosnick, 2010; see also Chapter 11). There are different levels of open questions. For example, highly open questions basically have no restrictions on the possibilities of answers. Moderately open questions have some limitations but generally give respondents freedom to answer. Open-ended questions are useful in interviews because they allow candidates the time and space to speak their mind and to offer up information. The length of time a respondent talks in response to a single question might show the interviewer how educated the person is. A few examples of this type of question include the following:

- Tell me about your experiences at your last job.
- Describe your experiences with employee motivation.
- Tell me about your ideal career.
- What led to your interest in management?

Be careful when answering open questions because sometimes responses can run longer than you might expect. You do not want a single question to take up the entire interview period!

Closed Questions

Closed questions are the opposite of open questions (see Chapter 12). They are narrow in focus and limited in terms of possible responses. As with open-ended questions, closed questions come in varying degrees. Highly closed questions generally induce a specific response. Moderately closed questions generally ask for specific pieces of information. An interviewer can use closed questions to better control the interview, but these types of questions do not allow for much information to be expressed. An interviewer might ask closed questions if the focus is on basic functions of the position. These basic functions can be addressed with brief responses. A few examples of closed questions include the following:

- Are you willing to travel?
- Do you know how to use Excel?
- Did you manage employees at your last job?
- Are you willing to manage more than one department?

The most extreme example of a closed question is the bipolar question, commonly known as a yes-or-no question. These questions have only two possible answers, which happen to be polar opposites, such as yes and no. Some examples of this type of question are

- Did you quit your last job?
- Are you going to attend the optional training today?
- Were you aware of cheating going on in this classroom?
- Did you read the job description carefully?

If you encounter bipolar questions, try to stay focused and provide honest and confident responses. Interviewers are not trying to set you up or make you fail the job interview, but keep in mind that questions are included for a reason—questions that seem awkward or difficult to respond to can often provide the interviewer with important information about you. This information may reflect the exact skill set needed to make a successful hiring decision.

Primary Questions

Primary questions are usually prepared prior to the meeting to introduce a list of key topics the interviewer wants to discuss with each candidate. Examples of primary questions can include the following:

- What led to your interest in training and development?
- In what ways has your business degree prepared you for this management position?
- What experience do you have with budget development?
- What is your leadership philosophy?

Depending on the career and industry you are interested in pursuing, you should do your best to anticipate primary questions that are directly related to the position. One quality of the Communication Age that makes it fairly easy to prepare for interviews is the ability to access sample interview questions online. Predicting interview formats and the exact questions you will encounter is difficult, but think about your strengths and weaknesses as well as what skills you bring to the table that will help you to succeed in the position for which you are interviewing. For example, if you are interviewing for a management position, you can probably anticipate primary questions about your management style or philosophy. Furthermore, if the job description mentions knowledge of particular types of computer software or research skills, you can expect primary questions about your competencies in those areas.

Probing Questions

Probing questions are used by interviewers to prod for additional information about the candidate. These questions typically follow a primary question. Probing questions are related to primary questions in that they are used to follow up on responses to primary questions. Job candidates can prepare for probing questions by preparing to offer more details about past work experience, education, and the like. For example, a primary question would be "Tell me what you know about our company." A probing question could take a spin on something the interviewee said in the initial response, such as "Tell me more about that." Review Figure A.1 to explore the variety of probing question types.

Silent Probes	Remaining silent for a few moments; use of nonverbals.
Nudging Probes	"And?" "So?" "Uh-huh?"
Clearinghouse Probes	Encourage respondents to volunteer information; "What else can you tell me about _____?" "Is there anything else I need to know about _____?"
Informational Probes	Attempt to get additional information; "What do you mean about that?" "What do you mean when you say _____?"
Restatement Probes	Restating all or part of the original question.
Reflective Probes	Reflects the answers just to verify or clarify.
Mirror Probes	Similar to the reflective probe but summarizes a series of answers.

FIGURE A.1
TYPES OF PROBING QUESTIONS

Neutral and Leading Questions

In addition to the probing questions covered in the previous section, you should be prepared to encounter neutral and leading questions. As you continue to review the different types of interview questions, realize that any interview will likely include a variety of questions. However, it is difficult to predict if every interview will present every type of question. Therefore, having an understanding of the wide variety of interview questions will only make you better prepared. *Neutral questions* allow the respondent freedom to answer without influence from the questioner (see Chapter 12). Examples of neutral questions can include the following:

- Why did you decide to major in chemistry?
- What are your thoughts on employee development opportunities?
- What do you think about our mission statement?
- Describe the qualities of your previous leadership team.

Leading questions exert some type of influence or pressure on the respondent to answer in a particular way allowing room for an interviewer bias (see Chapter 12). One type of leading question is the loaded question—extremely leading questions that provide strong direction toward the expected answer. Examples of leading questions include the following:

- Why didn't you major in biochemistry instead of chemistry?
- You support employment development opportunities, right?
- Don't you just love our mission statement?
- What did you dislike about your previous leadership team?

Hypothetical Questions

Hypothetical questions allow interviewers to present a possible situation and ask interviewees how they would react. Such questions allow the interviewer to determine how well the candidate can act under pressure and make a quick decision. It might be surprising to some of you that hypothetical questions are common during the interview process. As we have already said, it is difficult to predict the types of questions to expect during an interview. Keep the following examples of hypothetical questions in mind as you prepare for an interview:

- What would you do if you discovered that one of your employees was viewing porn on the company computer?

- What would you do if a coworker was texting you rumors about another colleague?

- If you received a Facebook friend invitation from one of your employees, would you accept it?

- How would you respond if several coworkers approached you regarding rumors about a workplace romance?

Illegal Questions

Hopefully you will never encounter an interviewer who asks illegal questions, but you should prepare just in case. These are questions related to factors about which

FIGURE A.2
ILLEGAL QUESTIONS

Illegal Job Interview Topics
NATIONALITY
Are you a U.S. citizen?
RELIGION
What is your religion?
AGE
How old are you?
MARITAL AND FAMILY STATUS
Do you have kids? Are you married?
GENDER
Do you think you can handle this job since you're a woman?
HEALTH AND PHYSICAL ABILITIES
Do you smoke or drink?

employers may not ask during the hiring process such as race, religion, or disability. Therefore, interviewers legally cannot ask questions related to these categories (review Figure A.2; see also Figure A.3 for a list of legal job interview questions).

This section focused on the different types of interview questions, including illegal questions. Having an understanding of the different types of interview questions will give you a general sense of what to expect during the process. Now that you have studied the basic types of interview questions, the next section explains the structure of the interview.

STRUCTURE OF THE INTERVIEW

As Monique prepares for her interview, she tries to envision each stage of the meeting. She plans on receiving an interview schedule, but will be sure to ask for clarity if times are not specified. Each stage of the interview serves a purpose, and the first few moments are crucial for a positive first impression, so being prepared is essential.

This is the moment where what you say and do matter the most. First impressions are extremely important when interviewing. Remember that you are being interviewed

FIGURE A.3
LEGAL QUESTIONS

Examples of Legal Job Interview Questions
PERSONAL INSIGHT
What really motivates you?
ADAPTING TO THE ENVIRONMENT
Describe a recent example of a challenging situation on the job. How did you respond?
LISTENING SKILLS
How would others describe your listening skills?
CONFLICT MANAGEMENT
How do you handle conflict?
CUSTOMER SERVICE
How do you problem-solve with angry customers?
PEOPLE SKILLS
What do you do to build rapport with your coworkers?
TIME MANAGEMENT
How do you manage your time when working on multiple projects?
TEAMWORK
How would others describe your contributions as a team member?

RESPECTING SELF AND OTHERS IN THE INTERVIEW CONTEXT

When an interviewer asked Marco, "I see you worked for the LGBTQ Teen Support Council—are you a homosexual?" he was not sure how to respond. There are several ways Marco could respond to such a question. First, he could answer it directly and move on by saying, "Yes, I am gay, but that will not interfere with my job performance." He could follow his response with a question of his own, such as, "Yes, I am gay. Why do you ask?" He could use humor to deflect the question: "Is this a test to see if I know which questions are illegal?" Or he could refuse to answer: "I don't see how a question about my sexual orientation is relevant to my qualifications." What's the correct way to handle it? Although many students might prefer to use one of the last three approaches, they may fear doing so will hurt their chances of getting the job. Regardless of how you answer the question, make note of what occurred from an ethical perspective. If you believe your answer negatively impacted your chances of being

hired, then you have a discrimination case on your hands. If offered the job, you may decide not to accept because the question indicated a hostile work environment. At the very least, you should report this behavior to someone higher up in the organization. Despite the choices new media provide in support of the hiring and job search process, Marco's experience with an unethical question during a face-to-face interview serves as a reminder that things can go wrong in any interview format.

QUESTIONS

1. In what ways did the interviewer's communication fail to respect self, others, and surroundings?

2. Can you think of other ways for Marco to represent self-ethically in response to a question about his sexual orientation?

during every interaction with the organization, whether it is with the official interviewer or not (Quintanilla & Wahl, 2014). The sections that follow explore the overall structure, including the opening, body, and closing of the interview experience.

The Opening

Two of the most important aspects of the interview opening are first impressions and establishing rapport. Let's take a moment to review these two important communication skills.

First Impressions

There is a sense of territoriality or control over particular spaces in interviews. If you are sent to someone's office for the interview, do not just walk in; knock first and wait to be called in. Physical appearance—the way your body and general appearance send messages to others, helping to form certain perceptions—is extremely important, especially for first impressions (Ivy & Wahl, 2014). Have you ever been told by your parents or a teacher to "dress for the job you want, not the job you have"? While many of us do not like to admit that our parents were right, it definitely is true. The way you look in an interview can either make you or break you, no matter how great your résumé is or how qualified you are for the position. Professional touch is also important during interviews. For example, as the interview begins, it is customary to shake hands with the interviewer. If you have a very weak handshake, the interviewer may see that as a sign that you are a weak person. However, you do not want to crush your potential employer's hand with a death grip. It may seem silly, but practicing handshakes may benefit you later on in life. Clearly, being aware of both your verbal and your nonverbal communication will help shape a positive first impression during the interview process (see the following "Communication How-To").

Establishing Rapport

Rapport is a process of establishing trust and comfort during the interview process using self-introductions and simple greetings, among other practices. The second phase is to orient the other party. This is where you become familiar with the other party by explaining the purpose of the interview, how the interview will work, and so on. An example of the rapport and orientation process is illustrated here:

Something as simple as a handshake in the first few moments of an interview can be extremely important.

Interviewer:	Good morning, Monique. Were you able to find the building without any problems?
Monique:	Good morning! Yes, I just followed the directions you e-mailed to me, and the traffic was not bad at all.
Interviewer:	Let's begin by you talking about why you are interested in the position.
Monique:	I am looking to learn from someone like you who has a lot of experience in the business. I am also attracted to the mission and core values of the company.
Interviewer:	That's good to hear. We are really proud of our mission and core values. Is there a particular value that stands out to you?
Monique:	Yes, community service is something I'm passionate about. I would be interested in the service programs that your business sponsors.

As you can see from this example, Monique and the interviewer have established some sort of rapport. This initial rapport and first impression are extremely important and should be maintained as the interview progresses.

COMMUNICATION HOW-TO

GETTING IN THE ZONE FOR YOUR INTERVIEW

 1. Arrive to the interview at least 10 minutes early.

 2. When waiting for your interview to begin, show patience and professionalism.

 3. Treat everyone from the receptionist to the general manager with the same level of professionalism and respect.

 4. When you meet the interviewer, make direct eye contact and be prepared to shake his or her hand.

 5. Turn your cell phone or smartphone to silent.

Images: istock.

Now that you have an understanding of the importance of first impressions and establishing rapport in the opening of this process, the next section examines the body of the interview.

The Body

The body of the interview experience provides information to the interviewer in terms of content, fit, demeanor, skills, motivation, and the like. This is where specific questions are asked and information is exchanged about the position. An interviewer might use an *interview guide*—an outline of topics used to maintain structure during the process (Stewart & Cash, 2008). The types of interview questions we reviewed earlier in this chapter can certainly be expected, but it also is important to pay attention to the "what" and "how" of your communication.

During the course of the interview, try to monitor the quality of both your verbal communication and your nonverbal communication (Ivy & Wahl, 2014; Quintanilla & Wahl, 2014). Avoid speaking too quickly and littering your responses with vocal fillers (e.g., "um," "ah," "like," "you know"). Sit up straight, and maintain eye contact. If you are asked a question that you need a moment to consider, take the time you need to gather a response. Remember, nonverbal cues do impact interviewer ratings in business and professional contexts.

Central to being a good interviewee is being an engaged listener (Ivy & Wahl, 2014; Quintanilla & Wahl, 2014; Wahl & Scholl, 2014). Focus on each question that is being asked. If you are unclear as to the meaning of a particular question, ask for clarification. If you are asked a question with multiple parts, make a mental note of each part and then begin to answer. If you have prepared and practiced, you will be ready to answer the questions. In your answers, include as much of the information you have practiced as possible. Ask the follow-up questions you have prepared. Know that your preparation and practice will make you stand out as a candidate.

Remember to remain positive about your qualifications, experiences, former employers, major/field, the job, and the organization. It is important to remain positive even when discussing weaknesses or failures. This can be accomplished by discussing a weakness or failure that will not affect you in this position.

The Closing

The closing is as important as the opening. During this stage, the interviewer will summarize the major points you have covered. Once this is accomplished, there generally is time to ask questions. If you are unsure of something that was discussed or if you have any questions about the position, the company, or anything else, this would be the time to ask. When the interview ends, be certain to thank your interviewer verbally. Once you return home, formalize your thank-you with a card. But remember that a handwritten thank-you card is not the only kind of touch that will make you stand out from others competing for the job. If you have been communicating with the interviewer electronically, then you can send the thank-you message using the same medium.

After a personal thank-you, it is a good idea to agree on some form of follow-up. Typically, employers will either arrange for another meeting or let you know of a decision in a few days. If this is the case, make sure you keep track of the days. If the interviewer does not get back to you, then call to follow up yourself. There are a lot of reasons for a delay: The interviewer may be interviewing more candidates or simply is busy. If any additional information was requested during the interview, get that information to your potential employer immediately. This will demonstrate your enthusiasm for the position and your attention to detail. Remember, the job search process can take time, so be patient as it may take a while for an employer to get back to you after an interview. Avoid calling and sending numerous e-mails or text messages if you have already followed up.

The previous section explained the basic structure of the interview. The section that follows looks at the importance of environment—that is, the context or location where the interview occurs.

THE INTERVIEW ENVIRONMENT

Context is everything when it comes to communication. Time, place, people, surroundings, and many other factors all influence the communication process (Quintanilla & Wahl, 2014; Wahl & Scholl, 2014). This is also the case for the interview environment—the built or natural spaces or settings where interviews take place (Ivy & Wahl, 2014). Before meeting, both parties already have some perception of what will happen and what the other party will be like, as well as some sense of where the interview will be conducted. Some interviewers may have a predetermined idea of what the candidates will be like just from reading their

Communication unplugged

TO IMPROVE JOB INTERVIEWS, STRIVE FOR NONMEDIATED COMMUNICATION EXCELLENCE

In the current landscape of the workplace, many job interviews begin online (electronically searching for a job, electronically uploading a résumé/cover letter, etc.) and end online as well. However, practicing effective nonmediated communication during the interview can mean the difference between landing a job or not. One study examined interviewee nonverbal cues during a simulated job interview. The feedback received from interviewers indicated that nonverbal behavior significantly predicts hiring decisions. Job applicants were more likely to be hired when gazing more at the recruiter and by having longer average speaking-time terms than other interviewees (Frauendorfer, Schmid, Nguyen, & Gatica-Perez, 2014). These, combined with other positive nonverbal cues, have been cited by more and more interviewers as having significant influence on their hiring decisions.

In this Communication Age, we run an alarming risk of relying too much on computer-mediated communication for our everyday needs. Despite an increasing focus on the "global

community" and the idea of online interconnectivity, many of our important relationships (social or professional) still rely on being effective face-to-face communicators.

WHAT TO DO NEXT

When participating in a face-to-face interview, remember to:

- Relax and lean forward a little toward the interviewer so you appear interested and engaged.

- Make eye contact with the interviewer for a few seconds at a time.

- Not sure what to do with your hands? Hold a pen and your notepad or rest an arm on the chair or on your lap, so you look comfortable.

- Be polite and keep an even tone to your speech. Don't be too loud or too quiet.

Interviews take place in many different environments and locations.

résumés or talking to them on the phone. Perceptions go beyond the person and include the other details of the event such as the place. The interview may take place in the interviewer's office, where he or she feels comfortable. On the other hand, the interviewee might not feel comfortable because of power differences.

There might be a certain time the interview will turn out best. For example, engaging in an interview at 4:30 p.m. might not be wise, considering that most people will consider the workday almost over. The interviewer might be more concerned about getting through the workday and getting home than actively engaging in the process. Mondays tend to be down periods because people are just getting back into the work cycle after the weekend. Fridays also tend to be down periods because of the impending weekend. The time of year and the place also affect certain types of interviews. Locations can be considered "turfs." Each party would prefer a "home field" advantage, but choosing a neutral location might lead to more interaction. Surroundings can also affect the interview. For example, a professor with all of her degrees on the wall behind her shows credibility to the candidate. Noise is generally a negative factor in interviews. Noise is something that interferes with the communication process. Examples of this would be the phone constantly ringing, cell phones vibrating, coworkers stopping by the office, or even an overly loud air-conditioning unit. Another force at play in the interview environment is proxemics (the communicative dimensions of space). Space- and distance-related seating arrangements during interviews can have a positive or negative influence. Think about what would make you comfortable in an interview setting.

As a job candidate or the person conducting the interview, remember the important role environment plays during the process. The next section examines the different types and styles of interviews.

TYPES OF INTERVIEWS

There are many different types and styles of interviews. Think about the different kinds of interviews you have experienced. Some of the most common interviews are employment interviews, mediated interviews, counseling interviews, information-gathering interviews, probing interviews, survey interviews, and performance interviews.

The Employment Interview

As a recent college graduate, the employment interview will be the most important to you. A bachelor's degree does not automatically guarantee you a job the day after you graduate. Employment interviews must be taken seriously, especially when they involve the job you want the most. As part of your preparation, attend job fairs on college campuses when they come around. During these fairs, career counselors sometimes offer sessions on interviewing and résumé writing. Typically the business schools, if your university has one, also offer sessions related to interviewing and preparation of your credentials. There are many other sources available to you related to interviewing, including books, business forums, and the Internet.

One of the main things you should do prior to your interview is your homework. This includes researching your field, the organization, the recruiter, the position, current events, and the hiring process. When researching your field, you want to keep an eye out for the education, training, and experience that are critical to the field you wish to enter. As part of your research, do a background check on each of the organizations so you will be familiar with them. The *recruiter* is the person who is attempting to recruit someone into a position. In other words, this is the person who will be conducting your interview. Though you may not be able to find out who will be doing this, if you can, try to find out as much professional information about the recruiter as you can. You definitely want to research the position for which you are applying. You will want to know just about everything this position will require of you, including duties, responsibilities, training, and so on. By doing this, you are better preparing yourself for potential questions that may arise during the interview. You should research current events because most employers want their employees to know what is going on in the world, especially if the event directly or indirectly affects the organization to which you are applying. A few good sources of current events are the news, online news, *Newsweek, Time, Bloomberg Businessweek, Fortune,* and *The Wall Street Journal,* plus many others. Last, it is important to research the interview process. Basically, you want to know what you are getting yourself into.

The manner in which you prepare your credentials can also affect whether or not you get the job. Interviewers can generally see how much time and effort you put into your résumé or portfolio just by looking at it. Consider your credentials an extension of yourself. They are you, only in print. Would you want yourself to look sloppy? Would you want to be seen as incomplete and incompetent by others? If you answer no to either of these questions, then you understand the importance of credentials.

Your résumé is the first chance an interviewer/recruiter has to see you. Remember, your résumé is a written sales pitch of you. This document provides a picture of who you are as an employee by highlighting your talents (see the following "Communication How-To"). An excellent résumé highlights the skills you possess that are relevant to the position for which you are applying. You might be thinking, "What's the best format for my résumé?" Remember, there is no one standard form for a résumé—there are a number of styles and formats you should consider. When selecting the format for your résumé, choose one that will highlight your strengths and downplay your weaknesses. Regardless of which format you select, you should customize your résumé to each position and organization. Although formats vary, every résumé should not exceed a single page and must be visually appealing.

More than likely, you will be applying for multiple positions while you are job searching. Therefore, it is important to develop a generic résumé that you can use as a starting point to work toward a customized résumé unique to each position for which you apply.

It is important to consider your résumé as an extension of self. This is the document that tells an employer why you are the right person for the job.

iStock

Mediated interviews are becoming more common in the
Communication Age.

If you work in the fields of photography, advertising, marketing, public relations, art, design, fashion, journalism, or architecture, your portfolio is an extension of your résumé. This is where you can actually include samples of your work for employers to view. In the portfolio you want to include a small sample consisting of your best work. The cover letter is the first thing employers will see (if you include one), so it must grab their attention and make them want to read it (see "Communication How-To: What Do I Include in My Cover Letter?"). It is best to address your cover letter to a specific person who will be involved in your interview process.

Mediated Interviews

In the Communication Age, mediated interviews are becoming more common with the technological advances that have been made in the past couple of decades (Chang & Krosnick, 2010; Toldi, 2011). With the emergence of telephone interviews, there is no longer a need to meet in person. Conference calls are one common practice that allows for multiple people to be in on a call at once. Telephone interviews are often used during the early screening phases of the interview process. Cell phone/smartphone interviews take place anywhere, anytime, allowing you to be in your dorm, in your office, or in just about any other location as long as you have cell phone reception. When doing a phone interview, remember to block the call-waiting feature if you have it. Using a landline is preferred to using a cell phone/smartphone. However, if you only have access to a cell phone, make sure the battery is charged. Never chew gum, smoke, eat, drink, or use the bathroom during a phone interview because the noise will be picked up on the other end of the line. When you have finished your answer, wait for the next question. Even if it takes the interviewer(s) a moment or two to ask the next question, do not try to fill that silence (Quintanilla & Wahl, 2011). The problem with telephone formats is that they seem impersonal and can be awkward—you cannot see the candidate's appearance or nonverbal cues.

 Videoconferencing has become a more common means to interview, especially for companies with locations across the globe (Chang & Krosnick, 2010; Toldi, 2011). With software like Skype or Google Hangouts, videoconferencing is relatively inexpensive, enables the parties to see one another, and allows interactions

COMMUNICATION**HOW-TO**
WHAT DO I INCLUDE IN MY RÉSUMÉ?

1. Name and contact information

2. Career objective

3. Education and training

4. Experiences

5. Skills

6. Activities

to occur globally. Rather than meeting face to face or voice to voice, people are meeting with a webcam connection and a simple mouse click. It allows people to communicate anytime and anywhere.

Other Interview Types

The selection interview may occur when you are being evaluated for promotion or selected for an academic award, a scholarship, or admittance to a graduate program. For example, if you apply for a scholarship and the selection committee needs to meet with each of the top applicants in order to choose a winner, this would be a selection interview.

Similar to a survey interview, an information-gathering interview occurs whenever you are seeking facts or opinions. For this type of interview, responses from a sample of a population are collected to disclose information about the larger population. Survey interviews must collect data from a representative sample of the population in question.

Performance interviews, also referred to as performance reviews, are usually conducted on an annual basis in a variety of industries to review employee performance. This type of interview usually involves a supervisor addressing both positive and negative aspects of the employee's performance.

If problems across organizational contexts emerge, problem-solving interviews are sometimes used by external consultants or members of the management team to describe a problem and work toward a solution. For example, if customer service ratings are low, an organization may choose to use problem-solving interviews with customers and/or employees. Information taken from these interviews about customer service breakdown can be utilized to help increase customer service scores.

Upon separation from the organization, exit interviews are conducted with the hopes that departing employees will provide candid feedback about their workplace experience. This feedback can then be used to improve the organization.

Last, helping interviews are always conducted by experts in a particular area. For example, design consultants could use a helping interview format to help homeowners having a difficult time selling a property. Counselors, doctors, and legal specialists all use helping interviews to take an inventory of a problem and then provide informed advice to help address the given concern.

COMMUNICATIONHOW-TO
WHAT DO I INCLUDE IN MY COVER LETTER?

1. Write the letter to a specific person

2. Refer to the position for which you are applying

3. Provide a summary of your qualifications and refer to your résumé

4. Emphasize interest in the position and ask for an interview

5. Conclude with a positive and professional tone

6. Education and training

7. Experiences

8. Skills

9. Activities

FIGURE A.4
SAMPLE RESUME

James T. Cox

1111 Airline Rd.

Corpus Christi, TX 78412

jtcox123@yahoo.com

Cell: 361-123-4367

Career Objective: To seek challenging assignment and responsibility, with an opportunity for growth and career advancement in the media industry.

SKILLS/TRAINING

Experienced writer for NCAA Division – I athletic programs

Experienced sports announcer and scorekeeper

Computer skills - Highly Proficient - 11+ Years Experience

Spanish (bilingual) - Proficient - 3 Years Experience

EDUCATION

Texas A&M University-Corpus Christi	Degree anticipated May 2016

Bachelor of Arts in Communication - Media Studies

Coursework:

Media News Writing and Performance	Web and Graphic Design
Technical Writing	Journalism
Voice and Diction	Media and Technology

RELEVANT WORK EXPERIENCE

United Championship Wrestling	Corpus Christi, TX
Ring Announcer/Commentator/Webmaster	May 2014-Present

Announcing wrestling competitors to/from arena and winners at the conclusion of the contest.

Conducting play-by-play commentary on wrestling matches for DVD purposes.

Light webpage design duties.

Maintaining the Facebook page and supporting websites with current information.

TAMU-CC Recreational Sports	Corpus Christi, TX
Official/Scorekeeper	Jan 2013 – Present

Officiating and scorekeeping games for Basketball, Dodgeball, Flag Football, and Volleyball.

TAMU-CC Island Waves Student Newspaper	Corpus Christi, TX
Sports Editor	July 2041-March 2015

Researched and wrote sports stories for NCAA Division – I athletic programs

Copy edited content

Light page designing duties

Worked effectively under heavy deadline pressure.

Source: Adapted from Quintanilla and Wahl, 2014

To: Rosalinda Garcia
From: James T. Cox
Date: January 17, 2016
RE: Network Studio Host, XYZ Studios

Dear Ms. Garcia,

    I am writing in regard to the position for a Network Studio Host at XYZ Studios in Laredo. Having reviewed the requirements and duties I believe I am an ideal candidate for this position.

    For the past four years, I studied Communication-Media at Texas A&M University-Corpus Christi. My education developed and honed the skills needed to be a successful on-air personality and an asset to your radio station. I will graduate in May 2013 with outstanding oral and written communication skills. In addition, I am highly proficient with computers, having demonstrated my web savvy both in the classroom and on the job.

    Clearly, my experience for this position extends beyond the classroom. While pursing my degree, I have worked as an on air announcer for United Championship Wrestling, broadcasting play-by-play commentary for DVD recordings. I have provided in-game scoreboard updates for a variety of sports. Furthermore, I am an experienced sports writer for an NCAA Division-I athletic program.

    By taking a full course load every semester and working full-time I have proven my strong work ethic and time management skills. I pride myself on my professionalism, dedication, and flexibility. I thoroughly enjoy working in the fast-paced environment provided by on-air sports broadcasting and I look forward to discussing my qualifications with you further. Thank you for this opportunity.

Sincerely,

James T. Cox

Source: Adapted from Quintanilla and Wahl, 2014

INTERVIEWING AND CONVERGENCE

Similar to every chapter you have read in this textbook, remember to connect your study of interviewing to convergence in the Communication Age. As you think back to Monique's experience preparing for a face-to-face interview, consider how new media can both help and hinder the interview experience. You learned from Monique's experience that new media can have a huge impact on interviews (both face-to-face and mediated ones).

The Communication Age enables employers to conduct searches of you online before they meet you face to face. Do your best to manage this blending of your virtual and face-to-face lives. As you get more familiar with the interviewing process in the Communication Age, consider how you present yourself online and face to face. Also, remember to prepare for a mediated interview in the same way you would a face-to-face one. As you prepare for mediated interviews in the Communication Age, consider the advantages and disadvantages. If you get nervous using new

Thinkstock

CAREER FRONTIER: BEHAVIORAL JOB INTERVIEWING STRATEGIES

BEHAVIORAL INTERVIEWING is a popular method of job interviewing. Companies such as AT&T and Accenture have used behavioral interviewing since the 1970s, and knowing how to excel in this situation is beneficial to the job hunt. The premise behind behavioral interviewing is that the most accurate predictor of future performance is assessing an interviewee's past performance in similar situations (Hansen, n.d.). In a traditional job interview, you generally tell an interviewer what they want to hear. Even when they do ask situational questions such as "How would you handle XYZ situation?" how can the interviewer know you would really react in a given situation the way you say you would?

In behavioral interviews, it's much more difficult to give responses that are untrue to your character. The employer structures very pointed questions to elicit detailed responses with the goal of determining if the candidate possesses the desired characteristics. Questions (often not even framed as questions) typically begin like: "Talk about

a time . . ." or "Describe a situation . . .", which are then evaluated using some type of rating system (Hansen, n.d.). Ideally, you should describe the situation, what specific action you took, and the positive result or outcome, usually a three-step process called an S-A-R statement:

1. Situation (or task, problem)

2. Action

3. Result/outcome

ISSUES TO CONSIDER

1. Given the huge number and variety of possible behavioral questions you could be asked, what strategies could you employ to be better prepared for most questions?

CONNECTING ORAL HISTORY TO INTERVIEWING

INTERVIEWING GOES BEYOND the function of landing a job. Your skills as an interviewer or experience as an interviewee can foster active engagement and participation with the past and present. Much of what we learn through history and scholarship comes from interviews with individuals who have firsthand experiences. If you are interested in finding out more information about yourself, your family, or other communities and cultures, you might consider learning more about oral history as an educational resource and research skill. The American Century Oral History Project is one example of an organization that celebrates oral history as a way to actively engage self, culture, and community. The interaction that takes place within interviews allows for an individual to

experience an aspect of another's history. When listening to the answers given, people then have a better understanding of the actual meaning being shared throughout the interview. As an interview continues, knowledge is shared between the communicators. The actual content of the information being shared is expressed through the unique voice of the individual. This brings forth a better understanding of another individual's standpoint. Interviews allow for a deeper understanding through nonverbal communication. We are able to pick up certain nonverbal cues that allow us to better understand the oral histories being shared during an interview. To learn more about oral history and the American Century Oral History Project, visit the organization's website, doingoralhistory.org.

media (e.g., social networking, Skype), remember to seek advice regarding how best to prepare. Can you think of other ways in which interviews are influenced by new media? Remember to carefully consider both the opportunities and the challenges convergence brings to the interviewing process. Your study of interviewing is applicable to both your face-to-face and your mediated communication experiences in the Communication Age.

WANT A BETTER GRADE?

Get the tools you need to sharpen your study skills.

Access practice quizzes, eFlashcards, video, and multimedia at **edge.sagepub.com/edwards2e.**

WHAT YOU'VE LEARNED

Now that you have studied this chapter, you should be able to:

1 Identify the basics of the interviewing process.

The interview process is relational. Interviewing is a form of communication that supports personal and professional success.

 Mock Job Interview Questions and Tips for a Successful Interview

 Seven Types of Nonverbal Communication at Your Job Interview

2 Explain how to prepare for and use common types of interview questions.

There are various types of interview questions (e.g., open-ended, closed, primary, probing, natural, leading, hypothetical, illegal). While it is difficult to predict the types of questions you will encounter in any employment interview, remember that the process of self-inventory is a good strategy to use in preparation.

 Interviewing Skills

 Common Interview Questions

3 Describe how an interview typically is structured.

Verbal and nonverbal communication are important during the opening, body, and conclusion of the interview process. Be prepared for a variety of interview environments and try to adapt if you run into the unexpected.

 How the Right Interview Closing Will Get You The Job Offer

 5 Tips to Look Confident in a Job Interview

4 Describe the factors that shape the interview environment and its influence on communication.

The different types of interviews are important to remember. Be ready to customize your résumé and/or portfolio to make the best impression possible.

 Could Video Games Be the Next Job Interview?

 4 Tips to Creating the Best Video Interview Environment

5 **Examine how best to prepare for different types of interview.**

Be ready for face-to-face as well as mediated interviews. There might be times when you have to be flexible regarding time, place, and format of the interview. If you are asked to participate in a videoconference interview, be sure to prepare.

🎙 10 Best Moments from Speaker John Boehner's Exit Interview

🎙 Behold the Entrenched (and Reviled) Annual Review

KEY TERMS

Review key terms with eFlashcards. **edge.sagepub.com/edwards2e**

Bipolar questions 427
Exit interviews 439
Helping interviews 439
Hypothetical questions 430

Illegal questions 430
Information-gathering
   interviews 439
Loaded questions 429

Performance interviews 439
Probing questions 428
Problem-solving interviews 439
Selection interviews 439

REFLECT

1. Discuss the experiences you have had interviewing. How did it go? Were you nervous? What will you do differently in preparation for interviews in the future?

2. Take a moment to think about your ideal job. Have you conducted an electronic search of the organization? What is it about the organization that makes you want to work there?

3. Discuss the resources your campus has in place to support the interviewing process. Would you consider participating in a mock interview to help prepare for the real deal?

4. Does your e-mail address appear professional? Have you thought about how your e-mail address could be perceived as being inappropriate or unprofessional?

5. What are some ethical dilemmas to consider related to interviewing?

6. What do you think about the display of tattoos and/or body piercings during a professional interview?

7. Think about social networking cites like Myspace, Facebook, and Twitter where you might maintain a profile. Is there any information that an employer could retrieve on the web that may be perceived as being inappropriate or unprofessional?

REVIEW

To check your answers go to **edge.sagepub.com/edwards2e**

1. What are open-ended questions?

2. What are closed questions?

3. The most extreme example of a closed question is the _____, commonly known as a yes-or-no question.

4. _____ are used by interviewers to prod for additional information about the candidate.

5. _____ allow interviewers to present a possible situation and ask interviewees how they would react.

6. List the relational dimensions of an interview.

7. The _____ may occur when you are being evaluated for promotion or selected for an academic award, a scholarship, or admittance to a graduate program.

8. Similar to a survey interview, an _____ occurs whenever you are seeking facts or opinions.

9. Upon separation from the organization, _____ are conducted with the hopes that departing employees will provide candid feedback about their workplace experience.

A

AD HOMINEM: A fallacy in which a speaker attacks the person instead of the argument or information.

ADAPTERS: Gestures we use to release tension.

AFFECT DISPLAYS: Nonverbal gestures, postures, and facial expressions that communicate emotions.

ANALOG CODE: A system of representations based on likeness or similarity.

ANDROGYNY: A blend of both feminine and masculine traits.

APPRECIATIVE LISTENING: Listening for pleasure.

ARGUMENT BY ANALOGY: Comparing different ideas or examples to reach a conclusion for a persuasive appeal.

ARGUMENT BY DEFINITION: Using the definition of an idea or a concept as part of a persuasive appeal.

ARGUMENT BY EXAMPLE: Using examples as the main support for a persuasive appeal.

ARGUMENT BY RELATIONSHIP: Using the relationship between two ideas or concepts as part of a persuasive appeal.

ARTIFACTS: The objects that employees can see, touch, or hear that provide them with an initial impression of how the organization operates.

ASSUMPTIONS: The ultimate sources of the values and actions of an organization; they offer an explanation for the artifacts displayed purposely, and they reinforce the strategies, goals, and philosophies that compose a workplace's values.

ATTENTION GETTER: The first part of the introduction in a presentation to get the audience's attention. This could be a statistic, an example or story, a rhetorical question, a reference to the past, a quotation, or anything that will draw the attention of the audience (as long as it is related to the topic).

ATTIRE: The clothing/dress chosen for a presentation.

ATTITUDES: Learned thought processes that guide behavior and thinking and represent likes or dislikes of a target.

AUDIENCE ANALYSIS: The process of gathering and analyzing information about an audience to make informed choices about content and delivery.

AUDIENCE RELEVANCE: A statement expressing why an audience should care about the topic.

AUDITORY LEARNER: A person who retains information best by hearing and speaking.

AUTONOMY AND CONNECTEDNESS: The dialectical tension resulting from simultaneous needs for independence and for togetherness in relationships.

AVATAR: A digital representation of self.

B

BANDWAGON: A fallacy in which a speaker expects the audience to make decisions based on the popularity and popular opinion of the position.

BAR GRAPH: A graph that uses vertical or horizontal bars to represent a certain quantity.

BELIEFS: Ideas that a person holds true or false and are formed from experiences in the world and significant relationships.

BIAS: Any assumption or attitude about a person, an issue, or a topic that is made before knowing all of the facts; a particular point of view that skews information.

BIPOLAR QUESTIONS: Commonly known as yes-or-no questions, or questions that require one of two answers.

BLOG: Allows users to disclose only the information that they desire at any given time.

BOUNDARY-SPANNING ROLE: A role in which a group member acts as a liaison between the group and the larger entity in which the group exists.

BRAINSTORMING: A process that allows group members to generate more ideas or solutions to problems by working together rather than working alone.

BUILDING AND MAINTENANCE ROLES: Group member roles used to develop and maintain the interpersonal and social development of the group.

C

CATEGORY QUESTION: Questions that limit the possible answers to groupings or categories (e.g., demographics).

CAUSATION: An argument based on the one thing causing another thing.

CAUSE-AND-EFFECT PATTERN: An organizational pattern that addresses a topic in terms of a cause and its effect on another entity.

CHRONEMICS: The study of the ways in which time is used to structure interactions.

CHRONOLOGICAL PATTERN: An organizational pattern that focuses on the exact ordering of information that matters for the topic.

CLOSED QUESTIONS: Questions that are very narrow in focus and impose many limitations on possible responses; for example, questions that require only a one- or two-word answer (e.g., yes or no).

CO-CULTURAL COMMUNICATION: The interactions among underrepresented and dominant group members.

CODING: Using programming language to instruct computers to perform specific functions.

COGNITIVE COMPLEXITY: The degree to which a person's system of interpersonal constructs are numerous, abstract, organized, and capable of handling contradictions.

COHESION: Group members feel a sense of belongingness to a group.

COLLECTIVIST CULTURES: Cultures where more emphasis is placed on the group rather than the individual to promote group cohesion and loyalty.

COMMUNICATION: The collaborative process of using messages to create and participate in social reality.

COMMUNICATION ACTIVISM: Direct energetic action in support of needed social change for individuals, groups, organizations, and communities.

COMMUNICATION AGE: The current period in which communication, technology, and media converge and deeply permeate daily life.

COMMUNICATION APPREHENSION: A person's level of fear or anxiety associated with a communication situation; can be either real or anticipated communication.

COMMUNICATION CHANNELS: The means through which workplace messages are transmitted between and among coworkers.

COMMUNICATION CLIMATE: A workplace environment where workplace members experience feelings of openness, trust, and support when interacting with one another.

COMMUNICATION COMPETENCE: The ability to communicate in a personally effective yet socially appropriate manner.

COMMUNICATION NETWORKS: The formal and informal patterns of interaction that regulate the extent to which and how organizational members talk with one another.

COMPREHENSIVE LISTENING: Listening to understand and make meaning of a message.

COMPUTER-MEDIATED COMMUNICATION: Human communication that is facilitated by a wide range of new media technologies such as chat rooms, e-mail message systems, message boards, and online games.

CONCLUDING DEVICE: The method used to end a presentation. Similar to the attention getter, concluding devices can be statistics, quotations, examples, or rhetorical questions, or even refer back to the attention getter in some way to demonstrate the end of the presentation.

CONFIRMING COMMUNICATION: Messages and interactions that make people feel valued and respected.

CONNECTING: The power of communication to link and relate us to

people, groups, communities, social institutions, and cultures.

CONNOTATIVE MEANING: Informal meanings associated with feelings and personal experiences.

CONSTITUTIVE RULES: Stipulations for what messages and behaviors count as and how they should be interpreted.

CONTACT CULTURES: Cultures that are frequent in touching.

CONTAMINATION: A type of intrusion in which someone's territory is marked with noise or pollution.

CONTENT: The actual information contained in a spoken or written message.

CONVERGENCE: The ways in which the many forms of technologically mediated and face-to-face communication overlap and intersect in daily life.

COOPERATIVE PRINCIPLE: The expectation that people will use messages that are appropriate and meet the demands of the type or nature of the conversation at hand.

COORDINATED MANAGEMENT OF MEANING: The theory focusing on how communicators move through eight levels of interpretation to coordinate their actions with one another and to make and manage meanings.

COORDINATION: The establishment of rules that help guide people through interactions.

CORRELATION: When two things happen at the same time but do not cause each other.

CREDIBILITY: A speaker's perceived level of knowledge, trustworthiness, and believability.

CRITICAL LISTENING: Listening to evaluate an argument or stance and develop an opinion based on evidence.

CROWDSOURCING: Asking other people about their opinions to help form our own ideas.

CULTURAL BACKGROUND: A person's race, ethnicity, or country of origin.

CULTURAL COMPETENCE: The level of knowledge a person has about others

who differ in some way in comparison to self.

CULTURAL RITUALS: Practices, behaviors, celebrations, and traditions common to people, organizations, and institutions.

CULTURAL VALUE DIMENSIONS: The idea of people having particular ways of thinking that developed from the time of childhood, including individualism versus collectivism, power distance, uncertainty avoidance, masculinity versus femininity, and long-term versus short-term orientation to time.

CULTURE: The rules of living and functioning in society.

CYBERSPACE: A place that collects all the information in the world and can be accessed and entered by any capable person.

DATA MINING: A complex system of computer programs used to predict people's future spending habits, opinions, or likes/dislikes.

DATAVEILLANCE: When companies like Facebook collect and aggregate personal data provided by users.

DECEPTION CUES: Things like avoiding eye contact, looking down at the floor, fidgeting, clearing the throat, and using lots of filled pauses like "um" and "er" commonly indicate that someone is lying. Breaking or being unable to sustain eye gaze is commonly believed to indicate deception.

DECISION-MAKING TALK: The group selects an option from a set of already selected options in which no externally correct option exists.

DEDUCTIVE REASONING: Using general conclusions to reach a specific conclusion.

DEFENSIVE COMMUNICATION: Messages and interactions that attempt to guard, or protect, one from an attack.

DEINTENSIFICATION: To reduce the intensity of our facial expression of a certain emotion.

DEMOGRAPHICS: Personal characteristics or attributes of the audience.

DEMONSTRATIVE INFORMATIVE PRESENTATION: A type of informative presentation that demonstrates how to perform a task.

DENOTATIVE MEANING: Formal and public word meanings often described as "dictionary definitions."

DESCRIPTIVE INFORMATIVE PRESENTATION: A type of informative presentation that describes people, places, or events.

DIGITAL CODE: A system of representations based on symbols.

DIGITAL IMMIGRANTS: People who have adopted and learned digital technologies later in life.

DIGITAL NATIVES: People for whom digital technologies such as computers, cell phones, video games, and digital cameras already existed when they were born.

DIRECT QUESTION: A question asked of an audience to encourage thinking about a topic that invites an actual audience response.

DISCONFIRMING COMMUNICATION: Messages and interactions that make people feel devalued and disrespected.

DISCRIMINATION: The act of excluding people from or denying them products, rights, and services based on their race, ethnicity, religion, gender, age, sexual orientation, or disability.

DISCRIMINATIVE LISTENING: Listening to understand the different stimuli in the environment in order to process their meanings.

DIVERSITY: A term used to describe the unique differences in people.

E

ECONOMIC IMPERATIVE: Countries are becoming more and more interdependent in shaping a global economy. Importing and exporting are important to countries across the globe.

EDUTAINMENT: Informative presentations that use entertainment to present social issues to an audience.

EITHER/OR ARGUMENTS: A fallacy that oversimplifies issues by offering only two solutions even though other options exist.

ELECTRONIC TRADITION (FIRST MEDIA AGE): Described media as a symbolic environment of any communicative act.

EMBLEMS: Specific, widely understood meanings in a given culture that may actually substitute for a word or phrase.

EMERGENT LEADER APPROACH TO LEADERSHIP: Leadership emerges through the communication that occurs among group members by choosing to eliminate those individuals who do not demonstrate leadership behaviors.

EMOJI: Means "picture letter" in Japanese. Used to show our feelings in the digital world.

EMOTICONS: A textual expression of emotions that show our feelings in the digital world. The use of :), :(, or :D demonstrates our feelings in text.

EMPATHIC LISTENING: Listening to another person by responding nonjudgmentally to his or her physical and/or emotional needs.

ENGAGING: The act of sharing in the activities of the group; in other words, participating.

ENVIRONMENT: The study of our surroundings; the physical setting of a presentation. The environment can shape the communication interaction.

EPIDEICTIC PRESENTATION: A type of presentation that occurs when a person is introducing him- or herself, introducing another person, celebrating an event, or commemorating a special occasion (e.g., award, funeral).

EPISODE: A broad communication situation created by conversational partners.

ETHICAL IMPERATIVE: Guides you in doing what is right versus what is wrong in various communication contexts.

ETHICS: A code of conduct based on respect for yourself, others, and your surroundings.

ETHNICITY: A social group that may be joined together by factors such as shared history, shared identity, shared geography, or shared culture.

ETHNOCENTRISM: Evaluating another culture using the standards of one's own culture.

ETHOS: The credibility and ethical appeal of a presentation.

EXIT INTERVIEWS: These are conducted with the hopes that departing employees will provide candid feedback about their workplace experience.

EXPLANATORY INFORMATIVE PRESENTATION: A type of informative presentation that explains a concept, an idea, or a phenomenon.

EXPLORATORY INFORMATIVE PRESENTATION: A type of informative presentation designed to invite the audience to learn or discover information about a topic.

EXTEMPORANEOUS PRESENTATION: A speech in which the speaker carefully prepares notes and an outline, and has thoroughly practiced.

EYE CONTACT: Looking at your audience in both live and virtual settings.

 F

FACE-TO-FACE COMMUNICATION: Situations in which the participants who are physically or bodily present speak directly to one another during the interaction.

FEEDBACK: A receiver's response to a sender's message.

FEMININITY: Behaviors associated with being caring or compassionate (what it means to be a woman).

FIELDS OF EXPERIENCE: The attitudes, perceptions, and backgrounds each person brings to the process of communication.

FLUENCY: The smoothness of vocal quality.

FORMAL COMMUNICATION NETWORKS: A network that is both prescribed and sanctioned by the workplace and occurs through downward communication, upward communication, and horizontal communication.

FRAMING: The structure of the presentation, argument, or information with regard to audience analysis.

FULL-SENTENCE OUTLINE: A formal outline that uses full and complete sentences.

FUNCTIONAL PERSPECTIVE OF SMALL GROUP COMMUNICATION: A group's performance is directly related to how well members engage in each of the five communicative functions necessary to make an informed choice.

G

GENDER: The psychological and emotional characteristics of individuals.

GENERAL PURPOSE: Large framing statements about the reason for the speech (to inform, to persuade, to entertain/celebrate [epideictic]).

GENERALIZED OTHER: The viewpoint of the entire society, including its values, rules, roles, and attitudes.

GESTURES: Hand movement used to emphasize and reinforce a message.

GLOBAL PLAGIARISM: A type of plagiarism that occurs when a person uses an entire document as his or her own.

GROUPHATE: The feelings of dread that arise when faced with the possibility of having to work in a group.

GROUP MEETING ENVIRONMENT: The time and place where a meeting is held.

GROUP MEMBER ROLE: An established and repetitive pattern of communicative behaviors that members expect from one another.

GROUP PRESENTATIONS: Consist of one speech with several people doing various parts.

GROUP SIZE: A minimum of 3 members and a maximum of 15 members, with the ideal small group size consisting of 5 to 7 members.

GROUP TALK: The specific types of communication in which group members engage.

GROUP TASK: An activity in which a decision or solution cannot be made without the input of all group members.

GROUPTHINK: When a group makes a faulty decision due to its members' collective inability to critically examine an issue.

H

HALO EFFECT: The tendency to allow perceptions of one positive trait to influence perceptions of other positive traits.

HAPTICS: The study of touch.

HASTY GENERALIZATION: A fallacy that occurs when someone uses one or two examples and then generalizes the examples to a much larger concept; accepting information that is not supported with evidence.

HATE SPEECH: General to uncivil discourse (talk), phrases, terms, cartoons, and entire campaigns used to humiliate people based on age, gender, race, ethnicity, culture, sexual orientation, social class, and more.

HEARING: The physical process in which the ear and brain receive sound waves.

HELPING INTERVIEWS: These are always conducted by experts in a particular area.

HETEROSEXIST: A view or an assumption that everyone is heterosexual.

HIGH-CONTEXT CULTURES: Cultures that place emphasis on the total environment or context where interactions occur.

HORNS EFFECT: The tendency to allow perceptions of one negative trait to influence perceptions of other negative traits.

HURIER: A six-step listening process of hearing, understanding, remembering, interpreting, evaluating, and responding.

HYPERPERSONAL COMMUNICATION: Communication situations in which the affection, emotion, and intimacy that develop through computer-mediated communication equal or surpass what happens face to face.

HYPOTHETICAL QUESTIONS: These questions allow interviewers to present a possible situation and ask interviewees how they would react.

I

IDENTITY: The psychological and/or physical boundaries that distinguish a group member from a non–group member.

ILLEGAL QUESTIONS: Questions related to factors employees may not consider such as race, religion, or disability during the hiring process.

ILLUSTRATORS: Gestures that complement, enhance, or substitute for the verbal message.

IMAGINED TRAJECTORIES: Personal understandings of the various paths relationships can follow and where those paths lead.

IMPRESSION MANAGEMENT: The formation of an impression, a perception, or a view of the other.

IMPROMPTU PRESENTATION: A speech in which the speaker has little or no preparation time.

INCLUSIVE LANGUAGE: Expressions and words that are broad enough to include all people; language that avoids expressions and words that exclude particular groups.

INDIVIDUALISTIC CULTURES: Cultures where emphasis is placed on individuals more than groups.

INDUCTIVE REASONING: Using specific conclusions to reach a general conclusion.

INFORMAL COMMUNICATION NETWORK: A network that is established through the social interactions that occur among coworkers.

INFORMANT: A person who generally knows about the speaking situation, the makeup of the potential audience, and even overall attitudes and beliefs about the audience.

INFORMATION-GATHERING INTERVIEW: Occurs whenever you are seeking facts or opinions.

INFORMATION OVERLOAD: The negative feelings resulting from being given too much information to process a topic.

INFORMATION SEEKING: The process by which workers proactively acquire feedback from one another.

INFORMATIVE PRESENTATION: A presentation designed to convey new information and/or to increase an audience's understanding about a topic.

INTENSIFICATION: To use an expression that exaggerates how we feel about something.

INTERACTION METAPHOR: The communication model that describes communication as a two-way process of reciprocal action, involving feedback and fields of experience.

INTERACTIVITY: The phenomenon of communication at a distance through new media.

INTERDEPENDENCE: The process by which a change in one part affects the other parts.

INTERNAL PREVIEW: A transition that lets the audience know the specific information that will be discussed next in the presentation.

INTERNAL SUMMARY: A transition that reminds the audience of what was just discussed in the presentation.

INTERNET OF THINGS: A scenario in which objects, animals, or people are equipped with unique identifiers and sensors, and the ability to transfer data over a network.

INTERPERSONAL COMMUNICATION: Communication with or between persons who approach one another as individuals in a relationship.

INTERPERSONAL CONSTRUCTS: Bipolar dimensions of judgment used to size up people or social situations.

INTERPRETATION: The process of giving meaning to information.

IN-TEXT CITATION: An abbreviated citation of a source appearing in an outline.

INTIMATE ZONE: Reserved for our significant others, family members, and closest friends (0 to 18 inches).

INVASION: An intense and typically permanent intrusion, in which the intention is to take over a given territory.

K

KEYWORD OUTLINE: An outline that uses words and phrases and is often used for speaking notes.

KINESICS: The study of body movement.

KINESTHETIC LEARNER: A person who retains information best through hands-on demonstrations.

L

LANGUAGE: A system of words represented by symbols, used for a common purpose by a group of people.

LATITUDE OF ACCEPTANCE: Arguments that are close to a person's already held beliefs and are accepted.

LATITUDE OF NONCOMMITMENT: Arguments that cause people not to shift their already held beliefs but to maintain their original beliefs.

LATITUDE OF REJECTION: Arguments that are not close to a person's already held beliefs and are rejected.

LEADING QUESTIONS: Questions asked in such a way that the interviewer expects or hopes for a specific answer, or that exert some type of influence or pressure on the respondent to answer in a particular way.

LEARNING STYLES: The different ways individuals like to obtain and process information.

LINE GRAPH: A graph showing how something changes over time by connecting line points.

LINGUISTIC RELATIVITY HYPOTHESIS: The idea that language creates and shapes social reality.

LISTENING: The active process of receiving and understanding spoken or written messages.

LISTENING ANXIETY: Apprehension associated with receiving messages that triggers the inability to process and interpret incoming information.

LISTENING GOAL: The objective a person aims to accomplish by listening in a particular context or situation.

LISTENING TOUR: A person's visit to one or more communities made with the specific purpose of listening to the concerns and ideas of those who live within them.

LOADED QUESTIONS: Questions that provide strong direction toward the expected answer.

LOGOS: The logical appeal of a presentation.

LONG-TERM TIME ORIENTATION: Emphasizes processes for accomplishing tasks not focused on a quick end result. A persistent and focused process is believed to achieve the best outcome.

LOOKING-GLASS SELF: The notion that the self arises from interpersonal interactions in which a person views himself or herself through the eyes of other people.

LOW-CONTEXT CULTURES: The message itself means everything, and it's more important to have a well-structured argument or a well-delivered presentation than it is to be a member of a high-status family or actually be related to the person by blood.

MANUSCRIPT PRESENTATION: A speech that is read from a script word for word.

MASCULINITY: Behaviors associated with being more assertive or aggressive (what it means to be a man).

MASKING: To hide an expression connected to a felt emotion and replace it with an expression more appropriate to the situation.

MASS COMMUNICATION: Messages transmitted by electronic and print media to large audiences that are distant and undifferentiated.

MASSPERSONAL COMMUNICATION: Communication involving the use of a traditionally mass communication channel for interpersonal interactions, or vice versa.

MATCHING HYPOTHESIS: The proposition that people tend to form relationships with others of comparable levels of physical attractiveness.

MEDIA AWARENESS: The ability to selectively attend to and evaluate messages in the media.

MEDIA MULTIPLEXITY: The phenomenon in which the closer a relationship dyad, the more means of communication they use to maintain their relationship with one another. Media multiplexity assumes that tie strength drives patterns of media use between individuals.

MEDIATED COMMUNICATION: Communication or messages that are transmitted through some type of medium, including writing, the telephone, e-mail, text messages, and the many forms of technological and computer-mediated interaction.

MEDIATED PRESENTATION: A speech that uses either manuscript, memorized, impromptu, or extemporaneous delivery but is viewed using some technological component.

MEDIUM DISTRACTIONS: Characteristics of the channel through which a message is delivered that obstruct the ability to receive messages clearly.

MEMORABLE MESSAGE: A short and simple yet serious statement uttered by a superior targeted toward a particular subordinate that is intended to reinforce appropriate work behavior and conduct.

MEMORIZED PRESENTATION: A speech given from memory without the use of notes.

MENTOR-PROTEGE RELATIONSHIPS: Workplace relationships that develop between an experienced colleague who has attained career success and a less advanced colleague who demonstrates the potential to become equally successful at work.

MESSAGE DESIGN LOGIC: Distinct ways of thinking about communication situations, choosing which thoughts to express, and deciding how to express them in order to achieve goals.

MICRO CHANGES: Asking an audience to adopt and make small changes in behavior instead of one or more large behavioral changes.

MINDFULNESS: The ability to remain in the present moment and be fully aware of the speaker, the environment, and the message.

MODEL OF INTERACTION STAGES: An account that explains the typical pattern of how communication progresses relationships through five stages of coming together and five stages of coming apart.

MONOCHRONIC: A time orientation that stresses being on time and maintaining a schedule for events.

MONROE'S MOTIVATED SEQUENCE: An organizational pattern used to persuade about the need, solution, advantages, and audience actions about a topic.

MORPHEMES: The smallest units of meaning in a language.

MOVEMENT: The use of the body during a presentation.

MULTIMEDIA PRESENTATIONAL AIDS: Objects and technology that reinforce your message, create emotion, or add new information using a variety of senses in a presentation.

MUTUAL RESPECT: When individuals and groups communicate with the goal of mutual understanding to avoid cultural tensions, misunderstandings, and conflict.

NARRATIVE COHERENCE: How well a story hangs together or makes sense.

NARRATIVE FIDELITY: How well a story matches personal lived experiences.

NETWORKING: Creating relationships with both work peers and acquaintances that can help you in your career.

NEUTRAL QUESTIONS: Questions that allow the respondent freedom to answer without influence from the questioner; there is no intended or expected answer.

NEUTRALIZATION: The process of using facial expression to erase or numb how we really feel.

NEW MEDIA: A technological interface that allows users to communicate, interact, personalize, and own media.

NEW MEDIA THEORY: Designed to describe the unique, customized communication styles of our generation with our media.

NEW MEDIA TRADITION (SECOND MEDIA AGE): From the early 1980s to the present day when the trends begin to move from broadcast media to new media, with the rise of popularity of the Internet.

NONCONTACT CULTURES: Cultures infrequent in touching.

NON SEQUITUR ARGUMENT: This fallacy does not follow a logical conclusion; the conclusion has no relationship to the statement.

NONVERBAL COMMUNICATION: All the ways we communicate without using words. Nonverbal communication can include our clothing, physical appearance, gestures, facial and eye expressions, and more.

NONVERBAL IMMEDIACY: The use of closeness-inducing nonverbal behavioral cues.

NONVERBAL TRANSITION: A transition that utilizes physical movement to indicate the move from one point to another point in a presentation.

NORMS: The guidelines or rules implemented by the group about not only how its members should behave, but also how the group should approach its tasks.

NOVELTY AND PREDICTABILITY: The dialectical tension resulting from simultaneous needs for new experiences and for routines in relationships.

OCCASION: The reason or event in which a person is speaking.

OPEN-ENDED QUESTIONS: Questions that allow the person to expand on the answers and not simply provide yes-or-no answers. These questions allow the respondent to specify on a topic but also allow for sufficient flexibility in answering the question.

OPENNESS AND CLOSEDNESS: The dialectical tension resulting from simultaneous needs for sharing information and for concealing information in relationships.

OPEN QUESTION: A question that allows the person to fully answer by giving perspective, insight, attitudes, and opinions.

ORAL TRADITION: Also referred to as Oral Culture or Oral Age; consists of cultural messages or traditions verbally transmitted across generations.

ORGANIZATIONAL COMMUNICATION: The process through which organization members develop, maintain, and modify practices through their communication with both internal superiors, subordinates, and peers and external clients, customers, and stakeholders.

ORGANIZATIONAL PATTERN: The specific pattern used to organize a presentation.

PANOPTICON: A hypothetical prison structure designed around a central surveillance tower from which the warden can see into each cell.

PATCHWORK PLAGIARISM: A type of plagiarism that occurs when several different documents are combined into one document and then used as a person's own.

PATHOS: The passion or emotional appeal of a presentation.

PEACE IMPERATIVE: Essential in understanding the foundations of communication, culture, and diversity. While conflict exists between various

cultures, it is a top priority to maintain overall peace.

PEAK COMMUNICATION EXPERIENCE: Individuals' greatest moments of mutual understanding, happiness, and fulfillment in interpersonal communication.

PEER RELATIONSHIPS: Workplace relationships that develop between two coworkers at the same hierarchical level who possess no formal authority over each other.

PERCEPTION: The process of being aware of and understanding the world.

PERCEPTION CHECKING: The practice of asking others to get a more informed sense of understanding.

PERCEPTUAL BARRIER: An influence on observation and interpretation that hinders effective communication.

PERFORMANCE INTERVIEWS: Interviews usually conducted on an annual basis in a variety of industries to review employee performance.

PERIODICAL: A publication, either printed or electronic, that is produced on a regular basis, such as newspapers, magazines, and journals.

PERIPHERAL INFORMATION: Relatively minor information about the self, usually on personal profiles, including things such as music interests or favorite movies.

PERSONAL BRANDING: Creating a self-package or brand of a person's identity.

PERSONAL PROFILES: Short descriptions about your age, sex, race, physical features, affiliations, and interests.

PERSONAL ZONE: Reserved for personal relationships with casual acquaintances and friends (18 inches to about 4 feet).

PERSUASION: The altering or modifying of a person's attitudes, beliefs, values, or outlook about a topic.

PERSUASIVE PRESENTATION: A type of presentation that seeks to change, alter, or modify an audience's attitudes, beliefs, values, or outlook about a topic.

PHONEMES: The sounds of a language.

PHYSICAL APPEARANCE: Observable traits of the body and its accessories and extensions.

PHYSICAL ATTRACTION: The degree to which a person finds the bodily traits of another pleasing and desirable.

PHYSICAL ATTRACTIVENESS: A perception of beauty derived from cultures.

PIE GRAPH: A graph in a circle form that is divided into sections illustrating frequencies or proportions.

PITCH: The amount of vocal inflections (highness or lowness) in a person's voice.

PLAGIARISM: Using someone else's words or ideas without giving credit to the source.

POLYCHRONIC: A time orientation that places less emphasis on keeping a tight schedule and values greater flexibility.

POLYSEMY: Multiple meanings associated with a single word or symbol.

POSSIBLE SELVES: Visions of what a person might become, what he or she would like to become, and what he or she is afraid of becoming.

POWER DISTANCE: The perceived equality or inequality felt between people in certain cultural or social contexts.

PREJUDICE: The dislike or hatred one has toward a particular group.

PREVIEW: The last step of the introduction that tells the audience the specific things that will be discussed in the presentation.

PRIMARY ORALITY: A culture that has no knowledge of technology beyond the spoken word.

PRIMARY SOURCE: Information obtained from a participant or an observer who witnessed the action.

PRINTING PRESS: A mechanical device that applies pressure from an inked surface to a print medium.

PRINT TRADITION: The creation and distribution of printed text; an identifiable period of technological development.

PROBING QUESTIONS: Used by interviewers to prod for additional information about the interviewee; typically follow a primary question.

PROBLEM-CAUSE-SOLUTION PATTERN: An organizational pattern used to show the problem and cause of a particular topic and then to persuade the audience about a particular solution.

PROBLEM-SOLVING INTERVIEWS: Interviews sometimes used by external consultants or members of the management team to describe a problem and work toward a solution.

PROBLEM-SOLVING TALK: The group defines and analyzes the problem, identifies several solutions, and chooses one solution.

PROTEUS EFFECT: The phenomenon in which the appearance of an avatar leads to behavioral changes in its user.

PROTOTYPES: A person's image of the best example of a particular category of message, person, or social situation.

PROXEMICS: The study of how we use space and distance to communicate.

PROXIMITY: The physical or virtual distance between two people.

PUBLIC COMMUNICATION: Situations in which a person delivers a message to an audience that is unified by some common interest.

PUBLIC ZONE: The distance typical of large, formal, public events (over 12 feet).

Q

QUESTIONS OF FACT: Questions that persuade that something is or is not true.

QUESTIONS OF POLICY: Questions that persuade for a change to an existing law, plan, or policy, or creating a new policy.

QUESTIONS OF VALUE: Questions that persuade for the relative merits—good/bad, moral/immoral—of a position.

R

RACE: The categorization of people based on physical characteristics such as skin color, dimensions of the human face, and hair.

RAPPORT TALK: Cooperative messages used to establish connection.

RATE: The speed (fast or slow) of speech.

READ/WRITE LEARNER: A person who retains information best through reading and writing about the topic.

REAL TIME: Activities or resources whose action and reactions occur immediately, without delay.

RED HERRING: A fallacy in which someone uses nonrelevant information to distract from important information.

REFERENCE LIST: A list of all the sources cited in the presentation that conforms to the specific guidelines of a reference system (e.g., APA).

REFERENT: The last point on the triangle of meaning, or actual object to which the word refers.

REGULATIVE RULES: Rules that guide how individuals respond or behave in interactions.

REGULATORS: Gestures used to control the turn-taking in conversations.

RELATIONAL CLIMATE: The overall emotional feeling, or temperature, of a relationship.

RELATIONAL CULTURE: The unique private world relationship partners create and maintain through their communication.

RELATIONAL DIALECTICS THEORY (RDT): The theory that the communication patterns in relationships arise from a series of tensions based on contradictory needs and conflicting core values held by relationship partners.

RELATIONAL SELF: A process of constantly changing and developing aspects of self as a result of togetherness with others.

REPORT TALK: Information-based messages used to establish status and gain power.

REWARD: Anything psychological or physical that the audience will obtain from listening to a presentation.

RHETORICAL QUESTION: A question asked of an audience to encourage thinking about a topic that does not invite an actual audience response.

S

SATURATED SELF: An identity infused with the numerous, and sometimes incompatible, views of others.

SCALED QUESTIONS: Questions that allow a person to make an answer between two points, usually found on surveys.

SCHEMAS: Mental structures developed from past experiences that help people respond to stimuli in the future.

SCREEN NAMES: The names people use to identify and locate others in a network.

SCREENCAST PRESENTATION: Occurs when a computer screen is recorded and shown in some format.

SCRIPTS: Organized sequences of action that define a well-known situation.

SECONDARY ORALITY: When verbal communication is sustained through other technologies, such as the telephone or Internet.

SECONDARY SOURCE: Research and information that is at least one step removed from the actual event. This would include textbooks, most scholarly books, news articles, and reference books.

SECTION TRANSITION: A transition to indicate that a speaker is moving from one main point to another main point.

SELECTION INTERVIEW: May occur when you are being evaluated for promotion or selected for an academic award, a scholarship, or admittance to a graduate program.

SELECTIVE ATTENTION: The process of concentrating on one part of the environment while not paying attention to the rest.

SELECTIVE EXPOSURE: The process of exposing oneself only to beliefs, values, and ideas that are similar to one's own.

SELECTIVE EXPOSURE THEORY: The theory that individuals prefer messages that support their own positions to messages supporting other positions.

SELECTIVE MEMORY: The process of retaining and recalling certain bits of information from past interactions, while forgetting the rest.

SELECTIVE PERCEPTION: The process in which individuals filter what they see and hear to make it suit their own needs, biases, or expectations.

SELF-AWARENESS IMPERATIVE: Encourages communicators to learn about other cultures. Not only do you learn about other cultures themselves, but by doing so, you learn more about your own culture.

SELF-CONCEPT: A person's general perception of who she or he is.

SELF-DISCLOSURE: The act of revealing information about oneself to others.

SELF-ESTEEM: The component of self-concept that refers to an individual's perception of her or his worth.

SELF-IMAGE: The component of self-concept that refers to an individual's mental picture of him- or herself.

SELF-PLAGIARISM: A type of plagiarism that occurs when a person uses his or her previous original work as new for another project, paper, or class.

SEMANTICS: The study of the meaning of words.

SEX: The chromosomal combinations that produce males, females, and the other possible, but rarer, sexes.

SEXUAL ORIENTATION: Identity typically based on the gender(s) or bodies of others to whom we're attracted sexually.

SHARED LEADERSHIP: The communicative behaviors any group member can enact to demonstrate leadership.

SHORT-TERM TIME ORIENTATION: Emphasizes efficiency, production, and fast results.

SIGNPOST: Brief phrases or words that let the audience know exactly where the speaker is in a presentation (e.g., *first, second, for example*).

SITUATIONAL DISTRACTIONS: Features of a particular environment, location, or setting that interfere with the ability to listen.

SLACKERS: Group members who fail to contribute equally or equitably to a group task.

SLIPPERY SLOPE: A fallacy that represents the notion that when a single step is made a host of other negative consequences follow.

SMALL GROUP COMMUNICATION: Communication among the members of a small group of people working together to achieve a common goal or purpose; three or more people working together interdependently for the purpose of accomplishing a task.

SMALL GROUP CONFLICT: The process that occurs when group members engage in an expressed struggle that impedes task accomplishment and usually arises due to the real and perceived differences that exist among group members.

SOCIAL ATTRACTIVENESS: The degree to which a person's actions and personality are deemed pleasing and desirable to others.

SOCIAL CONSTRUCTION METAPHOR: The communication model that stresses that communication shapes and creates the larger social realities in which people operate.

SOCIAL INFORMATION PROCESSING (SIP) THEORY: A theory that explains how computer-mediated and face-to-face communication are both successful in building relationships.

SOCIAL JUDGMENT THEORY: A persuasion theory that maintains that individuals can be persuaded on a topic by being convinced to accept changes that are close to their already held beliefs.

SOCIAL MEDIA: A web-based service that allows individuals to create a public profile and maintain and view a list of users who share a common interest.

SOCIAL PENETRATION THEORY: The theory that relationships progress toward intimacy as a result of self-disclosure from both partners.

SOCIAL REALITY: The set of social judgments upon which members of a group agree.

SOCIAL SURVEILLANCE: When people online eavesdrop, inquire into, and watch their peers' mediated communication practices.

SOCIAL ZONE: The distance at which we usually talk to strangers or conduct business (4 feet to 12 feet).

SOMATYPING: A system that classifies people according to their body type.

SOURCE: Research and information attained through others' work (newspapers, magazines, documentaries, books, government documents, online journals, news shows, interviews, and websites).

SOURCE DISTRACTIONS: Behaviors or mannerisms of the message source or the characteristics of a mediated message that detract from the ability to listen.

SPATIAL PATTERN: An organizational pattern used when information is grouped by space or location.

SPEAKER'S INTENT: The goal the speaker is trying to accomplish in a presentation.

SPEAKING SITUATION: Consists of the size of the audience, the environment, and the occasion.

SPECIFIC PURPOSE: The precise goals of the presentation including both the topic and the general purpose.

SPEECH ACT: A specific action like a promise, an apology, or a greeting performed through speech.

STANDPOINT THEORY: The theory that a person's point of view arises from the social groups to which he or she belongs and influences how he or she socially constructs the world.

STATE CA: Based on the particular context for the speaking occasion.

STEREOTYPES: Generalizations made to an entire group of people or situations on the basis of the observed traits of one or a few members of the group.

SUFFICIENCY OF EVIDENCE: Providing overwhelming evidence so that any reasonable person would have to accept a position.

SUPERIOR-SUBORDINATE RELATIONSHIPS: Workplace relationships that develop between two coworkers where one formally outranks the other by virtue of organizational role or title.

SURVEILLANCE: Focused, intentional, routine attention to personal details for purposes of influence or control.

SYMBOLIC INTERACTIONISM: The framework that positions communication as the primary means by which people internalize and use social values to guide how they see themselves, how they see others, and how they interact.

SYMBOLS: Things that represent or stand for something else.

SYNTAX: Meaning at the level of sentences.

SYSTEMATIC DESENSITIZATION: In terms of public speaking, the practicing of speaking in front of others as a way to lessen anxiety or fear.

T

TASK ROLES: Group member roles designated specifically to facilitate progress toward problem solving or decision making and attainment of group goals.

TEAM: Shares the same features as a small group, but is differentiated further by three defining characteristics: (1) Members hold one another mutually accountable for the task; (2) members demonstrate an extraordinary amount of involvement in, commitment to, and investment in the group; and (3) members are chosen carefully because they will be working together for an indefinite amount of time.

TECHNOLOGICAL IMPERATIVE: Important in today's society as technological advances make the world more easily accessible.

TELEWORKING: The practice of working off-site (i.e., away from the physical workplace) while remaining connected to the workplace through a host of communication technologies such as the Internet, e-mail, voice mail, cell phones, instant messaging, and virtual private networks.

TERRITORIALITY: The study of how people use space and objects to communicate occupancy or ownership of space.

TESTIMONY: A statement or declaration by a person who has a connection to the topic.

TETHERED SELF: A state of being in which one is always aware of and attuned to both the "real world" and life on the screen.

TEXT STEALING: A type of plagiarism that occurs when a person uses another person's words but does not give credit to the source.

THEORY OF SELF-PRESENTATION: Everyday settings are viewed as a stage, and people are considered actors who use performances to make an impression on an audience.

THESIS STATEMENT: Introduces your topic; provides the general purpose of your presentation.

TOPIC: The general subject of a presentation.

TOPICAL PATTERN: An organizational pattern used when information is grouped around central themes by subject matter.

TRAIT CA: The CA we possess in general on a daily basis across many different contexts.

TRANSACTION METAPHOR: The communication model that describes communication as a process in which participants, who are simultaneous senders and receivers, exchange meanings and influence their relationship.

TRANSITIONS: Sentences or phrases that connect what a speaker was just speaking about with what he or she will be speaking about next.

TRANSMISSION METAPHOR: The communication model that describes communication as a linear, one-way transfer of information in which a source sends a message through a channel or a medium to a receiver in an environment of noise that serves as interference with effective transmission of the message.

TURNING POINTS: Perceptions of events that transform relationships.

U

UNCERTAINTY AVOIDANCE: Deals with the way that a culture handles change and accepts uncertainty within social or cultural contexts.

V

VALUES: The strategies, goals, and philosophies that act as guidelines for work behavior.

VIOLATION: The use of or intrusion into primary territory without our permission.

VIRTUAL WORK TEAM: Tasks and professional projects that are traditionally accomplished face to face are completed through computer-mediated means to save time, travel, and energy.

VIRTUALITY: The general term for the reinvention of familiar physical space in cyberspace.

VISUAL LEARNER: A person who retains information best by seeing ideas and concepts through pictures or videos.

VOCAL FILLERS: Unnecessary words or phrases that create pauses and disrupt the flow in a speech.

VOCALICS: The study of the use of voice to express oneself.

VOLUME: The level and variety of loudness of a voice.

W

WARRANTING THEORY: Suggests that in the presence of anonymity, a person may potentially misrepresent information about his or her self.

WORK-LIFE BALANCE: When individuals are able to experience meaningful achievement and enjoyment across four areas of their lives (i.e., work, family, friends, and self) on a daily basis.

WORKPLACE BULLYING: The experience of at least two negative acts that occur at least weekly for 6 or more months in situations where the recipients find it difficult to defend against and stop abuse.

WORKPLACE COMMUNICATION: The communicative exchanges that occur among coworkers, managers, team members, committees, and task forces within an organization and that are aimed toward accomplishing company goals and objectives.

WORKPLACE CULTURE: The ways in which employees think, act, and behave that emerge as a result of their interactions with one another at work.

WORKPLACE DISSENT: When employees feel as if they no longer are a vital part of the company and they begin to disagree or express contradictory opinions about the organization, its policies and practices, and its employees.

WORKPLACE FRIENDSHIPS: A unique type of workplace relationship that blends the expectations associated with personal relationships with the expectations that govern work roles.

WORKPLACE RELATIONSHIPS: Sustained interactions that occur between coworkers as a direct result of employment at the same organization.

WORKPLACE ROMANTIC RELATIONSHIPS: When two employees, regardless of their status or position in the organization, acknowledge a mutual sexual attraction and physically act upon this attraction, whether it be through dating, cohabitation, or marriage.

WORKPLACE SOCIALIZATION: The process by which organizational newcomers learn about the values, norms, and expectations that will enable them to become fully contributing members of the workplace.

WRITTEN TRADITION: Early forms of written communication such as scribe and hieroglyphics; immediately follows the Oral Tradition.

A

Aarts, H., Custers, R., & Veltkamp, M. (2008). Goal priming and the affective-motivational route to nonconscious goal pursuit. *Social Cognition, 26,* 555–577.

Abedi, M., & Badragheh, A. (2011). Learning styles in adult education. *Journal of American Science, 7,* 142–146.

Acitelli, L. K., & Holmberg, D. (1993). Reflecting on relationships: The role of thoughts and memories. In D. Perlman & W. H. Jones (Eds.), *Advances in personal relationships* (Vol. 4, pp. 71–100). London, England: Kingsley.

Ahmad, A. (2010). Is Twitter a useful tool for journalists? *Journal of Media Practice, 11*(2), 145–155.

Allen, T. D., & Finkelstein, L. M. (2003). Beyond mentoring: Alternative sources and functions of developmental support. *Career Development Quarterly, 51,* 346–355.

Altman, I., & Taylor, D. A. (1973). *Social penetration: The development of interpersonal relationships.* New York, NY: Holt, Rinehart & Winston.

Alvarez, A. (2013, April 26). How j-setting is changing pop culture. Retrieved from http://abcnews.go.com/ABC_Univision/Entertainment/sette-dance-moves-loved-knowing/story?id=190 41546

Alvarez, L., & Buckley, C. (2013, July 13). Zimmerman is acquitted in Trayvon Martin killing. Retrieved from http://www.nytimes.com/2013/07/14/us/george-zimmerman-verdict-trayvon-martin.html?_r=0

The Amanda Todd story (2014, December 14). Retrieved May 14, 2015, from http://nobullying.com/amanda-todd-story/

Andersen, J. F. (1979). Teacher immediacy as a predictor of teaching effectiveness. In D. Nimmo (Ed.), *Communication yearbook 3* (pp. 543–559). New Brunswick, NJ: Transaction.

Anderson, J. G., & Taylor, A. G. (2011). Effects of healing touch in clinical practice: A systematic review of randomized clinical trials. *Journal of Holistic Nursing, 29,* 221–228.

Angel, C. (2005). Levitation [Television series episode]. *Mindfreak* [Season 1]. New York, NY: A&E.

Arceneaux, M. (2015, April 27). Here's why everyone's talking about the Prancing Elites. Retrieved from http://chicagodefender.com/2015/04/27/heres-why-everyones-talking-about-the-prancing-elites/

Aristotle. (1991). *On rhetoric* (G. A. Kennedy, trans.). New York, NY: Oxford University Press.

Arvidsson, A. (2006). "Quality singles": Internet dating and the work of fantasy. *New Media and Society, 8,* 671–690.

Atchley, R. A., Strayer, D. L., & Atchley, P. (2012). Creativity in the wild: Improving creative reasoning through immersion in natural settings. PLOS ONE. doi:10.1371/journal.pone.0051474

Ayers, I. (2007). *Super crunchers: Why thinking-by-numbers is the new way to be smart.* New York, NY: Bantam Dell.

Ayres, J. (1996). Speech preparation processes and speech apprehension. *Communication Education, 45,* 228–235.

Ayres, J. (2005). Performance visualization and behavioral disruption: A clarification. *Communication Reports, 18,* 55–63.

B

Baker, D. F., & Campbell, C. M. (2004). When is there strength in numbers? A study of undergraduate task groups. *College Teaching, 53,* 14–18.

Bales, R. F. (1950). *Interaction process analysis: A method for the study of small groups.* Chicago, IL: University of Chicago Press.

Bales, R. F. (1976). *Interaction process analysis.* Chicago: University of Illinois Press.

Barge, J. K., & Schlueter, D. W. (2004). Memorable messages and newcomer socialization. *Western Journal of Communication, 68,* 233–256.

Barnes, S. B. (2003). *Computer-mediated communication: Human-to-human communication across the Internet.* Boston, MA: Allyn & Bacon.

Barton, J., & Pretty, J. (2010). What is the best dose of nature and green exercise for improving mental health? A multi-study analysis. *Environmental Science & Technology, 44*(10), 3947–3955.

Bartsch, R. A., & Cobern, K. M. (2003). Effectiveness of PowerPoint presentations in lectures. *Computers & Education, 41,* 77–86.

Bass, A. N. (2010). From business dining to public speaking: Tips for acquiring professional presence and its role in the business curricula. *American Journal of Business Education, 3,* 57–63.

Bateson, M. C. (1994). *Peripheral visions: Learning along the way.* New York, NY: HarperCollins.

Bauer, T. N., Morrison, E. W., & Callister, R. R. (1998). Organizational socialization: A review and directions for future research. In G. R. Ferris (Ed.), *Research in personnel and human resources management* (Vol. 16, pp. 149–214). Greenwich, CT: JAI Press.

Bawden, D., & Robinson, L. (2009). The dark side of information: Overload, anxiety and other paradoxes and pathologies. *Journal of Informative Science, 35,* 180–191.

Baxter, L. A. (1987). Symbols of relationship identity in relationship cultures. *Journal of Social and Personal Relationships, 4,* 261–280.

Baxter, L. A. (1988). A dialectical perspective on communication strategies in relationship development. In S. W. Duck, D. F. Hay, S. E. Hobfoll, W. Ickes, & B. Montgomery (Eds.), *Handbook of personal relationships* (pp. 257–273). London, England: Wiley.

Baxter, L. A. (1990). Dialectical contradictions in relationships development. *Journal of Social and Personal Relationships, 7,* 69–88.

Baxter, L. A. (1993). The social side of personal relationships: A dialectical perspective. In S. Duck (Ed.), *Understanding relationship processes, 3: Social context and relationships* (pp. 139–165). Newbury Park, CA: Sage.

Baxter, L. A. (2004). Relationships as dialogues. *Personal Relationships, 11,* 1–22.

Baxter, L. A., & Bullis, C. (1986). Turning points in developing romantic relationships. *Human Communication Research, 12,* 469–493.

Baxter, L. A., & West, L. (2003). Couple perceptions of their similarities and differences: A dialectical analysis. *Journal of Social and Personal Relationships, 20,* 491–514.

Baym, N. (2000). *Tune in, log on: Soaps, fandom, and online community.* Thousand Oaks, CA: Sage.

Baym, N., Zhang, Y. B., & Lin, M.-C. (2004). Social interactions across media: Interpersonal communication on the Internet, telephone and face-to-face. *New Media & Society, 6,* 41–60.

Beatty, M. J., & Payne, S. K. (1984). Listening comprehension as a function of cognitive complexity: A research note. *Communication Monographs, 51,* 85–89.

Becker, J. A., Ellevold, B., & Stamp, G. H. (2008). The creation of defensiveness in social interaction II: A model of defensive communication among romantic couples. *Communication Monographs, 75,* 86–110.

Beehr, T. A., LeGro, K., Porter, K., Bowling, N. A., & Swader, W. M. (2010). Required volunteers: Community volunteerism among students in college classes. *Teaching of Psychology, 37,* 276–280. doi:10.1080/009 86283.2010.510965

Benne, K. D., & Sheats, P. (1948). Functional roles of group members. *Journal of Social Issues, 4,* 41–49.

Bentley, S. C. (2000). Listening in the 21st century. *International Journal of Listening, 14,* 129–143.

Berger, C. R. (2004, May). *Natural versus technological mediation: The insidious insinuation of technological mediation into natural mediation and face-to-face interaction.* Paper presented at the annual meeting of the International Communication Association, New Orleans, LA.

Berger, C. R. (2005). Interpersonal communication: Theoretical perspectives, future prospects. *Journal of Communication, 55,* 415–447.

Berger, P. L., & Luckmann, T. (1967). *The social construction of reality: A treatise in the sociology of knowledge.* New York, NY: Anchor Books.

Berman, M. G., Jonides, J., & Kaplan, S. (2008). The cognitive benefits of interacting with nature. *Psychological Science, 19,* 1207–1212. doi:10.1111/j.1467-9280.2008.02225.x

Berry, D. S., & Miller, K. M. (2001). When boy meets girl: Attractiveness and the five-factor model in opposite-sex interactions. *Journal of Research in Personality, 35,* 62–77.

Berry, G. R. (2011). Enhancing effectiveness on virtual teams: Understanding why traditional team skills are insufficient. *Journal of Business Communication, 48,* 186–206. doi:10.1177/0021943610397270

Berscheid, E., & Walster, E. H. (1969). *Interpersonal attraction.* Reading, MA: Addison-Wesley.

Bertcher, H. J., & Maple, F. F. (1996). *Creating groups* (2nd ed.). Thousand Oaks, CA: Sage.

Biemiller, L. (2007, June 8). Take me back to old main. *The Chronicle of Higher Education,* p. A40.

Bilton, N. (2014, December 3). Are gadget-free bedrooms the secret to a happy relationship? *New York Times.* Retrieved from http://www.nytimes.com

Blair, C. (2006). Communication as collective memory. In G. J. Shepherd, J. St. John, & T. Stripas (Eds.), *Communication as ... perspectives on theory* (pp. 51–59). Thousand Oaks, CA: Sage.

Bloomfield, S. (2006, January 16). The face of the future: Why Eurasians are changing the rules of attraction. *Independent on Sunday* (London), p. 3.

Bodie, G. D. (2010). Treating listening ethically. *International Journal of Listening, 24,* 185–188.

Bodie, G. D. (2011). The active-empathic listening scale (AELS): Conceptualization and evidence of validity within the interpersonal domain. *Communication Quarterly, 59,* 277–295.

Bodie, G. D., Powers, W. G., & Fitch-Hauser, M. (2006). Chunking, priming and active learning: Toward an innovative and blended approach to teaching communication-related skills. *Interactive Learning Environments, 14,* 119–135.

Bodie, G. D., Vickery, A. J., Cannava, K., & Jones, S. M. (2015). The role of "active listening" in informal helping conversations: Impact on perceptions of listener helpfulness, sensitivity, and supportiveness and discloser emotional improvement. *Western Journal of Communication, 79,* 151–173. doi:10.1080/10570314.2014.943429

Bodie, G. D., Vickery, A. J., & Gearhart, C. C. (2013). The nature of supportive listening, I: Exploring the relation between supportive listeners and supportive people. *International Journal of Listening, 27,* 39–49. doi:10.1080 /10904018.2013.732408

Bodie, G. D., Worthington, D., Imhof, M., & Cooper, L. O. (2008). What would a unified field of listening look like? A proposal linking past perspectives and future endeavors. *International Journal of Listening, 22,* 103–122.

Bolton, C. D. (1961). Mate selection as the development of a relationship. *Marriage and Family Living, 23,* 243–240.

Boltz, M. G., Dyer, R. L., & Miller, A. R. (2010). Are you lying to me? Temporal cues for deception. *Journal of Language and Social Psychology, 29,* 458–466.

Bormann, E. G. (1989). *Discussion and group methods: Theory and practice* (3rd ed.). New York, NY: Harper & Row.

Bosch, T. (2011, November 1). Would you trust your hospital care to a virtual nurse? Retrieved from http://www.slate.com/blogs/ future_tense/2011/11/01/virtual_nurses_ may_provide_patient_care_in_hospitals_in_ the_futu.html

Botelho, G., & Yan, H. (2013, July 14). George Zimmerman found not guilty of murder in Trayvon Martin's death. Retrieved from http://www.cnn.com/2013/07/13/ justice/zimmerman-trial/

Boyd, S. D. (1995). Executive speech coaching: An on-site, individualized, abbreviated course in public speaking. *Business Communication Quarterly, 58*(3), 58–60.

Boykoff, P. (2015, March 9). MH370 report: Search delayed by chaos and confusion. CNN. Retrieved May 1, 2015, from www .cnn.com/2015/03/09/asia/mh370-report-search-delays/

Braithwaite, D. O. (1991). "Just how much did that wheelchair cost?": Management of privacy boundaries by persons with disabilities. *Western Journal of Speech Communication, 55,* 254–274.

Braithwaite, D. O., & Braithwaite, C. A. (2009). "Which is my good leg?" Cultural communication of persons with disabilities. In L. W. Samovar, R. Porter, & E. R. McDaniel (Eds.), *Intercultural communication: A reader* (9th ed., pp. 207–218). Belmont, CA: Wadsworth.

Braithwaite, D. O., & Thompson, T. L. (2000). *Handbook of communication and people with disabilities: Research and application.* Mahwah, NJ: Erlbaum.

Brand-Gruwel, S., & Stadtler, M. (2011). Solving information-based problems: Evaluating sources and information. *Learning and Instruction, 21,* 175–179. doi:0959–4752, 10.1016/j. learninstruc.2010.02.008

Brehm, S. S. (1992). *Intimate relationships.* New York, NY: McGraw-Hill.

Bridge, K., & Baxter, L. A. (1992). Blended relationships: Friends as work associates. *Western Journal of Communication, 56,* 200–225. doi:10.1080/10570319209374414

Briñol, P., Rucker, D., & Petty, R. (2015). Naïve theories about persuasion: Implications for information processing and consumer attitude change. *International Journal of Advertising, 34,* 1–22. doi:10.1080/026504 87.2014.997080

Brock, A. (2011). When keeping it real goes wrong: *Resident Evil 5*, racial representation, and gamers. *Games and Culture, 6*(5), 429–452.

Bronstein, S., & Griffin, D. (2011, October 22). Teen murder suspect carried "backpack of hatred." Retrieved December 15, 2011, from http://www.cnn .com/2011/10/22/us/mississippi-hate-crime-teens/index.html

Brown, P., & Levinson, S. (1978). Universals in language usage: Politeness phenomena. In E. Goody (Ed.), *Questions and politeness* (pp. 56–311). Cambridge, England: Cambridge University Press.

Brown, R. (1973). *A first language.* Cambridge, MA: Harvard University Press.

Brownell, J. (1994). Creating strong listening environments: A key hospitality management task. *International Journal of Contemporary Hospitality Management, 6,* 3–10.

Bryant, E. M., & Sias, P. M. (2011). Sense making and relational consequences of peer co-worker deception. *Communication Monographs, 78,* 115–137.

Bureau of Labor Statistics. (2015, February 15). Volunteering in the United States, 2014. Retrieved from http://www.bls.gov/news .release/volun.nr0.htm

Burgoon, J. K., & Jones, S. B. (1976). Toward a theory of personal space expectations and their violations. *Human Communication Research, 2,* 131–146.

Burkard, A. W., Boticki, M. A., & Madson, M. B. (2002). Workplace discrimination, prejudice, and diversity measurement: A review of instrumentation. *Journal of Career Assessment, 10,* 343–361.

Burke, K. (1966). *Language as symbolic action.* Berkeley & Los Angeles: University of California Press.

Burleson, B. R., & Caplan, S. E. (1998). Cognitive complexity. In J. C. McCroskey, J. A. Daly, M. M. Martin, & M. J. Beatty (Eds.), *Communication and personality: Trait perspectives* (pp. 233–286). Creskill, NJ: Hampton Press.

Burns, K. (2011, March 10). 50 worst of the worst (and most common) job interview mistakes. *U.S. News & World Report.* Retrieved from http://money. usnews.com/money/blogs/outside-voices-careers/2010/03/10/50-worst-of-the-worst-job-interview-mistakes

Burtis, J. O., & Turman, P. D. (2006). *Group communication pitfalls: Overcoming barriers to an effective group experience.* Thousand Oaks, CA: Sage.

Caborn, J. (2007). On the methodology of dispositive analysis. *Critical Approaches to Discourse Analysis Across Disciplines, 1,* 115–123.

Cacioppo, J. T., Cacioppo, S., Gonzaga, G. C., Ogburn, E. L., & VanderWeele, T. J. (2013). Marital satisfaction and break-ups differ across on-line and off-line meeting venues. *Proceedings of the National Academy of Sciences, 110,* 18814–18819.

Cahill, D. J., & Sias, P. M. (1997). The perceived social costs and importance of seeking emotional support in the workplace: Gender differences and similarities. *Communication Research Reports, 14,* 231–240.

Calderwood, C., Ackerman, P. L., & Conklin, E. M. (2014). What else do college students "do" while studying? An investigation of multitasking. *Computers & Education, 75,* 19–29. doi:10.1016/j. compedu.2014.02.004

Cary, N. (2015, January 10). Clemson considers banning anonymous app Yik Yak. *WLTX19.* Retrieved from http://www .wltx.com

Cassidy, W., Jackson, M., & Brown, K. N. (2009). Sticks and stones can break my bones, but how can pixels hurt me? *School Psychology International, 30,* 383–402.

Caughlin, J. P., Brashers, D. E., Ramey, M. E., Kosenko, K. A., Donovan-Kicken, E., & Bute, J. J. (2008). The message design logics of responses to HIV disclosures. *Human Communication Research, 34,* 655–685.

Caughlin, J. P., Bute, J. J., Donovan-Kicken, E., Kosenko, K. A., Ramey, M. E., & Brashers, D. E. (2009). Do message features influence reactions to HIV disclosures? A multiple-goals perspective. *Health Communication, 24,* 270–283.

Caulfield, P. (2011, December 6). H&M uses virtual models for new lingerie, bikini ads. NYDailyNews.com. Retrieved from http://www.nydailynews.com/life-style/ fashion/h-m-virtual-models-lingerie-bikini-ads-article-1.987589

Caution: This office is a gossip-free zone. (2007, November 13). *Good Morning America.* Retrieved from http:// abcnews.go.com/GMA/WaterCooler/ story?id=3857737&page=1#.T3JFVexSTCo

Cenite, M., Detenber, B. H., Koh, A. W. K., Lim, A. H. L., & Soon, N. E. (2009). Doing

the right thing online: A survey of bloggers' ethical beliefs and practices. *New Media & Society, 11*(4), 575–597.

The challenges of working in virtual teams: Virtual teams survey report. (2010). Retrieved from http://rw-3.com/VTSReportv7.pdf

Chang, L., & Krosnick, J. A. (2010). Comparing oral interviewing with self-administered computerized questionnaires: An experiment. *Public Opinion Quarterly, 74*(1), 154–167.

Change.org. (2015). Facebook: Remove the "feeling fat emoticon." Retrieved from http://www.change.org/p/facebook-remove-the-feeling-fat-emoticon-fatisnotafeeling/ responses/27256

Chesebro, J. D., & McCroskey, J. C. (2001). The relationship of teacher clarity and immediacy with student state receiver apprehension, affect, and cognitive learning. *Communication Education, 50,* 59–68.

Chidambaram, L., & Bostrom, R. P. (1996). Group development (I): A review and synthesis of development models. *Group Decision and Negotiation, 6,* 159–187.

Christensen, L. J., & Menzel, K. E. (1998). The linear relationship between student reports of teacher immediacy behaviors and perceptions of state motivation, and of cognitive, affective, and behavioral learning. *Communication Education, 47,* 82–90.

Christian, J., Porter, L. W., & Moffit, G. (2006). Workplace diversity and group relations: An overview. *Group Process & Intergroup Relations, 9,* 459–466.

Cissna, K. N., & Sieburg, E. (1981). Patterns of interactional confirmation and disconfirmation. In C. Wilder-Mott & J. H. Weakland (Eds.), *Rigor and imagination: Essays from the legacy of Gregory Bateson* (pp. 253–282). New York, NY: Praeger.

Cissna, K. N., & Sieburg, E. (1995). Patterns of interactional confirmation and disconfirmation. In J. Redmond (Ed.), *Interpersonal communication: Readings in theory and research* (pp. 301–317). Fort Worth, TX: Harcourt Brace.

Clark, R. A., & Delia, J. G. (1977). Cognitive complexity, social perspective-taking, and functional persuasive skills in second- to ninth-grade children. *Human Communication Research, 3,* 128–134.

Clore, G. L. (1977). Reinforcement and affect in attraction. In S. W. Duck (Ed.), *Theory and practice in interpersonal attraction* (pp. 23–50). London, England: Academic Press.

CNN Wire Staff. (2011). Lady Gaga starts foundation to fight bullying, empower youth. Retrieved December 15, 2011, from http://www.cnn.com/2011/11/02/showbiz/lady-gaga-foundation/index.html

Coakley, A. B., & Duffy, M. E. (2010). The effect of therapeutic touch on postoperative patients. *Journal of Holistic Nursing, 28,* 193–200.

Coates, J. (1993). *Women, men and language.* London, England: Longman.

Comello, M. L. G. (2009). William James on "Possible Selves": Implications for studying identity in communication contexts. *Communication Theory, 19,* 337–350.

Conlee, C. J., & Olvera, J. (1993). The relationships among physician nonverbal immediacy and measures of patient satisfaction. *Communication Reports, 6,* 25–33.

Connelly, S. (2014, September 7). "Catfish" host Nev Schulman writes tell-all that details his online lies to warn others. *New York Daily News.* Retrieved from http://www.nydailynews.com/entertainment/nev-schulman-writes-tell-all-online-exploits-article-1

Cooley, C. (1902). *Human nature and the social order.* New York, NY: Scribner.

Coon, J. T., Boddy, K., Stein, K., Whear, R., Barton, J., & Depledge, M. H. (2011). Does participating in physical activity in outdoor natural environments have a greater effect on physical and mental well-being than physical activity indoors? A systemic review. *Environmental Science & Technology.* doi:10.1021/es102947t

Cooper, L. O., & Buchanan, T. (2010). Listening competency on campus: A psychometric analysis of student listening. *International Journal of Listening, 24,* 141–163.

Corporate Equality Index 2015: Rating American workplaces on lesbian, gay, bisexual, and transgender equality. (2014). Retrieved from www.hrc.org/cei

Corss, S. E., Bacon, P. L., & Morris, M. L. (2000). The relational-interdependent self-construal and relationships. *Journal of Personality and Social Psychology, 78,* 791–808. doi:10.1037/0022-3514.78.4.791

Costanza, D. P., Badger, J. M., Fraser, R. L., Severt, J. B., & Gade, P. (2012). Generational differences in work-related attitudes: A meta-analysis. *Journal of Business & Psychology, 27,* 375–394. doi:10.1007/s10869-012-0259-4

Couch, D., & Liamputtong, P. (2008). Online dating and mating: The use of the Internet to meet sexual partners. *Qualitative Health Research, 18,* 269–279.

Council of Writing Program Administrators. (2003, January). Defining and avoiding plagiarism: The WPA statement on best practices. Retrieved from http://www.wpacouncil.org/positions/WPAplagiarism.pdf

Cowan, R. L. (2011). "Yes, we have an anti-bullying policy, but . . .": HR professionals' understandings and experiences with workplace bullying policy. *Communication Studies, 62,* 307–327. doi:10.1080/105109 74.2011.553763

Cowan, R. L., & Bochantin, J. E. (2011). Blue-collar employees' work/life metaphors: Tough similarities, imbalance, separation, and opposition. *Qualitative Research Reports in Communication, 12,* 19–26.

Cowan, R., & Hoffman, M. F. (2007). The flexible organization: How contemporary employees construct the work/life border. *Qualitative Research Reports in Communication, 8,* 37–44. doi:10.1080/1745930701617895

Cragan, J. F., & Wright, D. W. (1999). *Communication in small groups: Theory, process, skills* (5th ed.). Belmont, CA: Wadsworth.

Craig, R. T. (1999). Communication theory as a field. *Communication Theory, 9,* 119–161.

Crockett, W. H. (1965). Cognitive complexity and impression formation. In B. A. Maher (Ed.), *Progress in experimental personality research* (Vol. 2, pp. 47–90). New York, NY: Academic Press.

Crockett, W. H., Mahood, S., & Press, A. N. (1975). Impressions of a speaker as a function of set to understand or to evaluate, of cognitive complexity, and of prior attitudes. *Journal of Personality, 43,* 168–178.

Cross, S. E., Bacon, P. L., & Morris, M. L. (2000). The relational-interdependent self-construal and relationships. *Journal of Personality and Social Psychology, 78,* 791–808.

Cruikshank, L. (2010). Digitizing race: Visual cultures of the Internet. *Information, Communication & Society, 13*(2), 278–280.

D

Dahlstrom, M. F. (2010). The role of causality in information acceptance in narratives: An example from science communication. *Communication Research, 37,* 857–875.

Dailey, R. M. (2006). Confirmation in parent-adolescent relationships and adolescent openness: Toward extending confirmation theory. *Communication Monographs, 73,* 434–458.

Daily Mail Reporter. (2011, May 26). "Space has lost its glamour": New tapes reveal how JFK fretted over selling Apollo moon mission to U.S. public. *Daily Mail.* Retrieved from http://www.dailymail.co.uk/news/article-1390928/New-tapes-reveal-JFK-fretted-selling-Apollo-moon-mission-US-public.html

Daniels, J. (2005). The art of making persuasive presentations. *Employment Relations Today, 31,* 39–49.

Darics, E. (2010). Politeness in computer-mediated discourse of a virtual team. *Journal of Politeness Research: Language, Behavior, Culture, 6*(1), 129–150.

Davis, K. (2011). Tensions of identity in a networked era: Young people's perspectives on the risks and rewards of online self-expression. *New Media & Society,* 1–18.

Deahl, R. (2011, December 5). Ethics in interviewing: The importance of ethics in interviewing. About.com. Retrieved from http://mediacareers.about.com/od/gettingthejob/a/Ethics.htm

Deal, T. E., & Kennedy, A. A. (2000). *Corporate cultures: The rites and rituals of corporate life.* New York, NY: Basic Books.

DeAndrea, D. C., Shaw, A. S., & Levine, T. R. (2010). Online language: The role of culture in self-expression and self-construal on Facebook. *Journal of Language & Social Psychology, 29*(4), 425–442.

Decision-making techniques: How to make better decisions. (1996–2015). Retrieved from http://www.mindtools.com

Delbecq, A., Van de Ven, A. H., & Gustafson, D. H. (1975). *Group techniques for program planning: A guide to nominal and Delphi processes.* Glenview, IL: Scott, Foresmen.

Delia, J. G., & Clark, R. A. (1977). Cognitive complexity, social perception, and the development of listener-adapted communication in six-, eight-, ten-, and twelve-year-old boys. *Communication Monographs, 44,* 326–345.

Denton, W. H., Burleson, B. R., & Sprenkle, D. H. (1995). Association of interpersonal cognitive complexity with communication skill in marriage: Moderating effects of marital distress. *Family Process, 34,* 101–111.

DePaulo, B. M., Lindsay, J. L., Malone, B. E., Muhlenbruck, L., Charlton, K., & Cooper, H.

(2003). Cues to deception. *Psychological Bulletin, 129,* 74–118.

Deterding, S., Sicart, M., Nacke, L., O'Hara, K., & Dixon, D. (2011). Gamification: Using game-design elements in non-gaming contexts. In *Proceedings of the 2011 Annual Conference Extended Abstracts on Human Factors in Computing Systems,* 2425–2428. doi:10.1145/1979742.1979575

Dewey, J. (1927). *The public and its problems.* Oxford, England: Holt.

Dewey, J. F. (1944). *Democracy and education: An introduction to the philosophy of education.* New York, NY: Free Press. (Original work published 1916)

Dillow, M. R., Malachowski, C. C., Brann, M., & Weber, K. D. (2011). An experimental examination of the effects of communicative infidelity motives on communication and relational outcomes in romantic relationships. *Western Journal of Communication, 75,* 473–499.

Distraction.gov. (2015a). One text or call could wreck it all: Distracted driving news. Retrieved May 17, 2015, from http://www.distraction.gov

Distraction.gov. (2015b). What is distracted driving? Key facts and statistics. Retrieved May 17, 2015, from http://distraction.gov/content/get-the-facts/facts-and-statistics.html

Docan-Morgan, S. (2011). "They don't know what it's like to be in my shoes": Topic avoidance about race in transracially adoptive families. *Journal of Social and Personal Relationships, 28,* 336–355.

Dodds, T. J., Mohler, B. J., & Bülthoff, H. H. (2011). Talk to the virtual hands: Self-animated avatars improve communication in head-mounted display virtual environments. *PLOS ONE, 6*(10), e25759. Retrieved from http://www.plosone.org/article/info%3Adoi%2F10.1371%2Fjournal.pone.0025759

Domenici, K., & Littlejohn, S. W. (2006). *Facework: Bridging theory and practice.* Thousand Oaks, CA: Sage.

Domingue, R., & Mollen, D. (2009). Attachment and conflict communication in adult romantic relationships. *Journal of Social & Personal Relationships, 26,* 678–696.

Donald, A. (2014). Girls against the world. *Screen Education, 76,* 60–67.

Dornburg, C. C., Stevens, S. M., Hendrickson, S. M. L., & Davidson, G. S. (2009). Improving extreme-scale problem solving: Assessing electronic brainstorming effectiveness in an industrial setting. *Human Factors, 51,* 519–527.

Dresner, E., & Herring, S. C. (2010). Functions of the nonverbal in CMC: Emoticons and illocutionary force. *Communication Theory, 20*(3), 249–268.

Driscoll, K., & Wiebe, E. (2007). Technical spirituality at work: Jacques Ellul on workplace spirituality. *Journal of Management Inquiry, 16,* 333–348.

Driskill, G. W., & Brenton, A. L. (2011). *Organizational culture in action: A cultural analysis workbook* (2nd ed.). Thousand Oaks, CA: Sage.

Drummond, D. K., & Orbe, M. P. (2009). "Who are you trying to be?": Identity gaps within intraracial encounters. *Qualitative Research Reports in Communication, 10,* 81–87.

Dube, L., & Robey, D. (2008). Surviving the paradoxes of virtual teamwork. *Information Systems Journal, 19,* 3–30. doi:10.111/j.1365-2575.2008.00313.x

Duck, S., & McMahan, D. (2010). *Communication in everyday life.* Los Angeles, CA: Sage.

Duran, R. L., & Kelly, L. (1988). The influence of communicative competence on perceived task, social, and physical attraction. *Communication Quarterly, 36,* 41–49.

Duran, R. L., & Wheeless, V. (1982). Social management: Towards a theory-based operationalization of communication competence. *Southern Speech Communication Journal, 48,* 51–64.

Eadie, W. F. (2009). In plain sight: Gay and lesbian communication and culture. In L. W. Samovar, R. Porter, & E. R. McDaniel (Eds.), *Intercultural communication: A reader* (9th ed., pp. 219–231). Belmont, CA: Wadsworth.

Eaves, M. H., & Leathers, D. G. (1991). Context as communication: McDonald's vs. Burger King. *Journal of Applied Communication Research, 19,* 263–289.

Edwards, C., & Edwards, A. (in press). Robotic communication. In *The SAGE Encyclopedia of Communication Research Methods.*

Edwards, C., Edwards, A., Myers, S., & Wahl, S. (2003). The relationship between student pre-performance concerns and evaluation apprehension. *Communication Research Reports, 20,* 54–61.

Edwards, C., Edwards, A., Qing, Q., & Wahl, S. T. (2007). The influence of computer-mediated word-of-mouth communication on student perceptions of instructors and attitudes toward learning course content. *Communication Education, 56,* 255–277.

Edwards, E., & Shepherd, G. J. (2007). An investigation of the relationship between implicit personal theories of communication and community behavior. *Communication Studies, 58,* 359–375.

Eisenstein, E. L. (1980). *The printing press as an agent of change.* Cambridge, England: Cambridge University Press.

Ekman, P., & Friesen, W. V. (1969a). Nonverbal leakage and clues to deception. *Psychiatry, 32,* 88–106.

Ekman, P., & Friesen, W. V. (1969b). The repertoire of nonverbal behavior: Categories, origins, usage, and coding. *Semiotica, 1,* 49–98.

Ekman, P., & Friesen, W. V. (1975). *Unmasking the face: A guide to recognizing emotions from facial cues.* Englewood Cliffs, NJ: Prentice Hall.

Ellis, K. (2000). Perceived teacher confirmation: The development and validation of an instrument and two studies of the relationship to cognitive and affective learning. *Human Communication Research, 26,* 264–291.

Ellis, K. (2002). Perceived parental confirmation: Development and validation of an instrument. *Southern Communication Journal, 67,* 319–334.

Ellison, N. B., Vitak, J., Gray, R., & Lampe, C. (2014). Cultivating social resources on social network sites: Facebook relationship maintenance behaviors and their role in social capital processes. *Journal of Computer-Mediated Communication, 19,* 855–870. doi:10.1111/jcc4.12078

Ephratt, M. (2011). "We try harder": Silence and Grice's cooperative principle, maxims and implicatures. *Language & Communication, 33,* 316–328.

Erdur-Baker, Ö. (2010). Cyberbullying and its correlation to traditional bullying, gender and frequent and risky usage of Internet-mediated communication tools. *New Media & Society, 12*(1), 109–125.

Erickson, I. (2010). Geography and community: New forms of interaction among people and places. *American Behavioral Scientist, 53,* 1194–1207.

Ertner, R. (2010, January 27). Under-aged texting: Usage and actual cost. Retrieved from http://blog.nielsen.com/nielsenwire/online_mobile/under-aged-texting-usage-and-actual-cost/

The evolution of the social media manager. (2014). *Communication World, 31*(1), 9–11.

F

Facebook. (2012). Fact sheet. Retrieved April 10, 2012, from http://www.facebook.com/press/info.php?factsheet

Facebook. (2015). Fact sheet. Retrieved April 9, 2012, from http://newsroom.fb.com/content/default.aspx?NewsAreaId=22

Fair, B. (2011). Constructing masculinity through penetration discourse: The intersection of misogyny and homophobia in high school wrestling. *Men and Masculinities, 14,* 491–504.

Fang, J. (2011, November 7). Virtual nurse provides comfort for hospital patients. Retrieved from http://www.smartplanet.com/blog/rethinking-healthcare/virtual-nurse-provides-comfort-for-hospital-patients/7383

Farmer, S. M., & Roth, J. (1998). Conflict-handling behavior in work groups: Effects of group structure, decision processes, and time. *Small Group Research, 29,* 669–713.

Fay, E., & Nyhan, J. (2015). Webbs on the Web: Libraries, digital humanities and collaboration. *Library Review, 64,* 118–134. doi:http://dx.doi.org/10.1108/LR-08-2014-0089

Feldman, D. C. (1984). The development and emergence of group norms. *Academy of Management Review, 9,* 47–53.

Ferguson unrest: From shooting to nationwide protests. (2015, March 12). *BBC News.* Retrieved from http://www.bbc.com/news/world-us-canada-30193354

Festinger, L, Schachter, S., & Back, K. W. (1950). *Social pressures in informal groups: A study of human factors in housing.* New York, NY: Harper.

Filley, A. C. (1975). *Interpersonal conflict resolution.* Glenview, IL: Scott, Foresman.

Fine, M. G. (1996). Cultural diversity in the workplace: The state of the field. *Journal of Business Communication, 33,* 485–502.

Fishbein, M., & Ajzen, I. (1975). *Belief, attitude, intention, and behavior: An introduction to theory and research.* Reading, MA: Addison-Wesley.

Fisher, B. A. (1971). Communication research and the task-oriented group. *Journal of Communication, 21,* 136–149.

Fisher, B. A. (1980). *Small group decision making: Communication and the group process* (2nd ed.). New York, NY: McGraw-Hill.

Fisher, W. R. (1984). Narration as a human communication paradigm: The case of public moral argument. *Communication Monographs, 51,* 1–22.

Fisher, W. R. (1987). *Human communication as narration: Toward a philosophy of reason, value, and action.* Columbia: University of South Carolina Press.

Fleming, N. D. (2001). *Teaching and learning styles: VARK strategies.* Christchurch, New Zealand: Author.

Fleming, P. (2007). Sexuality, power, and resistance in the workplace. *Organization Studies, 28,* 230–256.

Fleuriet, C., Cole, M., & Guerrero, L. (2014). Exploring Facebook: Attachment style and nonverbal message characteristics as predictors of anticipated emotional reactions to Facebook postings. *Journal of Nonverbal Behavior, 38*(4), 429–450.

Floyd, J. (2010). Provocation: Dialogic listening as reachable goal. *International Journal of Listening, 24,* 170–173.

Floyd, K. (2014). Empathic listening as an expression of interpersonal affection. *International Journal of Listening, 28,* 1–12.

Flynn, J., Valikoski, T., & Grau, J. (2008). Listening in the business context: Reviewing the state of research. *International Journal of Listening, 22,* 141–151.

Fong, T., Nourbakhsh, L., & Dautenhahn, K.(2003). A survey of socially interactive robots. *Robotics and Autonomous Systems, 42,*143–166.

Fonner, K. L., & Roloff, M. E. (2010). Why teleworkers are more satisfied than office-based workers: When less contact is beneficial. *Journal of Applied Communication Research, 38,* 336–361.

Fonner, K. L., & Timmerman, C. E. (2009). Organizational newc(ust)omers: Applying organizational newcomer assimilation concepts to customer information seeking and service outcomes. *Management Communication Quarterly, 23,* 244–271.

Ford, M. (2015, March 7). Obama's America. *The Atlantic.* Retrieved March 13, 2015, from http://www.theatlantic.com/politics/archive/2015/03/obama-at-selma-ferguson-exceptionalism/387169/

Fountain, H. M. (2005). Why Arab men hold hands. Retrieved from http://www.nytimes.com/2005/05/01/weekinreview/01basics.html

Frauendorfer, D., Schmid Mast, M., Nguyen, L., & Gatica-Perez, D. (2014). Nonverbal social sensing in action: Unobtrusive recording and extracting of nonverbal behavior in social interactions illustrated with a research example. *Journal of Nonverbal Behavior, 38*(2), 231–245.

Frey, L. R. (1997). Individuals in groups. In L. R. Frey & J. K. Barge (Eds.), *Managing group life: Communicating in decision-making groups* (pp. 52–79). Boston, MA: Houghton Mifflin.

Frey, L. R., & Carragee, K. M. (Eds.). (2007). *Communication activism: Volume 1. Communication for social change.* Cresskill, NJ: Hampton Press.

Fritz, J. H. (1997). Men's and women's organizational peer relationships: A comparison. *Journal of Business Communication, 34,* 27–46.

Fritz, J. M. H. (2002). How do I dislike thee? Let me count the ways: Constructing impressions of troublesome others at work. *Management Communication Quarterly, 15,* 410–438.

Fulford, C. P., & Zhang, S. (1993). Perceptions of interaction: The critical predictor in distance education. *American Journal of Distance Education, 7,* 8–21.

G

Gabler, N. (1998). *Life the movie: How entertainment conquered reality.* New York, NY: Knopf.

Gabriel, Y. (2008). Against the tyranny of PowerPoint: Technology-in-use and technology abuse. *Organization Studies, 29,* 255–276.

Gage, R. L., III, & Thapa, B. (2012). Volunteer motivations and constraints among college students: Analysis of the Volunteer Function Inventory and leisure constraints model. *Nonprofit and Voluntary Sector Quarterly, 41,* 405-430. doi:10.1177/0899764011406738

Galanes, G. A. (2003). In their own words: An exploratory study of bona fide group leaders. *Small Group Research, 34,* 741–770.

Galanes, G. J. (2009). Dialectical tensions of small group leadership. *Communication Studies, 60,* 409–425.

Gallagher, E. B., & Sias, P. M. (2009). The new employee as a source of uncertainty: Veteran employee information seeking about new hires. *Western Journal of Communication, 73,* 23–46.

Galliard, B. M., Myers, K. K., & Seibold, D. R. (2010). Organizational assimilation: A multidimensional reconceptualization and measure. *Management Communication Quarterly, 24,* 552–578.

Gallo, C. (2014, January 24). Mac 1984: Steve Jobs revolutionizes the art of corporate storytelling. *Forbes.* Retrieved April 3, 2015, from http://www.forbes.com/sites/carminegallo/2014/01/24/mac-1984-steve-jobs-revolutionizes-the-art-of-corporate-storytelling/

Generational differences chart. (n.d.). Westland Midland Family Center. Retrieved from http://www.wmfc.og/uploads.GenerationalDifferencesChart.pdf

Genova, G. L. (2009). No place to play: Current employee privacy rights in social networking sites. *Business Communication Quarterly, 72,* 97–101.

Gergen, K. (2001). *Social construction in context.* London, England: Sage.

Gergen, K. G. (1991). *The saturated self: Dilemmas of identity in contemporary life.* New York, NY: Basic Books.

Gergen, M. M. (2009). Framing lives: Therapy with women of a "certain age." *Women & Therapy, 32,* 252–266.

Gibb, J. R. (1961). Defensive communication. *Journal of Communication, 11,* 141–148.

Gibbs, J. L., Ellison, N. B., & Heino, R. D. (2006). Self-presentation in online personals: The role of anticipated future interaction, self-disclosure, and perceived success in Internet dating. *Communication Research, 33,* 152–177.

Giddings, S. (2011). *The new media and technocultures reader.* London, England: Routledge.

Gil de Zúñiga, H., Lewis, S., Willard, A., Valenzuela, S., Jae Kook, L., & Baresch, B. (2011). Blogging as a journalistic practice: A model linking perception, motivation, and behavior. *Journalism, 12*(5), 586–606.

Gillespie, D., Rosamond, S., & Thomas, E. (2006). Grouped out? Undergraduates' default strategies for participating in multiple small groups. *JGE: The Journal of General Education, 55,* 82–102.

Gilmour, J. B. (2011). Political theater or bargaining failure: Why presidents veto. *Presidential Studies Quarterly, 41,* 471–487.

Gittell, J. H. (2003). *The Southwest Airlines way: Using the power of relationships to achieve high performance.* New York, NY: McGraw-Hill.

Glowka, W., Barrett, G., Barnhart, D. K., Melancom, M., & Salter, M. (2009). Among new words. *American Speech, 84,* 83–101.

Goffman, E. (1952). On cooking the mark out: Some aspects of adaptation to failure. *Psychiatry, 15,* 451–463.

Goffman, E. (1959). *The presentation of self in everyday life.* Garden City, NJ: Doubleday Anchor Books.

Goffman, E. (1967). *Interaction ritual: Essays on face-to-face behavior.* New York, NY: Pantheon.

Goffman, E. (1971). *Relations in public: Microstudies of the public order.* New York, NY: Harper Colophon Books.

Golden, J. L, Berquist, G. F., & Coleman, W. E. (1997). *The rhetoric of Western thought.* Dubuque, IA: Kendall/Hunt.

Goldman, Z. W., & Myers, S. A. (2015). The relationship between organizational assimilation and employees' upward, lateral, and displaced dissent. *Communication Reports, 28,* 24–35. doi:10.1080/08934215.2014.902488

Gonzales, A. L., & Hancock, J. T. (2010, April). Identity shift in computer-mediated environments. *Media Psychology, 11,* 167–185.

Goodall, H. L. (1991). *Living in the rock n roll mystery.* Carbondale: Southern Illinois University Press.

Gordon, R. (1985). Dimensions of peak communication experiences: An exploratory study. *Psychological Reports, 57,* 824–826.

Gordon, T. (1970). *Parent effectiveness training: The "no-lose" program for raising responsible children.* New York, NY: Wyden.

Gosselin, P., Gilles, K., & Dore, F. Y. (1995). Components and recognition of facial expression in the communication of emotion by actors. *Journal of Personality and Social Psychology, 68,* 83–96.

Gouran, D. (1997). Effective versus ineffective group decision making. In L. R. Frey & J. K. Barge (Eds.), *Managing group life: Communicating in decision-making groups* (pp. 133–155). Boston, MA: Houghton Mifflin.

Gouran, D. S., & Hirokawa, R. Y. (1996). Functional theory and communication in decision-making and problem-solving groups: An expanded view. In R. Y. Hirokawa & M. S. Poole (Eds.), *Communication and group decision making* (2nd ed., pp. 55–80). Thousand Oaks, CA: Sage.

Gouran, D. S., Hirokawa, R. Y., Julian, K. M., & Leatham, G. B. (1993). The evolution and current status of the functional perspective on communication in decision-making and problem-solving groups. In S. A. Deetz (Ed.), *Communication yearbook* (Vol. 16, pp. 573–600). Newbury Park, CA: Sage.

Graham, E. E., Papa, M. J., & McPherson, M. B. (1997). An applied test of the functional communication perspective of small group decision-making. *Southern Communication Journal, 62,* 269–279.

Greenhow, C., & Robelia, B. (2009). Informal learning and identity formation in online social networks. *Learning, Media and Technology, 34*(2), 119–140.

Grice, P. (1975). Logic and conversation. In P. Cole & J. Morgan (Eds.), *Syntax and semantics 3: Speech acts.* New York, NY: Academic Press.

Grice, P. (1989). *Studies in the way of words.* Cambridge, MA: Harvard University Press.

Griesedieck, C. (2015). University hosts "teach-in": Event responds to recent ABC arrest. *The Cavalier Daily.* Retrieved from http://www.cavalierdaily.com/article/2015/04/university-hosts-teach-in

Griffin, A. M., & Langlois, J. H. (2006). Stereotype directionality and attractiveness stereotyping: Is beauty good or is ugly bad? *Social Cognition, 24,* 187–206.

Griffin, D. K., Mitchell, D., & Thompson, S. J. (2009). Podcasting by synchronizing PowerPoint and voice: What are the pedagogical benefits? *Computers & Education, 53,* 532–539.

Grisham, L. (2015, January 20). 13-year-old invents Lego Braille printer. *USA Today.* Retrieved from http://www.usatoday.com/story/tech/2015/01/20/braille-lego-printer/22055135/

Grosser, T. J., Lopez-Kidwell, V., & Labianca, G. (2010). A social network analysis of positive and negative gossip in organizational life. *Group & Organization Management, 35,* 177–212.

Grossman, L. (2009, June 17). Iran protests: Twitter, the medium of the movement. *Time World.* Retrieved from http://www.time.com/time/world/article/0,8599,1905125,00.html

Grossman, L., & McCracken, H. (2011, October 17). The inventor of the future. *Time, 178*(15), 36–44.

Grote, N. K., & Frieze, I. H. (1998). Remembrance of things past: Perceptions of marital love from its beginning to the present. *Journal of Social and Personal Relationships, 15,* 91–109.

Guerrero, L. K., & Floyd, K. (2006). *Nonverbal communication in close relationships.* Mahwah, NJ: Erlbaum.

Guiller, J., & Durndell, A. (2007). Students' linguistic behavior in online discussion groups: Does gender matter? *Computers in Human Behavior, 23,* 2240–2255.

Ha, Y., & Lennon, S. J. (2010). Online visual merchandising (VMD) cues and consumer pleasure and arousal: Purchasing versus browsing situation. *Psychology & Marketing, 27*(2), 141–165.

Habermas, J. (1979). *Communication and the evolution of society.* Boston, MA: Beacon Press.

Haines, R. (2014). Group development in virtual teams: An experimental reexamination. *Computers in Human Behavior, 39,* 213–222. doi:10.1016/j.chb.2014.07.019

Hale, C. L. (1980). Cognitive complexity-simplicity as a determinant of communication effectiveness. *Communication Monographs, 47,* 304–311.

Hale, C. L. (1982). An investigation of the relationship between cognitive complexity and listener-adapted communication. *Central States Speech Journal, 33,* 339–344.

Hale, C. L., & Delia, J. G. (1976). Cognitive complexity and social perspective taking. *Communication Monographs, 43,* 195–203.

Hall, E. T. (1963). A system for the notation of proxemic behavior. *American Anthropology, 65,* 1003–1026.

Hall, E. T. (1966). *The hidden dimension.* Garden City, NJ: Doubleday.

Hall, E. T. (1981). *Beyond culture.* New York, NY: Doubleday.

Hall, M. L. (2007). Communicating subjectivity: Leadership as situated construction. *Atlantic Journal of Communication, 15,* 194–213.

Hamilton, L. (2007). Trading on heterosexuality: College women's gender strategies and homophobia. *Gender & Society, 21,* 144–172.

Hammond, R. A., & Axelrod, R. (2006). The evolution of ethnocentrism. *Journal of Conflict Resolution, 50,* 926–936.

Hansen, K. (n.d.). Behavioral job interviewing strategies for job-seekers. Quintessential Careers. Retrieved from http://www.quintcareers.com/behavioral_interviewing.html

Hardaker, C. (2010). Trolling in asynchronous computer-mediated communication: From user discussions to academic definitions. *Journal of Politeness Research: Language, Behavior, Culture, 6*(2), 215–242.

Harris, P., & Sachau, D. (2005). Is cleanliness next to godliness? The role of housekeeping in impression formation. *Environment and Behavior, 37,* 81–99.

Harris, T. E. (1993). *Applied organizational communication: Perspectives, principles, and pragmatics.* Hillsdale, NJ: Erlbaum.

Hawk, T. F., & Shah, A. J. (2007). Using learning style instruments to enhance student learning. *Decision Sciences Journal of Innovative Education, 5,* 1–19.

Haythorthwaite, C. (2005). Social networks and Internet connectivity effects. *Information, Communication, & Society, 8,* 125–147.

Haywood, C. M. (1991). The Bill Crumby story. *St. Anthony Messenger, 99*(4), 17–20.

Heathfield, S. M. (2015). 20 ways Zappos reinforces its company culture. Retrieved from http://humanresources.about.com/od/organizationalculture/a/how-zappos-reinforces-its-company-culture.htm

Hecht, M. L. (1993). 2002—A research odyssey: Toward the development of a communication theory of identity. *Communication Monographs, 60,* 76–82.

Heffernan, V. (2009, January 23). Confession of a TED addict. *The New York Times.* Retrieved from http://www.nytimes.com/2009/01/25/magazine/25wwln-medium-t.html

Henderson, N. J. (2014). Online persona as hybrid-object: Tracing the problems and possibilities of persona in the short film *Noah. M/C Journal, 17*(3), 1.

Herman, B. (2015, April 24). Bruce Jenner's Diane Sawyer interview: A watershed moment for transgender and genderqueer visibility. *International Business Times.* Retrieved from http://www.ibtimes.com/bruce-jenners-diane-sawyer-interview-watershed-moment-transgender-genderqueer-1895969

Herring, S. C. (1993). Gender and democracy in computer-mediated communication. *Electronic Journal of Communication, 3*(2). Retrieved from http://www.cios.org/EJCPUBLIC/003/2/00328.HTML

Herrmann, A. F. (2007). "People get emotional about their money": Performing masculinity in a financial discussion board. *Journal of Computer-Mediated Communication, 12,* 165–188.

Heslin, R. (1974). *Steps toward a taxonomy of touching.* Paper presented at the meeting of the Midwestern Psychological Association, Chicago, IL.

Heyboer, K. (2011, December 4). Former Rutgers student says software-detecting plagiarism was wrong when it flagged her work, caused her to fail. *New Jersey Real-Time News.* Retrieved from http://www.nj.com/news/index.ssf/2011/12/former_rutgers_student_says_so.html

Heyman, R., & Pierson, J. (2013). Blending mass self-communication with advertising in Facebook and LinkedIn: Challenges for social media and user empowerment. *International Journal of Media & Cultural Politics, 9*(3), 229–245.

Hickson, M., III, Stacks, D. W., & Moore, N.-J. (2004). *Nonverbal communication: Studies and applications* (4th ed.). Los Angeles, CA: Roxbury.

Hiltz, S. R., & Turoff, M. (1993). *The network nation: Human communication via computer.* Reading, MA: Addison-Wesley.

Hinkle, L. L. (2001). Perceptions of supervisor nonverbal immediacy, vocalics, and subordinate liking. *Communication Research Reports, 18,* 128–136.

Hirokawa, R. Y. (1985). Discussion procedures and decision-making performance: A test of a functional perspective. *Human Communication Research, 12,* 203–224.

Hirokawa, R. Y., & Pace, R. (1983). A descriptive investigation of the possible communication-based reasons for effective and ineffective group decision making. *Communication Monographs, 50,* 363–379.

Hirokawa, R. Y., & Rost, K. M. (1992). Effective group decision making in organizations: Field test of the Vigilant Interaction Theory. *Management Communication Quarterly, 5,* 267–288.

Hirokawa, R. Y., & Salazar, A. J. (1997). An integrated approach to communication and group decision making. In L. R. Frey & J. K. Barge (Eds.), *Managing group life: Communicating in decision-making groups* (pp. 156–181). Boston, MA: Houghton Mifflin.

Hirsch, A. R., & Wolf, C. J. (2001). Practical methods for detecting mendacity: A case study. *Journal of the American Academy of Psychiatry and the Law, 29,* 438–444.

The history of ESA. (2011). Retrieved from http://www/epsilonsigmaalpha.org/about/ESA-International/history

Hitlin, P., Holcomb, J. (2015, April 6). From Twitter to Instagram, a different #Ferguson conversation. Pew Research Center. Retrieved from http://www.pewresearch.org/fact-tank/2015/04/06/from-twitter-to-instagram-a-different-ferguson/

Hobson, C. J., Delunas, L., & Kesic, D. (2001). Compelling evidence of the need for corporate work/life balance initiatives: Results from a national survey of stressful life-events. *Journal of Employment Counseling, 38,* 38–44.

Hocking, J. E., & Leathers, D. G. (1980). Nonverbal indicators of deception: A new theoretical perspective. *Communication Monographs, 47,* 119–131.

Hodge, R. D. (2015, October 4). A radical experiment at Zappos to end the office workplace as we know it. *New Republic.* Retrieved from http://www.newrepublic.com/article.122965

Hoffman, M. F., & Cowan, R. L. (2008). The meaning of work/life: A corporate ideology of work/life balance. *Communication Quarterly, 56,* 227–246. doi:10.1080.01463370802251053

Hofstede, G. (2001). *Culture's consequences: Comparing values, behaviors, institutions, and organizations across nations* (2nd ed.). Thousand Oaks, CA: Sage.

Hohmann, J. (2011). 10 best practices for social media: Helpful guidelines for news organizations. American Society of News Editors. Retrieved from http://asne.org/Files/pdf/10_Best_Practices_for_Social_Media.pdf

Holmberg, D., & Holmes, J. G. (1993). Reconstruction of relationship memoirs: A mental models approach. In N. Schwarz & S. Sudman (Eds.), *Autobiographical memory and the validity of retrospective reports* (pp. 267–288). New York, NY: Springer-Verlag.

Holohan, M. (2014, December 14). Put down that phone! "Technoference" may be hurting your relationship. *Today.* Retrieved from http://www.today.com

Honeycutt, J. M. (1993). Memory structures for the rise and fall of personal relationships. In S. W. Duck (Ed.), *Understanding relationship processes, 1: Individuals in relationships* (pp. 30–59). Newbury Park, CA: Sage.

Honeycutt, J. M., Choi, C. W., & DeBerry, J. R. (2009). Communication apprehension

and imagined interactions. *Communication Research Reports, 26,* 228–236.

Horton, P. (2011). School bullying and social and moral orders. *Children & Society, 25,* 268–277.

Howe, J. (2006). The rise of crowdsourcing. *Wired, 14*(6). Retrieved from http://www.wired.com/wired/archive/14.06/crowds.html

Hudson, M. B., & Irwin, Z. (2010). Uncovering organizational culture: A necessary skill for athletic trainers. *Athletic Therapy Today, 15*(1), 4–8.

Hughes, S. (2011, June 21). Ryan Dunn's death: Bam Margera slams Roger Ebert tweet. *The Washington Post.* Retrieved from http://www.washingtonpost.com/blogs/celebritology/post/ryan-dunns-death-bam-margera-slams-roger-ebert-tweet/2011/06/21/AG1kZFeH_blog.html

Hummert, M. L., Garstka, T., Shaner, J., & Strahm, S. (1994). Stereotypes of the elderly held by young, middle-aged, and elderly adults. *Journal of Gerontology, 49,* 240–245.

Infante, D. A., & Wigley, C. J. (1986). Verbal aggressiveness: An interpersonal model and measure. *Communication Monographs, 53,* 61–69.

Isaacson, W. (2011, October 17). American icon. *Time, 178*(15), 32–35.

Isquith, E. (2015, February 25). "More than just Wall Street": How the Occupy movement penetrated America—and what it means today. Salon.com. Retrieved March 2, 2015, from http://www.salon.com/2015/02/25/more_than_just_wall_street_how_the_occupy_movement_penetrated_america_and_what_it_means_today/

Ivy, D. K. (2012). *Genderspeak: Personal effectiveness in gender communication* (5th ed.). Boston, MA: Pearson.

Ivy, D. K., & Wahl, S. T. (2009). *The nonverbal self: Communication for a lifetime.* Boston, MA: Allyn & Bacon.

Ivy, D. K., & Wahl, S. T. (2014). *Nonverbal communication for a lifetime* (2nd ed.). Dubuque, IA: Kendall Hunt.

Jablin, F. (1987). Organizational entry, assimilation, and exit. In F. Jablin, L. Putnam, K. Roberts, & L. Porter (Eds.), *Handbook of*

organizational communication (pp. 679–740). Newbury Park, CA: Sage.

Jablin, F. M. (1985a). An exploratory study of vocational organizational communication socialization. *Southern Speech Communication Journal, 50,* 261–282.

Jablin, F. M. (1985b). Task/work relationships: A life-span perspective. In M. L. Knapp & G. R. Miller (Eds.), *Handbook of interpersonal communication* (pp. 615–654). Beverly Hills, CA: Sage.

Jablin, F. M. (1987). Organizational entry, assimilation, and exit. In F. M. Jablin, L. L. Putnam, K. H. Roberts, & L. W. Porter (Eds.), *Handbook of organizational communication: An interdisciplinary perspective* (pp. 679–740). Newbury Park, CA: Sage.

Jablin, F. M. (2001). Organizational entry, assimilation, and disengagement/exit. In F. M. Jablin & L. L. Putnam (Eds.), *The new handbook of organizational communication: Advances in theory, research, and methods* (pp. 732–819). Thousand Oaks, CA: Sage.

Jackson, H. (2005). Sitting comfortably? Then let's talk! *Psychologist, 18,* 691.

Jackson, L. (2013, July 23). The real secret behind Google's corporate culture. Retrieved from http://www.corporateculturepros.com/2013/07

Jacob, M., & Benzkofer, S. (2011, August 14). 10 things you might know about Wisconsin. *Chicago Tribune.* Retrieved from http://articles.chicagotribune.com/2011-08-14/news/ct-perspec-0814-things-20110814_1_america-s-dairyland-taliesin-house-wisconsin-dells

Jandt, F. (2010). *An introduction to intercultural communication.* Los Angeles, CA: Sage.

Janis, I. L. (1982). *Groupthink: Psychological studies of policy decisions and fiascoes* (2nd ed.). Boston, MA: Houghton Mifflin.

Janis, I. L. (1983). Groupthink. In H. H. Blumberg, A. P. Hare, V. Kent, & M. Davies (Eds.), *Small groups and social interaction* (Vol. 2, pp. 39–46). New York, NY: John Wiley & Sons.

Jansson, C., Marlow, N., & Bristow, M. (2004). The influence of color on visual search times in cluttered environments. *Journal of Marketing Communications, 10,* 183–193.

Jehn, K. A., Northcraft, G. B., & Neale, M. A. (1999). Why differences make a difference: A field study of diversity, conflict, and performance in groups. *Administrative Science Quarterly, 44,* 741–763.

Jensen, J. L. (2010). Augmentation of space: Four dimensions of spatial experiences of Google Earth. *Space and Culture, 13,* 121–133.

Job Outlook 2015. (2015). National Association of Colleges and Employers. Retrieved from http://www.naceweb.org

Johnson, D. W. (2006). *Reaching out: Interpersonal effectiveness and self-actualization.* Boston, MA: Allyn & Bacon.

Johnson, S. D., & Bechler, C. (1998). Examining the relationship between listening effectiveness and leadership emergence: Perceptions, behaviors, and recall. *Small Group Research, 29,* 452–471.

Johnston, M. K., Reed, K., & Lawrence, K. (2011). Team listening environment (TLE) scale: Development and validation. *Journal of Business Communication, 48,* 3–26. doi:10.1177/0021943610385655

Joinson, A. N. (2001, March–April). Self-disclosure in computer-mediated communication: The role of self-awareness and visual anonymity. *European Journal of Social Psychology, 31*(2), 177–192.

Jones, S. G. (1997). The Internet and its social landscape. In S. G. Jones (Ed.), *Virtual culture: Identity and communication in cyber society* (pp. 7–35). Thousand Oaks, CA: Sage.

Jones, S. M. (2011). Supportive listening. *International Journal of Listening, 25,* 85–103.

Jordan, J. W. (2005). A virtual death and a real dilemma: Identity, trust, and community in cyberspace. *Southern Communication Journal, 70,* 200–218.

Jordan, T. (1999). *Cyberpower: The culture and politics of cyberspace and the Internet.* London, England: Routledge.

Judge, T., Hurst, C., & Simon, L. S. (2009). Does it pay to be smart, attractive, or confident (or all three)? Relationships among general mental ability, physical attractiveness, core self-evaluations, and income. *Journal of Applied Psychology, 94,* 742–755.

Junco, R., & Cotton, S. R. (2011). Perceived academic effects of instant messaging use. *Computers & Education, 56,* 370–378.

K

Kalbfleisch, P. J. (2002). Communicating in mentoring relationships: A theory for enactment. *Communication Theory, 12,* 63–69.

Kalman, Y. M., & Rafaeli, S. (2011). Online pauses and silence: Chronemic expectancy

violations in written computer-mediated communication. *Communication Research, 38*(1), 54–69.

Kapidzic, S., & Herring, S. C. (2011). Gender, communication, and self-presentation in teen chat rooms revisited: Have patterns changed? *Journal of Computer-Mediated Communication, 17,* 39–59.

Kapoor, C., & Solomon, N. (2011). Understanding and managing generational differences in the workplace. *Worldwide Hospitality and Tourism Themes, 3,* 308–318. doi:10.1108/17554211111162435

Kassing, J. W. (1997). Articulating, antagonizing, and displacing: A model of employee dissent. *Communication Studies, 48,* 311–332.

Kassing, J. W. (1998). Development and validation of the organizational dissent scale. *Management Communication Quarterly, 12,* 183–229.

Kassing, J. W. (2000a). Exploring the relationship between workplace freedom of speech, organizational identification, and employee dissent. *Communication Research Reports, 17,* 387–396.

Kassing, J. W. (2000b). Investigating the relationship between superior–subordinate relationship quality and employee dissent. *Communication Research Reports, 17,* 58–70.

Kassing, J. W. (2001). From the looks of things: Assessing perceptions of organizational dissenters. *Management Communication Quarterly, 14,* 442–470.

Kassing, J. W. (2002). Speaking up: Identifying employees' upward dissent strategies. *Management Communication Quarterly, 16,* 187–209.

Kassing, J. W., & Armstrong, T. A. (2002). Someone's going to hear about this: Examining the association between dissent-triggering events and employees' dissent expression. *Management Communication Quarterly, 16,* 39–65.

Kassing, J. W., & Dicioccio, R. L. (2004). Testing a workplace experience explanation of displaced dissent. *Communication Reports, 17,* 113–120.

Kassing, J. W., & Kava, W. (2013). Assessing disagreement expressed to management: Development of the Upward Dissent Scale. *Communication Research Reports, 30,* 46–56. doi:10.1080/08824096.2012.746255

Kassing, J. W., Piemonte, N. M., Goman, C. C., & Mitchell, C. A. (2012). Dissent expression as an indicator of work

engagement and intention to leave. *Journal of Business Communication, 49,* 237–253. doi:10.1177/0021943612446751

Katz, J. (1999, Spring). Men, masculinities, and media: Some introductory notes. *WCW Research Report,* pp. 16–17.

Katz, J. (2006). *The macho paradox: Why some men hurt women and how all men can help.* Naperville, IL: Sourcebooks.

Katz, J. E., & Rice, R. E. (2002). *Social consequences of Internet use: Access, involvement, and interaction.* Cambridge, MA: MIT Press.

Katzenbach, J. R., & Smith, D. K. (1993). The discipline of teams. *Harvard Business Review, 71*(2), 111–120.

Kaufman, D. (2011). Battle workplace weight discrimination. Retrieved from http://career-advice.monster.com/in-the-office/workplace-issues/weight-discrimination/article.aspx

Kelly, G. A. (1955). *The psychology of personal constructs* (Vols. 1 and 2). New York, NY: Norton.

Kenny, D. (2007). Student plagiarism and professional practice. *Nurse Education Today, 27,* 14–18.

Ketrow, S. M. (1991). Communication role specializations and perceptions of leadership. *Small Group Research, 22,* 492–514.

Keyton, J. (1993). Group termination. *Small Group Research, 24,* 84–100.

Keyton, J. (1999). *Group communication: Process and analysis.* Mountain View, CA: Mayfield.

Keyton, J. (2011). *Communication and organizational culture: A key to understanding work experiences* (2nd ed.). Thousand Oaks, CA: Sage.

Keyton, J., Caputo, J. M., Ford, E. A., Fu, R., Leibowitz, S. A., Liu, T., Polasik, S. S., Ghosh, P., & Wu, C. (2013). Investigating verbal workplace communication behaviors. *Journal of Business Communication, 50,* 152–169. doi:10.1177/0021943612474990

Keyton, J., Harmon, K., & Frey, L. R. (1996, November). *Grouphate: Implications for teaching small group communication.* Paper presented at the meeting of the Speech Communication Association, San Diego, CA.

Kilbourne, J. (1979). *Killing us softly: Advertising's image of women.* Cambridge, MA: Cambridge Documentary Film.

Killmeier, M. A. (2009). The body medium and media ecology: Disembodiment in the theory and practice of modern media.

Proceedings of the Media Ecology Association, 10, 33–45. Retrieved from http://www.media-ecology.org/publications/MEA_proceedings/v10/5_body_Medium.pdf

Kim, Y. Y. (2007). Ideology, identity, and intercultural communication: An analysis of differing academic conceptions of cultural identity. *Journal of Intercultural Communication Research, 36*, 237–253.

Kingkade, T. (2015, January 14). Hate Yik Yak and anonymous gossip sites all you want, but they won't go away. *Huffington Post.* Retrieved from http://www.huffingtonpost.com

Kittler, M. G., Rygl, D., & MacKinnon, A. (2011). Beyond culture or beyond control? Reviewing the use of Hall's high-/low-context concept. *International Journal of Cross Cultural Management, 11*(1), 63–82.

Kjormo, O., & Halvari, H. (2002). Two ways related to performance in elite sport: The path of self-confidence and competitive anxiety and the path of group cohesion and group goal-clarity. *Perceptual and Motor Skills, 94*, 950–966.

Knapp, M. L., & Vangelisti, A. L. (2000). *Interpersonal communication and human relationships* (4th ed.). Boston, MA: Allyn & Bacon.

Kolb, D. (1984). *Experiential learning: Experience as the source of learning and development.* Englewood Cliffs, NJ: Prentice Hall.

Kolb, D. A. (2014). *Experiential learning: Experience as the source of learning and development.* Englewood Cliffs, N.J.: Prentice-Hall/FT Press.

Kolb, J. A. (1997). Are we still stereotyping leadership? A look at gender and other predictors of leader emergence. *Small Group Research, 28*, 370–393.

Kram, K. E., & Isabella, L. A. (1985). Mentoring alternatives: The role of peer relationships in career development. *Academy of Management Journal, 28*, 110–132.

Kramer, M. W. (2006). Shared leadership in a community theater group: Filling the leadership role. *Journal of Applied Communication Research, 34*, 141–162.

Kramer, M. W. (2010). *Organizational socialization: Joining and leaving organizations.* Cambridge, England: Polity Press.

Kuhn, T., & Poole, M. S. (2000). Do conflict management styles affect group decision-making? Evidence from a longitudinal field study. *Human Communication Research, 26*, 558–590.

Kumkale, G. T., Alabarracín, D., & Seignourel, P. J. (2010). The effects of source credibility in the presence or absence of prior attitudes: Implications for the design of persuasive communication campaigns. *Journal of Applied Social Psychology, 40*, 1325–1356. doi:10.1111/j.1559-1816.2010.00620.x

Kurland, N. B., & Pelled, L. H. (2000). Passing the word: Toward a model of gossip and power in the workplace. *Academy of Management Review, 25*, 428–438.

L

Labrecque, L. L., Markos, E., & Milne, G. R. (2010). Online personal branding: Processes, challenges, and implications. *Journal of Interactive Marketing, 25*, 37–50. doi:10.1016/j.intmar.2010.09.002

LaFasto, F., & Larson, C. (2001). *When teams work best: 6,000 team members and leaders tell what it takes to succeed.* Los Angeles, CA: Sage.

Laing, D. (1961). *The self and others.* New York, NY: Pantheon.

Lakoff, R. T. (1975). *Language and woman's place.* New York, NY: Harper & Row.

Lanham, R. A. (1993). *The electronic word: Democracy, technology, and the arts.* Chicago, IL: University of Chicago Press.

Lauricella, S. (2009). "Is this for real?": Web literacy for the web-savvy. *Communication Teacher, 23*, 137–141.

Ledbetter, A. M., Mazer, J. P., DeGroot, J. M., Meyer, K. R., Yuping, M., & Swafford, B. (2011). Attitudes toward online social connection and self-disclosure as predictors of Facebook communication and relational closeness. *Communication Research, 38*(1), 27–53.

Lees-Marshment, J. (2009). Marketing after the election: The potential and limitations of maintaining a market orientation in government. *Canadian Journal of Communication, 34*, 205–227.

Leggett, C., & Rossouw, P. (2014). The impact of technology use on couple relationships: A neuropsychological perspective. *International Journal of Neuropsychotherapy, 2*, 44–99. doi:10.12744/ijnpt.2014.0044-0099

Lenhart, A. (2012, March 19). Teens, smartphones, and texting. Pew Research Center. Retrieved from http://pewrsr.ch/1m8gDqR

Lenhart, A., & Fox, S. (2006, July 19). *Bloggers: A portrait of the Internet's new storytellers.* Washington, DC: Pew Internet & American Life Project.

Lenhart, A., Ling, R., Campbell, S., & Purcell, K. (2010, April 20). *Teens and mobile phones.* Retrieved from http://www.pewinternet.org/Reports/2010/Teens-and-Mobile-Phones/Chapter-3/Sleeping-with-the-phone-on-or-near-the-bed.aspx?r=1

Leonardi, P. M., Treem, J. W., & Jackson, M. H. (2010). The connectivity paradox: Using technology to both decrease and increase perceptions of distance in distributed work arrangements. *Journal of Applied Communication Research, 38*, 85–105.

Leung, R. (2009, February 11). Working the good life. CBS News. Retrieved from http://www.cbsnews.com/2100-18560_162-550102.html

Levine, D. (2000). Virtual attraction: What rocks your boat. *CyberPsychology & Behavior, 3*, 565–573.

Levinson, P. (1999). *Digital McLuhan: A guide to the information millennium.* London, England: Routledge.

Li, N., Jackson, M. H., & Trees, A. R. (2008). Relating online: Managing dialectical contradictions in massively multiplayer online role-playing game relationships. *Games and Culture, 3*, 76–97.

Liden, R. C., Wayne, S. J., Jaworski, R. A., & Bennett, N. (2004). Social loafing: A field investigation. *Journal of Management, 30*, 285–304.

Limbaugh, R. (2014, August 12). Occupy Wall Street justified looting—transcript. Rushlimbaugh.com. Retrieved March 16, 2015, from http://www.rushlimbaugh.com/daily/2014/08/12/occupy_wall_street_justified_looting

Lindgaard, G., Fernandes, G., Dudek, C., & Brown, J. (2006). Attention web designers: You have 50 milliseconds to make a good first impression! *Behaviour & Information Technology, 25*, 115–126.

Lipovsky, C. (2013). Negotiating one's expertise through appraisal in CVs. *Linguistics & the Human Sciences, 8*(3), 307–333.

Lippmann, W. (1922). *Public opinion.* New York, NY: Harcourt Brace.

Literat, I. (2014). Measuring new media literacies: Towards the development of a comprehensive assessment tool. *Journal of Media Literacy Education, 6.*

Littlejohn, S. W., & Foss, K. A. (2008). *Theories of human communication.* Belmont, CA: Thomson/Wadsworth.

Lodge, J. (2010). Communication with first-year students; so many channels but is anyone listening? A practice report. *The International Journal of the First Year in Higher Education, 1,* 100–105.

Loftus, E. F., & Palmer, J. C. (1974). Reconstruction of automobile destruction: An example of the interaction between language and memory. *Journal of Verbal Learning and Verbal Behavior, 13,* 585–589.

Loftus, E. F., & Pickrell, J. E. (1995). The formation of false memories. *Psychiatric Annals, 25,* 720–725.

Lohmann, A., Arriaga, X. B., & Goodfriend, W. (2003). Close relationships and placemaking: Do objects in a couple's home reflect couplehood? *Personal Relationships, 10,* 437–449.

Lorenzetti, L. (2014, October 27). Southwest Airlines is flying high. *Fortune, 170*(6), 38.

Louis, M. R., Posner, B. Z., & Powell, G. N. (1983). The availability and helpfulness of socialization practices. *Personnel Psychology, 36,* 857–866.

Lowry, P. B., Roberts, T. L., Romano, N. C., Jr., Cheney, P. D., & Hightower, P. D. (2006). The impact of group size and social presence on small-group communication: Does computer-mediated communication make a difference? *Small Group Research, 37,* 631–661.

Lutgen-Sandvik, P., Namie, G., & Namie, R. (2009). Workplace bullying: Causes, consequences, and corrections. In P. Lutgen-Sandvik & B. Davenport-Sypher (Eds.), *Destructive organizational communication: Processes, consequences, and constructive ways of organizing* (pp. 27–52). New York, NY: Routledge.

Lutgen-Sandvik, P., Tracy, S. J., & Alberts, J. K. (2007). Burned by bullying in the American workplace: Prevalence, perception, degree, and impact. *Journal of Management Studies, 44,* 837–862. doi:10.1111/j.1467-6486.2907.00715.x

Lyman, S. M., & Scott, M. B. (1967). Territoriality: A neglected social dimension. *Social Problems, 15,* 237–241.

Lyons, D. (2007). *Surveillance studies: An overview.* London, England: Polity Press.

Madlock, P. E., Kennedy-Lightsey, C. D., & Myers, S. A. (2007). Employees' communication attitudes and dislike for working in a group. *Psychological Reports, 101,* 1037–1040.

Madsen, S. R. (2011). The benefits, challenges, and implications of teleworking: A literature review. *Culture & Religion Journal, 1,* 148–158.

Magnuson, M. J., & Dundes, L. (2008). Gender differences in "social portraits" reflected in MySpace profiles. *CyberPsychology & Behavior, 11,* 239–241.

Mak, B. N., & Chui, H. L. (2013). A cultural approach to small talk: A double-edged sword of sociocultural reality during socialization into the workplace. *Journal of Multicultural Discourses, 8*(2), 118–133.

Malala Yousafzai becomes youngest-ever Nobel Prize winner. (2014, October 10). Associated Press. Retrieved from http://www.people.com/article/malala-yousafzai-wins-nobel-prize

Mangalindan, J. P. (2014, October 6). A healthier, more rewarding workplace: Clif Bar, the energy-bar and drink maker, ensures quality of life for employees. *Fortune, 170*(5), 49–50.

Manovich, L. (2003). New media from Borges to HTML. In N. Wardrip-Fruin & N. Montfort (Eds.), *The New Media Reader* (pp. 13–25). Cambridge, MA: MIT Press.

Maples, M. F. (1988). Group development: Extending Tuckman's theory. *Journal for Specialists in Group Work, 13,* 18–23.

Markey, P. M., & Markey, C. N. (2007). Romantic ideals, romantic obtainment, and relationship experiences: The complementarity of interpersonal traits among romantic partners. *Journal of Social and Personal Relationships, 24,* 517–533.

Markus, H., & Nurius, P. (1986). Possible selves. *American Psychologist, 41,* 954–969.

Martey, R. M., & Stromer-Galley, J. (2007). The digital dollhouse: Context and social norms in The Sims Online. *Games and Culture, 2,* 314–334.

Martin, J. N., & Nakayama, T. K. (2004). *Intercultural communication in context.* New York, NY: McGraw-Hill.

Martin, L. T., Schonlau, M., Haas, A., Derose, K. P., Rosenfeld, L., Buka, S. L., & Rudd, R.

(2011). Patient activation and advocacy: Which literacy skills matter most? *Journal of Health Communication, 16,* 177–190.

Marvin, C. (1988). *When old technologies were new: Thinking about electronic communication in the late nineteenth century.* Oxford, England: Oxford University Press.

Marwick, A. (2012). The public domain: Social surveillance in everyday life. *Surveillance & Society, 9,* 378–393. Retrieved from http://www.surveillance-and-society.org, ISSN: 1477-7487.

Mathes, E. W., & Moore, C. L. (1985). Reik's complementarity theory of romantic love. *Journal of Social Psychology, 125,* 321–327.

Mayer, M. E., Sonoda, K. T., & Gudykunst, W. B. (1997). The effect of time pressure and type of information on decision quality. *Southern Communication Journal, 62,* 280–292.

McCroskey, J. (1984). The communication apprehension perspective. In J. A. Daly & J. C. McCroskey (Eds.), *Avoiding communication: Shyness, reticence, and communication apprehension* (pp. 13–38). Beverly Hills, CA: Sage.

McCroskey, J. C., & Richmond, V. P. (1992). Increasing teacher influence through immediacy. In V. P. Richmond & J. C. McCroskey (Eds.), *Power in the classroom: Communication, control, and concern* (pp. 101–119). Hillsdale, NJ: Erlbaum.

McCroskey, J. C., & Teven, J. J. (1999). Goodwill: A reexamination of the construct and its measurement. *Communication Monographs, 66,* 90–103.

McDaniel, B. T., & Coyne, S. M. (2014). "Technoference": The interference of technology in couple relationships and implications for women's personal and relational well-being. *Psychology of Popular Media Culture.* doi:10.1037/ppm0000065

McDermott, V. M. (2004). Using motivated sequence in persuasive speaking: The speech for charity. *Communication Teacher, 18,* 13–14.

McDonald, S.N. (2014, August 29). Gaming vlogger Anita Sarkeesian is forced from her home after receiving harrowing death threats. *The Washington Post.* Retrieved from http://www.washingtonpost.com/news/morning-mix/wp/2014/08/29/gaming-vlogger-anita-sarkeesian-is-forced-from-home-after-receiving-harrowing-death-threats/

McDougall, M., & Beattie, R. S. (1997). Peer mentoring at work: The nature and outcomes of non-hierarchical developmental relationships. *Management Learning, 28,* 423–437.

McGregor, J. (2015, April 14). The worst question you could ask women in a job interview. *The Washington Post.* Retrieved from http://www.washingtonpost.com/blogs/on-leadership/wp/2015/04/14/the-worst-question-you-could-ask-women-in-a-job-interview/

McLuhan, M. (1964). *Understanding media: The extensions of man.* New York, NY: McGraw-Hill.

McQuail, D. (1997). *Audience analysis.* Thousand Oaks, CA: Sage.

Mead, G. H. (1934). *Mind, self, and society* (C. W. Morris, Ed.). Chicago, IL: University of Chicago Press.

Medved, C. E. (2007). Investigating family labor in communication studies: Threading across historical and contemporary discourses. *Journal of Family Communication, 7,* 225–243.

Men, L. R. (2014). Strategic internal communication: Transformational leadership, communication channels, and employee satisfaction. *Management Communication Quarterly, 28,* 264–284. doi:10.1177/0893318914524536

Merola, N., Penas, J., & Hancock, J. (2006). *Avatar color and social identity effects: On attitudes and group dynamics in virtual realities.* Paper presented at annual meeting of the International Communication Association, Dresden, Germany.

Metzger, M. J. (2007). Making sense of credibility on the Web: Models for evaluating online information and recommendations for future research. *Journal of the American Society for Information Science and Technology, 58,* 2078–2091. doi:10.1002/asi.20672

Michelson, G., van Iterson, A., & Waddington, K. (2010). Gossip in organizations: Contexts, consequences, and controversies. *Group & Organization Management, 35,* 371–390.

Mikkelson, A. C., Floyd, K., & Pauley, P. M. (2011). Differential solicitude of social support in different types of adult sibling relationships. *Journal of Family Communication, 11,* 220–236.

Millen, J. H. (2001). A model for delivery outlines: Empowering student speakers. *Communication Teacher, 15,* 4–6.

Miller, G. (1978). The current status of theory and research in interpersonal communication. *Human Communication Research, 4,* 164–178.

Miller, V. D., & Jablin, F. (1991). Information seeking during organizational entry: Influences, tactics, and a model of the process. *Academy of Management Review, 16,* 92–120.

Milliken, M. (2015, April 25). Olympian Bruce Jenner makes transgender history by identifying as a woman. Reuters.com. Retrieved from http://www.reuters.com/article/2015/04/25/us-people-brucejenner-interview-idUSKBN0NG02P20150425

Minagawa-Kawai, Y., Mori, K., Naoi, N., & Kojima, S. (2007). Neural attunement processes in infants during the acquisition of a language-specific phonemic contrast. *The Journal of Neuroscience, 27,* 315–321.

Misra, S., & Stokols, D. (2011). Psychological and health outcomes of perceived information overload. *Environment & Behavior.* Advanced online publication. doi:10.1177/0013916511404408

Mogg, T. (2015, February 26). Meet Robear, a Japanese robot nurse with the face of a bear. *Digital Trends.* Retrieved April 7, 2015, from http://www.digitaltrends.com/cool-tech/riken-robear/

Montagu, M. F. A. (1978). *Touching: The human significance of the skin* (2nd ed.). New York, NY: Harper & Row.

Moore, C. M. (1987). *Group techniques for idea building.* Newbury Park, CA: Sage.

Morris, D. (1985). *Body watching.* New York, NY: Crown.

Morrison, E. W. (1995). Information usefulness and acquisition during organizational encounter. *Management Communication Quarterly, 9,* 131–155.

Mudrack, P. E. (1989). Group cohesiveness and productivity: A closer look. *Human Relations, 42,* 771–785.

Mullaney, T. (2011, October 20). Protest spotlight a stressed middle class. *USA Today.* Retrieved from http://www.usatoday.com/money/markets/story/2011-10-19/occupy-wall-street-protests-profiles/50830924/1

Mumford, T. V., Campion, M. A., & Morgeson, F. P. (2006). Situational judgment in work teams: A team role typology. In J. A. Weekly & R. E. Polyhart (Eds.), *Situational judgment tests: Theory, measurement, and application* (pp. 319–343). Mahwah, NJ: Erlbaum.

Münzer, S., Seufert, T., & Brünken, R. (2009). Learning from multimedia presentations: Facilitation function of animations and spatial abilities. *Learning and Individual Differences, 19,* 481–485.

Murthy, D. (2011). Twitter: Microphone for the masses? *Media, Culture & Society, 33*(5), 779–789.

Myers, K. K., & Oetzel, J. G. (2003). Exploring the dimensions of organizational assimilation: Creating and validating a measure. *Communication Quarterly, 51,* 438–457.

Myers, K. K., & Sadaghiani, K. (2010). Millennials in the workplace: A communication perspective on Millennials' organization relationships and performance. *Journal of Business Psychology, 25,* 225–238. doi:10.1007/s10869-010-9172-7

Myers, S. A., & Anderson, C. M. (2008). *The fundamentals of small group communication.* Thousand Oaks, CA: Sage.

Myers, S. A., Cranmer, G. A., Goldman, Z. W., Sollitto, M., Gillen, H. G., & Ball, H. (2015). Differences in information seeking among organizational peers: Perceptions of appropriateness, importance, and frequency. *International Journal of Business Communication.* Advanced online publication. doi:10.1177/2329488415573928

Myers, S. A., Edwards, C., Wahl, S. T., & Martin, M. M. (2007). The relationship between perceived instructor aggressive communication and college student involvement. *Communication Education, 56,* 495–508.

Myers, S. A., & Goodboy, A. K. (2005). A study of group hate in a course on small group communication. *Psychological Reports, 97,* 381–386.

Myers, S. A., Goodboy, A. K., & Members of COMM 612. (2004, April). *An investigation of group hate in the small group communication course.* Paper presented at the meeting of the Central States Communication Association, Cleveland, OH.

Myers, S. A., & Johnson, A. D. (2004). Perceived solidarity, self-disclosure, and trust in organizational peer relationships. *Communication Research Reports, 21,* 75–83.

Myers, S. A., Knox, R. L., Pawlowski, D. R., & Ropog, B. L. (1999). Perceived communication openness and functional communication skills among organizational peers. *Communication Reports, 12,* 71–83.

Myers, S. A., Shimotsu, S., Byrnes, K., Frisby, B. N., Durbin, J., & Loy, B. N. (2010). Assessing the role of peer relationships in the small group communication course. *Communication Teacher, 24*, 43–57.

Myers, S. A., Smith, N. A., Eidsness, M. A., Bogdan, L. M., Zackery, B. A., Thompson, M. R., ... Johnson, A. N. (2009). Dealing with slackers in college classroom work groups. *College Student Journal, 43*, 592–598.

Namie, G., & Namie, R. (2009). *The bully at work: What you can do to stop the hurt and reclaim your dignity on the job* (2nd ed.). Naperville, IL: Sourcebooks, Inc.

Nelson, A., & Golant, S. K. (2004). *You don't say: Navigating nonverbal communication between the sexes.* New York, NY: Prentice Hall.

Nelson, K. (1981). Social cognition in a script framework. In J. H. Flavell & L. Ross (Eds.), *Social cognitive development: Frontiers and possible futures* (pp. 97–118). Cambridge, England: Cambridge University Press.

Nesterov, A. V. (2009). On semantic, pragmatic, and dialectic triangles. *Automatic Documentation and Mathematical Linguistics, 43*, 132–137.

Neuliep, J. W., & Hazelton, V., Jr. (1986). Enhanced conversational recall and reduced conversational interference as a function of cognitive complexity. *Human Communication Research, 13*, 211–224.

New Media Literacies, http://newmedialiteracies.org/

Newman, C. (2011, May 25). Red Frog reaps award for approach to office culture. Retrieved from http:www.nbcchicago.com/blogs/inc-well/Red-Frog-Reaps-Award-for-Approach-to-Office-Culture—122586414.html

Nguyen, M., Bin, Y. S., & Campbell, A. (2012). Comparing online and offline self-disclosure: A systematic review. *Cyberpsychology, Behavior & Social Networking, 15*(2), 103–111.

Nicolopoulou, A. (2008). The elementary forms of narrative coherence in young children's storytelling. *Narrative Inquiry, 18*, 299–325.

Nielsen Advertising and Audiences. (2014). Advertising and audiences: State of the media. Retrieved from http://www.nielsen.com

Nisbett, R. E., & Wilson, T. D. (1977). The halo effect: Evidence for unconscious alteration of judgments. *Journal of Personality and Social Psychology, 35*, 250–256.

Norton, W. I., Jr., Murfield, M. L. U., & Baucus, M. S. (2014). Leader emergence: The development of a theoretical framework. *Leadership & Organization Development Journal, 35*, 513–529. doi:10.1108/LODJ-08-2012-0109

Not in front of the telly: Warning over "listening" TV. (2015, February 9). BBC News. Retrieved from http://www.bbc.com/news/technology-31296188

Obama, B. (2015, March 7). *Our march is not yet finished*—speech transcript. *Los Angeles Times.* Retrieved March 13, 2015, from http://www.latimes.com/nation/la-na-obama-prepared-remarks-20150307-story.html#page=1

O'Connor, A., & Raile, A. N. W. (2015). Millenials "get a 'real job'": Exploring generational shifts in the colloquialism's characteristics and meanings. *Management Communication Quarterly, 29*, 276–290. doi:10.1177/0893318915580153

Odden, C. M., & Sias, P. M. (1997). Peer communication relationships and psychological climate. *Communication Quarterly, 45*, 153–166.

Ogden, C. K., & Richards, I. A. (1927). *The meaning of meaning: A study of the influence of language upon thought and of the science of symbolism.* London, England: Kegan Paul.

O'Hair, D., & Wiemann, M. O. (2004). *The essential guide to group communication.* Boston, MA: Bedford/St. Martin's.

Ohata, K. (2006). Auditory short-term memory in L2 listening comprehension processes. *Journal of Language and Learning, 5*, 21–28.

O'Keefe, B. J. (1988). The logic of message design: Individual differences in reasoning about communication. *Communication Monographs, 55*, 80–103.

O'Keefe, B. J. (1991). Message design logic and the management of multiple goals. In K. Tracy (Ed.), *Understanding face-to-face interaction: Issues linking goals and discourse* (pp. 101–117). Hillsdale, NJ: Erlbaum.

O'Keefe, B. J. (1997). Variation, adaptation, and functional explanation in the study of message design. In G. Philipsen & T. L. Albrecht (Eds.), *Developing communication theories* (pp. 85–118). Albany: State University of New York Press.

O'Keefe, B. J., Delia, J. G., & O'Keefe, D. J. (1977). Construct individuality, cognitive complexity, and the formation and remembering of interpersonal impressions. *Social Behavior and Personality, 5*, 229–240.

O'Keefe, B. J., & McCornack, S. A. (1987). Message design logic and message goal structure: Effects on perceptions of message quality in regulative communication situations. *Human Communication Research, 14*, 68–92.

O'Keefe, B. J., & Shepherd, G. J. (1989). The communication of identity during face-to-face persuasive interactions: Effects of perceiver's construct differentiation and target's message strategies. *Communication Research, 16*, 375–404.

O'Keefe, D. J. (2002). *Persuasion: Theory and research.* Thousand Oaks, CA: Sage.

Oliver, M. B. (2003). Mood management and selective exposure. In J. Bryant, D. Roskos-Ewoldsen, & J. Cantor (Eds.), *Communication and emotion: Essays in honor of Dolf Zillmann* (pp. 85–106). Mahwah, NJ: Erlbaum.

Olya, G. (2015, March 12). Facebook removes "feeling fat" option from status updates. *People.* Retrieved March 20, 2015, from http://www.people.com/article/facebook-removes-feeling-fat-status-update

Ong, W. J. (1982). *Orality and literacy: The technologizing of the word.* London, England: Methuen.

Orbe, M. (1998). *Constructing co-cultural theory: An explication of culture, power and communication.* Thousand Oaks, CA: Sage.

Osborn, A. F. (1953). *Applied imagination.* New York, NY: Scribner.

O'Sullivan, P. B. (1999). Bridging mass and interpersonal communication: Synthesis scholarship in HCR. *Human Communication Research, 25*, 569–588.

O'Sullivan, P. B. (2000). What you don't know won't hurt *me:* Impression management functions of communication channels in relationships. *Human Communication Research, 26*, 403–431.

O'Sullivan, P. B. (2005, May). *Mass personal communication: Rethinking the mass interpersonal divide.* Paper presented at the annual meeting of the International Communication Association, New York, NY.

P

Palomares, N. A., & Eun-Ju, L. (2010). Virtual gender identity: The linguistic assimilation to gendered avatars in computer-mediated communication. *Journal of Language & Social Psychology, 29*(1), 5–23.

Parker, M. (2000). *Organizational culture and identity: Unity and division at work.* Thousand Oaks, CA: Sage.

Payne, B. K., & Monk-Turner, B. (2006). Students' perceptions of group projects: The role of race, age, and slacking. *College Student Journal, 40,* 132–139.

Payne, H. J. (2007). The role of organization-based self-esteem in employee dissent expression. *Communication Research Reports, 24,* 235–240.

Payne, H. J. (2014). Examining the relationship between trust in supervisor–employee relationships and workplace dissent. *Communication Research Reports, 31,* 131–140. doi:10.1080/08824096.2014.90141

Payne, R. A. (2001). Persuasion, frames, and norm construction. *European Journal of International Relations, 7,* 37–61.

Pearce, W. B., & Cronen, V. E. (1980). *Communication, action, and meaning: The creation of social realities.* New York, NY: Praeger.

Pentecost, K. (2011). Imagined communities in cyberspace. *Social Alternatives, 30*(2), 44–47.

Perloff, R. M. (2010). *The dynamics of persuasion: Communication and attitudes in the 21st century.* New York, NY: Routledge.

Peter, J., & Valkenburg, P. M. (2007). Who looks for casual dates on the Internet? A test of the compensation and the recreation of hypotheses. *New Media and Society, 9,* 455–474.

Peters, J. D. (1999). *Speaking into the air: The history of the idea of communication.* Chicago, IL: University of Chicago Press.

Peterson, D. R. (1991). Interpersonal relationships as a link between person and environment. In W. B. Walsh, K. H. Craig, & R. H. Price (Eds.), *Person-environment psychology.* Hillsdale, NJ: Erlbaum.

Peterson, L. W., & Albrecht, T. L. (1996) Message design logic, social support, and mixed-status relationships. *Western Journal of Communication, 60,* 291–309.

Petroni, S. (2002). *Boundaries of privacy: Dialectics of disclosure.* Albany: State University of New York Press.

Petty, R. E., & Briñol, P. (2014). The elaboration likelihood and meta-cognitive models of attitudes: Implications for prejudice, the self, and beyond. In J. W. Sherman, B. Gawronski, & Y. Trope (Eds.), *Dual-process theories of the social mind* (pp. 172–187). New York, NY: Guilford.

Pew Research Center. (2010, February). Millennials: A portrait of generation next. Retrieved from http://pewsocialtrends.org/assets/pdf/millennials-confident-connected-open-to-change.pdf

Pew Research Center. (2010, July 2). The future of online socializing. Washington, DC: Pew Internet and American Life Project. Retrieved from http://pewresearch.org/pubs/1652/social-relations-online-experts-predict-future

Pew Research Center. (2011). Report of the Pew Internet and American Life Project, April 26–May 22, 2011, spring tracking survey. Retrieved from http://pewinternet.org/

Pierce, C. A., Byrne, D., & Aguinis, H. (1996). Attraction in organizations: A model of workplace romance. *Journal of Organizational Behavior, 17,* 5–32. doi:10.1002/(SICI)1099-1379(199601)

Plaugic, L. (2015, March 15). Studio promotes *Ex Machina* with a fake Tinder account. The Verge. Retrieved from http://www.theverge.com

Pollock, S. L. (2006). Internet counseling and its feasibility for marriage and family counseling. *The Family Journal: Counseling and Therapy for Couples and Families, 14,* 65–70.

Poole, M. S., & Roth, J. (1989). Decision development in small groups V: Test of a contingency model. *Human Communication Research, 15,* 549–589.

Poster, M. (1990). *The mode of information: Post-structuralism and social context.* Cambridge, England: Polity Press.

Potter, W. J., & Byrne, S. (2007). What are media literacy effects? In S. R. Mazzerella (Ed.), *Twenty questions about youth and the media* (pp. 197–210). New York, NY: Lang.

Prensky, M. (2001). Digital natives, digital immigrants. *On the Horizon, 9*(5), 1–6. Retrieved from http://www.marcprensky.com/writing/prensky%20-%20digital%20natives,%20digital%20immigrants%20-%20part1.pdf

Problem-solving techniques. (1996–2015). Retrieved from http://www.mindtools.com

Puhl, R. (2011). Chris Christie and our biases about weight. Retrieved from http://www.cnn.com/2011/10/07/opinion/puhl-christie-weight/index.html?iref=allsearch

Putnam, R. D. (2000). *Bowling alone: The collapse and revival of American community.* New York, NY: Simon & Schuster.

Q

Qualman, E. (2009). *Socialnomics: How social media transforms the way we live and do business.* Hoboken, NJ: Wiley.

Quan, Z. (2010). The multilingual Internet: Language, culture, and communication online. *Journal of Business & Technical Communication, 24*(2), 249–252.

Quinn, R. E. (1977). Coping with Cupid: The formation, impact, and management of romantic relationships in organizations. *Administrative Science Quarterly, 22,* 30–45. doi:10.2307/2391744

Quintanilla, K. M., & Wahl, S. T. (2011). *Business and professional communication: Keys for workplace excellence.* Thousand Oaks, CA: Sage.

Quintanilla, K. M., & Wahl, S. T. (2014). *Business and professional communication: Keys for workplace excellence* (2nd ed.). Thousand Oaks, CA: Sage.

R

Rabotin, M. B. (2014). The intricate web: Connecting virtual teams. *T+D, 68*(4), 32–35.

Rahim, M. A. (1983). A measure of styles of handling interpersonal conflict. *Academy of Management Journal, 26,* 368–376.

Rahim, M. A. (2002). Toward a theory of managing organizational conflict. *International Journal of Conflict Management, 13,* 206–235.

Rahim, M. A., & Bonoma, T. V. (1979). Managing organizational conflict: A model for diagnosis and intervention. *Psychological Reports, 44,* 1323–1344.

Rahim, M. A., Buntzman, G. F., & White, D. (1999). An empirical study of the stages of moral development and conflict management styles. *International Journal of Conflict Management, 10,* 154–171.

Rainie, L., & Anderson, J. (2008, December 14). The future of the Internet III. Retrieved from http:// www.pewinternet.org/Reports/2008/The-Future-of-the-Internet-III.aspx

Rains, S. A., & Keating, D. M. (2011). The social dimension of blogging about health: Health blogging, social support, and well-being. *Communication Monographs, 78,* 511–534.

Rankings of best top 10 social media optimization companies. (2010, July 28). Retrieved from http://www.topseos.com/rankings-of-best-social-media-optimization-companies

Rawlins, W. K. (2009). *The compass of friendship: Narratives, identities, and dialogues.* Thousand Oaks, CA: Sage.

The Red Frog way (n.d.). Culture statement. Retrieved from http://redfrogevents.com/rfe-way/

Redfield, R. (1953). *The primitive world and its transformation.* Ithaca, NY: Cornell University Press.

Reed, E. M. (1991). Electropolis: Communication and community on the Internet relay chat. Retrieved from http://www.ee.mu.oz.au/papers/emr/electropolis.html

Reiche, S. (2013, June 20). Managing virtual teams: Ten tips. Retrieved from http://www.forbes.com/sites/iese/2013/06/20/managing-virtual-teams-ten-tips/

Reid, P. J. (2009). Adapting to the human world: Dogs' responsiveness to our social cues. *Behavioural Processes, 80,* 325–333.

Reynolds, B. W. (2015, January 20). 100 top companies with remote jobs in 2015. Retrieved from http://www.flexjobs.com/blog/post/100-top-companies-with-remote-jobs-in-2015

Rhodan, M. (2014, June 13). 4 in 10 teens admit texting while driving. *Time.* Retrieved March 9, 2015, from http://time.com/2869683/kids-texting-driving/

Rice, S., & Burbules, N. C. (2010). Listening: A virtue account. *Teachers College Record, 112,* 2728–2742.

Richards, N. M. (2013). The dangers of surveillance. *Harvard Law Review,* 1935–1965.

Richmond, V. P., & Hickson, M. (2002). *Going public: Practical guide to public talk.* Boston, MA: Allyn & Bacon.

Richmond, V. P., McCroskey, J. C., & Johnson, A. D. (2003). Development of the nonverbal immediacy scale (NIS): Measures of self- and other-perceived nonverbal immediacy. *Communication Quarterly, 51,* 505–517.

Richtel, M. (2010, July 6). Attached to technology and paying a price. *The New York Times.* Retrieved from http://www.nytimes.com/2010/06/07/technology/07brain.html?pagewanted=all

Ridberg, R. (2004). *Spin the bottle: Sex, lies and alcohol.* Media Education Foundation.

Riessman, C. (1990). *Divorce talk: Women and men make sense of personal relationships.* New Brunswick, NJ: Rutgers University Press.

Ritter, E. M. (1979). Social perspective-taking ability, cognitive complexity and listener adapted communication early and late adolescence. *Communication Monographs, 46,* 40–51.

Ritts, V., Patterson, M. L., & Tubbs, M. E. (1992). Expectations, impressions, and judgments of physically attractive students: A review. *Review of Educational Research, 62,* 413–426.

Roberts, S. J., & Roach, T. (2009). Social networking web sites and human resource personnel: Suggestions for job searches. *Business Communication Quarterly, 72,* 110–114.

Robinson, K. (2010). Students' appraisal of emotional and relational experience whilst collaborating online using text based communication. *Computers & Education, 54*(3), 799–807.

Rogers, C. R. (1962). The interpersonal relationship: The core of guidance. *Harvard Educational Review, 32,* 416–429.

Roig-Franzia, M. (2013, July 14). Zimmerman found not guilty in killing of Trayvon Martin. *The Washington Post.* Retrieved from http://www.washingtonpost.com/national/zimmerman-trial-jurors-request-clarification-on-manslaughter-instructions/2013/07/13/3a26dbbe-ec0c-11e2-aa9f-c03a72e2d342_story.html

Romance in the workplace: The good, the bad, and the ugly. (2014). Retrieved from http://career.intelligence.com/romance-in-the-workplace-the-good-the-bad/

Rose, S. R. (1989). Members leaving groups: Theoretical and practical considerations. *Small Group Behavior, 20,* 524–535.

Rosen, D., Lafontaine, P., & Hendrickson, B. (2011). Couch surfing: Belonging and trust in a globally cooperative online social network. *New Media Society, 13*(6), 981–998.

Rosenfeld, M. J., & Thomas, R. J. (2009). How couples meet and stay together, wave I version 1.01 [machine readable data file]. Stanford, CA: Stanford University Libraries. Retrieved from http://data.stanford.edu/hcmst

Rosenfeld, M. J., & Thomas, R. J. (2011). How couples meet and stay together, waves 1, 2, and 3: Public version 3.04 [computer file]. Stanford, CA: Stanford University Libraries.

Rosenthal, R., & Jacobson, L. (1992). *Pygmalion in the classroom* (Expanded ed.). New York, NY: Irvington.

Roter, D. L. (2011). Oral literacy demand of health care communication: Challenges and solutions. *Nursing Outlook, 59,* 79–84.

Rothenbuhler, E. W. (2006). Communication as ritual. In G. J. Shepherd, J. St. John, & T. Striphas (Eds.), *Communication as . . . : Perspectives on theory* (pp. 13–21). Thousand Oaks, CA: Sage.

Royal, C. (2015, March 25). Why universities need to embrace coding across the curriculum. Retrieved from http://www.pbs.org/mediashift

Rubin, R. B., & Martin, M. M. (1994). Development of a measure of interpersonal communication competence. *Communication Research Reports, 11,* 33–44. doi:10.1080/08824099409359938

Rubin, R. B., Rubin, A. M., & Piele, L. J. (2005). *Communication research: Strategies and sources* (6th ed.). Belmont, CA: Wadsworth.

Rushkoff, D. (2012, November 13). Code literacy: A 21st-century requirement. Retrieved from www.edutopia.org

Sadri, G., & Lees, B. (2001). Developing corporate culture as a competitive advantage. *Journal of Management Development, 20,* 853–859.

Samovar, L., Porter, R. E., & McDaniel, E. R. (2009). *Communication between cultures* (7th ed.). Belmont, CA: Wadsworth.

Samter, W., Burleson, B. R., & Basden-Murphy, L. (1989). Behavioral complexity is in the eye of the beholder: Effects of cognitive complexity and message complexity on impressions of the source of comforting messages. *Human Communication Research, 15,* 612–629.

Sarno, D., & Goffard, C. (2011, October 6). Steve Jobs 1955–2011: American pioneer. *Chicago Tribune,* pp. A1, A12–13.

Sarri, R. C., & Galinsky, M. J. (1974). A conceptual framework for group development. In P. Glasser, R. Sarri, & R. Vinter (Eds.), *Individual change through small groups* (pp. 71–88). New York, NY: Free Press.

Saussure, F. de. (1959). *Course in general linguistics*. New York, NY: The Philosophical Library.

Savoy, A., Proctor, R. W., & Salvendy, G. (2009). Information retention from PowerPoint™ and traditional lectures. *Computers & Education, 52,* 858–867.

Schank, R., & Abelson, R. (1977). *Scripts, plans, goals, and understanding: An inquiry into human knowledge structure.* Hillsdale, NJ: Erlbaum.

Schein, E. H. (2004). *Organizational culture and leadership* (3rd ed.). San Francisco, CA: Jossey-Bass.

Schofield, A., Torr, J., & Perrett, B. (2014, March 20). MH370 search coordination lapses echo global issues. *Aviation Week.* Retrieved May 16, 2015, from http:// aviationweek.com/commercial-aviation/ mh370-search-coordination-lapses-echo-global-issues

Schramm, W. (1954). How communication works. In W. Schramm (Ed.), *The process and effects of mass communication* (pp. 3–26). Urbana: University of Illinois Press.

Schrodt, P., & Wheeless, L. R. (2001). Aggressive communication and informational reception apprehension: The influence of listening anxiety and intellectual inflexibility on trait argumentativeness and verbal aggressiveness. *Communication Quarterly, 49,* 53–69.

Schrodt, P., Wheeless, L. R., & Ptacek, K. M. (2000). Informational reception apprehension, educational motivation, and achievement. *Communication Quarterly, 48,* 60–73.

Schultz, M. C., & Schultz, J. T. (2004). Interpreting the learning styles of traditional and distance learning students. *Journal of College Teaching & Learning, 1,* 19–28.

Schultz, N. J., Hoffman, M. F., Fredman, A. J., & Bainbridge, A. L. (2012). The work and life of young professionals: Rationale and strategy for balance. *Qualitative Research Reports in Communication, 13,* 44–52. doi:1 0.1080/17459435.2012.719208

Schutz, W. (1958). *FIRO: A three-dimensional theory of interpersonal behavior.* New York, NY: Holt, Rinehart & Winston.

Shannon, C. E., & Weaver, W. (1949). *A mathematical model of communication.* Urbana: University of Illinois Press.

Shaw, M. E. (1981). *Group dynamics: The psychology of small group behavior* (3rd ed.). New York, NY: McGraw-Hill.

Sheldon, W. H., Stevens, S. S., & Tucker, S. (1942). *The varieties of temperament: A psychology of constitutional differences.* New York, NY: Harper & Row.

Shepherd, G. J. (2001). Community as the interpersonal accomplishment of communication. In G. J. Shepherd & E. W. Rothenbuhler (Eds.), *Communication and community* (pp. 23–35). Mahwah, NJ: Erlbaum.

Shepherd, G. J., St. John, J., & Striphas, T. (Eds.). (2006). *Communication as . . . : Perspectives on theory.* Thousand Oaks, CA: Sage.

Sherif, M., & Hovland, C. I. (1961). *Social judgment: Assimilation and contrast effects in communication and attitude change.* New Haven, CT: Yale University Press.

Shirazi, F. (2012). Information and communication technology and women empowerment in Iran. *Telematics & Informatics, 29,* 45–55.

Shulruf, B., Hattie, J., & Dixon, R. (2007). Development of a new tool for individualism and collectivism. *Journal of Psychoeducational Assessment, 25*(4), 385–401.

Sias, P. M. (2005). Workplace relationship quality and employee information experiences. *Communication Studies, 56,* 375–395.

Sias, P. M. (2009). *Organizing relationships: Traditional and emerging perspectives on workplace relationships.* Thousand Oaks, CA: Sage.

Sias, P. M., & Cahill, D. J. (1998). From coworkers to friends: The development of peer friendships in the workplace. *Western Journal of Communication, 62,* 273–299.

Sias, P. M., Heath, R. G., Perry, T., Silva, D., & Fix, B. (2004). Narratives of workplace friendship deterioration. *Journal of Social and Personal Relationships, 21,* 321–340.

Sias, P. M., Krone, K. K., & Jablin, F. M. (2002).An ecological systems perspective on workplace relationships. In M. L. Knapp & J. A. Daly (Eds.), *Handbook of interpersonal communication* (3rd ed., pp. 615–642). Thousand Oaks, CA: Sage.

Sias, P. M., Pedersen, H., Gallagher, E. B., & Kopaneva, I. (2012). Workplace friendship in the electronically connected organization. *Human Communication Research, 38,* 253–279. doi:10.1111/j.1468-2958.2012.01428.x

Sias, P. M., & Perry, T. (2004). Disengaging from workplace relationships: A research note. *Human Communication Research, 30,* 589–602.

Sias, P. M., Smith, G., & Avdeyeva, T. (2003). Sex and sex-composition differences and similarities in peer workplace friendship development. *Communication Studies, 54,* 322–340.

Silverman, C. (2014, May 16). CNN serial plagiarist primarily lifted from her old employer, Reuters. Poynter.org. Retrieved March 11, 2015, from http://www.poynter. org/news/mediawire/252458/cnn-serial-plagiarist-primarily-lifted-from-her-old-employer-reuters/

Simha, A., Topuzova, L. N., & Albert, J. F. (2011).V for volunteer(ing)—The journeys of undergraduate volunteers. *Journal of Academic Ethics, 9,* 107–126.

Simons, D. (2010). Monkeying around with the gorillas in our midst: Familiarity with an inattentional-blindness task does not improve the detection of unexpected events. *i-Perception, 1,* 3–6.

Simons, D. J., & Chabris, C. F. (1999). Gorillas in our midst: Sustained inattentional blindness for dynamic events. *Perception, 28,* 1059.

Sinclair-James, L., & Stohl, C. (1997). Group endings and new beginnings. In L. R. Frey & J. K. Barge (Eds.), *Managing group life: Communicating in decision-making groups* (pp. 308–334). Boston, MA: Houghton Mifflin.

Singer, J. B. (1996). Virtual anonymity: Online accountability and the virtuous virtual journalist. *Journal of Mass Media Ethics, 11,* 95–106.

Slackman, S. (2009, June 4). Varying responses to speech in Mideast highlight divisions. *The New York Times.* Retrieved April 4, 2012, from http://www.nytimes. com/2009/06/05/world/middleeast/ 05reax.html

Sloan, G. (2015, March 16). Why marketers shouldn't be seduced into using believable bots. *Adweek.* Retrieved from http://www. adweek.com

Smidts, A., Pruyn, A. T. H., & van Riel, C. B. M. (2001). The impact of employee communication and perceived external prestige on organizational identification. *Academy of Management Journal, 49,* 1051–1062.

Smith, G. (2001). Group development: A review of the literature and a commentary on future research directions. *Group Facilitation: A Research and Applications Journal, 3,* 14–46.

Smith, G. (2004). An evaluation of the corporate culture of Southwest Airlines. *Measuring Business Excellence, 8*(4), 26–33.

Socha, T. J. (1997). Group communication across the life span. In L. R. Frey & J. K. Barge (Eds.), *Managing group life: Communicating in decision-making groups* (pp. 3–28). Boston, MA: Houghton Mifflin.

Solebello, N., & Elliot, S. (2011). "We want them to be as heterosexual as possible": Fathers talk about their teen children's sexuality. *Gender & Society, 25,* 293–315.

Soliz, J., Ribarsky, E., Harrigan, M., & Tye-Williams, S. (2010). Perceptions of communication with gay and lesbian family members: Predictors of relational satisfaction and implications for out group attitudes. *Communication Quarterly, 58,* 77–95.

Sollitto, M., & Myers, S. A. (2015). Peer coworker relationships: Influences on the expression of lateral dissent. *Communication Reports, 28,* 36–47. doi:10.1080/08934215.2014.925569

Soloman, K. (2013, November 22). LG admits that some TVs are watching you—but not for long. Retrieved from www.Techradar.com

Sorensen, R. L., & Savage, G. T. (1989). Signaling participation through relational communication: A test of the leader interpersonal influence model. *Group & Organization Studies, 14,* 325–354.

Sorensen, S. M. (1981, May). *Grouphate.* Paper presented at the annual meeting of the International Communication Association, Minneapolis, MN.

Soroker, A. (2014, October 16). The real reasons for telecommuting. Retrieved from http://recode.net/2014/10/6/the-real-reasons-for-telecommuting

Soukup, C. (2004). Multimedia performance in computer-mediated community: Communication as a virtual drama. *Journal of Computer-Mediated Communication* [online], *9*(4). Retrieved from http://jcmc.indiana.edu/vo19/issue4/soukup.html

Soukup, C. (2006). Computer-mediated communication as a virtual third place: Building Oldenburg's great good places on the World Wide Web. *New Media and Society, 8,* 421–440.

Southwest Airlines. (2015). About Southwest. Retrieved from https://www.southwest.com/html/about-southwest

Spitzberg, B. H. (2006). Preliminary development of a model and measure of computer-mediated communication (CMC) competence. *Journal of Computer-Mediated Communication, 11*(2), 629–666.

Sproull, L., & Kiesler, S. (1991). *Connections: New ways of working in the networked organization.* Cambridge, MA: Nelson Hall.

Steimel, S. (2013). Connecting with volunteers: Memorable messages and volunteer identification. *Communication Research Reports, 30,* 12–21. doi:10.1080/08824096.2012.746220

Steinmann, S. (2013, December 22). All-male dance group stirs controversy in Semmes Christmas parade. Retrieved from http://blog.al.com/live/2013/12/all-male_dancers_stir_controve.html

Stephens, K. K., Sornes, J. O., Rice, R. E., Browning, L. D., & Saetre, A. S. (2010). Discrete, sequential, and follow-up use of information and communication technology by experienced ICT users. *Management Communication Quarterly, 22,* 197–231.

Stewart, C. J., & Cash, W. B., Jr. (2008). *Interviewing: Principles and practices* (12th ed.). Boston, MA: McGraw-Hill.

Stiffler, D., Stoten, S., & Cullen, D. (2011). Podcasting as an instructional supplement to online learning: A pilot study. *CIN: Computers, Informatics, Nursing, 29,* 144–148.

Stohl, C. (1986). The role of memorable messages in the process of organizational socialization. *Communication Quarterly, 34,* 231–249.

Stoolmacher, I. S. (2015, March 11). Opinion: Wedge issues such as immigration lure voters over the fence. New Jersey On-Line. Retrieved March 17, 2015, from http://www.nj.com/opinion/index.ssf/2015/03/opinion_wedge_issues_lure_voters_over_the_fence.html

Stone, B., & Cohen, N. (2009, June 15). Social networks spread defiance online. *The New York Times.* Retrieved from http://www.nytimes.com/2009/06/16/world/middleeast/16media.html

Stritzke, W. K., Nguyen, A., & Durkin, K. (2004). Shyness and computer-mediated communication: A self-presentational theory perspective. *Media Psychology, 6,* 1–22.

Stuever, H. (2015, April 21). "The Prancing Elites Project": Loved from afar, but unwelcome at home. Retrieved from http://www.washingtonpost.com/entertainment/tv/the-prancing-elites-project-loved-from-afar-but-unwelcome-at-home/2015/04/21/6f4f7ef4-e845-11e4-9767-6276fc9b0ada_story.html

Suicide in youth. (2011, November 7). National Alliance on Mental Illness. Retrieved from www.nami.org

Sumner, W. G. (1906). *Folkways.* Boston, MA: Ginn.

Sung, K. H., & Lee, M. J. (2015). Do online comments influence the public's attitudes toward an organization? Effects of online comments based on individuals' prior attitudes. *The Journal of Psychology: Interdisciplinary and Applied, 149,* 325–338. doi:10.1080/00223980.2013.879847

Sunwolf. (2002). Getting to "groupaha!": Provoking creative processes in task groups. In L. R. Frey (Ed.), *New directions in group communication* (pp. 203–217). Thousand Oaks, CA: Sage.

Sunwolf. (2008). *Peer groups: Expanding our study of small group communication.* Los Angeles, CA: Sage.

Surowiecki, J. (2004). *The wisdom of crowds: Why the many are smarter than the few and how collective wisdom shapes business, economies, societies, and nations.* New York, NY: Doubleday.

Surra, C. A. (1985). Courtship types: Variations in interdependence between partners and social networks. *Journal of Personality and Social Psychology, 49,* 357–375.

Swami, V., Furnham, A., Chamorro-Premuzic, T., Akbar, K., Gordon, N., Harris, T., . . . Tovée, M. J. (2010). More than just skin deep? Personality information influences men's ratings of the attractiveness of women's body sizes. *Journal of Social Psychology, 150,* 628–674.

Tan, S. (2011, September 27). Teenager struggled with bullying before taking his life. *Buffalo News.* Retrieved from http://www.buffalonews.com/city/schools/article563538.ece

Tannen, D. (1990). *You just don't understand: Women and men in conversation.* New York, NY: HarperCollins.

Tannen, D. (1994). *Gender and discourse.* New York, NY: Oxford University Press.

Tannen, D. (2001). *You just don't understand: Women and men in conversation.* New York, NY: Quill.

Taylor, L. S., Fiore, A. T., Mendelsohn, G. A., & Cheshire, C. (2011). "Out of my league": A real-world test of the matching hypothesis. *Personality and Social Psychology Bulletin, 37,* 942–954.

TED. (n.d.). About TED. Retrieved from http://www.ted.com/pages/about

TED. (2012). TED reaches its billionth video view! Retrieved June 8, 2015, from http://blog.ted.com/ted-reaches-its-billionth-video-view/

Tekleab, A. G., Quigley, N. R., & Tesluk, P. E. (2009). A longitudinal study of team conflict, conflict management, cohesion, and team effectiveness. *Group & Organization Management, 34,* 170–205.

Thibaut, J. W., & Kelley, H. H. (1959). *The social psychology of groups.* New York, NY: John Wiley & Sons.

Thomas, M., Hariharan, M., Rana, S., Swain, S., & Andrew, A. (2014). Medical jargons as hindrance in doctor–patient communication. *Psychological Studies, 59,* 394–400. doi:10.1007/s12646-014-0262-x

Thompson, C. (2012, December). Sensors everywhere. *WIRED.* Retrieved from http://www.wired.com/opinion/2012/12/20-12-st_thompson/

Thomson, R., & Murachver, T. (2001). Predicting gender from electronic discourse. *British Journal of Social Psychology, 40,* 193–208.

Thorndike, E. L. (1920). A constant error on psychological rating. *Journal of Applied Psychology, IV,* 25–29.

Tian, Y. (2010). Organ donation on Web 2.0: Content and audience analysis of organ donation videos on YouTube. *Health Communication, 25,* 238–246.

Tidwell, L. C., & Walther, J. B. (2002). Computer-mediated effects of disclosure, impressions, and interpersonal evaluations: Getting to know one another a bit at a time. *Human Communication Research, 28,* 317–348.

Tiffan, B. (2014). The art of team leadership. *American Journal of Health-System Pharmacy, 71,* 799–801. doi:10.2146/sp140005

Ting-Toomey, S., & Chung, L. (2005). *Understanding intercultural communication.* New York, NY: Oxford University Press.

Tolbize, A. (2008). *Generational differences in the workplace.* Minneapolis, MN: Research and Training Center on Community Living.

Toldi, N. L. (2011). Job applicants favor video interviewing in the candidate-selection process. *Employment Relations Today, 38*(3), 19–27.

Tompkins, P. S. (2009). Rhetorical listening and moral sensitivity. *The International Journal of Listening, 23,* 60–79.

Tomsho, R. (2009, July 30). White House "Beer Summit" becomes something of a brouhaha. *The Wall Street Journal.* Retrieved from http://online.wsj.com/article/SB124891169018991961.html

Tong, S. T., Van Der Heide, B., Lanwell, L., & Walther, J. B. (2008). Too much of a good thing? The relationship between number of friends and interpersonal impressions on Facebook. *Journal of Computer-Mediated Communication, 13,* 531–549.

Transforming our jobs, our cities, our hospitals. (2014). *Equality,* 18–19.

Treem, J. W., Dailey, S. L., Pierce, C. S., & Leonardi, P. M. (2015). Bringing technological frames to work: How previous experience with social media shapes the technology's meaning in an organization. *Journal of Communication, 65,* 396–422. doi:10.1111/jcom.12149

Tuckman, B. W. (1965). Developmental sequence in small groups. *Psychological Bulletin, 63,* 384–399.

Tuckman, B. W., & Jensen, M. A. C. (1977). Stages of small-group development revisited. *Group & Organization Studies, 2,* 419–427.

Tullis Owen, J. A., McRae, C., Adams, T. E., & Vitale, A. (2009). Truth troubles. *Qualitative Inquiry, 15,* 178–200.

Turkle, S. (1995). *Life on the screen: Identity in the age of the Internet.* New York, NY: Simon & Schuster.

Turkle, S. (1996). Parallel lives: Working on identity in virtual space. In D. Grodin & T. R. Lindlof (Eds.), *Constructing the self in a mediated world* (pp. 156–175). London, England: Sage.

Turman, P. D. (2008). Coaches' immediacy behaviors as predictors of athletes' perceptions of satisfaction and team cohesion. *Western Journal of Communication, 72,* 162–179.

Tversky, B. (1997). Memory for pictures, maps, environments, and graphs. In D. G. Payne & F. G. Conrad (Eds.), *Intersections in basic and applied memory research* (pp. 257–277). Hillsdale, NJ: Erlbaum.

Twitter firing Jet's Pizza: Texas teenager gets fired on Twitter after complaining about her new job. (2015, February 12). Retrieved from http://www.jobsnhire.com/articles/18852/20150212/twitter-firing-jets-pizza-texas-teenager-gets-fired-on-twitter-after-complaining-about-her-new-job.htm

U.S. Department of Transportation, Federal Motor Carrier Safety Administration (2009). Driver distraction in commercial vehicle operations (Report No. FMCSA-RRR-09-042). Retrieved from http://mcsac.fmcsa.dot.gov/documents/DriverDistractionStudy.pdf

Utz, S. (2010). Show me your friends and I will tell you what type of person you are: How one's profile, number of friends, and type of friends influence impression formation on social network sites. *Journal of Computer-Mediated Communication, 15,* 314–335.

Vaidyanathan, G., & Climatewire (2015, January 30). Big gap between what scientists say and Americans think about climate change. *Scientific American.* Retrieved April 8, 2015, from http://www.scientificamerican.com/article/big-gap-between-what-scientists-say-and-americans-think-about-climate-change/

Van de Vord, R. (2010). Distance students and online research: Promoting information literacy through media literacy. *The Internet and Higher Education, 13,* 170–175.

Vansina, J. M. (1985). *Oral tradition as history.* Madison: University of Wisconsin Press.

Vivian, G. (2006). Neoliberal epideictic: Rhetorical form and commemorative politics on September 11, 2002. *Quarterly Journal of Speech, 92,* 1–26.

Vogel, E. A., Rose, J. P., Roberts, L. R., & Eckles, K. (2014). Social comparison, social media, and self-esteem. *Psychology of Popular Media Culture, 3,* 206–222. Retrieved from http://dx.doi.org/10.1037/ppm0000047

Wagner, M. (2015, February 9). Texas tween fired from pizza shop for complaining about "f—k a-ss" new job on Twitter before her first day. *New York Daily News.* Retrieved from http://www.nydailynews.com/news/texas-teen-fired-f-k-a-pizza-shop-job-tweets-articles-1.2108603

Wahl, S. T., & Scholl J. C. (2014). *Communication and culture in your life.* Dubuque, IA: Kendall Hunt.

Waldron, V. R., & Kassing, J. W. (2011). *Managing RISK in communication encounters: Strategies for the workplace.* Thousand Oaks, CA: Sage.

Walker, J. (2014, May 10). Another Dolphin in Twitter trouble. ESPN. Retrieved from http://abcnews.go.com/Sports/dolphin-twitter-trouble/story?id=23670999

Wall, V. D., Jr., & Galanes, G. J. (1986). The SYMLOG dimensions and small group conflict. *Central States Speech Journal, 37,* 61–78.

Wall, V. D., Jr., Galanes, G. J., & Love, S. B. (1987). Small, task-oriented groups: Conflict, conflict management, satisfaction, and decision quality. *Small Group Behavior, 18,* 31–55.

Walmart Corporate. (2015). Our business. Retrieved from http://corporate.walmart.com/our-story/our-business/

Walsh, P. (2010, March 10). Lakeville man sues TV show over segment about his genital blemishes. *Star Tribune.* Retrieved from http://www.startribune.com/lifestyle/87109677.html?source=error

Walther, J. B. (1995). Relational aspects of computer-mediated communication: Experimental observations over time. *Organizational Science, 6,* 186–202.

Walther, J. B. (1996). Computer-mediated communication: Impersonal, interpersonal, and hyper-personal interaction. *Communication Research, 23,* 3–43.

Walther, J. B., & D'Addario, K. P. (2001). The impacts of emoticons on message interpretation in computer-mediated communication. *Social Science Computer Review, 19*(3), 324–347.

Walther, J. B., Loh, T., & Granka, L. (2005). Let me count the ways: The interchange of verbal and nonverbal cues in computer-mediated and face-to-face affinity. *Journal of Language and Social Psychology, 24,* 36–65.

Walther, J. B., & Parks, M. R. (2002). Cues filtered out, cues filtered in: Computer-mediated communication and relationships. In M. L. Knapp & J. A. Daly (Eds.), *Handbook of interpersonal communication* (3rd ed., pp. 539–563). Thousand Oaks, CA: Sage.

Walther, J. B., Van Der Heide, B., Kim, S.-Y., Westerman, D., & Tong, S. T. (2008). The role of friends' appearance and behavior on evaluations of individuals on Facebook: Are we known by the company we keep? *Human Communication Research, 34,* 28–49.

Wang, S. S., Moon, S.-I., Kwon, K. H., Evans, C. A., & Stefanone, M. A. (2010). Face

off: Implications of visual cues on initiating friendship on Facebook. *Computers in Human Behavior, 26,* 226–234.

Warnick, B. (2007). *Rhetoric online: Persuasion and politics of the World Wide Web.* New York, NY: Peter Lang.

Watzlavick, P., Beavin, J. G., & Jackson, D. D. (1967). *Pragmatics of human communication: A study of interactional patterns, pathologies and paradoxes.* New York, NY: Norton.

Webb, L. M., Ledbetter, A. M., & Norwood, K. M. (2015). Families and technologically assisted communication. In L. H. Turner & R. West (Eds.), *The SAGE handbook of family communication* (pp. 354–370). Los Angeles, CA: Sage.

Weger, H., Jr., Castle, G. R., & Emmett, M. C. (2010). Active listening in peer interviews: The influence of message paraphrasing on perceptions of listening skill. *International Journal of Listening, 24,* 34–49.

Wemple, E. (2014, May 16). CNN fires news editor Marie-Louise Gumuchian for plagiarism. *The Washington Post.* Retrieved March 9, 2015, from http://www.washingtonpost.com/blogs/erik-wemple/wp/2014/05/16/cnn-fires-news-editor-marie-louise-gumuchian-for-plagiarism/

Wheelan, S. A. (2016). *Creating effective teams: A guide for members and leaders* (5th ed.). Los Angeles, CA: Sage.

Wheelan, S. A., & Burchill, C. (1999). Take teamwork to new heights. *Nursing Management, 30*(4), 28–31.

Wheelan, S. A., Davidson, B., & Tilin, F. (2003). Group development across time: Reality or illusion? *Small Group Research, 34,* 223–245.

Wheelan, S. A., & Hochberger, J. M. (1996). Validation studies of the Group Development Questionnaire. *Small Group Research, 27,* 143–170.

Wheelan, S. A., & McKeage, R. L. (1993). Developmental patterns in small and large groups. *Small Group Research, 24,* 60–83.

Wheeler, Jacob. (2013, March 27). Dancing for justice . . .. An UpTake leadership profile: Ananya Chatterjea. Retrieved from http://theuptake.org/2013/03/27/dancing-for-social-justicean-uptake-leadership-profile-ananya-chatterjea/

Wheeless, L. R. (1975). An investigation of receiver apprehension and social context dimensions of communication apprehension. *Speech Teacher, 24,* 261–268.

Wheeless, L. R., Preiss, R. W., & Gayle, B. M. (1997). Receiver apprehension, informational receptivity, and cognitive processing. In J. A. Daly, J. C. McCroskey, J. Ayres, T. Hopf, & D. M. Ayres (Eds.), *Avoiding communication: Shyness, reticence, and communication apprehension* (pp. 151–187). Cresskill, NJ: Hampton Press.

White, K. (2014, December 24). Controversial Yik Yak "gossip" app gains popularity. *USA Today.* Retrieved from http://www.usatoday.com

Wilkie, D. (2013, September 24). Forbidden love: Workplace-romance policies now stricter. Retrieved from http://www.shm.org/hrdisciplines/employeerelations/articles/pages/forbideen-love-workplace-romance-oloicies-stricter.aspx

Whorf, B. L. (1956). Discussion of Hopi linguistics. In John B. Carroll (Ed.), *Language, thought, and reality: Selected writings of Benjamin Lee Whorf* (pp. 102–111). Cambridge, MA: MIT Press.

Wittgenstein, L. (1922). *Tractatus Logico-Philosophicus.* New York, NY: Harcourt.

Wolf, N. (1991). *The beauty myth.* New York, NY: Bantam Doubleday Dell.

Wollan, M. (2011, September 26). A "diversity bake sale" backfires on campus. *The New York Times.* Retrieved from http://www.nytimes.com/2011/09/27/us/campus-diversity-bake-sale-is-priced-by-race-and-sex.html?ref=discrimination

Wolvin, A., & Coakley, C.G. (1996). *Listening.* Boston, MA: McGraw-Hill.

Wood, J. T. (1982). Communication and relational culture: Bases for study of human relationships. *Communication Quarterly, 30,* 75–84.

Wood, J. T. (1992). Gender and the moral voice: Moving from woman's nature to standpoint epistemology. *Women's Studies in Communication, 15,* 1–24.

Wood, J. T. (2009). *Gendered lives: Communication, gender, and culture.* Boston, MA: Wadsworth.

WorkLifeBalance.com. (2003). Work-life balance defined. Retrieved from http://www.worklifebalance.com/work-life-balance-defined.html

Workplace Bullying Institute. (2014). 2014 WBI U.S. workplace bullying survey. Retrieved from http://www.workplacebullying.org

Wright, K. (2004). On-line relational maintenance strategies and perceptions of partners with exclusively Internet-based and primarily Internet-based relationships. *Communication Studies, 55,* 239–253.

Wright, K. B., Abendschein, B., Wombacher, K., O'Connor, M., Hoffman, M., Dempsey, M., Krull, C., Dewes, A., & Shelton, A. (2014). Work-related communication technology use outside of regular work hours and work life conflict: The influence of communication technologies on perceived work life conflict, burnout, job satisfaction, and turnover intentions. *Management Communication Quarterly, 28,* 507–530. doi:10.1177/0893318914533332

Wright, K. B., Rosenberg, J., Egbert, N., Ploeger, N. A., Bernard, D. R., & King, S. (2013). Communication competence, social support, and depression among college students: A model of Facebook and face-to-face support network influence. *Journal of Health Communication, 18*(1), 41–57.

Xun, L. (2010). Online posting anxiety: Impacts on blogging. *Chinese Journal of Communication, 3*(2), 202–222.

Yang, J., & Trap, P. (2011, October 26). Top reasons why someone hired would not work out in the position. *USA Today,* B1.

Yee, N., & Bailenson, J. (2007). The Proteus effect: The effect of transformed self-representation on behavior. *Human Communication Research, 33,* 271–290.

Yee, N., & Bailenson, J. N. (2009). The difference between being and seeing: The relative contribution of self-perception and priming to behavioral changes via digital self-representation. *Media Psychology, 12,* 195–209.

Yee, N., Bailenson, J. N., & Ducheneaut, N. (2009). The Proteus effect: Implications of transformed digital self-representation on online and offline behavior. *Communication Research, 36,* 285–312.

Yeung, K., & Martin, J. L. (2003). The looking glass self: An empirical test and elaboration. *Social Forces, 81,* 843–879.

Young, J. R. (2008, March 17). How to combat a campus gossip web site (and why you shouldn't). *The Chronicle of Higher Education.*

Yu, C-P., & Kuo, F-Y. (2012). Investigating the development of work-oriented groups in an e-learning environment. *Educational Technology & Society, 15,* 164–176. doi:10.XX

Yu, J., King, K., & Hye Jun, Y. (2010). How much are health websites influenced by culture? Content analysis of online diet programs in the United States, the United Kingdom, and Korea. *Journal of Promotion Management, 16*(3), 331–359.

Zarefsky, D. (2007). Strategic maneuvering through persuasive definitions: Implications for dialectic and rhetoric. *Argumentation: An International Journal on Reasoning, 20,* 399–416.

Zeidan, F., Johnson, S. K., Diamond, B. J., David, Z., & Goolkasian, P. (2010). Mindfulness meditation improves cognition: Evidence of brief mental training. *Consciousness and Cognition, 19,* 597–605.

Zelizer, B. (1995). Reading the past against the grain: The shape of memory studies. *Critical Studies in Mass Communication, 12,* 214–239.

Zhang, X. (2008). On perspectives of audience studies. *Asian Social Science, 4,* 38–41.

Ziek, P., & Smulowitz, S. (2014). The impact of emergent virtual leadership competencies on team effectiveness. *Leadership & Organization Development Journal, 35,* 106–120. doi:10.1108/LODJ-03-2012-0043

Zillmann, D. (2000). Mood management in the context of selective exposure theory. In M. F. Roloff (Ed.), *Communication yearbook 23* (pp. 103–123). Thousand Oaks, CA: Sage.

Zillmann, D., & Bryant, J. (1985). *Selective exposure to communication.* Hillsdale, NJ: Erlbaum.

Zompetti, J. (2010). Freaking the mind: Exploring the rhetoric of magic in Criss Angel's *Mindfreak. Lore, 8.1,* 1–20.

Zorn, T., Hector, C., & Gibson, J. (2008, May). *Perceived effects of information and communication technology adoption on quality of work life: An exploratory study.* Paper presented at the annual meeting of the International Communication Association, Montreal, Quebec, Canada.